GO!
Premium Media Site

D0072547

Improve your grade with hands-on tools and resources!

- Master *Key Terms* to expand your vocabulary.
- Assess your knowledge with fun *Crossword Puzzles* and *Flipboards*, which let you flip through the definitions of the key terms and match them with the correct term.
- Prepare for exams by taking practice quizzes in the *Online Chapter Review*.
- Download *Student Data Files* for the application projects in each chapter.
- Answer matching and multiple choice questions to test what you learned in each chapter.

And for even more tools, you can access the following Premium Resources using your Access Code. Register now to get the most out of *GO!*.

- *Student Training Videos* for each Objective have been created by the author - a real instructor teaching the same types of courses that you take.*
- *GO! to Work* videos are short interviews with workers showing how they use Office in their job.*
- *GO! for Job Success* videos related to the projects in the chapter cover such important topics as Dressing for Success, Time Management, and Making Ethical Choices.*

*Access code required for these premium resources

Your Access Code is:

Note: If there is no silver foil covering the access code, it may already have been redeemed, and therefore may no longer be valid. In that case, you can purchase online access using a major credit card or PayPal account. To do so, go to **www.pearsonhighered.com/go**, select your book cover, click on "Buy Access" and follow the on-screen instructions.

To Register:

- To start you will need a valid email address and this access code.
- Go to **www.pearsonhighered.com/go** and scroll to find your text book.
- Once you've selected your text, on the Home Page for the book, click the link to access the Student Premium Content.
- Click the Register button and follow the on-screen instructions.
- After you register, you can sign in any time via the log-in area on the same screen.

System Requirements

Windows 7 Ultimate Edition; IE 8
Windows Vista Ultimate Edition SP1; IE 8
Windows XP Professional SP3; IE 7
Windows XP Professional SP3; Firefox 3.6.4
Mac OS 10.5.7; Firefox 3.6.4
Mac OS 10.6; Safari 5

Technical Support

http://247pearsoned.custhelp.com

Photo credits: Goodluz/wrangler/Elena Elisseeva/Shutterstock

GO!

with Microsoft®

PowerPoint 2013

Comprehensive

GO!

with Microsoft®

PowerPoint 2013
Comprehensive

Shelley Gaskin, Alicia Vargas, and Suzanne Marks

Boston   Columbus   Indianapolis   New York   San Francisco   Upper Saddle River
Amsterdam   Cape Town   Dubai   London   Madrid   Milan   Munich   Paris   Montréal   Toronto
Delhi   Mexico City   São Paulo   Sydney   Hong Kong   Seoul   Singapore   Taipei   Tokyo

Editor in Chief: Michael Payne
Executive Acquisitions Editor: Jenifer Niles
Editorial Project Manager: Carly Prakapas
Product Development Manager: Laura Burgess
Development Editor: Cheryl Slavik
Editorial Assistant: Andra Skaalrud
Director of Marketing: Maggie Leen
Marketing Manager: Brad Forrester
Marketing Coordinator: Susan Osterlitz
Marketing Assistant: Darshika Vyas
Managing Editor: Camille Trentacoste
Senior Production Project Manager: Rhonda Aversa

Operations Specialist: Maura Zaldivar-Garcia
Senior Art Director: Jonathan Boylan
Cover Photo: © photobar/Fotolia
Associate Director of Design: Blair Brown
Director of Media Development: Taylor Ragan
Media Project Manager, Production: Renata Butera
Full-Service Project Management: PreMediaGlobal
Composition: PreMediaGlobal
Printer/Binder: Webcrafters, Inc.
Cover Printer: Lehigh-Phoenix Color/Hagerstown
Text Font: MinionPro

Credits and acknowledgments borrowed from other sources and reproduced, with permission, in this textbook appear on the appropriate page within text. Microsoft and/or its respective suppliers make no representations about the suitability of the information contained in the documents and related graphics published as part of the services for any purpose. All such documents and related graphics are provided "as is" without warranty of any kind.

Microsoft and/or its respective suppliers hereby disclaim all warranties and conditions with regard to this information, including all warranties and conditions of merchantability, whether express, implied or statutory, fitness for a particular purpose, title and non-infringement. In no event shall Microsoft and/or its respective suppliers be liable for any special, indirect or consequential damages or any damages whatsoever resulting from loss of use, data or profits, whether in an action of contract, negligence or other tortious action, arising out of or in connection with the use or performance of information available from the services.

The documents and related graphics contained herein could include technical inaccuracies or typographical errors. Changes are periodically added to the information herein. Microsoft and/or its respective suppliers may make improvements and/or changes in the product(s) and/or the program(s) described herein at any time.

Microsoft® and Windows® are registered trademarks of the Microsoft Corporation in the U.S.A. and other countries. This book is not sponsored or endorsed by or affiliated with the Microsoft Corporation.

Copyright © 2014 by Pearson Education, Inc. as Prentice Hall. All rights reserved. Manufactured in the United States of America. This publication is protected by Copyright, and permission should be obtained from the publisher prior to any prohibited reproduction, storage in a retrieval system, or transmission in any form or by any means, electronic, mechanical, photocopying, recording, or likewise. To obtain permission(s) to use material from this work, please submit a written request to Pearson Education, Inc., Permissions Department, One Lake Street, Upper Saddle River, New Jersey 07458, or you may fax your request to 201-236-3290.

Many of the designations by manufacturers and sellers to distinguish their products are claimed as trademarks. Where those designations appear in this book, and the publisher was aware of a trademark claim, the designations have been printed in initial caps or all caps.

Library of Congress data on file

10 9 8 7 6 5 4 3 2

ISBN 10: 0-13-341506-6
ISBN 13: 978-0-13-341506-3

Brief Contents

Table of Contents

PowerPoint Introduction to Microsoft PowerPoint 2013   49

Chapter 1   Getting Started with Microsoft PowerPoint..51

Chapter 3   Enhancing a Presentation with Animation, Video, Tables, and Charts 165

Chapter 4 Creating Templates and Reviewing, Publishing, Comparing, Combining, and Protecting Presentations...................223

Chapter 8 Presentations Using Tables and Publishing Presentations 467

About the Authors

Shelley Gaskin, Series Editor, is a professor in the Business and Computer Technology Division at Pasadena City College in Pasadena, California. She holds a bachelor's degree in Business Administration from Robert Morris College (Pennsylvania), a master's degree in Business from Northern Illinois University, and a doctorate in Adult and Community Education from Ball State University (Indiana). Before joining Pasadena City College, she spent 12 years in the computer industry, where she was a systems analyst, sales representative, and director of Customer Education with Unisys Corporation. She also worked for Ernst & Young on the development of large systems applications for their clients. She has written and developed training materials for custom systems applications in both the public and private sector, and has also written and edited numerous computer application textbooks.

This book is dedicated to my students, who inspire me every day.

Alicia Vargas is a faculty member in Business Information Technology at Pasadena City College. She holds a master's and a bachelor's degree in Business Education from California State University, Los Angeles, and has authored several textbooks and training manuals on Microsoft Word, Microsoft Excel, and Microsoft PowerPoint.

This book is dedicated with all my love to my husband Vic, who makes everything possible; and to my children Victor, Phil, and Emmy, who are an unending source of inspiration and who make everything worthwhile.

Suzanne Marks is a faculty member in Business Technology Systems at Bellevue Community College, Bellevue, Washington. She holds a bachelor's degree in Business Education from Washington State University, and was project manager for the first IT Skills Standards in the United States.

This book is dedicated to my sister, Janet Curtis, for her unfailing support.

GO! with PowerPoint 2013

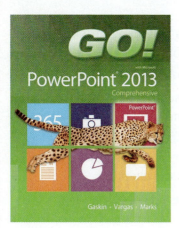

GO! with PowerPoint 2013 is the right solution for you and your students in today's fast-moving, mobile environment. The GO! Series content focuses on the real-world job skills students need to succeed in the workforce. They learn Office by working step-by-step through practical job-related projects that put the core functionality of Office in context. And as has always been true of the GO! Series, students learn the important concepts when they need them, and they never get lost in instruction, because the GO! Series uses Microsoft procedural syntax. Students learn how and learn why—at the teachable moment.

After completing the instructional projects, students are ready to apply the skills in a wide variety of progressively challenging projects that require them to solve problems, think critically, and create projects on their own. And, for those who want to go beyond the classroom and become certified, GO! provides clear MOS preparation guidelines so students know what is needed to ace the Core exam!

What's New

New Design reflects the look of Windows 8 and Office 2013 and enhances readability.

Enhanced Chapter Opener now includes a deeper introduction to the A and B instructional projects and more highly defined chapter Objectives and Learning Outcomes.

New Application Introductions provide a brief overview of the application and put the chapters in context for students.

Coverage of New Features of Office 2013 ensures that students are learning the skills they need to work in today's job market.

New Application Capstone Projects ensure that students are ready to move on to the next set of chapters. Each Application Capstone Project can be found on the Instructor Resource Center and is also a Grader project in MyITLab.

More Grader Projects based on the E, F, and G mastering-level projects, both homework and assessment versions! These projects are written by our GO! authors, who are all instructors in colleges like yours!

New Training & Assessment Simulations are now written by the authors to match the book one-to-one!

New MOS Map on the Instructor Resource Site and in the Annotated Instructor's Edition indicates clearly where each required MOS Objective is covered.

Three Types of Videos help students understand and succeed in the real world:

- *Student Training Videos* are broken down by Objective and created by the author—a real instructor teaching the same types of courses that you do. Real personal instruction.
- *GO! to Work* videos are short interviews with workers showing how they use Office in their jobs.
- *GO! for Job Success* videos relate to the projects in the chapter and cover important career topics such as *Dressing for Success*, *Time Management*, and *Making Ethical Choices*. **Available for Chapters 1–3 only**.

New GO! Learn It Online Section at the end of the chapter indicates where various student learning activities can be found, including multiple choice and matching activities.

New Styles for In-Text Boxed Content: Another Way, Notes, More Knowledge, Alerts, and **new *By Touch* instructions** are included in line with the instruction and not in the margins so that the student is more likely to read this information.

Clearly Indicated Build from Scratch Projects: GO! has always had many projects that begin "from scratch," and now we have an icon to really call them out!

New Visual Summary focuses on the four key concepts to remember from each chapter.

New Review and Assessment Guide summarizes the end-of-chapter assessments for a quick overview of the different types and levels of assignments and assessments for each chapter.

New Skills and Procedures Summary Chart (online at the Instructor Resource Center) summarizes all of the shortcuts and commands covered in the chapter.

New End-of-Chapter Key Term Glossary with Definitions for each chapter, plus a comprehensive end-of-book glossary.

New Flipboards and Crossword Puzzles enable students to review the concepts and key terms learned in each chapter by completing online challenges.

Teach the Course You Want in Less Time

A Microsoft® Office textbook designed for student success!

- **Project-Based** – Students learn by creating projects that they will use in the real world.

- **Microsoft Procedural Syntax** – Steps are written to put students in the right place at the right time.

- **Teachable Moment** – Expository text is woven into the steps—at the moment students need to know it—not chunked together in a block of text that will go unread.

- **Sequential Pagination** – Students have actual page numbers instead of confusing letters and abbreviations.

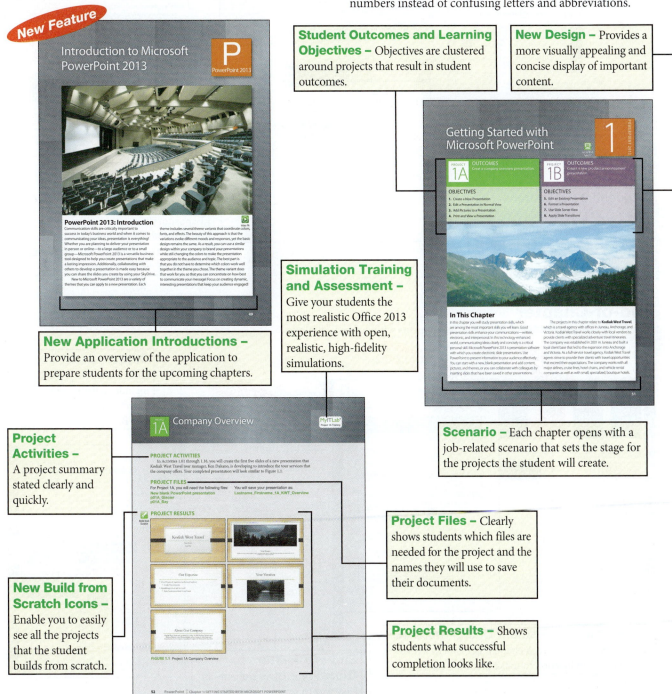

Student Outcomes and Learning Objectives – Objectives are clustered around projects that result in student outcomes.

New Design – Provides a more visually appealing and concise display of important content.

New Application Introductions – Provide an overview of the application to prepare students for the upcoming chapters.

Simulation Training and Assessment – Give your students the most realistic Office 2013 experience with open, realistic, high-fidelity simulations.

Scenario – Each chapter opens with a job-related scenario that sets the stage for the projects the student will create.

Project Activities – A project summary stated clearly and quickly.

Project Files – Clearly shows students which files are needed for the project and the names they will use to save their documents.

New Build from Scratch Icons – Enable you to easily see all the projects that the student builds from scratch.

Project Results – Shows students what successful completion looks like.

In-Text Features
Another Way, Notes, More Knowledge, Alerts, and By Touch Instructions

Microsoft Procedural Syntax – Steps are written to put the student at the right place at the right time.

Color Coding – Each chapter has two instructional projects, which is less overwhelming for students than one large chapter project. The two projects are differentiated by different colored numbering and headings.

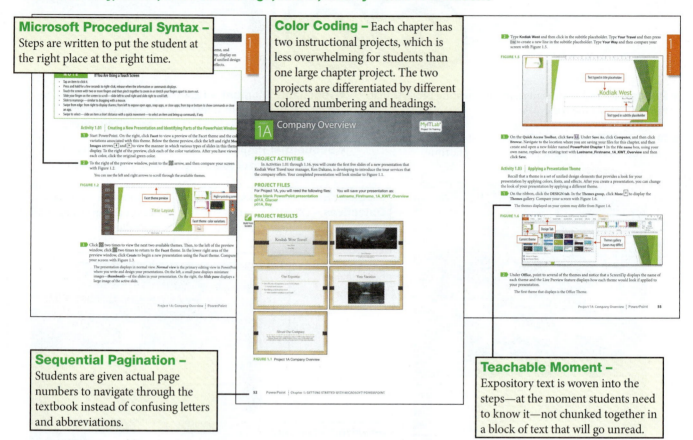

Sequential Pagination – Students are given actual page numbers to navigate through the textbook instead of confusing letters and abbreviations.

Teachable Moment – Expository text is woven into the steps—at the moment students need to know it—not chunked together in a block of text that will go unread.

End-of-Chapter
Content-Based Assessments – Assessments with defined solutions.

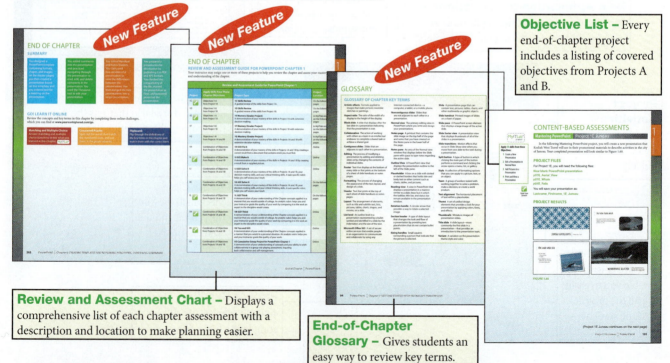

New Feature

New Feature

New Feature

Objective List – Every end-of-chapter project includes a listing of covered objectives from Projects A and B.

Review and Assessment Chart – Displays a comprehensive list of each chapter assessment with a description and location to make planning easier.

End-of-Chapter Glossary – Gives students an easy way to review key terms.

End-of-Chapter

Content-Based Assessments – Assessments with defined solutions. (continued)

Grader Projects – Each chapter has six MyITLab Grader projects—three homework and three assessment—clearly indicated by the MyITLab logo.

Task-Specific Rubric – A matrix specific to the GO! Solve It projects that states the criteria and standards for grading these defined-solution projects.

End-of-Chapter

Outcomes-Based Assessments – Assessments with open-ended solutions.

Sample Solution – Outcomes-based assessments include a sample solution so the instructor can compare student work with an example of expert work.

Outcomes Rubric – A matrix specific to the GO! Think projects that states the criteria and standards for grading these open-ended assessments.

GO! with Microsoft Office 365 – A collaboration project for each chapter teaches students how to use the cloud-based tools of Office 365 to communicate and collaborate from any device, anywhere. **Available for Chapters 1–3 only**.

Office Web Apps – For each instructional project, students can create the same or similar result in the corresponding Office Web Apps - 24 projects in all! **Available for Chapters 1–3 only**.

GO! with MyITLab

Gives you a completely integrated solution

Instruction ▪ Training ▪ Assessment

All of the content in the book and MyITLab is written by the authors, who are instructors, so the instruction works seamlessly with the simulation trainings and grader projects — true 1:1. eText, Training and Assessment Simulations, and Grader Projects

Student Materials

Student Data Files – All student data files are available to all on the companion website: www.pearsonhighered.com/go.

Three Types of Videos help students understand and succeed in the real world:

- **Student Training Videos** are by Objective and created by the author—a real instructor teaching the same types of courses that you teach.
- **GO! to Work** videos are short interviews with workers showing how they use Office in their job.
- **GO! for Job Success** videos related to the projects in the chapter cover important career topics such as *Dressing for Success*, *Time Management*, and *Making Ethical Choices*. **Available for Chapters 1–3 only.**

Flipboards and Crossword Puzzles provide a variety of review options for content in each chapter.
Available on the companion website using the access code included with your book.
pearsonhighered.com/go.

All Instructor and Student materials available at pearsonhighered. com/go

Instructor Materials

Annotated Instructor Edition – An instructor tool includes a full copy of the student textbook and a guide to implementing your course in three different ways, depending on the emphasis you want to place on digital engagement. Also included are teaching tips, discussion topics, and other useful pieces for teaching each chapter.

Student Assignment Tracker (previously called Assignment Sheets) – Lists all the assignments for the chapter. Just add the course information, due dates, and points. Providing these to students ensures they will know what is due and when.

Scripted Lectures – A script to guide your classroom lecture of each instructional project.

Annotated Solution Files – Coupled with the scorecards, these create a grading and scoring system that makes grading easy and efficient.

PowerPoint Lectures – PowerPoint presentations for each chapter.

Audio PowerPoints – Audio versions of the PowerPoint presentations for each chapter.

Scoring Rubrics – Can be used either by students to check their work or by you as a quick check-off for the items that need to be corrected.

Syllabus Templates – For 8-week, 12-week, and 16-week courses.

MOS Map – Provided at the Instructor Resource Center site and in the Annotated Instructor's Edition, showing where each required MOS Objective is covered either in the book or via additional instructional material provided.

Test Bank – Includes a variety of test questions for each chapter.

Companion Website – Online content such as the Online Chapter Review, Glossary, and Student Data Files are all at www.pearsonhighered.com/go.

Reviewers

GO! Focus Group Participants

Kenneth Mayer	Heald College
Carolyn Borne	Louisiana State University
Toribio Matamoros	Miami Dade College
Lynn Keane	University of South Carolina
Terri Hayes	Broward College
Michelle Carter	Paradise Valley Community College

GO! Reviewers

Abul Sheikh	Abraham Baldwin Agricultural College
John Percy	Atlantic Cape Community College
Janette Hicks	Binghamton University
Shannon Ogden	Black River Technical College
Karen May	Blinn College
Susan Fry	Boise State University
Chigurupati Rani	Borough of Manhattan Community College / CUNY
Ellen Glazer	Broward College
Kate LeGrand	Broward College
Mike Puopolo	Bunker Hill Community College
Nicole Lytle-Kosola	California State University, San Bernardino
Nisheeth Agrawal	Calhoun Community College
Pedro Diaz-Gomez	Cameron
Linda Friedel	Central Arizona College
Gregg Smith	Central Community College
Norm Cregger	Central Michigan University
Lisa LaCaria	Central Piedmont Community College
Steve Siedschlag	Chaffey College
Terri Helfand	Chaffey College
Susan Mills	Chambersburg
Mandy Reininger	Chemeketa Community College
Connie Crossley	Cincinnati State Technical and Community College
Marjorie Deutsch	City University of New York - Queensborough Community College
Mary Ann Zlotow	College of DuPage
Christine Bohnsak	College of Lake County
Gertrude Brier	College of Staten Island
Sharon Brown	College of The Albemarle
Terry Rigsby	Columbia College
Vicki Brooks	Columbia College
Donald Hames	Delgado Community College
Kristen King	Eastern Kentucky University
Kathie Richer	Edmonds Community College
Gary Smith	Elmhurst College
Wendi Kappersw	Embry-Riddle Aeronautical University
Nancy Woolridge	Fullerton College
Abigail Miller	Gateway Community & Technical College
Deep Ramanayake	Gateway Community & Technical College
Gwen White	Gateway Community & Technical College
Debbie Glinert	Gloria K School
Dana Smith	Golf Academy of America
Mary Locke	Greenville Technical College
Diane Marie Roselli	Harrisburg Area Community College
Linda Arnold	Harrisburg Area Community College - Lebanon
Daniel Schoedel	Harrisburg Area Community College - York Campus
Ken Mayer	Heald College
Xiaodong Qiao	Heald College
Donna Lamprecht	Hopkinsville Community College
Kristen Lancaster	Hopkinsville Community College
Johnny Hurley	Iowa Lakes Community College
Linda Halverson	Iowa Lakes Community College
Sarah Kilgo	Isothermal Community College
Chris DeGeare	Jefferson College
David McNair	Jefferson College
Diane Santurri	Johnson & Wales University
Roland Sparks	Johnson & Wales University
Ram Raghuraman	Joliet Junior College
Eduardo Suniga	Lansing Community College
Kenneth A. Hyatt	Lone Star College - Kingwood
Glenn Gray	Lone Star College - North Harris
Gene Carbonaro	Long Beach City College
Betty Pearman	Los Medanos College
Diane Kosharek	Madison College
Peter Meggison	Massasoit Community College
George Gabb	Miami Dade College
Lennie Alice Cooper	Miami Dade College
Richard Mabjish	Miami Dade College
Victor Giol	Miami Dade College
John Meir	Midlands Technical College
Greg Pauley	Moberly Area Community College
Catherine Glod	Mohawk Valley Community College
Robert Huyck	Mohawk Valley Community College
Kevin Engellant	Montana Western
Philip Lee	Nashville State Community College
Ruth Neal	Navarro College
Sharron Jordan	Navarro College
Richard Dale	New Mexico State University
Lori Townsend	Niagara County Community College
Judson Curry	North Park University
Mary Zegarski	Northampton Community College
Neal Stenlund	Northern Virginia Community College
Michael Goeken	Northwest Vista College
Mary Beth Tarver	Northwestern State University
Amy Rutledge	Oakland University
Marcia Braddock	Okefenokee Technical College
Richard Stocke	Oklahoma State University - OKC
Jane Stam	Onondaga Community College
Mike Michaelson	Palomar College
Kungwen (Dave) Chu	Purdue University Calumet
Wendy Ford	City University of New York - Queensborough Community College
Lewis Hall	Riverside City College
Karen Acree	San Juan College
Tim Ellis	Schoolcraft College
Dan Combellick	Scottsdale Community College
Pat Serrano	Scottsdale Community College
Rose Hendrickson	Sheridan College
Kit Carson	South Georgia College
Rebecca Futch	South Georgia State College
Brad Hagy	Southern Illinois University Carbondale
Mimi Spain	Southern Maine Community College
David Parker	Southern Oregon University
Madeline Baugher	Southwestern Oklahoma State University
Brian Holbert	St. Johns River State College
Bunny Howard	St. Johns River State College
Stephanie Cook	State College of Florida
Sharon Wavle	Tompkins Cortland Community College
George Fiori	Tri-County Technical College
Steve St. John	Tulsa Community College
Karen Thessing	University of Central Arkansas
Richard McMahon	University of Houston-Downtown
Shohreh Hashemi	University of Houston-Downtown
Donna Petty	Wallace Community College
Julia Bell	Walters State Community College
Ruby Kowaney	West Los Angeles College
Casey Thompson	Wiregrass Georgia Technical College
DeAnnia Clements	Wiregrass Georgia Technical College

Introduction to Microsoft Office 2013 Features

1

OFFICE 2013

PROJECT 1A

OUTCOMES
Create, save, and print a Microsoft Office 2013 document.

OBJECTIVES

1. Use File Explorer to Download, Extract, and Locate Files and Folders
2. Use Start Search to Locate and Start a Microsoft Office 2013 Desktop App
3. Enter, Edit, and Check the Spelling of Text in an Office 2013 Program
4. Perform Commands from a Dialog Box
5. Create a Folder and Name and Save a File
6. Insert a Footer, Add Document Properties, Print a File, and Close a Desktop App

---

PROJECT 1B

OUTCOMES
Use the ribbon and dialog boxes to perform commands in Microsoft Office 2013.

OBJECTIVES

7. Open an Existing File and Save It with a New Name
8. Sign In to Office and Explore Options for a Microsoft Office Desktop App
9. Perform Commands from the Ribbon and Quick Access Toolbar
10. Apply Formatting in Office Programs
11. Compress Files and Use the Microsoft Office 2013 Help System
12. Install Apps for Office and Create a Microsoft Account

etse1112/Fotolia

In This Chapter

In this chapter, you will use File Explorer to navigate the Windows folder structure, create a folder, and save files in Microsoft Office 2013 programs. You will also practice using features in Microsoft Office 2013 that work similarly across Word, Excel, Access, and PowerPoint. These features include managing files, performing commands, adding document properties, signing in to Office, applying formatting, and using Help. You will also practice compressing files and installing Apps for Office from the Office Store. In this chapter, you will also learn how to set up a free Microsoft account so that you can use SkyDrive.

The projects in this chapter relate to **Skyline Metro Grill**, which is a chain of 25 casual, full-service restaurants based in Boston. The Skyline Metro Grill owners are planning an aggressive expansion program. To expand by 15 additional restaurants in Chicago, San Francisco, and Los Angeles by 2018, the company must attract new investors, develop new menus, develop new marketing strategies, and recruit new employees, all while adhering to the company's quality guidelines and maintaining its reputation for excellent service. To succeed, the company plans to build on its past success and maintain its quality elements.

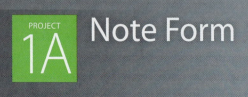

Note Form

MyITLab®
Project 1A Training

PROJECT ACTIVITIES

In Activities 1.01 through 1.09, you will create a note form using Microsoft Word, save it in a folder that you create by using File Explorer, and then print the note form or submit it electronically as directed by your instructor. Your completed note form will look similar to Figure 1.1.

PROJECT FILES

For Project 1A, you will need the following file: You will save your file as:

New blank Word document   **Lastname_Firstname_1A_Note_Form**

PROJECT RESULTS

Build from
Scratch

Skyline Metro Grill, Chef's Notes
Executive Chef, Sarah Jackson

Lastname_Firstname_1A_Note_Form

FIGURE 1.1 Project 1A Note Form

NOTE   If You Are Using a Touchscreen

- Tap an item to click it.
- Press and hold for a few seconds to right-click; release when the information or commands displays.
- Touch the screen with two or more fingers and then pinch together to zoom in or stretch your fingers apart to zoom out.
- Slide your finger on the screen to scroll—slide left to scroll right and slide right to scroll left.
- Slide to rearrange—similar to dragging with a mouse.
- Swipe from edge: from right to display charms; from left to expose open apps, snap apps, or close apps; from top or bottom to show commands or close an app.
- Swipe to select—slide an item a short distance with a quick movement to select an item and bring up commands, if any.

Objective 1   Use File Explorer to Download, Extract, and Locate Files and Folders

Video OF1-1

A **file** is a collection of information stored on a computer under a single name, for example, a Word document or a PowerPoint presentation. A file is stored in a **folder**—a container in which you store files—or a **subfolder**, which is a folder within a folder. The Windows operating system stores and organizes your files and folders, which is a primary task of an operating system.

You **navigate**—explore within the organizing structure of Windows—to create, save, and find your files and folders by using the **File Explorer** program. File Explorer displays the files and folders on your computer and is at work anytime you are viewing the contents of files and folders in a **window**. A window is a rectangular area on a computer screen in which programs and content appear; a window can be moved, resized, minimized, or closed.

Activity 1.01 │ Using File Explorer to Download, Extract, and Locate Files and Folders

ALERT!   You Will Need a USB Flash Drive

You will need a USB flash drive for this activity to download the Student Data Files for this chapter. If your instructor is providing the files to you, for example by placing the files at your learning management system, be sure you have downloaded them to a location where you can access the files and then skip to Activity 1.02.

NOTE   Creating a Microsoft Account

Use a free Microsoft account to sign in to Windows 8 and Office 2013 so that you can work on different PCs and use your SkyDrive. You need not use the Microsoft account as your primary email address unless you want to do so. To create a Microsoft account, go to **www.outlook.com**.

1 ▸ Sign in to Windows 8 with your Microsoft account—or the account provided by your instructor—to display the Windows 8 **Start screen**, and then click the **Desktop** tile. Insert a **USB flash drive** in your computer; **Close** ✗ any messages or windows that display.

The **desktop** is the screen in Windows that simulates your work area. A **USB flash drive** is a small data storage device that plugs into a computer USB port.

2 ▸ On the taskbar, click **Internet Explorer** 🖻. Click in the **address bar** to select the existing text, type **www.pearsonhighered.com/go** and press [Enter]. Locate and click the name of this textbook, and then click the **STUDENT DATA FILES tab**.

The **taskbar** is the area along the lower edge of the desktop that displays buttons representing programs—also referred to as desktop apps. In the desktop version of Internet Explorer 10, the **address bar** is the area at the top of the Internet Explorer window that displays, and where you can type, a **URL—Uniform Resource Locator**—which is an address that uniquely identifies a location on the Internet.

3 On the list of files, move your mouse pointer over—*point* to—**Office Features Chapter 1** and then *click*—press the left button on your mouse pointing device one time.

4 In the **Windows Internet Explorer** dialog box, click **Save As**.

A *dialog box* is a small window that contains options for completing a task.

5 In the **Save As** dialog box, on the left, locate the **navigation pane**, and point to the vertical **scroll bar**.

The Save As dialog box is an example of a *common dialog box*; that is, this dialog box looks the same in Excel and in PowerPoint and in most other Windows-based desktop applications—also referred to as programs.

Use the *navigation pane* on the left side of the Save As dialog box to navigate to, open, and display favorites, libraries, folders, saved searches, and an expandable list of drives. A *pane* is a separate area of a window.

A *scroll bar* displays when a window, or a pane within a window, has information that is not in view. You can click the up or down scroll arrows—or the left and right scroll arrows in a horizontal scroll bar—to scroll the contents up and down or left and right in small increments.

You can also drag the *scroll box*—the box within the scroll bar—to scroll the window or pane in either direction.

This is a *compressed folder*—also called a *zipped folder*—which is a folder containing one or more files that have been reduced in size. A compressed folder takes up less storage space and can be transferred to other computers faster.

N O T E | **Comparing Your Screen with the Figures in This Textbook**

Your screen will match the figures shown in this textbook if you set your screen resolution to 1280 × 768. At other resolutions, your screen will closely resemble, but not match, the figures shown. To view your screen's resolution, on the desktop, right-click in a blank area, and then click Screen resolution.

---

6 In the **navigation pane**, if necessary, on the scroll bar click ⌄ to scroll down. If necessary, to the left of **Computer**, click ▷ to expand the list. Then click the name of your **USB flash drive**.

7 With *Office_Features* displayed in the **File name** box, in the lower right corner click **Save**.

At the bottom of your screen, the *Notification bar* displays information about pending downloads, security issues, add-ons, and other issues related to the operation of your computer.

8 In the **Notification bar**, when the download is complete, click **Open folder** to display the folder window for your **USB flash drive**.

A *folder window* displays the contents of the current location—folder, library, or drive—and contains helpful parts so that you can navigate within the file organizing structure of Windows.

9 With the compressed **Office_Features** folder selected, on the ribbon, click the **Extract tab** to display the **Compressed Folder Tools**, and then click **Extract all**.

The *ribbon* is a user interface in both Office 2013 and Windows 8 that groups the commands for performing related tasks on tabs across the upper portion of a window.

In the dialog box, you can *extract*—decompress or pull out—files from a compressed folder.

You can navigate to some other location by clicking the Browse button and navigating within your storage locations.

10 In the **Extract Compressed (Zipped) Folders** dialog box, click to the right of the selected text, and then press Backspace until only the drive letter of your USB and the colon following it display—for example G:—and then click **Extract**. Notice that a progress bar indicates the progress of the extract process, and that when the extract is complete, the **Office_Features** folder displays on the file list of your **USB flash drive**.

> In a dialog box or taskbar button, a *progress bar* indicates visually the progress of a task such as a download or file transfer.
>
> The *address bar* in File Explorer displays your current location in the folder structure as a series of links separated by arrows, which is referred to as the *path*—a sequence of folders that leads to a specific file or folder.
>
> By pressing Backspace in the Extract dialog box, you avoid creating an unneeded folder level.

11 Because you no longer need the compressed (zipped) version of the folder, be sure it is selected, click the **Home tab**, and then click **Delete**. In the upper right corner of the **USB drive** folder window, click **Close** ❌. **Close** ❌ the **Internet Explorer** window and in the Internet Explorer message, click **Close all tabs**.

> Your desktop redisplays.

Objective 2   Use Start Search to Locate and Start a Microsoft Office 2013 Desktop App

Video OF1-2

The term *desktop app* commonly refers to a computer program that is installed on your computer and requires a computer operating system such as Microsoft Windows or Apple OS to run. The programs in Microsoft Office 2013 are considered to be desktop apps. Apps that run from the *device software* on a smartphone or a tablet computer—for example, iOS, Android, or Windows Phone—or apps that run from *browser software* such as Internet Explorer, Safari, Firefox, or Chrome on a desktop PC or laptop PC are referred to simply as *apps*.

Activity 1.02   Using Start Search to Locate and Start a Microsoft Office 2013 Desktop App

The easiest and fastest way to search for an app is to use the **Start search** feature—simply display the Windows 8 Start screen and start typing. By default, Windows 8 searches for apps; you can change it to search for files or settings.

1 With your desktop displayed, press ⊞ to display the Windows 8 **Start screen**, and then type **word 2013** With *word 2013* bordered in white in the search results, press Enter to return to the desktop and open Word. If you want to do so, in the upper right corner, sign in with your Microsoft account, and then compare your screen with Figure 1.2.

> Documents that you have recently opened, if any, display on the left. On the right, you can select either a blank document or a *template*—a preformatted document that you can use as a starting point and then change to suit your needs.

🔄 **BY TOUCH**   Swipe from the right edge of the screen to display the charms, and then tap Search. Tap in the Apps box, and then use the onscreen keyboard that displays to type *word 2013*. Tap the selected Word 2013 app name to open Word.

FIGURE 1.2

Recently opened documents, if any, display here

Start a blank document here

User signed in; this is optional

Templates to start different types of documents

2 ▶ Click **Blank document**. Compare your screen with Figure 1.3, and then take a moment to study the description of these screen elements in the table in Figure 1.4.

N O T E   **Displaying the Full Ribbon**

If your full ribbon does not display, click any tab, and then at the right end of the ribbon, click ⊞ to pin the ribbon to keep it open while you work.

FIGURE 1.3

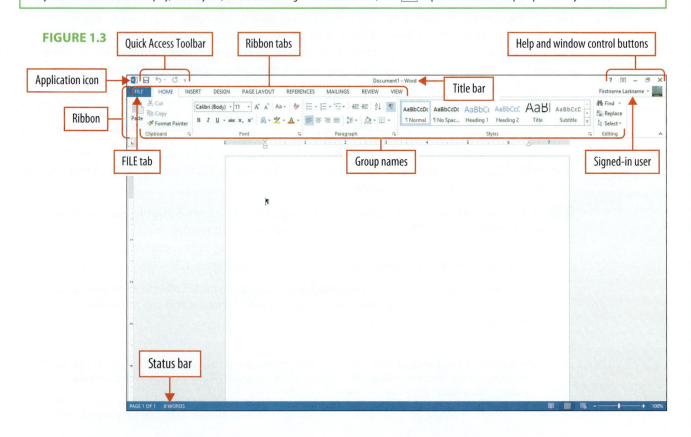

Quick Access Toolbar

Ribbon tabs

Help and window control buttons

Application icon

Title bar

Ribbon

FILE tab

Group names

Signed-in user

Status bar

FIGURE 1.4

MICROSOFT OFFICE SCREEN ELEMENTS	
SCREEN ELEMENT	**DESCRIPTION**
FILE tab	Displays Microsoft Office Backstage view, which is a centralized space for all of your file management tasks such as opening, saving, printing, publishing, or sharing a file—all the things you can do *with* a file.
Group names	Indicate the names of the groups of related commands on the displayed tab.
Help and window control buttons	Display Word Help and Full Screen Mode and enable you to Minimize, Restore Down, or Close the window.
Application icon	When clicked, displays a menu of window control commands including Restore, Minimize, and Close.
Quick Access Toolbar	Displays buttons to perform frequently used commands and use resources with a single click. The default commands include Save, Undo, and Redo. You can add and delete buttons to customize the Quick Access Toolbar for your convenience.
Ribbon	Displays a group of task-oriented tabs that contain the commands, styles, and resources you need to work in an Office 2013 desktop app. The look of your ribbon depends on your screen resolution. A high resolution will display more individual items and button names on the ribbon.
Ribbon tabs	Display the names of the task-oriented tabs relevant to the open program.
Status bar	Displays file information on the left; on the right displays buttons for Read Mode, Print Layout, and Web Layout views; on the far right displays Zoom controls.
Title bar	Displays the name of the file and the name of the program. The Help and window control buttons are grouped on the right side of the title bar.
Signed-in user	Name of the Windows 8 signed-in user.

Objective 3 | Enter, Edit, and Check the Spelling of Text in an Office 2013 Program

Video OF1-3

All of the programs in Office 2013 require some typed text. Your keyboard is still the primary method of entering information into your computer. Techniques to enter text and to *edit*—make changes to—text are similar among all of the Office 2013 programs.

Activity 1.03 | Entering and Editing Text in an Office 2013 Program

1 On the ribbon, on the HOME tab, in the Paragraph group, if necessary, click Show/Hide ¶ so that it is active—shaded. If necessary, on the VIEW tab, in the Show group, select the Ruler check box so that rulers display below the ribbon and on the left side of your window.

The *insertion point*—a blinking vertical line that indicates where text or graphics will be inserted—displays. In Office 2013 programs, the mouse *pointer*—any symbol that displays on your screen in response to moving your mouse device—displays in different shapes depending on the task you are performing and the area of the screen to which you are pointing.

When you press Enter, Spacebar, or Tab on your keyboard, characters display to represent these keystrokes. These screen characters do not print and are referred to as *formatting marks* or *nonprinting characters*.

NOTE | **Activating Show/Hide in Word Documents**

When Show/Hide is active—the button is shaded—formatting marks display. Because formatting marks guide your eye in a document—like a map and road signs guide you along a highway—these marks will display throughout this instruction. Many expert Word users keep these marks displayed while creating documents.

2 Type **Skyline Grille Info** and notice how the insertion point moves to the right as you type. Point slightly to the right of the letter *e* in *Grille* and click to place the insertion point there. Compare your screen with Figure 1.5.

> A *paragraph symbol* (¶) indicates the end of a paragraph and displays each time you press Enter. This is a type of formatting mark and does not print.

FIGURE 1.5

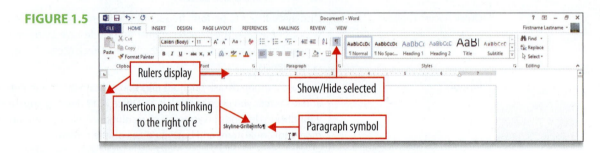

3 On your keyboard, locate and then press the Backspace key to delete the letter *e*.

> Pressing Backspace removes a character to the left of the insertion point.

4 Press → one time to place the insertion point to the left of the *I* in *Info*. Type **Chef's** and then press Spacebar one time.

> By *default*, when you type text in an Office program, existing text moves to the right to make space for new typing. Default refers to the current selection or setting that is automatically used by a program unless you specify otherwise.

5 Press Del four times to delete *Info* and then type **Notes**

> Pressing Del removes a character to the right of the insertion point.

6 With your insertion point blinking after the word *Notes*, on your keyboard, hold down the Ctrl key. While holding down Ctrl, press ← three times to move the insertion point to the beginning of the word *Grill*.

> This is a *keyboard shortcut*—a key or combination of keys that performs a task that would otherwise require a mouse. This keyboard shortcut moves the insertion point to the beginning of the previous word.

> A keyboard shortcut is commonly indicated as Ctrl + ← (or some other combination of keys) to indicate that you hold down the first key while pressing the second key. A keyboard shortcut can also include three keys, in which case you hold down the first two and then press the third. For example, Ctrl + Shift + ← selects one word to the left.

7 With the insertion point blinking at the beginning of the word *Grill*, type **Metro** and press Spacebar.

8 Press Ctrl + End to place the insertion point after the letter *s* in *Notes*, and then press Enter one time. With the insertion point blinking, type the following and include the spelling error:
Exective Chef, Madison Dunham

With your mouse, point slightly to the left of the *M* in *Madison*, hold down the left mouse button, and then **drag**—hold down the left mouse button while moving your mouse—to the right to select the text *Madison Dunham* but not the paragraph mark following it, and then release the mouse button. Compare your screen with Figure 1.6.

The **mini toolbar** displays commands that are commonly used with the selected object, which places common commands close to your pointer. When you move the pointer away from the mini toolbar, it fades from view.

Selecting refers to highlighting, by dragging or clicking with your mouse, areas of text or data or graphics so that the selection can be edited, formatted, copied, or moved. The action of dragging includes releasing the left mouse button at the end of the area you want to select.

The Office programs recognize a selected area as one unit to which you can make changes. Selecting text may require some practice. If you are not satisfied with your result, click anywhere outside of the selection, and then begin again.

BY TOUCH Tap once on *Madison* to display the gripper—small circle that acts as a handle—directly below the word. This establishes the start gripper. If necessary, with your finger, drag the gripper to the beginning of the word. Then drag the gripper to the end of Dunham to select the text and display the end gripper.

FIGURE 1.6

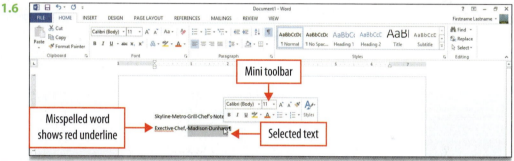

10 ▶ With the text *Madison Dunham* selected, type **Sarah Jackson**

In any Windows-based program, such as the Microsoft Office 2013 programs, selected text is deleted and then replaced when you begin to type new text. You will save time by developing good techniques for selecting and then editing or replacing selected text, which is easier than pressing the Del key numerous times to delete text.

Activity 1.04 │ Checking Spelling

Office 2013 has a dictionary of words against which all entered text is checked. In Word and PowerPoint, words that are not in the dictionary display a wavy red line, indicating a possible misspelled word or a proper name or an unusual word—none of which are in the Office 2013 dictionary.

In Excel and Access, you can initiate a check of the spelling, but red underlines do not display.

1 ▶ Notice that the misspelled word *Exective* displays with a wavy red underline.

2 ▶ Point to *Exective* and then **right-click**—click your right mouse button one time.

A **shortcut menu** displays, which displays commands and options relevant to the selected text or object. These are **context-sensitive commands** because they relate to the item you right-clicked. These types of menus are also referred to as **context menus**. Here, the shortcut menu displays commands related to the misspelled word.

BY TOUCH Tap and hold a moment to select the misspelled word, then release your finger to display the shortcut menu.

3 ▶ Press Esc to cancel the shortcut menu, and then in the lower left corner of your screen, on the **status bar**, click the **Proofing** icon ⬚ᵪ, which displays an *X* because some errors are detected. Compare your screen with Figure 1.7.

> The Spelling pane displays on the right. Here you have many more options for checking spelling than you have on the shortcut menu. The suggested correct word, *Executive*, is highlighted.
>
> You can click the speaker icon to hear the pronunciation of the selected word. You can also see some synonyms for *Executive*. Finally, if you have not already installed a dictionary, you can click *Get a Dictionary*—if you are signed in to Office with a Microsoft account—to find and install one from the online Office store; or if you have a dictionary app installed, it will display here and you can search it for more information.
>
> In the Spelling pane, you can ignore the word one time or in all occurrences, change the word to the suggested word, select a different suggestion, or add a word to the dictionary against which Word checks.

FIGURE 1.7

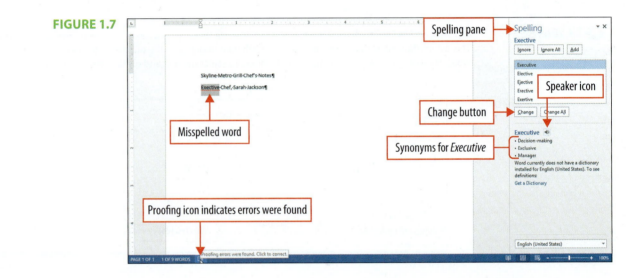

 ANOTHER WAY   Press F7 to display the Spelling pane; or, on the Review tab, in the Proofing group, click Spelling & Grammar.

4 ▶ In the **Spelling** pane, click **Change** to change the spelling to *Executive*. In the message box that displays, click **OK**.

Objective 4   Perform Commands from a Dialog Box

▶ **Video OF1-4**

In a dialog box, you make decisions about an individual object or topic. In some dialog boxes, you can make multiple decisions in one place.

Activity 1.05 | Performing Commands from a Dialog Box

1 ▶ On the ribbon, click the **DESIGN tab**, and then in the **Page Background group**, click **Page Color**.

2 ▶ At the bottom of the menu, notice the command **Fill Effects** followed by an **ellipsis** (…). Compare your screen with Figure 1.8.

> An *ellipsis* is a set of three dots indicating incompleteness. An ellipsis following a command name indicates that a dialog box will display when you click the command.

FIGURE 1.8

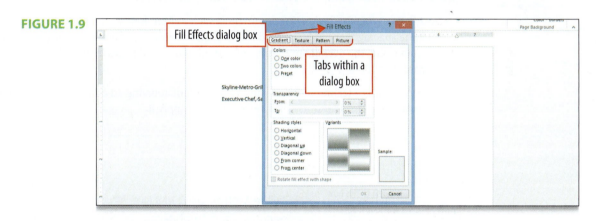

DESIGN tab active

Page Color button

Fill Effects followed by ellipsis

3 Click **Fill Effects** to display the **Fill Effects** dialog box. Compare your screen with Figure 1.9.

Fill is the inside color of a page or object. The Gradient tab is active. In a ***gradient fill***, one color fades into another. Here, the dialog box displays a set of tabs across the top from which you can display different sets of options. Some dialog boxes display the option group names on the left.

FIGURE 1.9

Fill Effects dialog box

Tabs within a dialog box

4 Under **Colors**, click the **One color** option button.

The dialog box displays settings related to the One color option. An ***option button*** is a round button that enables you to make one choice among two or more options.

5 Click the **Color 1 arrow**—the arrow under the text *Color 1*—and then in the third column, point to the second color to display the ScreenTip *Gray-25%, Background 2, Darker 10%*.

A ***ScreenTip*** displays useful information about mouse actions, such as pointing to screen elements or dragging.

6 Click **Gray-25%, Background 2, Darker 10%**, and then notice that the fill color displays in the **Color 1** box. In the **Dark Light** bar, click the **Light arrow** as many times as necessary until the scroll box is all the way to right. Under **Shading styles**, click the **Diagonal down** option button. Under **Variants**, click the upper right variant. Compare your screen with Figure 1.10.

FIGURE 1.10

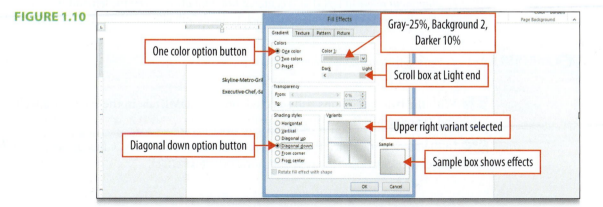

Gray-25%, Background 2, Darker 10%

One color option button

Scroll box at Light end

Diagonal down option button

Upper right variant selected

Sample box shows effects

BY TOUCH
In a dialog box, you can tap option buttons and other commands just as you would click them with a mouse. When you tap an arrow to display a color palette, a larger palette displays than if you used your mouse. This makes it easier to select colors in a dialog box.

7 At the bottom of the dialog box, click **OK**, and notice the subtle page color.

In Word, the gray shading page color will not print—even on a color printer—unless you set specific options to do so. However a subtle background page color is effective if people will be reading the document on a screen. Microsoft's research indicates that two-thirds of people who open Word documents never edit them; they only read them.

Activity 1.06 | Using Undo

1 Point to the *S* in *Skyline*, and then drag down and to the right to select both paragraphs of text and include the paragraph marks. On the mini toolbar, click **Styles,** and then *point to* but do not click **Title**. Compare your screen with Figure 1.11.

A *style* is a group of *formatting* commands, such as font, font size, font color, paragraph alignment, and line spacing that can be applied to a paragraph with one command. Formatting is the process of establishing the overall appearance of text, graphics, and pages in an Office file—for example, in a Word document.

Live Preview is a technology that shows the result of applying an editing or formatting change as you point to possible results—before you actually apply it.

FIGURE 1.11

Live Preview shows how style will look if applied

Title style

2 In the **Styles** gallery, click **Title**.

A *gallery* is an Office feature that displays a list of potential results.

3 On the ribbon, on the **HOME tab**, in the **Paragraph group**, click **Center** ☰ to center the two paragraphs.

Alignment refers to the placement of paragraph text relative to the left and right margins. *Center alignment* refers to text that is centered horizontally between the left and right margins. You can also align text at the left margin, which is the default alignment for text in Word, or at the right.

 ANOTHER WAY
Press Ctrl + E to use the Center command.

4 With the two paragraphs still selected, on the **HOME tab**, in the **Font Group**, click **Text Effects and Typography** Ⓐ ▾ to display a gallery.

5 In the second row, click the first effect—**Gradient Fill – Gray**. Click anywhere to *deselect*—cancel the selection—the text and notice the text effect.

6 Because this effect might be difficult to read, in the upper left corner of your screen, on the **Quick Access Toolbar**, click **Undo** ⟲.

The **Undo** command reverses your last action.

🔄 **ANOTHER WAY**   Press Ctrl + Z as the keyboard shortcut for the Undo command.

7 Display the **Text Effects and Typography** gallery again, and then in the second row, click the second effect—**Gradient Fill – Blue, Accent 1, Reflection**. Click anywhere to deselect the text and notice the text effect. Compare your screen with Figure 1.12.

As you progress in your study of Microsoft Office, you will practice using many dialog boxes and applying interesting effects such as this to your Word documents, Excel worksheets, Access database objects, and PowerPoint slides.

FIGURE 1.12

Text formatted with blue reflective text effect → Skyline·Metro·Grill·Chef's·Notes¶
Executive·Chef·Sarah·Jackson¶

Gray page fill effects →

Objective 5   Create a Folder and Name and Save a File

Video OF1-5

A *location* is any disk drive, folder, or other place in which you can store files and folders. Where you store your files depends on how and where you use your data. For example, for your college classes, you might decide to store on a removable USB flash drive so that you can carry your files to different locations and access your files on different computers.

If you do most of your work on a single computer, for example your home desktop system or your laptop computer that you take with you to school or work, then you can store your files in one of the Libraries—Documents, Music, Pictures, or Videos—that the Windows 8 operating system creates on your hard drive.

The best place to store files if you want them to be available anytime, anywhere, from almost any device is on your *SkyDrive*, which is Microsoft's free *cloud storage* for anyone with a free Microsoft account. Cloud storage refers to online storage of data so that you can access your data from different places and devices. *Cloud computing* refers to applications and services that are accessed over the Internet, rather than to applications that are installed on your local computer.

Because many people now have multiple computing devices—desktop, laptop, tablet, smartphone—it is common to store data *in the cloud* so that it is always available. *Synchronization*, also called *syncing*—pronounced SINK-ing—is the process of updating computer files that are in two or more locations according to specific rules. So if you create and save a Word document on your SkyDrive using your laptop, you can open and edit that document on your tablet. And then when you close the document again, the file is properly updated to reflect your changes.

You need not be connected to the Internet to access documents stored on SkyDrive because an up-to-date version of your content is synched to your local system and available on SkyDrive. You must, however, be connected to the Internet for the syncing to occur. Saving to SkyDrive will keep the local copy on your computer and the copy in the cloud synchronized for as long as you need it. If you open and edit on a different computer, log into the SkyDrive website, and then edit using Office 2013, Office 2010, or the **Office Web Apps**, you can save any changes back to SkyDrive. Office Web Apps are the free online companions to Microsoft Word, Excel, PowerPoint, Access, and OneNote. These changes will be synchronized back to any of your computers that run the SkyDrive for Windows application, which you get for free simply by logging in with your Microsoft account at skydrive.com.

The Windows operating system helps you to create and maintain a logical folder structure, so always take the time to name your files and folders consistently.

Activity 1.07 | Creating a Folder and Naming and Saving a File

A Word document is an example of a file. In this activity, you will create a folder on your USB flash drive in which to store your files. If you prefer to store on your SkyDrive or in the Documents library on your hard drive, you can use similar steps.

1 If necessary, insert your **USB flash drive** into your computer.

As the first step in saving a file, determine where you want to save the file, and if necessary, insert a storage device.

2 At the top of your screen, in the title bar, notice that *Document1 – Word* displays.

The Blank option on the opening screen of an Office 2013 program displays a new unsaved file with a default name—*Document1, Presentation1*, and so on. As you create your file, your work is temporarily stored in the computer's memory until you initiate a Save command, at which time you must choose a file name and a location in which to save your file.

3 In the upper left corner of your screen, click the **FILE tab** to display **Backstage** view. Compare your screen with Figure 1.13.

Backstage view is a centralized space that groups commands related to *file* management; that is why the tab is labeled *FILE*. File management commands include opening, saving, printing, publishing, or sharing a file. The **Backstage tabs**—*Info, New, Open, Save, Save As, Print, Share, Export,* and *Close*—display along the left side. The tabs group file-related tasks together.

Here, the **Info tab** displays information—*info*—about the current file, and file management commands display under Info. For example, if you click the Protect Document button, a list of options that you can set for this file that relate to who can open or edit the document displays.

On the right, you can also examine the **document properties**. Document properties, also known as **metadata**, are details about a file that describe or identify it, such as the title, author name, subject, and keywords that identify the document's topic or contents. To close Backstage view and return to the document, you can click ⊙ in the upper left corner or press [Esc].

FIGURE 1.13

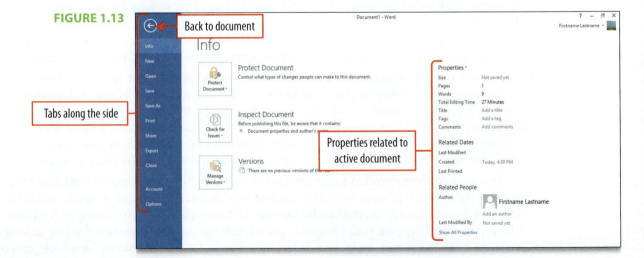

4 On the left, click **Save As**, and notice that the default location for storing Office files is your **SkyDrive**—if you are signed in. Compare your screen with Figure 1.14.

> When you are saving something for the first time, for example a new Word document, the Save and Save As commands are identical. That is, the Save As commands will display if you click Save or if you click Save As.

FIGURE 1.14

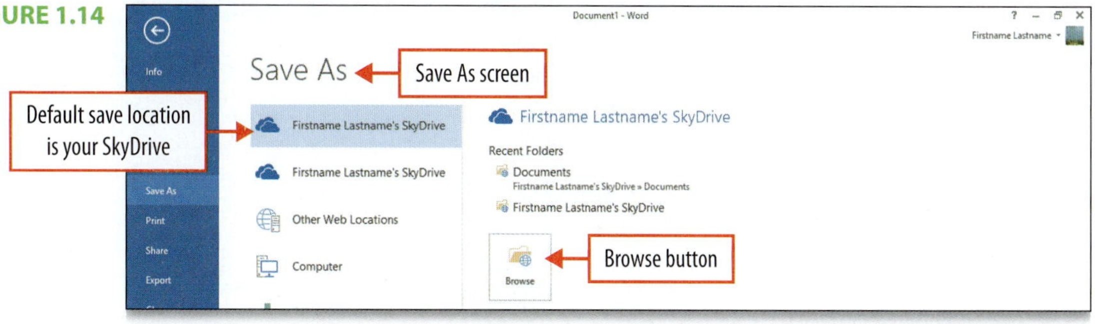

NOTE   **Saving after Your File Is Named**

After you name and save a file, the Save command on the Quick Access Toolbar saves any changes you make to the file without displaying Backstage view. The Save As command enables you to name and save a *new* file based on the current one—in a location that you choose. After you name and save the new document, the original document closes, and the new document—based on the original one—displays.

---

5 To store your Word file on your **USB flash drive**—instead of your SkyDrive—click the **Browse** button to display the **Save As** dialog box. On the left, in the navigation pane, scroll down, and then under **Computer**, click the name of your **USB flash drive**. Compare your screen with Figure 1.15.

> In the Save As dialog box, you must indicate the name you want for the file and the location where you want to save the file. When working with your own data, it is good practice to pause at this point and determine the logical name and location for your file.

> In the Save As dialog box, a ***toolbar*** displays. This is a row, column, or block of buttons or icons, that usually displays across the top of a window and that contains commands for tasks you perform with a single click.

FIGURE 1.15

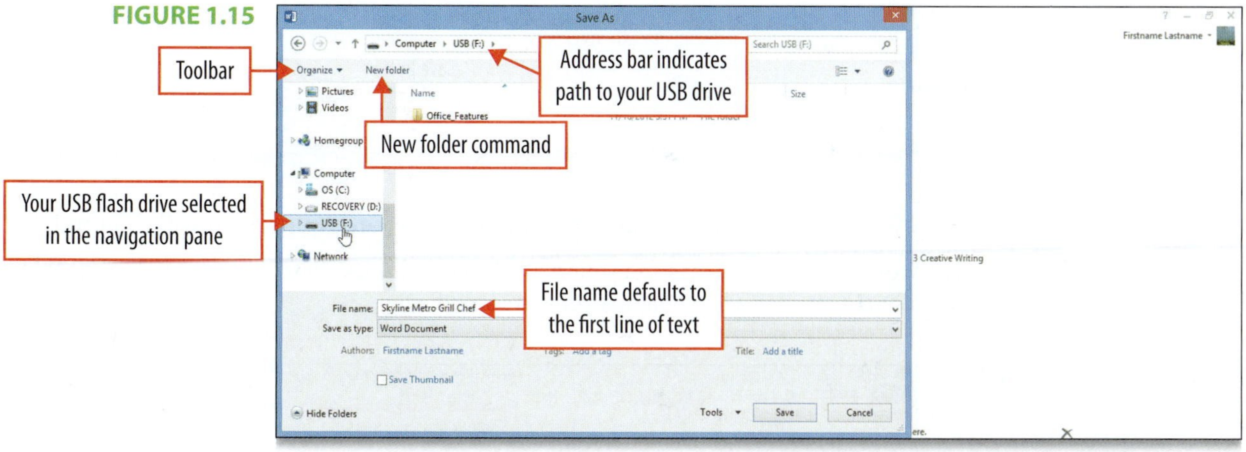

6 On the toolbar, click **New folder**.

In the file list, Word creates a new folder, and the text *New folder* is selected.

7 Type **Office Features Chapter 1** and press Enter. Compare your screen with Figure 1.16.

In Windows-based programs, the Enter key confirms an action.

FIGURE 1.16

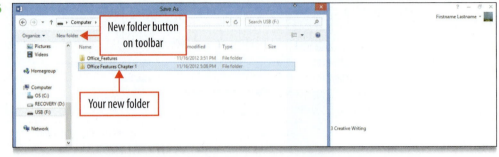

8 In the **file list**, double-click the name of your new folder to open it and display its name in the **address bar**.

9 In the lower portion of the dialog box, click in the **File name** box to select the existing text. Notice that Office inserts the text at the beginning of the document as a suggested file name.

10 On your keyboard, locate the hyphen — key. Notice that the Shift of this key produces the underscore character. With the text still selected and using your own name, type **Lastname_Firstname_1A_Note_Form** and then compare your screen with Figure 1.17.

You can use spaces in file names, however, some people prefer not to use spaces. Some programs, especially when transferring files over the Internet, may insert the extra characters *%20* in place of a space. This can happen in *SharePoint*, so using underscores instead of spaces can be a good habit to adopt. SharePoint is Microsoft's collaboration software with which people in an organization can set up team sites to share information, manage documents, and publish reports for others to see. In general, however, unless you encounter a problem, it is OK to use spaces. In this textbook, underscores are used instead of spaces in file names.

FIGURE 1.17

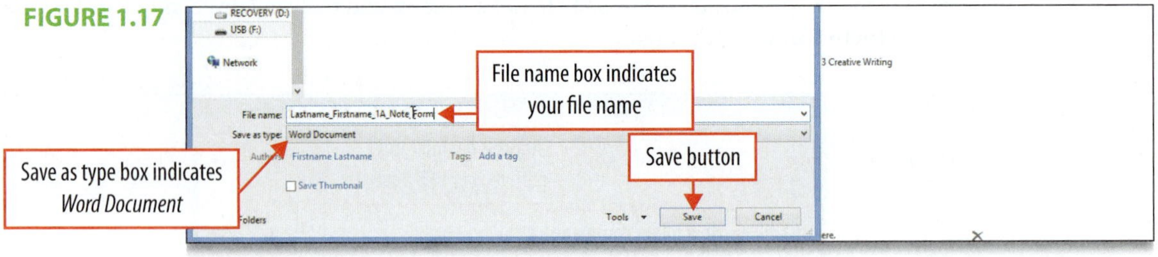

| Save as type box indicates *Word Document* | File name box indicates your file name | Save button |

11 In the lower right corner, click **Save** or press Enter. Compare your screen with Figure 1.18.

The Word window redisplays and your new file name displays in the title bar, indicating that the file has been saved to a location that you have specified.

FIGURE 1.18

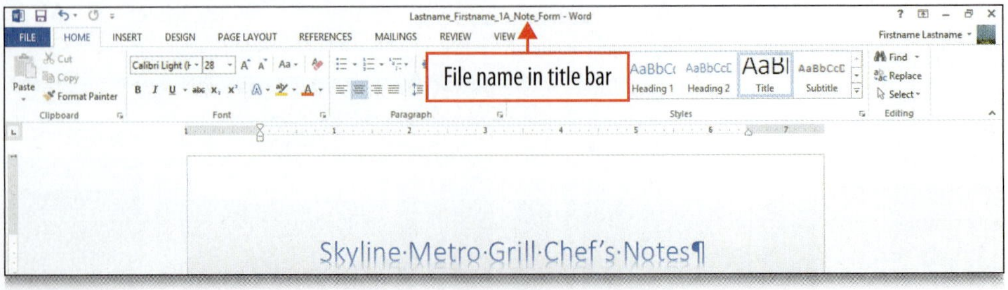

File name in title bar

Skyline·Metro·Grill·Chef's·Notes¶

12 In the first paragraph, click to place the insertion point after the word *Grill* and type **,** (a comma). In the upper left corner of your screen, on the **Quick Access Toolbar**, click **Save** 🖫.

> After a document is named and saved in a location, you can save any changes you have made since the last Save operation by using the Save command on the Quick Access Toolbar. When working on a document, it is good practice to save your changes from time to time.

Objective 6 Insert a Footer, Add Document Properties, Print a File, and Close a Desktop App

Video OF1-6

For most of your files, especially in a workplace setting, it is useful to add identifying information to help in finding files later. You might also want to print your file on paper or create an electronic printout. The process of printing a file is similar in all of the Office applications.

Activity 1.08 | **Inserting a Footer, Inserting Document Info, and Adding Document Properties**

> **N O T E** **Are You Printing or Submitting Your Files Electronically?**
>
> In this activity, you can either produce a paper printout or create an electronic file to submit to your instructor if required.

1 On the ribbon, click the **INSERT tab**, and then in the **Header & Footer group**, click **Footer**.

2 At the bottom of the list, click **Edit Footer**. On the ribbon, notice that the **HEADER & FOOTER TOOLS** display.

> The *Header & Footer Tools Design* tab displays on the ribbon. The ribbon adapts to your work and will display additional tabs like this one—referred to as **contextual tabs**—when you need them.
>
> A **footer** is a reserved area for text or graphics that displays at the bottom of each page in a document. Likewise, a **header** is a reserved area for text or graphics that displays at the top of each page in a document. When the footer (or header) area is active, the document area is dimmed, indicating it is unavailable.

3 On the ribbon, under **HEADER & FOOTER TOOLS**, on the **DESIGN tab**, in the **Insert group**, click **Document Info**, and then click **File Name** to insert the name of your file in the footer, which is a common business practice. Compare your screen with Figure 1.19.

> Ribbon commands that display ▼ will, when clicked, display a list of options for the command.

FIGURE 1.19

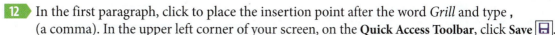

Callouts: HEADER & FOOTER TOOLS on ribbon; DESIGN tab added; Document Info button; arrow indicates more options available; Close Header and Footer button; Footer area with your file name

Lastname_Firstname_1A_Note_Form

4 At the right end of the ribbon, click **Close Header and Footer**.

ANOTHER WAY Double-click anywhere in the dimmed document to close the footer.

5 Click the **FILE tab** to display **Backstage** view. On the right, at the bottom of the **Properties** list, click **Show All Properties**.

ANOTHER WAY Click the arrow to the right of Properties, and then click Show Document Panel to show and edit properties at the top of your document window.

6 On the list of **Properties**, click to the right of **Tags** to display an empty box, and then type **chef, notes, form**

> *Tags*, also referred to as *keywords*, are custom file properties in the form of words that you associate with a document to give an indication of the document's content. Adding tags to your documents makes it easier to search for and locate files in File Explorer and in systems such as Microsoft SharePoint document libraries.

BY TOUCH Tap to the right of Tags to display the Tags box and the onscreen keyboard.

7 Click to the right of **Subject** to display an empty box, and then type your course name and section #; for example *CIS 10, #5543*.

8 Under **Related People**, be sure that your name displays as the author. If necessary, right-click the author name, click Edit Property, type your name, click outside of the Edit person dialog box, and then click OK. Compare your screen with Figure 1.20.

FIGURE 1.20

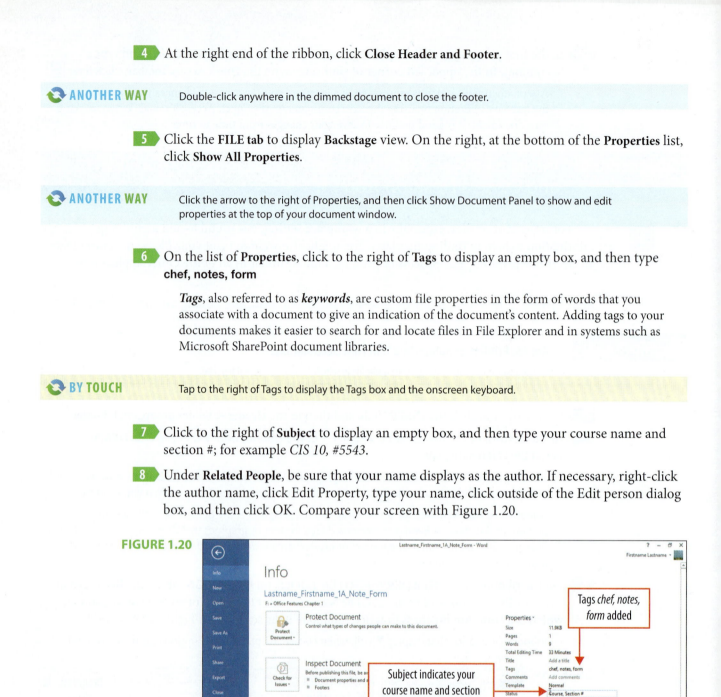

Activity 1.09 | Printing a File and Closing a Desktop App

1 On the left, click **Print**, and then compare your screen with Figure 1.21.

Here you can select any printer connected to your system and adjust the settings related to how you want to print. On the right, the *Print Preview* displays, which is a view of a document as it will appear on paper when you print it.

At the bottom of the Print Preview area, in the center, the number of pages and page navigation arrows with which you can move among the pages in Print Preview display. On the right, the Zoom slider enables you to shrink or enlarge the Print Preview. *Zoom* is the action of increasing or decreasing the viewing area of the screen.

ANOTHER WAY   From the document screen, press Ctrl + P or Ctrl + F2 to display Print in Backstage view.

FIGURE 1.21

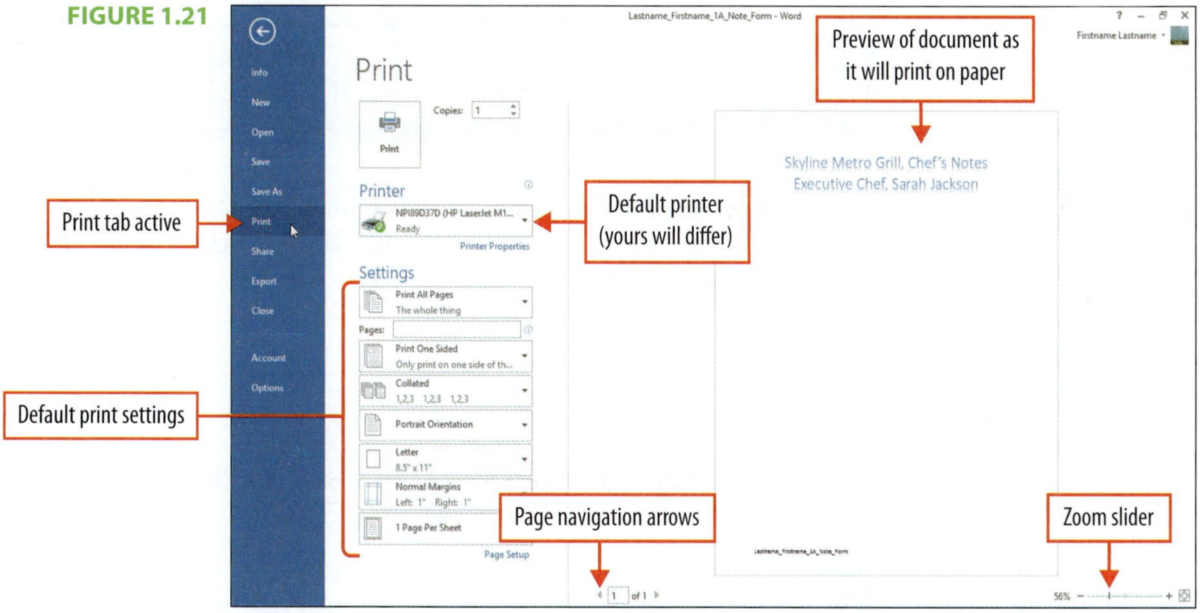

2 To submit your file electronically, skip this step and continue to Step 3. To print your document on paper using the default printer on your system, in the upper left portion of the screen, click the **Print** button.

The document will print on your default printer; if you do not have a color printer, the blue text will print in shades of gray. The gray page color you applied to the document does not display in Print Preview nor does it print unless you specifically adjust some of Word's options. Backstage view closes and your file redisplays in the Word window.

3 To create an electronic file, on the left click **Export**. On the right, click the **Create PDF/XPS** button to display the **Publish as PDF or XPS** dialog box.

PDF stands for *Portable Document Format*, which is a technology that creates an image that preserves the look of your file. This is a popular format for sending documents electronically, because the document will display on most computers.

XPS stands for *XML Paper Specification*—a Microsoft file format that also creates an image of your document and that opens in the XPS viewer.

4 On the left in the **navigation pane**, if necessary expand ▷ Computer, and then navigate to your **Office Features Chapter 1** folder on your **USB flash drive**. Compare your screen with Figure 1.22.

FIGURE 1.22

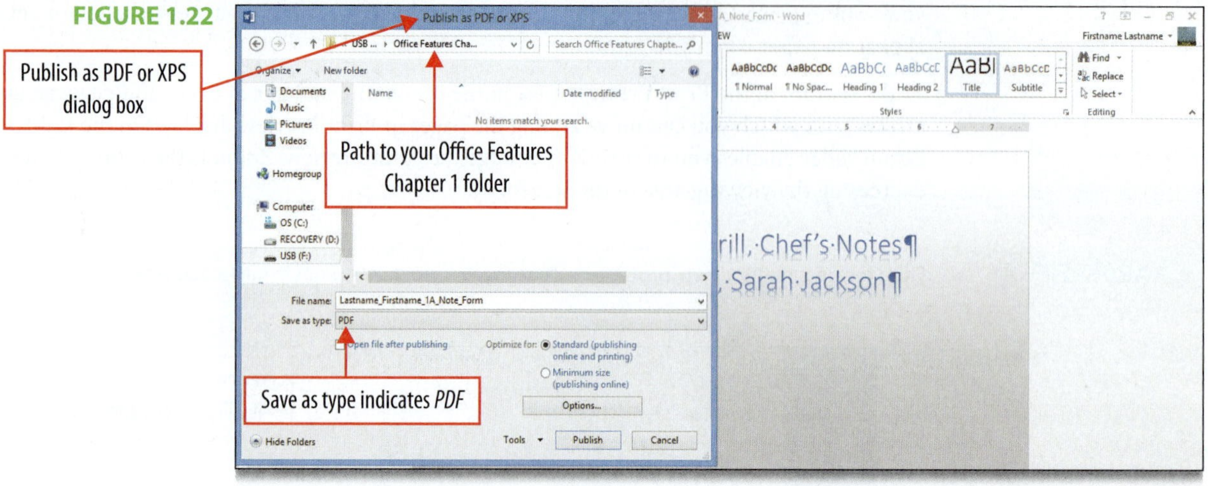

Publish as PDF or XPS dialog box

Path to your Office Features Chapter 1 folder

Save as type indicates *PDF*

5 In the lower right corner of the dialog box, click **Publish**; if your Adobe Acrobat or Adobe Reader program displays your PDF, in the upper right corner, click Close ☒. Notice that your document redisplays in Word.

↻ **ANOTHER WAY**   In Backstage view, click Save As, navigate to the location of your Chapter folder, click the Save as type arrow, on the list click PDF, and then click Save.

6 Click the **FILE tab** to redisplay **Backstage** view. On the left, click **Close**, if necessary click Save, and then compare your screen with Figure 1.23.

FIGURE 1.23

Word window with all documents closed

Close button

7 In the upper right corner of the Word window, click **Close** ☒. If directed by your instructor to do so, submit your paper or electronic file.

END | You have completed Project 1A

Memo

PROJECT ACTIVITIES

In Activities 1.10 through 1.21, you will open, edit, and then compress a Word file. You will also use the Office Help system and install an app for Office. Your completed document will look similar to Figure 1.24.

PROJECT FILES

For Project 1B, you will need the following file:

of01B_Rehearsal_Dinner

You will save your file as:

Lastname_Firstname_1B_Rehearsal_Dinner

PROJECT RESULTS

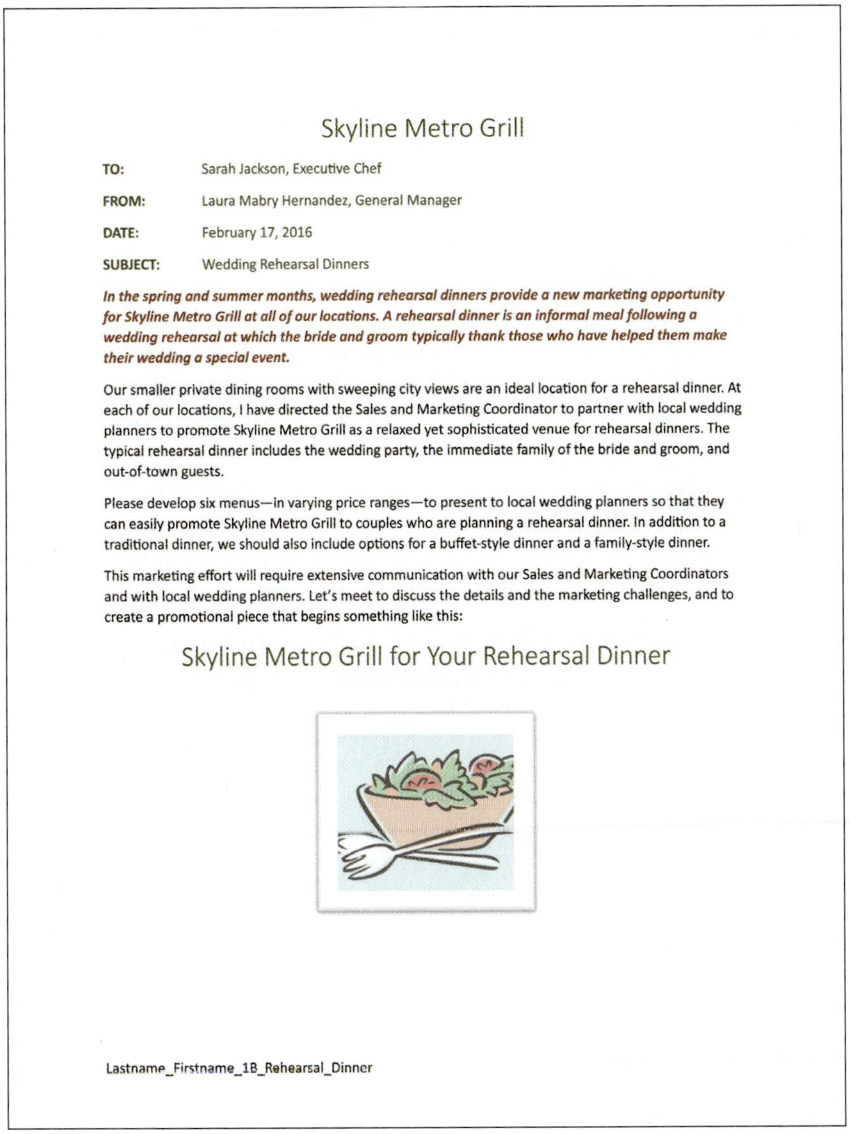

Skyline Metro Grill

TO:	Sarah Jackson, Executive Chef
FROM:	Laura Mabry Hernandez, General Manager
DATE:	February 17, 2016
SUBJECT:	Wedding Rehearsal Dinners

In the spring and summer months, wedding rehearsal dinners provide a new marketing opportunity for Skyline Metro Grill at all of our locations. A rehearsal dinner is an informal meal following a wedding rehearsal at which the bride and groom typically thank those who have helped them make their wedding a special event.

Our smaller private dining rooms with sweeping city views are an ideal location for a rehearsal dinner. At each of our locations, I have directed the Sales and Marketing Coordinator to partner with local wedding planners to promote Skyline Metro Grill as a relaxed yet sophisticated venue for rehearsal dinners. The typical rehearsal dinner includes the wedding party, the immediate family of the bride and groom, and out-of-town guests.

Please develop six menus—in varying price ranges—to present to local wedding planners so that they can easily promote Skyline Metro Grill to couples who are planning a rehearsal dinner. In addition to a traditional dinner, we should also include options for a buffet-style dinner and a family-style dinner.

This marketing effort will require extensive communication with our Sales and Marketing Coordinators and with local wedding planners. Let's meet to discuss the details and the marketing challenges, and to create a promotional piece that begins something like this:

Skyline Metro Grill for Your Rehearsal Dinner

Lastname_Firstname_1B_Rehearsal_Dinner

FIGURE 1.24 Project 1B Memo

Video OF1-7

In any Office program, you can display the **Open dialog box**, from which you can navigate to and then open an existing file that was created in that same program.

The Open dialog box, along with the Save and Save As dialog boxes, is a common dialog box. These dialog boxes, which are provided by the Windows programming interface, display in all Office programs in the same manner. So the Open, Save, and Save As dialog boxes will all look and perform the same regardless of the Office program in which you are working.

Activity 1.10 | Opening an Existing File and Saving It with a New Name

In this activity, you will display the Open dialog box, open an existing Word document, and then save it in your storage location with a new name.

1 Sign in to your computer, and then on the Windows 8 Start screen, type **word 2013** Press Enter to open Word on your desktop. If you want to do so, on the taskbar, right-click the **Word icon**, and then click **Pin this program to taskbar** to keep the Word program available from your desktop.

2 On Word's opening screen, on the left, click **Open Other Documents**. Under **Open**, click **Computer**, and then on the right click **Browse**.

3 In the **Open** dialog box, on the left in the **navigation pane**, scroll down, if necessary expand ▷ Computer, and then click the name of your **USB flash drive**. In the **file list**, double-click the **Office_Features** folder that you downloaded.

4 Double-click **of01B_Rehearsal_Dinner**. If **PROTECTED VIEW** displays at the top of your screen, in the center click **Enable Editing**.

In Office 2013, a file will open in **Protected View** if the file appears to be from a potentially risky location, such as the Internet. Protected View is a security feature in Office 2013 that protects your computer from malicious files by opening them in a restricted environment until you enable them. **Trusted Documents** is another security feature that remembers which files you have already enabled.

You might encounter these security features if you open a file from an email or download files from the Internet; for example, from your college's learning management system or from the Pearson website. So long as you trust the source of the file, click Enable Editing or Enable Content—depending on the type of file you receive—and then go ahead and work with the file.

5 With the document displayed in the Word window, be sure that **Show/Hide** is active; if necessary, on the HOME tab, in the Paragraph group, click Show/Hide to activate it. Compare your screen with Figure 1.25.

FIGURE 1.25

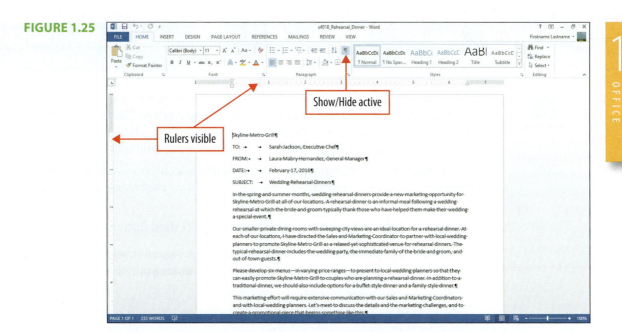

Show/Hide active

Rulers visible

6 ▸ Click the **FILE tab** to display **Backstage** view, and then on the left, click **Save As**. On the right, click the folder under **Current Folder** to open the **Save As** dialog box. Notice that the current folder is the **Office_Features** folder you downloaded.

🔄 **ANOTHER WAY**   Press [F12] to display the Save As dialog box.

7 ▸ In the upper left corner of the **Save As** dialog box, click the **Up** button ⬆ to move up one level in the File Explorer hierarchy. In the **file list**, double-click your **Office Features Chapter 1** folder to open it.

8 ▸ Click in the **File name** box to select the existing text, and then, using your own name, type **Lastname_Firstname_1B_Rehearsal_Dinner** Compare your screen with Figure 1.26.

FIGURE 1.26

Save As dialog box

Up button

Path to your folder on your USB flash drive

File name (your own name displays)

9 ▸ Click **Save** or press [Enter]; notice that your new file name displays in the title bar.

The original document closes, and your new document, based on the original, displays with the name in the title bar.

More Knowledge   **Read-Only**

Some files might display **Read-Only** in the title bar, which is a property assigned to a file that prevents the file from being modified or deleted; it indicates that you cannot save any changes to the displayed document unless you first save it with a new name.

Objective 8 Sign In to Office and Explore Options for a Microsoft Office Desktop App

Video OF1-8

If you sign in to Windows 8 with a Microsoft account, you may notice that you are also signed in to Office. This enables you to save files to and retrieve files from your SkyDrive and to ***collaborate*** with others on Office files when you want to do so. To collaborate means to work with others as a team in an intellectual endeavor to complete a shared task or to achieve a shared goal.

Within each Office application, an ***Options dialog box*** enables you to select program settings and other options and preferences. For example, you can set preferences for viewing and editing files.

Activity 1.11 | Signing In to Office and Viewing Application Options

1 In the upper right corner of your screen, if you are signed in with a Microsoft account, click the arrow to the right of your name, and then compare your screen with Figure 1.27.

Here you can change your photo, go to About me to edit your profile, examine your Account settings, or switch accounts to sign in with a different Microsoft account.

FIGURE 1.27

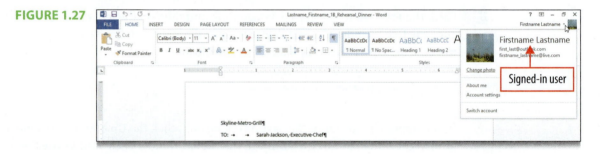

2 Click the **FILE tab** to display **Backstage** view. On the left, click the last tab—**Options**.

3 In the **Word Options** dialog box, on the left, click **Display**, and then on the right, locate the information under **Always show these formatting marks on the screen**.

4 Under **Always show these formatting marks on the screen**, be sure the last check box, **Show all formatting marks**, is selected—select it if necessary. Compare your screen with Figure 1.28.

FIGURE 1.28

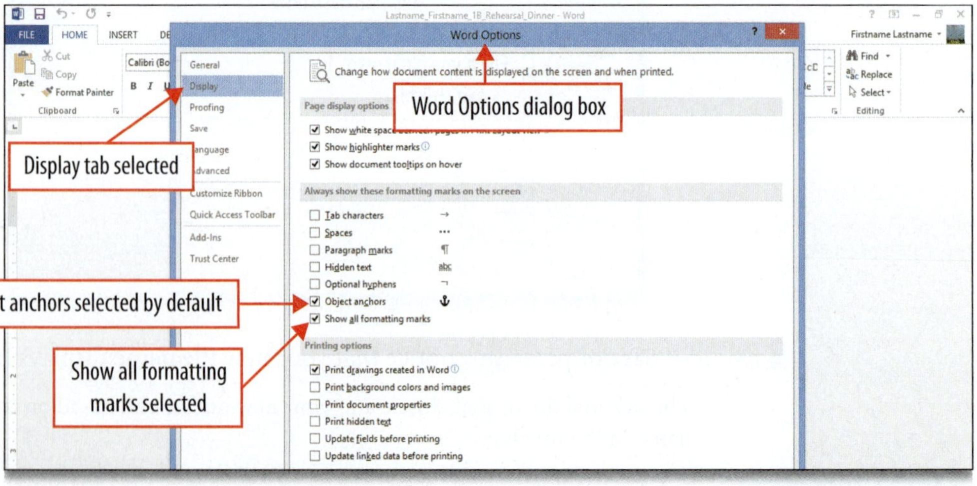

5 In the lower right corner of the dialog box, click **OK**.

Video OF1-9

The ribbon that displays across the top of the program window groups commands in a manner that you would most logically use them. The ribbon in each Office program is slightly different, but all contain the same three elements: ***tabs***, ***groups***, and ***commands***.

Tabs display across the top of the ribbon, and each tab relates to a type of activity; for example, laying out a page. Groups are sets of related commands for specific tasks. Commands—instructions to computer programs—are arranged in groups and might display as a button, a menu, or a box in which you type information.

You can also minimize the ribbon so only the tab names display, which is useful when working on a smaller screen such as a tablet computer where you want to maximize your screen viewing area.

Activity 1.12 | Performing Commands from and Customizing the Ribbon and the Quick Access Toolbar

1 Take a moment to examine the document on your screen. If necessary, on the ribbon, click the VIEW tab, and then in the Show group, click to place a check mark in the Ruler check box. Compare your screen with Figure 1.29.

This document is a memo from the General Manager to the Executive Chef regarding a new restaurant promotion for wedding rehearsal dinners.

When working in Word, display the rulers so that you can see how margin settings affect your document and how text and objects align. Additionally, if you set a tab stop or an indent, its location is visible on the ruler.

FIGURE 1.29

Ruler checkbox selected

VIEW tab active

Show group

Rulers display

2 In the upper left corner of your screen, above the ribbon, locate the **Quick Access Toolbar**.

Recall that the Quick Access Toolbar contains commands that you use frequently. By default, only the commands Save, Undo, and Redo display, but you can add and delete commands to suit your needs. Possibly the computer at which you are working already has additional commands added to the Quick Access Toolbar.

3 At the end of the **Quick Access Toolbar**, click the **Customize Quick Access Toolbar** button ⏷, and then compare your screen with Figure 1.30.

A list of commands that Office users commonly add to their Quick Access Toolbar displays, including New, Open, Email, Quick Print, and Print Preview and Print. Commands already on the Quick Access Toolbar display a check mark. Commands that you add to the Quick Access Toolbar are always just one click away.

Here you can also display the More Commands dialog box, from which you can select any command from any tab on the ribbon to add to the Quick Access Toolbar.

BY TOUCH   Tap once on Quick Access Toolbar commands.

FIGURE 1.30

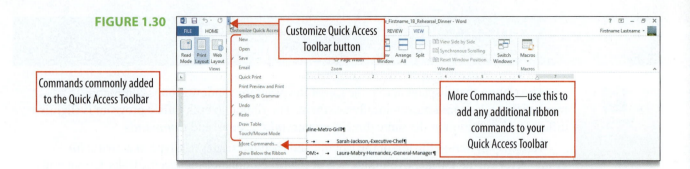

Customize Quick Access Toolbar button

Commands commonly added to the Quick Access Toolbar

More Commands—use this to add any additional ribbon commands to your Quick Access Toolbar

4 ▸ On the list, click **Print Preview and Print**, and then notice that the icon is added to the **Quick Access Toolbar**. Compare your screen with Figure 1.31.

The icon that represents the Print Preview command displays on the Quick Access Toolbar. Because this is a command that you will use frequently while building Office documents, you might decide to have this command remain on your Quick Access Toolbar.

🔄 **ANOTHER WAY**   Right-click any command on the ribbon, and then on the shortcut menu, click Add to Quick Access Toolbar.

FIGURE 1.31

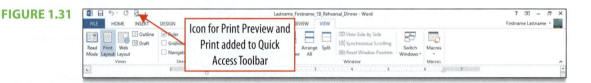

Icon for Print Preview and Print added to Quick Access Toolbar

5 ▸ In the first line of the document, if necessary, click to the left of the *S* in *Skyline* to position the insertion point there, and then press Enter one time to insert a blank paragraph. Press ↑ one time to position the insertion point in the new blank paragraph. Compare your screen with Figure 1.32.

FIGURE 1.32

Insertion point blinking in new blank paragraph

6 ▸ On the ribbon, click the **INSERT tab**. In the **Illustrations group**, *point* to the **Online Pictures** button to display its ScreenTip.

Many buttons on the ribbon have this type of *enhanced ScreenTip*, which displays useful descriptive information about the command.

7 ▸ Click **Online Pictures**, and then compare your screen with Figure 1.33.

In the Insert Pictures dialog box you can search for online pictures using Microsoft's Clip Art collection. *Clip art* refers to royalty-free photos and illustrations you can download from Microsoft's Office.com site.

Here you can also search for images using the Bing search engine, and if you are signed in with your Microsoft account, you can also find images on your SkyDrive or on your computer by clicking Browse. At the bottom, you can click the Flickr logo and download pictures from your Flickr account if you have one.

FIGURE 1.33

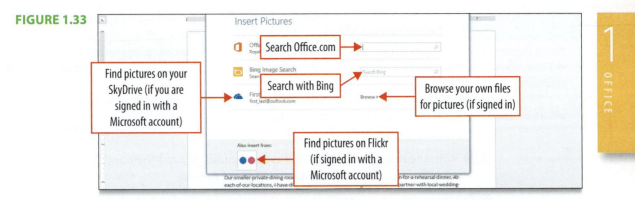

8 ▶ Click **Office.com Clip Art** and in the box that displays to the right, type **salad in a bowl** and press Enter. As shown in Figure 1.34, point to the illustration of the salad bowl to display its keywords.

> You can use various keywords to find clip art that is appropriate for your documents.

FIGURE 1.34

9 ▶ Click the illustration of the salad to select it, and then in the lower right corner, click **Insert**. In the upper right corner of the picture, point to the **Layout Options** button 📷 to display its ScreenTip, and then compare your screen with Figure 1.35. If you cannot find the image, select a similar image, and then drag one of the corner sizing handles to match the approximate size shown in the figure.

> Inserted pictures anchor—attach to—the paragraph at the insertion point location—as indicated by the anchor symbol. *Layout Options* enable you to choose how the *object*—in this instance an inserted picture—interacts with the surrounding text. An object is a picture or other graphic such as a chart or table that you can select and then move and resize.

> When a picture is selected, the PICTURE TOOLS become available on the ribbon. Additionally, *sizing handles*—small squares that indicate an object is selected—surround the selected picture.

FIGURE 1.35

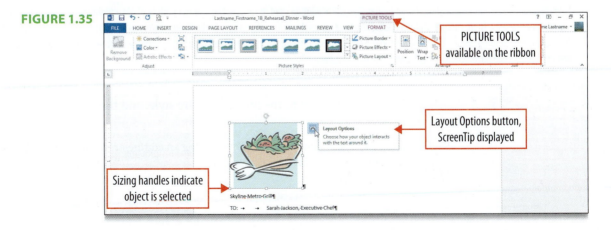

More Knowledge   **Customizing the Ribbon**

You can customize the ribbon in any Office application to make it the way you want it. To do so, right-click in any empty space on the ribbon, and then click Customize the Ribbon. Click the Choose commands from arrow, and then select the commands you want to see in the list below. For example click All Commands to see every command available.

On the left, click the Customize the Ribbon arrow, click the set of tabs you want to customize, for example the Main Tabs, and then use the list below to add, remove, rename, and reorder tabs, groups, and commands.

10 ▶ With the image selected, click **Layout Options** 🖼, and then under **With Text Wrapping**, in the second row, click the first layout—**Top and Bottom**.

11 ▶ Point to the image to display the 🔀 pointer, hold down the left mouse button to display a green line at the left margin, and then drag the image to the right and slightly upward until a green line displays in the center of the image and at the top of the image, as shown in Figure 1.36, and then release the left mouse button. If you are not satisfied with your result, on the Quick Access Toolbar, click Undo 🔄 and begin again.

Alignment Guides are green lines that display to help you align objects with margins or at the center of a page.

FIGURE 1.36

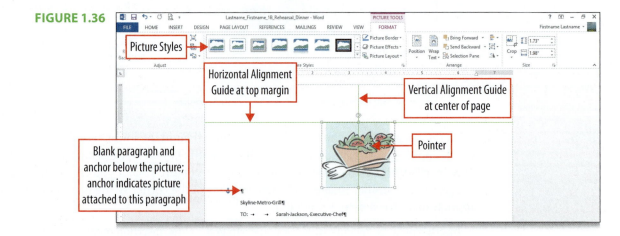

12 ▶ On the ribbon, in the **Picture Styles group**, point to the first style to display the ScreenTip *Simple Frame, White,* and notice that the image displays with a white frame.

N O T E   **The Size of Groups on the Ribbon Varies with Screen Resolution**

Your monitor's screen resolution might be set higher than the resolution used to capture the figures in this book. At a higher resolution, the ribbon expands some groups to show more commands than are available with a single click, such as those in the Picture Styles group. Or, the group expands to add descriptive text to some buttons, such as those in the Adjust group. Regardless of your screen resolution, all Office commands are available to you. In higher resolutions, you will have a more robust view of the ribbon commands.

13 ▶ Watch the image as you point to the second picture style, and then to the third, and then to the fourth.

Recall that Live Preview shows the result of applying an editing or formatting change as you point to possible results—*before* you actually apply it.

14 In the **Picture Styles group**, click the second style—**Beveled Matte, White**—and then click anywhere outside of the image to deselect it. Notice that the *PICTURE TOOLS* no longer display on the ribbon. Compare your screen with Figure 1.37.

Contextual tabs on the ribbon display only when you need them.

FIGURE 1.37

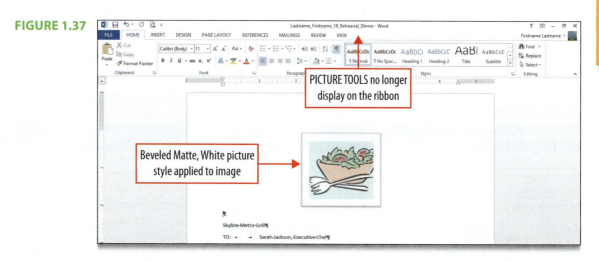

15 On the **Quick Access Toolbar**, click **Save** to save the changes you have made.

Activity 1.13 | Minimizing and Using the Keyboard to Control the Ribbon

Instead of a mouse, some individuals prefer to navigate the ribbon by using keys on the keyboard.

1 On your keyboard, press Alt, and then on the ribbon, notice that small labels display. Press N to activate the commands on the **INSERT tab**, and then compare your screen with Figure 1.38.

Each label represents a *KeyTip*—an indication of the key that you can press to activate the command. For example, on the INSERT tab, you can press F to open the Online Pictures dialog box.

FIGURE 1.38

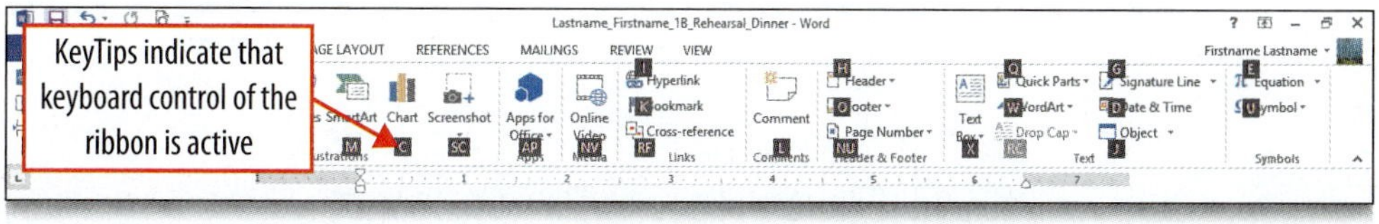

2 Press Esc to redisplay the KeyTips for the tabs. Then, press Alt or Esc again to turn off keyboard control of the ribbon.

3 Point to any tab on the ribbon and right-click to display a shortcut menu.

Here you can choose to display the Quick Access Toolbar below the ribbon or collapse the ribbon to maximize screen space. You can also customize the ribbon by adding, removing, renaming, or reordering tabs, groups, and commands, although this is not recommended until you become an expert Office user.

4 Click **Collapse the Ribbon**. Notice that only the ribbon tabs display. Click the **HOME tab** to display the commands. Click anywhere in the document, and notice that the ribbon goes back to the collapsed display.

5 Right-click any ribbon tab, and then click **Collapse the Ribbon** again to remove the check mark from this command.

Many expert Office users prefer the full ribbon display.

6 Point to any tab on the ribbon, and then on your mouse device, roll the mouse wheel. Notice that different tabs become active as you roll the mouse wheel.

You can make a tab active by using this technique instead of clicking the tab.

Objective 10 | Apply Formatting in Office Programs

Video OF1-10

Activity 1.14 | Changing Page Orientation and Zoom Level

In this activity, you will practice common formatting techniques used in Office applications.

1 On the ribbon, click the **PAGE LAYOUT tab**. In the **Page Setup group**, click **Orientation**, and notice that two orientations display—*Portrait* and *Landscape*. Click **Landscape**.

In *portrait orientation*, the paper is taller than it is wide. In *landscape orientation*, the paper is wider than it is tall.

2 In the lower right corner of the screen, locate the **Zoom slider** .

Recall that to zoom means to increase or decrease the viewing area. You can zoom in to look closely at a section of a document, and then zoom out to see an entire page on the screen. You can also zoom to view multiple pages on the screen.

3 Drag the **Zoom slider** to the left until you have zoomed to approximately *60%*. Compare your screen with Figure 1.39.

FIGURE 1.39

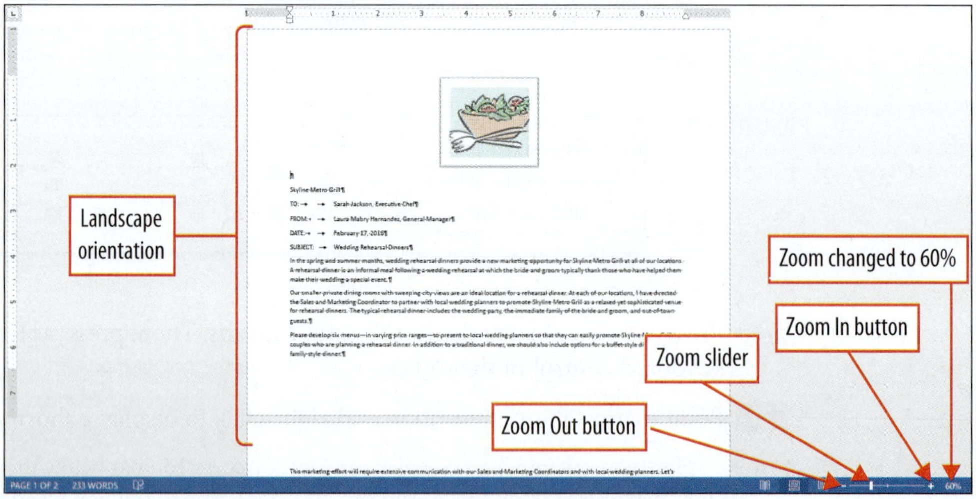

Landscape orientation

Zoom changed to 60%

Zoom In button

Zoom slider

Zoom Out button

🔄 **BY TOUCH**   Drag the Zoom slider with your finger.

4 Use the technique you just practiced to change the **Orientation** back to **Portrait**.

The default orientation in Word is Portrait, which is commonly used for business documents such as letters and memos.

5 In the lower right corner, click the **Zoom In** button ➕ as many times as necessary to return to the **100%** zoom setting.

Use the zoom feature to adjust the view of your document for editing and for your viewing comfort.

🔄 **ANOTHER WAY**   You can also control Zoom from the ribbon. On the VIEW tab, in the Zoom group, you can control the Zoom level and also zoom to view multiple pages.

6 On the **Quick Access Toolbar**, click **Save** 💾.

More Knowledge   **Zooming to Page Width**

Some Office users prefer Page Width, which zooms the document so that the width of the page matches the width of the window. Find this command on the VIEW tab, in the Zoom group.

Activity 1.15 | Formatting Text by Using Fonts, Alignment, Font Colors, and Font Styles

1 If necessary, on the right side of your screen, drag the vertical scroll box to the top of the scroll bar. To the left of *Skyline Metro Grill*, point in the margin area to display the 𝄃 pointer and click one time to select the entire paragraph. Compare your screen with Figure 1.40.

Use this technique to select complete paragraphs from the margin area—drag downward to select multiple-line paragraphs—which is faster and more efficient than dragging through text.

FIGURE 1.40

2 On the ribbon, click the **HOME tab**, and then in the **Paragraph group**, click **Center** ≡ to center the paragraph.

3 On the **HOME tab**, in the **Font group**, click the **Font button arrow** [Calibri (Body) ▾]. On the alphabetical list of font names, scroll down and then locate and *point to* **Cambria**.

A *font* is a set of characters with the same design and shape. The default font in a Word document is Calibri, which is a *sans serif* font—a font design with no lines or extensions on the ends of characters.

The Cambria font is a *serif font*—a font design that includes small line extensions on the ends of the letters to guide the eye in reading from left to right.

The list of fonts displays as a gallery showing potential results. For example, in the Font gallery, you can point to see the actual design and format of each font as it would look if applied to text.

4 Point to several other fonts and observe the effect on the selected text. Then, scroll back to the top of the **Font** gallery. Under **Theme Fonts**, click **Calibri Light**.

A *theme* is a predesigned combination of colors, fonts, line, and fill effects that look good together and is applied to an entire document by a single selection. A theme combines two sets of fonts—one for text and one for headings. In the default Office theme, Calibri Light is the suggested font for headings.

5 With the paragraph *Skyline Metro Grill* still selected, on the **HOME tab**, in the **Font group**, click the **Font Size button arrow** [11 ▾], point to **36**, and then notice how Live Preview displays the text in the font size to which you are pointing. Compare your screen with Figure 1.41.

FIGURE 1.41

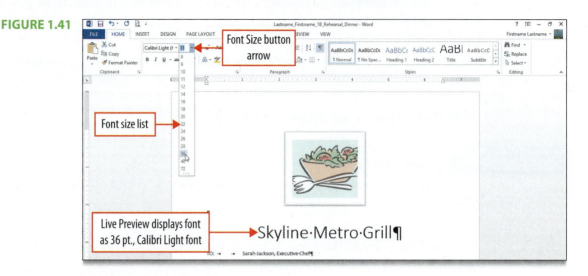

6 On the list of font sizes, click **20**.

Fonts are measured in *points*, with one point equal to 1/72 of an inch. A higher point size indicates a larger font size. Headings and titles are often formatted by using a larger font size. The word *point* is abbreviated as *pt*.

7 With *Skyline Metro Grill* still selected, on the **HOME tab**, in the **Font group**, click the **Font Color button arrow** [A ▾]. Under **Theme Colors**, in the last column, click the last color—**Green, Accent 6, Darker 50%**. Click anywhere to deselect the text.

8 To the left of *TO:*, point in the left margin area to display the [pointer], hold down the left mouse button, and then drag down to select the four memo headings. Compare your screen with Figure 1.42.

Use this technique to select complete paragraphs from the margin area—drag downward to select multiple paragraphs—which is faster and more efficient than dragging through text.

🔁 **BY TOUCH**   Tap once on TO: to display the gripper, then with your finger, drag to the right and down to select the four paragraphs.

FIGURE 1.42

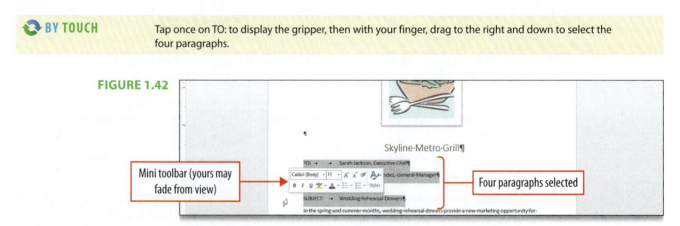

9 With the four paragraphs selected, on the mini toolbar, click the **Font Color** button ⬛A ▾, and notice that the text color of the four paragraphs changes.

The font color button retains its most recently used color—Green, Accent 6, Darker 50%. As you progress in your study of Microsoft Office, you will use other buttons that behave in this manner; that is, they retain their most recently used format. This is commonly referred to as *MRU*—most recently used.

Recall that the mini toolbar places commands that are commonly used for the selected text or object close by so that you reduce the distance that you must move your mouse to access a command. If you are using a touchscreen device, most commands that you need are close and easy to touch.

10 On the right, drag the vertical scroll box down slightly to position more of the text on the screen. Click anywhere in the paragraph that begins *In the spring*, and then ***triple-click***—click the left mouse button three times—to select the entire paragraph. If the entire paragraph is not selected, click in the paragraph and begin again.

11 With the entire paragraph selected, on the mini toolbar, click the **Font Color button arrow** ⬛A ▾, and then under **Theme Colors**, in the sixth column, click the last color— **Orange, Accent 2, Darker 50%.**

12 In the memo headings, select the guide word *TO:* and then on the mini toolbar, click **Bold** B and **Italic** I .

Font styles include bold, italic, and underline. Font styles emphasize text and are a visual cue to draw the reader's eye to important text.

13 On the mini toolbar, click **Italic** I again to turn off the Italic formatting.

A ***toggle button*** is a button that can be turned on by clicking it once, and then turned off by clicking it again.

Activity 1.16 | Using Format Painter

Use the Format Painter to copy the formatting of specific text or of a paragraph and then apply it in other locations in your document.

1 With *TO:* still selected, on the mini toolbar, click **Format Painter** 🖌. Then, move your mouse under the word *Sarah*, and notice the 🖌I mouse pointer. Compare your screen with Figure 1.43.

The pointer takes the shape of a paintbrush, and contains the formatting information from the paragraph where the insertion point is positioned. Information about the Format Painter and how to turn it off displays in the status bar.

FIGURE 1.43

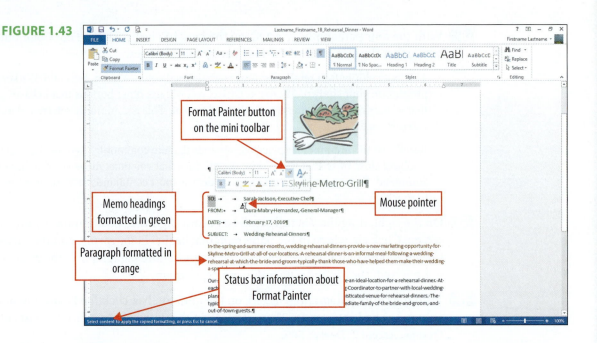

2 > With the pointer, drag to select the guide word *FROM:* and notice that Bold formatting is applied. Then, point to the selected text *FROM:* and on the mini toolbar, *double-click* **Format Painter** .

3 > Select the guide word *DATE:* to copy the Bold formatting, and notice that the pointer retains the shape.

> When you *double-click* the Format Painter button, the Format Painter feature remains active until you either click the Format Painter button again, or press Esc to cancel it—as indicated on the status bar.

4 > With Format Painter still active, select the guide word *SUBJECT:*, and then on the ribbon, on the **HOME tab**, in the **Clipboard group**, notice that **Format Painter** is selected, indicating that it is active. Compare your screen with Figure 1.44.

FIGURE 1.44

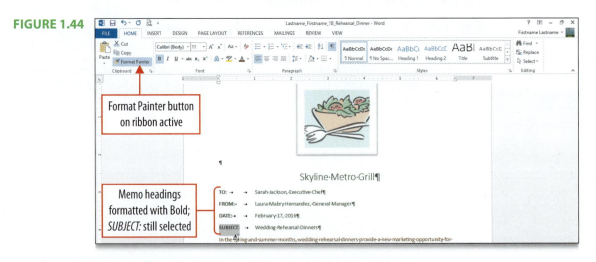

5 > On the ribbon, click **Format Painter** to turn the command off.

🔄 **ANOTHER WAY**   Press Esc to turn off Format Painter.

6 In the paragraph that begins *In the spring*, triple-click again to select the entire paragraph. On the mini toolbar, click **Bold** B and **Italic** I. Click anywhere to deselect.

7 On the **Quick Access Toolbar**, click **Save** 🖫 to save the changes you have made to your document.

Activity 1.17 | Using Keyboard Shortcuts and Using the Clipboard to Copy, Cut, and Paste

The *Clipboard* is a temporary storage area that holds text or graphics that you select and then cut or copy. When you *copy* text or graphics, a copy is placed on the Clipboard and the original text or graphic remains in place. When you *cut* text or graphics, a copy is placed on the Clipboard, and the original text or graphic is removed—cut—from the document.

After copying or cutting, the contents of the Clipboard are available for you to *paste*—insert—in a new location in the current document, or into another Office file.

1 Hold down Ctrl and press Home to move to the beginning of your document, and then take a moment to study the table in Figure 1.45, which describes similar keyboard shortcuts with which you can navigate quickly in a document.

FIGURE 1.45

KEYBOARD SHORTCUTS TO NAVIGATE IN A DOCUMENT	
TO MOVE	**PRESS**
To the beginning of a document	Ctrl + Home
To the end of a document	Ctrl + End
To the beginning of a line	Home
To the end of a line	End
To the beginning of the previous word	Ctrl + ←
To the beginning of the next word	Ctrl + →
To the beginning of the current word (if insertion point is in the middle of a word)	Ctrl + ←
To the beginning of the previous paragraph	Ctrl + ↑
To the beginning of the next paragraph	Ctrl + ↓
To the beginning of the current paragraph (if insertion point is in the middle of a paragraph)	Ctrl + ↑
Up one screen	PgUp
Down one screen	PgDn

2 To the left of *Skyline Metro Grill*, point in the left margin area to display the pointer, and then click one time to select the entire paragraph. On the **HOME tab**, in the **Clipboard group**, click **Copy** 🗐.

Because anything that you select and then copy—or cut—is placed on the Clipboard, the Copy command and the Cut command display in the Clipboard group of commands on the ribbon. There is no visible indication that your copied selection has been placed on the Clipboard.

🔁 **ANOTHER WAY** Right-click the selection, and then click Copy on the shortcut menu; or, use the keyboard shortcut Ctrl + C.

3 On the **HOME tab**, in the **Clipboard group**, to the right of the group name *Clipboard*, click the **Dialog Box Launcher** button, and then compare your screen with Figure 1.46.

The Clipboard pane displays with your copied text. In any ribbon group, the ***Dialog Box Launcher*** displays either a dialog box or a pane related to the group of commands. It is not necessary to display the Clipboard in this manner, although sometimes it is useful to do so.

FIGURE 1.46

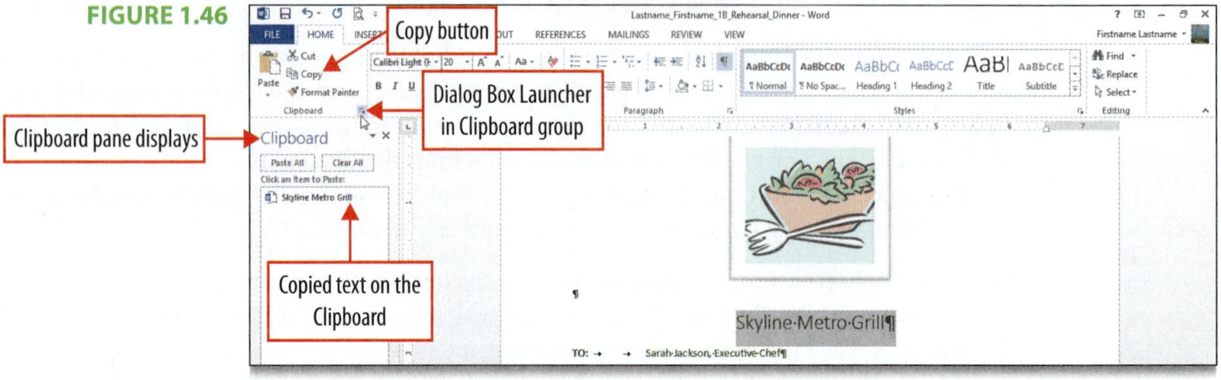

4 In the upper right corner of the **Clipboard** pane, click **Close** ✕.

5 Press Ctrl + End to move to the end of your document. Press Enter one time to create a new blank paragraph. On the **HOME tab**, in the **Clipboard group**, point to **Paste**, and then click the *upper* portion of this split button.

The Paste command pastes the most recently copied item on the Clipboard at the insertion point location. If you click the lower portion of the Paste button, a gallery of Paste Options displays. A ***split button*** is divided into two parts; clicking the main part of the button performs a command, and clicking the arrow displays a list or gallery with choices.

🔄 **ANOTHER WAY**   Right-click, on the shortcut menu under Paste Options, click the desired option button; or, press Ctrl + V.

6 Below the pasted text, click **Paste Options** as shown in Figure 1.47.

Here you can view and apply various formatting options for pasting your copied or cut text. Typically you will click Paste on the ribbon and paste the item in its original format. If you want some other format for the pasted item, you can choose another format from the ***Paste Options gallery***.

The Paste Options gallery provides a Live Preview of the various options for changing the format of the pasted item with a single click. The Paste Options gallery is available in three places: on the ribbon by clicking the lower portion of the Paste button—the Paste button arrow; from the Paste Options button that displays below the pasted item following the paste operation; or on the shortcut menu if you right-click the pasted item.

FIGURE 1.47

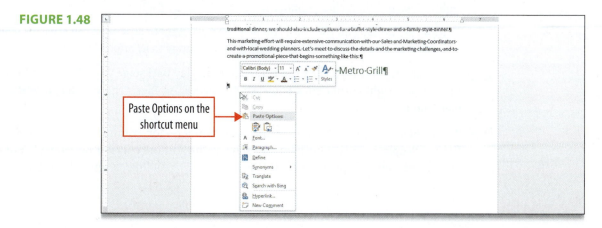

Upper portion of Paste button

Paste button arrow on the ribbon

Pasted text → Skyline·Metro·Grill¶

Paste Options button

Paste Options gallery

7 In the **Paste Options** gallery, *point* to each option to see the Live Preview of the format that would be applied if you clicked the button.

The contents of the Paste Options gallery are contextual; that is, they change based on what you copied and where you are pasting.

8 Press Esc to close the gallery; the button will remain displayed until you take some other screen action.

9 Press Ctrl + Home to move to the top of the document, and then click the **salad image** one time to select it. While pointing to the selected image, right-click, and then on the shortcut menu, click **Cut**.

Recall that the Cut command cuts—removes—the selection from the document and places it on the Clipboard.

ANOTHER WAY   On the HOME tab, in the Clipboard group, click the Cut button; or, use the keyboard shortcut Ctrl + X.

10 Press Del one time to remove the blank paragraph from the top of the document, and then press Ctrl + End to move to the end of the document.

11 With the insertion point blinking in the blank paragraph at the end of the document, right-click, and notice that the **Paste Options** gallery displays on the shortcut menu. Compare your screen with Figure 1.48.

FIGURE 1.48

Paste Options on the shortcut menu

12 On the shortcut menu, under **Paste Options**, click the first button—**Keep Source Formatting**.

13 Point to the picture to display the pointer, and then drag to the right until the center green **Alignment Guide** displays and the blank paragraph is above the picture, as shown in Figure 1.49. Release the left mouse button.

🔄 BY TOUCH   Drag the picture with your finger to display the Alignment Guide.

FIGURE 1.49

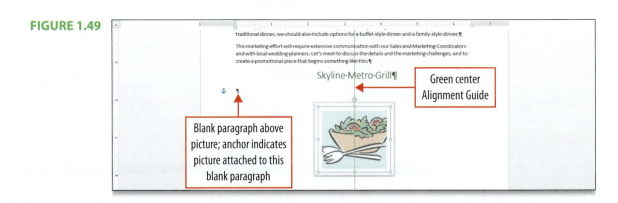

14 Above the picture, click to position the insertion point at the end of the word *Grill*, press Spacebar one time, type **for Your Rehearsal Dinner** and then **Save** your document. Compare your screen with Figure 1.50.

FIGURE 1.50

15 On the **INSERT tab**, in the **Header & Footer group**, click **Footer**. At the bottom of the list, click **Edit Footer**, and then with the **HEADER & FOOTER Design tab** active, in the **Insert group**, click **Document Info**. Click **File Name** to add the file name to the footer.

16 On the right end of the ribbon, click **Close Header and Footer**.

17 On the **Quick Access Toolbar**, point to the **Print Preview and Print icon** you placed there, right-click, and then click **Remove from Quick Access Toolbar**.

> If you are working on your own computer and you want to do so, you can leave the icon on the toolbar; in a lab setting, you should return the software to its original settings.

18 Click **Save** and then click the **FILE tab** to display **Backstage** view. With the **Info tab** active, in the lower right corner click **Show All Properties**. As **Tags**, type **weddings, rehearsal dinners, marketing**

19 As the **Subject**, type your course name and number—for example *CIS 10, #5543*. Under **Related People**, be sure your name displays as the author (edit it if necessary), and then on the left, click **Print** to display the Print Preview. Compare your screen with Figure 1.51.

FIGURE 1.51

20 ▶ On the left side of **Backstage** view, click **Save**. As directed by your instructor, print or submit your file electronically as described in Project 1A, and then in the upper right corner of the Word window, click **Close** [**×**].

21 ▶ If a message indicates *Would you like to keep the last item you copied?* click **No**.

> This message displays if you have copied some type of image to the Clipboard. If you click Yes, the items on the Clipboard will remain for you to use in another program or document.

Objective 11 | Compress Files and Use the Microsoft Office 2013 Help System

A ***compressed file*** is a file that has been reduced in size. Compressed files take up less storage space and can be transferred to other computers faster than uncompressed files. You can also combine a group of files into one compressed folder, which makes it easier to share a group of files.

Within each Office program, the Help feature provides information about all of the program's features and displays step-by-step instructions for performing many tasks.

Video OF1-11

Activity 1.18 | Compressing Files

In this activity, you will combine the two files you created in this chapter into one compressed file.

1 ▶ On the Windows taskbar, click **File Explorer** . On the left, in the **navigation pane**, navigate to your **USB flash drive**, and then open your **Office Features Chapter 1** folder. Compare your screen with Figure 1.52.

FIGURE 1.52

2 In the **file list**, click your **Lastname_Firstname_1A_Note_Form** Word file one time to select it. Then, hold down ⌃Ctrl, and click your **Lastname_Firstname_1B_Rehearsal_Dinner** file to select the files in the list.

In any Windows-based program, holding down ⌃Ctrl while selecting enables you to select multiple items.

3 On the **File Explorer** ribbon, click **Share**, and then in the **Send group**, click **Zip**. Compare your screen with Figure 1.53.

Windows creates a compressed folder containing a *copy* of each of the selected files. The folder name is selected—highlighted in blue—so that you can rename it.

 BY TOUCH Tap the ribbon commands.

FIGURE 1.53

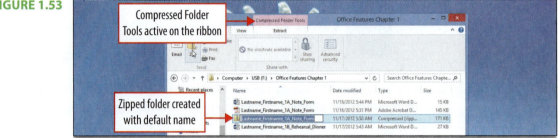

 ANOTHER WAY Point to the selected files in the File List, right-click, point to Send to, and then click Compressed (zipped) folder.

---

4 Using your own name, type **Lastname_Firstname_Office_Features_Chapter_1** and press Enter.

The compressed folder is ready to attach to an email or share in some other format.

5 In the upper right corner of the folder window, click **Close** ⊠.

Activity 1.19 | Using the Microsoft Office 2013 Help System in Excel

In this activity, you will use the Microsoft Help feature to find information about formatting numbers in Excel.

1 Press ⊞ to display the Windows 8 **Start screen**, and then type **excel 2013** Press Enter to open the Excel desktop app.

2 On Excel's opening screen, click **Blank workbook**, and then in the upper right corner, click **Microsoft Excel Help** ⃝.

 ANOTHER WAY Press F1 to display Help in any Office program.

---

3 In the **Excel Help** window, click in the **Search online help** box, type **formatting numbers** and then press Enter.

4 On the list of results, click **Format numbers as currency**. Compare your screen with Figure 1.54.

FIGURE 1.54

5 If you want to do so, at the top of the **Excel Help** window, click Print 🖶 to print a copy of this information for your reference.

6 In the upper right corner of the Help window, click **Close** ⊠ .

7 Leave Excel open for the next activity.

Objective 12   Install Apps for Office and Create a Microsoft Account

> **ALERT!   Working with Web-Based Applications and Services**
>
> Computer programs and services on the web receive continuous updates and improvements. Thus, the steps to complete the following web-based activities may differ from the ones shown. You can often look at the screens and the information presented to determine how to complete the activity.

Video OF1-12

Apps for Office 2013 and SharePoint 2013 are a collection of downloadable apps that enable you to create and view information within your familiar Office programs. Some of these apps are developed by Microsoft, but many more are developed by specialists in different fields. As new apps are developed, they will be available from the online Office Store.

An *app for Office* is a webpage that works within one of the Office applications, such as Excel, that you download from the Office Store. Office apps combine cloud services and web technologies within the user interface of Office and SharePoint. For example, in Excel, you can use an app to look up and gather search results for a new apartment by placing the information in an Excel worksheet, and then use maps to determine the distance of each apartment to work and to family members.

Activity 1.20 | Installing Apps for Office

> **ALERT!   You Must Be Signed In to Office with a Microsoft Account to Complete This Activity**
>
> To download an Office app, you must be signed in to Office with a free Microsoft account. If you do not have a Microsoft account, refer to the next activity to create one by using Microsoft's outlook.com email service, which includes free SkyDrive cloud storage.

1 On the Excel ribbon, click the **INSERT tab**. In the **Apps group**, click the **Apps for Office** arrow, and then click **See All**.

2 Click **FEATURED APPS**, and then on the right, click in the **Search for apps on the Office Store** box, type **Bing Maps** and press Enter.

3 Click the **Bing logo**, and then click the **Add** button, and then if necessary, click Continue.

4 **Close** ⊠ Internet Explorer, and then **Close** ⊠ the **Apps for Office** box.

5 On the **INSERT tab**, in the **Apps group**, click **Apps for Office**, click **See All**, click **MY APPS**, click the **Bing Maps** app, and then in the lower right corner, click **Insert**.

6 On the Welcome message, click **Insert Sample Data**.

Here, the Bing map displays information related to the sample data. Each state in the sample data displays a small pie chart that represents the two sets of data. Compare your screen with Figure 1.55.

This is just one example of many apps downloadable from the Office store.

FIGURE 1.55

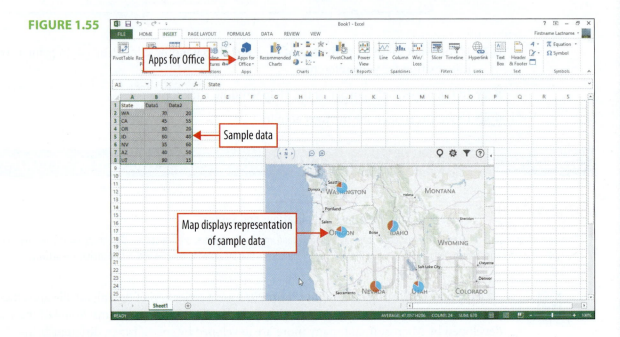

7 **Close** ☒ Excel without saving.

Activity 1.21 | Creating a Microsoft Account

> **ALERT!**   **This Is an Optional Activity**
>
> You will find both Windows 8 and Office 2013 to be much more useful if you sign in with a Microsoft account. If you already have an email account from msn.com, hotmail.com, live.com, or outlook.com, then you already have a Microsoft account. If you do not, you can create a free Microsoft account by following the steps in this activity.

In Windows 8, you can create a Microsoft account, and then use that account to sign in to *any* Windows 8 PC. Signing in with a Microsoft account is recommended because you can:

- Download Windows 8 apps from the Windows Store.
- Get your online content—email, social network updates, updated news—automatically displayed in an app on the Windows 8 Start screen when you sign in.
- Synch settings online to make every Windows 8 computer you use look and feel the same.
- Sign in to Office so that you can store documents on your SkyDrive and download Office apps.

1 Open Internet Explorer 🖉, and then go to **www.outlook.com**

2 Locate and click **Sign up now** to display a screen similar to Figure 1.56. Complete the form to create your account.

FIGURE 1.56

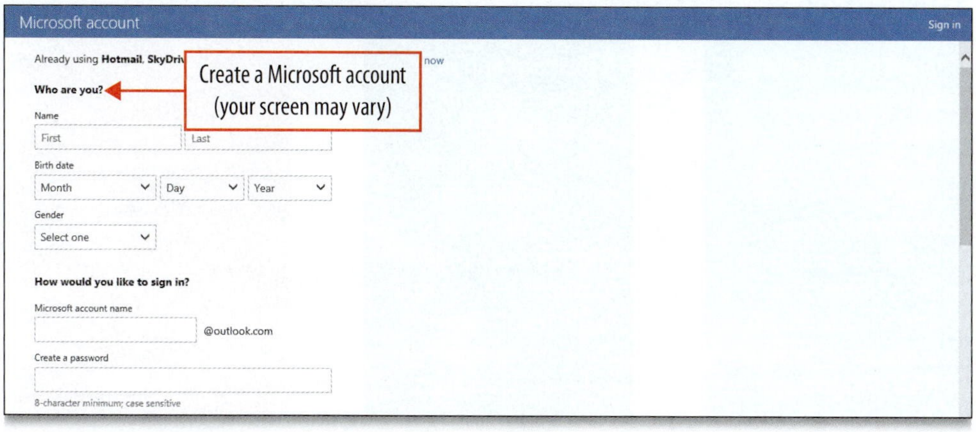

3 **Close** ⊠ Internet Explorer.

END | You have completed Project 1B

END OF CHAPTER

SUMMARY

Many Office features and commands, such as the Open and Save As dialog boxes, performing commands from the ribbon and from dialog boxes, and using the Clipboard are the same in all Office desktop apps.

A desktop app is installed on your computer and requires a computer operating system such as Microsoft Windows or Apple OS to run. The programs in Microsoft Office 2013 are considered to be desktop apps.

Apps that run on a smartphone or tablet computer—for example, iOS, Android, or Windows Phone—or apps that run from browser software such as Internet Explorer or Chrome on a PC, are referred to as apps.

Within each Office app, you can install additional Apps for Office from the Office Store. You must have a Microsoft account, which includes free SkyDrive storage, to download Windows 8 or Office apps.

GO! LEARN IT ONLINE

Review the concepts and key terms in this chapter by completing these online challenges, which you can find at **www.pearsonhighered.com/go**.

Matching and Multiple Choice:
Answer matching and multiple choice questions to test what you learned in this chapter. **MyITLab®**

Crossword Puzzle:
Spell out the words that match the numbered clues, and put them in the puzzle squares.

Flipboard:
Flip through the definitions of the key terms in this chapter and match them with the correct term.

GLOSSARY

GLOSSARY OF CHAPTER KEY TERMS

Address bar (Internet Explorer) The area at the top of the Internet Explorer window that displays, and where you can type, a URL—Uniform Resource Locator—which is an address that uniquely identifies a location on the Internet.

Address bar (Windows) The bar at the top of a folder window with which you can navigate to a different folder or library, or go back to a previous one.

Alignment The placement of text or objects relative to the left and right margins.

Alignment guides Green lines that display when you move an object to assist in alignment.

App The term that commonly refers to computer programs that run from the device software on a smartphone or a tablet computer—for example, iOS, Android, or Windows Phone—or computer programs that run from the browser software on a desktop PC or laptop PC—for example Internet Explorer, Safari, Firefox, or Chrome.

App for Office A webpage that works within one of the Office applications, such as Excel, and that you download from the Office Store.

Apps for Office 2013 and SharePoint 2013 A collection of downloadable apps that enable you to create and view information within your familiar Office programs.

Backstage tabs The area along the left side of Backstage view with tabs to display screens with related groups of commands.

Backstage view A centralized space for file management tasks; for example, opening, saving, printing, publishing, or sharing a file. A navigation pane displays along the left side with tabs that group file-related tasks together.

Center alignment The alignment of text or objects that is centered horizontally between the left and right margins.

Click The action of pressing and releasing the left button on a mouse pointing device one time.

Clip art Downloadable predefined graphics available online from Office.com and other sites.

Clipboard A temporary storage area that holds text or graphics that you select and then cut or copy.

Cloud computing Refers to applications and services that are accessed over the Internet, rather than to applications that are installed on your local computer.

Cloud storage Online storage of data so that you can access your data from different places and devices.

Collaborate To work with others as a team in an intellectual endeavor to complete a shared task or to achieve a shared goal.

Commands An instruction to a computer program that causes an action to be carried out.

Common dialog boxes The set of dialog boxes that includes Open, Save, and Save As, which are provided by the Windows programming interface, and which display and operate in all of the Office programs in the same manner.

Compressed file A file that has been reduced in size and thus takes up less storage space and can be transferred to other computers quickly.

Compressed folder A folder that has been reduced in size and thus takes up less storage space and can be transferred to other computers quickly; also called a *zipped* folder.

Context menus Menus that display commands and options relevant to the selected text or object; also called *shortcut menus*.

Context-sensitive commands Commands that display on a shortcut menu that relate to the object or text that you right-clicked.

Contextual tabs Tabs that are added to the ribbon automatically when a specific object, such as a picture, is selected, and that contain commands relevant to the selected object.

Copy A command that duplicates a selection and places it on the Clipboard.

Cut A command that removes a selection and places it on the Clipboard.

Default The term that refers to the current selection or setting that is automatically used by a computer program unless you specify otherwise.

Deselect The action of canceling the selection of an object or block of text by clicking outside of the selection.

Desktop In Windows, the screen that simulates your work area.

Desktop app The term that commonly refers to a computer program that is installed on your computer and requires a computer operating system like Microsoft Windows or Apple OS to run.

Dialog box A small window that contains options for completing a task.

Dialog Box Launcher A small icon that displays to the right of some group names on the ribbon, and which opens a related dialog box or pane providing additional options and commands related to that group.

Document properties Details about a file that describe or identify it, including the title, author name, subject, and keywords that identify the document's topic or contents; also known as *metadata*.

Drag The action of holding down the left mouse button while moving your mouse.

Edit The process of making changes to text or graphics in an Office file.

Ellipsis A set of three dots indicating incompleteness; an ellipsis following a command name indicates that a dialog box will display if you click the command.

Enhanced ScreenTip A ScreenTip that displays more descriptive text than a normal ScreenTip.

Extract To decompress, or pull out, files from a compressed form.

File A collection of information stored on a computer under a single name, for example, a Word document or a PowerPoint presentation.

File Explorer The program that displays the files and folders on your computer, and which is at work anytime you are viewing the contents of files and folders in a window.

Fill The inside color of an object.

Folder A container in which you store files.

Folder window In Windows, a window that displays the contents of the current folder, library, or device, and contains helpful parts so that you can navigate the Windows file structure.

Font A set of characters with the same design and shape.

Font styles Formatting emphasis such as bold, italic, and underline.

Footer A reserved area for text or graphics that displays at the bottom of each page in a document.

Formatting The process of establishing the overall appearance of text, graphics, and pages in an Office file—for example, in a Word document.

Formatting marks Characters that display on the screen, but do not print, indicating where the Enter key, the Spacebar, and the Tab key were pressed; also called *nonprinting characters*.

Gallery An Office feature that displays a list of potential results instead of just the command name.

Gradient fill A fill effect in which one color fades into another.

Groups On the Office ribbon, the sets of related commands that you might need for a specific type of task.

Header A reserved area for text or graphics that displays at the top of each page in a document.

Info tab The tab in Backstage view that displays information about the current file.

Insertion point A blinking vertical line that indicates where text or graphics will be inserted.

Keyboard shortcut A combination of two or more keyboard keys, used to perform a task that would otherwise require a mouse.

KeyTip The letter that displays on a command in the ribbon and that indicates the key you can press to activate the command when keyboard control of the ribbon is activated.

Keywords Custom file properties in the form of words that you associate with a document to give an indication of the document's content; used to help find and organize files. Also called *tags*.

Landscape orientation A page orientation in which the paper is wider than it is tall.

Layout Options A button that displays when an object is selected and that has commands to choose how the object interacts with surrounding text.

Live Preview A technology that shows the result of applying an editing or formatting change as you point to possible results—*before* you actually apply it.

Location Any disk drive, folder, or other place in which you can store files and folders.

Metadata Details about a file that describe or identify it, including the title, author name, subject, and keywords that identify the document's topic or contents; also known as *document properties*.

Mini toolbar A small toolbar containing frequently used formatting commands that displays as a result of selecting text or objects.

MRU Acronym for *most recently used*, which refers to the state of some commands that retain the characteristic most recently applied; for example, the Font Color button retains the most recently used color until a new color is chosen.

Navigate The process of exploring within the organizing structure of Windows.

Navigation pane In a folder window, the area on the left in which you can navigate to, open, and display favorites, libraries, folders, saved searches, and an expandable list of drives.

Nonprinting characters Characters that display on the screen, but do not print, indicating where the Enter key, the Spacebar, and the Tab key were pressed; also called *formatting marks*.

Notification bar An area at the bottom of an Internet Explorer window that displays information about pending downloads, security issues, add-ons, and other issues related to the operation of your computer.

Object A text box, picture, table, or shape that you can select and then move and resize.

Office Web Apps The free online companions to Microsoft Word, Excel, PowerPoint, Access, and OneNote.

Open dialog box A dialog box from which you can navigate to, and then open on your screen, an existing file that was created in that same program.

Option button In a dialog box, a round button that enables you to make one choice among two or more options.

Options dialog box A dialog box within each Office application where you can select program settings and other options and preferences.

Pane A separate area of a window.

Paragraph symbol The symbol ¶ that represents the end of a paragraph.

Paste The action of placing text or objects that have been copied or cut from one location to another location.

Paste Options gallery A gallery of buttons that provides a Live Preview of all the Paste options available in the current context.

Path A sequence of folders that leads to a specific file or folder.

PDF The acronym for Portable Document Format, which is a file format that creates an image that preserves the look of your file; this is a popular format for sending documents electronically because the document will display on most computers.

Point The action of moving your mouse pointer over something on your screen.

Pointer Any symbol that displays on your screen in response to moving your mouse.

Points A measurement of the size of a font; there are 72 points in an inch.

Portable Document Format A file format that creates an image that preserves the look of your file, but that cannot be easily changed; a popular format for sending documents electronically, because the document will display on most computers.

Portrait orientation A page orientation in which the paper is taller than it is wide.

Print Preview A view of a document as it will appear when you print it.

Progress bar In a dialog box or taskbar button, a bar that indicates visually the progress of a task such as a download or file transfer.

Protected View A security feature in Office 2013 that protects your computer from malicious files by opening them in a restricted environment until you enable them; you might encounter this feature if you open a file from an email or download files from the Internet.

pt The abbreviation for *point*; for example, when referring to a font size.

Quick Access Toolbar In an Office program window, the small row of buttons in the upper left corner of the screen from which you can perform frequently used commands.

Read-Only A property assigned to a file that prevents the file from being modified or deleted; it indicates that you cannot save any changes to the displayed document unless you first save it with a new name.

Ribbon A user interface in both Office 2013 and File Explorer that groups the commands for performing related tasks on tabs across the upper portion of the program window.

Right-click The action of clicking the right mouse button one time.

Sans serif font A font design with no lines or extensions on the ends of characters.

ScreenTip A small box that that displays useful information when you perform various mouse actions such as pointing to screen elements or dragging.

Scroll bar A vertical or horizontal bar in a window or a pane to assist in bringing an area into view, and which contains a scroll box and scroll arrows.

Scroll box The box in the vertical and horizontal scroll bars that can be dragged to reposition the contents of a window or pane on the screen.

Selecting Highlighting, by dragging with your mouse, areas of text or data or graphics, so that the selection can be edited, formatted, copied, or moved.

Serif font A font design that includes small line extensions on the ends of the letters to guide the eye in reading from left to right.

SharePoint Collaboration software with which people in an organization can set up team sites to share information, manage documents, and publish reports for others to see.

Shortcut menu A menu that displays commands and options relevant to the selected text or object; also called a *context menu*.

Sizing handles Small squares that indicate a picture or object is selected.

SkyDrive Microsoft's free cloud storage for anyone with a free Microsoft account.

Split button A button divided into two parts and in which clicking the main part of the button performs a command and clicking the arrow opens a menu with choices.

Start search The search feature in Windows 8 in which, from the Start screen, you can begin to type and by default, Windows 8 searches for apps; you can adjust the search to search for files or settings.

Status bar The area along the lower edge of an Office program window that displays file information on the left and buttons to control how the window looks on the right.

Style A group of formatting commands, such as font, font size, font color, paragraph alignment, and line spacing that can be applied to a paragraph with one command.

Subfolder A folder within a folder.

Synchronization The process of updating computer files that are in two or more locations according to specific rules—also called *syncing*.

Syncing The process of updating computer files that are in two or more locations according to specific rules—also called *synchronization*.

Tabs (ribbon) On the Office ribbon, the name of each activity area.

Tags Custom file properties in the form of words that you associate with a document to give an indication of the document's content; used to help find and organize files. Also called *keywords*.

Taskbar The area along the lower edge of the desktop that displays buttons representing programs.

Template A preformatted document that you can use as a starting point and then change to suit your needs.

Theme A predesigned combination of colors, fonts, and effects that look good together and is applied to an entire document by a single selection.

Title bar The bar at the top edge of the program window that indicates the name of the current file and the program name.

Toggle button A button that can be turned on by clicking it once, and then turned off by clicking it again.

Toolbar In a folder window, a row of buttons with which you can perform common tasks, such as changing the view of your files and folders or burning files to a CD.

Triple-click The action of clicking the left mouse button three times in rapid succession.

Trusted Documents A security feature in Office that remembers which files you have already enabled; you might encounter this feature if you open a file from an email or download files from the Internet.

Uniform Resource Locator An address that uniquely identifies a location on the Internet.

URL The acronym for Uniform Resource Locator, which is an address that uniquely identifies a location on the Internet.

USB flash drive A small data storage device that plugs into a computer USB port.

Window A rectangular area on a computer screen in which programs and content appear, and which can be moved, resized, minimized, or closed.

XML Paper Specification A Microsoft file format that creates an image of your document and that opens in the XPS viewer.

XPS The acronym for XML Paper Specification—a Microsoft file format that creates an image of your document and that opens in the XPS viewer.

Zipped folder A folder that has been reduced in size and thus takes up less storage space and can be transferred to other computers quickly; also called a *compressed* folder.

Zoom The action of increasing or decreasing the size of the viewing area on the screen.

Introduction to Microsoft PowerPoint 2013

P PowerPoint 2013

alexandre zveiger/Fotolia

PowerPoint 2013: Introduction

Communication skills are critically important to success in today's business world and when it comes to communicating *your* ideas, presentation is everything! Whether you are planning to deliver your presentation in person or online—to a large audience or to a small group—Microsoft PowerPoint 2013 is a versatile business tool designed to help you create presentations that make a lasting impression. Additionally, collaborating with others to develop a presentation is made easy because you can share the slides you create by using your SkyDrive.

New to Microsoft PowerPoint 2013 are a variety of themes that you can apply to a new presentation. Each

theme includes several theme variants that coordinate colors, fonts, and effects. The beauty of this approach is that the variations evoke different moods and responses, yet the basic design remains the same. As a result, you can use a similar design within your company to brand your presentations while still changing the colors to make the presentation appropriate to the audience and topic. The best part is that you do not have to determine which colors work well together in the theme you chose. The theme variant does that work for you so that you can concentrate on how best to communicate your message! Focus on creating dynamic, interesting presentations that keep your audience engaged!

Video PA

Getting Started with Microsoft PowerPoint

GO! to Work
Video P1

PROJECT 1A

OUTCOMES
Create a company overview presentation.

PROJECT 1B

OUTCOMES
Create a new product announcement presentation.

OBJECTIVES

1. Create a New Presentation
2. Edit a Presentation in Normal View
3. Add Pictures to a Presentation
4. Print and View a Presentation

OBJECTIVES

5. Edit an Existing Presentation
6. Format a Presentation
7. Use Slide Sorter View
8. Apply Slide Transitions

Caleb Foster/Fotolia

In This Chapter

In this chapter you will study presentation skills, which are among the most important skills you will learn. Good presentation skills enhance your communications—written, electronic, and interpersonal. In this technology-enhanced world, communicating ideas clearly and concisely is a critical personal skill. Microsoft PowerPoint 2013 is presentation software with which you create electronic slide presentations. Use PowerPoint to present information to your audience effectively. You can start with a new, blank presentation and add content, pictures, and themes, or you can collaborate with colleagues by inserting slides that have been saved in other presentations.

The projects in this chapter relate to **Kodiak West Travel**, which is a travel agency with offices in Juneau, Anchorage, and Victoria. Kodiak West Travel works closely with local vendors to provide clients with specialized adventure travel itineraries. The company was established in 2001 in Juneau and built a loyal client base that led to the expansion into Anchorage and Victoria. As a full-service travel agency, Kodiak West Travel agents strive to provide their clients with travel opportunities that exceed their expectations. The company works with all major airlines, cruise lines, hotel chains, and vehicle rental companies as well as with small, specialized, boutique hotels.

Company Overview

MyITLab®
Project 1A Training

PROJECT ACTIVITIES

In Activities 1.01 through 1.16, you will create the first five slides of a new presentation that Kodiak West Travel tour manager, Ken Dakano, is developing to introduce the tour services that the company offers. Your completed presentation will look similar to Figure 1.1.

PROJECT FILES

For Project 1A, you will need the following files:

New blank PowerPoint presentation
p01A_Glacier
p01A_Bay

You will save your presentation as:

Lastname_Firstname_1A_KWT_Overview

PROJECT RESULTS

Build from
Scratch

FIGURE 1.1 Project 1A Company Overview

Objective 1 | Create a New Presentation

Video P1-1

You can edit and format a blank presentation by adding text, a presentation theme, and pictures. When you start PowerPoint, presentations you have recently opened, if any, display on the left. On the right you can select either a blank presentation or a *theme*—a set of unified design elements that provides a look for your presentation by applying colors, fonts, and effects.

> **NOTE** **If You Are Using a Touch Screen**
>
> • Tap an item to click it.
> • Press and hold for a few seconds to right-click; release when the information or commands displays.
> • Touch the screen with two or more fingers and then pinch together to zoom in or stretch your fingers apart to zoom out.
> • Slide your finger on the screen to scroll—slide left to scroll right and slide right to scroll left.
> • Slide to rearrange—similar to dragging with a mouse.
> • Swipe from edge: from right to display charms; from left to expose open apps, snap apps, or close apps; from top or bottom to show commands or close an app.
> • Swipe to select—slide an item a short distance with a quick movement—to select an item and bring up commands, if any.

Activity 1.01 | Creating a New Presentation and Identifying Parts of the PowerPoint Window

1 Start PowerPoint. On the right, click **Facet** to view a preview of the Facet theme and the color variations associated with this theme. Below the theme preview, click the left and right **More Images** arrows ◀ and ▶ to view the manner in which various types of slides in this theme display. To the right of the preview, click each of the color variations. After you have viewed each color, click the original green color.

2 To the right of the preview window, point to the ▶ arrow, and then compare your screen with Figure 1.2.

You can use the left and right arrows to scroll through the available themes.

FIGURE 1.2

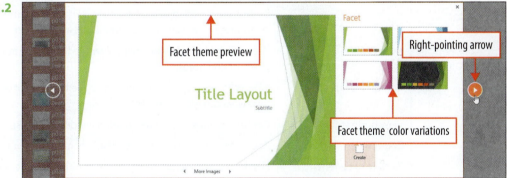

3 Click ▶ two times to view the next two available themes. Then, to the left of the preview window, click ◀ two times to return to the **Facet** theme. In the lower right area of the preview window, click **Create** to begin a new presentation using the Facet theme. Compare your screen with Figure 1.3.

The presentation displays in normal view. *Normal view* is the primary editing view in PowerPoint where you write and design your presentations. On the left, a small pane displays miniature images—*thumbnails*—of the slides in your presentation. On the right, the *Slide pane* displays a large image of the active slide.

FIGURE 1.3

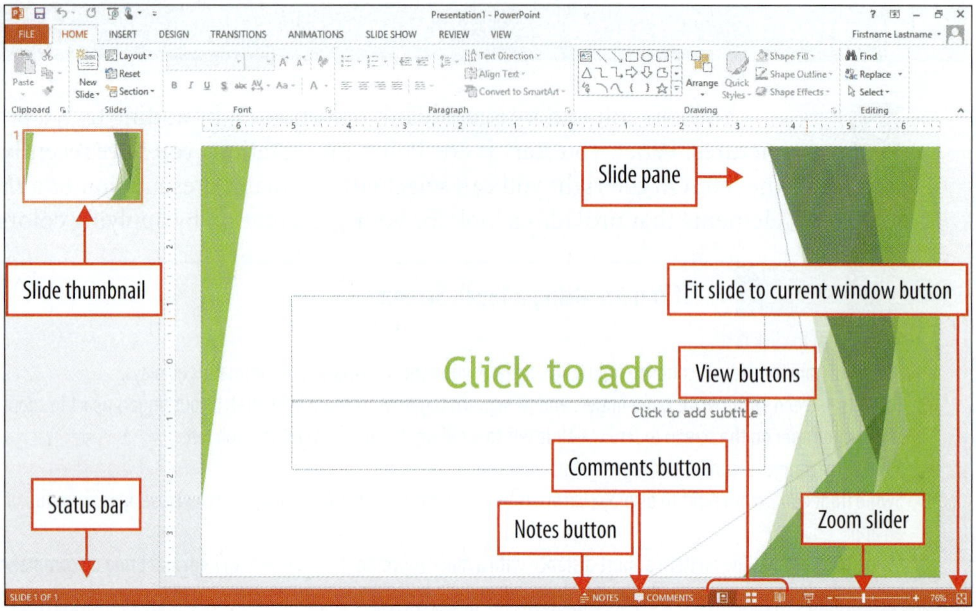

4 ▷ Take a moment to study the parts of the PowerPoint window described in the table in Figure 1.4.

FIGURE 1.4

MICROSOFT POWERPOINT SCREEN ELEMENTS	
SCREEN ELEMENT	**DESCRIPTION**
Slide pane	Displays a large image of the active slide.
Slide thumbnails	Miniature images of each slide in the presentation. Clicking a slide thumbnail displays the slide in the Slide pane.
Status bar	Displays, in a horizontal bar at the bottom of the presentation window, the current slide number, number of slides in a presentation, Notes button, Comments button, View buttons, Zoom slider, and Fit slide to current window button; you can customize this area to include additional information.
Notes button	When clicked, displays an area below the Slide pane in which you can type presentation notes.
Comments button	When clicked, displays a Comments pane to the right of the Slide pane, in which reviewers can type comments.
View buttons	Control the look of the presentation window with a set of commands.
Zoom slider	Zooms the slide displayed in the Slide pane, in and out.
Fit slide to current window button	Fits the active slide to the maximum view in the Slide pane.

Activity 1.02 | Entering Presentation Text

When a new presentation is created, PowerPoint displays a new blank presentation with a single slide—a title slide in Normal view. A presentation *slide*—similar to a page in a document—can contain text, pictures, tables, charts, and other multimedia or graphic objects. The *title slide* is most commonly the first slide in a presentation and provides an introduction to the presentation topic.

1 ▷ In the **Slide pane**, click in the text *Click to add title*, which is the title placeholder.

A *placeholder* is a box on a slide with dotted or dashed borders that holds title and body text or other content such as charts, tables, and pictures. This slide contains two placeholders, one for the title and one for the subtitle.

2 ▶ Type **Kodiak West** and then click in the subtitle placeholder. Type **Your Travel** and then press Enter to create a new line in the subtitle placeholder. Type **Your Way** and then compare your screen with Figure 1.5.

FIGURE 1.5

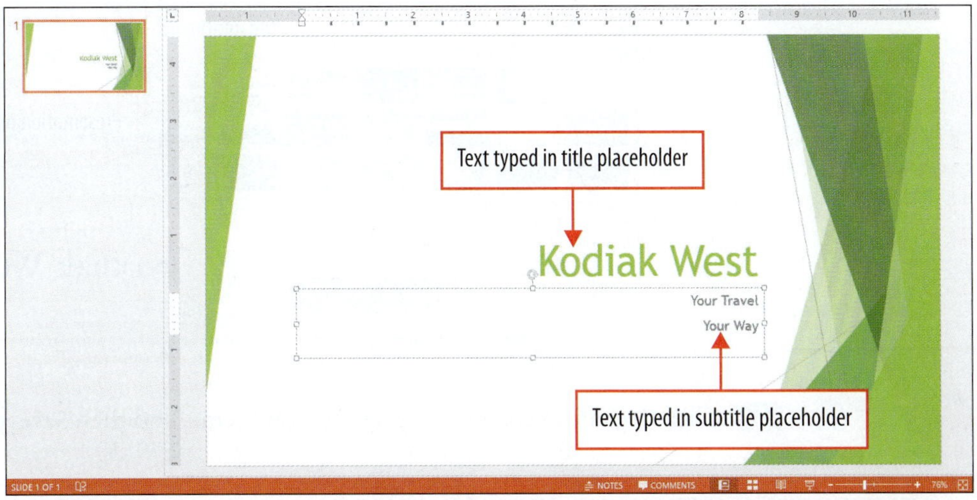

Text typed in title placeholder

Kodiak West

Your Travel
Your Way

Text typed in subtitle placeholder

3 ▶ On the **Quick Access Toolbar**, click **Save** 🖫. Under **Save As**, click **Computer**, and then click **Browse**. Navigate to the location where you are saving your files for this chapter, and then create and open a new folder named **PowerPoint Chapter 1** In the **File name** box, using your own name, replace the existing text with **Lastname_Firstname_1A_KWT_Overview** and then click **Save**.

Activity 1.03 | Applying a Presentation Theme

Recall that a theme is a set of unified design elements that provides a look for your presentation by applying colors, fonts, and effects. After you create a presentation, you can change the look of your presentation by applying a different theme.

1 ▶ On the ribbon, click the **DESIGN tab**. In the **Themes group**, click **More** ⊡ to display the **Themes** gallery. Compare your screen with Figure 1.6.

The themes displayed on your system may differ from Figure 1.6.

FIGURE 1.6

Design Tab

Current theme

Themes gallery
(yours may differ)

2 ▶ Under **Office**, point to several of the themes and notice that a ScreenTip displays the name of each theme and the Live Preview feature displays how each theme would look if applied to your presentation.

The first theme that displays is the Office Theme.

3 ⟩ Use the ScreenTips to locate the **Organic** theme shown in Figure 1.7.

FIGURE 1.7

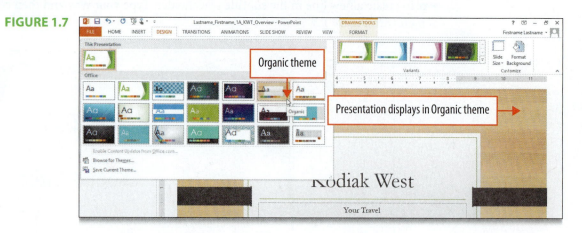

4 ⟩ Click **Organic** to change the presentation theme, and then **Save** 🖫 your presentation.

Video P1-2

Objective 2 | Edit a Presentation in Normal View

Editing is the process of modifying a presentation by adding and deleting slides or by changing the contents of individual slides.

Activity 1.04 | Inserting a New Slide

To insert a new slide in a presentation, display the slide that will precede the slide that you want to insert.

1 ⟩ On the **HOME tab**, in the **Slides group**, point to the **New Slide arrow**—the lower part of the New Slide button. Compare your screen with Figure 1.8.

The New Slide button is a *split button*—a type of button in which clicking the main part of the button performs a command and clicking the arrow opens a menu, list, or gallery. The upper, main part of the New Slide button, when clicked, inserts a slide without displaying any options. The lower part—the New Slide arrow—when clicked, displays a gallery of slide *layouts*— the arrangement of elements, such as title and subtitle text, lists, pictures, tables, charts, shapes, and movies, on a slide.

FIGURE 1.8

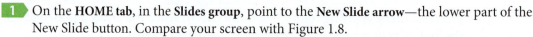

2 ⟩ In the **Slides group**, click the lower portion of the New Slide button—the **New Slide arrow**—to display the gallery, and then compare your screen with Figure 1.9.

FIGURE 1.9

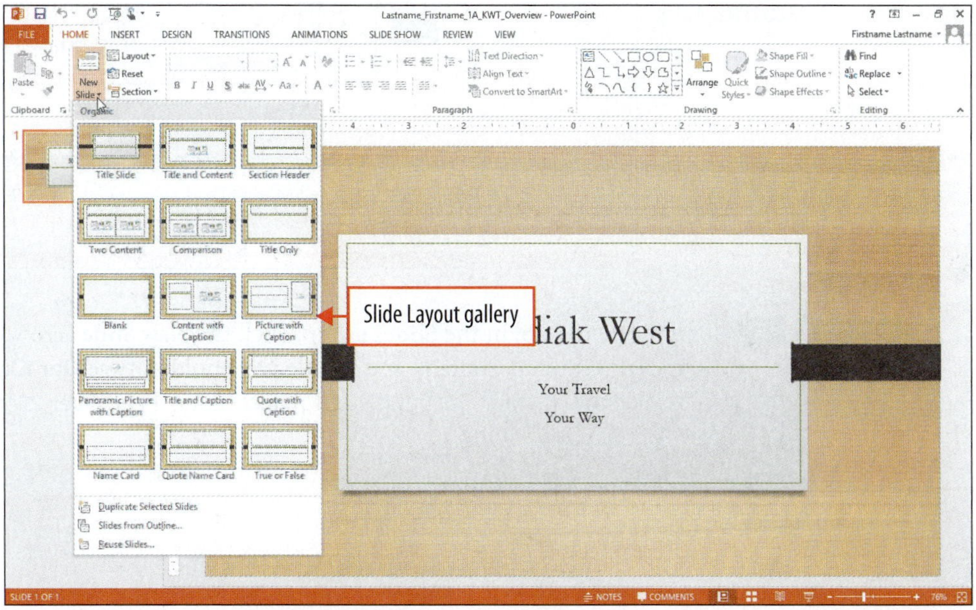

FIGURE 1.9

Slide Layout gallery

3 ▶ In the gallery, in the fourth row, click the first layout—**Panoramic Picture with Caption**—to insert a new slide. Notice that the new blank slide displays in the **Slide pane** and a slide thumbnail displays at the left. Compare your screen with Figure 1.10.

🔄 **BY TOUCH** In the gallery, tap the desired layout to insert a new slide.

FIGURE 1.10

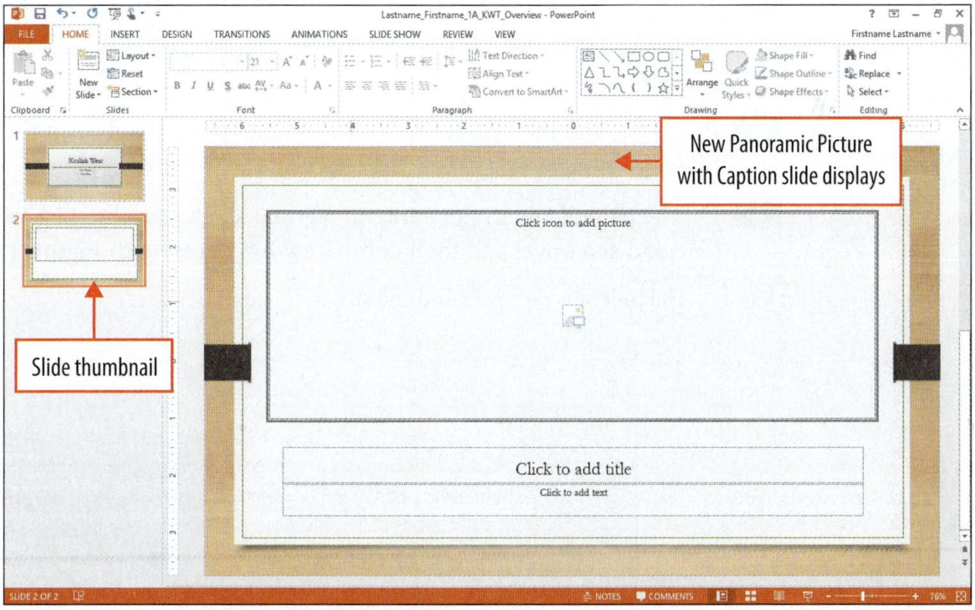

New Panoramic Picture with Caption slide displays

Slide thumbnail

4 ▶ On the slide, below the large picture placeholder, click the text *Click to add title*, and then type **Your Dreams**

5 ▶ Below the title placeholder, click in the text placeholder. Type **Whether you want to trek on a glacier or spend your time in quiet solitude, Kodiak West Travel can make your dream a reality.** Compare your screen with Figure 1.11.

FIGURE 1.11

Slide title

Text typed in text placeholder

Your Dreams

Whether you want to trek on a glacier or spend your time in quiet solitude, Kodiak West Travel can make your dream a reality.

---

6 On the **HOME tab**, in the **Slides group**, click the **New Slide arrow** to display the gallery, and then click **Title and Content**. In the title placeholder, type **Our Expertise** and then below the title placeholder, click in the content placeholder. Type **Over 20 years of experience in the travel industry**

7 Save 🖫 your presentation.

Activity 1.05 | Increasing and Decreasing List Levels

Text in a PowerPoint presentation can be organized according to *list levels*. List levels, each represented by a bullet symbol, are similar to outline levels. On a slide, list levels are identified by the bullet style, indentation, and the size of the text. The first level on an individual slide is the title. Increasing the list level of a bullet point increases its indent and results in a smaller text size. Decreasing the list level of a bullet point decreases its indent and results in a larger text size.

1 On **Slide 3**, if necessary, click at the end of the last bullet point after the word *industry*, and then press Enter to insert a new bullet point.

2 Press Tab, and then notice that the bullet is indented. Type **Certified Travel Associates**

> By pressing Tab at the beginning of a bullet point, you can increase the list level and indent the bullet point.

3 Press Enter, and then notice that a new bullet point displays at the same level as the previous bullet point.

4 On the **HOME tab**, in the **Paragraph group**, click **Decrease List Level** 🔄. Type **Specializing in land and sea travel** and then compare your screen with Figure 1.12.

> The indent is removed and the size of the text increases.

FIGURE 1.12

Our Expertise

- Over 20 years of experience in the travel industry
  - Certified Travel Associates

List level increased

- Specializing in land and sea travel

List level decreased

5 Press Enter, and then on the **HOME tab**, click **Increase List Level** 🔄. Type **Pacific Northwest including U.S. and Canada**

> You can use the Increase List Level button to indent the bullet point.

6 Compare your screen with Figure 1.13, and then **Save** 🖫 your presentation.

FIGURE 1.13

List level increased

Activity 1.06 | Adding Speaker's Notes to a Presentation

The **Notes pane** is an area of the Normal view window that displays below the Slide pane with space to type notes regarding the active slide. You can refer to these printouts while making a presentation, thus reminding you of the important points that you want to discuss.

1 With **Slide 3** displayed, in the **Status bar**, click **NOTES**, and then notice that below the Slide pane, the Notes pane displays. Click in the **Notes pane**, and then type **Kodiak West Travel has locations in Juneau, Anchorage, and Victoria.**

2 Compare your screen with Figure 1.14, and then **Save** 🖫 your presentation.

FIGURE 1.14

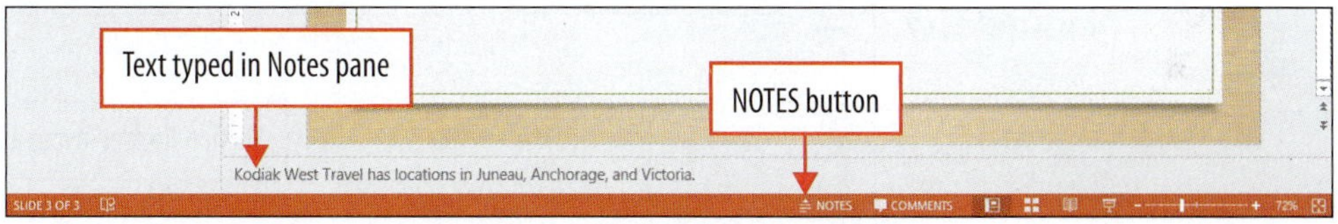

Text typed in Notes pane

NOTES button

Kodiak West Travel has locations in Juneau, Anchorage, and Victoria.

Activity 1.07 | Displaying and Editing Slides in the Slide Pane

1 At the left side of the PowerPoint window, look at the slide thumbnails, and then notice that the presentation contains three slides. At the right side of the PowerPoint window, in the vertical scroll bar, point to the scroll box, and then hold down the left mouse button to display a ScreenTip indicating the slide number and title.

2 Drag the scroll box up until the ScreenTip displays *Slide: 2 of 3 Your Dreams*. Compare your slide with Figure 1.15, and then release the mouse button to display **Slide 2**.

FIGURE 1.15

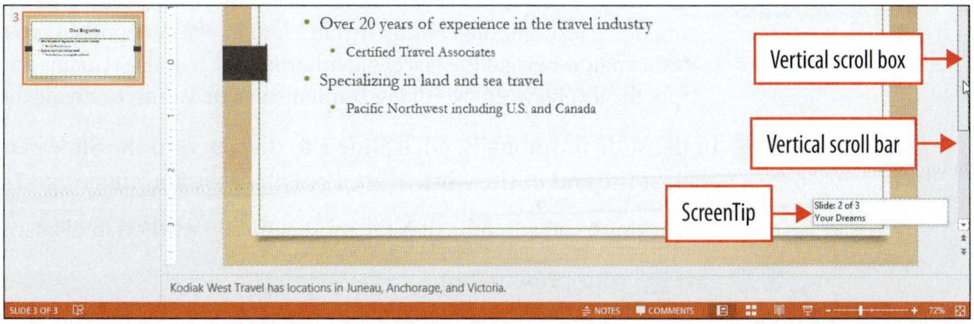

Our Expertise

- Over 20 years of experience in the travel industry
  - Certified Travel Associates
- Specializing in land and sea travel
  - Pacific Northwest including U.S. and Canada

Vertical scroll box

Vertical scroll bar

ScreenTip

Slide: 2 of 3
Your Dreams

Kodiak West Travel has locations in Juneau, Anchorage, and Victoria.

3 At the bottom of the slide, in the content placeholder, click at the end of the sentence, after the period. Press Spacebar, and then type **If you can dream it, we can help you get there.**

4 On the left side of the PowerPoint window, in the slide thumbnails, point to **Slide 3**, and then notice that a ScreenTip displays the slide title. Compare your screen with Figure 1.16.

FIGURE 1.16

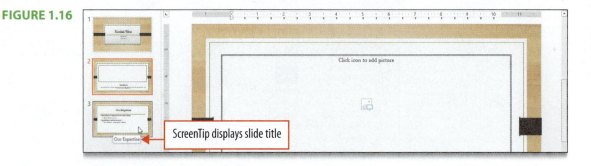

5 Click **Slide 3** to display it in the Slide pane. On the **HOME tab**, in the **Slides group**, click the **New Slide arrow** to display the **Slide Layout** gallery, and then click **Section Header**.

A *section header* is a type of slide layout that changes the look and flow of a presentation by providing text placeholders that do not contain bullet points.

6 Click in the title placeholder, and then type **About Our Company**

7 Click in the content placeholder below the title, and then type **Kodiak West Travel was established in May of 2001 by Ken Dakona and Mariam Dorner, two Alaska residents whose sense of adventure and commitment to ecotourism is an inherent aspect of their travel itineraries.** Compare your screen with Figure 1.17.

The placeholder text resizes to fit within the placeholder. The AutoFit Options button displays.

FIGURE 1.17

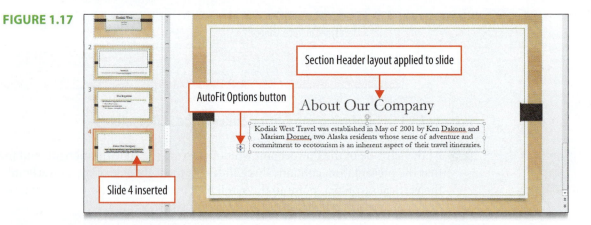

8 Click **AutoFit Options** ⬍, and then if necessary, click AutoFit Text to Placeholder.

The *AutoFit Text to Placeholder* option keeps the text contained within the placeholder by reducing the size of the text. The *Stop Fitting Text to This Placeholder* option turns off the AutoFit option so that the text can flow beyond the placeholder border; the text size remains unchanged. You can also choose to split the text between two slides, continue on a new slide, or divide the text into two columns.

9 In the slide thumbnails, click **Slide 1** to display it in the **Slide pane**, and then in the slide title, click at the end of the word *West*. Press Spacebar, and then type **Travel**

Clicking a slide thumbnail is the most common method to display a slide in the Slide pane.

10 **Save** 💾 your presentation.

Objective 3   Add Pictures to a Presentation

Video P1-3

Photographic images add impact to a presentation and help the audience visualize your message.

Activity 1.08 | Inserting a Picture from a File

Many slide layouts in PowerPoint accommodate digital picture files so that you can easily add pictures you have stored on your system or on a portable storage device.

1 ▶ Display **Slide 2**, and then compare your screen with Figure 1.18.

In the center of the large picture placeholder, the *Pictures* button displays.

FIGURE 1.18

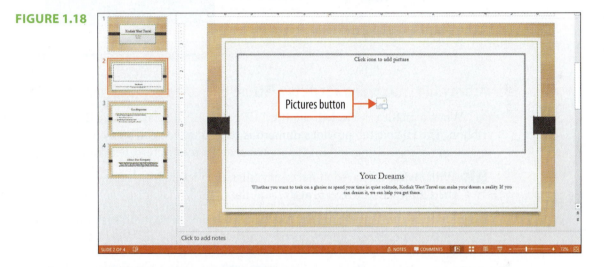

2 ▶ In the picture placeholder, click **Pictures** to open the **Insert Picture** dialog box. Navigate to the location in which your student data files are stored, click **p01A_Glacier**, and then click **Insert** to insert the picture in the placeholder. Compare your screen with Figure 1.19.

Small squares—*sizing handles*—surround the inserted picture and indicate that the picture is selected and can be modified or formatted. The *rotation handle*—a circular arrow above the picture—provides a way to rotate a selected image. The PICTURE TOOLS are added to the ribbon, providing picture formatting options.

FIGURE 1.19

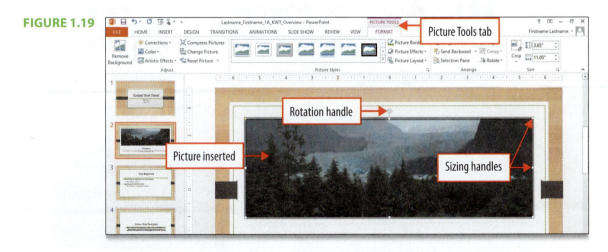

3 ▶ Display **Slide 3**. On the **HOME tab**, in the **Slides group**, click the **New Slide arrow**, and then click **Title and Content**. In the title placeholder, type **Your Vacation**

4 In the content placeholder, click **Pictures** 🖻. Navigate to your student data files, and then click **p01A_Bay**. Click **Insert**, and then compare your screen with Figure 1.20. **Save** 🖫 the presentation.

FIGURE 1.20

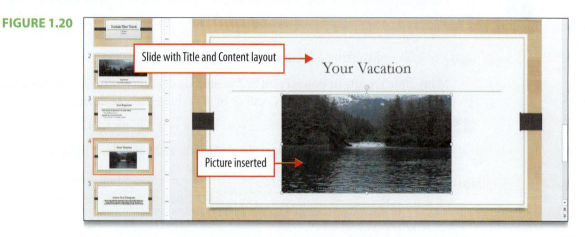

Activity 1.09 | Applying a Style to a Picture

When a picture is selected, the PICTURE TOOLS display, adding the Format tab to the ribbon. The Format tab provides numerous styles that you can apply to your pictures. A *style* is a collection of formatting options that you can apply to a picture, text, or an object.

1 With **Slide 4** displayed, if necessary, click the picture to select it. On the ribbon, notice that the *PICTURE TOOLS* are active and the *FORMAT* tab displays.

2 On the **FORMAT tab**, in the **Picture Styles group**, click **More** ⏷ to display the **Picture Styles** gallery, and then compare your screen with Figure 1.21.

FIGURE 1.21

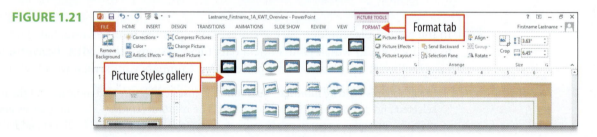

3 In the gallery, point to several of the picture styles to display the ScreenTips and to view the effect on your picture. In the second row, click the second style—**Simple Frame, Black**. Click in a blank area of the slide, compare your screen with Figure 1.22, and then **Save** 🖫 the presentation.

FIGURE 1.22

Activity 1.10 | Applying and Removing Picture Artistic Effects

Artistic effects are formats applied to images that make pictures resemble sketches or paintings.

1 On **Slide 4**, select the picture. Click the **FORMAT tab**, and then in the **Adjust group**, click **Artistic Effects** to display the **Artistic Effects** gallery. Compare your screen with Figure 1.23.

FIGURE 1.23

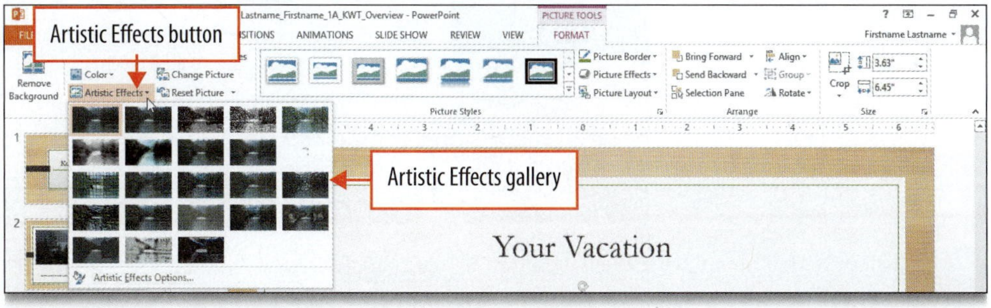

2 In the gallery, point to several of the artistic effects to display the ScreenTips and to have Live Preview display the effect on your picture. Then, in the second row, click the **Glow Diffused** effect.

3 With the picture still selected, on the **FORMAT tab**, in the **Adjust group**, click **Artistic Effects** again to display the gallery. In the first row, click the first effect—**None**—to remove the effect from the picture and restore the previous formatting.

4 **Save** 🖫 the presentation.

Objective 4 Print and View a Presentation

Video P1-4

There are several print options in PowerPoint. For example, you can print full page images of your slides, presentation handouts to provide your audience with copies of your slides, or Notes pages displaying speaker's notes below an image of the slide.

Activity 1.11 | Viewing a Slide Show

When you view a presentation as an electronic slide show, the entire slide fills the computer screen, and an audience can view your presentation if your computer is connected to a projection system.

1 On the ribbon, click the **SLIDE SHOW tab**. In the **Start Slide Show group**, click **From Beginning**. Compare your screen with Figure 1.24.

The first slide fills the screen, displaying the presentation as the audience would see it if your computer was connected to a projection system.

> **🔁 ANOTHER WAY** Press F5 to start the slide show from the beginning. Or, display the first slide you want to show and click the Slide Show button on the lower right side of the status bar.

FIGURE 1.24

Kodiak West Travel

Your Travel

Your Way

2 ▶ Click the left mouse button or press $\boxed{\text{Spacebar}}$ to advance to the second slide.

3 ▶ Continue to click or press $\boxed{\text{Spacebar}}$ until the last slide displays, and then click or press $\boxed{\text{Spacebar}}$ one more time to display a ***black slide***—a slide that displays after the last slide in a presentation indicating that the presentation is over.

4 ▶ With the black slide displayed, click the left mouse button to exit the slide show and return to the presentation.

Activity 1.12 | Using Presenter View

Presenter View shows the full-screen slide show on one monitor while enabling the presenter to view a preview of the next slide, notes, and a timer on another monitor. Your audience will be able to view only the current slide.

1 ▶ On the **SLIDE SHOW tab**, in the **Monitors** group, be sure that the **Use Presenter View** check box is selected. Hold down $\boxed{\text{Alt}}$ and press $\boxed{\text{F5}}$. Compare your screen with Figure 1.25.

If you do not have two monitors, you can practice using Presenter View by pressing $\boxed{\text{Alt}}$+$\boxed{\text{F5}}$. Above the upper left corner of the slide, a timer displays. Below the timer, the current slide displays. Below the current slide are slide show option buttons. In the upper right corner, the next slide displays. In the lower right corner, any notes that you typed in the notes pane for the current slide display. Below the notes are buttons that enable you to make the notes smaller or larger. Below the current slide, navigation buttons display.

FIGURE 1.25

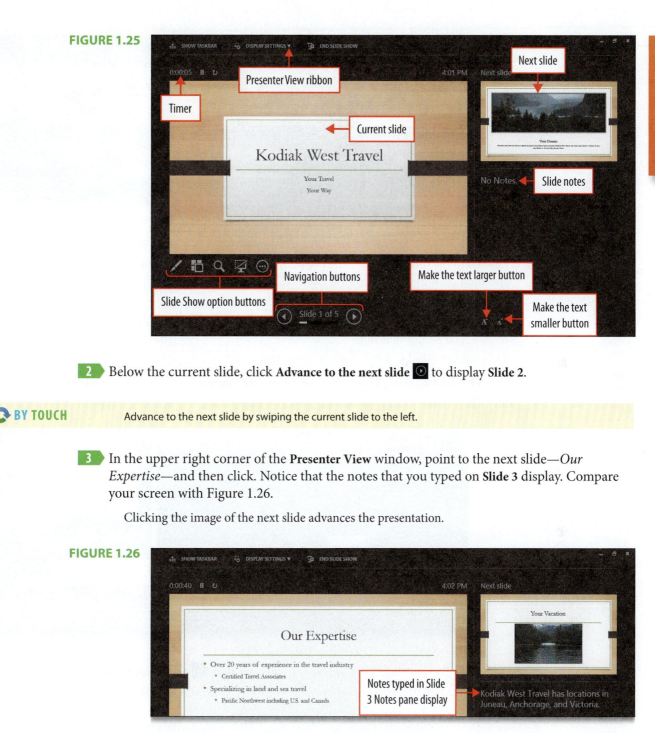

2 Below the current slide, click **Advance to the next slide** ⊙ to display **Slide 2**.

🔄 **BY TOUCH**   Advance to the next slide by swiping the current slide to the left.

3 In the upper right corner of the **Presenter View** window, point to the next slide—*Our Expertise*—and then click. Notice that the notes that you typed on **Slide 3** display. Compare your screen with Figure 1.26.

Clicking the image of the next slide advances the presentation.

FIGURE 1.26

4 Below the notes, click **Make the text larger** 🄰 one time to increase the font size of the notes in Presenter view, thus increasing readability.

5 Below the current slide, click **See all slides** ▦. Compare your screen with Figure 1.27.

A thumbnail view of all of the slides in your presentation displays. Here you can quickly move to another slide; for example, if you want to review a concept or answer a question related to a slide other than the current slide.

FIGURE 1.27

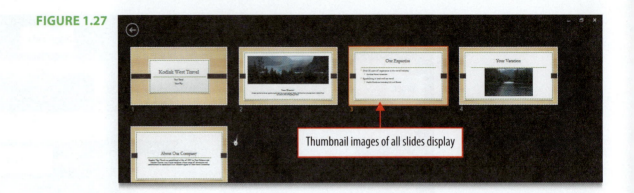

Thumbnail images of all slides display

6 ▶ Click **Slide 4** to make Slide 4 the current slide in Presenter View. Below the current slide, click **Zoom into the slide** 🔍. Move the 🔍 pointer to the middle of the picture on the current slide, and then click to zoom in on the picture. Notice that the ✋ pointer displays. Compare your slide with Figure 1.28.

With the ✋ pointer displayed, you can move the zoomed image to draw close-up attention to a particular part of your slide.

🔁 **BY TOUCH**   Touch the current slide with two fingers and then pinch together to zoom in or stretch your fingers apart to zoom out.

FIGURE 1.28

No Notes.

Pointer

Zoom button

Zoomed-in image

7 ▶ Below the current slide, click **Advance to the next slide** ⊙ to display **Slide 5.** At the top of the Presenter View window, click **END SLIDE SHOW** to return to your presentation.

Activity 1.13 | Inserting Headers and Footers on Slide Handouts

A **_header_** is text that prints at the top of each sheet of **_slide handouts_** or **_notes pages_**. Slide handouts are printed images of slides on a sheet of paper. Notes pages are printouts that contain the slide image on the top half of the page and notes that you have created on the Notes pane in the lower half of the page.

In addition to headers, you can insert **_footers_**—text that displays at the bottom of every slide or that prints at the bottom of a sheet of slide handouts or notes pages.

1 ▶ Click the **INSERT tab**, and then in the **Text group**, click **Header & Footer** to display the **Header and Footer** dialog box.

2 ▶ In the **Header and Footer** dialog box, click the **Notes and Handouts tab**. Under **Include on page**, select the **Date and time** check box, and as you do so, watch the Preview box in the upper right corner of the Header and Footer dialog box.

The Preview box indicates the placeholders on the printed Notes and Handouts pages. The two narrow rectangular boxes at the top of the Preview box indicate placeholders for the header text and date. When you select the Date and time check box, the placeholder in the upper right corner is outlined, indicating the location in which the date will display.

3 ▶ Be sure that the **Update automatically** option button is selected so that the current date prints on the notes and handouts each time you print the presentation. If it is not selected, click the Update automatically option button.

4 ▶ If necessary, *clear* the Header check box to omit this element. Notice that in the **Preview** box, the corresponding placeholder is not selected.

5 ▶ Verify that the **Page number** check box is selected and select it if it is not. Select the **Footer** check box, and then click in the **Footer** box. Using your own name, type **Lastname_Firstname_1A_KWT_Overview** so that the file name displays as a footer, and then compare your dialog box with Figure 1.29.

FIGURE 1.29

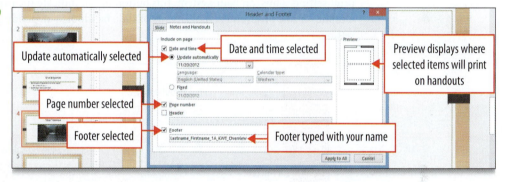

6 ▶ In the lower right corner of the dialog box, click **Apply to All**. **Save** 🖫 your presentation.

Activity 1.14 | Inserting Slide Numbers on Slides

In this activity, you will insert the slide numbers on the presentation slides.

1 ▶ Display **Slide 1**. On the **INSERT tab**, in the **Text group**, click **Header & Footer** to display the **Header and Footer** dialog box.

2 ▶ In the **Header and Footer** dialog box, if necessary, click the Slide tab. Under **Include on slide**, select the **Slide number** check box, and then select the **Don't show on title slide** check box. Verify that all other check boxes are cleared, and then compare your screen with Figure 1.30.

Selecting the *Don't show on title slide* check box omits the slide number from the first slide in a presentation.

FIGURE 1.30

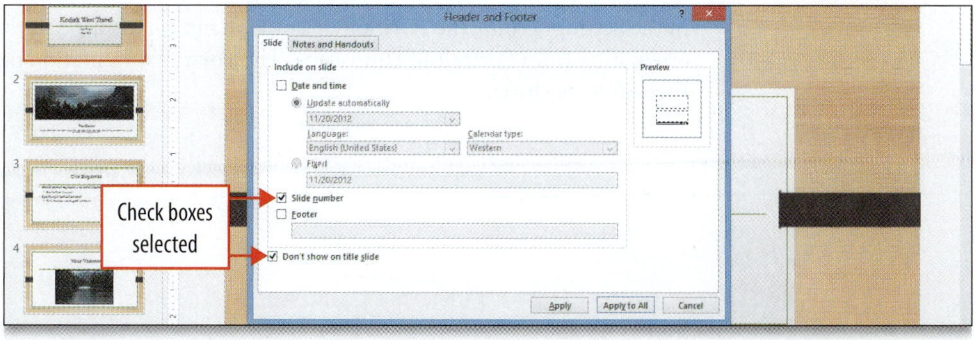

3 Click **Apply to All**, and then notice that on the first slide, the side number does not display.

4 Display **Slide 2**, and then notice that the slide number displays in the lower right area of the slide. Display each slide in the presentation and notice the placement of the slide number.

The position of the slide number and other header and footer information is determined by the theme applied to the presentation.

Activity 1.15 | Printing Presentation Handouts

Use Backstage view to preview the arrangement of slides and to print your presentation.

1 Display **Slide 1**. Click the **FILE tab** to display **Backstage** view, and then click **Print**.

The Print tab in Backstage view displays the tools you need to select your settings and also to view a preview of your presentation. On the right, Print Preview displays your presentation exactly as it will print. If your system is not connected to a color printer, your slide may display in black and white.

2 Under **Settings**, click **Full Page Slides**, and then compare your screen with Figure 1.31.

The gallery displays either the default print setting—Full Page Slides—or the most recently selected print setting. Thus, on your system, this button might indicate the presentation Notes Pages, Outline, or one of several arrangements of slide handouts—depending on the most recently used setting.

FIGURE 1.31

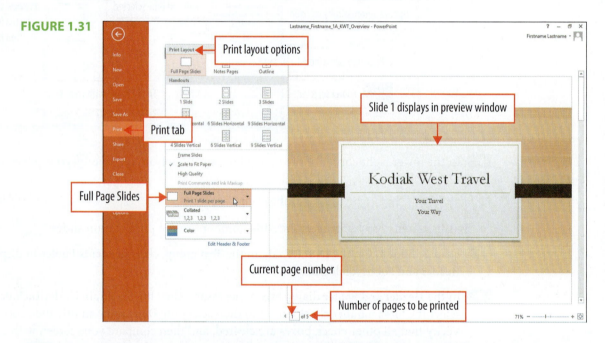

3 In the gallery, under **Handouts**, click **6 Slides Horizontal**. Notice that the **Print Preview** on the right displays the slide handout, and that the current date, file name, and page number display in the header and footer. Compare your screen with Figure 1.32.

In the Settings group, the Portrait Orientation option displays so that you can change the print orientation from Portrait to Landscape. The Portrait Orientation option does not display when Full Page Slides is chosen.

FIGURE 1.32

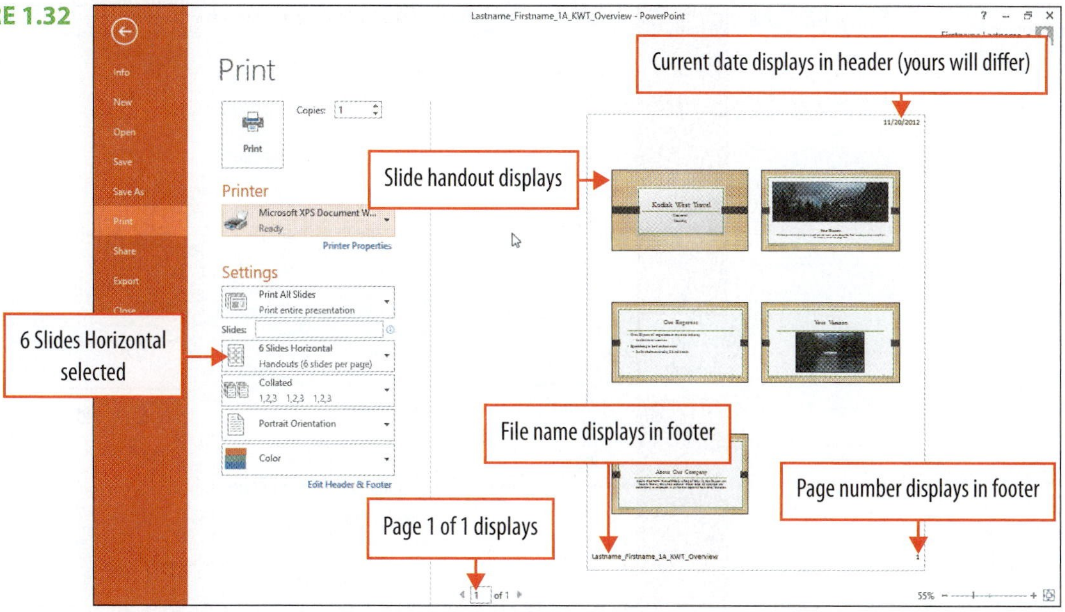

4 To submit your file electronically, skip this step and move to Step 5. To print your document on paper using the default printer on your system, in the upper left portion of the screen, click **Print**.

The handout will print on your default printer—on a black and white printer, the colors will print in shades of gray. Backstage view closes and your file redisplays in the PowerPoint window.

5 To create an electronic file, on the left click **Export**. On the right, click **Create PDF/XPS**. In the **Publish as PDF or XPS** dialog box, navigate to your **PowerPoint Chapter 1** folder, and then click **Publish**. If your Adobe Acrobat or Adobe Reader program displays your PDF, close the program.

> **More Knowledge** **Print a Presentation in Grayscale**
>
> To save toner and ink, you can print a presentation in shades of gray using the grayscale setting. To do so, on the FILE tab, click Print. Under Settings, click the Color arrow, and then click Grayscale.

Activity 1.16 | Printing Speaker Notes

1 Click the **FILE tab**, and then click **Print**. Under **Settings**, click **6 Slides Horizontal**, and then under **Print Layout**, click **Notes Pages** to view the presentation notes for **Slide 1**; recall that you created notes for **Slide 3**.

Indicated below the Notes page are the current slide number and the number of pages that will print when Notes Pages is selected. You can use the Next Page and Previous Page arrows to display each Notes page in the presentation.

2 At the bottom of the **Print Preview**, click **Next Page** two times so that **Page 3** displays. Notice that the notes you typed for Slide 3 display below the image of the slide. Compare your screen with Figure 1.33.

FIGURE 1.33

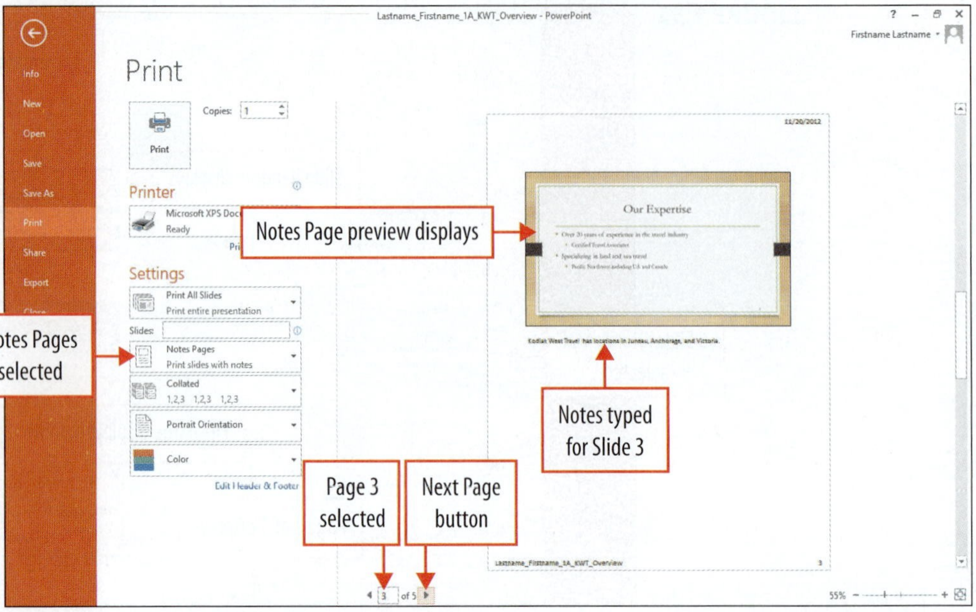

3 ▸ Under **Settings**, click in the **Slides box**. Type **3** and then click **Notes Pages**. In the lower section, select **Frame Slides**. To print the notes page, click **Print**.

4 ▸ Click the **FILE tab** to display **Backstage** view. On the right, at the bottom of the **Properties** list, click **Show All Properties**. On the list of **Properties**, click to the right of **Tags** to display an empty box, and then type **company overview**

5 ▸ Click to the right of **Subject** to display an empty box, and then type your course name and section number. Under **Related People**, be sure that your name displays as the author, and edit if necessary.

6 ▸ In the lower right corner, scroll down if necessary, click **Show Fewer Properties**, and then on the left, click **Save**. On the right end of the title bar, click **Close** **✕** to close the presentation and close PowerPoint.

END | You have completed Project 1A

GO! with Office Web Apps

Objective | Create a Company Overview Presentation in the PowerPoint Web App

> **ALERT!** | **Working with Web-Based Applications and Services**
>
> Computer programs and services on the web receive continuous updates and improvements, so the steps to complete this web-based activity may differ from the ones shown. You can often look at the screens and the information presented to determine how to complete the activity.

Activity | Creating a Company Overview Presentation in the PowerPoint Web App

In this activity, you will use the PowerPoint Web App to create a presentation similar to the one you created in Project 1A.

1 From the desktop, start Internet Explorer. Navigate to **http://skydrive.com**, and then sign in to your Microsoft account. Open your **GO! Web Projects** folder—or create and then open this folder if necessary.

2 On the SkyDrive menu bar, click **Create**, and then click **PowerPoint presentation**. Using your own name, as the file name, type **Lastname_Firstname_PPT_1A_Web** and then click **Create** to start a new file in the PowerPoint Web app.

3 In the **Select Theme** window, click **Organic**, and then click **Apply**.

4 In the title placeholder, type **Kodiak West Travel** and then in the subtitle placeholder type **Your Travel** and press ⏎. Type **Your Way** and then click anywhere on the slide outside of the subtitle placeholder to enter the text.

5 On the **HOME Tab**, in the **Slides group**, click **New Slide**. Scroll the **New Slide gallery**, and then click **Panoramic Picture with Caption**. Click **Add Slide**.

6 In the picture placeholder, click **Pictures** 🖼, navigate to your student data files, and then click **p01A_Glacier**. Click **Open**.

7 Click in the title placeholder. Type **Your Dreams** and then click in the text placeholder. Type **Let Kodiak West Travel assist you with all of your travel arrangements!** Compare your screen with Figure A.

8 Click outside of the text placeholder. On the **HOME tab**, click **New Slide**, and then click **Title and Content**. Click **Add Slide**. In the title placeholder type **Our Expertise**

FIGURE A

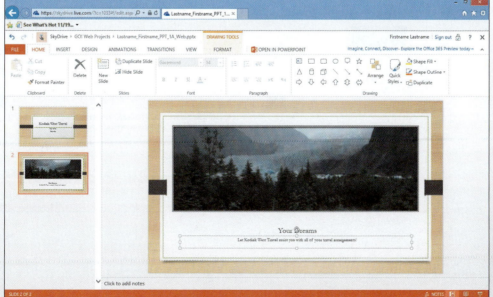

(GO! with Office Web Apps continues on the next page)

9 In the content placeholder, type **Over 20 years of experience in the travel industry** and then press ⏎. Press ⇥. Type **Certified Travel Associates** and then press ⏎. On the **HOME tab**, in the **Paragraph group**, click **Decrease List Level** ⇤. Type **Specializing in land and sea travel** and then press ⏎. Press ⇥ and then type **Pacific Northwest including U.S. and Canada**

10 Click outside the content placeholder, and then insert a **New Slide** with the **Title and Content** layout. In the title placeholder type **Your Vacation** and then in the content placeholder click **Pictures** 🖼. From your student data files, insert **p01A_Bay**. On the **PICTURE TOOLS FORMAT** tab, in the **Picture Styles group**, click the **down arrow**, and then in the second row, click the first style **Simple Frame, Black**.

11 Insert a **New Slide** with the **Section Header** layout. In the title placeholder, type **About Our Company** and then click in the text placeholder. Type **Kodiak West**

Travel was founded in May of 2001 by Ken Dakona and Mariam Dorner.

12 Click anywhere in a blank area of the slide, and then compare your screen with Figure B.

13 Click **Slide 3**, and then below the slide, click in the Notes pane. Type **Kodiak West Travel has locations in Juneau, Anchorage, and Victoria.**

14 Display **Slide 1**. On the **VIEW tab**, in the **Presentation Views group**, click **Slide Show**. If a Security warning displays at the bottom of your screen, click Allow once. Click the left mouse button to progress through the presentation. When the black slide displays, click the mouse button.

15 On the ribbon, click the **FILE tab** and click **Exit**. Sign out of your Microsoft account. Submit as instructed by your instructor. If you are instructed to submit your file, create a PDF as indicated in the Note box below.

N O T E **Creating a PDF from the PowerPoint Web App**

To print on paper, click the File tab, click Print, and then click Print to PDF. In the Microsoft PowerPoint Web App message box, click Click here to view the PDF of your document. In the message bar at the bottom of your screen, click the Save arrow, and then click Save as. In the Save As dialog box, navigate to your PowerPoint Chapter 1 folder, and then save the file. Click Close.

FIGURE B

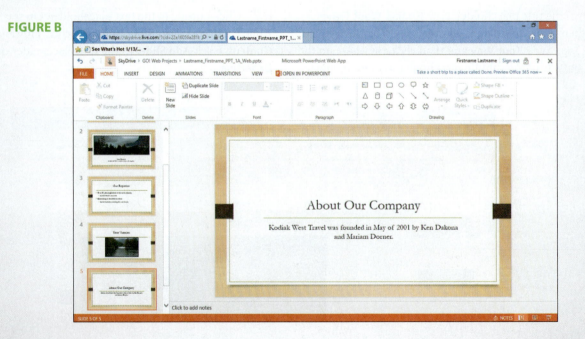

Itinerary Presentation

PROJECT ACTIVITIES

In Activities 1.17 through 1.33, you will combine two presentations that the marketing team at Kodiak West Travel developed describing itinerary ideas when visiting Seattle before or after a cruise. You will insert slides from one presentation into another, and then you will rearrange and delete slides. You will also apply font formatting and slide transitions to the presentation. Your completed presentation will look similar to Figure 1.34.

PROJECT FILES

For Project 1B, you will need the following files: You will save your presentation as:

p01B_Seattle   **Lastname_Firstname_1B_Seattle**
p01B_Slides

PROJECT RESULTS

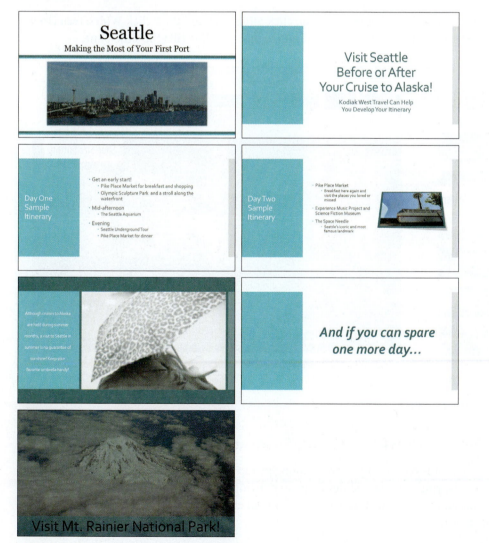

FIGURE 1.34 Project 1B Itinerary Presentation

Video P1-5

Recall that editing refers to the process of adding, deleting, and modifying presentation content. You can edit presentation content in either the Slide pane or in the presentation outline.

Activity 1.17 | Changing Slide Size

Presentations that you create with some of the newer themes in PowerPoint 2013 default to a widescreen format using a 16:9 *aspect ratio*—the ratio of the width of a display to the height of the display. This slide size is similar to most television and computer monitor screens. Previous versions of PowerPoint used a squarer format with a 4:3 aspect ratio. The widescreen format utilizes screen space more effectively.

1 Start PowerPoint. On the left, under the list of recent presentations, click **Open Other Presentations**. Under **Open**, click **Computer** and then click **Browse**. Navigate to your student data files, and then click **p01B_Seattle**. Click **Open**. On the **FILE tab**, click **Save As**, navigate to your **PowerPoint Chapter 1** folder, and then using your own name, save the file as **Lastname_Firstname_1B_Seattle**

2 Notice that **Slide 1** displays in a square format and that in the **Slide pane**, there is white space on the left and right slides of the slide.

3 On the **DESIGN tab**, in the **Customize group**, click **Slide Size**, and then click **Widescreen (16:9)**. Compare your screen with Figure 1.35 and notice that the slide fills the slide pane.

FIGURE 1.35

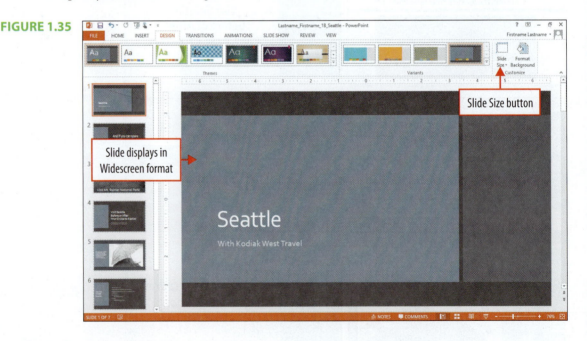

4 Save the presentation.

Activity 1.18 | Inserting Slides from an Existing Presentation

Presentation content is commonly shared among group members in an organization. Rather than re-creating slides, you can insert slides from an existing presentation into the current presentation. In this activity, you will insert slides from an existing presentation into your 1B_Seattle presentation.

1 With **Slide 1** displayed, on the **HOME tab**, in the **Slides group**, click the **New Slide arrow** to display the **Slide Layout** gallery and additional commands for inserting slides. Compare your screen with Figure 1.36.

FIGURE 1.36

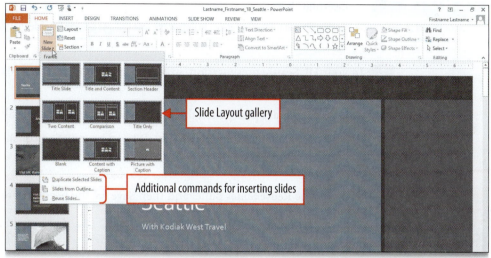

2 Below the gallery, click **Reuse Slides** to open the Reuse Slides pane on the right side of the PowerPoint window.

3 In the **Reuse Slides** pane, click **Browse**, and then click **Browse File**. In the **Browse** dialog box, navigate to the location where your student data files are stored, and then double-click **p01B_Slides** to display the slides from this presentation in the **Reuse Slides** pane.

4 At the bottom of the **Reuse Slides** pane, be sure that the **Keep source formatting** check box is *cleared*, and then compare your screen with Figure 1.37.

When the *Keep source formatting* check box is cleared, the theme formatting of the presentation in which the slides are inserted is applied. When the *Keep source formatting* check box is selected, you retain the formatting applied to the slides when inserted into the existing presentation.

FIGURE 1.37

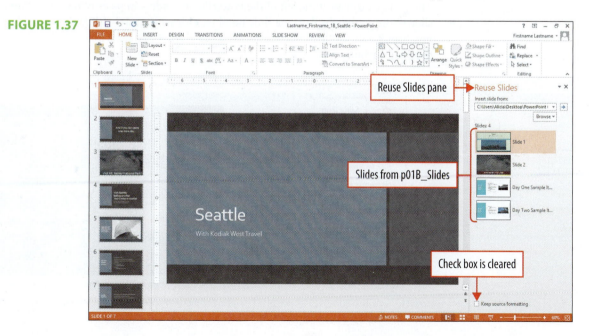

5 In the **Reuse Slides** pane, point to each slide to view a ScreenTip displaying the file name and the slide title.

6 In the **Reuse Slides** pane, click the first slide to insert the slide after Slide 1. Notice that the inserted slide adopts the color of the presentation theme into which the slide was inserted.

NOTE **Inserting Slides**

You can insert slides into your presentation in any order; remember to display the slide that will precede the slide that you want to insert.

7 In your **1B_Seattle** presentation, in the slide thumbnails, click **Slide 7** to display it in the **Slide pane**.

8 In the **Reuse Slides** pane, click the fourth slide to insert it after Slide 7.

Your presentation contains nine slides. When a presentation contains a large number of slides, a scroll box displays to the right of the slide thumbnails so that you can scroll and then select the thumbnails.

9 **Close** ☒ the **Reuse Slides** pane, and then **Save** 🖫 the presentation.

***More* Knowledge** **Inserting All Slides**

You can insert all of the slides from an existing presentation into the current presentation at one time. In the Reuse Slides pane, right-click one of the slides that you want to insert, and then click Insert All Slides.

Activity 1.19 | Displaying and Editing the Presentation Outline

Outline View displays the presentation outline to the left of the Slide pane. You can use the outline to edit the presentation text. Changes that you make in the outline are immediately displayed in the Slide pane.

1 To the right of the slide thumbnails, drag the scroll box up, and then click **Slide 1** to display it in the Slide pane. On the **VIEW tab**, in the **Presentation Views group**, click **Outline View**. Compare your screen with Figure 1.38.

The outline displays at the left of the PowerPoint window in place of the slide thumbnails. Each slide in the outline displays the slide number, slide icon, and the slide title in bold. Slides that do not display a slide title in the outline use a slide layout that does not include a title, for example, the Blank layout.

FIGURE 1.38

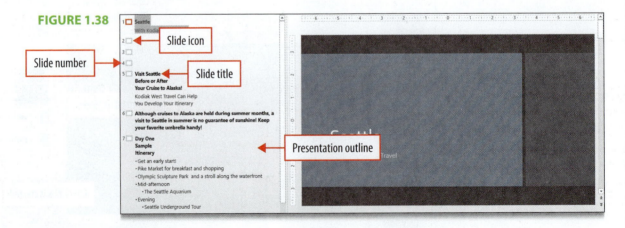

2 In the **Outline**, in **Slide 7**, drag to select the second and third bullet points—*Pike Market for breakfast and shopping*, and *Olympic Sculpture Park and a stroll along the waterfront*. Compare your screen with Figure 1.39.

FIGURE 1.39

3 On the **HOME tab**, in the **Paragraph group**, click **Increase List Level** one time to increase the list level of the selected bullet points.

When you type in the outline or change the list level, the changes also display in the Slide pane.

4 In the **Outline**, in **Slide 7**, click at the end of the last bullet point after the word *Tour*. Press Enter to create a new bullet point at the same list level as the previous bullet point. Type **Pike Place Market for dinner** and then compare your screen with Figure 1.40.

FIGURE 1.40

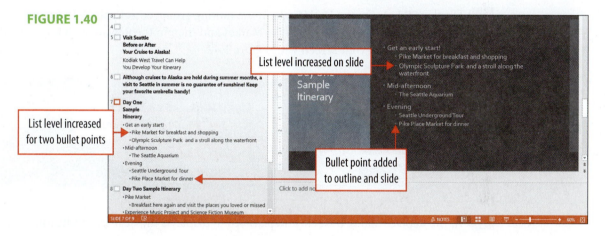

5 In the **Status bar**, click **Normal** to display the slide thumbnails, and then **Save** the presentation.

You can type text in the Slide pane or in the Outline. Displaying the Outline enables you to view the entire flow of the presentation.

Activity 1.20 | Deleting and Moving a Slide

1 To the right of the slide thumbnails, locate the vertical scroll bar and scroll box. If necessary, drag the scroll box down so that **Slide 9** displays in the slide thumbnails. Click **Slide 9** to display it in the Slide pane. Press Del to delete the slide from the presentation.

Your presentation contains eight slides.

2 If necessary, scroll the slide thumbnails so that **Slide 4** displays. Point to **Slide 4**, hold down the left mouse button, and then drag down to position the **Slide 4** thumbnail below the **Slide 8** thumbnail. Release the mouse button and then compare your screen with Figure 1.41.

You can easily rearrange your slides by dragging a slide thumbnail to a new location in the presentation.

BY TOUCH Use your finger to drag the slide you want to move to a new location in the presentation.

FIGURE 1.41

Slide 4 moved to end of presentation

Mt. Rainier National Park!

3 Save the presentation.

Activity 1.21 | Finding and Replacing Text

The Replace command enables you to locate all occurrences of specified text and replace it with alternative text.

1 Display **Slide 1**. On the **HOME tab**, in the **Editing group**, click **Replace**. In the **Replace** dialog box, in the **Find what** box, type **Pike Market** and then in the **Replace with** box, type **Pike Place Market** Compare your screen with Figure 1.42.

FIGURE 1.42

Text typed in Replace with box

Text typed in Find what box

Seattle

2 In the **Replace** dialog box, click **Replace All** to display a message box indicating that two replacements were made.

3 In the message box, click **OK**. **Close** the **Replace** dialog box, and then click **Save** .

Objective 6 | Format a Presentation

Video P1-6

Formatting refers to changing the appearance of the text, layout, and design of a slide.

Activity 1.22 | Applying a Theme Variant

Recall that a theme is a set of unified design elements that provides a look for your presentation by applying colors, fonts, and effects. Each PowerPoint theme includes several ***variants***—variations on the theme style and color.

1 On the **DESIGN tab**, In the **Variants group**, notice that four variants of the current theme—*Frame*—display.

2 Point to each of the variants to view the change to **Slide 1**.

3 With **Slide 1** displayed, in the **Variants group**, point to the **third variant**, and then right-click. Compare your screen with Figure 1.43.

The shortcut menu displays options for applying the variant.

FIGURE 1.43

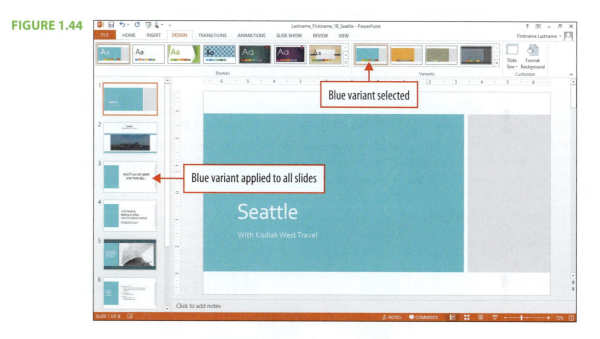

> **Shortcut menu displays options for applying Variant**

> 4 Click **Apply to Selected Slides** to apply the variant to **Slide 1** only.

> 5 In the **Variants group**, right-click the **blue variant**. On the shortcut menu, click **Apply to All Slides** so that the blue color is applied to all of the slides in the presentation. Compare your screen with Figure 1.44.

FIGURE 1.44

> **Blue variant selected**

> **Blue variant applied to all slides**

Seattle

With Kodiak West Travel

> 6 Save your presentation.

Activity 1.23 | Changing Fonts and Font Sizes

Recall that a font is a set of characters with the same design and shape and that fonts are measured in points. Font styles include bold, italic, and underline, and you can apply any combination of these styles to presentation text. Font styles and font color are useful to provide emphasis and are a visual cue to draw the reader's eye to important text.

> 1 Display **Slide 2**. Select all of the text in the title placeholder, point to the mini toolbar, and then click the **Font button arrow** to display the available fonts. Scroll the font list, and then click **Georgia**.

> 2 Select the first line of the title—*Seattle*. On the mini toolbar, click the **Font Size button arrow** and then click **80**.

> 3 Select the second line of the title—*Making the Most of Your First Port*. On the **HOME tab**, in the **Font group**, click the **Font Size button arrow**, and then click **36**. Click in a blank area of the slide to cancel your selection, and then compare your screen with Figure 1.45. **Save** your presentation.

FIGURE 1.45

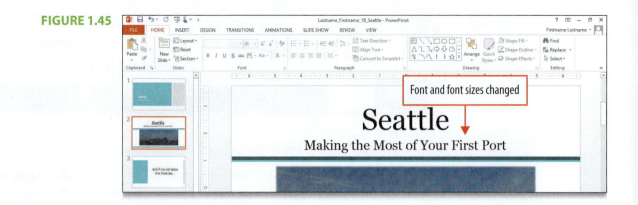

Activity 1.24 | Changing Font Styles and Font Colors

Font styles include bold, italic, and underline, and you can apply any combination of these styles to presentation text. Font styles and font color are useful to provide emphasis and are a visual cue to draw the reader's eye to important text.

1 Display **Slide 3**, and then select both lines of text. On the **HOME tab**, in the **Font group**, click the **Font Color button arrow** and then compare your screen with Figure 1.46.

The colors in the top row of the color gallery are the colors associated with the presentation theme—*Frame*. The colors in the rows below the first row are light and dark variations of the theme colors.

FIGURE 1.46

2 Point to several of the colors and notice that a ScreenTip displays the color name and Live Preview displays the selected text in the color to which you are pointing.

3 In the fifth column of colors, click the last color—**Turquoise, Accent 1, Darker 50%**—to change the font color. Notice that on the **HOME tab**, the lower part of the **Font Color** button displays the most recently applied font color—*Turquoise, Accent 1, Darker 50%*.

When you click the Font Color button instead of the Font Color button arrow, the color displayed in the lower part of the Font Color button is applied to selected text without displaying the color gallery.

4 Display **Slide 4**, and then select the title—*Visit Seattle Before or After Your Cruise to Alaska!* On the mini toolbar, click **Font Color** to apply the font color **Turquoise, Accent 1, Darker 50%** to the selection. Select the subtitle—*Kodiak West Travel Can Help You Develop Your Itinerary*—and then change the **Font Color** to **Turquoise, Accent 1, Darker 50%**. Click anywhere on the slide to cancel the selection, and then compare your screen with Figure 1.47.

FIGURE 1.47

5 ▶ Display **Slide 3**, and then select the two lines of text. From the mini toolbar, apply **Bold** [B] and **Italic** [I], and then **Save** [💾] your presentation.

Activity 1.25 | Aligning Text

In PowerPoint, **text alignment** refers to the horizontal placement of text within a placeholder. You can align left, centered, right, or justified.

1 ▶ Display **Slide 5**, and then on the left side of the slide, click anywhere in the paragraph. On the **HOME tab**, in the **Paragraph group**, click **Center** [≡] to center the text within the placeholder.

2 ▶ Display **Slide 4**, and then click anywhere in the slide title. Press [Ctrl] + [E] to use the keyboard shortcut to center the text.

3 ▶ On **Slide 4**, using one of the methods that you practiced, **Center** the subtitle. Click in a blank area of the slide. Compare your screen with Figure 1.48, and then **Save** [💾] the presentation.

FIGURE 1.48

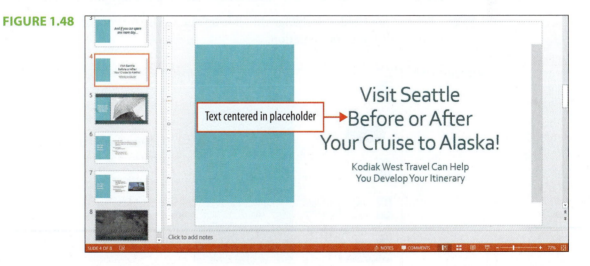

Activity 1.26 | Changing Line Spacing

1 ▶ Display **Slide 5**, and then click anywhere in the paragraph. On the **HOME tab**, in the **Paragraph group**, click **Line Spacing** [≡▾]. On the list, click **2.0** to change from single spacing to double spacing between lines of text. Compare your screen with Figure 1.49.

FIGURE 1.49

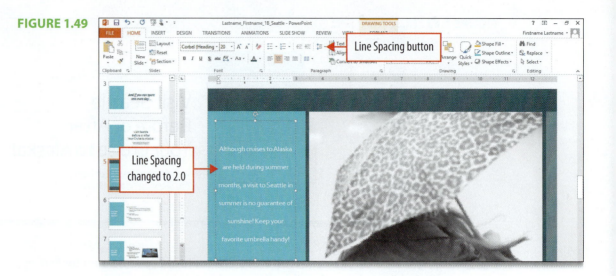

Line Spacing button

Line Spacing changed to 2.0

Although cruises to Alaska are held during summer months, a visit to Seattle in summer is no guarantee of sunshine! Keep your favorite umbrella handy!

2 ▶ **Save** 🖫 your presentation.

Activity 1.27 | Changing the Slide Layout

Recall that the slide layout defines the placement of the content placeholders on a slide. PowerPoint includes predefined layouts that you can apply to your slide for the purpose of arranging slide elements. For example, a Title Slide contains two placeholder elements—the title and the subtitle. When you design your slides, consider the content that you want to include, and then choose a layout with the elements that will display the message you want to convey in the best way.

1 ▶ Display **Slide 1**. On the **HOME tab**, in the **Slides group**, click **Layout** to display the **Slide Layout** gallery. Notice that *Title Slide* is selected, indicating the layout of the current slide.

2 ▶ Click **Section Header** to change the slide layout. Compare your screen with Figure 1.50, and then **Save** 🖫 your presentation.

FIGURE 1.50

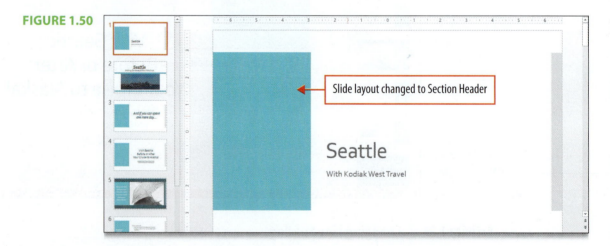

Slide layout changed to Section Header

Seattle

With Kodiak West Travel

Objective 7 Use Slide Sorter View

Video P1-7

Slide Sorter view displays thumbnails of all of the slides in a presentation. Use Slide Sorter view to rearrange and delete slides and to apply formatting to multiple slides.

Activity 1.28 | Deleting Slides in Slide Sorter View

1 In the lower right corner of the PowerPoint window, click **Slide Sorter** ⊞ to display all of the slide thumbnails. Compare your screen with Figure 1.51.

> Your slides may display larger or smaller than those shown in Figure 1.51.

🔄 **ANOTHER WAY**   On the VIEW tab, in the Presentation Views group, click Slide Sorter.

FIGURE 1.51

2 Click **Slide 1**, and notice that a thick outline surrounds the slide, indicating that it is selected. On your keyboard, press Delete to delete the slide. Click **Save** 💾.

Activity 1.29 | Moving a Single Slide in Slide Sorter View

1 With the presentation displayed in Slide Sorter view, point to **Slide 2**. Hold down the left mouse button, and then drag to position the slide to the right of **Slide 6**, as shown in Figure 1.52.

FIGURE 1.52

2 ▶ Release the mouse button to move the slide to the **Slide 6** position in the presentation. **Save** 🖫 your presentation.

Activity 1.30 | Selecting Contiguous and Noncontiguous Slides and Moving Multiple Slides

Contiguous slides are slides that are adjacent to each other in a presentation. *Noncontiguous slides* are slides that are not adjacent to each other in a presentation.

1 ▶ Click **Slide 2**, hold down Ctrl, and then click **Slide 4**. Notice that both slides are selected.

The noncontiguous slides—Slides 2 and 4—are outlined, indicating that both are selected. By holding down Ctrl, you can select noncontiguous slides.

2 ▶ Click **Slide 3**, so that only Slide 3 is selected. Hold down Shift, and then click **Slide 5**. Compare your screen with Figure 1.53.

The contiguous slides—Slides 3, 4, and 5—are outlined, indicating that all three slides are selected. By holding down Shift, you can create a group of contiguous selected slides.

FIGURE 1.53

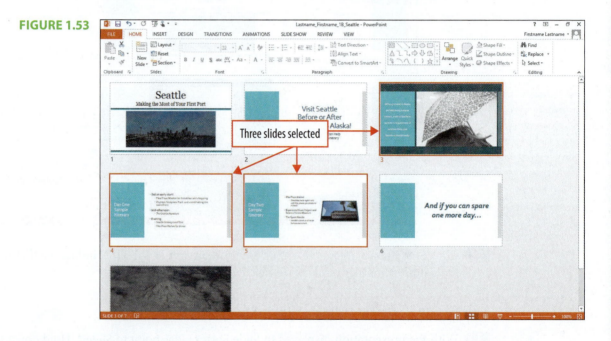

3 ▶ With Slides 3, 4, and 5 selected, hold down Ctrl, and then click **Slide 3**. Notice that only slides 4 and 5 are selected.

When a group of slides is selected, you can press Ctrl and then click a selected slide to deselect it.

4 ▶ Point to either of the selected slides, hold down the left mouse button, and then drag to position the two slides to the right of **Slide 2**, and then compare your screen with Figure 1.54.

The selected slides are dragged as a group and the number 2 in the upper left area of the selected slides indicates the number of slides that you are moving.

FIGURE 1.54

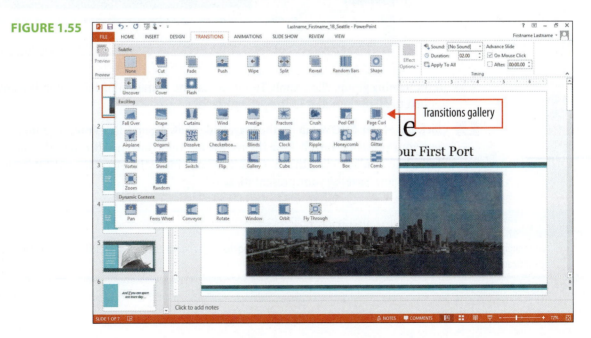

5 ▶ Release the mouse button to move the two slides. In the status bar, click **Normal** to return to Normal view. **Save** 🖫 your presentation.

Objective 8 | Apply Slide Transitions

Slide transitions are the motion effects that occur in Slide Show view when you move from one slide to the next during a presentation. You can choose from a variety of transitions, and you can control the speed and method with which the slides advance.

Video P1-8

Activity 1.31 | Applying Slide Transitions to a Presentation

1 ▶ Display **Slide 1**. On the **TRANSITIONS tab**, in the **Transition to This Slide group**, click **More** 🔽 to display the **Transitions** gallery. Compare your screen with Figure 1.55.

FIGURE 1.55

2 Under **Exciting**, click **Doors** to apply and view the transition. In the **Transition to This Slide group**, click **Effect Options** to display the directions from which the slide enters the screen. Click **Horizontal**. In the **Timing group**, click **Apply To All** to apply the *Doors*, *Horizontal* transition to all of the slides in the presentation. **Save** your presentation 🖫.

The Effect Options vary depending upon the selected transition and include the direction from which the slide enters the screen or the shape in which the slide displays during the transition. In the slide thumbnails, a star displays below the slide number providing a visual cue that a transition has been applied to the slide.

Activity 1.32 | Setting Slide Transition Timing Options

1 In the **Timing group**, notice that the **Duration** box displays *01.40*, indicating that the transition lasts 1.40 seconds. Click the **Duration up spin arrow** two times so that *01.75* displays. Under **Advance Slide**, verify that the **On Mouse Click** check box is selected; select it if necessary. Compare your screen with Figure 1.56.

When the On Mouse Click option is selected, the presenter controls when the current slide advances to the next slide by clicking the mouse button or by pressing [Spacebar].

FIGURE 1.56

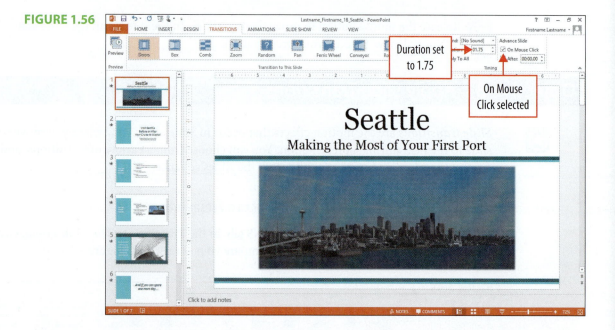

2 In the **Timing group**, click **Apply To All** so that the Duration of *1.75* seconds transition is applied to all of the slides in the presentation.

3 Click the **SLIDE SHOW tab**. In the **Start Slide Show group**, click **From Beginning**, and then view your presentation, clicking the mouse button to advance through the slides. When the black slide displays, click the mouse button one more time to display the presentation in Normal view. **Save** 🖫 your presentation.

More Knowledge | **Applying Multiple Slide Transitions**

You can apply more than one type of transition in your presentation by displaying the slides one at a time, and then clicking the transition that you want to apply instead of clicking Apply To All.

Activity 1.33 | Displaying a Presentation in Reading View

Organizations frequently conduct online meetings when participants are unable to meet in one location. The **Reading view** in PowerPoint displays a presentation in a manner similar to a slide show but the taskbar, title bar, and status bar remain available in the presentation window. This feature enables a presenter to facilitate an online conference easily by switching to another window without closing the slide show.

1 In the lower right corner of the PowerPoint window, click **Reading View** 📖. Compare your screen with Figure 1.57.

In Reading View, the status bar contains the Next and Previous buttons with which you can navigate in the presentation, and the Menu button from which you can print, copy, and edit slides.

ANOTHER WAY   On the VIEW tab, in the Presentation Views group, click Reading View.

FIGURE 1.57

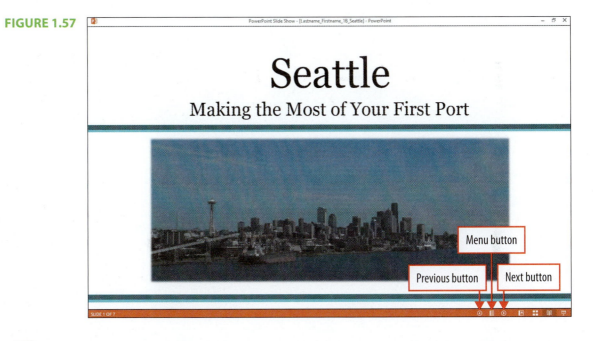

2 Press Spacebar to display **Slide 2**. Click the left mouse button to display **Slide 3**. In the status bar, click **Previous** ◄ to display **Slide 2**.

3 In the status bar, click **Menu** 📋 to display the Reading view menu, and then click **End Show** to return to Normal view.

ANOTHER WAY   Press Esc to exit Reading view and return to Normal view.

4 On the **INSERT tab**, in the **Text group**, click **Header & Footer**, and then click the **Notes and Handouts tab**. Under **Include on page**, select the **Date and time** check box, and if necessary, select **Update automatically**. Clear the **Header** check box if necessary, and then select the **Page number** and **Footer** check boxes. In the **Footer** box, using your own name, type **Lastname_Firstname_1B_Seattle** and then click **Apply to All**.

5 Display **Backstage** view, and then on the right, at the bottom of the **Properties** list, click **Show All Properties**. On the list of properties, click to the right of **Tags**, and type **Seattle** To the right of **Subject**, type your course name and section number. Under **Related People**, be sure that your name displays as the author and edit if necessary.

6 On the left, click **Save**. Submit your presentation electronically or print **Handouts, 4 Slides Horizontal**, as directed by your instructor.

7 **Close** [**x**] PowerPoint.

More Knowledge   **Present a Presentation Online**

You can use the Office Presentation Service to present to people who can watch the presentation in a web browser. You will need a Microsoft account to use this free service. To present online, on the SLIDE SHOW tab, in the Start Slide Show group, click Present Online, and then follow the instructions in the Present Online window.

END | You have completed Project 1B

GO! with Office Web Apps

Objective | Create an Itinerary Presentation in the PowerPoint Web App

> **A L E R T !** | **Working with Web-Based Applications and Services**
>
> Computer programs and services on the web receive continuous updates and improvements, so the steps to complete this web-based activity may differ from the ones shown. You can often look at the screens and the information presented to determine how to complete the activity.

Activity | Creating an Itinerary Presentation in the PowerPoint Web App

In this activity, you will use the PowerPoint Web App to create a presentation similar to the one you created in Project 1B.

1 From the desktop, start Internet Explorer. Navigate to **http://skydrive.com**, and then sign in to your Microsoft account. Open your **GO! Web Projects** folder—or create and then open this folder if necessary.

2 In the SkyDrive menu bar, click **Upload**. Navigate to your student data files, click **p01_1B_Web**, and then click **Open**.

3 Point to the uploaded file **p01_1B_Web**, and then right-click. On the shortcut menu, click **Rename**. Using your own last name and first name, type **Lastname_Firstname_PPT_1B_Web** and then press Enter to rename the file.

4 Click the file that you just renamed, and then click **EDIT PRESENTATION**. On the list, click **Edit in PowerPoint Web App**.

5 On the **DESIGN tab**, in the **Variants group**, click the variant that includes a light blue background and

notice that the variant is applied to all of the slides in the presentation.

6 On **Slide 1**, double-click in the title, and then drag to select the two lines of text. On the **HOME tab**, in the **Font group**, click the **Font button arrow**, and then click **Georgia**.

7 Select the text *Making the Most of Your First Port*. On the **HOME tab**, in the **Font group**, click the **Font Size button arrow**, and then click **27**. Click in a blank area of the slide, and then compare your screen with Figure A.

8 Click **Slide 2**. On the **HOME tab**, in the **Delete group**, Click **Delete** to remove the slide from the presentation.

9 With **Slide 2**—*Seattle Weather*—displayed, press Delete to remove the slide from your presentation. Notice that the Status bar indicates that the presentation contains 7 slides.

FIGURE A

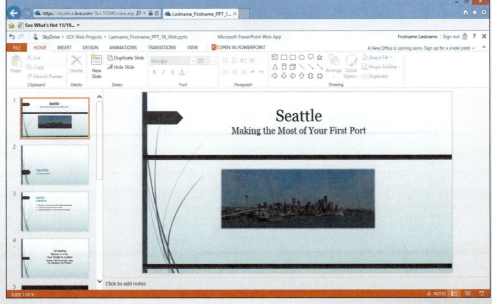

(GO! with Office Web Apps continues on the next page)

Display **Slide 3**, and then double-click in the paragraph on the left side of the slide. Drag to select the text, and then on the **HOME tab**, in the **Font group**, click the **Font Color button arrow**. In the first column, click the first color—**White, Background 1**. With the paragraph still selected, in the **Font group**, click **Bold** **B** and **Italic** *I*. In the **Paragraph group**, click **Center** .

 Click anywhere in a blank area of the slide to cancel the selection and view your formatting changes. Compare your screen with Figure B.

 In the slide thumbnails, point to **Slide 4**, hold down the left mouse button, and then drag up slightly. Notice that a black bar displays above Slide 4. Continue to drag up until the black bar displays above **Slide 3**. Release the mouse button to move the slide.

 Using the technique that you just practiced, move **Slide 5** to position it above **Slide 4**.

 Display **Slide 6**. Double-click anywhere in the slide text, and then triple-click to select all three lines of text. On the **HOME tab**, in the **Paragraph group**, click **Center** . Click anywhere on the slide to cancel the selection.

 Display **Slide 1**. On the **TRANSITIONS tab**, in the **Transition to This Slide group**, click **Push**. Click **Effect Options**, and then click **From Left**. In the **Transitions group**, click **Apply To All**.

 Click the **VIEW tab**, and then in the **Presentation Views group**, click **Slide Show**. If a security warning displays at the bottom of your screen, click Allow once. Press Spacebar or click the left mouse button to advance through the slides in the presentation. When the black slide displays, click one more time to return to the presentation.

 On the ribbon, click the **File tab**, and then click **Exit**. Sign out of your Microsoft account. Submit as instructed by your instructor.

FIGURE B

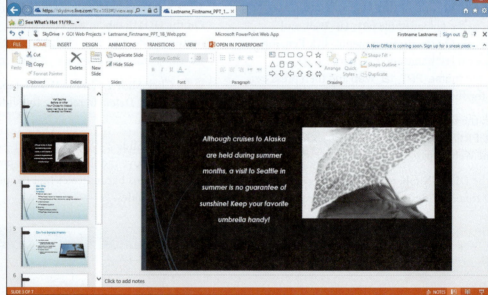

Andrew Rodriguez / Fotolia; FotolEdhar/ Fotolia; apops/ Fotolia; Yuri Arcurs/ Fotolia

In every job, you must work and communicate with other people. A group of workers tasked with working together to solve a problem, make a decision, or create a work product is referred to as a *team*. For a team to succeed, the team members must be able to communicate with one another easily.

If all the team members work at the same location and work the same hours, communication is easy. You schedule face-to-face meetings and exchange documents and information among yourselves. But that is a rare arrangement in today's organizations. Rather, it is more likely that the members of your team work in different locations—even different countries—and work different hours or travel extensively away from the headquarters location. Also, for specific projects, teams are frequently organized across different departments of an organization or even across different organizations entirely. Then when the project is complete, the team disbands.

Collaboration is when you work together with others as a team in an intellectual endeavor to complete a shared task or achieve a shared goal; for example, when you and one or more of your classmates work together on a class project. Collaboration involves giving feedback to and receiving feedback from others on the team, and then revising the strategies to achieve the goal or produce the work product based on the feedback.

Microsoft Office 365 is a set of secure online services that enables people in an organization to communicate and collaborate by using any Internet-connected device—a computer, a tablet, or a mobile phone. Because Office 365 offers access from anywhere to email, web conferencing, documents, and calendars, everyone on a team can work together easily. Office 365 is intended for use by multiple users in an organization.

Activity | Using the Exchange Online Outlook Meeting Tool to Collaborate

This group project relates to the **Bell Orchid Hotels**. If your instructor assigns this project to your class, you can expect to use the **Outlook Meeting tool** in **Office 365 Exchange Online** to collaborate on the following tasks for this chapter:

- If you are in the **Accounting Group**, you and your teammates will meet virtually to create the text and initial formatting for a Loan Presentation to be presented by the Director to the Loan Officers of San Diego's SoCal Bank.

- If you are in the **Engineering Group**, you and your teammates will meet virtually to create the text and initial formatting for a Safety Presentation to be presented to all hotel department heads.

- If you are in the **Food and Beverage Group**, you and your teammates will meet virtually to create the text and initial formatting for a New Menu Item Presentation to be presented by the Director of the F&B Department to restaurant, banquet, and room service managers.

- If you are in the **Human Resources Group**, you and your teammates will meet virtually to create the text and initial formatting for a New Employees Orientation presentation to be presented to new staff hired by the hotel.

- If you are in the **Operations Group**, you and your teammates will meet virtually to create the text and initial formatting for a Front Desk Clerk Training Presentation as part of the hotel's on-the-job training program for Front Desk staff.

- If you are in the **Sales and Marketing Group**, you and your teammates will meet virtually to create the text and initial formatting for a Marketing Plan Presentation to be presented to all department heads and the Executive Office.

FIGURE A

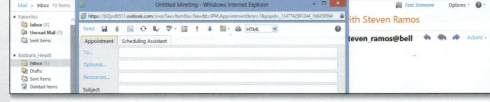

END OF CHAPTER

SUMMARY

When communicating your ideas, PowerPoint is a versatile business tool that will help you create presentations that make a lasting impression. Additionally, you can share slides you create on your SkyDrive.

Use a presentation theme to establish a unified presentation design. You can change the color of the presentation theme by applying one of the predefined variants that are supplied with each theme.

Presentations are often organized in a manner similar to how outline levels are organized. List levels represent outline levels and are identified by the bullet style, indentation, and text size.

Slide layout defines the placement of content placeholders on a slide. Each presentation theme includes predefined layouts that you can apply to slides for the purpose of arranging slide elements.

GO! LEARN IT ONLINE

Review the concepts and key terms in this chapter by completing these online challenges, which you can find at **www.pearsonhighered.com/go**.

Matching and Multiple Choice: Answer matching and multiple choice questions to test what you learned in this chapter. MyITLab®

Crossword Puzzle: Spell out the words that match the numbered clues, and put them in the puzzle squares.

Flipboard: Flip through the definitions of the key terms in this chapter and match them with the correct term.

GO! FOR JOB SUCCESS

Video: Managing Priorities and Workspace

Your instructor may assign this video to your class, and then ask you to think about, or discuss with your classmates, these questions:

FotolEdhar / Fotolia

What kind of scheduling tool do you use? Is it on your computer, your cell phone, or other electronic device, or do you write in a notebook or physical calendar? Which kind of scheduling tool will be most effective for you and why?

Name one lifestyle change that you can make today that will help you create more time for your work projects.

What is the *one touch rule* and how do you think it will help you be more efficient?

END OF CHAPTER

REVIEW AND ASSESSMENT GUIDE FOR POWERPOINT CHAPTER 1

Your instructor may assign one or more of these projects to help you review the chapter and assess your mastery and understanding of the chapter.

Review and Assessment Guide for PowerPoint Chapter 1			
Project	**Apply Skills from These Chapter Objectives**	**Project Type**	**Project Location**
1C	Objectives 1-4 from Project 1A	**1C Skills Review** A guided review of the skills from Project 1A.	On the following pages
1D	Objectives 5-8 from Project 1B	**1D Skills Review** A guided review of the skills from Project 1B.	On the following pages
1E	Objectives 1-4 from Project 1A	**1E Mastery (Grader Project)** A demonstration of your mastery of the skills in Project 1A with extensive decision making.	In MyITlab and on the following pages
1F	Objectives 5-8 from Project 1B	**1F Mastery (Grader Project)** A demonstration of your mastery of the skills in Project 1B with extensive decision making.	In MyITlab and on the following pages
1G	Objectives 1-8 from Projects 1A and IB	**1G Mastery (Grader Project)** A demonstration of your mastery of the skills in Projects 1A and 1B with extensive decision making.	In MyITlab and on the following pages
1H	Combination of Objectives from Projects 1A and 1B	**1H GO! Fix It** A demonstration of your mastery of the skills in Projects 1A and 1B by creating a correct result from a document that contains errors you must find.	Online
1I	Combination of Objectives from Projects 1A and 1B	**1I GO! Make It** A demonstration of your mastery of the skills in Projects 1A and 1B by creating a result from a supplied picture.	Online
1J	Combination of Objectives from Projects 1A and 1B	**1J GO! Solve It** A demonstration of your mastery of the skills in Projects 1A and 1B, your decision-making skills, and your critical thinking skills. A task-specific rubric helps you self-assess your result.	Online
1K	Combination of Objectives from Projects 1A and 1B	**1K GO! Solve It** A demonstration of your mastery of the skills in Projects 1A and 1B, your decision-making skills, and your critical thinking skills. A task-specific rubric helps you self-assess your result.	On the following pages
1L	Combination of Objectives from Projects 1A and 1B	**1L GO! Think** A demonstration of your understanding of the Chapter concepts applied in a manner that you would outside of college. An analytic rubric helps you and your instructor grade the quality of your work by comparing it to the work an expert in the discipline would create.	On the following pages
1M	Combination of Objectives from Projects 1A and 1B	**1M GO! Think** A demonstration of your understanding of the Chapter concepts applied in a manner that you would outside of college. An analytic rubric helps you and your instructor grade the quality of your work by comparing it to the work an expert in the discipline would create.	Online
1N	Combination of Objectives from Projects 1A and 1B	**1N You and GO!** A demonstration of your understanding of the Chapter concepts applied in a manner that you would in a personal situation. An analytic rubric helps you and your instructor grade the quality of your work.	Online
1O	Combination of Objectives from Projects 1A and 1B	**1O Cumulative Group Project for PowerPoint Chapter 1** A demonstration of your understanding of concepts and your ability to work collaboratively in a group role-playing assessment, requiring both collaboration and self-management.	Online

GLOSSARY

GLOSSARY OF CHAPTER KEY TERMS

Artistic effects Formats applied to images that make pictures resemble sketches or paintings.

Aspect ratio The ratio of the width of a display to the height of the display.

Black slide A slide that displays after the last slide in a presentation indicating that the presentation is over.

Collaboration The action of working with others as a team in an intellectual endeavor to complete a shared task or achieve a shared goal.

Contiguous slides Slides that are adjacent to each other in a presentation.

Editing The process of modifying a presentation by adding and deleting slides or by changing the contents of individual slides.

Footer Text that displays at the bottom of every slide or that prints at the bottom of a sheet of slide handouts or notes pages.

Formatting The process of changing the appearance of the text, layout, and design of a slide.

Header Text that prints at the top of each sheet of slide handouts or notes pages.

Layout The arrangement of elements, such as title and subtitle text, lists, pictures, tables, charts, shapes, and movies, on a slide.

List level An outline level in a presentation represented by a bullet symbol and identified in a slide by the indentation and the size of the text.

Microsoft Office 365 A set of secure online services that enable people in an organization to communicate and collaborate by using any Internet-connected device—a computer, a tablet, or a mobile phone.

Noncontiguous slides Slides that are not adjacent to each other in a presentation.

Normal view The primary editing view in PowerPoint where you write and design your presentations.

Notes page A printout that contains the slide image on the top half of the page and notes that you have created on the Notes pane in the lower half of the page.

Notes pane An area of the Normal view window that displays below the Slide pane with space to type notes regarding the active slide.

Outline View A PowerPoint view that displays the presentation outline to the left of the Slide pane.

Placeholder A box on a slide with dotted or dashed borders that holds title and body text or other content such as charts, tables, and pictures.

Reading view A view in PowerPoint that displays a presentation in a manner similar to a slide show but in which the taskbar, title bar, and status bar remain available in the presentation window.

Rotation handle A circular arrow that provides a way to rotate a selected image.

Section header A type of slide layout that changes the look and flow of a presentation by providing text placeholders that do not contain bullet points.

Sizing handles Small squares surrounding a picture that indicate that the picture is selected.

Slide A presentation page that can contain text, pictures, tables, charts, and other multimedia or graphic objects.

Slide handout Printed images of slides on a sheet of paper.

Slide pane A PowerPoint screen element that displays a large image of the active slide.

Slide Sorter view A presentation view that displays thumbnails of all of the slides in a presentation.

Slide transitions Motion effects that occur in Slide Show view when you move from one slide to the next during a presentation.

Split button A type of button in which clicking the main part of the button performs a command and clicking the arrow opens a menu, list, or gallery.

Style A collection of formatting options that you can apply to a picture, text, or an object.

Team A group of workers tasked with working together to solve a problem, make a decision, or create a work product.

Text alignment The horizontal placement of text within a placeholder.

Theme A set of unified design elements that provides a look for your presentation by applying colors, fonts, and effects.

Thumbnails Miniature images of presentation slides.

Title slide A slide layout—most commonly the first slide in a presentation—that provides an introduction to the presentation topic.

Variant A variation on the presentation theme style and color.

CHAPTER REVIEW

Skills Review | Project 1C Glaciers

Apply **1A** skills from these Objectives:

1 Create a New Presentation

2 Edit a Presentation in Normal View

3 Add Pictures to a Presentation

4 Print and View a Presentation

Build from Scratch

In the following Skills Review, you will create a new presentation by inserting content and pictures, adding notes and footers, and applying a presentation theme. Your completed presentation will look similar to Figure 1.58.

PROJECT FILES

For Project 1C, you will need the following files:

New blank PowerPoint presentation
p01C_Glacier_Bay
p01C_Ice
p01C_Ship

You will save your presentation as:

Lastname_Firstname_1C_Glaciers

PROJECT RESULTS

FIGURE 1.58

(Project 1C Glaciers continues on the next page)

CHAPTER REVIEW

1 Start PowerPoint. On the right, click **Celestial**, and then click **Create**. In the **Slide pane**, click in the text *Click to add title*. Type **Glacier Bay** and then click in the subtitle placeholder. Type **Part One in a Series of Alaskan Passage Adventures** Notice that the font uses all uppercase letters.

a. On the **Quick Access Toolbar**, click **Save** 🖫. Under **Save As**, click **Computer**, and then click **Browse**. Navigate to your **PowerPoint Chapter 1** folder. In the **File name** box, using your own name, replace the existing text with **Lastname_Firstname_1C_Glaciers** and then click **Save**.

b. On the **HOME tab**, in the **Slides group**, click the **New Slide arrow**, and then in the gallery, click **Two Content**. Click the text *Click to add title*, and then type **About the Park**

2 On the left side of the slide, click in the content placeholder. Type **Located in the Southeast Alaskan Wilderness** and then press **Enter**. Press **Tab**. Type **3.3 million acres** and then press **Enter**. Type **A national park and preserve** and then press **Enter**

a. On the **HOME tab**, in the **Paragraph group**, click **Decrease List Level**. Type **Visitor season** and then press **Enter**. On the **HOME tab**, in the **Paragraph group**, click **Increase List Level**. Type **May to September**

b. On the **HOME tab**, in the **Slides group**, click the **New Slide arrow**, and then in the gallery, click **Panoramic Picture with Caption**. In the lower portion of the slide, click the text *Click to add title*, and then type **Prepare to be Amazed!**

c. Click in the text placeholder. Type **Before you reach Glacier Bay, walk around your cruise ship to find the best viewing locations. Make sure your camera battery is charged!**

d. On the **HOME tab**, in the **Slides group**, click the **New Slide arrow**, and then in the gallery, click **Content with Caption**. In the title placeholder, type **Learn More!**

e. Click in the text placeholder, and then type **A national park ranger will board your ship during your visit to Glacier Bay. Check your ship's itinerary for presentation information and locations.**

3 With **Slide 4** displayed, in the **Status bar**, click **NOTES**. Click in the **Notes pane**, and then type **Your cruise ship will spend between 6 and 8 hours in Glacier Bay.**

a. On the left side of the PowerPoint window, in the slide thumbnails, click **Slide 1**. Click in the subtitle placeholder after the *n* in *Alaskan*. Press **Spacebar**, and then type **Inside**

b. In the slide thumbnails, click **Slide 2**, and then click at the end of the last bullet point after the word *September*. Press **Enter**, and then type **Be prepared for rain**

4 With **Slide 2** displayed, in the placeholder on the right side of the slide, click **Pictures**. Navigate to your student data files, and then click **p01C_Glacier_Bay**. Click **Insert**.

a. With the picture selected, on the **FORMAT tab**, in the **Picture Styles group**, click **More** to display the **Picture Styles** gallery. In the second row, click the third style—**Beveled Oval, Black**.

b. Display **Slide 3**. In the Picture placeholder, click **Pictures**. Navigate to your student data files, and then click **p01C_Ice**. Click **Insert**.

c. Display **Slide 4**. In the content placeholder on the right side of the slide, click **Pictures**. Navigate to your student data files, and then insert **p01C_Ship**. On the **FORMAT tab**, in the **Picture Styles group**, click **More** to display the **Picture Styles** gallery. In the third row, click the sixth style—**Soft Edge Oval**.

d. With the picture still selected, on the **FORMAT tab**, in the **Adjust group**, click **Artistic Effects** to display the gallery. In the fourth row, click the third effect—**Crisscross Etching**.

5 On the ribbon, click the **SLIDE SHOW tab**. In the **Start Slide Show group**, click **From Beginning**.

a. Click the left mouse button or press **Spacebar** to advance to the second slide. Continue to click or press **Spacebar** until the last slide displays, and then click or press **Spacebar** one more time to display a black slide.

b. With the black slide displayed, click the left mouse button or press **Spacebar** to exit the slide show and return to the presentation.

(Project 1C Glaciers continues on the next page)

6 Click the **INSERT tab**, and then in the **Text group**, click **Header & Footer** to display the **Header and Footer** dialog box.

a. In the **Header and Footer** dialog box, click the **Notes and Handouts tab**. Under **Include on page**, select the **Date and time** check box. If necessary, click the Update automatically option button so that the current date prints on the notes and handouts.

b. If necessary, clear the Header check box to omit this element. Select the **Page number** and **Footer** check boxes. In the **Footer** box, using your own name, type **Lastname_Firstname_1C_Glaciers** and then click **Apply to All**.

c. In the upper left corner of your screen, click the **FILE** tab to display **Backstage** view. On the right, at the bottom of the **Properties list**, click **Show All Properties**.

d. On the list of Properties, click to the right of **Tags** to display an empty box, and then type **Glacier Bay** Click to the right of **Subject** to display an empty box, and then type your course name and section number. Under **Related People**, be sure that your name displays as the author; edit if necessary.

e. **Save** your presentation. Submit your presentation electronically or print **Handouts, 4 Slides Horizontal** as directed by your instructor. **Close** PowerPoint.

END | You have completed Project 1C

CHAPTER REVIEW

Apply 1B skills from these Objectives:

5 Edit an Existing Presentation

6 Format a Presentation

7 Use Slide Sorter View

8 Apply Slide Transitions

Skills Review Project 1D Photography

In the following Skills Review, you will edit an existing presentation by inserting slides from another presentation, applying font and slide formatting, and applying slide transitions. Your completed presentation will look similar to Figure 1.59.

PROJECT FILES

For Project 1D, you will need the following files:

p01D_Photography
p01D_Photography_Slides

You will save your presentation as:

Lastname_Firstname_1D_Photography

PROJECT RESULTS

FIGURE 1.59

(Project 1D Photography continues on the next page)

1 Start PowerPoint. On the left, under the list of recent presentations, click **Open Other Presentations**. Under **Open**, click **Computer** and then click **Browse**. Navigate to your student data files, and then click **p01D_Photography**. Click **Open**. On the **FILE tab**, click **Save As**, navigate to your **PowerPoint Chapter 1** folder, and then using your own name, save the file as **Lastname_Firstname_1D_Photography**

  a. On the **DESIGN tab**, in the **Customize group**, click **Slide Size**, and then click **Widescreen (16:9)**.

  b. With **Slide 1** displayed, on the **HOME tab**, in the **Slides group**, click the **New Slide arrow**, and then click **Reuse Slides**. In the **Reuse Slides** pane, click **Browse**, and then click **Browse File**. In the **Browse** dialog box, navigate to your student data files, and then double-click **p01D_Photography_Slides** to display the slides from this presentation in the Reuse Slides pane.

  c. At the bottom of the **Reuse Slides** pane, be sure that the **Keep source formatting** check box is *cleared*. In the **Reuse Slides** pane, click the first slide to insert the slide after Slide 1.

  d. At the left of your screen, in the slide thumbnails, click **Slide 6** to display it in the **Slide pane**. In the **Reuse Slides** pane, click the second slide to insert it after Slide 6. **Close** the **Reuse Slides** pane.

2 Display **Slide 1**. On the **VIEW tab**, in the **Presentation Views group**, click **Outline View**.

  a. In the **Outline**, in **Slide 7**, drag to select the second and third bullet points—beginning with *Never approach* and ending with *animal's home.*

  b. On the **HOME tab**, in the **Paragraph group**, click **Decrease List Level** one time.

  c. In the **Outline**, in the same slide, click at the end of the first bullet point after the word *sense*. Press Spacebar, and then type **when photographing wildlife**

  d. In the **Status bar**, click **Normal** to display the slide thumbnails.

3 Display **Slide 8**, and then press Delete to delete the slide from the presentation.

  a. Display **Slide 1**. On the **HOME tab**, in the **Editing group**, click **Replace**. In the **Replace** dialog box, in the **Find what** box, type **home** and then in the **Replace with** box, type **habitat**

  b. In the **Replace** dialog box, click **Replace All** to display a message box indicating that one replacement was made. In the message box, click **OK**. **Close** the **Replace** dialog box.

  c. On the **DESIGN tab**, in the **Variants group**, right-click the green variant. On the shortcut menu, click **Apply to All Slides** so that the green color is applied to all of the slides in the presentation.

4 Display **Slide 5**. Select all of the text in the placeholder. On the **HOME tab**, in the **Font group**, click the **Font button arrow**, scroll the font list, and then click **Arial Black**. Click the **Font Size button arrow**, and then click **32**. In the **Paragraph group**, click **Line Spacing**, and then click **1.5**.

  a. Display **Slide 2**. On the **HOME tab**, in the **Slides group**, click **Layout** to display the **Slide Layout** gallery. Click **Title Slide** to change the slide layout.

  b. On **Slide 2**, select the title—*Alaskan Wildlife*. On the **HOME tab**, in the **Font group**, click the **Font Color button arrow**. In the fifth column, click the first color—**Dark Teal, Accent 1**.

  c. Display **Slide 3**, and then select the title—*Lights, Camera, Action*. On the mini toolbar, click **Font Color** to apply the font color **Dark Teal, Accent 1**.

  d. Display **Slide 4**, and then, click anywhere in the text. On the **HOME tab**, in the **Paragraph group**, click **Center** to center the text within the placeholder.

  e. Display **Slide 6**, and then select the subtitle. From the mini toolbar, apply **Bold** and **Italic**.

  f. In the slide thumbnails, point to **Slide 7**, hold down the left mouse button, and then drag up to position the slide between **Slides 3** and **4**.

5 In the lower right corner of the PowerPoint window, click **Slide Sorter** to display all of the slide thumbnails. Click **Slide 1**, so that it is selected. Press Delete to delete the slide.

  a. Click **Slide 4**, and then hold down Ctrl and click **Slide 5**. With both slides selected, point to either of the selected slides, hold down the left mouse button, and then drag to position the two slides to the right of **Slide 6**. Release the mouse button to move the two slides. In the status bar, click **Normal** to return to Normal view.

(Project 1D Photography continues on the next page)

CHAPTER REVIEW

b. Display **Slide 1**. On the **TRANSITIONS tab**, in the **Transition to This Slide group**, click **More** to display the **Transitions** gallery.

c. Under **Exciting**, click **Gallery** to apply and view the transition. In the **Transition to This Slide group**, click **Effect Options**, and then click **From Left**. In the **Timing group**, click **Apply To All** to apply the *Gallery, From Left* transition to all of the slides in the presentation.

d. In the **Timing group**, click the **Duration up spin arrow** so that *01.75* displays. Under **Advance Slide**, verify that the **On Mouse Click** check box is selected; select it if necessary. In the **Timing group**, click **Apply To All**.

e. Click the **SLIDE SHOW tab**. In the **Start Slide Show group**, click **From Beginning**, and then view your presentation, clicking the mouse button to advance through the slides. When the black slide displays, click the mouse button one more time to display the presentation in Normal view.

6 ▸ Click the **INSERT tab**, and then in the **Text group**, click **Header & Footer** to display the **Header and Footer** dialog box.

a. In the **Header and Footer** dialog box, click the **Notes and Handouts tab**. Under **Include on page**, select the **Date and time** check box. If necessary, click the Update automatically option button so that the current date prints on the notes and handouts.

b. If necessary, clear the Header check box to omit this element. Select the **Page number** and **Footer** check boxes. In the **Footer** box, type **Lastname_Firstname_1D_Photography** and then click **Apply to All**.

c. In the upper left corner of your screen, click the **FILE** tab to display **Backstage** view. On the right, at the bottom of the **Properties list**, click **Show All Properties**.

d. On the list of Properties, click to the right of **Tags** to display an empty box, and then type **photography** Click to the right of **Subject** to display an empty box, and then type your course name and section number. Under **Related People**, be sure that your name displays as the author; edit if necessary.

e. **Save** your presentation. Submit your presentation electronically or print **Handouts, 6 Slides Horizontal** as directed by your instructor. **Close** PowerPoint.

END | You have completed Project 1D

CONTENT-BASED ASSESSMENTS

Mastering PowerPoint Project 1E Juneau

In the following Mastering PowerPoint project, you will create a new presentation that Kodiak West Travel will use in their promotional materials to describe activities in the city of Juneau. Your completed presentation will look similar to Figure 1.60.

Apply 1A skills from these Objectives:

1 Create a New Presentation

2 Edit a Presentation in Normal View

3 Add Pictures to a Presentation

4 Print and View a Presentation

Build from Scratch

PROJECT FILES

For Project 1E, you will need the following files:

New blank PowerPoint presentation
p01E_Aerial_View
p01E_Whale
p01E_Falls

You will save your presentation as:

Lastname_Firstname_1E_Juneau

PROJECT RESULTS

FIGURE 1.60

(Project 1E Juneau continues on the next page)

CONTENT-BASED ASSESSMENTS

1 Start PowerPoint and create a presentation using the **Integral** theme. Use the first color variation. As the title of this presentation type **Juneau Highlights** and as the subtitle type **Kodiak West Travel** Save the presentation in your **PowerPoint Chapter 1** folder as **Lastname_Firstname_1E_Juneau**

2 Insert a **New Slide** using the **Content with Caption** layout. In the title placeholder, type **The View from Above** In the content placeholder on the right side of the slide, from your student data files, insert the picture **p01E_Aerial_View**. Format the picture with the **Bevel Rectangle** picture style and the **Paint Brush** artistic effect.

3 In the text placeholder on the left, type **View a glacial ice field from above by plane or helicopter. If you are more adventurous, try glacier trekking in Juneau where you can land on a glacier and climb an ice wall.**

4 Insert a **New Slide** using the **Two Content** layout. In the title placeholder, type **On Land and Sea** In the content placeholder on the left, type the following text, increasing and decreasing the list level as shown below. In this presentation theme, the first level bullet points do not include a bullet symbol.

On the water
> **Whale watching**
> **Kayaking**

Mount Roberts tramway
> **Spectacular views of Juneau**
> **Recreational hiking trails**

5 In the content placeholder on the right, from your student data files, insert the picture **p01D_Whale**. Apply the **Rotated, White** picture style.

6 Insert a new slide with the **Picture with Caption** layout. In the title placeholder, type **Mendenhall Glacier** and then in the picture placeholder, from your student data files, insert the picture **p01E_Falls**.

7 In the text placeholder, type **Walk to Mendenhall Glacier from the Visitor Center to get a close-up view of Nugget Falls.**

8 In the **Notes pane**, type **Mendenhall Glacier is the most famous glacier in Juneau and in some years is visited by over 400,000 people.**

9 Insert a **Header & Footer** on the **Notes and Handouts**. Include the **Date and time** updated automatically, the **Page number**, and a **Footer**—using your own name—with the text **Lastname_Firstname_1E_ Juneau** and apply to all the slides.

10 Display the **Document Properties**. As the **Tags** type **Juneau** As the **Subject** type your course and section number. Be sure your name is indicated as the author.

11 **Save** your presentation, and then view the slide show from the beginning. Submit your presentation electronically or print **Handouts, 4 Slides Horizontal** as directed by your instructor. **Close** PowerPoint.

> **END | You have completed Project 1E**

CONTENT-BASED ASSESSMENTS

Apply 1B skills from these Objectives:

5 Edit an Existing Presentation

6 Format a Presentation

7 Use Slide Sorter View

8 Apply Slide Transitions

In the following Mastering PowerPoint project, you will edit a presentation regarding a wildlife refuge where Kodiak West Travel conducts tours. Your completed presentation will look similar to Figure 1.61.

PROJECT FILES

For Project 1F, you will need the following files:

p01F_Refuge

p01F_Excursions

You will save your presentation as:

Lastname_Firstname_1F_Refuge

PROJECT RESULTS

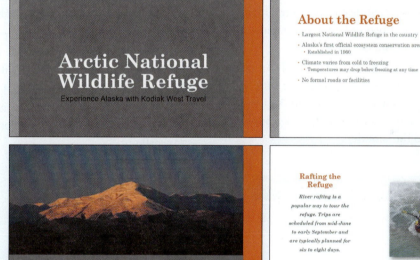

FIGURE 1.61

(Project 1F Refuge continues on the next page)

CONTENT-BASED ASSESSMENTS

1 Start PowerPoint, and then from your student data files, open the file **p01F_Refuge**. In your **PowerPoint Chapter 1** folder, **Save** the file as **Lastname_Firstname_1F_Refuge**

2 Change the **Slide Size** to **Widescreen (16:9)**, and then change the **Variant** for all the slides to the option with the orange bar on the right side.

3 Display the presentation **Outline**. In the **Outline**, on **Slide 2**, increase the list level of the third and the fifth bullet points. Click at the end of the last bullet point after the word *roads*, and then type **or facilities**

4 Return the presentation to **Normal view**, and then display **Slide 4**. Display the **Reuse Slides** pane. Browse to your student data files, and then open **p01F_Excursions**. Make sure the **Keep source formatting** check box is *cleared*. With **Slide 4** in your presentation displayed, insert the last two slides from the **Reuse Slides** pane, and then close the pane.

5 Display **Slide 1**, and then change the layout to **Title Slide**. Select the subtitle—*Experience Alaska with Kodiak West Travel*. Change the **Font** to **Arial**, and the **Font Size** to **28**. Change the **Font Color** to **Black, Background 1**. **Center** the title and the subtitle.

6 Display **Slide 5**, and then select the paragraph in the content placeholder. Apply **Bold** and **Italic**, and then change the **Font Size** to **18**. **Center** the text, and then change the **Line Spacing** to **1.5**. **Center** the slide title.

7 In **Slide Sorter** view, delete **Slide 3**. Move **Slide 5** to position it after **Slide 2**. Move **Slide 4** to the end of the presentation.

8 In **Normal** view, display **Slide 1**. Apply the **Split** transition and change the **Effect Options** to **Horizontal Out**. Change the **Duration** to **1.75**, and the apply the transition to all of the slides in the presentation. View the slide show from the beginning.

9 **Insert** a **Header & Footer** on the **Notes and Handouts**. Include the **Date and time** updated automatically, the **Page number**, and a **Footer** with the text **Lastname_Firstname_1F_Refuge**

10 Display the **Document Properties**. As the **Tags** type **refuge, tours** As the **Subject** type your course and section number. Be sure your name is indicated as the author.

11 **Save** your presentation, and then submit your presentation electronically or print **Handouts, 6 Slides Horizontal** as directed by your instructor. **Close** PowerPoint.

END | You have completed Project 1F

CONTENT-BASED ASSESSMENTS

MyITLab grader

Apply 1A and 1B skills from these Objectives:

1. Create a New Presentation
2. Edit a Presentation in Normal View
3. Add Pictures to a Presentation
4. Print and View a Presentation
5. Edit an Existing Presentation
6. Format a Presentation
7. Use Slide Sorter View
8. Apply Slide Transitions

Mastering PowerPoint Project 1G Northern Lights

In the following Mastering PowerPoint project, you will edit an existing presentation that describes the Northern Lights and ideal viewing areas. Your completed presentation will look similar to Figure 1.62.

PROJECT FILES

For Project 1G, you will need the following files:

p01G_Northern_Lights
p01G_Lights
p01G_Slides

You will save your presentation as:

Lastname_Firstname_1G_Northern_Lights

PROJECT RESULTS

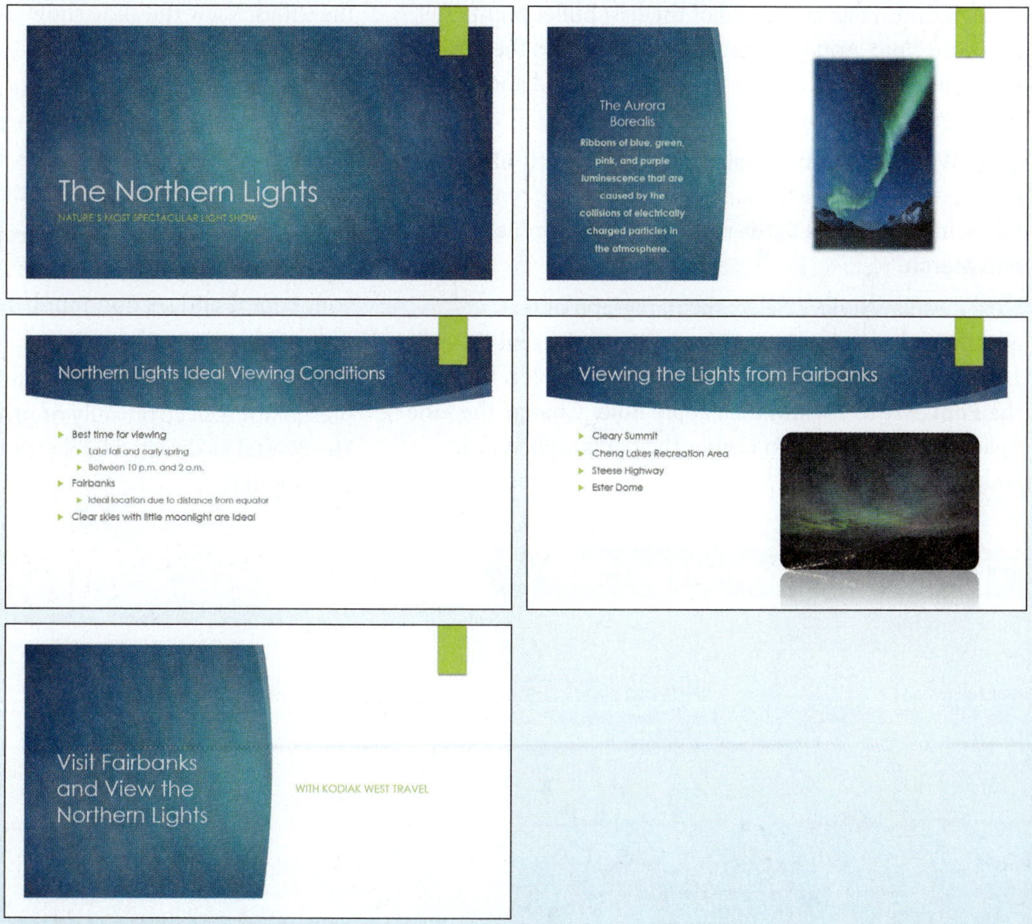

FIGURE 1.62

(Project 1G Northern Lights continues on the next page)

CONTENT-BASED ASSESSMENTS

1 Start PowerPoint, and then from your student data files, open the file **p01G_Northern_Lights**. In your **PowerPoint Chapter 1** folder, **Save** the file as **Lastname_Firstname_1G_Northern_Lights**

2 Replace all occurrences of the text **North** with **Northern** and then change the layout of **Slide 1** to **Title Slide**. Apply the **Ion Boardroom** theme, and then change the **Variant** to the blue variant option. Change the **Slide Size** to **Widescreen (16:9)**.

3 Display **Slide 2**, open the **Reuse Slides** pane, and then from your student data files browse for and open the presentation **p01G_Slides**. If necessary, clear the Keep source formatting check box, and then insert the last two slides from the **p01G_Slides** file.

4 Display **Slide 2**. In either the slide pane or in the slide outline, click at the end of the first bullet point after the word *time*. Add the words **for viewing** and then in the same slide, increase the list level of the second and third bullet points.

5 With **Slide 2** still displayed, select the title and change the **Font Size** to **32**. In the **Notes pane**, type the following notes: **The lights reach their peak in September and March.**

6 Display **Slide 3**. Select the paragraph of text, and then change the **Font Color** to **Green, Accent 6, Lighter 60%**—in the last column, the third color. Change the **Font Size** to **18**, and then apply **Bold**. Change the **Line Spacing** to **1.5**, and then **Center** the paragraph and the slide title.

7 With **Slide 3** still displayed, format the picture with the **Soft Edge Rectangle** picture style and the **Marker** artistic effect.

8 Display **Slide 4**. In the content placeholder on the right, from your student data files, insert the picture **p01G_Lights**. Apply the **Reflected Rounded Rectangle** picture style.

9 Move **Slide 3** between **Slides 1** and **2**, and then display **Slide 4**. Insert a **New Slide** with the **Section Header** layout. In the title placeholder type **Visit Fairbanks and View the Northern Lights!** In the text placeholder type **With Kodiak West Travel**

10 Apply the **Uncover** transition and change the **Effect Options** to **From Top**. Change the **Timing** by increasing the **Duration** to **01.25**. Apply the transition effect to all of the slides. View the slide show from the beginning.

11 **Insert** a **Header & Footer** on the **Notes and Handouts**. Include the **Date and time** updated automatically, the **Page number**, and a **Footer**, using your own name, with the text **Lastname_Firstname_1G_Northern_Lights**

12 Display the **Document Properties**. As the **Tags** type **northern lights, Fairbanks** As the **Subject** type your course and section number. Be sure your name is indicated as the author.

13 **Save** your presentation, and then submit your presentation electronically or print **Handouts, 6 Slides Horizontal** as directed by your instructor. **Close** PowerPoint.

END | You have completed Project 1G

CONTENT-BASED ASSESSMENTS

Apply a combination of the 1A and 1B skills.

Build from Scratch

| GO! Fix It | Project 1H Rain Forest | Online |

| GO! Make It | Project 1I Eagles | Online |

| GO! Solve It | Project 1J Packrafting | Online |

| GO! Solve It | Project 1K Packing |

PROJECT FILES

For Project 1K, you will need the following file:

p01K_Packing

You will save your presentation as:

Lastname_Firstname_1K_Packing

Open the file p01K_Packing and save it as **Lastname_Firstname_1K_Packing** Complete the presentation by applying a theme and changing the variant. Format the presentation attractively by applying appropriate font formatting and by changing text alignment and line spacing. Change the layout of Slide 4 to an appropriate layout. On Slide 2, insert a picture that you have taken yourself, or use one of the pictures in your student data files that you inserted in other projects in this chapter. Apply a style to the picture. Apply slide transitions to all of the slides in the presentation, and then insert a header and footer that includes the date and time updated automatically, the file name in the footer, and the page number. Add your name, your course name and section number, and the tags **packing, weather** to the properties. Save and print or submit as directed by your instructor.

Performance Level

Performance Criteria		Exemplary	Proficient	Developing
	Apply a theme and a variant	An appropriate theme and variant were applied to the presentation.	A theme was applied but the variant was not changed.	Neither a theme nor the variant theme were applied.
	Apply font and slide formatting	Font and slide formatting is attractive and appropriate.	Adequately formatted but difficult to read or unattractive.	Inadequate or no formatting.
	Use appropriate pictures and apply styles attractively	An appropriate picture was inserted and a style is applied attractively.	A picture was inserted but a style was not applied.	Picture was not inserted.
	Apply appropriate slide layout to Slide 4	An appropriate layout was applied to the last slide.	The slide layout was changed but is not appropriate for the type of slide.	The slide layout was not changed.

END | You have completed Project 1K

OUTCOMES-BASED ASSESSMENTS

RUBRIC

The following outcomes-based assessments are open-ended assessments. That is, there is no specific correct result; your result will depend on your approach to the information provided. Make Professional Quality your goal. Use the following scoring rubric to guide you in how to approach the problem and then to evaluate how well your approach solves the problem.

The *criteria*—Software Mastery, Content, Format and Layout, and Process—represent the knowledge and skills you have gained that you can apply to solving the problem. The *levels of performance*—Professional Quality, Approaching Professional Quality, or Needs Quality Improvements—help you and your instructor evaluate your result.

	Your completed project is of Professional Quality if you:	Your completed project is Approaching Professional Quality if you:	Your completed project Needs Quality Improvements if you:
1-Software Mastery	Choose and apply the most appropriate skills, tools, and features and identify efficient methods to solve the problem.	Choose and apply some appropriate skills, tools, and features, but not in the most efficient manner.	Choose inappropriate skills, tools, or features, or are inefficient in solving the problem.
2-Content	Construct a solution that is clear and well organized, contains content that is accurate, appropriate to the audience and purpose, and is complete. Provide a solution that contains no errors in spelling, grammar, or style.	Construct a solution in which some components are unclear, poorly organized, inconsistent, or incomplete. Misjudge the needs of the audience. Have some errors in spelling, grammar, or style, but the errors do not detract from comprehension.	Construct a solution that is unclear, incomplete, or poorly organized; contains some inaccurate or inappropriate content; and contains many errors in spelling, grammar, or style. Do not solve the problem.
3-Format & Layout	Format and arrange all elements to communicate information and ideas, clarify function, illustrate relationships, and indicate relative importance.	Apply appropriate format and layout features to some elements, but not others. Overuse features, causing minor distraction.	Apply format and layout that does not communicate information or ideas clearly. Do not use format and layout features to clarify function, illustrate relationships, or indicate relative importance. Use available features excessively, causing distraction.
4-Process	Use an organized approach that integrates planning, development, self-assessment, revision, and reflection.	Demonstrate an organized approach in some areas, but not others; or, use an insufficient process of organization throughout.	Do not use an organized approach to solve the problem.

OUTCOMES-BASED ASSESSMENTS

Apply a combination of the 1A and 1B skills.

Build from
Scratch

GO! Think Project 1L Bears

PROJECT FILES

For Project 1L, you will need the following files:

New blank PowerPoint presentation
p01L_Bear

You will save your presentation as:

Lastname_Firstname_1L_Bears

Cindy Barrow, Tour Operations Manager for Kodiak West Travel, is developing a presentation describing brown bear viewing travel experiences that the company is developing. In the presentation, Cindy will be describing the brown bear habitat and viewing opportunities.

Kodiak bears are the largest known size of brown bears on record; they can weigh as much as 2,000 pounds and can get as large as polar bears. Kodiak bears are active during the day and are generally solitary creatures. The Kodiak Bear Travel Experience is a small, personalized travel adventure available to only eight participants at a time. It is an opportunity to peer into the life of these majestic mammals.

The adventure takes place on Kodiak Island near a lake with a high concentration of salmon, making it the perfect natural feeding ground for the Kodiak bears. Travelers can view the bears from boats, kayaks, and recently constructed viewing platforms and guides are available.

This is a true wildlife experience because the area is home to deer, fox, and river otter. Accommodations are available at the Kodiak West Breakfast Inn from mid-June to the end of August. Peak season is early August and reservations can be made up to one year in advance. The cost is $1,800 per person for one week, and includes all meals, use of watercraft, and guided tours.

Using the preceding information, create a presentation that Cindy can show at a travel fair. The presentation should include four to six slides describing the travel experience. Apply an appropriate theme and use slide layouts that will effectively present the content. Insert at least one picture and apply appropriate picture formatting. You may use a picture of your choosing or from your student data files, use the file p01L_Bear. Apply font formatting and slide transitions, and modify text alignment and line spacing as necessary.

Save the file as **Lastname_Firstname_1L_Bears** and then insert a header and footer that include the date and time updated automatically, the file name in the footer, and the page number. Add your name, your course name and section number, and the tags **bears, tours** to the properties. Save and print or submit as directed by your instructor.

END | You have completed Project 1L

OUTCOMES-BASED ASSESSMENTS

Build from
Scratch

| GO! Think | Project 1M Sitka | Online |

Build from
Scratch

| You and GO! | Project 1N Travel | Online |

| GO! Cumulative Group Project | Project 1O Bell Orchid Hotels |
| Online |

Formatting PowerPoint Presentations

GO! to Work
Video P2

OUTCOMES
Format a presentation to add visual interest and clarity.

OBJECTIVES

1. Format Numbered and Bulleted Lists
2. Insert Online Pictures
3. Insert Text Boxes and Shapes
4. Format Objects

OUTCOMES
Enhance a presentation with WordArt and SmartArt.

OBJECTIVES

5. Remove Picture Backgrounds and Insert WordArt
6. Create and Format a SmartArt Graphic

shinta / Fotolia

In This Chapter

A PowerPoint presentation is a visual aid in which well-designed slides help the audience understand complex information while keeping them focused on the message. Color is an important element that enhances your slides and draws the audience's interest by creating focus. When designing the background and element colors for your presentation, be sure that the colors you use provide contrast so that the text is visible on the background. Graphic elements such as pictures, SmartArt, and shapes can illustrate important information. Choose elements that work well with the presentation design and colors.

The projects in this chapter relate to **Sensation Park Entertainment Group**, an entertainment company that operates 15 regional theme parks across the United States, Mexico, and Canada. Park types include traditional theme parks, water parks, and animal parks. This year the company will launch three of its new "Sensation Parks" where attractions combine fun and the discovery of math and science information, and where teens and adults enjoy the free Friday night concerts. The company focuses on safe and imaginative attractions that appeal to guests with a variety of entertainment interests, including adventure, science, and the arts.

Employee Training Presentation

PROJECT ACTIVITIES

In Activities 2.01 through 2.21, you will format a presentation for Marc Johnson, Director of Operations for Sensation Park Entertainment Group, that describes important safety guidelines for employees. Your completed presentation will look similar to Figure 2.1.

PROJECT FILES

For Project 2A, you will need the following file:

p02A_Safety

You will save your presentation as:

Lastname_Firstname_2A_Safety

PROJECT RESULTS

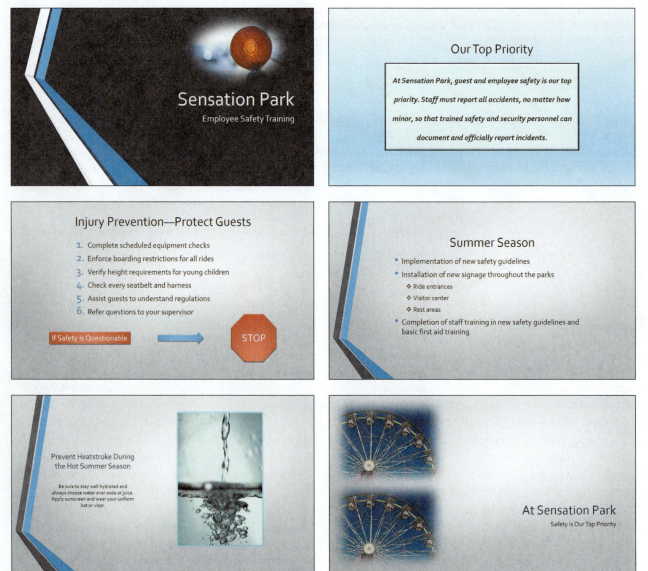

FIGURE 2.1 Project 2A Employee Training Presentation

Video P2-1

The font, color, and style of a numbered or bulleted list are determined by the presentation theme. You can format slide content by changing the bulleted and numbered list styles and colors.

Activity 2.01   Selecting Placeholder Text

Recall that a placeholder is a box on a slide with dotted or dashed borders that holds title and body text or other content such as charts, tables, and pictures. You can format placeholder contents by selecting text or by selecting the entire placeholder.

1 Start PowerPoint. From the student data files that accompany this textbook, locate and open **p02A_Safety**. Display the **Save As** dialog box, create a **New Folder** with the name **PowerPoint Chapter 2** and then using your own name, save the file in the folder you created as **Lastname_Firstname_2A_Safety**

2 Display **Slide 2**, and then click anywhere in the content placeholder with the single bullet point.

3 Point to the dashed border surrounding the placeholder to display the pointer, and then click one time to display the border as a solid line. Compare your screen with Figure 2.2.

When a placeholder's border displays as a solid line, all of the text in the placeholder is selected, and any formatting changes that you make will be applied to *all* of the text in the placeholder.

FIGURE 2.2

4 With the border of the placeholder displaying as a solid line, change the **Font Size** [20] to **24**. Notice that the font size of *all* of the placeholder text increases.

5 **Save** your presentation.

Activity 2.02   Changing a Bulleted List to a Numbered List

1 Display **Slide 3**, and then click anywhere in the bulleted list. Point to the placeholder dashed border to display the pointer, and then click one time to display the border as a solid line indicating that all of the text is selected.

2 On the **HOME tab**, in the **Paragraph group**, click **Numbering**, and then compare your slide with Figure 2.3.

All of the bullet symbols are converted to numbers. The color of the numbers is determined by the presentation theme.

FIGURE 2.3

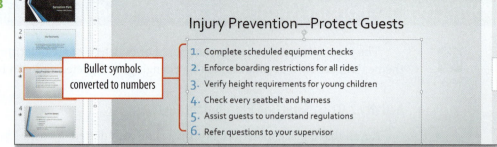

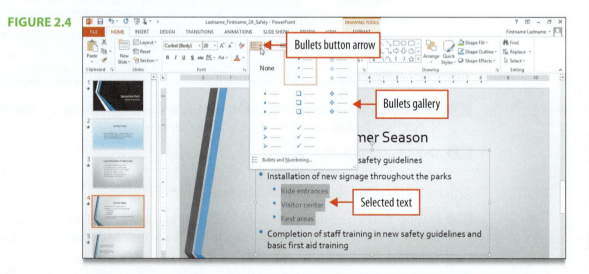

ALERT!   **Did You Display the Numbering Gallery?**

If you clicked the Numbering button arrow instead of the Numbering button, the Numbering gallery displays. Click the Numbering button arrow again to close the gallery, and then click the Numbering button to convert the bullets to numbers.

3 ▸ **Save** 🖫 your presentation.

Activity 2.03 | Changing the Shape and Color of a Bulleted List Symbol

The presentation theme includes default styles for the bullet points in content placeholders. You can customize a bullet by changing its style, color, and size.

1 ▸ Display **Slide 4**, and then select the three second-level bullet points—*Ride entrances*, *Visitor center*, and *Rest areas*.

2 ▸ On the **HOME tab**, in the **Paragraph group**, click the **Bullets button arrow** ⬚▾ to display the **Bullets** gallery, and then compare your screen with Figure 2.4.

FIGURE 2.4

ALERT!   **Were the Bullets Removed?**

If the bullets were removed, then you clicked the Bullets button instead of the Bullets button arrow. Click the Bullets button arrow, and then continue with Step 3.

3 ▸ Below the **Bullets** gallery, click **Bullets and Numbering**. In the **Bullets and Numbering** dialog box, point to each bullet style to display its ScreenTip. Then, in the second row, click **Star Bullets**. If the Star Bullets are not available, in the second row of bullets, click the second bullet style, and then click the Reset button.

4 Below the gallery, click the **Color** button. Under **Theme Colors**, in the eighth column, click the last color—**Red, Accent 4, Darker 50%**. In the **Size** box, select the existing number, type **100** and then compare your dialog box with Figure 2.5.

FIGURE 2.5

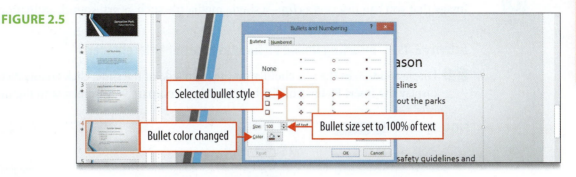

Selected bullet style

Bullet color changed

Bullet size set to 100% of text

5 Click **OK** to apply the bullet style, and then **Save** 🔲 your presentation.

> ***More* Knowledge** | **Using Other Symbols as Bullet Characters**
>
> Many bullets styles are available to insert in your presentation. In the Bullets and Numbering dialog box, click Customize to view additional bullet styles.

Activity 2.04 | Removing a Bullet Symbol from a Bullet Point

The Bullets button is a toggle, enabling you to turn the bullet symbol on and off. A slide that contains a single bullet point can be formatted as a single paragraph *without* a bullet symbol.

1 Display **Slide 2**, and then click in the paragraph. On the **HOME tab**, in the **Paragraph group**, click **Bullets** ⌄. Compare your screen with Figure 2.6.

The bullet symbol no longer displays, and the Bullets button is no longer selected. Additionally, the indentation associated with the list level is removed.

FIGURE 2.6

Our Top Priority

Bullet symbol removed

At Sensation Park, guest and employee safety is our top priority. Staff must report all accidents, no matter how minor, so that trained safety and security personnel can document and officially report incidents.

2 **Center** ≣ the paragraph. Click the dashed border to display the solid border and to select all of the text in the paragraph, and then apply **Bold** **B** and **Italic** *I*. On the **HOME tab**, in the **Paragraph group**, click **Line Spacing** ⌄, and then click **2.0**.

3 **Save** 🔲 your presentation.

Video P2-2

There are many sources from which you can insert images into a presentation. One type of image that you can insert is a *clip*—a single media file such as art, sound, animation, or a movie.

Activity 2.05 | Inserting Online Pictures in a Content Placeholder

1 Display **Slide 5**. In the placeholder on the right side of the slide, click **Online Pictures** to display the **Insert Pictures** dialog box, and then compare your screen with Figure 2.7.

FIGURE 2.7

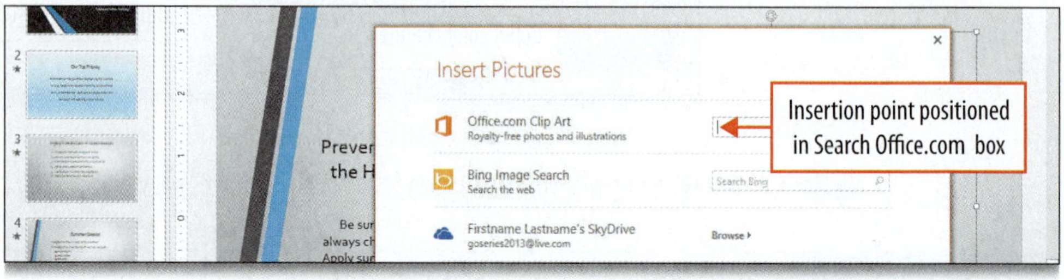

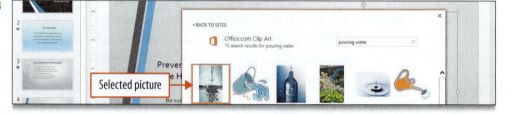

2 With the insertion point in the Search Office.com box, type **pouring water** and then press Enter to search for images that contain the keywords *pouring water*. Click the grayish-blue picture of water being poured. Compare your screen with Figure 2.8. If you are unable to locate the picture, choose another image.

FIGURE 2.8

3 With the water picture selected, click **Insert**. Compare your screen with Figure 2.9, and then **Save** your presentation.

On the ribbon, the Picture Tools display, and the water bottle image is surrounded by sizing handles, indicating that the image is selected.

BY TOUCH   Tap the picture that you want to insert, and then tap Insert.

FIGURE 2.9

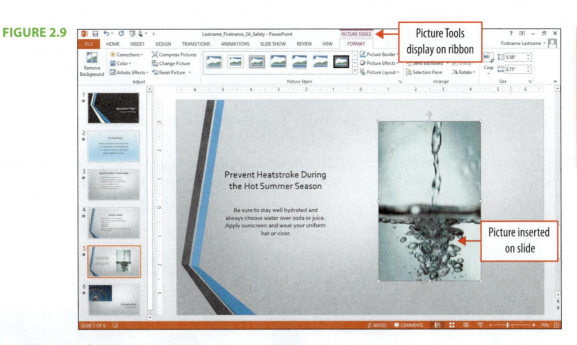

Picture Tools display on ribbon

Picture inserted on slide

Activity 2.06 | Inserting Online Pictures in Any Location on a Slide

1 Display **Slide 1**. Click the **INSERT tab**, and then in the **Images group**, click **Online Pictures**.

2 In the **Insert Pictures** dialog box, in the **Search Office.com** box, type **red lights** and then press Enter. Click the picture of the single red warning light, and then click **Insert**. Compare your screen with Figure 2.10. If you cannot locate the picture, select another image.

> When you use the Online Pictures button on the ribbon instead of the Online Pictures button in a content placeholder, PowerPoint inserts the image in the center of the slide.

FIGURE 2.10

Picture inserted

3 **Save** 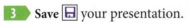 your presentation.

Activity 2.07 | Sizing a Picture

Recall that a selected image displays sizing handles that you can drag to resize the image. You can also resize an image using the Shape Height and Shape Width boxes on the FORMAT tab.

1 If necessary, select the picture of the red light. On the **FORMAT tab**, in the **Size group**, click in the **Shape Height** box 🔲, and then replace the selected number with **3.5**

2 Press Enter to resize the image. Notice that the picture is resized proportionately, and the **Width** box displays *5.26*. Compare your screen with Figure 2.11.

> When a picture is resized in this manner, the width adjusts in proportion to the picture height.

FIGURE 2.11

🔄 **BY TOUCH**   Drag the corner sizing handle with your finger or mouse to resize the picture proportionately.

---

3 **Save** 🔲 your presentation.

Activity 2.08 | Using Smart Guides and the Ruler to Position a Picture

Smart Guides are dashed lines that display on your slide when you are moving an object to assist you with alignment.

1 On **Slide 1**, on the **VIEW tab**, in the **Show group**, verify that the **Ruler** check box is selected and if necessary, select the check box. On the horizontal and vertical rulers, notice that *0* displays in the center.

> Horizontally, the PowerPoint ruler indicates measurements from the center of the slide *out* to the left and to the right. Vertically, the PowerPoint ruler indicates measurements from the center up and down.

2 Point to the picture to display the 🔼 pointer. Hold down Shift, and then very slowly, drag the picture to the right and notice that dashed red Smart Guides periodically display along the right edge of the picture. When the dashed red Smart Guide displays on the right edge of the picture at approximately **6 inches to the right of zero on the horizontal ruler**, compare your screen with Figure 2.12, and then release the mouse button.

> Smart Guides display when you move an object and the object is aligned with another object on the slide. Here, the Smart Guide displays because the right edge of the picture is aligned with the right edge of the title placeholder. Pressing Shift while dragging an object constrains object movement in a straight line either vertically or horizontally. Here, pressing Shift maintains the vertical placement of the picture at the top edge of the slide.

FIGURE 2.12

3 ▸ **Save** 🖫 the presentation.

More **Knowledge**   **Moving an Object by Using the Arrow Keys**

You can use the directional arrow keys on your keyboard to move a picture, shape, or other object in small increments. Select the object so that its outside border displays as a solid line. Then, on your keyboard, hold down the Ctrl key and press the directional arrow keys to move the selected object in small, precise increments.

Activity 2.09 │ Cropping a Picture

When you *crop* a picture you remove unwanted or unnecessary areas of the picture.

1 ▸ Display **Slide 6**, and then select the ferris wheel picture. On the **FORMAT tab**, in the **Size group**, click the upper portion of the **Crop** button to display the crop handles. Compare your screen with Figure 2.13.

Use the *crop handles* like sizing handles to remove unwanted areas of the picture.

FIGURE 2.13

2 ▸ Point to the center right crop handle to display the Crop pointer 🔖. Compare your screen with Figure 2.14.

The *crop pointer* is the mouse pointer that enables you to crop areas of a picture.

FIGURE 2.14

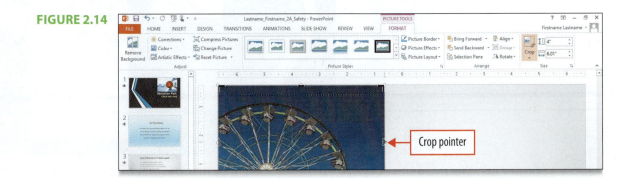

3 With the crop pointer displayed, hold down the left mouse button and drag to the left to approximately **1.5 inches to the left of 0 on the horizontal ruler**, and then release the mouse button. Compare your screen with Figure 2.15.

The portion of the picture to be removed by the crop displays in gray.

FIGURE 2.15

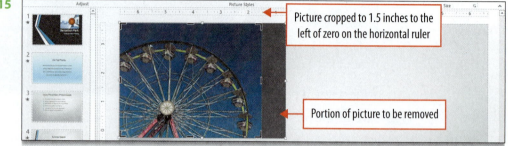

Picture cropped to 1.5 inches to the left of zero on the horizontal ruler

Portion of picture to be removed

4 Click anywhere on the slide outside of the image to apply the crop, and then **Save** 🔲 your presentation.

Activity 2.10 │ Using Crop to Shape to Change the Shape of a Picture

An inserted picture is rectangular in shape; however, you can modify a picture by changing its shape.

1 Display **Slide 1**, and then select the picture. On the **FORMAT tab**, in the **Size group**, click the lower portion of the Crop button—the **Crop button arrow**—and then compare your screen with Figure 2.16.

FIGURE 2.16

Crop button arrow

2 Point to **Crop to Shape** to display a gallery of shapes. Compare your screen with Figure 2.17.

FIGURE 2.17

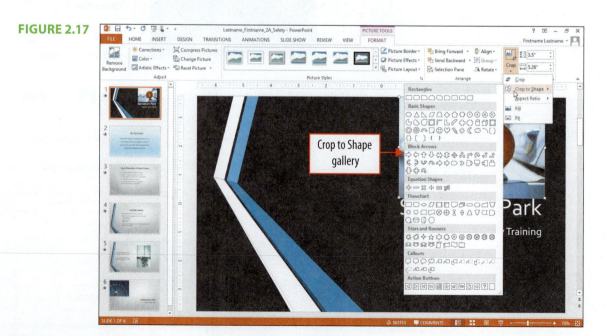

Crop to Shape gallery

3 Under **Basic Shapes**, in the first row, click the first shape—**Oval**—to change the picture's shape to an oval. **Save** your presentation.

Objective 3 | Insert Text Boxes and Shapes

Video P2-3

You can use objects, including text boxes and shapes, to draw attention to important information or to serve as containers for slide text. Many shapes, including lines, arrows, ovals, and rectangles, are available to insert and position anywhere on your slides.

Activity 2.11 | Inserting a Text Box

A *text box* is an object with which you can position text anywhere on a slide.

1 Display **Slide 3** and verify that the rulers display. Click the **INSERT tab**, and then in the **Text group**, click **Text Box**.

2 Move the pointer to several different places on the slide, and as you do so, in the horizontal and vertical rulers, notice that *ruler guides*—dotted red vertical and horizontal lines that display in the rulers indicating the pointer's position—move also.

Use the ruler guides to help you position objects on a slide.

3 Position the pointer so that the ruler guides are positioned on the **left half of the horizontal ruler at 4.5 inches** and on the **lower half of the vertical ruler at 2 inches**, and then compare your screen with Figure 2.18.

FIGURE 2.18

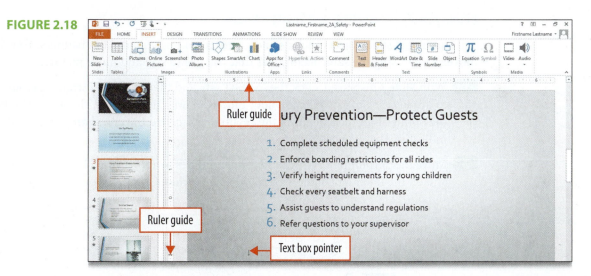

4 Click one time to create a narrow rectangular text box. With the insertion point blinking inside the text box, type **If Safety is Questionable** Notice that as you type, the width of the text box expands to accommodate the text. Compare your screen with Figure 2.19.

Do not be concerned if your text box is not positioned exactly as shown in Figure 2.19.

FIGURE 2.19

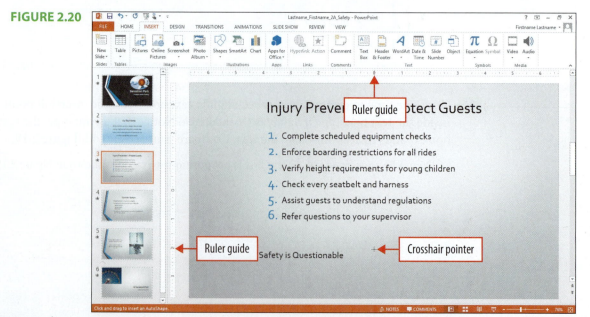

Injury Prevention—Protect Guests

1. Complete scheduled equipment checks
2. Enforce boarding restrictions for all rides
3. Verify height requirements for young children
4. Check every seatbelt and harness
5. Assist guests to understand regulations
6. Refer questions to your supervisor

If Safety is Questionable ← Text box inserted on slide

A L E R T ! **Does the Text in the Text Box Display Vertically, One Character at a Time?**

If you move the pointer when you click to create the text box, PowerPoint sets the width of the text box and does not widen to accommodate the text. If this happens, your text may display vertically instead of horizontally or the text may display on two lines. Click Undo, and then repeat the steps again, being sure that you do not move the mouse when you click to insert the text box.

---

5 ▸ Select the text that you typed, change the **Font Size** to **24** and then **Save** 🖫 your presentation.

You can format the text in a text box by using the same techniques that you use to format text in any other placeholder. For example, you can change the font, font style, font size, and font color.

Activity 2.12 | Inserting and Sizing a Shape

Shapes are slide objects such as lines, arrows, boxes, callouts, and banners. You can size and move shapes using the same techniques that you use to size and move pictures.

1 ▸ With **Slide 3** displayed, click the **INSERT tab**, and then in the **Illustrations group**, click **Shapes** to display the **Shapes** gallery. Under **Block Arrows**, click the first shape—**Right Arrow**. Move the pointer into the slide until the ➕ pointer—called the *crosshair pointer*—displays, indicating that you can draw a shape.

2 ▸ Move the ➕ pointer to position the ruler guides at approximately **0 on the horizontal ruler** and on the **lower half of the vertical ruler at 2 inches**. Compare your screen with Figure 2.20.

FIGURE 2.20

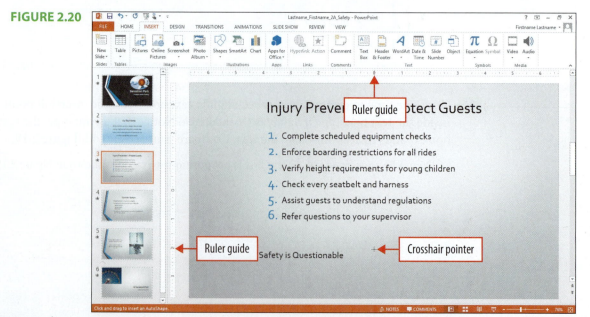

Injury Prevei Ruler guide **otect Guests**

1. Complete scheduled equipment checks
2. Enforce boarding restrictions for all rides
3. Verify height requirements for young children
4. Check every seatbelt and harness
5. Assist guests to understand regulations
6. Refer questions to your supervisor

Ruler guide ← Safety is Questionable ＋ → Crosshair pointer

3 Click to insert the arrow. On the **FORMAT tab**, in the **Size group**, click in the **Shape Height** box ⬍ to select the number. Type **0.5** and then click in the **Shape Width** box ↔. Type **2** and then press Enter to resize the arrow. Compare your screen with Figure 2.21.

FIGURE 2.21

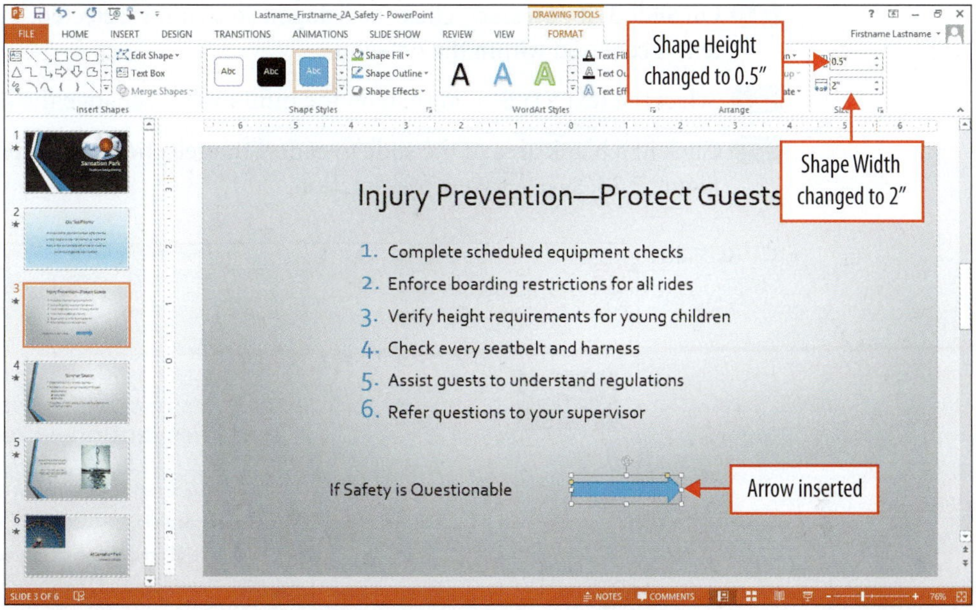

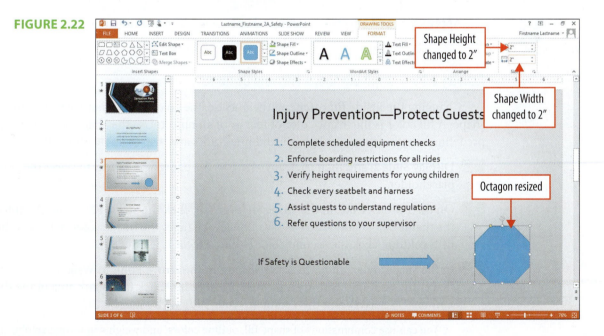

4 On the **FORMAT tab**, in the **Insert Shapes group**, click **More** ▼. In the gallery, under **Basic Shapes**, in the first row, click the second to last shape—**Octagon**.

5 Move the ✛ pointer to position the ruler guides on the **right half of the horizontal ruler at 3.5 inches** and on the **lower half of the vertical ruler at 1 inch**, and then click one time to insert an octagon.

6 On the **FORMAT tab**, in the **Size group**, click in the **Shape Height** box ⬍ to select the number. Type **2** and then click in the **Shape Width** box ↔. Type **2** and then press Enter to resize the octagon. Compare your slide with Figure 2.22. Do not be concerned if your shapes are not positioned exactly as shown in the figure.

FIGURE 2.22

7 **Save** 🖫 your presentation.

Activity 2.13 | Adding Text to Shapes

Shapes can serve as a container for text. After you add text to a shape, you can change the font and font size, apply font styles, and change text alignment.

1 On **Slide 3**, if necessary, click the octagon so that it is selected. Type **STOP** and notice that the text is centered within the octagon.

2 Select the text *STOP*, and then on the mini toolbar, change the **Font Size** to **32**.

3 Click in a blank area of the slide to cancel the selection, and then compare your screen with Figure 2.23. **Save** your presentation.

FIGURE 2.23

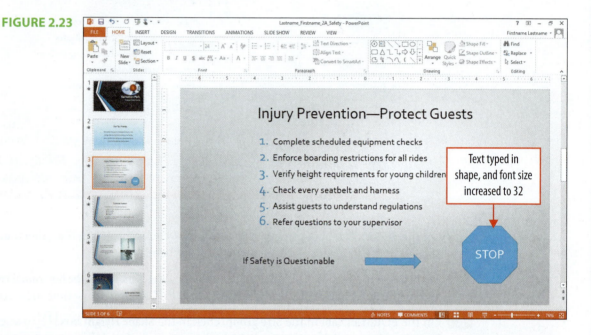

Objective 4 | Format Objects

Apply styles and effects to pictures, shapes, and text boxes to complement slide backgrounds and colors.

Video P2-4

Activity 2.14 | Applying Shape Fills and Outlines

Changing the inside *fill color* and the outside line color is a distinctive way to format a shape. A fill color is the inside color of text or of an object. Use the Shape Styles gallery to apply predefined combinations of these fill and line colors and also to apply other effects.

1 Display **Slide 2**, and then click anywhere in the paragraph of text to select the content placeholder.

2 On the **FORMAT tab**, in the **Shape Styles group**, click the **Shape Fill arrow**. Point to several of the theme colors and watch as Live Preview changes the inside color of the text box. In the fifth column, click the second color—**Blue, Accent 1, Lighter 80%**.

3 In the **Shape Styles group**, click the **Shape Outline arrow**. Point to **Weight**, click **3 pt**, and notice that a thick outline surrounds the text placeholder. Click in a blank area of the slide so that nothing is selected, and then compare your slide with Figure 2.24.

You can use combinations of shape fill, outline colors, and weights to format an object.

FIGURE 2.24

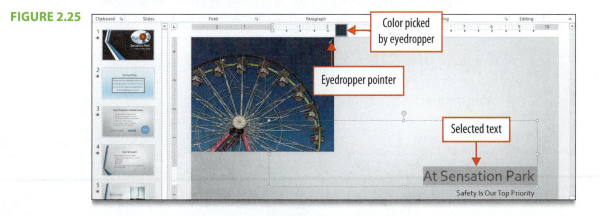

Shape fill applied to content placeholder

Shape outline applied

Our Top Priority

At Sensation Park, guest and employee safety is our top priority. Staff must report all accidents, no matter how minor, so that trained safety and security personnel can document and officially report incidents.

4 ▸ **Save** 🖫 your presentation.

Activity 2.15 │ Using the Eyedropper to Change Color

The **eyedropper** is a tool that captures the exact color from an object on your screen and then applies the color to any shape, picture, or text. You can use the eyedropper to give your presentation a cohesive look by matching a font color, fill color, border color, or other slide element to any color on any slide.

1 ▸ Display **Slide 6**, and then select the title text—*At Sensation Park*.

2 ▸ On the **HOME tab**, in the **Font group**, click the **Font Color button arrow**. Below the gallery, click **Eyedropper**, and then move the 🖉 pointer into the upper right corner of the Ferris wheel picture. Compare your screen with Figure 2.25.

A small square displays next to the pointer indicating the exact color to which you are pointing. When you hover over a color, it's **RGB** color coordinates display. RGB is a color model in which the colors red, green, and blue are added together to form another color.

FIGURE 2.25

Color picked by eyedropper

Eyedropper pointer

Selected text

At Sensation Park

Safety Is Our Top Priority

3 ▸ With the 🖉 pointer in the upper right corner of the picture, click one time. Notice that the color is applied to the selected text. Compare your screen with Figure 2.26.

FIGURE 2.26

Color from picture applied to selected text

At Sensation Park

Safety Is Our Top Priority

4 Display **Slide 5**, and then select the title. On the mini toolbar, click the **Font Color button arrow**. Under **Recent Colors**, notice that the color you selected with the eyedropper displays. Point to the color to display the ScreenTip—*Dark Blue*. Click **Dark Blue** to apply the color to the selection.

> After a color has been selected with the eyedropper, the color remains available in the presentation each time the color gallery is displayed. When you use the eyedropper in this manner, you can consistently apply the same color throughout your presentation.

5 **Save** 🖫 your presentation.

Activity 2.16 | Applying Shape Styles

1 Display **Slide 3**, and then select the **arrow shape**. On the **FORMAT tab**, in the **Shape Styles group**, click **More** ▾ to display the **Shape Styles** gallery. In the last row, click the second style—**Intense Effect - Blue, Accent 1**.

2 Click anywhere in the text *If Safety is Questionable* to select the text box. On the **FORMAT tab**, in the **Shape Styles group**, click **More** ▾.

3 In the last row, click the fifth style—**Intense Effect - Red, Accent 4**.

4 Select the **octagon** shape, and then apply the same style you applied to the text box—**Intense Effect - Red, Accent 4**.

5 Compare your screen with Figure 2.27, and then **Save** 🖫 your presentation.

FIGURE 2.27

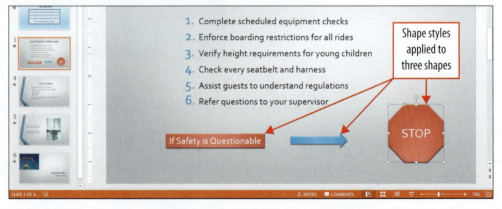

1. Complete scheduled equipment checks
2. Enforce boarding restrictions for all rides
3. Verify height requirements for young children
4. Check every seatbelt and harness
5. Assist guests to understand regulations
6. Refer questions to your supervisor

Shape styles applied to three shapes

If Safety is Questionable

STOP

Activity 2.17 | Applying Shape and Picture Effects

1 Display **Slide 1**, and then select the picture. On the **FORMAT tab**, in the **Picture Styles group**, click **Picture Effects**.

A list of effects that you can apply to pictures displays. These effects can also be applied to shapes and text boxes.

2 Point to **Soft Edges**, and then in the **Soft Edges** gallery, point to each style to view its effect on the picture. Click the last **Soft Edges** effect—**50 Point**, and then compare your screen with Figure 2.28.

The soft edges effect softens and blurs the outer edge of the picture so that the picture blends into the slide background.

FIGURE 2.28

3 Display **Slide 2**, and then select the light blue content placeholder. On the **FORMAT tab**, in the **Shape Styles group**, click **Shape Effects**. Point to **Bevel** to display the **Bevel** gallery. Point to each bevel to view its ScreenTip and to use Live Preview to examine the effect of each bevel on the content placeholder. In the last row, click the last bevel—**Art Deco**.

4 Click in a blank area of the slide and then compare your screen with Figure 2.29.

FIGURE 2.29

5 Display **Slide 5**, and then select the picture. On the **FORMAT tab**, in the **Picture Styles group**, click **Picture Effects**, and then point to **Glow**.

6 Point to several of the effects to view the effect on the picture, and then under **Glow Variations**, in the second row, click the first glow effect—**Blue, 8 pt glow, Accent color 1**.

The glow effect applies a colored, softly blurred outline to the selected object.

7 **Save** your presentation.

Activity 2.18 | Duplicating Objects

1 ▸ Display **Slide 6**, and then select the picture.

2 ▸ Press and hold down Ctrl, and then press D one time. Release Ctrl.

Ctrl + D is the keyboard shortcut to duplicate an object. A duplicate of the picture overlaps the original picture and the duplicated image is selected.

3 ▸ Click in a blank area of the slide, and then compare your screen with Figure 2.30. **Save** 💾 your presentation.

FIGURE 2.30

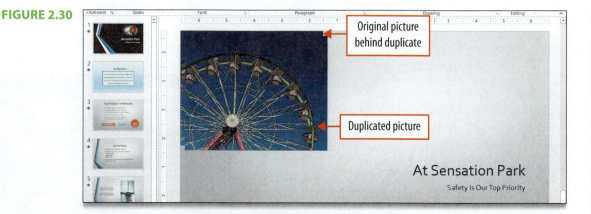

Activity 2.19 | Aligning and Distributing Objects Relative to the Slide

You can select multiple slide objects, and then use ribbon commands to align and distribute the objects precisely.

1 ▸ With **Slide 6** displayed, position the pointer in the gray area of the Slide pane just outside the upper left corner of the slide to display the 🖾 pointer. Drag down and to the right to draw a transparent, gray, selection rectangle that encloses both pictures. Compare your slide with Figure 2.31.

🔄 **ANOTHER WAY**   Hold down Shift and then click each object that you want to select.

FIGURE 2.31

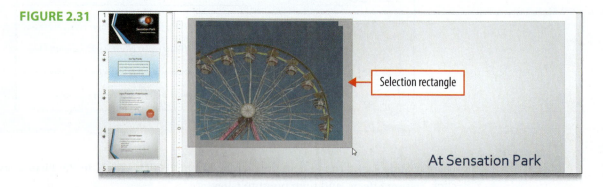

2 ▸ Release the mouse button to select the objects, and then compare your screen with Figure 2.32.

Objects completely enclosed by a selection rectangle are selected when the mouse button is released.

FIGURE 2.32

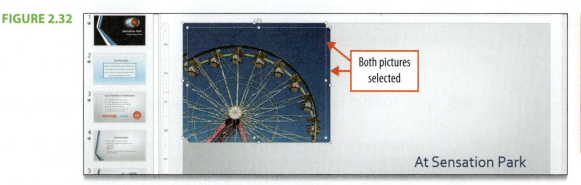

Both pictures selected

At Sensation Park

3 Click the **FORMAT tab**, and then in the **Arrange group**, click **Align**. Toward the bottom of the menu, click **Align to Slide** to activate this setting. On the **FORMAT tab**, in the **Arrange group**, click **Align** again, and then click **Align Left**.

> The Align to Slide option, in combination with the Align Left option, aligns the left edge of each picture with the left edge of the slide.

4 With both pictures still selected, on the **FORMAT tab**, in the **Arrange group**, click **Align** again, and then click **Distribute Vertically**. Compare your screen with Figure 2.33.

> The pictures are distributed evenly down the left edge of the slide between the top and bottom edges of the slide.

FIGURE 2.33

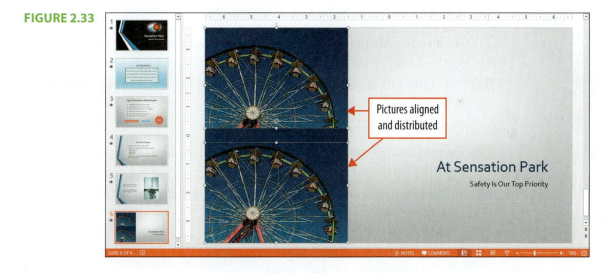

Pictures aligned and distributed

At Sensation Park

Safety Is Our Top Priority

5 With both pictures selected, on the **FORMAT tab**, in the **Picture Styles group**, click the **Picture Effects** button. Point to **Soft Edges**, and then click **50 Point** to apply the picture effect to both images.

6 Save 💾 the presentation.

Activity 2.20 | Aligning and Distributing Objects Relative to Each Other

1 Display **Slide 3**, hold down Shift, and then at the bottom of the slide, click the **text box**, the **arrow**, and the **octagon** to select all three objects.

🔄 **BY TOUCH**   Tap the text box, hold down Shift, and then tap the arrow and the octagon.

2 With the three objects selected, on the **FORMAT tab**, in the **Arrange group**, click **Align**. Click **Align Selected Objects**.

The *Align Selected Objects* option will cause the objects that you select to align relative to each other, rather than relative to the edges of the slide.

3 On the **FORMAT tab**, in the **Arrange group**, click **Align**, and then click **Align Middle**. Click the **Align** button again, and then click **Distribute Horizontally**.

The midpoint of each object aligns and the three objects are distributed evenly between the left edge of the leftmost object—the text box—and the right edge of the rightmost object—the octagon.

4 Click anywhere on the slide so that none of the objects are selected. Compare your screen with Figure 2.34, and then **Save** 💾 the presentation.

FIGURE 2.34

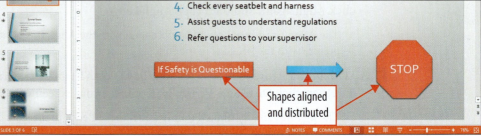

Activity 2.21 | Grouping Objects

You can select multiple objects and group them so that they can be formatted and edited as one object.

1 With **Slide 3** displayed, click the text box, hold down Shift, and then click the arrow and the octagon so that all three objects are selected.

Sizing handles surround each individual object.

2 On the **FORMAT tab**, in the **Arrange group**, click **Group**, and then click **Group**. Compare your screen with Figure 2.35.

The sizing handles surround all three shapes as one, indicating that the three shapes are grouped into one object. The individual objects are not selected. The grouped object can be formatted, aligned, and moved as one object.

FIGURE 2.35

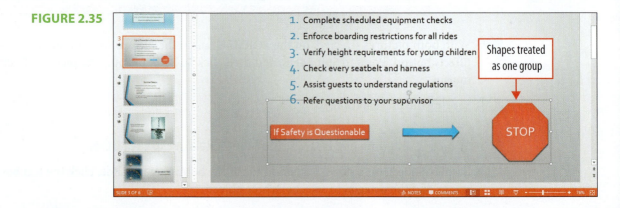

3 On the **FORMAT tab**, in the **Arrange group**, click **Align**, and then click **Align Center**.

The group is centered horizontally on the slide.

4 On the **Slide Show tab**, in the **Start Slide Show group**, click the **From Beginning** button, and then view the slide show. When the black slide displays, press Esc.

5 On the **INSERT tab**, in the **Text group**, click **Header & Footer** to display the **Header and Footer** dialog box. Click the **Notes and Handouts** tab. Under **Include on page**, select the **Date and time** check box, and then select **Update automatically**. If necessary, clear the Header check box. Select the **Page number** and **Footer** check boxes. In the **Footer** box, using your own name, type **Lastname_Firstname_2A_Safety** and then click **Apply to All**.

6 Display the document properties. As the **Tags** type **safety presentation** and as the **Subject** type your course and section number. Be sure your name displays as the author, and then **Save** your file. Print **Handouts 6 Slides Horizontal**, or submit your presentation electronically as directed by your instructor.

7 **Close** PowerPoint.

END | You have completed Project 2A

2

POWERPOINT

GO! with Office Web Apps

Objective | Create an Informational Presentation in the PowerPoint Web App

A L E R T !   **Working with Web-Based Applications and Services**

Computer programs and services on the web receive continuous updates and improvements, so the steps to complete this web-based activity may differ from the ones shown. You can often look at the screens and the information presented to determine how to complete the activity.

Activity | Creating an Informational Presentation in the PowerPoint Web App

In this activity, you will use the PowerPoint Web App to create a presentation similar to the one you created in Project 2A.

1 From the desktop, start Internet Explorer. Navigate to **http://skydrive.com**, and then sign in to your Microsoft account. Open your **GO! Web Projects** folder—or create and then open this folder if necessary.

2 On the SkyDrive menu bar, click **Upload**, and then navigate to your student data files and select **p02_2A_Web**. Click **Open**. When the upload is complete, right click **p02_2A_Web**, and then click **Rename**. Using your own name, as the file name type **Lastname_Firstname_PPT_2A_Web** and then press Enter. Click your file, and then click **EDIT PRESENTATION**. Click **Edit in PowerPoint Web App**.

3 Display **Slide 5**. In the content placeholder, click the third button—**Online Pictures** ⧉. In the **Search** box, type **pouring water** and then press Enter. Insert the picture that you inserted in Project 2A. If the picture is not available, choose another appropriate image.

4 Display **Slide 2**, and then click the paragraph to activate the content placeholder. Click in the paragraph again so that you can edit the paragraph. On the **HOME tab**, in the **Paragraph group**, click **Bullets** to remove the bullet symbol from the paragraph.

5 On the **HOME tab**, in the **Paragraph group**, click **Center** and then select the entire paragraph. Change the **Font Size** to **24** and apply **Bold**.

6 With **Slide 2** displayed and the paragraph selected, click the outer edge of the content placeholder so that the outer edge displays as a solid line. On the **DRAWING TOOLS FORMAT tab**, in the **Shape Styles group**, click the small down arrow. In the last row, click the second style—**Intense Effect – Blue, Accent 1**. In the **Shape Styles group**, click **Shape Outline**, in the second column, click the first color—**Black, Text 1**. Click **Shape Outline** again, point to **Weight**, and then click **4 1/2 pt**.

7 Click outside the content placeholder to apply your changes, and then compare your screen with Figure A.

FIGURE A

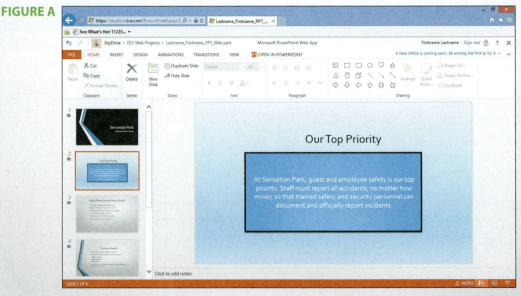

(GO! with Office Web Apps continues on the next page)

8 Display **Slide 3**, and then double-click in the bulleted list. On the **HOME tab**, in the **Paragraph group**, click **Numbering** to apply numbers to all of the bullet points. It is not necessary to select the text; in the PowerPoint Web App, bullets and numbering are applied to all of the bullet points in a content placeholder.

9 Click outside of the content placeholder to deselect it. With **Slide 3** still displayed, on the **INSERT tab**, in the **Text group**, click **Text Box** to insert a text box in the middle of your slide. Point to the text box border, and then drag down and to the left to position the text box so that the circular rotation handle above the center of the text box is positioned below the number 6.

10 Click in the text box and then drag to select *Click to add text*. Type **If Safety is Questionable** and then on the **FORMAT tab**, in the **Shape Styles group**, click the small down arrow. In the last row, click the fifth style—**Intense Effect – Red, Accent 4**.

11 On the **INSERT tab**, in the **Illustrations group**, click **Right Arrow** to insert an arrow in the middle of your slide. Drag the arrow so that it is aligned horizontally with the text box and its left edge aligns with the *y* in *your*.

12 Click outside of the arrow to deselect it. On the **INSERT tab**, in the **Illustrations group**, click **Rounded Rectangle** to insert a 1 × 1 rounded rectangle in the middle of your slide. Drag the rectangle so that so that its center sizing handle aligns with the arrow point and its left edge aligns with the *s* in *regulations*. On the **FORMAT tab**, in the **Shape Styles group**, click the small down arrow. In the last row, click the fifth style—**Intense Effect – Red, Accent 4**.

13 Click in the rectangle. Type **STOP** and then click in a blank area of the slide. Compare your screen with Figure B and make adjustments to the position of the shapes as necessary.

14 If you are instructed to submit your file, create a PDF as indicated in the Note box below. On the ribbon, click the **FILE tab** and click **Exit**. Sign out of your Microsoft account and close the browser. Submit as instructed by your instructor.

N O T E   **Creating a PDF from the PowerPoint Web App**

To print on paper, click the File tab, click Print, and then click Print to PDF. In the Microsoft PowerPoint Web App message box, click Click here to view the PDF of your document. In the message bar at the bottom of your screen, click the Save arrow, and then click Save As. In the Save As dialog box, navigate to your PowerPoint Chapter 2 folder, and then save the file.

FIGURE B

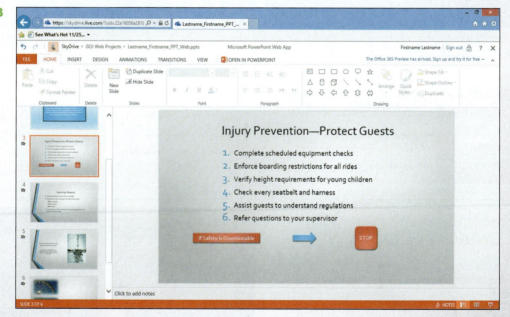

Event Announcement

PROJECT ACTIVITIES

In Activities 2.22 through 2.34, you will format slides in a presentation for the Sensation Park Entertainment Group's Marketing Director that informs employees about upcoming events at the company's amusement parks. You will enhance the presentation using SmartArt and WordArt graphics. Your completed presentation will look similar to Figure 2.36.

PROJECT FILES

For Project 2B, you will need the following files:

p02B_Celebrations
p02B_Canada_Contact
p02B_Mexico_Contact
p02B_US_Contact

You will save your presentation as:

Lastname_Firstname_2B_Celebrations

PROJECT RESULTS

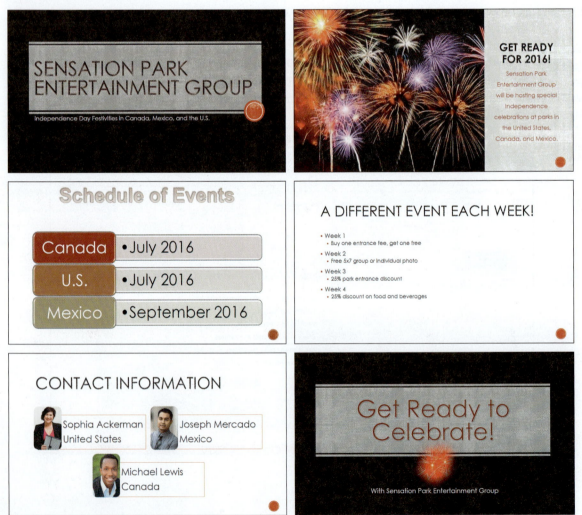

FIGURE 2.36 Project 2B Event Announcement

Video P2-5

To avoid the boxy look that results when you insert an image into a presentation, use **Background Removal** to flow a picture into the content of the presentation. Background Removal removes unwanted portions of a picture so that the picture does not appear as a self-contained rectangle.

WordArt is a gallery of text styles with which you can create decorative effects, such as shadowed or mirrored text. You can choose from the gallery of WordArt styles to insert a new WordArt object or you can customize existing text by applying WordArt formatting.

Activity 2.22 | Removing the Background from a Picture and Applying Soft Edge Options

1 Start PowerPoint. From your student data files, open **p02B_Celebrations**. On the **VIEW tab**, in the **Show group**, if necessary, select the Ruler check box. In your **PowerPoint Chapter 2** folder, **Save** the file as **Lastname_Firstname_2B_Celebrations**

2 Display **Slide 6**. Click the picture to select it, and then on the **FORMAT tab**, in the **Adjust group**, click **Remove Background**. Compare your screen with Figure 2.37.

PowerPoint determines what portion of the picture is the foreground—the portion to keep—and which portion is the background—the portion to remove. The background is overlaid in magenta, leaving the remaining portion of the picture as it will look when the background removal is complete. A rectangular selection area displays that you can move and size to select additional areas of the picture. The Background Removal options display in the Refine group on the ribbon.

FIGURE 2.37

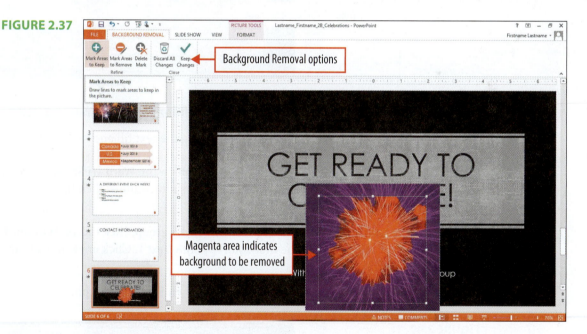

3 On the **Background Removal tab**, in the **Close group**, click **Keep Changes** to remove the background.

4 With the picture selected, on the **FORMAT tab**, in the **Picture Styles group**, click **Picture Effects**, point to **Soft Edges**, and then click **50 Point**. Compare your slide with Figure 2.38, and then **Save** your presentation.

FIGURE 2.38

Background removed, and soft edge picture style applied

Activity 2.23 | Applying WordArt Styles to Existing Text

1 On **Slide 6**, click anywhere in the word *Get* to activate the title placeholder, and then select the title—*Get Ready to Celebrate!* Click the **FORMAT tab**, and then in the **WordArt Styles group**, click **More** ⬇ to display the WordArt gallery.

2 Point to several WordArt styles to view the change to the slide title. In the first row, click the first style—**Fill – White, Text 1, Shadow**. Click anywhere on the slide to cancel the selection.

3 Compare your screen with Figure 2.39, and then **Save** 🖫 your presentation.

FIGURE 2.39

WordArt style applied to title

Activity 2.24 | Changing the Text Fill and Text Outline Colors of a WordArt Object

A WordArt object can be modified by changing the text fill and text outline colors.

1 On **Slide 6**, select the title. On the **FORMAT tab**, in the **WordArt Styles group**, click the **Text Fill button arrow**. Under **Theme Colors**, in the sixth column, click the fifth color—**Dark Red, Accent 2, Darker 25%.**

2 With the text still selected, in the **WordArt Styles group**, click the **Text Outline button arrow**. In the second column, click the first color—**White, Text 1**. Click anywhere on the slide to cancel the selection.

3 Compare your screen with Figure 2.40, and then **Save** 🖫 your presentation.

FIGURE 2.40

WordArt text fill and text outline colors changed

Activity 2.25 | Inserting and Aligning a WordArt Object

In addition to formatting existing text using WordArt, you can insert a new WordArt object anywhere on a slide.

1 ▶ Display **Slide 3**. On the **INSERT tab**, in the **Text group**, click **WordArt**. In the gallery, in the second row, click the third WordArt style—**Gradient Fill – Brown, Accent 4, Outline – Accent 4**.

In the center of your slide, a WordArt placeholder displays *Your text here*. Text that you type will replace this text and the placeholder will expand to accommodate the text. The WordArt is surrounded by sizing handles with which you can adjust its size.

2 ▶ Type **Schedule of Events** to replace the WordArt placeholder text. Compare your screen with Figure 2.41.

FIGURE 2.41

3 ▶ With the WordArt selected, on the **FORMAT tab**, in the **Arrange group**, click **Align**, and then click **Align Top** to move the WordArt to the top of the slide.

4 ▶ Click in a blank area of the slide, and then compare your screen with Figure 2.42.

FIGURE 2.42

5 ▶ **Save** 🖫 your presentation.

Activity 2.26 | Adding Text Effects to a WordArt

Text effects are formats applied to text that include shadows, reflections, glows, bevels, and 3-D rotations.

1 With **Slide 3** displayed, select the **WordArt** text. On the mini toolbar, change the **Font** to **Arial** and the **Font Size** to **66**.

2 On the **FORMAT tab**, in the **WordArt Styles group**, click **Text Effects**. Point to **Shadow**, and then compare your screen with Figure 2.43.

FIGURE 2.43

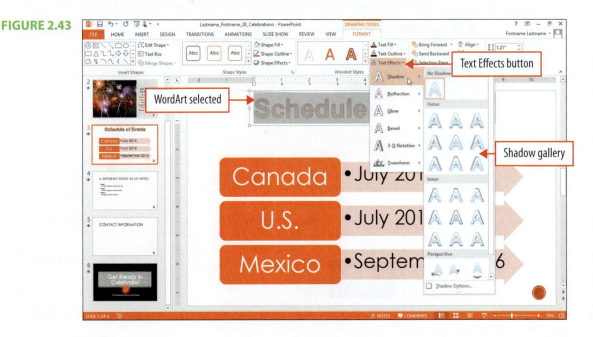

3 Under **Outer**, in the third row, click the third style—**Offset Diagonal Top Left**. Click in a blank area of the slide, and then compare your screen with Figure 2.44.

FIGURE 2.44

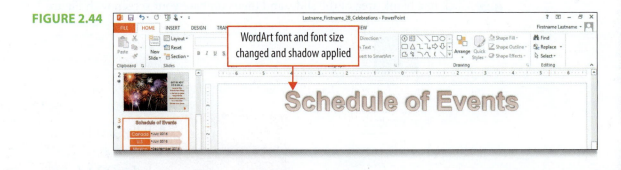

4 Save your presentation.

Objective 6 | Create and Format a SmartArt Graphic

Video P2-6

A *SmartArt graphic* is a visual representation of information that you create by choosing from among various layouts to communicate your message or ideas effectively. SmartArt graphics can illustrate processes, hierarchies, cycles, lists, and relationships. You can include text and pictures in a SmartArt graphic, and you can apply colors, effects, and styles that coordinate with the presentation theme.

Activity 2.27 | Creating a SmartArt Graphic from Bulleted Points

You can convert an existing bulleted list into a SmartArt graphic. When you create a SmartArt graphic, consider the message that you are trying to convey, and then choose an appropriate layout. The table in Figure 2.45 describes types of SmartArt layouts and suggested purposes.

FIGURE 2.45

MICROSOFT POWERPOINT SMARTART GRAPHIC TYPES	
GRAPHIC TYPE	**PURPOSE OF GRAPHIC**
List	Shows non-sequential information
Process	Shows steps in a process or timeline
Cycle	Shows a continual process
Hierarchy	Shows a decision tree or displays an organization chart
Relationship	Illustrates connections
Matrix	Shows how parts relate to a whole
Pyramid	Shows proportional relationships with the largest component on the top or bottom
Picture	Includes pictures in the layout to communicate messages and ideas
Office.com	Additional layouts available from Office.com

1 Display **Slide 4**, and then click anywhere in the bulleted list placeholder. On the **HOME tab**, in the **Paragraph group**, click **Convert to SmartArt**. Below the gallery, click **More SmartArt Graphics**.

Three sections comprise the Choose a SmartArt Graphic dialog box. The left section lists the SmartArt graphic types. The center section displays the SmartArt layouts according to type. The third section displays the selected SmartArt graphic, its name, and a description of its purpose.

🔄 **ANOTHER WAY**   Right-click in a bulleted list to display the shortcut menu, point to Convert to SmartArt, and then click More SmartArt Graphics.

2 On the left side of the **Choose a SmartArt Graphic** dialog box, click **List**. Use the ScreenTips to locate and then click **Vertical Box List**. Compare your screen with Figure 2.46.

FIGURE 2.46

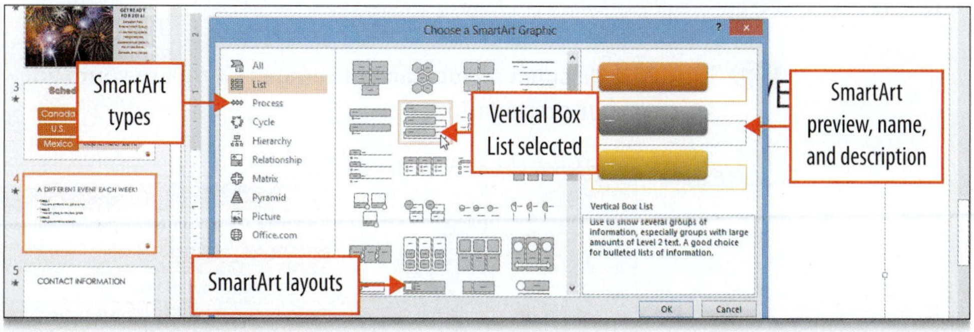

3 In the **Choose a SmartArt Graphic** dialog box, click **OK**. Compare your screen with Figure 2.47, and then **Save** 🖫 your presentation.

It is not necessary to select all of the text in the list. By clicking in the list, PowerPoint converts all of the bullet points to the selected SmartArt graphic. On the ribbon, the SmartArt contextual tools display two tabs—Design and Format. The thick border surrounding the SmartArt graphic indicates that the SmartArt graphic is selected and displays the area that the object will cover on the slide.

FIGURE 2.47

4 Save ⊟ your presentation.

Activity 2.28 | Adding Shapes in a SmartArt Graphic

If a SmartArt graphic does not have enough shapes to illustrate a concept or display the relationships, you can add more shapes.

1 Click in the shape that contains the text *Week 3*. In the **SMARTART TOOLS**, click the **DESIGN tab**. In the **Create Graphic group**, click the **Add Shape arrow**, and then click **Add Shape After** to insert a shape at the same level. Type **Week 4**

The text in each of the SmartArt shapes resizes to accommodate the added shape.

🔄 **ANOTHER WAY**   Right-click the shape, point to Add Shape, and then click Add Shape After.

2 On the **DESIGN tab**, in the **Create Graphic group**, click **Add Bullet** to add a bullet below the *Week 4* shape.

3 Type **25% discount on food and beverages** Compare your slide with Figure 2.48, and then Save ⊟ your presentation.

FIGURE 2.48

Activity 2.29 | Inserting a SmartArt Graphic Using a Content Layout

1 Display **Slide 5**. In the center of the content placeholder, click **Insert a SmartArt Graphic** 📊 to open the **Choose a SmartArt Graphic** dialog box.

2 On the left, click **Picture**, and then scroll as necessary and use the ScreenTips to locate **Picture Strips**. Click **Picture Strips** and then compare your screen with Figure 2.49.

FIGURE 2.49

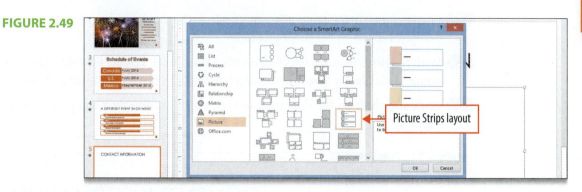

3 Click **OK** to insert the SmartArt graphic.

You can type text directly into the shapes or you can type text in the Text Pane, which may display to the left of your SmartArt graphic. You can display the Text Pane by clicking the Text Pane tab on the left side of the SmartArt graphic border, or by clicking the Text Pane button in the Create Graphic group. Depending on your software settings, the Text Pane may display.

Activity 2.30 | Inserting Pictures and Text in a SmartArt Graphic

1 In the SmartArt graphic, in the upper left text rectangle shape, type **Sophia Ackerman** and then press Enter. Type **United States** and then click in the text rectangle on the right. Type **Joseph Mercado** and then press Enter. Type **Mexico** and then click in the lower text rectangle. Type **Michael Lewis** and then press Enter. Type **Canada**

2 In the top left picture placeholder, click **Insert Picture** 🖼. In the **Insert Pictures** dialog box, to the right of **From a file**, click **Browse**. Navigate to your student data files, click **p02B_US_Contact**, and then click **Insert** to insert the picture.

3 Using the technique you just practiced, in the right picture placeholder, insert **p02B_Mexico_Contact**. In the lower picture placeholder, insert **p02B_Canada_Contact**.

4 Compare your screen with Figure 2.50, and then **Save** 💾 your presentation.

FIGURE 2.50

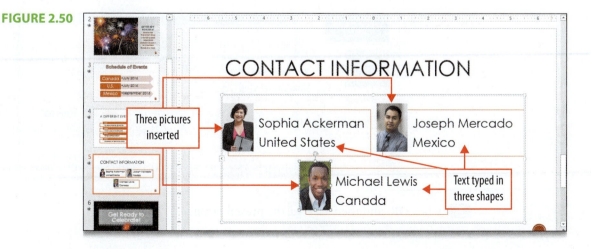

Activity 2.31 | Changing the Size and Shape of SmartArt Elements

You can select individual or groups of shapes in a SmartArt graphic and make them larger or smaller, and you can change selected shapes to another type of shape.

1 With **Slide 5** displayed, click the picture of *Sophia Ackerman*. Hold down Shift, and then click the pictures of *Joseph Mercado* and *Michael Lewis* so that all three pictures are selected.

2 On the **SMARTART TOOLS FORMAT tab**, in the **Shapes group**, click **Larger** two times to increase the size of the three pictures.

3 With the three pictures selected, on the **SMARTART TOOLS FORMAT tab**, in the **Shapes group**, click **Change Shape**. Under **Rectangles**, click the second shape—**Rounded Rectangle**.

4 Click anywhere on the slide to cancel the selection, and then compare your screen with Figure 2.51.

FIGURE 2.51

5 Save 💾 your presentation.

Activity 2.32 | Changing the SmartArt Layout

1 Display **Slide 3**, and then click anywhere in the SmartArt graphic. On the **SMARTART TOOLS DESIGN tab**, in the **Layouts group**, click **More** ⬇, and then click **More Layouts**. In the **Choose a SmartArt Graphic** dialog box, click **List**. Scroll up or down as necessary to locate and then click **Vertical Block List**. Compare your screen with Figure 2.52.

FIGURE 2.52

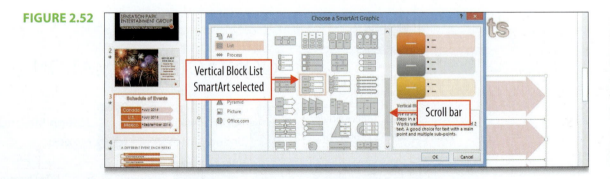

2 Click **OK**, and then Save 💾 the presentation.

Activity 2.33 | Changing the Color and Style of a SmartArt Graphic

SmartArt Styles are combinations of formatting effects that you can apply to SmartArt graphics.

1 With **Slide 3** displayed, if necessary, select the SmartArt. On the **SMARTART TOOLS DESIGN tab**, in the **SmartArt Styles group**, click **Change Colors**. In the color gallery, under **Colorful**, click the second style—**Colorful Range - Accent Colors 2 to 3**—to change the colors.

2 On the **DESIGN tab**, in the **SmartArt Styles group**, click **More** to display the **SmartArt Styles gallery**. Under **3-D**, click the third style, **Cartoon**. Compare your slide with Figure 2.53.

FIGURE 2.53

3 Save 🖫 the presentation.

Activity 2.34 | Converting a SmartArt to Text

1 Display **Slide 4**, and then click anywhere in the SmartArt graphic. On the **SMARTART TOOLS DESIGN tab**, in the **Reset group**, click **Convert**, and then click **Convert to Text** to convert the SmartArt graphic back to a bulleted list. Compare your screen with Figure 2.54.

FIGURE 2.54

2 Insert a **Header & Footer** on the **Notes and Handouts**. Include the **Date and time updated automatically**, the **Page number**, and a **Footer** with the text **Lastname_Firstname_2B_Celebrations**

3 Display the document properties. As the **Tags** type **independence day, celebrations** and as the **Subject** type your course and section number. Be sure your name displays as the author, and then **Save** your file.

4 View the slide show from the beginning, and then make any necessary adjustments. **Save** 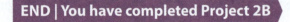 your presentation. Print **Handouts 6 Slides Horizontal**, or submit your presentation electronically as directed by your instructor.

5 **Close** PowerPoint.

END | You have completed Project 2B

GO! with Office Web Apps

Objective   Create an Advertisement Presentation in the PowerPoint Web App

> **ALERT!**   **Working with Web-Based Applications and Services**
>
> Computer programs and services on the web receive continuous updates and improvements, so the steps to complete this web-based activity may differ from the ones shown. You can often look at the screens and the information presented to determine how to complete the activity.

Activity | Creating an Advertisement Presentation in the PowerPoint Web App

In this activity, you will use the PowerPoint Web App to format a presentation similar to the one you created in Project 2B.

1 From the desktop, start Internet Explorer. Navigate to **http://skydrive.com**, and then sign in to your Microsoft account. Open your **GO! Web Projects** folder—or create and then open this folder if necessary.

2 On the SkyDrive menu bar, click **Upload**, and then navigate to your student data files and select **p02_2B_Web**. Click **Open**. When the upload is complete, right click **p02_2B_Web**, and then click **Rename**. Using your own name, as the file name type **Lastname_Firstname_PPT_2B_Web** and then press [Enter]. Click your file, and then click **EDIT PRESENTATION**. Click **Edit in PowerPoint Web App**.

3 Display **Slide 3**. In the content placeholder, click the first button—**Insert a SmartArt Graphic** . On the **SMARTART TOOLS DESIGN tab**, in the **Layouts group**, click the second layout—**Horizontal Bullet List** to change the SmartArt style.

4 Click in the upper left orange rectangle and notice that the content placeholder displays a bulleted list. Here you can type the SmartArt text. Type **Canada** and then click in the hollow circle indented bullet point below the text you typed. Type **July 2016** and then press [Delete] to remove the second bullet point.

5 Click to the right of the second solid bullet, and then type **U.S.** Click in the hollow circle indented bullet point below the text you typed. Type **July 2016** and then press [Delete]. Using the technique you practiced, in the third set of bullet points, type **Mexico** and **September 2016**

6 Compare your screen with Figure A.

7 Click outside the content placeholder to display the SmartArt graphic.

FIGURE A

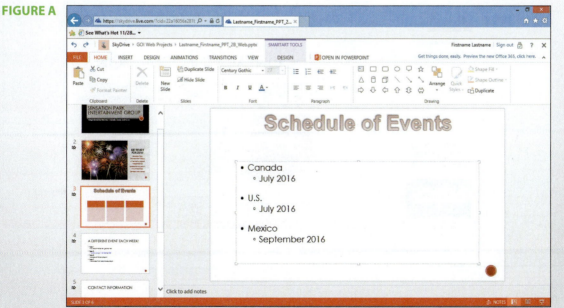

(GO! with Office Web Apps continues on the next page)

8 Select the SmartArt graphic, and then on the **SMARTART TOOLS DESIGN tab**, in the **SmartArt Styles group**, click **Change Colors**. Under **Colorful**, click the first style— **Colorful – Accent Colors**. In the **SmartArt Styles group**, click the small down arrow to display more styles, and then in the second row, click the third style—**Cartoon**.

9 Display **Slide 5**. In the content placeholder, click the first button—**Insert a SmartArt Graphic**. On the **SMARTART TOOLS DESIGN tab**, in the **Layouts group**, click the **More Layouts arrow**, and then in the third row, click the eighth layout—**Grouped List** to change the SmartArt style.

10 Click in the upper left shape. To the right of the first solid bullet, type **Sophia Ackerman** and then click in the hollow circle indented bullet point below the text you typed. Type **United States** and then press Delete to remove the second bullet point.

11 Click to the right of the second solid bullet, and then type **Joseph Mercado** Click in the hollow circle

indented bullet point below the text you typed. Type **Mexico** and then press Delete. Using the technique you practiced, in the third set of bullet points, type **Michael Lewis** and **Canada**

12 Click outside the content placeholder to display the SmartArt graphic.

13 Select the SmartArt graphic, and then on the **SMARTART TOOLS DESIGN tab**, in the **SmartArt Styles group**, click **Change Colors**. Under **Colorful**, click the first style— **Colorful – Accent Colors**. In the **SmartArt Styles group**, click the **More Styles arrow**, and then in the second row, click the third style—**Cartoon**.

14 Click in a blank area of the slide and then compare your screen with Figure B.

15 If you are instructed to submit your file, create a PDF as indicated in the Note box below. On the ribbon, click the **FILE tab** and click **Exit**. Sign out of your Microsoft account and close the browser. Submit as instructed by your instructor.

N O T E   **Creating a PDF from the PowerPoint Web App**

To print on paper, click the File tab, click Print, and then click Print to PDF. In the Microsoft PowerPoint Web App message box, click Click here to view the PDF of your document. In the message bar at the bottom of your screen, click the Save arrow, and then click Save as. In the Save As dialog box, navigate to your PowerPoint Chapter 2 folder, and then save the file.

FIGURE B

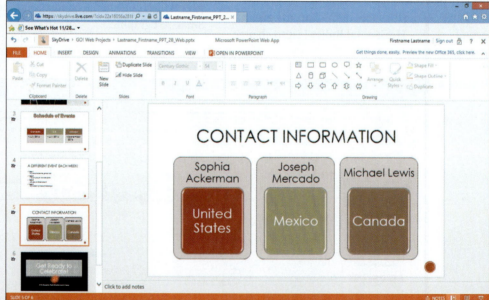

Andrew Rodriguez / Fotolia; FotolEdhar/ Fotolia; apops/ Fotolia; Yuri Arcurs/ Fotolia

Office 365 combines tools for collaboration and productivity and delivers them to multiple users in an organization by using *cloud computing*—applications and services that are accessed over the Internet with multiple devices. For example, one cloud service with which you might be familiar is *SkyDrive*, a free web-based application with which you can save, store, organize, and share files online. This cloud service is available for anyone who has a free Microsoft account.

Another cloud service from Microsoft is *Office Web Apps*. These are the online companions to the desktop versions of Microsoft Office Word, Excel, PowerPoint, and OneNote that enable you to create, access, share, and perform light editing on Microsoft Office documents from any device that connects to the Internet and uses a supported *web browser*. A web browser is software, such as Internet Explorer, Firefox, Safari, or Chrome, that displays web pages.

For an organization, cloud computing enables the addition of services without investing in additional hardware and software. For you as a team member, you can use your web browser to access, edit, store, and share files. You do not need to have a full version of Office installed on your computer to do this. You have all the tools and security that large organizations have!

When you use Office 365, your email and storage servers are hosted by Microsoft. Your organization gets business-class security from Microsoft—a large, well-established company. Sophisticated security and data management features are built into Office 365 so that you can control *permissions*—access rights that define the ability of an individual or group to view or make changes to documents—and provide secure email and communications.

Activity | Using Lync to Collaborate by Using a Video Call

This group project relates to the **Bell Orchid Hotels**. If your instructor assigns this project to your class, you can expect to use **Lync** in **Office 365** to collaborate on the following tasks for this chapter:

- If you are in the **Accounting Group**, you and your teammates will conduct a video call to discuss and agree on the format of the drawing objects, slide transitions, comments, and graphics in your Loan Presentation.

- If you are in the **Engineering Group**, you and your teammates will conduct a video call to discuss and agree on the format of the drawing objects, slide transitions, comments, and graphics in your Safety Presentation.

- If you are in the **Food and Beverage Group**, you and your teammates will conduct a video call to discuss and agree on the format of the drawing objects, slide transitions, comments, and graphics in your New Menu Item Presentation.

- If you are in the **Human Resources Group**, you and your teammates will conduct a video call to discuss and agree on the format of the drawing objects, slide transitions, comments, and graphics in your New Employees Presentation.

- If you are in the **Operations Group**, you and your teammates will conduct a video call to discuss and agree on the format of the drawing objects, slide transitions, comments, and graphics in your Front Desk Clerk Training Presentation.

- If you are in the **Sales and Marketing Group**, you and your teammates will conduct a video call to discuss and agree on the format of the drawing objects, slide transitions, comments, and graphics in your Marketing Plan Presentation.

FIGURE A

END OF CHAPTER

SUMMARY

Use numbered and bulleted lists in a presentation to focus attention on specific items. The theme that you select includes default styles for bullets, but you can change the shape and color of the symbols.

Use pictures to illustrate an idea. The Online Pictures feature enables you to search Office.com for images that emphasize important points. Using good keywords is critical to a successful search to find a great picture!

Objects are easily modified in PowerPoint. Removing the picture background and cropping eliminate unnecessary picture parts. Smart guides and alignment options are used to position pictures and shapes.

Use SmartArt graphics to present information and to illustrate processes, hierarchies, cycles, lists, and relationships. SmartArt graphics may include text and pictures, and can be formatted with styles and color combinations for maximum impact.

GO! LEARN IT ONLINE

Review the concepts and key terms in this chapter by completing these online challenges, which you can find at **www.pearsonhighered.com/go**.

Matching and Multiple Choice:
Answer matching and multiple choice questions to test what you learned in this chapter. MyITLab®

Crossword Puzzle:
Spell out the words that match the numbered clues, and put them in the puzzle squares.

Flipboard:
Flip through the definitions of the key terms in this chapter and match them with the correct term.

GO! FOR JOB SUCCESS

Video: Business Lunch Interpersonal Communications
Your instructor may assign this video to your class, and then ask you to think about, or discuss with your classmates, these questions:

FotolEdhar / Fotolia

In what specific ways did Sara and Jordan demonstrate improper interpersonal communication during their lunch with Karen?

As a manager, did Chris follow the rules of interpersonal communication with his client? Explain your answer.

In what ways did Sara, Jordan, and Theo demonstrate proper or improper *nonverbal* communication skills?

END OF CHAPTER

REVIEW AND ASSESSMENT GUIDE FOR POWERPOINT CHAPTER 2

Your instructor may assign one or more of these projects to help you review the chapter and assess your mastery and understanding of the chapter.

	Review and Assessment Guide for PowerPoint Chapter 2		
Project	**Apply Skills from These Chapter Objectives**	**Project Type**	**Project Location**
2C	Objectives 1-4 from Project 2A	**2C Skills Review** A guided review of the skills from Project 2A.	On the following pages
2D	Objectives 5-6 from Project 2B	**2D Skills Review** A guided review of the skills from Project 2B.	On the following pages
2E	Objectives 1-4 from Project 2A	**2E Mastery (Grader Project)** A demonstration of your mastery of the skills in Project 2A with extensive decision making.	In MyITLab and on the following pages
2F	Objectives 5-6 from Project 2B	**2F Mastery (Grader Project)** A demonstration of your mastery of the skills in Project 2B with extensive decision making.	In MyITLab and on the following pages
2G	Objectives 1-6 from Projects 2A and 2B	**2G Mastery (Grader Project)** A demonstration of your mastery of the skills in Projects 2A and 2B with extensive decision making.	In MyITLab and on the following pages
2H	Combination of Objectives from Projects 2A and 2B	**2H GO! Fix It** A demonstration of your mastery of the skills in Projects 2A and 2B by creating a correct result from a document that contains errors you must find.	Online
2I	Combination of Objectives from Projects 2A and 2B	**2I GO! Make It** A demonstration of your mastery of the skills in Projects 2A and 2B by creating a result from a supplied picture.	Online
2J	Combination of Objectives from Projects 2A and 2B	**2J GO! Solve It** A demonstration of your mastery of the skills in Projects 2A and 2B, your decision-making skills, and your critical thinking skills. A task-specific rubric helps you self-assess your result.	Online
2K	Combination of Objectives from Projects 2A and 2B	**2K GO! Solve It** A demonstration of your mastery of the skills in Projects 2A and 2B, your decision-making skills, and your critical thinking skills. A task-specific rubric helps you self-assess your result.	On the following pages
2L	Combination of Objectives from Projects 2A and 2B	**2L GO! Think** A demonstration of your understanding of the Chapter concepts applied in a manner that you would outside of college. An analytic rubric helps you and your instructor grade the quality of your work by comparing it to the work an expert in the discipline would create.	On the following pages
2M	Combination of Objectives from Projects 2A and 2B	**2M GO! Think** A demonstration of your understanding of the Chapter concepts applied in a manner that you would outside of college. An analytic rubric helps you and your instructor grade the quality of your work by comparing it to the work an expert in the discipline would create.	Online
2N	Combination of Objectives from Projects 2A and 2B	**2N You and GO!** A demonstration of your understanding of the Chapter concepts applied in a manner that you would in a personal situation. An analytic rubric helps you and your instructor grade the quality of your work.	Online
2O	Combination of Objectives from Projects 2A and 2B	**2O Cumulative Group Project for PowerPoint Chapter 2** A demonstration of your understanding of concepts and your ability to work collaboratively in a group role-playing assessment, requiring both collaboration and self-management.	Online

GLOSSARY

Background Removal A feature that removes unwanted portions of a picture so that the picture does not appear as a self-contained rectangle.

Clip A single media file, such as art, sound, animation, or a movie.

Crop A command that removes unwanted or unnecessary areas of a picture.

Crop handles Handles used to remove unwanted areas of a picture.

Crop pointer The pointer used to crop areas of a picture.

Crosshair pointer The pointer used to draw a shape.

Eyedropper A tool that captures the exact color from an object on your screen and then applies the color to any shape, picture, or text.

Fill color The inside color of text or of an object.

RGB A color model in which the colors red, green, and blue are added together to form another color.

Ruler guides Dotted red vertical and horizontal lines that display in the rulers indicating the pointer's position.

Shape A slide object such as a line, arrow, box, callout, or banner.

Smart Guides Dashed lines that display on your slide when you are moving an object to assist you with alignment.

SmartArt graphic A visual representation of information that you create by choosing from among various layouts to communicate your message or ideas effectively.

SmartArt Styles Combinations of formatting effects that you can apply to SmartArt graphics.

Text Box An object with which you can position text anywhere on a slide.

Text effects Formats applied to text that include shadows, reflections, glows, bevels, and 3-D rotations.

WordArt A gallery of text styles with which you can create decorative effects, such as shadowed or mirrored text.

CHAPTER REVIEW

Skills Review Project 2C Concerts

Apply **2A** skills from these
Objectives:

1 Format Numbered and
Bulleted Lists

2 Insert Online Pictures

3 Insert Text Boxes and
Shapes

4 Format Objects

In the following Skills Review, you will format a presentation that describes annual Concerts in the Park events at several Sensation Park Entertainment Group amusement parks. Your completed presentation will look similar to Figure 2.55.

PROJECT FILES

For Project 2C, you will need the following file:

p02C_Concerts

You will save your presentation as:

Lastname_Firstname_2C_Concerts

PROJECT RESULTS

FIGURE 2.55

(Project 2C Concerts continues on the next page)

CHAPTER REVIEW

1 ▸ Start PowerPoint. From the student data files that accompany this textbook, locate and open **p02C_ Concerts**. On the **FILE tab**, click **Save As**, navigate to your **PowerPoint Chapter 2** folder, and then using your own name, save the file as **Lastname_Firstname_2C_Concerts**

a. If necessary, display the Rulers. With **Slide 1** displayed, on the **INSERT tab**, in the **Illustrations group**, click **Shapes**, and then under **Basic Shapes**, in the second row, click the fifth shape—**Frame**.

b. Move the pointer to align the ruler guides with the **left half of the horizontal ruler at 3 inches** and with the **upper half of the vertical ruler at 2.5 inches**, and then click to insert the Frame.

c. On the **FORMAT tab**, in the **Size group**, click in the **Shape Height** box to select the number, and then type **1.7** Click in the **Shape Width** box. Replace the selected number with **5.5** and then press [Enter] to resize the shape.

d. With the frame selected, type **Sensation Park Entertainment Group** and then change the **Font Size** to **28**. On the **FORMAT tab** in the **Shape Styles group**, click **Shape Fill**, and then under **Theme Colors**, in the fourth column, click the first color— **Gray-25%, Text 2.**

2 ▸ On the **INSERT tab**, in the **Images group**, click **Online Pictures**. In the **Office.com Search** box, type **sheet music close up** and then press [Enter].

a. Click the picture of the two lines of music on a music sheet, and then click **Insert**.

b. On the **FORMAT tab**, in the **Size group**, click in the **Shape Height** box. Replace the selected number with **2.5** and then press [Enter] to resize the image.

c. Drag the picture down and to the right until intersecting red dashed Smart Guides display, indicating that the picture is center aligned with the title and its top edge aligns with the bottom edge of the title placeholder.

d. With the picture selected, on the **FORMAT tab**, in the **Size group**, click the **Crop arrow**, and then point to **Crop to Shape**. Under **Basic Shapes**, click the first shape—**Oval**. In the **Picture Styles group**, click **Picture Effects**, point to **Soft Edges**, and then click **25 Point**.

e. With the picture selected, hold down [Shift], and then click the **frame shape** and the **title placeholder** so that all three objects are selected. Under **DRAWING TOOLS**, on the **FORMAT tab**, in the **Arrange group**, click **Align**, and then click **Align to Slide**. Click **Align** again, and then click **Align Center**. **Save** the presentation.

3 ▸ Display **Slide 2**. On the right side of the slide, in the content placeholder, click **Online Pictures**. In the **Search Office.com** box, type **drum kit** and then press [Enter]. Insert the picture of the drum set on a white background. If the picture is not available, choose another image.

a. On the **FORMAT tab**, in the **Picture Styles group**, click **Picture Effects**, point to **Soft Edges**, and then click **50 Point**.

b. Click in the placeholder containing the text *Every Friday in June and July*. On the **HOME tab**, in the **Paragraph group**, click **Bullets** to remove the bullet symbol from the title.

c. Select the text *Every Friday in June and July*. On the **HOME tab**, in the **Font group**, click the **Font Color button arrow**. Below the gallery, click **Eyedropper**, and then move the eyedropper pointer so that it is pointing to the bright gold area of the drum on the right side of the picture. Click one time to apply the color to the selected text. Apply **Bold** and **Italic** and change the **Font Size** to **28**.

4 ▸ Display **Slide 3**, and then select the third and fourth bullet points—*Seating is limited* and *Reserved seating is available*.

a. On the **HOME tab**, in the **Paragraph group**, click the **Bullets button arrow**, and then click **Bullets and Numbering**. In the second row, click the first style—**Hollow Square Bullets**. Replace the number in the **Size** box with **90** and then click the **Color arrow**. Under **Recent Colors**, apply the color chosen using the eyedropper on Slide 2—**Tan**. Click **OK**.

b. Display **Slide 4**, and then click the bulleted list placeholder. Click the dashed border so that the border displays as a solid line, and then on the **HOME tab**, in the **Paragraph group**, click **Numbering** to change the bullet symbols to numbers.

(Project 2C Concerts continues on the next page)

CHAPTER REVIEW

c. On the left side of the slide, select the title text, and then on the mini toolbar, click the **Font Color button arrow**. Under **Recent Colors**, click **Tan**.

5 ▶ Display **Slide 5**. On the **INSERT tab**, in the **Images group**, click **Online Pictures**. In the **Office.com search** box, type **electric guitar** and then press Enter. Insert the picture of the black electric guitar on the white, blue, and black background. If you cannot locate the picture, choose another image.

a. Change the picture **Height** to **4.75** and then drag the picture so that its upper left corner aligns with the upper left corner of the purple area on the slide. On the **FORMAT tab**, in the **Picture Styles group**, click **Picture Effects**, and then point to **Soft Edges**. Click **2.5 Point**.

b. Press Ctrl + D and then drag the duplicated picture to the right about 1 inch. Press Ctrl + D to insert a third picture.

c. Point to the third guitar picture that you inserted and then drag to the right so that its upper right corner aligns with the upper right corner of the purple area on the slide.

d. Hold down Shift and then click the first two guitar pictures so that all three pictures are selected. On the **FORMAT tab**, in the **Arrange group**, click **Align**, and then click **Align to Slide**. Click **Align** again, and then click **Align Middle**.

e. With the three pictures selected, click **Align**, and then click **Align Selected Objects**. Click **Align** again, and then click **Distribute Horizontally**.

6 ▶ With **Slide 5** displayed, on the **INSERT tab**, in the **Text group**, click **Text Box**. Move the pointer to align the ruler guides with the **left half of the horizontal ruler at 2 inches** and with the **lower half of the vertical ruler at 2.5 inches**, and then click to insert the text box.

a. Type **Concerts Begin on June 21!** Select the text and then change the **Font Size** to **32**. On the **FORMAT tab**, in the **Arrange group**, click **Align**, and then click **Align Center**.

b. Insert a **Header & Footer** on the **Notes and Handouts tab**. Include the **Date and time updated automatically**, the **Page number**, and a **Footer** with the text **Lastname_Firstname_2C_Concerts**

c. Display the document properties. As the **Tags**, type **concerts** and as the **Subject**, type your course and section number. Be sure your name displays as the author, and then **Save** your file.

d. View the slide show from the beginning. Print **Handouts 6 Slides Horizontal**, or submit your presentation electronically as directed by your instructor. **Close** the presentation.

END | You have completed Project 2C

CHAPTER REVIEW

Skills Review | Project 2D Corporate Events

In the following Skills Review, you will format a presentation by inserting and formatting WordArt and SmartArt graphics. Your completed presentation will look similar to Figure 2.56.

PROJECT FILES

For Project 2D, you will need the following file:

p02D_Corporate_Events

You will save your presentation as:

Lastname_Firstname_2D_Corporate_Events

PROJECT RESULTS

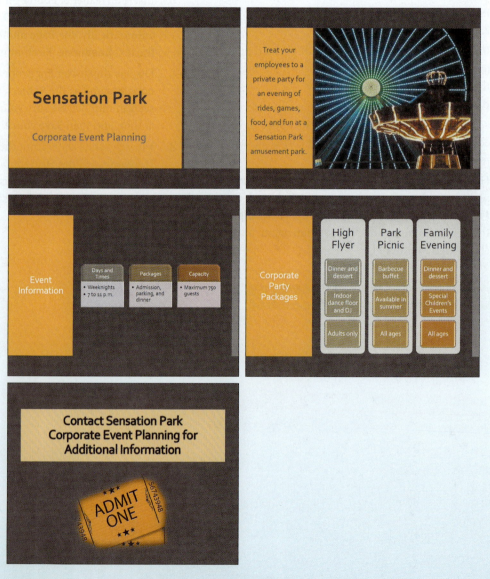

FIGURE 2.56

(Project 2D Corporate Events continues on the next page)

CHAPTER REVIEW

1 Start PowerPoint. From the student data files that accompany this textbook, locate and open **p02D_Corporate_Events**. **Save** the presentation in your **PowerPoint Chapter 2** folder as **Lastname_Firstname_2D_Corporate_Events**

a. With **Slide 1** displayed, select the text **Corporate Event Planning**. On the **FORMAT tab**, in the **WordArt Styles group**, click **More**. In the second row, click the last style—**Fill – Brown, Accent 3, Sharp Bevel**. Click outside the placeholder.

b. On the **INSERT tab**, in the **Text group**, click **WordArt**. In the **WordArt gallery**, in the third row, click the last style—**Fill - Brown, Background 2, Inner Shadow**. With the text *Your text here* selected, type **Sensation Park**

c. With the WordArt selected, hold down [Shift], and then click the subtitle. On the **FORMAT tab**, in the **Arrange group**, click **Align**, and then click **Align Selected Objects**. Click **Align** again, and then click **Align Left**.

2 Display **Slide 3**. In the center of the content placeholder, click **Insert a SmartArt Graphic** to open the **Choose a SmartArt Graphic** dialog box. On the left, click **List**, and then scroll as necessary and locate and click **Horizontal Bullet List**. Click **OK**.

a. In the SmartArt graphic, in the first gold rectangle, click *Text*. Type **Days and Times** and then click in the rectangle below the text you typed. Type **Weeknights** and then click in the second bullet point. Type **7 to 11 p.m.**

b. In the second gold rectangle, type **Packages** and then click in the rectangle below the text you typed. Type **Admission, parking, and dinner** and then delete the second text bullet point in the rectangle.

c. In the third gold rectangle, type **Capacity** and then click in the rectangle below the text you typed. Type **Maximum 750 guests** and then delete the second text bullet point in the rectangle.

d. On the **SMARTART TOOLS DESIGN tab**, in the **SmartArt Styles group**, click **Change Colors**, and then under **Colorful**, click the last style **Colorful Range - Accent Colors 5 to 6**. In the **SmartArt Styles group**, click **More**, and then under **3-D**, in the first row, click the fourth style—**Powder**.

e. Click in the **Days and Times** rectangle, hold down [Shift], and then click the **Packages** and **Capacity**

rectangles. On the **SMARTART TOOLS FORMAT tab**, in the **Shapes group**, click **Change Shape**. Under **Rectangles**, click the fourth shape—**Snip Same Side Corner Rectangle**.

3 Display **Slide 4**, and then click anywhere in the bulleted list. On the **HOME tab**, in the **Paragraph group**, click **Convert to SmartArt**. At the bottom of the gallery, click **More SmartArt Graphics**. On the left side of the **Choose a SmartArt Graphic** dialog box, click **List**. Locate and click **Grouped List**, and then click **OK** to convert the list to a SmartArt graphic.

a. Under **Family Evening**, click in the **Dinner and dessert** shape, and then on the **SMARTART TOOLS DESIGN tab**, in the **Create Graphic group**, click **Add Shape**. In the inserted shape, type **Special Children's Events**

b. With the *Special Children's Events* shape selected, add another shape, and then type **All ages**

c. On the **SMARTART TOOLS DESIGN tab**, in the **SmartArt Styles group**, click **Change Colors**. In the **Color** gallery, under **Colorful**, click the last style—**Colorful Range - Accent Colors 5 to 6**.

d. On the **DESIGN tab**, in the **SmartArt Styles group**, click **More** to display the **SmartArt Styles gallery**. Under **3-D**, in the first row, click the third style—**Cartoon**.

4 Display **Slide 5**. Select the picture of the admission tickets, and then on the **FORMAT tab**, in the **Adjust group**, click **Remove Background**. In the **Close group**, click **Keep Changes**.

a. With the picture selected, on the **FORMAT tab**, in the **Picture Styles group**, click **Picture Effects**. Point to **Soft Edges**, and then click **25 Point**.

b. Insert a **Header & Footer** on the **Notes and Handouts**. Include the **Date and time updated automatically**, a **Page number**, and a **Footer** with the text **Lastname_Firstname_2D_Corporate_Events**

c. Display the document properties. As the **Tags** type **corporate events** and as the **Subject** type your course and section number. Be sure your name displays as the author, and then **Save** your file.

d. View the slide show from the beginning. Print **Handouts 6 Slides Horizontal**, or submit your presentation electronically as directed by your instructor. **Close** the presentation.

END | You have completed Project 2D

CONTENT-BASED ASSESSMENTS

Mastering PowerPoint	Project 2E Coasters

Apply 2A skills from these Objectives:

1 Format Numbered and Bulleted Lists
2 Insert Online Pictures
3 Insert Text Boxes and Shapes
4 Format Objects

In the following Mastering PowerPoint project, you will format a presentation describing new roller coasters under construction at several Sensation Park Entertainment Group amusement parks. Your completed presentation will look similar to Figure 2.57.

PROJECT FILES

For Project 2E, you will need the following file:

p02E_Coasters

You will save your presentation as:

Lastname_Firstname_2E_Coasters

PROJECT RESULTS

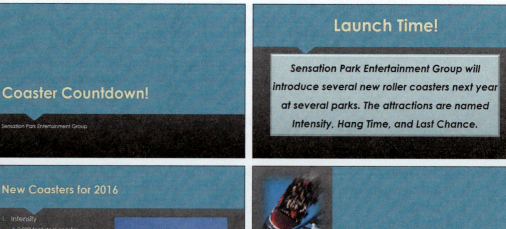

FIGURE 2.57

(Project 2E Coasters continues on the next page)

CONTENT-BASED ASSESSMENTS

1 Start PowerPoint. From the student data files that accompany this textbook, locate and open **p02E_Coasters**. In your **PowerPoint Chapter 2** folder, **Save** the file as **Lastname_Firstname_2E_Coasters**

2 On **Slide 2**, remove the bullet symbol from the paragraph, and then **Center** the paragraph. With the content placeholder selected, display the **Shape Styles** gallery, and then in the fourth row, apply the sixth style—**Subtle Effect – Blue-Gray, Accent 5**. Apply the **Art Deco** beveled shape effect to the placeholder.

3 On **Slide 3**, apply **Numbering** to the first-level bullet points—*Intensity, Hang Time,* and *Last Chance.* Under each of the numbered items, change all of the circle bullet symbols to **Star Bullets**, and then change the bullet color to **Aqua, Accent 1, Lighter 40%**—in the fifth column, the fourth color.

4 On **Slide 3**, select the title. Change the **Font Color** using the **Eyedropper**. With the eyedropper pointer, click anywhere in the thick, light yellow stripe on the roller coaster car at the right side of the picture to apply the light yellow color to the title. If necessary, use the Zoom slider to zoom in on the picture. On **Slides 1** and **2**, apply the same light yellow color to the slide title on each slide.

5 Display **Slide 3**, and then apply an **Aqua, 5 pt glow, Accent color 2** picture effect to the picture.

6 Display **Slide 4**. Insert an **Online Picture** by searching for **roller coaster** and then insert the close-up picture of the roller coaster with the red cars and the people raising their hands in the air. If you cannot locate the picture, choose another image. **Crop** the picture by dragging the bottom-center crop handle up so that the crop handle is positioned on the **lower half of the vertical ruler at 1 inch**.

7 Align the upper left corner of the picture with the top left corner of the slide, and then change the **Height** to **4.5** Modify the picture effect by applying a **50 Point Soft Edges** effect.

8 Duplicate the picture, and then use the **Align to Slide** option to align the pictures with the left edge of the slide and to distribute the pictures vertically.

9 Insert a **Text Box** aligned with the **horizontal ruler at 0 inches** and with the **lower half of the vertical ruler at 1 inch**. In the text box, type **Starting Summer 2016!** Change the **Font Size** to **28**. Change the **Shape Fill** to the last color in the last column—**Blue, Accent 6, Darker 50%**.

10 Select the title and the text box, and then, using the **Align Selected Objects** option, apply **Align Right** alignment. Apply the **Box** transition to all of the slides in the presentation, and then view the slide show from the beginning.

11 Insert a **Header & Footer** on the **Notes and Handouts**. Include the **Date and time updated automatically**, the **Page number**, and a **Footer** with the text **Lastname_Firstname_2E_Coasters**

12 Display the document properties. As the **Tags** type **coasters** and as the **Subject** type your course and section number. Be sure your name displays as the author, and then **Save** your file.

13 **Save** your presentation. Submit your presentation electronically or print **Handouts 4 Slides Horizontal** as directed by your instructor. **Close** PowerPoint.

END | You have completed Project 2E

CONTENT-BASED ASSESSMENTS

MyITLab® grader

Mastering PowerPoint | Project 2F Attractions

Apply 2B skills from these Objectives:

5 Remove Picture Backgrounds and Insert WordArt

6 Create and Format a SmartArt Graphic

In the following Mastering PowerPoint project, you will format a presentation describing new attractions at several of the Sensation Park Entertainment Group amusement parks. Your completed presentation will look similar to Figure 2.58.

PROJECT FILES

For Project 2F, you will need the following file:

p02F_Attractions

You will save your presentation as:

Lastname_Firstname_2F_Attractions

PROJECT RESULTS

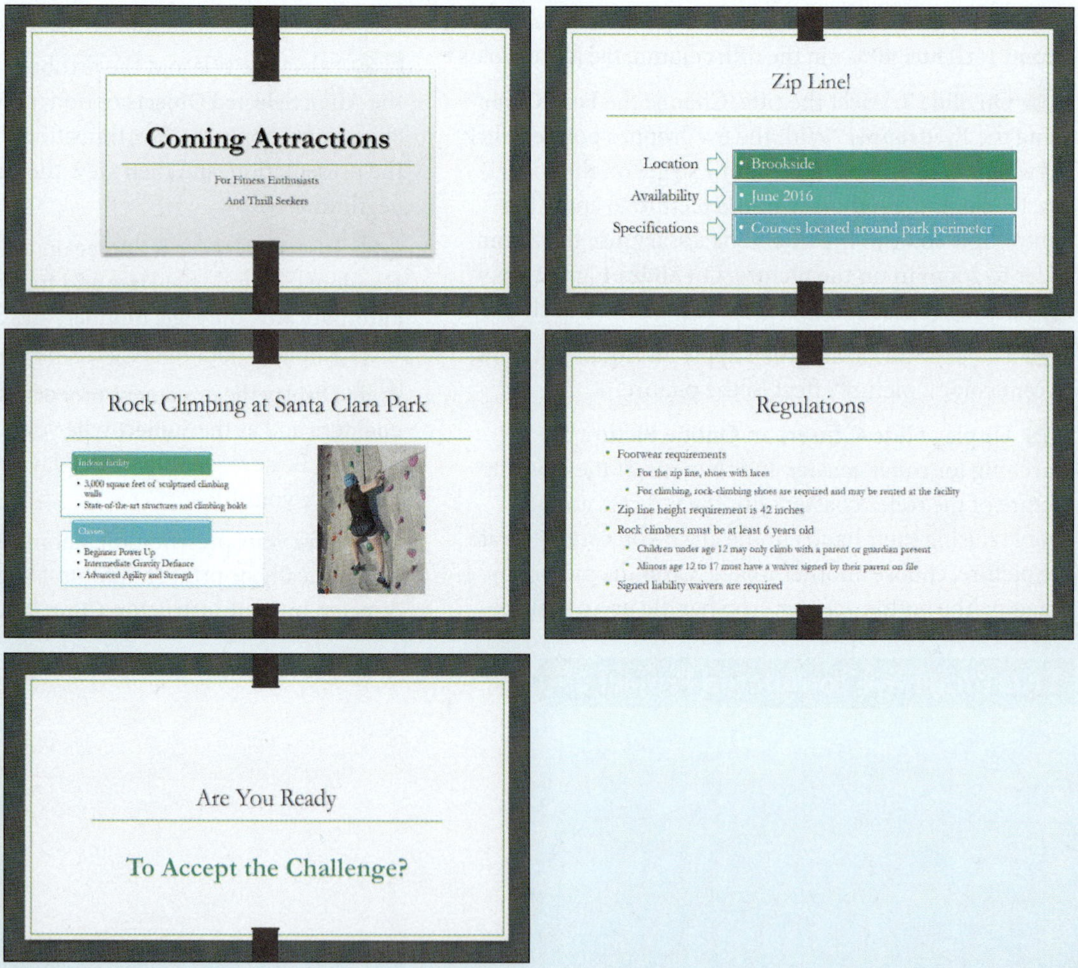

FIGURE 2.58

(Project 2F Attractions continues on the next page)

CONTENT-BASED ASSESSMENTS

1 Start PowerPoint. From the student data files that accompany this textbook, open **p02F_Attractions**, and then **Save** the file in your **PowerPoint Chapter 2** folder as **Lastname_Firstname_2F_Attractions**

2 On **Slide 1**, select the title and display the **WordArt Styles** gallery. In the third row, apply the first WordArt style—**Fill – Black, Text 1, Outline – Background 1, Hard Shadow – Background 1**. Change the **Text Outline** by applying, in the fourth column, the fourth color—**Dark Green, Text 2, Lighter 40%**.

3 On **Slide 2**, in the content placeholder, insert a **List** type **SmartArt** graphic using **Vertical Bracket List**. In the upper-left Text placeholder, type **Location** and then in the bullet point to the right of *Location*, type **Brookside** In the lower text placeholder, type **Availability** and then in the rectangle to the right of *Availability*, type **June 2016**

4 Click the *Availability* placeholder, and then add a shape after the placeholder. In the new placeholder, type **Specifications** and then add a bullet. Type **Courses located around park perimeter**

5 Change the SmartArt color to **Colorful Range - Accent Colors 4 to 5**, and then apply the **3-D Cartoon** style. Select the three bracket shapes, and then change the shapes to the **Right Arrow** shape. On the **FORMAT tab**, in the **Shapes group**, click the **Smaller** button two times to decrease the size of the arrows.

6 On **Slide 3**, convert the bulleted list to a **SmartArt** graphic by applying the **Vertical Box List** graphic. Change the SmartArt color to **Colorful Range - Accent Colors 4 to 5**, and then apply the **Polished 3-D** SmartArt style.

7 On **Slide 5**, insert a **WordArt**—in the first row, the last style—**Fill – Dark Teal, Accent 4, Soft Bevel**. Replace the WordArt text with **To Accept the Challenge?** Change the **Font Size** to **48**.

8 Hold down Shift and then drag the WordArt down so that its upper edge is positioned on the **lower half of the vertical ruler at 1**.

9 Apply the **Peel Off** transition to all the slides, and then view the slide show from the beginning.

10 **Insert** a **Header & Footer** on the **Notes and Handouts**. Include the **Date and time updated automatically**, the **Page number**, and a **Footer** with the text **Lastname_Firstname_2F_Attractions**

11 Display the document properties. As the **Tags** type **zip line, rock wall** and as the **Subject,** type your course and section number. Be sure your name displays as the author, and then **Save** your file.

12 **Save** your presentation. Submit your presentation electronically or print **Handouts 6 Slides Horizontal** as directed by your instructor. **Close** the presentation and exit PowerPoint.

END | You have completed Project 2F

CONTENT-BASED ASSESSMENTS

In the following Mastering PowerPoint project, you will edit an existing presentation that is shown to Sensation Park Entertainment Group employees on their first day of a three-day orientation. Your completed presentation will look similar to Figure 2.59.

Apply 2A and 2B skills from these Objectives:

1 Format Numbered and Bulleted Lists
2 Insert Online Pictures
3 Insert Text Boxes and Shapes
4 Format Objects
5 Remove Picture Backgrounds and Insert WordArt
6 Create and Format a SmartArt Graphic

PROJECT FILES

For Project 2G, you will need the following file:

p02G_Orientation

You will save your presentation as:

Lastname_Firstname_2G_Orientation

PROJECT RESULTS

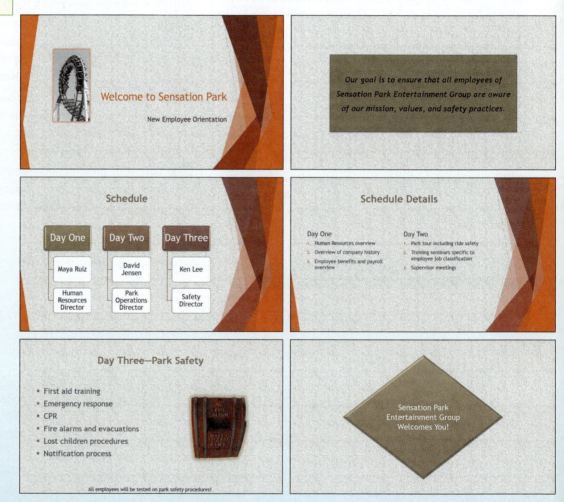

FIGURE 2.59

(Project 2G Orientation continues on the next page)

CONTENT-BASED ASSESSMENTS

1 Start PowerPoint, and then from your student data files, open the file **p02G_Orientation**. In your **PowerPoint Chapter 2** folder, **Save** the file as **Lastname_Firstname_2G_Orientation**

2 On **Slide 1**, format the subtitle—*New Employee Orientation*—with a **WordArt Style** using the second style in the first row—**Fill - Orange, Accent 1, Shadow**. Change the **Text Fill** to **Dark Red, Accent 2, Darker 50%**.

3 Select the picture and then **Crop** the image from the left side so that the center-left crop handle aligns with the **left half of the horizontal ruler at 5 inches**. Size the picture **Height** to **3.5** and then apply an **Orange, 8 pt glow, Accent color 1** picture effect to the image. Use the **Align Selected Objects** command to apply **Align Middle** to the title and the picture.

4 On **Slide 2**, remove the bullet symbol from the paragraph, and then change the **Shape Fill** to **Tan, Background 2, Darker 50%**, and the **Shape Outline** to **Black, Text 1**.

5 On **Slide 3**, convert the bulleted list to the **Hierarchy** type **SmartArt** graphic—**Hierarchy List**. Change the color to **Colorful Range - Accent Colors 3 to 4**, and then apply the **3-D Inset** style.

6 On **Slide 4**, change the two bulleted lists to **Numbering**. On **Slide 5**, change the bullet symbols to **Filled Square Bullets**, change the **Color** to **Tan, Background 2, Darker 50%**, and then change the **Size** to **100**

7 On **Slide 5**, in the placeholder on the right, insert an **Online Picture** by searching for **fire pull** and then insert the picture of the fire alarm on a white background.

Remove the background from the picture, and then apply the **Brown, 18 pt glow, Accent color 3** picture effect.

8 On **Slide 5**, insert a **Text Box** below the content placeholder on the left side of the slide. In the text box, type **All employees will be tested on park safety procedures!** Using the **Align to Slide** option **Align Center** the text box and apply **Align Bottom**.

9 On **Slide 6**, from the **Shapes** gallery, under **Basic Shapes**, insert a **Diamond** of any size anywhere on the slide. Resize the diamond so that its **Shape Height** is **6** and its **Shape Width** is **8**

10 Using the **Align to Slide** option, apply the **Align Center**, and **Align Middle** alignment commands to the diamond shape. Apply the **Moderate Effect - Brown, Accent 3** shape style, and then in the diamond, type **Sensation Park Entertainment Group Welcomes You!** Change the **Font Size** to **28**, and then apply the **Art Deco Bevel** shape effect to the diamond shape.

11 Insert a **Header & Footer** on the **Notes and Handouts**. Include the **Date and time updated automatically**, the **Page number**, and a **Footer** with the text **Lastname_Firstname_2G_Orientation** Apply to all.

12 Display the document properties. As the **Tags** type **orientation** and as the **Subject** type your course and section number. Be sure your name displays as the author, and then **Save** your file.

13 **Save** your presentation. Submit your presentation electronically or print **Handouts 6 Slides Horizontal** as directed by your instructor. **Close** PowerPoint.

END | You have completed Project 2G

CONTENT-BASED ASSESSMENTS

Apply a combination of the **2A** and **2B** skills.

GO! Fix It	Project 2H Summer Jobs	Online

GO! Make It	Project 2I Renovation Plans	Online

GO! Solve It	Project 2J Business Summary	Online

GO! Solve It	Project 2K Hotel	

PROJECT FILES

For Project 2K, you will need the following file:

p02K_Hotel

You will save your presentation as:

Lastname_Firstname_2K_Hotel

Open the file p02K_Hotel and save it as **Lastname_Firstname_2K_Hotel** Complete the presentation by inserting an online picture on the first slide and applying appropriate picture effects. On Slide 2, format the bullet point as a single paragraph and apply a shape style, and then on Slide 3, convert the bulleted list to an appropriate SmartArt graphic. Change the SmartArt color and apply a style. On Slide 4, insert and attractively position a WordArt with the text Save the Date! Insert a header and footer that includes the date and time updated automatically, the file name in the footer, and the page number. Add your name, your course name and section number, and the tags **hotel, accommodations** to the Properties area. Save your presentation. Print or submit as directed by your instructor.

Performance Level

Performance Criteria	Exemplary	Proficient	Developing
Insert and format an appropriate online picture	An appropriate online picture was inserted and formatted in the presentation.	An online picture was inserted but was not appropriate for the presentation or was not formatted.	An online picture was not inserted.
Insert and format appropriate SmartArt graphic	Appropriate SmartArt graphic was inserted and formatted in the presentation.	SmartArt graphic was inserted but was not appropriate for the presentation or was not formatted.	SmartArt graphic was not inserted.
Insert and format appropriate WordArt	Appropriate WordArt was inserted and formatted in the presentation.	WordArt was inserted but was not appropriate for the presentation or was not formatted.	WordArt was not inserted.
Remove bullet point and apply appropriate shape style	Bullet point was removed and an appropriate shape style was applied.	Either the bullet point was not removed or the shape style was not applied.	Bullet point was not removed and a shape style was not applied.

END | You have completed Project 2K

OUTCOMES-BASED ASSESSMENTS

RUBRIC

The following outcomes-based assessments are open-ended assessments. That is, there is no specific correct result; your result will depend on your approach to the information provided. Make Professional Quality your goal. Use the following scoring rubric to guide you in how to approach the problem and then to evaluate how well your approach solves the problem.

The *criteria*—Software Mastery, Content, Format and Layout, and Process—represent the knowledge and skills you have gained that you can apply to solving the problem. The *levels of performance*—Professional Quality, Approaching Professional Quality, or Needs Quality Improvements—help you and your instructor evaluate your result.

	Your completed project is of Professional Quality if you:	Your completed project is Approaching Professional Quality if you:	Your completed project Needs Quality Improvements if you:
1-Software Mastery	Choose and apply the most appropriate skills, tools, and features and identify efficient methods to solve the problem.	Choose and apply some appropriate skills, tools, and features, but not in the most efficient manner.	Choose inappropriate skills, tools, or features, or are inefficient in solving the problem.
2-Content	Construct a solution that is clear and well organized, contains content that is accurate, appropriate to the audience and purpose, and is complete. Provide a solution that contains no errors in spelling, grammar, or style.	Construct a solution in which some components are unclear, poorly organized, inconsistent, or incomplete. Misjudge the needs of the audience. Have some errors in spelling, grammar, or style, but the errors do not detract from comprehension.	Construct a solution that is unclear, incomplete, or poorly organized; contains some inaccurate or inappropriate content; and contains many errors in spelling, grammar, or style. Do not solve the problem.
3-Format & Layout	Format and arrange all elements to communicate information and ideas, clarify function, illustrate relationships, and indicate relative importance.	Apply appropriate format and layout features to some elements, but not others. Overuse features, causing minor distraction.	Apply format and layout that does not communicate information or ideas clearly. Do not use format and layout features to clarify function, illustrate relationships, or indicate relative importance. Use available features excessively, causing distraction.
4-Process	Use an organized approach that integrates planning, development, self-assessment, revision, and reflection.	Demonstrate an organized approach in some areas, but not others; or, use an insufficient process of organization throughout.	Do not use an organized approach to solve the problem.

OUTCOMES-BASED ASSESSMENTS

Apply a combination of the **2A** and **2B** skills.

Build from Scratch

GO! Think Project 2L Interactive Ride

PROJECT FILES

For Project 2L, you will need the following file:

New blank PowerPoint presentation

You will save your presentation as:

Lastname_Firstname_2L_Interactive_Ride

As part of its mission to combine fun with the discovery of math and science, Sensation Park Entertainment Group is opening a new, interactive roller coaster at its South Lake Tahoe location. Sensation Park's newest coaster is designed for maximum thrill and minimum risk. In a special interactive exhibit located next to the coaster, riders can learn about the physics behind this powerful coaster and even try their hand at building a coaster.

Guests will begin by setting the height of the first hill, which determines the coaster's maximum potential energy to complete its journey. Next they will set the exit path, and build additional hills, loops, and corkscrews. When completed, riders can submit their coaster for a safety inspection to find out whether the ride passes or fails.

In either case, riders can also take a virtual tour of the ride they created to see the maximum speed achieved, the amount of negative G-forces applied, the length of the track, and the overall thrill factor. They can also see how their coaster compares with other Sensation Park coasters, and they can email the coaster simulation to their friends.

Using the preceding information, create a presentation that Marketing Director, Annette Chosek, will present at a travel fair describing the new attraction. The presentation should include four to six slides with at least one SmartArt graphic and one online picture. Apply an appropriate theme and use slide layouts that will effectively present the content, and use text boxes, shapes, and WordArt styles if appropriate. Apply font formatting and slide transitions, and modify text alignment and line spacing as necessary. Save the file as **Lastname_Firstname_2L_Interactive_Ride** and then insert a header and footer that includes the date and time updated automatically, the file name in the footer, and the page number. Add your name, your course name and section number, and the tags **roller coaster, new rides** to the Properties area. Print or submit as directed by your instructor.

END | You have completed Project 2L

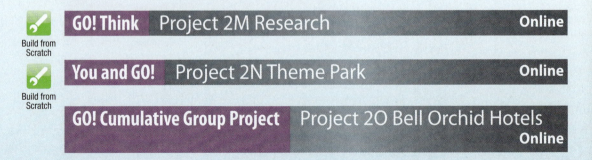

Build from Scratch

GO! Think Project 2M Research   **Online**

Build from Scratch

You and GO! Project 2N Theme Park   **Online**

GO! Cumulative Group Project Project 2O Bell Orchid Hotels
                                                                           Online

Enhancing a Presentation with Animation, Video, Tables, and Charts

GO! to Work
Video P3

PROJECT 3A	OUTCOMES
	Customize a presentation with animation and video.

OBJECTIVES

1. Customize Slide Backgrounds and Themes
2. Animate a Slide Show
3. Insert a Video

PROJECT 3B	OUTCOMES
	Create a presentation that includes data in tables and charts.

OBJECTIVES

4. Create and Modify Tables
5. Create and Modify Charts

forcdan / Fotolia

In This Chapter

In this chapter, you will learn how to customize a presentation by modifying the theme, formatting the slide background, and applying animation to slide elements. Additionally, you will learn how to enhance your presentations by inserting tables and charts that help your audience understand numeric data and trends just as pictures and diagrams help illustrate a concept. The data that you present should determine whether a table or a chart would most appropriately display your information. Styles applied to your tables and charts unify these slide elements by complementing your presentation theme.

The projects in this chapter relate to the city of **Pacifica Bay**, a coastal city south of San Francisco. The city's access to major transportation provides both residents and businesses an opportunity to compete in the global marketplace. The city's mission is to create a more beautiful and more economically viable community for its residents. Each year the city welcomes a large number of tourists who enjoy exploring the rocky coastline and seeing the famous landmarks in San Francisco. The city encourages best environmental practices and partners with cities in other countries to promote sound government at the local level.

PROJECT ACTIVITIES

In Activities 3.01 through 3.17, you will edit and format a presentation that Carol Lehman, Director of Pacifica Bay Parks and Recreation, is creating to inform residents about the benefits of using the city's parks and trails. Your completed presentation will look similar to Figure 3.1.

PROJECT FILES

For Project 3A, you will need the following files:

p03A_Hills
p03A_Trails
p03A_Video

You will save your presentation as:

Lastname_Firstname_3A_Trails

PROJECT RESULTS

FIGURE 3.1 Project 3A Informational Presentation

Video P3-1

You have practiced customizing presentations by applying themes with unified design elements, backgrounds, and colors that provide a consistent look in your presentation. Additional ways to customize a slide include changing theme fonts and colors, applying a background style, modifying the background color, or inserting a picture on the slide background.

N O T E	If You Are Using a Touchscreen

- Tap an item to click it.
- Press and hold for a few seconds to right-click; release when the information or commands display.
- Touch the screen with two or more fingers and then pinch together to zoom in or stretch your fingers apart to zoom out.
- Slide your finger on the screen to scroll—slide left to scroll right and slide right to scroll left.
- Slide to rearrange—similar to dragging with a mouse.
- Swipe from edge: from right to display charms; from left to expose open apps, snap apps, or close apps; from top or bottom to show commands or close an app.
- Swipe to select—slide an item a short distance with a quick movement—to select an item and bring up commands, if any.

Activity 3.01 | Changing Theme Colors

Recall that the presentation theme is a coordinated, predefined set of colors, fonts, lines, and fill effects. In this activity, you will open a presentation in which the Retrospect theme is applied, and then you will change the *theme colors*—a set of coordinating colors that are applied to the backgrounds, objects, and text in a presentation.

1 From the student data files that accompany this textbook, locate and open **p03A_Trails**. Display the **Save As** dialog box, create a **New Folder** with the name **PowerPoint Chapter 3** and then using your own name, **Save** the file in the folder you created as **Lastname_Firstname_3A_Trails**

2 Click the **DESIGN tab**, and then in the **Variants group**, click **More** ⊽. Point to **Colors** to display the sets of theme colors. Point to several sets and notice the color changes on **Slide 1**.

3 Click **Green** to change the presentation colors, and then compare your screen with Figure 3.2.

Changing the colors does not change the overall design of the presentation. In this presentation, the *Retrospect* presentation theme is still applied to the presentation. By modifying the theme colors, you retain the design of the *Retrospect* theme but apply colors that coordinate with the pictures in the presentation, and that are available as text, accent, and background colors.

FIGURE 3.2

Green color applied to all sides

Take a Hike!

4 Save 🖫 your presentation.

Activity 3.02 | Changing Theme Fonts

In addition to theme colors, every presentation theme includes *theme fonts* that determine the font to apply to two types of slide text—headings and body. The *Headings font* is applied to slide titles and the *Body font* is applied to all other text. When you apply a new theme font to the presentation, the text on every slide is updated with the new heading and body fonts.

1 With **Slide 1** displayed, click anywhere in the title placeholder. Click the **HOME tab**, and then in the **Font group**, click the **Font button arrow**. Notice that at the top of the **Font** list, under **Theme Fonts**, Calibri Light (Headings) and Calibri (Body) display. Compare your screen with Figure 3.3.

FIGURE 3.3

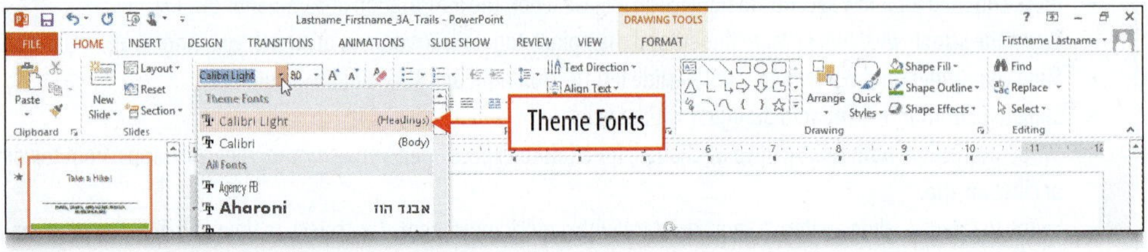

2 Click anywhere on the slide to close the Font list. Click the **DESIGN tab**, and then in the **Variants group**, click **More**. Point to **Fonts**.

> This list displays the name of each theme and the pair of fonts in the theme. The first and larger font in each pair is the Headings font and the second and smaller font in each pair is the Body font.

3 Point to several of the themes and watch as Live Preview changes the title and subtitle font. Scroll to the bottom of the **Fonts** list, and then click **Trebuchet MS**. Compare your screen with Figure 3.4, and then **Save** your presentation.

FIGURE 3.4

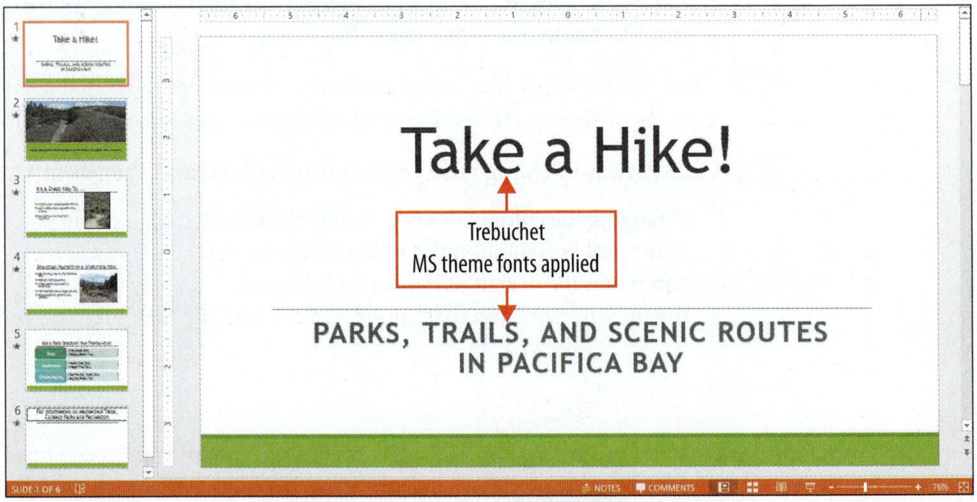

Activity 3.03 | Applying a Background Style

1 With **Slide 1** displayed, on the **DESIGN tab**, in the **Variants group**, click **More**. Point to **Background Styles**, and then compare your screen with Figure 3.5.

> A *background style* is a predefined slide background fill variation that combines theme colors in different intensities or patterns.

FIGURE 3.5

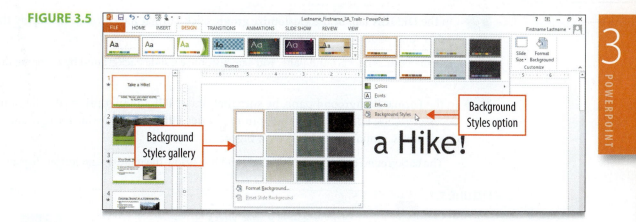

2 ▶ Point to each of the background styles to view the style on **Slide 1**. Then, in the first row, click **Style 2**. Compare your screen with Figure 3.6.

The background style is applied to all the slides in the presentation.

FIGURE 3.6

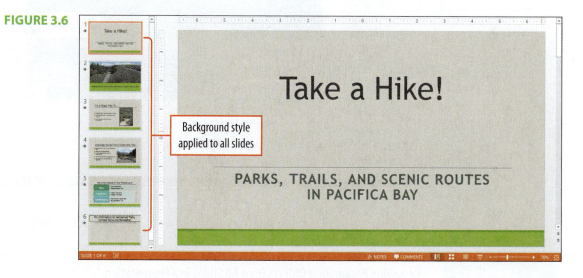

3 ▶ Display **Slide 5**. On the **DESIGN tab**, in the **Variants group**, click **More** ▾. Point to **Background Styles**, and then in the third row, *right-click* the third style—**Style 11**—to display the shortcut menu. On the shortcut menu, click **Apply to Selected Slides** to apply the style to Slide 5.

Use this technique to apply a background style to individual slides.

4 ▶ Save ▣ your presentation.

Activity 3.04 | Hiding Background Graphics

Many of the PowerPoint 2013 themes contain graphic elements that display on the slide background. In the Retrospect theme applied to this presentation, the background includes a rectangle shape and line. Sometimes the background graphics interfere with or clash with the slide content. When this happens, you can hide the background graphics.

1 ▶ Display **Slide 2**, and notice the bright green rectangle and line at the bottom of the slide.

You cannot delete these objects because they are a part of the slide background; however, you can hide them.

2 On the **DESIGN tab**, in the **Customize group**, click **Format Background** to display the **Format Background** pane.

In the Format Background pane, you can customize a slide background by changing the formatting options.

3 In the **Format Background** pane, be sure that under **Fill**, the fill options display, and if necessary, click Fill to display the options. Under **Fill**, select the **Hide Background Graphics** check box. Compare your slide with Figure 3.7.

The background objects—the rectangle and line below the picture—no longer display.

FIGURE 3.7

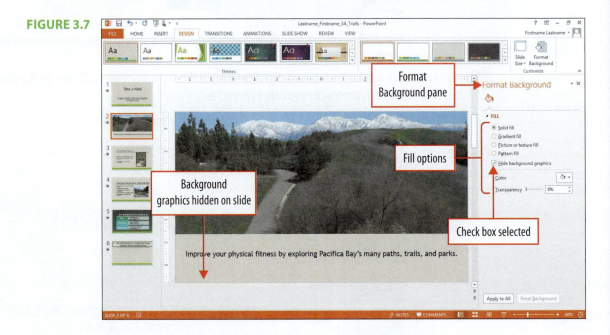

4 **Close** ☒ the **Format Background** pane, and then **Save** 🖫 your presentation.

More **Knowledge**   **Removing Background Objects from All Slides in a Presentation**

To remove the background objects from all of the slides in a presentation, in the Format Background pane, select the Hide background graphics check box, and then at the bottom of the Format Background pane, click Apply to All.

Activity 3.05 │ Applying a Background Fill Color to a Slide

In addition to applying predefined background styles, you can apply a fill color to one or all of the slides in your presentation.

1 Display **Slide 1**. On the **DESIGN tab**, in the **Customize group**, click **Format Background**.

2 In the **Format Background** pane, under **Fill**, verify that **Solid fill** is selected, and select it if it is not. To the right of **Color**, click **Fill Color** 🎨. Under **Theme Colors**, in the third column, click the second color—**Tan, Background 2, Darker 10%**. Compare your screen with Figure 3.8.

The solid fill color is applied to the slide background.

FIGURE 3.8

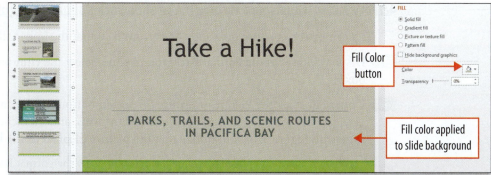

Fill Color button

Fill color applied to slide background

> **3** Leave the **Format Background** pane open for the next Activity. **Save** 🖫 your presentation.

More Knowledge | **Applying a Fill Color to All the Slides in a Presentation**

To apply a fill color to all of the slides in a presentation, in the Format Background pane, select the fill color that you want to apply, and then at the bottom of the Format Background pane, click Apply to All.

Activity 3.06 | Applying a Background Texture

> **1** Display **Slide 2**, and then in the slide thumbnails, hold down ⇧Shift and click **Slide 4** to select **Slides 2**, **3**, and **4**.

Recall that you can select contiguous slides in this manner.

> **2** In the **Format Background** pane, under **Fill**, click **Picture or texture fill**.

A background picture or fill that is part of the Retrospect theme may display on the slide background of the three selected slides.

> **3** Under **Insert picture from**, to the right of **Texture**, click **Texture** 🖾 ▼. In the **Texture gallery**, in the third row, point to the fourth texture—**Recycled Paper**. Compare your screen with Figure 3.9.

FIGURE 3.9

Recycled paper texture

Texture gallery

Texture button

> **4** Click **Recycled Paper** to apply the textured background to the three selected slides.

> **5** Leave the **Format Background** pane open for the next Activity, and then **Save** 🖫 your presentation.

Activity 3.07 | Applying a Picture to the Slide Background and Adjusting Transparency

You can insert a picture on a slide background so that the image fills the entire slide.

1 Display **Slide 6**. In the **Format Background** pane, select the **Hide background graphics** check box.

2 Under **Fill**, click the **Picture or texture fill** option button. Under **Insert picture from**, click **File**. Navigate to your student data files, click **p03A_Hills**, and then click **Insert**. Compare your slide with Figure 3.10, and notice that the picture displays as the background of Slide 6.

When a picture is applied to a slide background using the Format Background option, the picture is not treated as an object. The picture fills the entire background and you cannot move it or size it.

FIGURE 3.10

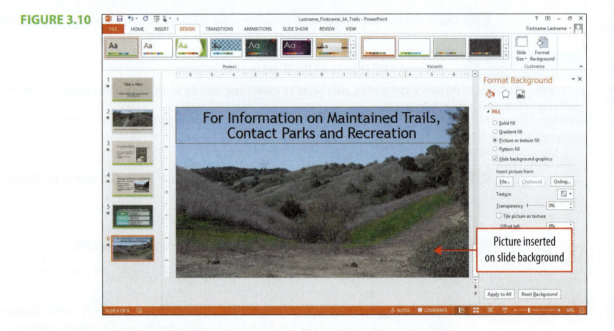

Picture inserted on slide background

3 In the **Format Background** pane, to the right of **Transparency**, notice that *0%* displays, indicating that the picture is inserted in full color. Click in the **Transparency box**, and then replace the number with **50**

The transparency setting lightens the picture on the slide background. You can use the transparency option when there are other objects on the slide that do not display well against the slide background.

BY TOUCH — Drag the Transparency slider to the left or right with your finger to adjust the transparency of the figure.

4 Replace the number in the **Transparency box** with **10%**.

The 10% transparency setting provides good contrast for the title while still displaying the picture in a vibrant color.

5 Click in the title placeholder. On the **FORMAT tab**, in the **Shape Styles group**, click **More**. In the fourth row, click the second style—**Subtle Effect – Green, Accent 1**. Click anywhere on the slide outside of the title placeholder. Compare your screen with Figure 3.11.

Adequate contrast between the slide background and slide text is important because it improves slide readability. Use combinations of transparency and text placeholder styles and fills to improve contrast.

FIGURE 3.11

For Information on Maintained Trails, Contact Parks and Recreation

Shape Style applied to title placeholder

Transparency set to 10%

6 ▶ Leave the **Format Background** pane open for the next Activity, and then **Save** 🖫 your presentation.

Activity 3.08 | Resetting a Slide Background

1 ▶ Display **Slide 5**. At the bottom of the **Format Background** pane, click **Reset Background**, and then compare your slide with Figure 3.12.

After making changes to a slide background, you may decide that the original formatting is the best choice for displaying the text and graphics on a slide. The Reset Background feature restores the theme and color theme formatting to a slide.

FIGURE 3.12

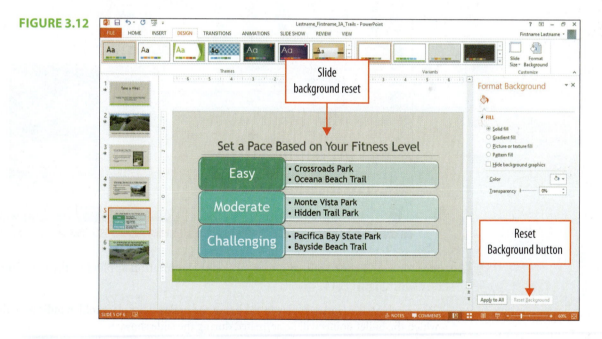

Slide background reset

Set a Pace Based on Your Fitness Level

Easy	• Crossroads Park • Oceana Beach Trail
Moderate	• Monte Vista Park • Hidden Trail Park
Challenging	• Pacifica Bay State Park • Bayside Beach Trail

Reset Background button

2 ▶ **Close** ☒ the **Format Background** pane, and then **Save** 🖫 your presentation.

Video P3-2

Animation is a visual or sound effect added to an object or text on a slide. Animation can focus the audience's attention, providing the speaker with an opportunity to emphasize important points using the slide element as an effective visual aid.

Activity 3.09 | Applying Animation Entrance Effects and Effect Options

Entrance effects are animations that bring a slide element onto the screen. You can modify an entrance effect by using the animation Effect Options command.

1 ▶ Display **Slide 3**, and then click anywhere in the bulleted list placeholder. On the **ANIMATIONS tab**, in the **Animation group**, click **More** ▾, and then compare your screen with Figure 3.13.

> Recall that an entrance effect is animation that brings an object or text onto the screen. An *emphasis effect* is animation that emphasizes an object or text that is already displayed. An *exit effect* is animation that moves an object or text off the screen.

FIGURE 3.13

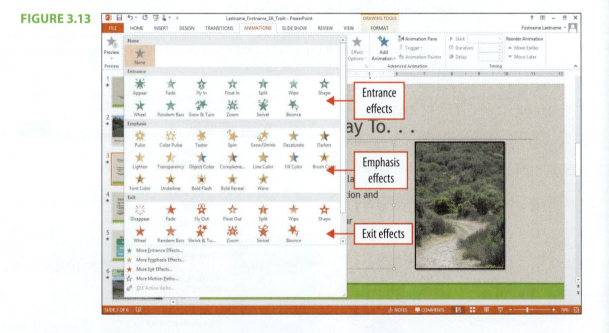

2 ▶ Under **Entrance**, click **Split**, and then notice the animation applied to the list. Compare your screen with Figure 3.14.

> The numbers *1*, *2*, and *3* display to the left of the bulleted list placeholder, indicating the order in which the bullet points will be animated during the slide show.

FIGURE 3.14

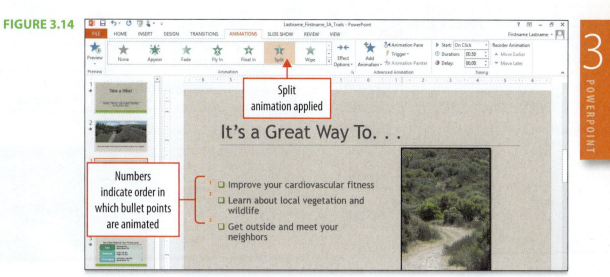

Split animation applied

Numbers indicate order in which bullet points are animated

3 Select the bulleted list placeholder. In the **Animation group**, click **Effect Options**, and then compare your screen with Figure 3.15.

The Effect Options control the direction and sequence in which the animation displays. Additional options may be available with other entrance effects.

FIGURE 3.15

Effect options

4 Click **Vertical Out** and notice the direction from which the animation is applied.

5 Select the picture. In the **Animation group**, click **More** [▾], and then below the gallery, click **More Entrance Effects**. In the lower left corner of the **Change Entrance Effect** dialog box, verify that the **Preview Effect** check box is selected. Compare your screen with Figure 3.16.

The Change Entrance Effect dialog box displays additional entrance effects grouped in four categories: Basic, Subtle, Moderate, and Exciting.

FIGURE 3.16

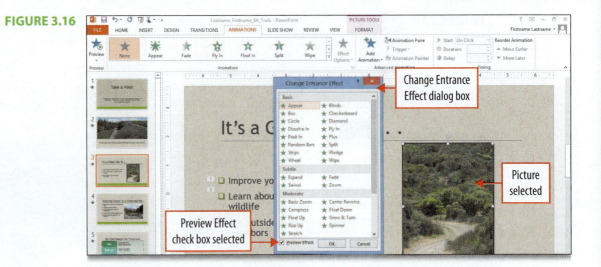

6 ▶ Under **Basic**, click **Dissolve In**, and then watch as Live Preview displays the picture with the selected entrance effect. Click **OK**.

> The number *4* displays next to the picture, indicating that it is fourth in the slide animation sequence.

7 ▶ Select the title. On the **ANIMATIONS tab**, in the **Animation group**, click **More** ▼, and then under **Entrance**, click **Split** to apply the animation to the title.

> The number *5* displays next to the title, indicating that it is fifth in the slide animation sequence.

8 ▶ **Save** 🖫 the presentation.

Activity 3.10 | Reordering Animation

1 ▶ With **Slide 3** displayed, on the **ANIMATIONS tab**, in the **Preview group**, click **Preview**.

> The list displays first, followed by the picture, and then the title. The order in which animation is applied is the order in which objects display during the slide show.

2 ▶ Select the title. On the **ANIMATIONS tab**, in the **Timing group**, under **Reorder Animation**, click the **Move Earlier** button two times, and then compare your screen with Figure 3.17.

> To the left of the title placeholder, the number *1* displays. You can use the Reorder Animation buttons to change the order in which text and objects are animated during the slide show.

FIGURE 3.17

Activity 3.11 | Setting Animation Start Options

Timing options control when animated items display in the animation sequence.

1 With the title selected, on the **ANIMATIONS tab**, in the **Timing group**, click the **Start button arrow** to display three options—*On Click*, *With Previous*, and *After Previous*. Compare your screen with Figure 3.18.

> The **On Click** option begins the animation sequence for the selected slide element when the mouse button is clicked or the Spacebar is pressed. The **With Previous** option begins the animation sequence at the same time as the previous animation or slide transition. The **After Previous** option begins the animation sequence for the selected slide element immediately after the completion of the previous animation or slide transition.

FIGURE 3.18

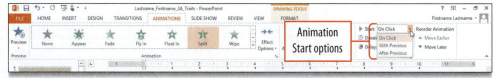

2 Click **After Previous**, and then notice that next to the title, the number *1* is changed to *0*, indicating that the animation will begin immediately after the slide transition; the presenter does not need to click the mouse button or press Spacebar to display the title.

3 Select the picture, and then in the **Timing group**, click the **Start arrow**. Click **With Previous** and notice that the number is changed to *3*, indicating that the animation will begin at the same time as the third bullet point in the bulleted list.

4 On the **ANIMATIONS tab**, in the **Preview group**, click **Preview** and notice that the title displays first, and that the picture displays at the same time as the third bullet point.

5 Display **Slide 1**, and then click in the title placeholder. On the **ANIMATIONS tab**, in the **Animation group**, click the **Entrance** effect **Fly In**, and then click the **Effect Options button**. Click **From Top**. In the **Timing group**, click the **Start arrow**, and then click **After Previous**.

> The number *0* displays to the left of the title indicating that the animation will begin immediately after the slide transition.

6 **Save** your presentation.

Activity 3.12 | Setting Animation Duration and Delay Timing Options

1 On **Slide 1**, if necessary, select the title. In the **Timing group**, click the **Duration arrows** as necessary so that *00.75* displays in the **Duration** box. Compare your screen with Figure 3.19.

> Duration controls the speed of the animation. You can set the duration of an animation by typing a value in the Duration box, or you can use the spin box arrows to increase and decrease the duration in 0.25-second increments. When you decrease the duration, the animation speed increases. When you increase the duration, the animation is slowed.

FIGURE 3.19

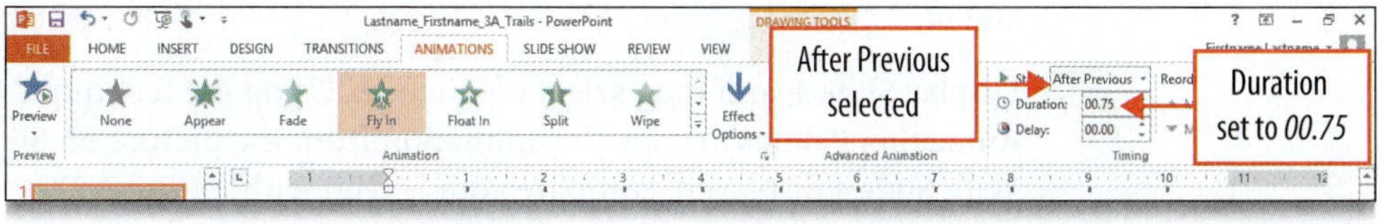

2 ▷ Select the subtitle, and then in the **Animation group**, apply the **Fly In** entrance effect. In the **Timing group**, click the **Start arrow**, and then click **After Previous**. In the **Timing group**, select the value in the **Delay** box, type **00.50** and then press ⏎. Compare your screen with Figure 3.20.

> You can use Delay to begin a selected animation after a specified amount of time has elapsed. Here, the animation is delayed by one-half of a second after the completion of the previous animation—the title animation. You can type a value in the Delay or Duration boxes, or you can use the up and down arrows to change the timing.

FIGURE 3.20

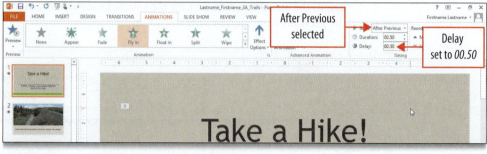

3 ▷ View the slide show from the beginning and notice the animation on Slides 1 and 3. When the black slide displays, press ⎋ to return to Normal view, and then **Save** 🖫 your presentation.

Activity 3.13 | Using Animation Painter and Removing Animation

Animation Painter is a feature that copies animation settings from one object to another.

1 ▷ Display **Slide 3**, and then click anywhere in the bulleted list. On the **ANIMATIONS tab**, in the **Advanced Animation group**, click **Animation Painter**. Display **Slide 4**, and then point anywhere in the bulleted list placeholder to display the Animation Painter pointer 🖫. Compare your screen with Figure 3.21.

FIGURE 3.21

2 ▷ Click the bulleted list to copy the animation settings from the list on **Slide 3** to the list on **Slide 4**.

3 ▷ Display **Slide 3**, and then select the picture. Using the technique that you just practiced, use **Animation Painter** to copy the animation from the picture on **Slide 3** to the picture on **Slide 4**. With **Slide 4** displayed, compare your screen with Figure 3.22.

> The numbers displayed to the left of the bulleted list and the picture indicate that animation is applied to the objects.

FIGURE 3.22

4 Display **Slide 3**, and then click in the title placeholder. On the **ANIMATIONS tab**, in the **Animation group**, click **More** ⬇. At the top of the gallery, click **None** to remove the animation from the title placeholder. Compare your screen with Figure 3.23, and then **Save** 🔲 your presentation.

FIGURE 3.23

Objective 3 | Insert a Video

Video P3-3

You can insert, size, and move videos in a PowerPoint presentation, and you can format videos by applying styles and effects. Video editing features in PowerPoint 2013 enable you to trim parts of a video and to compress the video to make the presentation easier to share.

Activity 3.14 | Inserting a Video and Using Media Controls

1 Display **Slide 1**. On the **INSERT tab**, in the **Media group**, click **Video**, and then click **Video on My PC**. In the **Insert Video** dialog box, navigate to your student data files, and then click **p03A_Video**. Click **Insert**, and then compare your screen with Figure 3.24.

The video displays in the center of the slide, and media controls display in the control panel below the video. VIDEO TOOLS for FORMAT and PLAYBACK display on the Ribbon.

FIGURE 3.24

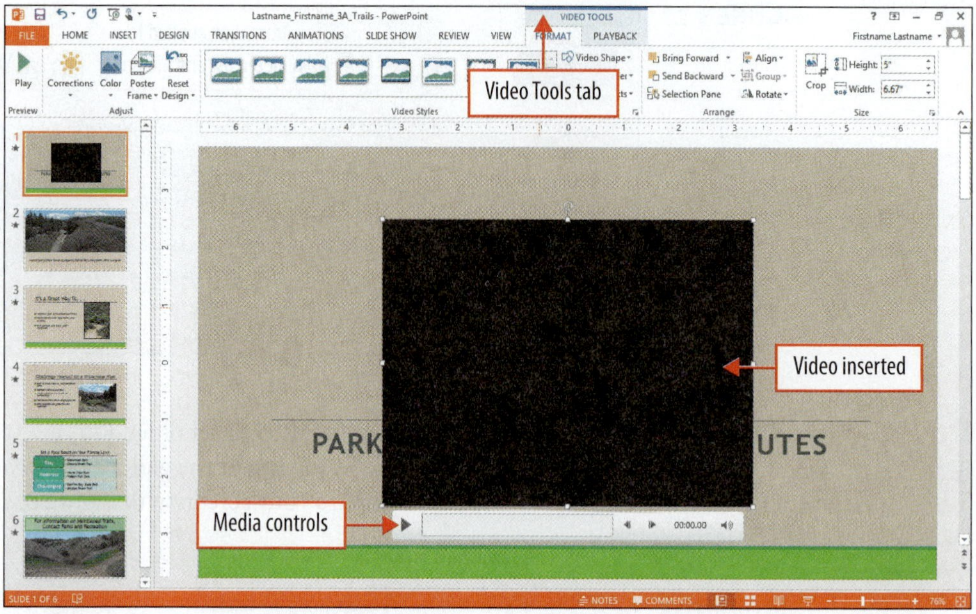

Video Tools tab

Video inserted

Media controls

2 Below the video, in the media controls, click **Play/Pause** ▶ to view the video and notice that as the video plays, the media controls display the time that has elapsed since the start of the video.

3 View the slide show from the beginning. On **Slide 1**, after the subtitle displays, point to the video to display the 👆 pointer, and then compare your screen with Figure 3.25.

When you point to the video during the slide show, the media controls display.

FIGURE 3.25

Pointer

PARK   UTES

Media controls

4 With the 👆 pointer displayed, click the mouse button to view the video. Move the pointer away from the video and notice that the media controls no longer display. When the video is finished, press Esc to exit the slide show.

5 Save 💾 your presentation.

Activity 3.15 | Sizing and Aligning a Video

1 With the video selected, on the **FORMAT tab**, in the **Size group**, click in the **Height** box. Type **2** and then press Enter. Notice that the video width adjusts proportionately.

2 On the **FORMAT tab**, in the **Arrange group**, click **Align**, and then click **Align Center**. Click **Align** again, and then click **Align Middle**. Compare your screen with Figure 3.26.

The video is centered horizontally and vertically on the slide.

FIGURE 3.26

3 ▶ **Save** 🖫 your presentation.

Activity 3.16 | Changing the Style and Shape of a Video

You can apply styles and effects to a video and change the video shape and border. You can also recolor a video so that it coordinates with the presentation theme.

1 ▶ With **Slide 1** displayed, if necessary, select the video. On the **FORMAT tab**, in the **Video Styles group**, click **More** ▾ to display the **Video Styles** gallery.

2 ▶ Using the ScreenTips to view the style name, under **Subtle**, in the second row, click the last style—**Drop Shadow Rectangle**. Compare your screen with Figure 3.27.

FIGURE 3.27

3 ▶ In the **Video Styles group**, click **Video Shape**, and then under **Rectangles**, click the second shape—**Rounded Rectangle**. Compare your screen with Figure 3.28.

You can format a video with any combination of styles, shapes, and effects.

FIGURE 3.28

Activity 3.17 | Trimming and Compressing a Video and Setting Playback Options

You can *trim*—delete parts of a video to make it shorter—and you can compress a video file to reduce the file size of your PowerPoint presentation.

1 If necessary, select the video. On the **PLAYBACK tab**, in the **Editing group**, click **Trim Video**, and then compare your screen with Figure 3.29.

At the top of the Trim Video dialog box, the file name and the video duration display. Below the video, a timeline displays with start and end markers indicating the video start and end time. Start Time and End Time boxes display the current start and end of the video. The Previous Frame and Next Frame buttons move the video forward and backward one frame at a time.

FIGURE 3.29

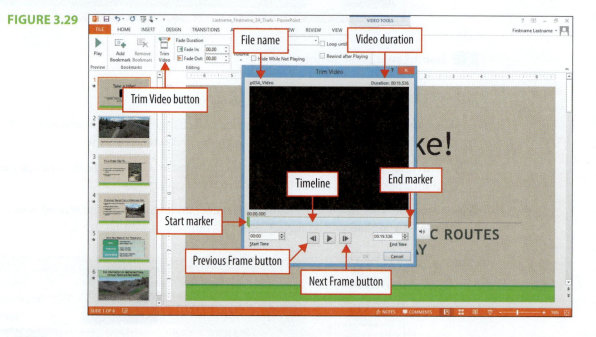

2 In the **End Time** box, replace the number with **00:16.865**. Compare your screen with Figure 3.30.

The blue section of the timeline indicates the portion of the video that will play during the slide show. The gray section indicates the portion of the video that is trimmed. The image in the Trim Video dialog box displays the last frame in the video based on the trim setting.

FIGURE 3.30

🔄 **BY TOUCH**   Drag the red ending marker with your finger until its ScreenTip displays the ending time that you want.

3 ▶ Click **OK** to apply the trim settings.

4 ▶ Click **FILE**, and then on the **Info tab**, click **Compress Media**. Read the description of each video quality option, and then click **Low Quality**. Compare your screen with Figure 3.31.

The Compress Media dialog box displays the slide number on which the selected video is inserted, the video file name, the original size of the video file, and when compression is complete, the amount that the file size was reduced.

FIGURE 3.31

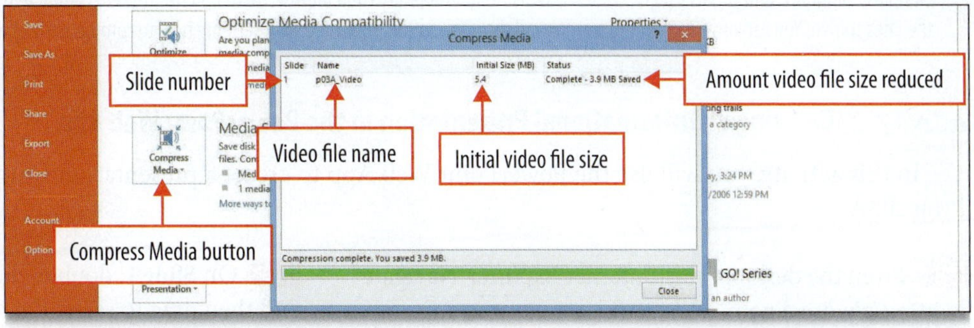

5 ▶ In the **Compress Media** dialog box, click **Close**, and then on the left, click **Save**.

6 ▶ If necessary, select the video. On the **PLAYBACK tab**, in the **Video Options group**, click the **Start arrow**, and then click **Automatically** so that during the slide show, the video will begin automatically. Compare your screen with Figure 3.32.

FIGURE 3.32

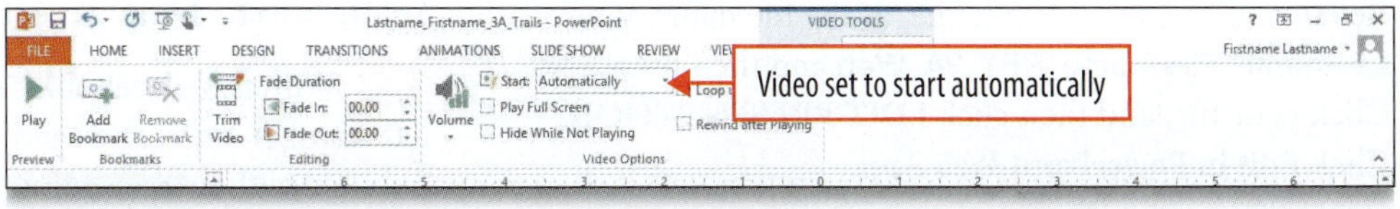

7 ▶ Click the **SLIDE SHOW tab**, in the **Start Slide Show group**, click the **From Beginning** button, and then view the slide show. Notice that on Slide 1, the video begins playing immediately after the subtitle displays. After you view the video, click the mouse button to advance to the next slide and then continue to view the presentation. Press Esc when the black slide displays.

8 ▶ Insert a **Header & Footer** on the **Notes and Handouts**. Include the **Date and time** updated automatically, the **Page Number**, and a **Footer**. In the **Footer** box, using your own name, type **Lastname_Firstname_3A_Trails** and then click **Apply to All**.

9 ▶ Display the document properties. As the **Tags**, type **walking trails** and as the **Subject**, type your course and section number. Be sure your name displays as the author, and then **Save** your file.

10 ▶ Print **Handouts 6 Slides Horizontal**, or submit your presentation electronically as directed by your instructor.

11 ▶ **Close** the presentation.

> **END | You have completed Project 3A**

GO! with Office Web Apps

<table>
<tr><td>ALERT!</td><td>**Working with Web-Based Applications and Services**</td></tr>
</table>

Computer programs and services on the web receive continuous updates and improvements, so the steps to complete this web-based activity may differ from the ones shown. You can often look at the screens and the information presented to determine how to complete the activity.

Objective | Create an Informational Presentation in the PowerPoint Web App

Activity | Creating an Informational Presentation in the PowerPoint Web App

In this activity, you will use the PowerPoint Web App to create a presentation similar to the one you created in Project 3A.

1 From the desktop, start Internet Explorer. Navigate to **http://skydrive.com**, and then sign in to your Microsoft account. Open your **GO! Web Projects** folder—or create and then open this folder if necessary.

2 On the SkyDrive menu bar, click **Upload**, and then navigate to your student data files and select **p03_3A_Web**. Click **Open**. When the upload is complete, right-click **p03_3A_Web**, and then click **Rename**. Using your own name, as the file name, type **Lastname_Firstname_PPT_3A_Web** and then press [Enter]. Click your file, and then click **EDIT PRESENTATION**. Click **Edit in PowerPoint Web App**.

3 On the **DESIGN tab**, in the **Variants group**, click **Variant 2** to apply the green variant to the entire presentation.

4 On **Slide 1**, double-click in the title placeholder, and then drag to select the title text—*Take a Hike!* On the **HOME tab**, in the **Font Group**, click the **Font arrow**, and then click **Candara**.

5 Display **Slide 2**, and then at the bottom of the slide, click in the text placeholder. On the **FORMAT tab**, in the **Shape Styles group**, click the **Quick Styles arrow**, and then in the fourth row, click the second style—**Subtle Effect – Lime, Accent 1**. Change the **Font Size** to **48**.

6 With the placeholder selected, point to the center-left sizing handle, and then drag as far to the left as possible without exceeding the left edge of the slide. Repeat this process on the right side of the slide, and then click outside of the placeholder. Compare your screen with Figure A.

FIGURE A

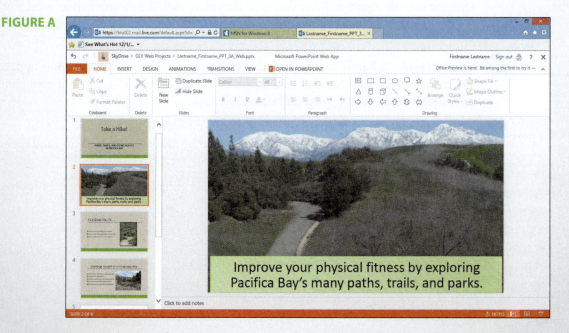

(GO! with Office Web Apps continues on the next page)

7 Display **Slide 3**, and then click the bulleted list. On the **ANIMATIONS tab**, in the **Animation group**, click **Fly In**. Click **Effect Options**, and then click **From Right**. Click the picture, and then in the **Animation group**, click **Appear**. Click the title, and then in the **Animation group**, click **Fly In**. Click **Effect Options**, and then click **From Top**. Notice the animation sequencing numbers that display on the slide, which indicate that the title will display last.

8 With **Slide 3** displayed and the title selected, in the **Timing group**, under **Reorder Animation**, click **Move Earlier** several times until the number *1* displays above the title, indicating that it will display first. Compare your screen with Figure B.

9 Display **Slide 4**, and then click the title. On the **ANIMATIONS tab**, in the **Animation group**, click **Fly In**. Click **Effect Options**, and then click **From Top**. Click the bulleted list, and then in the **Animation group**, click **Fly In**. Click **Effect Options**, and then click **From Right**. Click the **Picture**, and then in the **Animation group**, click **Appear**.

10 Display **Slide 6**, and then click in the title. On the **ANIMATIONS tab**, in the **Animation group**, click **Fly In**. Click **Effect Options**, and then click **From Top**.

11 On the **TRANSITIONS tab**, in the **Transition to This slide group**, click **Push**. Click **Effect Options**, and then click **From Left**. Click **Apply to All**.

12 On the **VIEW tab**, click **Slide Show**, and then view the presentation. If a security warning displays, click Allow once. Click the mouse button to advance through the slides.

13 If you are instructed to submit your file, create a PDF as indicated in the Note box below. On the ribbon, click the **FILE tab** and click **Exit**. Sign out of your Microsoft account and close the browser. Submit the file as directed by your instructor.

N O T E   **Creating a PDF from the PowerPoint Web App**

To print on paper, click the File tab, click Print, and then click Print to PDF. In the Microsoft PowerPoint Web App message box, click Click here to view the PDF of your document. In the message bar at the bottom of your screen, click the Save arrow, and then click Save as. In the Save As dialog box, navigate to your PowerPoint Chapter 3 folder, and then save the file.

FIGURE B

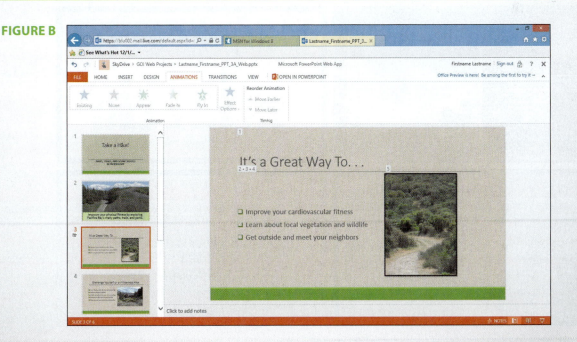

Summary and Analysis Presentation

MyITLab®
Project 3B Training

PROJECT ACTIVITIES

In Activities 3.18 through 3.29, you will add a table and two charts to a presentation that Mindy Walker, Director of Parks and Recreation, is creating to inform the City Council about enrollment trends in Pacifica Bay recreation programs. Your completed presentation will look similar to Figure 3.33.

PROJECT FILES

For Project 3B, you will need the following file:

p03B_Enrollment

You will save your presentation as:

Lastname_Firstname_3B_Enrollment

PROJECT RESULTS

FIGURE 3.33 Project 3B Summary and Analysis Presentation

Video P3-4

A **table** is a format for information that organizes and presents text and data in columns and rows. The intersection of a column and row is referred to as a **cell** and is the location in which you type text in a table.

Activity 3.18 | Creating a Table

There are several ways to insert a table in a PowerPoint slide. For example, you can insert a slide with a Content Layout and then click the Insert Table button. Or, click the Insert tab and then click Table.

1 Start PowerPoint. From your student data files, open **p03B_Enrollment**, and then **Save** the presentation in your **PowerPoint Chapter 3** folder as **Lastname_Firstname_3B_Enrollment**

2 Display **Slide 2**. In the content placeholder, click **Insert Table** ▦ to display the **Insert Table** dialog box. In the **Number of columns** box, type **3** and then press Tab. In the **Number of rows** box, type **2** and then compare your screen with Figure 3.34.

Here you enter the number of columns and rows that you want the table to contain.

FIGURE 3.34

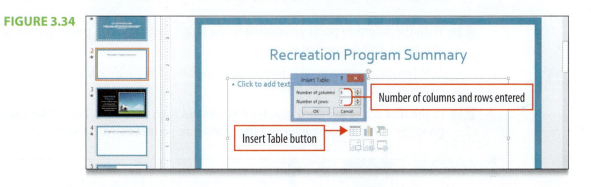

3 Click **OK** to create a table with three columns and two rows. Notice that the insertion point is blinking in the upper left cell of the table.

The table extends from the left side of the content placeholder to the right side, and the three columns are equal in width. By default, a style is applied to the table.

4 With the insertion point positioned in the first cell of the table, type **Athletics** and then press Tab.

Pressing Tab moves the insertion point to the next cell in the same row.

ALERT!   **Did You Press** Enter **Instead of** Tab **?**

In a table, pressing Enter creates another line in the same cell. If you press Enter by mistake, you can remove the extra line by pressing Backspace.

---

5 With the insertion point positioned in the second cell of the first row, type **Leisure** and then press Tab. Type **Arts** and then press Tab to move the insertion point to the first cell in the second row. Compare your table with Figure 3.35.

FIGURE 3.35

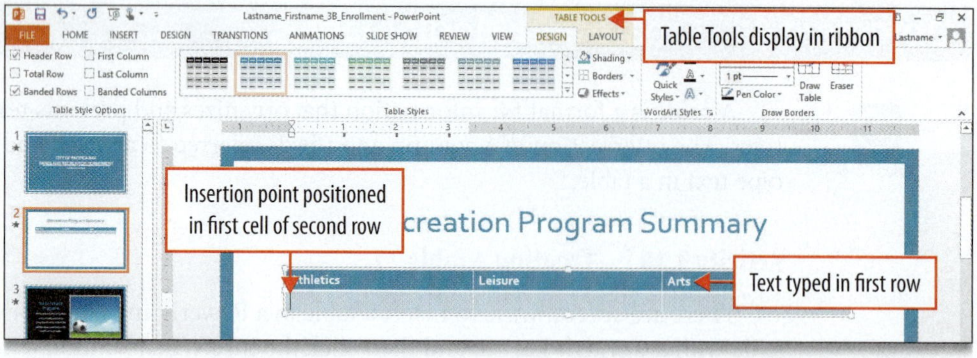

Table Tools display in ribbon

Insertion point positioned in first cell of second row

creation Program Summary

Athletics   Leisure   Arts

Text typed in first row

6 With the insertion point positioned in the first cell of the second row, type **Team sports** and then press [Tab]. Type **Personal development classes** and then press [Tab]. Type **Music and dance classes**

7 Save 🖫 your presentation.

Activity 3.19 │ Inserting Rows and Columns in a Table

You can modify the layout of a table by inserting or deleting rows and columns.

1 With the insertion point positioned in the last cell of the table, press [Tab] and notice that a new blank row is inserted.

When the insertion point is positioned in the last cell of a table, pressing [Tab] inserts a new blank row at the bottom of the table.

2 In the first cell of the third row, type **Youth** and then press [Tab]. Type **Older adults** and then press [Tab]. Type **Young adults** and then compare your table with Figure 3.36.

FIGURE 3.36

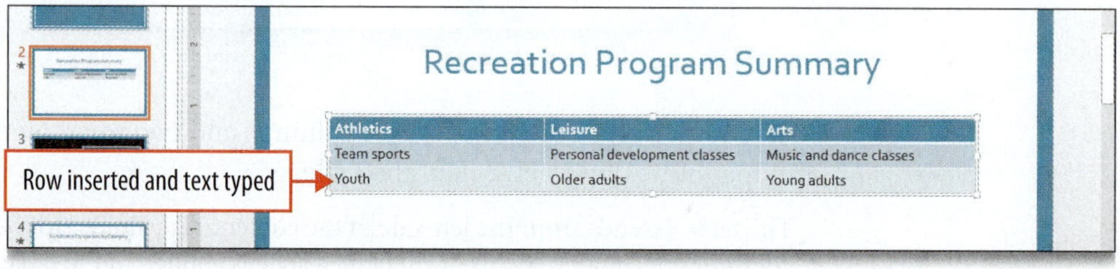

Recreation Program Summary

Athletics	Leisure	Arts
Team sports	Personal development classes	Music and dance classes
Youth	Older adults	Young adults

Row inserted and text typed

ALERT!   **Did You Add an Extra Row to the Table?**

Recall that when the insertion point is positioned in the last cell of the table, pressing [Tab] inserts a new blank row. If you inadvertently inserted a blank row in the table, on the Quick Access Toolbar, click Undo.

---

3 Click in any cell in the first column, and then click the **LAYOUT tab**. In the **Rows & Columns group**, click **Insert Left**.

A new first column displays and the width of the columns adjust so that all four columns are the same width.

4 In the *second* row, click in the first cell, and then type **Largest Enrollments**

5 In the third row, click in the first cell, and then type **Primary Market** Compare your table with Figure 3.37.

FIGURE 3.37

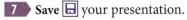

Column inserted and text typed → Program Summary

	Athletics	Leisure	Arts
Largest Enrollments	Team sports	Personal development classes	Music and dance classes
Primary Market	Youth	Older adults	Young adults

6 ▶ With the insertion point positioned in the third row, on the **LAYOUT tab**, in the **Rows & Columns group**, click **Insert Above** to insert a new third row. In the first cell of the new row, type **Average Enrollment** and then press ⎡Tab⎤. Type the remaining three entries, pressing ⎡Tab⎤ to move from cell to cell: **85% of capacity** and **62% of capacity** and **78% of capacity**

More Knowledge **Deleting Rows and Columns**

To delete a row or column from a table, click in the row or column that you want to delete. Click the LAYOUT tab, and then in the Rows & Columns group, click Delete. In the displayed list, click Delete Columns or Delete Rows.

---

7 ▶ **Save** 🔲 your presentation.

Activity 3.20 │ Sizing a Table

A selected table is surrounded by sizing handles and can be resized in the same manner in which a shape or picture is resized.

1 ▶ Point to the bottom, center sizing handle to display the ⬍ pointer. Compare your screen with Figure 3.38.

FIGURE 3.38

	Athletics	Leisure	Arts
Largest Enrollments	Team sports	Personal development classes	Music and dance classes
Average Enrollment	85% of capacity	62% of capacity	78% of capacity
Primary Market	Youth	Older a...	

Pointer positioned over sizing handle

2 ▶ Drag down until the ruler guide is positioned on the **lower half of the vertical ruler at 2 inches**. Compare your screen with Figure 3.39.

A dim border and the red dotted ruler guides display, indicating the size of the table.

FIGURE 3.39

	Athletics	Leisure	Arts
Largest Enrollments	Team sports	Personal development classes	Music and dance classes
Average Enrollment	85% of capacity	62% of capacity	78% of capacity
Primary Market	Youth	Older adults	Young adults

Ruler guide on lower half of vertical ruler at 2 inches

Border indicates new table size

3 ▶ Release the mouse button to size the table, and then **Save** 🔲 your presentation.

 **ANOTHER WAY**   On the LAYOUT tab, in the Table Size group, type an exact measurement in the Height or Width boxes.

Activity 3.21 | Distributing Rows and Aligning Table Text

1 Click in the first cell of the table. On the **LAYOUT tab**, in the **Cell Size group**, click **Distribute Rows**. Compare your table with Figure 3.40.

> The Distribute Rows command adjusts the height of the rows in the table so that they are equal.

FIGURE 3.40

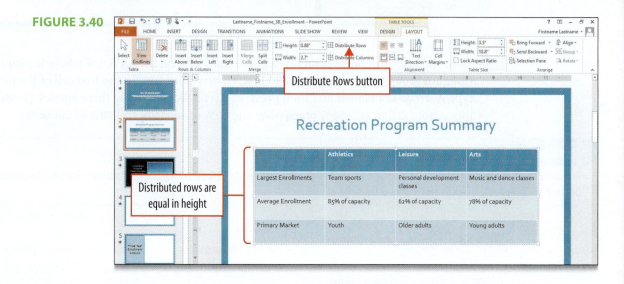

Distribute Rows button

Distributed rows are equal in height

Recreation Program Summary

	Athletics	Leisure	Arts
Largest Enrollments	Team sports	Personal development classes	Music and dance classes
Average Enrollment	85% of capacity	62% of capacity	78% of capacity
Primary Market	Youth	Older adults	Young adults

2 On the **LAYOUT tab**, in the **Table group**, click **Select**, and then click **Select Table**. In the **Alignment group**, click **Center** ☰, and then click **Center Vertically** ▤.

> All of the table text is centered horizontally and vertically within the cells.

3 Save 🖫 your presentation.

> **More Knowledge**   **Distributing Columns**
>
> To distribute columns, click anywhere in the table, and then on the LAYOUT tab, in the Cell Size group, click Distribute Columns.

Activity 3.22 | Applying and Modifying a Table Style

You can modify the design of a table by applying a *table style*. A table style formats the entire table so that it is consistent with the presentation theme. There are color categories within the table styles—Best Match for Document, Light, Medium, and Dark.

1 Click in any cell in the table. Under the **TABLE TOOLS**, click the **DESIGN tab**, and then in the **Table Styles group**, click **More** ▾. In the displayed **Table Styles** gallery, point to several of the styles to view the Live Preview of the style.

2 Under **Light**, in the third row, click the fourth style—**Light Style 3 – Accent 3**—to apply the style to the table.

3 On the **TABLE TOOLS DESIGN tab**, in the **Table Style Options group**, clear the **Banded Rows** check box, and then select the **Banded Columns** check box. Compare your screen with Figure 3.41.

> The check boxes in the Table Style Options group control where Table Style formatting is applied.

FIGURE 3.41

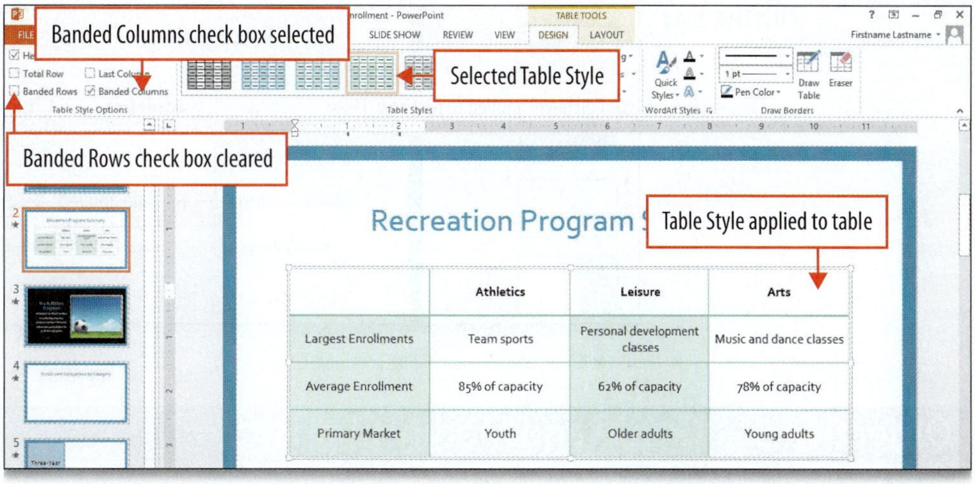

Figure 3.41 — Banded Columns check box selected, Banded Rows check box cleared, Selected Table Style, Table Style applied to table. Recreation Program Summary table:

	Athletics	Leisure	Arts
Largest Enrollments	Team sports	Personal development classes	Music and dance classes
Average Enrollment	85% of capacity	62% of capacity	78% of capacity
Primary Market	Youth	Older adults	Young adults

4 ▸ **Save** 🖫 the presentation.

Activity 3.23 | Applying Table Effects and Font Formatting

1 ▸ Move the pointer outside of the table so that it is positioned to the left of the first row in the table to display the ➡ pointer, as shown in Figure 3.42.

FIGURE 3.42

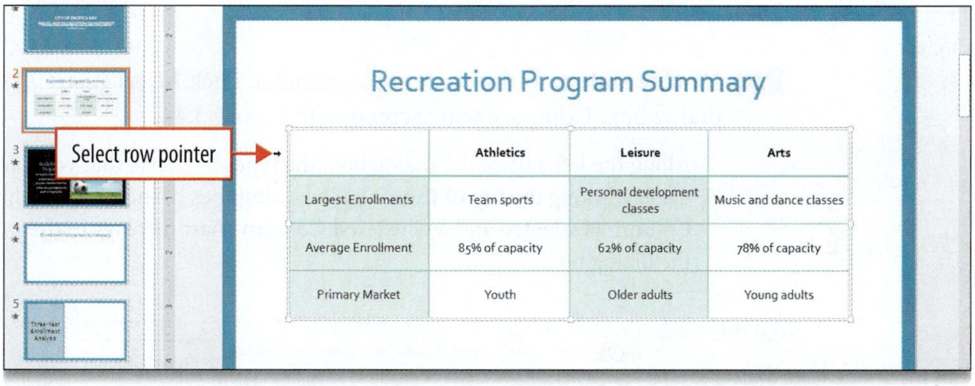

Figure 3.42 — Select row pointer. Recreation Program Summary table:

	Athletics	Leisure	Arts
Largest Enrollments	Team sports	Personal development classes	Music and dance classes
Average Enrollment	85% of capacity	62% of capacity	78% of capacity
Primary Market	Youth	Older adults	Young adults

2 ▸ With the ➡ pointer pointing to the first row in the table, click the mouse button to select the entire row so that you can apply formatting to the selection. Move the pointer into the selected row, and then right-click to display the mini toolbar and shortcut menu. On the mini toolbar, change the **Font Size** to **28**.

3 ▸ With the first row still selected, on the **TABLE TOOLS DESIGN tab**, in the **Table Styles group**, click **Effects**. Point to **Cell Bevel**, and then under **Bevel**, click the first bevel—**Circle**.

4 ▸ Position the pointer above the first column to display the ⬇ pointer, and then right-click to select the first column and display the mini toolbar and shortcut menu. Apply **Bold**.

5 ▸ Click in a blank area of the slide, and then compare your slide with Figure 3.43. **Save** 🖫 the presentation.

FIGURE 3.43

Recreation Program

Font size changed for text in first row

Cell bevel applied to first row

	Athletics	Leisure	Arts
Largest Enrollments	Team sports	Personal development classes	Music and dance classes
Average Enrollment		2% of capacity	78% of capacity
Primary Market	Youth	Older adults	Young adults

Bold applied

Objective 5 | Create and Modify Charts

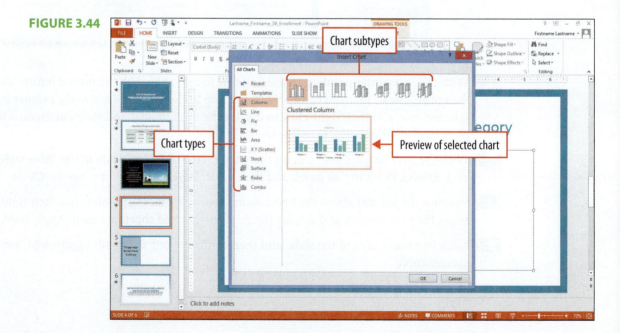

Video P3-5

A *chart* is a graphic representation of numeric data. Commonly used chart types include bar and column charts, pie charts, and line charts. A chart that you create in PowerPoint is stored in an Excel worksheet that is incorporated into the PowerPoint file.

Activity 3.24 | Inserting a Column Chart

A *column chart* is useful for illustrating comparisons among related numbers. In this activity, you will create a column chart that compares enrollment in each category of recreation activities by season.

1 Display **Slide 4**. In the content placeholder, click **Insert Chart** to display the **Insert Chart** dialog box. Compare your screen with Figure 3.44.

Along the left side of the dialog box, the types of charts that you can insert in your presentation display. Along the top of the dialog box, subtypes of the selected chart type display. By default, Column is selected and a Clustered Column chart displays in the preview area on the right side of the dialog box.

FIGURE 3.44

Chart subtypes

Chart types

Preview of selected chart

2 Along the top of the dialog box, point to each column chart to view the ScreenTip. Then, with the **Clustered Column** chart selected, click **OK**. Compare your screen with Figure 3.45.

The PowerPoint window displays a column chart in the content placeholder. Above the chart, a *Chart in Microsoft PowerPoint* worksheet window displays with cells, columns, and rows. A cell is identified by the intersecting column letter and row number, forming the ***cell reference***.

The worksheet contains sample data from which the chart on the PowerPoint slide is generated. The column headings—*Series 1*, *Series 2*, and *Series 3* display in the chart ***legend*** and the row headings—*Category 1*, *Category 2*, *Category 3*, and *Category 4*—display as ***category labels***. The legend identifies the patterns or colors that are assigned to the data series in the chart. The category labels display along the bottom of the chart to identify the categories of data.

FIGURE 3.45

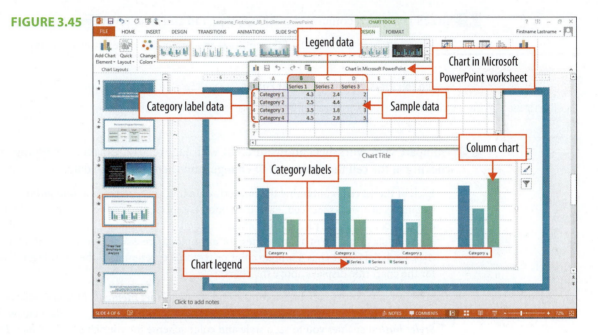

Activity 3.25 | Entering Chart Data

1 In the *Chart in Microsoft PowerPoint* worksheet window, click in cell **B1**, which contains the text *Series 1*. Type **Athletics** and then press Tab to move to cell **C1**.

Below the chart, the chart legend is updated to reflect the change in the Excel worksheet.

2 In cell **C1**, which contains the text *Series 2*, type **Leisure** and then press Tab to move to cell **D1**. Type **Arts** and then press Tab. Notice that cell **A2**, which contains the text *Category 1*, is selected. Compare your screen with Figure 3.46.

The outlined cells define the area in which you are entering data. When you press Tab in the rightmost cell, the first cell in the next row becomes active.

FIGURE 3.46

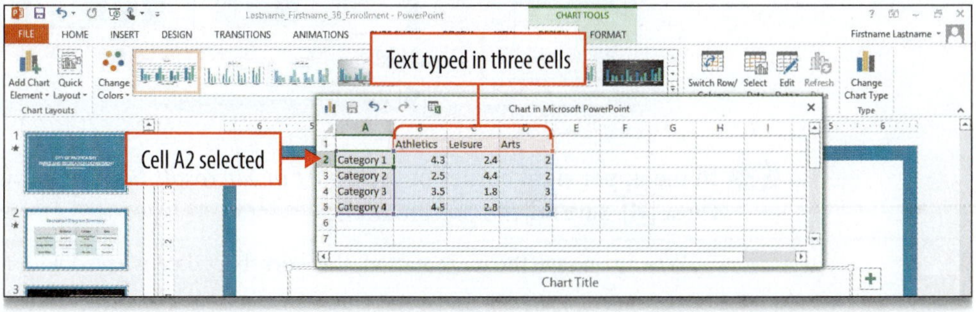

3 ▶ Beginning in cell **A2**, type the following data (starting with *Spring*), pressing [Tab] to move from cell to cell. Notice that as you enter the data, the chart columns resize to display the entered amounts.

	ATHLETICS	LEISURE	ARTS
Spring	895	630	720
Summer	1250	350	820
Fall	1490	585	690
Winter	1130	750	

4 ▶ In cell **D5**, which contains the value 5, type **710** and then press [Enter].

Pressing [Enter] in the last cell of the outlined area maintains the existing data range.

ALERT!   **Did You Press [Tab] After the Last Entry?**

If you pressed [Tab] after entering the data in cell D5, you expanded the chart range. In the Excel window, click Undo.

---

5 ▶ Compare your worksheet and your chart with Figure 3.47. Correct any typing errors by clicking in the cell that you want to change, and then retype the data.

Each of the 12 cells containing the numeric data that you entered is a *data point*—a value that originates in a worksheet cell. Each data point is represented in the chart by a *data marker*—a column, bar, area, dot, pie slice, or other symbol in a chart that represents a single data point. Related data points form a *data series*; for example, there is a data series for *Athletics*, *Leisure*, and *Arts*. Each data series has a unique color or pattern represented in the chart legend. A placeholder for the chart title displays above the chart.

To the right of the chart, three buttons display. The *Chart Elements button* enables you to add, remove, or change chart elements such as the title, legend, gridlines, and data labels. The *Chart Styles button* enables you to set a style and color scheme for your chart. The *Chart Filters button* enables you to change which data displays in the chart.

FIGURE 3.47

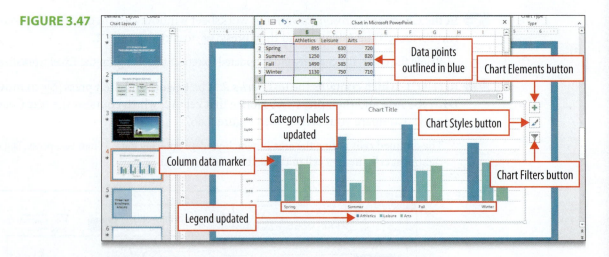

6 ▶ In the upper right corner of the *Chart in Microsoft PowerPoint* worksheet window, click **Close** [X]. **Save** [💾] the presentation.

When you save the presentation, the worksheet data is saved with it.

More Knowledge | Editing the Chart Data After Closing the Worksheet

You can redisplay the worksheet and make changes to the data after you have closed it. To do so, click the chart to select it, and then on the CHART TOOLS DESIGN tab in the Data group, click Edit Data.

Activity 3.26 | Applying a Chart Style and Modifying Chart Elements

A *chart style* is set of predefined formats applied to a chart, including colors, backgrounds, and effects. *Chart elements* are the various components of a chart, including the chart title, axis titles, data series, legend, chart area, and plot area.

1 Be sure the chart is selected; click the outer edge of the chart if necessary to select it. On the **CHART TOOLS DESIGN tab**, in the **Chart Styles group**, click **More** ⊡ to display the **Chart Styles** gallery.

2 In the **Chart Styles** gallery, point to each style to Live Preview the style. Notice that as you point to a chart style, a ScreenTip indicates the chart style number. Click **Style 5**. Compare your screen with Figure 3.48.

> This style includes lightly shaded column data markers. Horizontal gridlines display behind the columns.

FIGURE 3.48

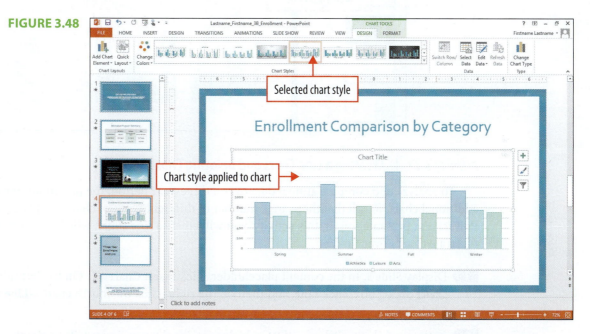

3 To the right of the chart, click **Chart Elements** ⊞, and then compare your screen with Figure 3.49.

> A list of chart elements displays to the left of the chart. Here, you can select the chart elements that you wish to display in your chart. In this slide, the slide title describes the chart. Thus, chart title is not necessary.

FIGURE 3.49

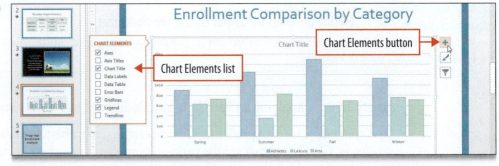

4 ▶ Under **Chart Elements**, click **Chart Title** to clear the check box and remove the chart title placeholder from the chart. Click **Chart Elements** ⊞ to close the Chart Elements list.

5 ▶ Click in a blank area of the slide, and then compare your screen with Figure 3.50. **Save** 🖫 your presentation.

FIGURE 3.50

Activity 3.27 | Creating a Line Chart and Deleting Chart Data

To analyze and compare annual data over a three-year period, the presentation requires an additional chart. Recall that there are a number of different types of charts that you can insert in a PowerPoint presentation. In this activity, you will create a *line chart*, which is commonly used to illustrate trends over time.

1 ▶ Display **Slide 5**. In the content placeholder, click **Insert Chart** 📊. On the left side of the **Insert Chart** dialog box, click **Line**, and then on the right, click the fourth chart—**Line with Markers**. Click **OK**.

2 ▶ In the worksheet, click in cell **B1**, which contains the text *Series 1*. Type **Youth** and then press Tab. Type **Adult** and then press Tab. Type **Senior** and then press Tab.

3 ▶ Beginning in cell **A2**, type the following data, pressing Tab to move from cell to cell. If you make any typing errors, click in the cell that you want to change, and then retype the data.

	YOUTH	ADULT	SENIOR
2015	3822	1588	2240
2016	4675	1833	2534
2017	4535	1925	2897

4 ▶ In the worksheet, position the pointer over **row heading 5** so that the ➡ pointer displays. Compare your screen with Figure 3.51.

FIGURE 3.51

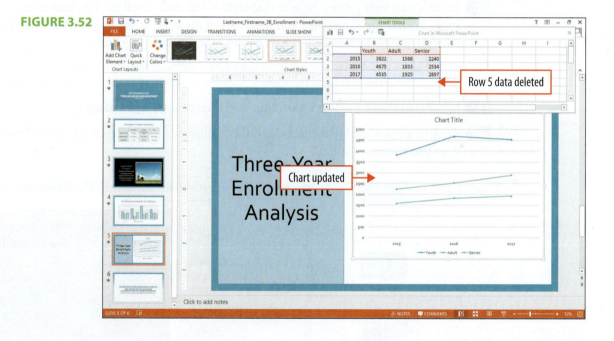

5 With the ➡ pointer displayed, *right-click* to select the row and display the shortcut menu. On the shortcut menu, click **Delete** to delete the extra row from the worksheet, and then compare your screen with Figure 3.52.

The data in the worksheet contains four columns and four rows, and the outline area defining the chart data range is resized. You must delete columns and rows from the sample worksheet data that you do not want to include in the chart. You can add additional rows and columns by typing column and row headings and then entering additional data. When data is typed in cells adjacent to the chart range, the range is resized to include the new data.

FIGURE 3.52

Three Year Enrollment Analysis

Activity 3.28 | Formatting a Line Chart

1 **Close** ✖ the worksheet window. To the right of the chart, click **Chart Styles** 🖌. Compare your screen with Figure 3.53.

The Chart Style gallery displays on the left side of the chart and the Style tab is active. The chart styles display in a vertical gallery.

FIGURE 3.53

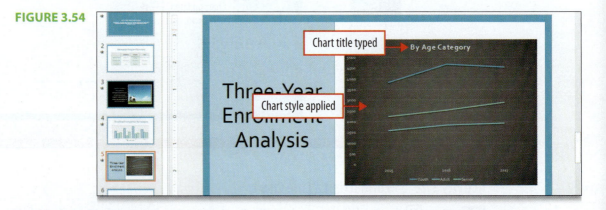

2 ▶ In the **Chart Style** gallery, be sure that **Style** is selected. Scroll the list, and point to various styles to view the ScreenTips and the effect of the style on the chart. Click **Style 6** and then click anywhere outside of the chart to close the Chart Style gallery.

The styles that display when you click the Chart Styles button are the same as those that display in the Chart Styles gallery on the ribbon. Apply chart styles using the technique that you prefer.

3 ▶ In the chart, click the text **Chart Title**, and then type **By Age Category**

4 ▶ Click in a blank area of the slide, and then compare your screen with Figure 3.54. **Save** 🖫 your presentation.

FIGURE 3.54

Activity 3.29 | Animating a Chart

1 ▶ Display **Slide 4**, and then click anywhere in the column chart to select it. On the **ANIMATIONS tab**, in the **Animation group**, click **More** ⯆, and then under **Entrance**, click **Split**.

2 ▶ In the **Animation group**, click **Effect Options**, and then under **Sequence**, click **By Series**. Compare your screen with Figure 3.55.

The By Series option displays the chart one data series at a time, and the numbers 1, 2, 3, and 4 to the left of the chart indicate the four parts of the chart animation sequence. The chart animation sequence includes the background, followed by the Athletics data series for each season, and then the Leisure series, and then the Arts series.

FIGURE 3.55

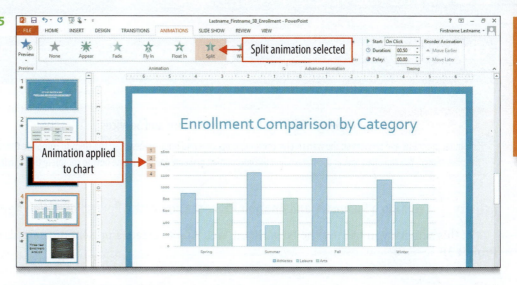

3 ▶ View the slide show from the beginning. On **Slide 4**, notice the chart animation sequence.

4 ▶ Insert a **Header & Footer** on the **Notes and Handouts**. Include the **Date and time** updated automatically, the **Page Number**, and a **Footer**. In the Footer box, using your own name, type **Lastname_Firstname_3B_Enrollment** and then click **Apply to All**.

5 ▶ Display the document properties. As the **Tags**, type **recreation enrollment** and as the **Subject**, type your course and section number. Be sure your name displays as the author, and then **Save** your file.

6 ▶ Print **Handouts 6 Slides Horizontal**, or submit your presentation electronically as directed by your instructor.

7 ▶ **Close** the presentation.

END | You have completed Project 3B

GO! with Office Web Apps

Objective	Create a Summary and Analysis Presentation in the PowerPoint Web App

> **ALERT!** **Working with Web-Based Applications and Services**
>
> Computer programs and services on the web receive continuous updates and improvements, so the steps to complete this web-based activity may differ from the ones shown. You can often look at the screens and the information presented to determine how to complete the activity.

Activity | Creating a Summary and Analysis Presentation in the PowerPoint Web App

In this activity, you will use the PowerPoint Web App to create a presentation similar to the one you created in Project 3B.

1 From the desktop, start Internet Explorer. Navigate to **http://skydrive.com**, and then sign in to your Microsoft account. Open your **GO! Web Projects** folder—or create and then open this folder if necessary.

2 On the SkyDrive menu bar, click **Upload**, and then navigate to your student data files and select **p03_3B_Web**. Click **Open**. When the upload is complete, right-click **p03_3B_Web**, and then click **Rename**. Using your own name, as the file name, type **Lastname_Firstname_PPT_3B_Web** and then press Enter. Click your file, and then click **EDIT PRESENTATION**. Click **Edit in PowerPoint Web App**.

3 Display **Slide 3**. In the text placeholder on the left side of the slide, type **The largest enrollment numbers in Pacifica Bay recreation programs continue to be in the athletic area, particularly in the youth soccer program.** Click outside of the placeholder to enter the text.

4 On the right side of the slide, click **Insert Picture**. From your student data files, insert **p03B_Web_Picture**.

5 With the picture selected, on the **FORMAT tab**, in the **Picture Styles group**, click the third style—**Metal Frame**.

6 Click in a blank area of the slide, and then compare your screen with Figure A.

FIGURE A

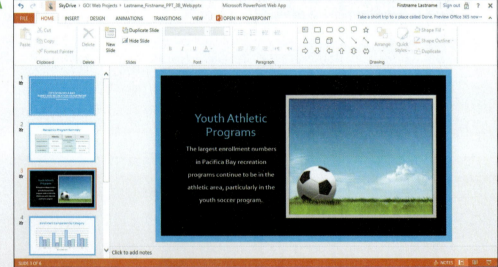

(GO! with Office Web Apps continues on the next page)

7 Display **Slide 4**, and then select the title. On the **ANIMATIONS tab**, in the **Animation group**, click **Fly In**. Click **Effect Options**, and then click **From Top**. In the **Timing group**, click **Move Earlier** several times until the title animation number displays as *1*.

8 Display **Slide 5**, and then click in the title placeholder. Type **Three-Year Enrollment Analysis** and then click outside of the placeholder to enter the text.

9 On **Slide 5**, select the chart. On the **ANIMATIONS tab**, in the **Animation group**, click **Fade In**.

10 Compare your screen with Figure B.

11 Display **Slide 6**. In the title placeholder, type **Recreation Program Enrollments Are Expected to Increase** and then click outside of the placeholder to enter the text.

12 On the **VIEW tab**, click **Slide Show**, and then view the presentation. If a security warning displays, click Allow once. Click the mouse button to advance through the slides.

13 If you are instructed to submit your file, create a PDF as indicated in the Note box below. On the ribbon, click the **FILE tab** and click **Exit**. Sign out of your Microsoft account and close the browser. Submit as directed by your instructor.

NOTE **Creating a PDF from the PowerPoint Web App**

To print on paper, click the File tab, click Print, and then click Print to PDF. In the Microsoft PowerPoint Web App message box, click Click here to view the PDF of your document. In the message bar at the bottom of your screen, click the Save arrow, and then click Save as. In the Save As dialog box, navigate to your PowerPoint Chapter 3 folder, and then save the file.

FIGURE B

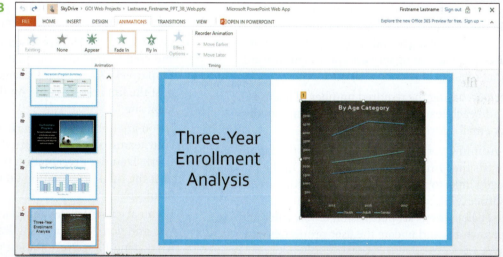

GO! with Microsoft Office 365

Andrew Rodriguez / Fotolia; FotolEdhar/ Fotolia; apops/ Fotolia; Yuri Arcurs/ Fotolia

The advantage of using Office 365 is that your organization does not have to purchase and install server hardware and software for sophisticated business applications and does not need a full-time IT person or staff just to manage the technology your teams need.

By using Office 365, you are able to have business-class services for your employees without investing in expensive hardware, software, and personnel. However, at least one person in an organization must be designated as the *Office 365 Administrator*—the person who creates and manages the account, adds new users, sets up the services your organization wants to use, sets permission levels, and manages the SharePoint team sites. You can have more than one Administrator if you want to share these tasks with others.

Microsoft provides easy-to-use instructions and videos to get you started, and you might also have contact with a Microsoft representative. You will probably find, however, that subscribing to and setting up the account, adding users, and activating services is a straightforward process that requires little or no assistance.

After purchasing the required number of licenses, you will add each team member as a user that includes his or her email address.

The Admin Overview page, as shown in the Figure below, assists the Office 365 Administrator. On the left there are links to manage the users and domains in your Office 365 account. This is where you can add new users, delete users, set permission levels, enter and change passwords, and update the user properties and the licenses.

In the center, you can see the various services available to you in Office 365. In the site shown in the Figure, Outlook, Lync, SharePoint (team sites), and a public-facing website are all part of the services.

Activity | Using a Team Site to Collaborate

This group project relates to the **Bell Orchid Hotels**. If your instructor assigns this project to your class, you can expect to use a SharePoint team site in **Office 365** to collaborate on the following tasks for this chapter:

- If you are in the **Accounting Group**, you and your teammates will finalize the Loan Presentation and post the final presentation on the SharePoint team site.
- If you are in the **Engineering Group**, you and your teammates will finalize the Safety Presentation and post the final presentation on the SharePoint team site.
- If you are in the **Food and Beverage Group**, you and your teammates will finalize the New Menu Item presentation and post the final presentation on the SharePoint team site.
- If you are in the **Human Resources Group**, you and your teammates will finalize the New Employees Orientation presentation and post the final presentation on the SharePoint team site.
- If you are in the **Operations Group**, you and your teammates will finalize the Front Desk Clerk Training Presentation presentation and post the final presentation on the SharePoint team site.
- If you are in the **Sales and Marketing Group**, you and your teammates will finalize the Marketing Plan Presentation presentation and post the final presentation on the SharePoint team site.

(GO! with Microsoft Office 365 continues on the next page)

Andrew Rodriguez / Fotolia; FotolEdhar/ Fotolia; apops/ Fotolia; Yuri Arcurs/ Fotolia

FIGURE A

END OF CHAPTER

SUMMARY

There are many ways to modify a presentation theme and customize a presentation. You can apply background styles, insert pictures and textures on slide backgrounds, and change theme fonts and colors.

One way to enhance a presentation and engage an audience is by inserting interesting and informative video. Styles, shapes, and effects can be applied to videos. A video can be trimmed and compressed to make the file size smaller.

Use animation to focus audience attention on a particular slide element in order to draw attention to important points. Apply animation to slide elements in the order in which you want them to display.

Use tables to present information in an organized and attractive manner. Use charts to visually represent data. Apply styles to charts and tables to give your presentations a consistent and informative look.

GO! LEARN IT ONLINE

Review the concepts and key terms in this chapter by completing these online challenges, which you can find at **www.pearsonhighered.com/go**.

Matching and Multiple Choice: Answer matching and multiple choice questions to test what you learned in this chapter. MyITLab®

Crossword Puzzle: Spell out the words that match the numbered clues, and put them in the puzzle squares.

Flipboard: Flip through the definitions of the key terms in this chapter and match them with the correct term.

GO! FOR JOB SUCCESS

Video: Making Ethical Choices

Your instructor may assign this video to your class, and then ask you to think about, or discuss with your classmates, these questions:

FotolEdhar / Fotolia

Which behaviors in this video do you think were unethical?

Is it unethical to "borrow" things from your employer? Why? What would you do if you saw this behavior going on?

What do you think an employer could do to prevent unethical behavior?

END OF CHAPTER

REVIEW AND ASSESSMENT GUIDE FOR POWERPOINT CHAPTER 3

Your instructor may assign one or more of these projects to help you review the chapter and assess your mastery and understanding of the chapter.

Project	Apply Skills from These Chapter Objectives	Project Type	Project Location
		Review and Assessment Guide for PowerPoint Chapter 3	
3C	Objectives 1-3 from Project 3A	**3C Skills Review** A guided review of the skills from Project 3A.	On the following pages
3D	Objectives 4-5 from Project 3B	**3D Skills Review** A guided review of the skills from Project 3B.	On the following pages
3E	Objectives 1-3 from Project 3A	**3E Mastery (Grader Project)** A demonstration of your mastery of the skills in Project 3A with extensive decision making.	In MyITLab and on the following pages
3F	Objectives 4-5 from Project 3B	**3F Mastery (Grader Project)** A demonstration of your mastery of the skills in Project 3B with extensive decision making.	In MyITLab and on the following pages
3G	Objectives 1-5 from Projects 3A and 3B	**3G Mastery (Grader Project)** A demonstration of your mastery of the skills in Projects 3A and 3B with extensive decision making.	In MyITLab and on the following pages
3H	Combination of Objectives from Projects 3A and 3B	**3H GO! Fix It** A demonstration of your mastery of the skills in Projects 3A and 3B by creating a correct result from a document that contains errors you must find.	Online
3I	Combination of Objectives from Projects 3A and 3B	**3I GO! Make It** A demonstration of your mastery of the skills in Projects 3A and 3B by creating a result from a supplied picture.	Online
3J	Combination of Objectives from Projects 3A and 3B	**3J GO! Solve It** A demonstration of your mastery of the skills in Projects 3A and 3B, your decision-making skills, and your critical thinking skills. A task-specific rubric helps you self-assess your result.	Online
3K	Combination of Objectives from Projects 3A and 3B	**3K GO! Solve It** A demonstration of your mastery of the skills in Projects 3A and 3B, your decision-making skills, and your critical thinking skills. A task-specific rubric helps you self-assess your result.	On the following pages
3L	Combination of Objectives from Projects 3A and 3B	**3L GO! Think** A demonstration of your understanding of the Chapter concepts applied in a manner that you would outside of college. An analytic rubric helps you and your instructor grade the quality of your work by comparing it to the work an expert in the discipline would create.	On the following pages
3M	Combination of Objectives from Projects 3A and 3B	**3M GO! Think** A demonstration of your understanding of the Chapter concepts applied in a manner that you would outside of college. An analytic rubric helps you and your instructor grade the quality of your work by comparing it to the work an expert in the discipline would create.	Online
3N	Combination of Objectives from Projects 3A and 3B	**3N You and GO!** A demonstration of your understanding of the Chapter concepts applied in a manner that you would in a personal situation. An analytic rubric helps you and your instructor grade the quality of your work.	Online
3O	Combination of Objectives from Projects 3A and 3B	**3O Cumulative Group Project for PowerPoint Chapter 3** A demonstration of your understanding of concepts and your ability to work collaboratively in a group role-playing assessment, requiring both collaboration and self-management.	Online
Capstone Project for PowerPoint Chapters 1-3	Combination of Objectives from Projects 1A, 1B, 2A, 2B, 3A, and 3B	A demonstration of your mastery of the skills in Chapters 1-3 with extensive decision making. **(Grader Project)**	In MyITLab and online

GLOSSARY

GLOSSARY OF CHAPTER KEY TERMS

After Previous An animation option that begins the animation sequence for the selected slide element immediately after the completion of the previous animation or slide transition.

Animation A visual or sound effect added to an object or text on a slide.

Animation Painter A feature that copies animation settings from one object to another.

Background style A predefined slide background fill variation that combines theme colors in different intensities or patterns.

Body font A font that is applied to all slide text except slide titles.

Category labels Text that displays along the bottom of a chart to identify the categories of data.

Cell The intersection of a column and row in a table.

Cell reference The intersecting column letter and row number that identify a cell.

Chart A graphic representation of numeric data.

Chart elements The various components of a chart, including the chart title, axis titles, data series, legend, chart area, and plot area.

Chart Elements button A button that displays options for adding, removing, or changing chart elements.

Chart Filters button A button that displays options for changing the data displayed in a chart.

Chart style A set of predefined formats applied to a chart, including colors, backgrounds, and effects.

Chart Styles button A button that displays options for setting the style and color scheme for a chart.

Column chart A type of chart used for illustrating comparisons among related numbers.

Data marker A column, bar, area, dot, pie slice, or other symbol in a chart that represents a single data point.

Data point A chart value that originates in a worksheet cell.

Data series A group of related data points.

Emphasis effect Animation that emphasizes an object or text that is already displayed.

Entrance effect Animation that brings a slide element onto the screen.

Exit effect Animation that moves an object or text off the screen.

Headings font A font that is applied to all slide title text.

Legend A chart element that identifies the patterns or colors that are assigned to the data series in the chart.

Line chart A type of chart commonly used to illustrate trends over time.

On Click An animation option that begins the animation sequence for the selected slide element when the mouse button is clicked or the Spacebar is pressed.

Table A format for Information that organizes and presents text and data in columns and rows.

Table style A format applied to a table that is consistent with the presentation theme.

Theme colors A set of coordinating colors that are applied to the backgrounds, objects, and text in a presentation.

Theme fonts The fonts applied to two types of slide text—headings and body.

Timing options Animation options that control when animated items display in the animation sequence.

Trim A command that deletes parts of a video to make it shorter.

With Previous An animation option that begins the animation sequence at the same time as the previous animation or slide transition.

CHAPTER REVIEW

Apply 3A skills from these Objectives:

1 Customize Slide Backgrounds and Themes
2 Animate a Slide Show
3 Insert a Video

In the following Skills Review, you will format a presentation by applying slide background styles, colors, pictures, and animation. Your completed presentation will look similar to Figure 3.56.

PROJECT FILES

For Project 3C, you will need the following files:

p03C_Park
p03C_Park_Scenery
p03C_Park_Video

You will save your presentation as:

Lastname_Firstname_3C_Park

PROJECT RESULTS

FIGURE 3.56

(Project 3C Park continues on the next page)

CHAPTER REVIEW

1 Start PowerPoint, from your student data files, open **p03C_Park**, and then **Save** the presentation in your **PowerPoint Chapter 3** folder as **Lastname_Firstname_3C_Park**

a. On the **DESIGN tab**, in the **Variants group**, click **More**, point to **Colors**, and then click **Orange Red** to change the theme colors.

b. On the **DESIGN tab**, in the **Variants group**, click **More**, point to **Fonts**, and then click **Candara** to change the theme fonts.

c. On the **DESIGN tab**, in the **Customize group**, click **Format Background**. In the **Format Background** pane, under **Fill**, click **Picture or texture fill**. Under **Insert picture from**, to the right of **Texture**, click the **Texture** button, and then in the third row, click the fourth texture—**Recycled Paper**.

d. **Close** the **Format Background** pane.

2 Display **Slide 2**. Hold down Ctrl and click **Slide 4** so that both **Slides 2** and **4** are selected. On the **DESIGN tab**, in the **Variants group**, click **More**, and then point to **Background Styles**. In the second row, *right-click* the third style—**Style 7**, and then on the shortcut menu, click **Apply to Selected Slides**.

a. Display **Slide 3**. On the **DESIGN tab**, in the **Customize group**, click **Format Background**. Select the **Hide Background Graphics** check box.

b. In the **Format Background** pane, under **Fill**, click the **Picture or texture fill** option button. Under **Insert picture from**, click **File**, and then navigate to your student data files. Click **p03C_Park_Scenery**, and then click **Insert**.

c. In the **Transparency** box, type **10%**

3 Display **Slide 5**. If necessary, display the **Format Background** pane.

a. In the **Format Background** pane, under **Fill**, verify that **Solid Fill** is selected.

b. To the right of **Color**, click **Fill Color**. In the third column, click the first color—**Tan, Background 2**.

c. **Close** the **Format Background** pane.

4 With **Slide 5** displayed, on the **INSERT tab**, in the **Media group**, click **Video**, and then click **Video on My PC**. Navigate to your student data files, and then click **p03C_Park_Video**. Click **Insert** to insert the video.

a. With the video selected, on the **FORMAT tab**, in the **Size group**, replace the value in the **Height** box with **2.5** and then press Enter.

b. On the **FORMAT tab**, in the **Arrange group**, click **Align**, and then click **Align Center**. Click **Align** again, and then click **Align Bottom** so that the video is centered and aligned with the lower edge of the slide.

c. With the video selected, on the **FORMAT tab**, in the **Video Styles** group, click **More**, and then under **Subtle**, click the third style—**Soft Edge Rectangle**.

d. In the **Video Styles group**, click **Video Shape**, and then under **Rectangles**, click the second shape—**Rounded Rectangle**.

e. With the video selected, on the **PLAYBACK tab**, in the **Video Options group**, click the **Start arrow**, and then click **Automatically**.

f. On the **PLAYBACK tab**, in the **Editing group**, click **Trim Video**. Select the number in the **End Time** box, and then type **00:14** and notice that the video ends with a picture of the park. Click **OK** to apply the trim settings.

5 Display **Slide 2**, and then select the text in the in the bulleted list placeholder. On the **HOME tab**, in the **Font group**, click the **Font Color button arrow**, and then in the second column, click the first color—**White, Text 1** so that the text displays with more contrast against the slide background.

a. With the bulleted list selected, on the **ANIMATIONS tab**, in the **Animation group**, click **More**, and then under **Entrance**, click **Split**.

b. In the **Animation group**, click **Effect Options**, and then click **Vertical Out**.

c. In the **Timing group**, click the **Start arrow**, and then click **After Previous** so that the list displays after the slide transition.

d. In the **Timing group**, click the **Duration up arrow** two times so that *01.00* displays in the **Duration** box. Click the **Delay up arrow** one time so that *00.25* displays in the **Delay** box.

(Project 3C Park continues on the next page)

CHAPTER REVIEW

6 ▶ Display **Slide 3**, and then click in the title placeholder. On the **ANIMATIONS tab**, in the **Animation group**, click **More**, and then under **Entrance**, click **Wipe**. In the **Timing group**, click the **Start arrow**, and then click **After Previous** so that the title displays immediately after the slide transition.

a. With the title selected, in the **Advanced Animation group**, click **Animation Painter**. Click **Slide 1**, and then click the subtitle—*Remodel Update*—to apply the animation effect to the subtitle.

b. On **Slide 1**, select the title. Notice that in the Animation group, the Bounce animation is applied. On the **ANIMATIONS tab**, in the **Animation group**, click **More**, and then click **None** to remove the animation from the title.

c. Insert a **Header & Footer** for the **Notes and Handouts**. Include the **Date and time updated automatically**, the **Page number**, and a **Footer** with the file name **Lastname_Firstname_3C_Park**

d. On the **SLIDE SHOW tab**, in the **Start Slide Show group**, click **From Beginning**, and then view your presentation, clicking the mouse button to advance through the slides. When the video on Slide 5 finishes, press Esc to return to the presentation.

7 ▶ Click the **FILE tab**, and then on the **Info tab**, click **Compress Media**. Click **Low Quality** to make the presentation size smaller and easier to submit. When the compression is complete, in the **Compress Media** dialog box, click **Close**.

a. Display the document properties. As the **Tags** type **park remodel** and as the **Subject** type your course and section number. Be sure your name displays as the author, and then **Save** your file.

b. Print **Handouts 6 Slides Horizontal**, or submit your presentation electronically as directed by your instructor. **Close** the presentation.

END | You have completed Project 3C

CHAPTER REVIEW

Apply 3B skills from these Objectives:

4 Create and Modify Tables

5 Create and Modify Charts

Skills Review   Project 3D Budget

In the following Skills Review, you will format a presentation by inserting and formatting a table, a column chart, and a line chart. Your completed presentation will look similar to Figure 3.57.

PROJECT FILES

For Project 3D, you will need the following file:

p03D_Budget

You will save your presentation as:

Lastname_Firstname_3D_Budget

PROJECT RESULTS

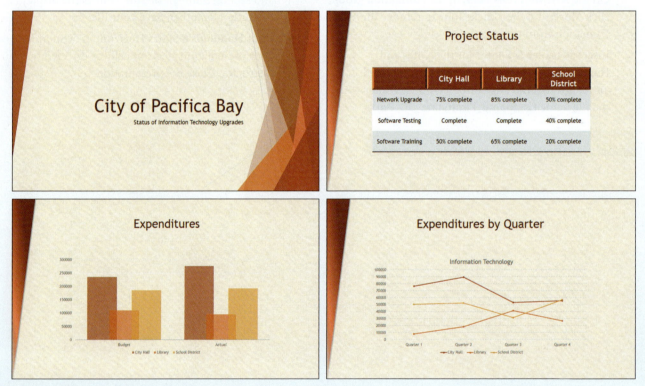

FIGURE 3.57

(Project 3D Budget continues on the next page)

Skills Review Project 3D Budget (continued)

1 ▸ Start PowerPoint, from your student data files, open **p03D_Budget**, and then **Save** the presentation in your **PowerPoint Chapter 3** folder as **Lastname_Firstname_3D_Budget**

a. Display **Slide 2**. In the content placeholder, click **Insert Table** to display the **Insert Table** dialog box. In the **Number of columns box**, type **3** and then press Tab. In the **Number of rows** box, type **2** and then click **OK** to create the table.

b. In the first row of the table, click in the second cell. Type **City Hall** and then press Tab. Type **School District** and then press Tab to move the insertion point to the first cell in the second row.

c. With the insertion point positioned in the first cell of the second row, type **Network Upgrade** and then press Tab. Type **75% complete** and then press Tab. Type **50% complete** and then press Tab to insert a new blank row. In the first cell of the third row, type **Software Training** and then press Tab. Type **50% complete** and then press Tab. Type **20% complete**

d. With the insertion point positioned in the last column, on the **LAYOUT tab**, in the **Rows & Columns group**, click **Insert Left** to insert a new column. Click in the top cell of the inserted column, and then type **Library** In the second and third rows of the inserted column, type **85% complete** and **65% complete**

e. With the insertion point positioned in the third row, on the **LAYOUT tab**, in the **Rows & Columns group**, click **Insert Above**. Click in the first cell of the row you inserted, type **Software Testing** and then press Tab. Type the remaining three entries in the row as follows: **Complete** and **Complete** and **40% complete**

2 ▸ At the center of the lower border surrounding the table, point to the sizing handle, and make the table larger by dragging down until the lower edge of the table aligns **on the lower half of the vertical ruler at 2 inches**.

a. Click in the first cell of the table. On the **LAYOUT tab**, in the **Cell Size group**, click **Distribute Rows**.

b. On the **LAYOUT tab**, in the **Table group**, click **Select**, and then click **Select Table**. In the **Alignment group**, click **Center**, and then click **Center Vertically**.

c. Click in any cell in the table. Under **TABLE TOOLS**, click the **DESIGN tab**, and then in the **Table Styles group**, click **More**. Under **Medium**, in the third row, click the second style—**Medium Style 3 – Accent 1**— to apply the style to the table.

d. Move the pointer outside of the table so that is positioned to the left of the first row in the table to display the ➜ pointer, and then click one time to select the entire row. On the **DESIGN tab**, in the **Table Styles group**, click **Effects**. Point to **Cell Bevel**, and then under **Bevel**, click the first bevel—**Circle**. Change the **Font Size** of the text in the first row to **24**.

3 ▸ Display **Slide 3**. In the content placeholder, click **Insert Chart** to display the **Insert Chart** dialog box. With the *Clustered* **Column** chart selected, click **OK**.

a. In the worksheet window, click in cell **B1**, which contains the text *Series 1*. Type **City Hall** and then press Tab to move to cell **C1**.

b. In cell **C1**, which contains the text *Series 2*, type **Library** and then press Tab to move to cell **D1**, which contains the text *Series 3*. Type **School District** and then press Tab.

c. Beginning in cell **A2**, type the following data, pressing Tab to move from cell to cell.

	City Hall	Library	School District
Budget	235650	110500	185635
Actual	275895	95760	192570

d. In the worksheet window, position the pointer over **row heading 4** so that the ➜ pointer displays. Then, drag down to select both **rows 4** and **5**. *Right-click* in one of the selected the rows to display the shortcut menu. On the shortcut menu, click **Delete**. **Close** the worksheet window.

e. With the chart selected, under **CHART TOOLS**, on the **DESIGN tab**, in the **Chart Styles group**, click **More**. In the **Chart Styles** gallery, in the second row, click **Style 13** to apply the style to the chart.

f. To the right of the chart, click **Chart Elements** ➕, and then *clear* the **Chart Title** box to remove it from the chart.

(Project 3D Budget continues on the next page)

g. With the chart selected, click the **ANIMATIONS tab**, and then in the **Animation group**, click **More**. Under **Entrance**, click **Split**. In the **Animation group**, click **Effect Options**, and then under **Sequence**, click **By Series**.

4 ▶ Display **Slide 4**. In the content placeholder, click **Insert Chart**. On the left side of the **Insert Chart** dialog box, click **Line**, and then under **Line**, click the fourth chart—**Line with Markers**. Click **OK**.

a. In the worksheet, click in cell **B1**, which contains the text *Series 1*. Type **City Hall** and then press Tab. Type **Library** and then press Tab. Type **School District** and then press Tab.

b. Beginning in cell **A2**, type the following data, pressing Tab to move from cell to cell. After you finish entering the data, close the worksheet window.

	City Hall	Library	School District
Quarter 1	76575	8265	50665
Quarter 2	89670	18675	52830
Quarter 3	53620	41730	31560
Quarter 4	56030	27090	57515

END | You have completed Project 3D

c. Click in the **Chart Title**, and then type **Information Technology**

d. Insert a **Header & Footer** for the **Notes and Handouts**. Include the **Date and time updated automatically**, the **Page number**, and a **Footer** with the file name **Lastname_Firstname_3D_Budget**

e. Display the document properties. As the **Tags** type **technology budget** and as the **Subject** type your course and section number. Be sure your name displays as the author, and then **Save** your file.

f. Print **Handouts 4 Slides Horizontal**, or submit your presentation electronically as directed by your instructor. **Close** the presentation.

CONTENT-BASED ASSESSMENTS

MyITLab® grader

Mastering PowerPoint | Project 3E Gardens

In the following Mastering PowerPoint project, you will format a presentation created by the Pacifica Bay Public Relations department that describes the City of Pacifica Bay Botanical Gardens. Your completed presentation will look similar to Figure 3.58.

Apply 3A skills from these Objectives:

1 Customize Slide Backgrounds and Themes

2 Animate a Slide Show

3 Insert a Video

PROJECT FILES

For Project 3E, you will need the following files:

p03E_Garden
p03E_Flower
p03E_Video

You will save your presentation as:

Lastname_Firstname_3E_Garden

PROJECT RESULTS

FIGURE 3.58

(Project 3E Gardens continues on the next page)

CONTENT-BASED ASSESSMENTS

1 Start PowerPoint. From the student data files that accompany this textbook, locate and open **p03E_ Garden**. Save the presentation in your **PowerPoint Chapter 3** folder as **Lastname_Firstname_3E_Garden**

2 Change the **Colors** for the presentation to **Violet**, and the **Fonts** to **Cambria**. On **Slide 1**, format the background by changing the **Color** of the Solid fill to **Gray – 25%, Text 2, Darker 90%**—in the fourth column, the last color.

3 Select **Slides 2** and **3**, and then format the background of the two selected slides with the **Green marble** texture.

4 On **Slide 2**, select the paragraph on the right side of the slide, and then apply the **Split** entrance effect. Change the **Effect Options** to **Horizontal Out**. Change the **Start** setting to **After Previous**, and then change the **Duration** to **01.00**.

5 Use **Animation Painter** to apply the same animation from the paragraph on **Slide 2** to the bulleted list on **Slide 3**. Then, on **Slide 3**, remove the animation from the title.

6 On **Slide 4**, hide the background graphics, and then format the background with a picture from your student data files—**p03E_Flower**. Change the **Transparency** to **50%**

7 Format the title placeholder with a **Shape Fill** color—in the fifth column, the last color—**Lavender, Accent 1, Darker 50%**.

8 From your student data files, insert the video **p03E_Video**. Change the **Video Height** to **6.25** and then using the **Align to Slid**e option, apply the **Align Center** and **Align Bottom** options. Format the video by applying, from the **Video Styles** gallery, an **Intense** style—**Bevel Rectangle**.

9 Change the video **Start** setting to **Automatically**, and then trim the video to **00:14** Compress the video using the **Low Quality** setting.

10 Insert a **Header & Footer** on the **Notes and Handouts**. Include the **Date and time updated automatically**, the **Page number**, and a **Footer** with the text **Lastname_Firstname_3E_Garden**

11 Display the document properties. As the **Tags** type **botanical garden** and as the **Subject** type your course and section number. Be sure your name displays as the author, and then **Save** your file.

12 View the slide show from the beginning, and then print **Handouts 4 Slides Horizontal**, or submi t your presentation electronically as directed by your instructor. **Close** the presentation.

END | You have completed Project 3E

CONTENT-BASED ASSESSMENTS

In the following Mastering PowerPoint project, you will format several of the slides in a presentation that the City Manager is developing for an upcoming City Council meeting. Your completed presentation will look similar to Figure 3.59.

Apply 3B skills from these Objectives:

4 Create and Modify Tables

5 Create and Modify Charts

PROJECT FILES

For Project 3F, you will need the following file:

p03F_Report

You will save your presentation as:

Lastname_Firstname_3F_Report

PROJECT RESULTS

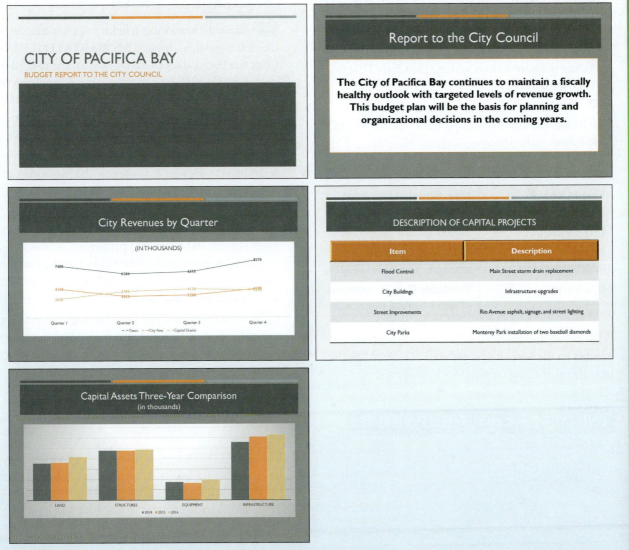

FIGURE 3.59

(Project 3F Report continues on the next page)

1 Start PowerPoint. From your student data files, open **p03F_Report**, and then **Save** the presentation in your **PowerPoint Chapter 3** folder as **Lastname_Firstname_3F_Report**

2 On **Slide 3**, in the content placeholder, insert a **Line with Markers** chart. In the worksheet, in cell **B1**, type **Taxes** and then enter the following data:

	Taxes	City Fees	Capital Grants
Quarter 1	7480	4154	2650
Quarter 2	6380	3092	3785
Quarter 3	6695	3260	4150
Quarter 4	8370	4190	3970

3 **Close** the worksheet window. Apply **Chart Style 7**, and then apply the **Wipe** entrance effect to the chart. Including the parentheses, change the **Chart Title** to **(In Thousands)**

4 On **Slide 4**, in the content placeholder, insert a **Table** with **2 columns** and **5 rows**, and then type the text in the table below

Item	Description
Flood Control	Main Street storm drain replacement
City Buildings	Infrastructure upgrades
Street Improvements	Rio Avenue asphalt, signage, and street lighting
City Parks	Monterey Park installation of two baseball diamonds

5 Resize the table so that its lower edge extends to **3 inches on the lower half of the vertical ruler**. Align the table text so that it is centered horizontally and vertically within the cells. Apply table style **Medium Style 3 - Accent 2**, and then to the first row, apply a **Cell Bevel** using the **Circle** effect. Change the **Font Size** of the text in the first row to **24**.

6 On **Slide 5**, in the content placeholder, insert a **Clustered Column** chart. In the worksheet, in cell **B1**, type **2014** and then enter the following data:

	2014	2015	2016
Land	71534	72823	83653
Structures	95746	95920	97812
Equipment	35042	33465	39767
Infrastructure	111586	121860	125873

7 **Close** the worksheet window. Apply **Chart Style 4** to the chart, and then display the **CHART ELEMENTS** list. Clear the **Data Labels** check box so that the data labels do not display at the top of each column. Apply the **Wipe** entrance effect to the chart. Change the **Effect Options** so that the animation is applied **By Series**. Change the **Timing** so that the animation starts **After Previous**. Remove the **Chart Title** element.

8 Insert a **Header & Footer** on the **Notes and Handouts**. Include the **Date and time updated automatically**, the **Page number**, and a **Footer** with the text **Lastname_Firstname_3F_Report**

9 Display the document properties. As the **Tags**, type **city council report** and as the **Subject**, type your course and section number. Be sure your name displays as the author, and then **Save** your file.

10 View the slide show from the beginning, and then print **Handouts 6 Slides Horizontal**, or submit your presentation electronically as directed by your instructor. **Close** the presentation.

END | You have completed Project 3F

CONTENT-BASED ASSESSMENTS

MyITLab®
grader

Mastering PowerPoint   Project 3G Travel

In the following Mastering PowerPoint project, you will format a presentation that the Pacifica Bay Travel and Tourism Director will show at a conference for travel agents in California. Your completed presentation will look similar to Figure 3.60.

Apply 3A and 3B skills from these Objectives:

1 Customize Slide Backgrounds and Themes
2 Animate a Slide Show
3 Insert a Video
4 Create and Modify Tables
5 Create and Modify Charts

PROJECT FILES

For Project 3G, you will need the following files:

p03G_Travel
p03G_Video
p03G_Background

You will save your presentation as:

Lastname_Firstname_3G_Travel

PROJECT RESULTS

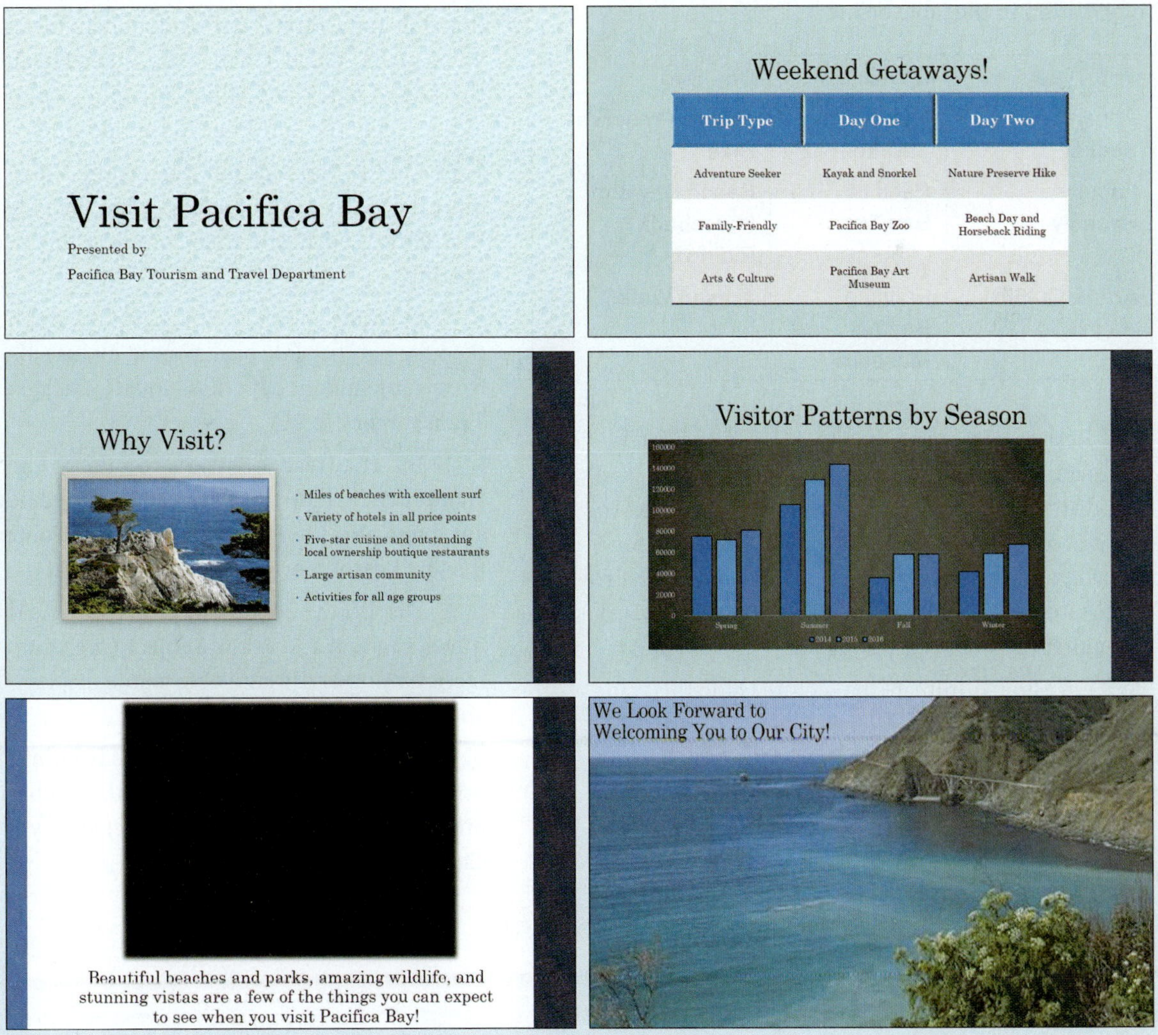

FIGURE 3.60

(Project 3G Travel continues on the next page)

CONTENT-BASED ASSESSMENTS

1 Start PowerPoint. From the student data files that accompany this textbook, locate and open **p03G_ Travel**. Save the presentation in your **PowerPoint Chapter 3** folder as **Lastname_Firstname_3G_Travel**

2 Change the **Colors** for the presentation to **Blue Warm**. On **Slide 1**, format the background with the **Water droplets Texture**, and then change the **Transparency** to **50%**

3 Select **Slides 2 through 4**, and then format the background of the selected slides with a **Solid fill** using the color **Teal, Accent 5, Lighter 60%**—in the second to last column, the third color.

4 On **Slide 2**, hide the background graphics, and then insert a **Table** with **3 columns** and **4 rows**. Apply table style **Medium Style 3 - Accent 3**, and then type the information in the table below.

Trip Type	Day One	Day Two
Adventure Seeker	Kayak and Snorkel	Nature Preserve Hike
Family-Friendly	Pacifica Bay Zoo	Beach Day and Horseback Riding
Arts & Culture	Pacifica Bay Art Museum	Artisan Walk

5 Resize the table so that its lower edge extends to **3 inches on the lower half of the vertical ruler**, and then distribute the table rows. Align the table text so that it is centered horizontally and vertically within the cells, and then change the **Font Size** of the first row of the table text to **24**. Apply a **Circle** style **Cell Bevel** to the first row.

6 On **Slide 3**, animate the picture using the **Wipe** entrance effect starting **After Previous**. Change the **Duration** to **01:00**. Apply the **Split** entrance effect to the bulleted list placeholder, and then change the **Effect Options** to **Vertical Out**.

7 On **Slide 4**, insert a **Clustered Column** chart. In the worksheet, in cell **B1** type **2014** and then enter the following data:

	2014	2015	2016
Spring	75600	72300	81460
Summer	105300	128730	143600
Fall	35900	58300	58320
Winter	41600	58430	67300

8 **Close** the worksheet window, apply **Chart Style 8** to the chart, and then remove the **Chart Title** element. Apply the **Wipe** entrance effect to the chart and change the **Effect Options** to **By Series**.

9 On **Slide 5**, apply the **Style 1** background style to this slide only. From your student data files, insert the video **p03G_Video**. Change the **Video Height** to **6** and use the **Align Center** and **Align Top** options to position the video. Apply the **Soft Edge Rectangle** video style.

10 On the **Playback tab**, change the **Video Options** to **Start** the video **Automatically**. **Trim** the video so that the **End Time** is **00:22** and then compress the media in **Low Quality**.

11 On **Slide 6**, hide the background graphics, and then format the slide background by inserting a picture from your student data files—**p03G_Background**. Set the **Transparency** to **0%**

12 Insert a **Header & Footer** on the **Notes and Handouts**. Include the **Date and time updated automatically**, the **Page number**, and a **Footer** with the text **Lastname_Firstname_3G_Travel**

13 Display the document properties. As the **Tags** type **travel, tourism** and as the **Subject** type your course and section number. Be sure your name displays as the author, and then **Save** your file.

14 View the slide show from the beginning, and then print **Handouts 6 Slides Horizontal**, or submit your presentation electronically as directed by your instructor. **Close** PowerPoint.

END | You have completed Project 3G

CONTENT-BASED ASSESSMENTS

Apply a combination of the **3A** and **3B** skills.

GO! Fix It	Project 3H Housing Developments	Online
GO! Make It	Project 3I Water Usage	Online
GO! Solve It	Project 3J Aquatic Center	Online
GO! Solve It	Project 3K Power	

PROJECT FILES

For Project 3K, you will need the following files:

p03K_Power
p03K_Tower

You will save your presentation as:

Lastname_Firstname_3K_Power

Open the file p03K_Power and save it as **Lastname_Firstname_3K_Power** Apply a theme and then format the slide background of the title slide with the picture found in your student data files—p03K_Tower. Format the title slide so that the title text displays attractively against the background. Format the background of at least one other slide using a background style, solid fill color, or texture. On Slide 3, insert a table with the following information:

Power Sources	Percent Used by City
Natural gas	32%
Hydroelectric	17%
Renewables	18%
Coal	23%
Nuclear	10%

On Slide 4, insert and format an appropriate chart to demonstrate the revenue collected from residential power sales over the past three years. Revenue in 2014 was 35.5 million dollars, in 2015 revenue was 42.6 million dollars, and in 2016 revenue was 48.2 million dollars. Apply appropriate animation and and insert an appropriate header and footer. Add your name, your course name and section number, and the tags **power sources, revenue** to the Properties. Save and then print or submit the presentation as directed by your instructor.

(Project 3K Power continues on the next page)

CONTENT-BASED ASSESSMENTS

Performance Level

Performance Elements	Exemplary	Proficient	Developing
	You consistently applied the relevant skills	You sometimes, but not always, applied the relevant skills.	You rarely or never applied the relevant skills.
Format two slide backgrounds with pictures and styles	Two slide backgrounds were formatted attractively and text displayed with good contrast against backgrounds.	Slide backgrounds were formatted but text did not display well, or only one slide background was formatted.	Slide backgrounds were not formatted with pictures or styles.
Insert and format appropriate table and chart	Appropriate table and chart were inserted and formatted and the entered data was accurate.	A table and a chart were inserted but were not appropriate for the presentation or either a table or a chart was omitted.	Table and chart were not inserted.
Apply appropriate animation	Appropriate animation was applied to the presentation.	Animation was applied but was not appropriate for the presentation.	Animation was not applied.

END | You have completed Project 3K

OUTCOMES-BASED ASSESSMENTS

RUBRIC

The following outcomes-based assessments are open-ended assessments. That is, there is no specific correct result; your result will depend on your approach to the information provided. Make Professional Quality your goal. Use the following scoring rubric to guide you in how to approach the problem and then to evaluate how well your approach solves the problem.

The *criteria*—Software Mastery, Content, Format and Layout, and Process—represent the knowledge and skills you have gained that you can apply to solving the problem. The *levels of performance*—Professional Quality, Approaching Professional Quality, or Needs Quality Improvements—help you and your instructor evaluate your result.

	Your completed project is of Professional Quality if you:	Your completed project is Approaching Professional Quality if you:	Your completed project Needs Quality Improvements if you:
1-Software Mastery	Choose and apply the most appropriate skills, tools, and features and identify efficient methods to solve the problem.	Choose and apply some appropriate skills, tools, and features, but not in the most efficient manner.	Choose inappropriate skills, tools, or features, or are inefficient in solving the problem.
2-Content	Construct a solution that is clear and well organized, contains content that is accurate, appropriate to the audience and purpose, and is complete. Provide a solution that contains no errors in spelling, grammar, or style.	Construct a solution in which some components are unclear, poorly organized, inconsistent, or incomplete. Misjudge the needs of the audience. Have some errors in spelling, grammar, or style, but the errors do not detract from comprehension.	Construct a solution that is unclear, incomplete, or poorly organized; contains some inaccurate or inappropriate content; and contains many errors in spelling, grammar, or style. Do not solve the problem.
3-Format & Layout	Format and arrange all elements to communicate information and ideas, clarify function, illustrate relationships, and indicate relative importance.	Apply appropriate format and layout features to some elements, but not others. Overuse features, causing minor distraction.	Apply format and layout that does not communicate information or ideas clearly. Do not use format and layout features to clarify function, illustrate relationships, or indicate relative importance. Use available features excessively, causing distraction.
4-Process	Use an organized approach that integrates planning, development, self-assessment, revision, and reflection.	Demonstrate an organized approach in some areas, but not others; or, use an insufficient process of organization throughout.	Do not use an organized approach to solve the problem.

OUTCOMES-BASED ASSESSMENTS

Apply a combination of the **3A** and **3B** skills.

Build from Scratch

GO! Think   Project 3L Animal Sanctuary

PROJECT FILES

For Project 3L, you will need the following file:

New blank PowerPoint presentation

You will save your presentation as:

Lastname_Firstname_3L_Animal_Sanctuary

The Pacifica Bay Animal Sanctuary, a non-profit organization, provides shelter and care for animals in need, including dogs, cats, hamsters, and guinea pigs. The Sanctuary, which celebrates its tenth anniversary in July, has cared for more than 12,000 animals since it opened and is a state-of-the-art facility. Funding for the Sanctuary comes in the form of business sponsorships, individual donations, and pet adoption fees. The following table indicates revenue generated by the Sanctuary during the past three years.

	Fees	Donations	Sponsorships
2014	125,085	215,380	175,684
2015	110,680	256,785	156,842
2016	132,455	314,682	212,648

In addition to shelter services, the Sanctuary offers community service and training programs, veterinarian services, and vaccine clinics. Examples of these services include Canine Obedience classes, microchipping ($25 fee), and the Healthy Pet Hotline (free). Canine Obedience classes are for puppies and adult dogs to improve obedience, socialization, and behavior. Classes last two, three, or four months and cost $150 to $250.

Using the preceding information, create the first five slides of a presentation that the director of the Pacifica Bay Animal Sanctuary will show at an upcoming pet fair. Apply an appropriate theme and use slide layouts that will effectively present the content. Include a line chart with the revenue data, a table with the community service programs information, and at least one slide formatted with a dog or cat on the slide background. Apply styles to the table and chart, and apply animation and slide transitions to the slides. Use the techniques that you practiced in this chapter so that your presentation is professional and attractive. Save the file as **Lastname_Firstname_3L_Animal_Sanctuary** and then insert a header and footer that includes the date and time updated automatically, the file name in the footer, and the page number. Add your name, your course name and section number, and the keywords **animals, pets** to the properties. Save and then print or submit the presentation as directed by your instructor.

END | You have completed Project 3L

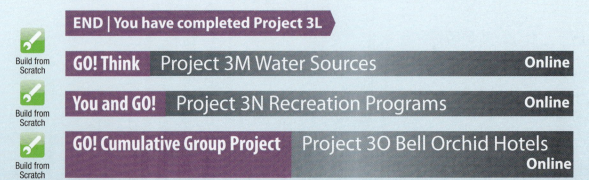

Build from Scratch

GO! Think   Project 3M Water Sources   **Online**

Build from Scratch

You and GO!   Project 3N Recreation Programs   **Online**

Build from Scratch

GO! Cumulative Group Project   Project 3O Bell Orchid Hotels   **Online**

Creating Templates and Reviewing, Publishing, Comparing, Combining, and Protecting Presentations

GO! to Work
Video P4

PROJECT 4A

OUTCOMES
Create and Apply a Custom Template.

OBJECTIVES
1. Create a Custom Template by Modifying Slide Masters
2. Apply a Custom Template to a Presentation

PROJECT 4B

OUTCOMES
Review, Publish, Compare, Combine, and Protect Presentations.

OBJECTIVES
3. Create and Edit Comments
4. Compare and Combine Presentations
5. Prepare a Presentation for Distribution
6. Protect a Presentation

Luis Louro/Fotolia

In This Chapter

PowerPoint provides built-in templates to use when creating a new presentation. You can create your own customized templates and reuse them. You can review and comment on the content of a presentation by inserting and editing comments in the file. You can compare two versions of a presentation to view the differences between the presentations. PowerPoint also provides several ways to share presentations with others: converting to PDF or XPS format or printing handouts. You can check a presentation for compatibility with other versions, protect the presentation from further editing by marking it as Final, and password protect it.

Attorneys at **Thompson Henderson Law Partners** counsel their clients on a wide variety of issues, including contracts, licensing, intellectual property, and taxation, with emphasis on the unique needs of the entertainment and sports industries. Entertainment clients include production companies, publishers, talent agencies, actors, writers, artists—anyone involved in creating or doing business in the entertainment industry. Sports clients include colleges and universities, professional sports teams, and athletes. Increasingly, sports coaches and organizations with concerns about liability are also seeking the firm's counsel.

Instructional Presentation

PROJECT ACTIVITIES

In Activities 4.01 through 4.10, you will design a template for the Thompson Henderson Law Partners to use to create presentations for meetings with the partners and clients. The template will contain formatting for the slide masters and shapes and images to add interest. Then you will use the template to create a presentation. You will also edit slide masters in an existing presentation in order to maintain uniformity in the slide designs. Your completed presentation will look similar to Figure 4.1.

PROJECT FILES

Build from Scratch

For Project 4A, you will need the following files:

New blank PowerPoint presentation
p04A_Law1.jpg

You will save your presentations as:

Lastname_Firstname_4A_Meeting_Template.potx
Lastname_Firstname_4A_Filing_Procedures.pptx

PROJECT RESULTS

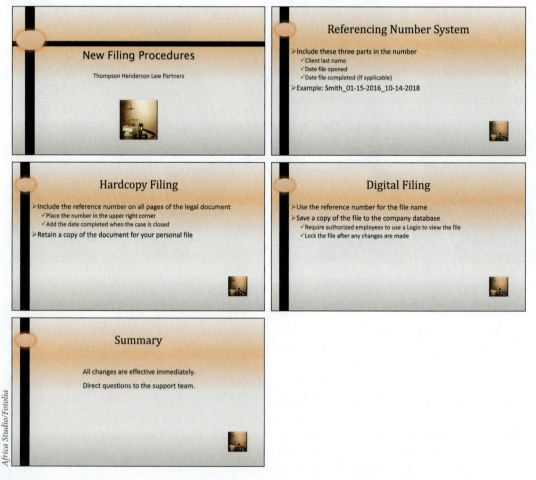

FIGURE 4.1 Project 4A Instructional Presentation

Video P4-1

A PowerPoint *template* is a predefined layout for a group of slides and is saved as a .potx file. You use a template to standardize the design of the slides in a presentation. A ***slide master*** is part of a template that stores information about the formatting and text that displays on every slide in a presentation. The stored information includes such items as the placement and size of text and object placeholders.

For example, if your company or organization has a logo that should be displayed on all slides of a presentation, the logo can be inserted one time on the slide master. That logo will then display in the same location on all slides of the presentation.

Activity 4.01 | Displaying and Editing Slide Masters

In this activity, you will change the Office Theme Slide Master background and the Title Slide Layout font and font size. You will start with a blank PowerPoint presentation file.

1 Start PowerPoint and then click **Blank Presentation**. On the Ribbon, click the **VIEW tab**. In the **Master Views group**, point to, but do not click, **Slide Master**. Read the **ScreenTip**: *Master slides control the look of your entire presentation, including colors, fonts, backgrounds, effects, and just about everything else. You can insert a shape or a logo on a slide master, for example, and it will show up on all your slides automatically.* Compare your screen with Figure 4.2.

In the Master Views group, notice the three views available—Slide Master, Handout Master, and Notes Master.

FIGURE 4.2

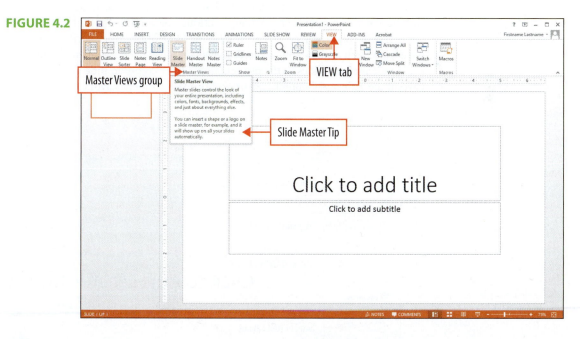

2 Click **Slide Master**. Take a moment to study the options associated with the **SLIDE MASTER tab**, as described in the table shown in Figure 4.3.

You are already familiar with editing themes, fonts, and colors by using the Edit Theme group, customizing a background by using the Background group, and modifying page setup and orientation by using the Size group. From the SLIDE MASTER tab, you can apply these changes to certain layouts or to the entire theme.

FIGURE 4.3

OPTIONS ON THE SLIDE MASTER TAB	
SCREEN ELEMENT	**DESCRIPTION**
Edit Master group	**Enables you to:**
Insert Slide Master	Add a new Slide Master to the presentation.
Insert Layout	Add a custom layout to the master slide set.
Delete	Remove this slide from your presentation.
Rename	Rename your custom layout so you can find it easily in the layout gallery.
Preserve	Preserve the selected master so that it remains with the presentation even if it is not used.
Master Layout group	**Enables you to:**
Master Layout	Choose the elements to include in the slide master.
Insert Placeholder	Add a placeholder to the slide layout to hold content, such as a picture, table, media, or text.
Title	Show or hide the title placeholder on this slide.
Footers	Show or hide the footer placeholders.

3 If necessary, scroll up, and then point to the first thumbnail to display the ScreenTip—**Office Theme Slide Master: used by slide(s) 1**. Compare your screen with Figure 4.4. Locate the **Title Slide Layout: used by slide(s) 1**, **Title and Content Layout: used by no slides**, and **Two Content Layout: used by no slide(s)** thumbnails.

In the Slide Master view, in the thumbnail pane, the larger slide image represents the slide master, and the associated layouts are smaller, positioned beneath it. The slide master is referred to as the Office Theme Slide Master. The **Office Theme Slide Master** is a specific slide master that contains the design, such as the background that displays on all slide layouts in the presentation. Changes made to it affect all slides in the presentation. Other common slide layouts include the Title Slide Layout, the Title and Content Layout, and the Two Content Layout.

FIGURE 4.4

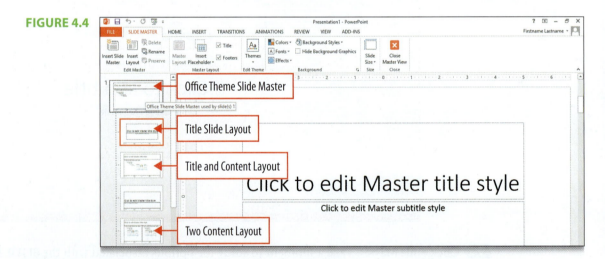

4 Click the first thumbnail—**Office Theme Slide Master**. In the **Background group**, click **Background Styles**. In the **Background Styles gallery**, locate **Style 10**, and then click it.

Notice that all slide layouts display with the same background style.

More Knowledge   **Slide Master - Add New Layouts**

You can create a custom layout in Slide Master view. In the Edit Master group, click Insert Layout. From there, you can make custom choices about four placeholders—Title, Date, Footer and Slide Number. In the Edit Master group, click the Rename button to assign a new name to your custom layout. Your custom layout is now available for use in a presentation and will display in the New Slide gallery.

5 Click the second thumbnail—**Title Slide Layout**. On the slide, click anywhere on the dashed border on the Master title style placeholder to display the border as a solid line. Click the **HOME tab**. In the **Font group**, change the font to **Lucida Sans Unicode**. Change the font size to **40**. Compare your screen with Figure 4.5.

The font and font size change affects only the Title Slide.

BY TOUCH   Tap to select second thumbnail—Title Slide Layout. On the slide, tap anywhere on the dashed border on the Master title style placeholder to display the border as a solid line. Tap the HOME tab. In the Font group, slide the arrow to select the font to Lucida Sans Unicode. Tap and slide the arrow to change the font size to 40.

ANOTHER WAY   You can also triple-click the text in the Master title style placeholder to select the text.

FIGURE 4.5

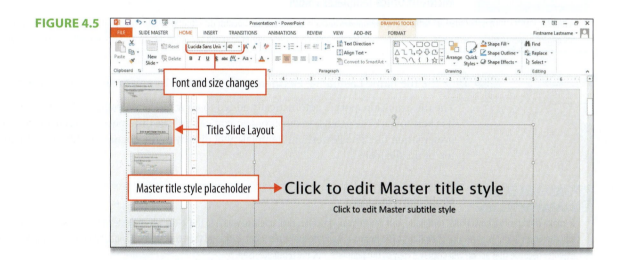

Activity 4.02 | Saving a Presentation as a Template

In this activity, you will save your design as a template.

1 Press F12 to display the **Save As** dialog box. At the right side of the **Save as type** box, click the **arrow** to display the file types. Point to, but do not click, **PowerPoint Template (*.potx)**. Compare your screen with Figure 4.6. Your display may differ slightly.

FIGURE 4.6

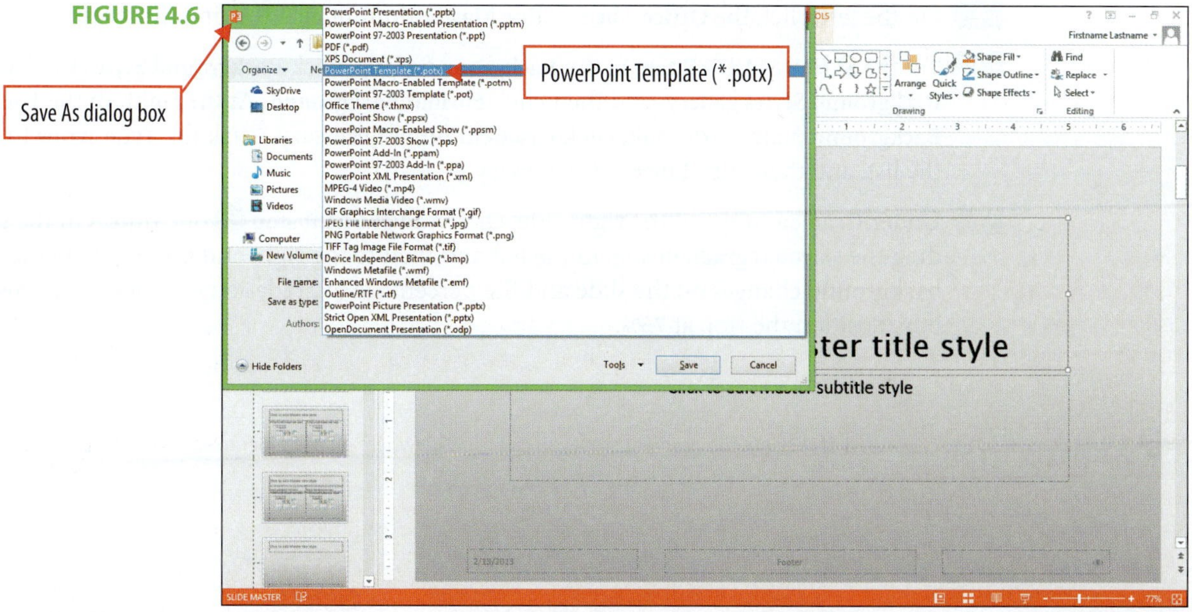

2 From the list of file types, click **PowerPoint Template (*.potx).**

N O T E   **Displaying File Extensions in Windows**

If the extension does not display after the file name, go to File Explorer. In Libraries, click the VIEW tab, and then in the Show/hide group, select the File name extensions check box.

3 Navigate to the location where you are saving your work and create a new folder named **PowerPoint Chapter 4**

Your PowerPoint Chapter 4 folder is created. You will use this folder to store your templates.

More Knowledge   **Microsoft Office Templates Folder**

When Microsoft Office is installed, a Custom Office Templates folder is created in the Documents Library. You can save your templates to the Custom Office Templates folder to make them easier to find. However, for the projects in this chapter, you will save your files to your PowerPoint Chapter 4 folder.

4 Type the file name **Lastname_Firstname_4A_Meeting_Template** and then click **Save.**

The file extension .potx is automatically added to your file name. When working with templates, it is best to have the extension displayed so you can tell the difference between a template and a presentation file. The PowerPoint template will display in file documents library with gold at the top of the file icon.

More Knowledge   **Modifying a Template**

To make changes to a PowerPoint template, start PowerPoint, click FILE, click Open, navigate to the folder where the template is saved, click the file name, and then click Open. You can also open it from File Explorer. Navigate to the file, right-click, and then click Open. Do not double-click on the file name in File Explorer because that action will display a copy of the template, not the template itself.

Activity 4.03 | Formatting a Slide Master with a Gradient Fill

In this activity, you will modify a gradient fill to the slide master background. A ***gradient fill*** is a gradual progression of several colors blending into each other or shades of the same color blending into each other. A ***gradient stop*** allows you to apply different color combinations to selected areas of the background.

1 On the left, click the **Office Theme Slide Master** thumbnail—the first thumbnail.

2 On the **SLIDE MASTER tab, in** the **Background group,** click **Background Styles** to display the **Background Styles gallery,** and then click **Format Background.** At the right, in the **Format Background** pane, under **Fill,** click **Gradient fill,** if necessary. Click the **Type arrow** to display the list, and then click **Linear,** if necessary.

3 Under **Gradient stops,** at the right side, click **Add gradient stop** one time. On the slider, drag the selected **gradient stop** to the left and then to the right and observe how the background changes on the slide and the percentage of gradation changes in the **Position** box. Position the stop at **75%.**

ANOTHER WAY   Instead of clicking Add gradient stop, you can click anywhere on the slider to add a gradient stop.

4 Click **Add gradient stop** 🔲 again to add another **gradient stop**, and then position it at **25%**. Click the **Color arrow**, and then, under **Theme Colors**, in the sixth column, fourth row, click **Orange, Accent 2, Lighter 40%**. Compare your screen with Figure 4.7.

Applying a gradient stop to the background makes the color vary smoothly from a darker to a lighter shade. The additional stop with a different color provides more interest.

🔄 **ANOTHER WAY**   You can position the gradient stop by typing the value or using the spin arrows in the Position spin box.

FIGURE 4.7

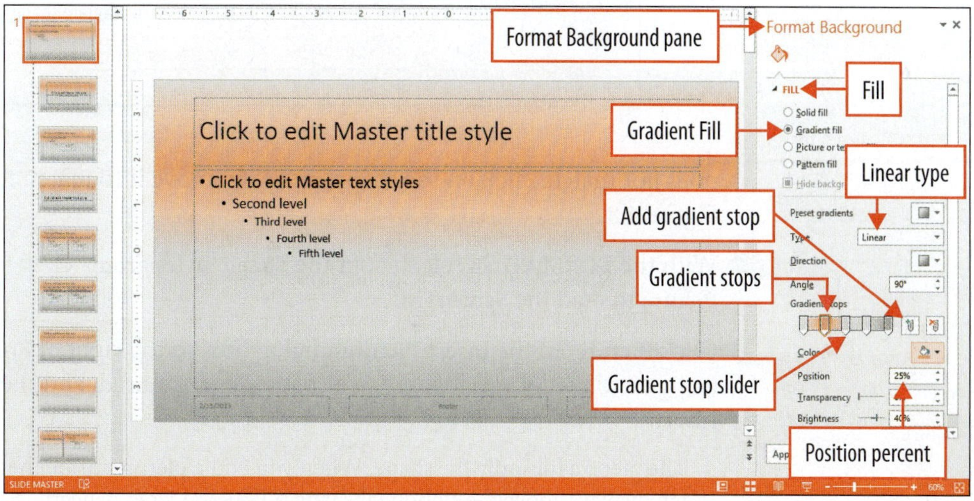

5 At the bottom of the **Format Background** pane, click **Apply to All**. At the top of the pane, click **Close** ❌.

All slide layout thumbnails are displayed with the gradient fill.

6 Save 💾 the template.

Activity 4.04 | Formatting Slide Masters by Adding Pictures and Shapes

In this activity, you will add and format a shape, and then insert a picture into the shape. Then you will duplicate the shape, move the copied shape to a different slide layout, resize and recolor it.

1 Click the **Title Slide Layout** thumbnail—the second thumbnail—to make the **Title Slide Layout Master** the active slide layout.

2 On the **VIEW tab**, in the **Show group**, select the **Ruler** check box to display the horizontal and vertical rulers, if necessary. Click the **INSERT tab**. In the **Illustrations group**, click **Shapes**. From the list, under **Rectangles**, click the **Rectangle** shape—the first shape. Position the pointer at **2 inches on the right side of the horizontal ruler** and **3 inches on the upper half of the vertical ruler**, and then click to insert the shape. It looks like a square.

When you insert a shape, a DRAWING TOOLS tab is displayed above the ribbon tabs. A context-sensitive FORMAT tab is displayed under the DRAWING TOOLS tab. When you deselect the shape, the DRAWING TOOLS and FORMAT tabs disappear.

3 With the shape still selected, on the ribbon, on the **DRAWING TOOLS FORMAT tab**, in the **Shapes Styles group**, click **Shape Effects**. From the list, click **Bevel**. Point to some of the effects and note the changes made to the rectangle. In the first row, under **Bevel**, click the first effect—**Circle**. In the **Shapes Styles group**, click **Shape Outline**, and then click **No Outline**.

Removing the border softens the appearance of the shape.

4 With the rectangle still selected, in the **Size group**, change the **Shape Height** to **2"** and the **Shape Width** to **2"**. Compare your screen with Figure 4.8. If the placement of your rectangle

FIGURE 4.8

does not match, click on the shape, and then move it to match the position shown in Figure 4.8.

5 With the **FORMAT tab** selected, in the **Shape Styles group**, click **Shape Fill**, and then point to **Picture** to read the **ScreenTip**.

6 Click **Picture**. In the **Insert Pictures** dialog box, to the right of **From a file**, click **Browse**, navigate to the location where your data files are stored, and then click **p04A_Law1.jpg** Click **Insert**.

> The picture fills only the shape. When you add a picture inside the shape, a PICTURE TOOLS tab displays above the ribbon tabs with a FORMAT tab beneath it. One FORMAT tab is for the DRAWING TOOLS for the shape. The other FORMAT tab is for the PICTURE TOOLS for the picture you inserted. When you deselect the shape, both the DRAWING TOOLS and PICTURE TOOLS tabs disappear.

7 With the shape still selected, in the **Arrange group**, click **Align** to see the alignment options. Click **Align Center**. Click **Align** again, and then click **Align Bottom**.

> The shape with the picture aligns in the horizontal center at the bottom of the slide.

8 With the shape still selected, on the **HOME tab**, in the **Clipboard group**, click **Copy**. Click the **Title and Content Layout** thumbnail, which is the third thumbnail. In the **Clipboard group**, click **Paste**.

> The copied shape maintains the same format and position.

9 From the Ribbon, on the **DRAWING TOOLS FORMAT tab**, in the **Size group**, change the **Shape Height** to **1"** and the **Shape Width** to **1"**.

> The copied shape is resized.

10 With the shape still selected, hold down the Shift key, and then click on the dashed border of the content placeholder. In the **Arrange group**, click **Align**, and then click **Align Right**. Click **Align** again, and then click **Align Bottom**.

11 On the ribbon, on the **PICTURE TOOLS FORMAT tab**, in the **Adjust group**, click **Color**. Under **Recolor**, in the second row, click the third color—**Orange, Accent color 2 Dark**. Compare your screen with Figure 4.9.

> The logo now appears on the first slide of your presentation and then displays in a smaller format on slides using the title and content layout. If you wanted to have the logo on other slide layouts, you could copy the small logo to those layouts as well.

FIGURE 4.9

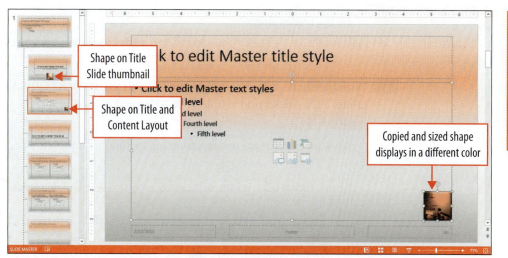

Shape on Title Slide thumbnail

Shape on Title and Content Layout

Copied and sized shape displays in a different color

12 Save 🖫 the template. At the top of the **Format Shape** pane, click **Close** ☒ , if necessary.

Activity 4.05 | Formatting Slide Masters by Adding Shapes and Shape Effects

In this activity, you will add and format shapes, and then add a glow effect to shapes.

1 Click the **Office Theme Slide Master** thumbnail—the first thumbnail. On the **VIEW tab**, in the **Show group**, select the **Guides** check box to display the horizontal and vertical guides, if not already checked.

Light orange dotted guide lines display on the slide on both the horizontal and vertical rulers at zero.

2 At the top of the slide, move your mouse pointer over the orange dotted line until the mouse pointer changes into a double arrow ⟺ . Drag the light orange dotted **vertical guide line** ⟺ to the left to **5.5 inches on the left side of the horizontal ruler**. Click the light orange dotted **horizontal guide line** ⇕ and drag it up to **2 inches on upper half of the vertical ruler**.

3 Click the **Title Slide Layout** thumbnail—the second thumbnail. Click the **INSERT tab**. In the **Illustrations group**, click **Shapes**. From the list, under **Rectangles**, click the **Rectangle** shape—the first shape. To insert the rectangle, position the pointer at **6 inches on the left side of the horizontal ruler**, aligning it with the top edge of the slide. Click and **drag across the top edge of the slide 0.5 inch to 5.5 inches on the horizontal ruler** to the edge of the vertical guide line, continue holding, and then **drag down along the vertical guide line** to the bottom edge of the slide, aligning it with the bottom edge of the slide, and then release. Compare your screen with Figure 4.10.

FIGURE 4.10

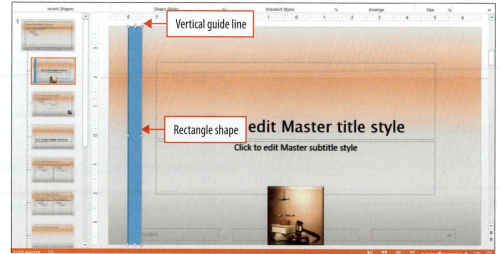

Vertical guide line

Rectangle shape

edit Master title style

Click to edit Master subtitle style

ALERT!   **Are the Guides Visible?**

If you cannot see the light orange dotted guide line, deselect the Guides check box, and then reselect the Guides check box.

4 With the shape still selected, on the **DRAWING TOOLS FORMAT tab**, in the **Shapes Styles group**, click the second visible style—**Colored Fill – Black, Dark 1**. Compare your screen with Figure 4.11.

A black vertical shape displays from top to bottom on the left side of the slide.

BY TOUCH Tap the FORMAT tab. In the Shapes Styles group, tap to select the second visible style—Colored Fill – Black, Dark 1.

FIGURE 4.11

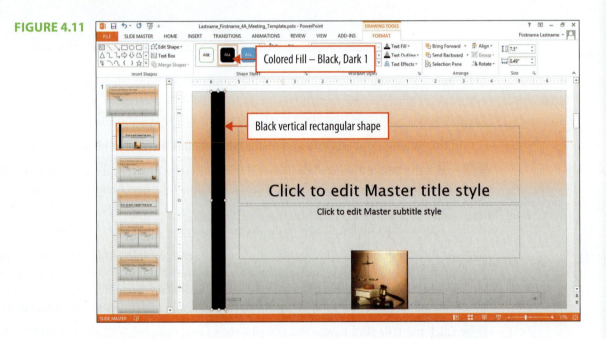

Black vertical rectangular shape

5 Click the **INSERT tab**. In the **Illustrations group**, click **Shapes**. From the list, under **Rectangles**, click the **Rectangle** shape. Position the pointer at **1.75 inches on the upper half of the vertical ruler**, aligning it with the left edge of the slide. **Drag up the edge of the slide .25 inches to 2.0 inches on the vertical ruler** to the edge of the horizontal guide line, continue holding, and then **drag to the right along the horizontal guide line**, aligning it with the right edge of the slide, and then release. With the shape still selected, on the ribbon, on the **DRAWING TOOLS FORMAT tab**, in the **Shapes Styles group**, click the second visible style—**Colored Fill – Black, Dark 1**. Compare your screen with Figure 4.12.

FIGURE 4.12

Horizontal rectangle shape, Colored Fill – Black, Dark 1

6 ▶ Click the **INSERT tab**. In the **Illustrations group**, click **Shapes**. From the list, under **Basic Shapes**, click the **Oval** shape—the second shape. Point to the intersection of the two black lines and click one time to insert the shape. With the oval still selected, in the **Size group**, change the **Shape Height** to **1"** and the **Shape Width** to **1.5"**. In the **Size group**, click the **dialog launcher** ⬜. Click **Position** to expand. In the **Horizontal position** box, type **0.2** and then press ⏎. In the **Vertical position** box, type **1.2** and then press ⏎.

The oval shape is positioned over the intersection of the two black lines.

7 ▶ With the shape still selected, on the ribbon, in the **Shapes Styles group**, click the **More arrow** ⬇. From the list, in the fourth row, click the third item—**Subtle Effect – Orange, Accent 2**. With the shape still selected, click the **Shape Effects arrow**. From the list, click **Glow**, and then under **Glow Variations**, in the second column, click the last item—**Orange, 18 pt glow, Accent color 2**. Compare your screen with Figure 4.13.

A black horizontal and vertical shape line with a soft glowing oval shape display on the upper portion of the slide.

FIGURE 4.13

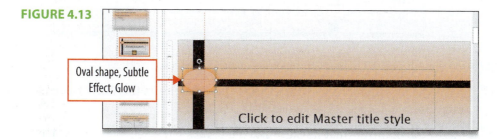

Oval shape, Subtle Effect, Glow

Click to edit Master title style

8 ▶ Click the **Office Theme Slide Master** thumbnail—the first thumbnail. Click the light orange dotted **vertical guide line** and drag to the left to **5.75 inches on the left side of the horizontal ruler**.

9 ▶ Click the **Title and Content Layout** thumbnail—the third thumbnail. Click the **INSERT tab**. In the **Illustrations group**, click **Shapes**. From the list, under **Rectangles**, click the **Rectangle** shape—the first shape. Position the pointer at **6.25 inches on the left side of the horizontal ruler**, aligning it with the top edge of the slide. Click and **drag across the top edge of the slide 0.5 inch to 5.75 inches on the horizontal ruler** to the edge of the vertical guide line, continue holding, and then **drag down along the vertical guide line** to the bottom edge of the slide, aligning it with the bottom edge of the slide, and then release. With the shape still selected, on the **DRAWING TOOLS FORMAT tab**, in the **Shapes Styles group,** click the second visible style—**Colored Fill – Black, Dark 1**. Compare your screen with Figure 4.14.

FIGURE 4.14

Vertical black rectangle shape

Click to edit Master text styles
· Second level

10 ▶ Click the **INSERT tab**. In the **Illustrations group**, click **Shapes**. From the list, under **Basic Shapes**, click the **Oval** shape. Click to insert the oval shape near the intersecting guide lines. With the oval shape selected, in the **Size group**, change the **Shape Height** to **0.7"** and the **Shape Width** to **1"**. In the **Size group**, click the **dialog launcher** ⬜. In the **Format Shape** pane, under **Position**, in the **Horizontal position** box, type **0.2** and then press ⏎. In the **Vertical position** box, type **0.8** and then press ⏎. Compare your screen with Figure 4.15.

FIGURE 4.15

11 With the shape still selected, on the **DRAWING TOOLS FORMAT tab**, in the **Shapes Styles group**, click the **More arrow** ▼. From the list, in the fourth row, click the third column—**Subtle Effect – Orange, Accent 2**. With the shape still selected, on the **DRAWING TOOLS FORMAT tab**, in the **Shapes Styles group**, click **Shape Effects**. From the list, click **Glow**, and then under **Glow Variations**, in the second column, click the last item—**Orange, 18 pt glow, Accent color 2**. Compare your screen with Figure 4.16.

FIGURE 4.16

12 At the top of the **Format Shape** pane, click **Close** ⊠.

13 Click the first thumbnail—**Office Theme Slide Master**. On the **VIEW tab**, in the **Show group**, select the **Guides** check box to deselect.

14 At the top of the **Format Background** pane, click **Close** ⊠. **Save** 🖫 the template.

Activity 4.06 | Customizing Placeholders on a Slide Master

In this activity, you will change the size and position of the placeholders on the Title Slide master, format the footer placeholder, and then change the bullet types on the Title and Content Slide master.

1 Click the **Title Slide Layout** thumbnail to make it the active slide. Click anywhere on the dashed border for the **title placeholder**, hold down the Shift key, and then drag the entire placeholder so the top border is at **3.5 inches on the upper half of the vertical ruler**. Release the Shift key. Click anywhere on the dashed border for the **subtitle placeholder**, hold down the Shift key, and then drag the entire placeholder so the top border is at **0.5 inch on the upper half of the vertical ruler**. Release the Shift key.

Moving a placeholder does not change the size of it. Using the Shift key while dragging the placeholder constrains the placeholder to either perfect vertical movement or perfect horizontal movement.

2 With the **subtitle placeholder** still selected, drag the **bottom middle sizing handle** to **0.5 inches on the lower half of the vertical ruler** to decrease the size of the placeholder. Compare your screen with Figure 4.17.

Using the sizing handle changes the size of the placeholder.

FIGURE 4.17

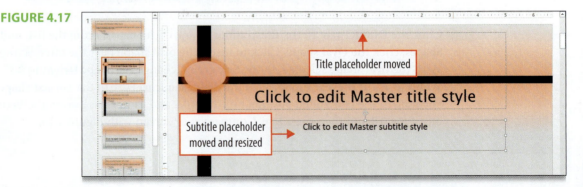

3 ▶ Click the **Office Theme Slide Master** thumbnail to make it the active slide. Click anywhere in the first bulleted line. On the **HOME tab**, in the **Paragraph group**, click the **Bullets button arrow**, and then click **Bullets and Numbering**. In the **Bullets and Numbering** dialog box, click the **Bulleted tab** if necessary. Click **Arrow Bullets**. At the bottom left, click the **Color button arrow**. Under **Theme Colors**, in the sixth column, click the last color—**Orange, Accent 2, Darker 50%**. Compare your screen with Figure 4.18. Click **OK**.

FIGURE 4.18

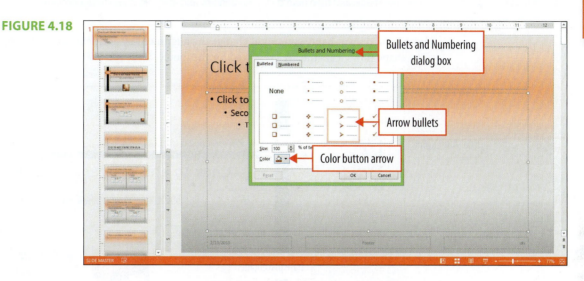

4 ▶ Click anywhere in the second bulleted line. Using the procedure that you used for the first bulleted line, display the **Bullets and Numbering** dialog box. Click the **Filled Square Bullets**. Click the **Color button arrow**, and then in the sixth row, last column, click **Orange, Accent 2, Darker 50%**. Click **OK**. Compare your screen with Figure 4.19.

All slides in the presentation will automatically display these custom bullets for the first two levels of the outline. If you intend to have more levels in your outline, you can continue customizing them.

FIGURE 4.19

More Knowledge   **Customizing Bullets on Different Slide Masters**

When you customize the bullets on the Office Theme Slide Master, the customized bullets are available on all slides. If you want different bullets on some of the slide masters, customize the slide masters, separately. For example, you could change the bullets on the Title and Content Layout and then change the bullets on the Two Content Layout.

---

5 ▶ With the first thumbnail, the **Office Theme Slide Master,** selected, click anywhere on the dashed border of the date placeholder, at the bottom left of the slide, to select the date. On the **HOME tab**, change the **font size** to **10**.

↻ **ANOTHER WAY**   Highlight the date to select the date placeholder.

6 Click the **Title Slide Layout** thumbnail. Select and drag the rectangle picture shape so the top of the rectangle aligns at **1.0 inches on the lower half of the vertical ruler**. On the **DRAWING TOOLS FORMAT tab**, in the **Arrange group**, click **Align**, and then select **Align Center**. Click outside to deselect the shape. Compare your screen with Figure 4.20.

ANOTHER WAY   Select the shape, and then hold down the Shift key and drag the shape to the desired location.

When you drag a shape, you might change the alignment by accident, so set the alignment again. The shape now clears the area reserved for the footer.

FIGURE 4.20

7 With the **SLIDE MASTER tab** selected, in the **Close group**, click **Close Master View**.

ANOTHER WAY   On the status bar, click Normal to close the Master View.

8 Save 🖫 the template.

Activity 4.07 | Displaying and Editing the Handout Master

In this activity, you will edit the Handout Master for the meeting template you are building for the Thompson Henderson Law Partners. You can print your presentation in the form of handouts that your audience can use to follow along as you give your presentation, or keep for future reference. The *Handout Master* specifies the design of presentation handouts for an audience. You will learn how to change from landscape to portrait orientations, set the number of slides on a page, and specify whether you want to include the header, footer, date, and page number placeholders. Because you are working in a template file rather than a presentation file, the changes to the master affect presentations created from this template. You may change the settings in each presentation if you wish.

1 With the **Lastname_Firstname_4A_Meeting_Template** open, click the **VIEW tab**, and then in the **Master Views group**, click **Handout Master**. In the **Page Setup group**, click **Handout Orientation**, and then notice that the default orientation is **Portrait**. Click **Slide Size**, and then notice that the default orientation is **Widescreen**. Leave the settings as they are. Compare your screen with Figure 4.21.

The Portrait handout orientation means that the slides will print on paper that is 8.5" wide by 11" long. The Landscape handout orientation means that the slides will print on paper that is 11" wide by 8.5" long.

FIGURE 4.21

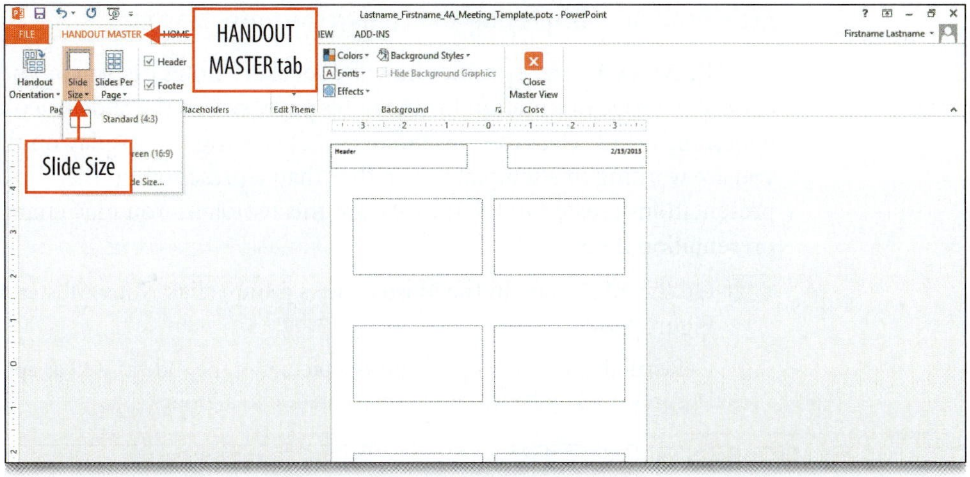

2 In the **Page Setup group**, click **Slides Per Page**. Click **3 Slides**. Compare your screen with Figure 4.22.

You can print the handouts with 1, 2, 3, 4, 6, or 9 slides per page.

FIGURE 4.22

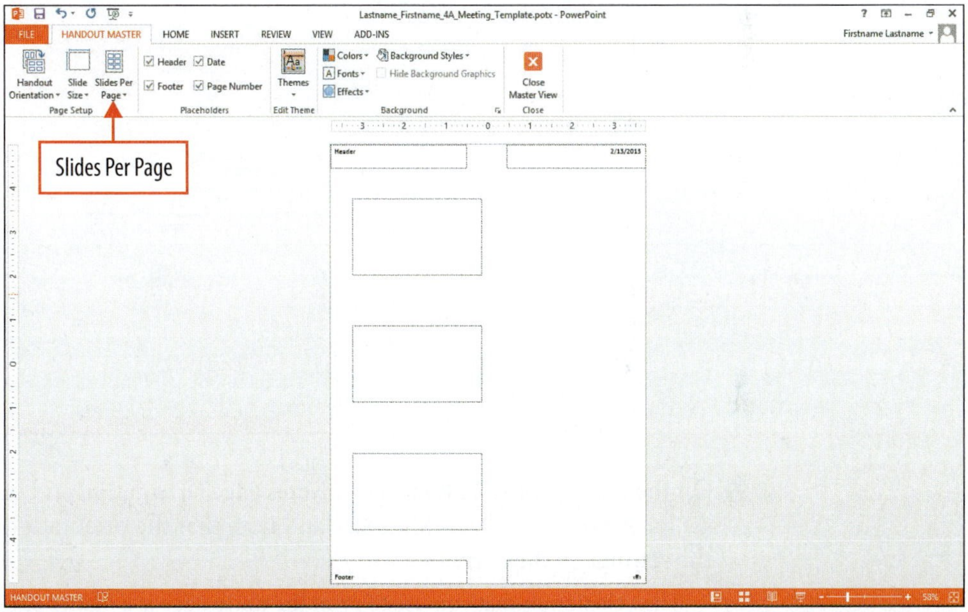

3 In the **Placeholders group**, click **Header** to clear the check mark. Compare your screen with Figure 4.23.

Notice that the Header placeholder disappears. The placeholders for the notes master include Header, Footer, Date, and Page Number.

FIGURE 4.23

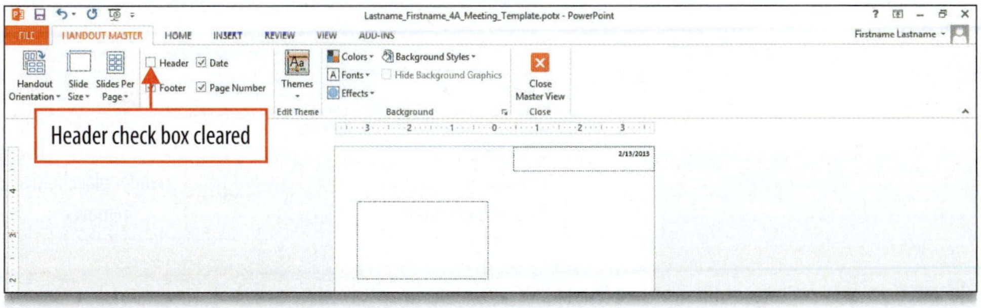

4 In the **Close group**, click **Close Master View**.

5 **Save** 🖫 the template.

Activity 4.08 | Displaying and Editing the Notes Master

The *Notes Master* specifies how the speaker's notes display on the printed page. You can choose the page orientation for the notes page, switch the slide orientation between standard and widescreen, and select the placeholders that you want to display on the printed page. Because you are working in a template file rather than a presentation file, the changes to the master affect presentations created in the future from this template. You may change the settings in each presentation if you wish.

1 On the **VIEW tab**, in the **Master Views group**, click **Notes Master**. Compare your screen with Figure 4.24.

Recall that the Notes page shows a picture of the slide as well as appropriate notes to assist the speaker when delivering the presentation to a group.

FIGURE 4.24

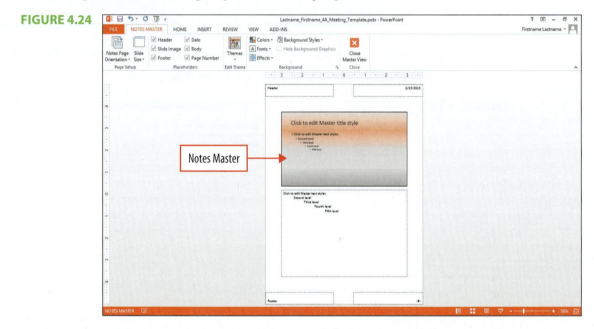

2 On the **NOTES MASTER tab**, click **Notes Page Orientation** and observe that the orientation is set for **Portrait**. Click the **Slide Size** and note that the orientation is set for **Widescreen**. Leave the settings as they are.

The orientation that you use to print the notes page is a matter of personal preference and what works best for the content of the presentation.

3 In the **Placeholders group**, click **Header** to clear the check mark. Compare your screen with Figure 4.25.

Notice that the Header placeholder disappears. The placeholders for the notes master include Header, Slide Image, Footer, Date, Body, and Page Number.

FIGURE 4.25

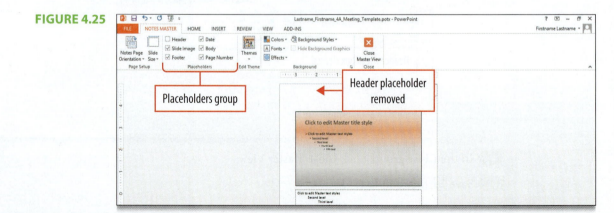

4 ▸ In the **Close group**, click **Close Master View**.

5 ▸ On the **INSERT tab**, in the **Text group** click **Header & Footer** to display the Header and Footer dialog box. click the **Notes and Handouts tab**. Under **Include on page**, select the **Date and time** check box, and then select **Fixed**. If necessary, clear the **Header** check box, and then select the **Page number** and **Footer** check boxes. In the footer box, using your own name, type **Lastname_Firstame_4A_Meeting_Template** and then click **Apply to All**.

6 ▸ Click the **FILE tab**, and then in the lower right portion of the screen, click **Show All Properties**. In the **Tags** box, type **template, meeting** and in the **Subject** box type, your course name and section number. In the **Author** box, right-click the existing author name, click **Edit Property**, replace the existing text with your first and last name, click outside the text box to deselect, and then click **OK**.

7 ▸ **Save** 🖫 the template, and then close the template file but leave PowerPoint open.

Objective 2 Apply a Custom Template to a Presentation

Video P4-2

Activity 4.09 | Applying a Template to a Presentation

In this activity, you will use the meeting template to create a slide presentation that explains the new filing procedures to the law partners. Recall that you are saving your template in your PowerPoint Chapter 4 folder.

1 ▸ Click **FILE**, and then click **New**. Compare your screen with Figure 4.26. For complete descriptions of the templates and themes, see Figure 4.27.

> Several template options display—search online template and themes, categories for suggested searches, a blank presentation, and other pre-built themes. Recall that a PowerPoint template is a file that contains layouts, theme colors, theme fonts, theme effects, background styles, and content. It contains the complete blueprint for slides pertaining to a specific kind of presentation. A theme includes coordinated colors and matched backgrounds, fonts, and effects.

FIGURE 4.26

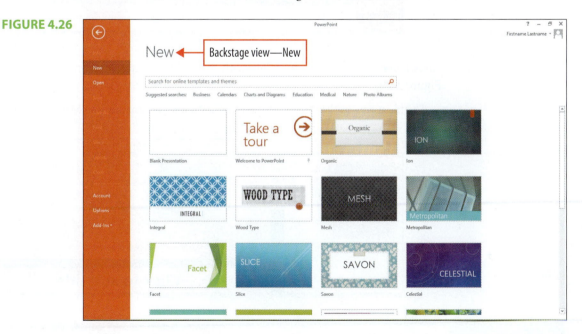

FIGURE 4.27

AVAILABLE TEMPLATES AND THEMES	
AVAILABLE TEMPLATES AND THEMES	**DESCRIPTION**
Search box	Search online templates and themes.
Suggested searches	Templates designed for specific uses, such as a Business, Calendars, Charts and Diagrams, Education, Medical, Nature, and Photo Albums.
Blank presentation	Default template that contains no content.
Themes	Templates with themes already added.

2 ▶ Click **Open**, and then navigate to the location where you are saving your files. Locate **Lastname_Firstname_4A_Meeting_Template.potx** Click the file name one time, and then compare your screen with Figure 4.28.

The extension for a PowerPoint template is *.potx* and the extension for a PowerPoint presentation is *.pptx*.

FIGURE 4.28

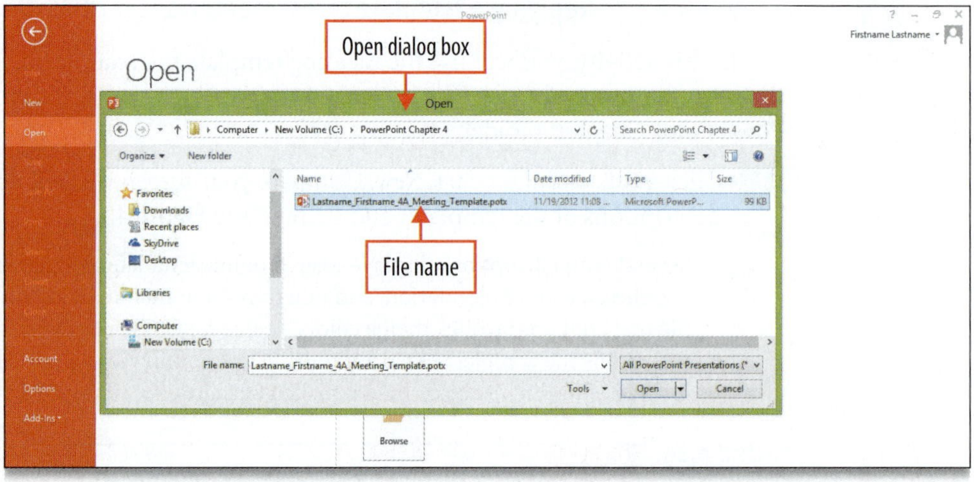

3 ▶ Click **Open** to display the template with the Title slide active. Compare your screen with Figure 4.29.

The file name on the title bar displays as Lastname_Firstname_4A_Meeting_Template.potx

FIGURE 4.29

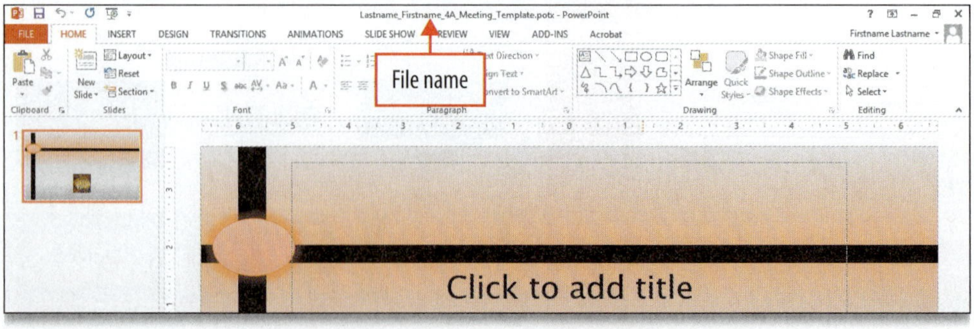

More Knowledge   **Opening a Template**

If you need to edit a template, start PowerPoint. Click FILE, click Open, navigate to your storage location, and then open the file. You can also open a template by navigating to it in File Explorer, right-clicking the file name, and then clicking Open. Make sure that you see the .potx at the end of the file name in the title bar. To open a template saved in the Template folder on your computer, you have to know the path to the template.

4 ▸ Press F12 to display the **Save As** dialog box. Navigate to the location where you are saving your files, if necessary, and then at the right side of the **Save as type** box, click the arrow to display the file types. Click **PowerPoint Presentation (*.pptx),** and then save the file as **Lastname_Firstname_4A_Filing_Procedures**

> The file name on the title bar displays as Lastname_Firstname_4A_Filing_Procedures.pptx.

5 ▸ Click the title placeholder, and then type **New Filing Procedures** Click the subtitle placeholder, and then type **Thompson Henderson Law Partners**

🔄 **ANOTHER WAY**   Press the keyboard shortcut Ctrl + Enter to move to the subtitle placeholder.

6 ▸ On the **HOME tab**, in the **Slides group**, click the **New Slide button arrow**. The gallery shows the formatting you created for the slide layouts. Compare your screen with Figure 4.30.

FIGURE 4.30

7 ▸ Click **Title and Content** to add the slide and make it the active slide. In the title placeholder, press Ctrl + E to center the text. Type **Referencing Number System** Press Ctrl + Enter to move to the content placeholder. In the content placeholder, type **Include these three parts in the number** and then press Enter. In the **Paragraph group**, click **Increase List Level** 📇 to increase the outline level. Type **Client last name** Press Enter, and then type **Date file opened** Press Enter, type **Date file completed (if applicable)** and then press Enter.

> When you increase an outline level, the text moves to the right. When you press Enter, the same outline level continues. When you press Ctrl + E, the text centers. When you press Ctrl + Enter, the cursor moves to the next placeholder.

🔄 **ANOTHER WAY**   Use the Tab key to increase the outline level. Use the Shift + Tab key combination to decrease the outline level.

8 ▸ In the **Paragraph group**, click **Decrease List Level** 📇 to decrease the outline level. Type **Example: Smith_01-15-2016_10-14-2018**

> To move the text to the left, you need to decrease the outline level.

9 ▸ In the **Slides group**, click the **New Slide button arrow**, and then click **Title and Content** to add a third slide. Click in the title placeholder, press Ctrl + E, type **Hardcopy Filing** and then press Ctrl + Enter. Following the procedure explained for the previous slide, type the following bulleted items for the Hardcopy Filing slide in the content placeholder.

Include the reference number on all pages of the legal document

    Place the number in the upper right corner

    Add the date completed when the case is closed

Retain a copy of the document for your personal file

 **ANOTHER WAY**   To add a slide with the same layout as the previous slide, you can click New Slide without displaying the gallery.

10 At the bottom of the PowerPoint window, on the **status bar**, click **NOTES** ⬒ to activate the notes pane, if necessary. In the **NOTES pane**, click in the placeholder and type **The ending date is the actual date that the case is closed. Until then, leave the ending date blank.** Compare your screen with Figure 4.31.

FIGURE 4.31

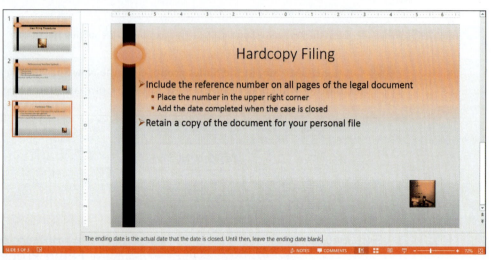

11 In the **Slides group**, click the **New Slide button arrow**, and then click **Title and Content** to add another slide. In the title placeholder, press Ctrl + E, type **Digital Filing** and then press Ctrl + Enter. In the content placeholder, type the following bulleted items, and then compare your screen with Figure 4.32:

Use the reference number for the file name

Save a copy of the file to the company database

    Require authorized employees to use a Login to view the file

    Lock the file after any changes are made

FIGURE 4.32

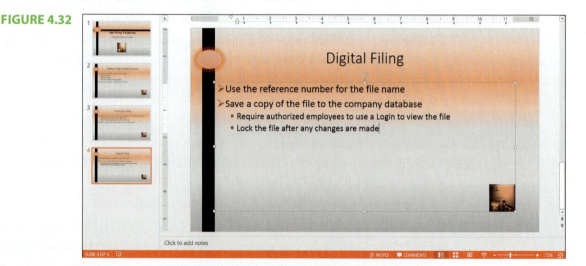

12 In the **Slides group**, click the **New Slide button arrow**, and then click **Title and Content** to add another slide. In the title placeholder, press Ctrl + E, type **Summary** In the content placeholder, type **All changes are effective immediately. Direct questions to the support team.** On the **HOME tab**, in the **Paragraph group**, click **Bullets** to remove the bullet. In the **Paragraph group**, click **Center**.

13 With the content placeholder selected, on the left side of the content placeholder, click the **middle sizing handle**, and then drag the sizing handle to **3.5 inches on the left side of the horizontal ruler**. On the right side of the content placeholder, drag the **middle sizing handle** to **3.5 inches on the right side of the horizontal ruler**. With the content placeholder still selected, at the bottom of the content placeholder, drag the **middle sizing handle** to **0.5 inches on the lower half of the vertical ruler** to reduce the size of the placeholder. Hold down the Shift key, and then click the top border of the content placeholder. Drag the entire placeholder down so the top is aligned at **1.5 inches on the upper half of the vertical ruler**. Release the Shift key. In the **Paragraph group**, click **Line Spacing**, and then click **1.5**. Compare your screen with Figure 4.33.

FIGURE 4.33

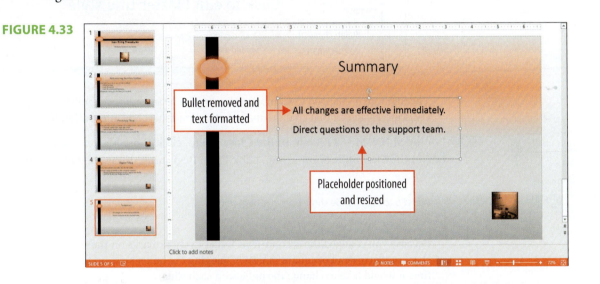

14 On the **INSERT tab**, in the **Text group**, click **Header & Footer** to display the **Header and Footer** dialog box. Click the **Notes and Handouts tab**. Under **Include on page**, select the **Date and time** check box, and then select **Fixed** and type today's date. If necessary, clear the **Header** check box, and then select the **Page number** and **Footer** check boxes. In the **Footer** box, using your own name, type **Lastname_Firstname_4A_Filing_Procedures** and then click **Apply to All**.

15 Click the **FILE tab**, and then in the lower right portion of the screen, click **Show All Properties**. In the **Tags** box, type **filing, number, system** and in the **Subject** box type your course name and section number. In the **Author** box, right-click the existing author name, click **Edit Property**, replace the existing text with your first and last name, click outside text box to deselect, and then click **OK**.

16 Save 💾 the presentation.

Activity 4.10 | Editing Slide Masters in an Existing Presentation

Occasionally, you might want to change the master design for a presentation created from your custom template. In this activity, you will change the bullet style on the Title and Content Layout slide master.

1 With **Lastname_Firstname_4A_Filing_Procedures** open, on the **VIEW tab**, in the **Master Views group**, click **Slide Master**.

2 Scroll up as necessary, and click the first thumbnail— **Office Theme Slide Master**. On the **SLIDE MASTER tab**, in **Background group**, click **Fonts**, and then click **Office 2007-2010**.

3 In the content placeholder, click the second bulleted line. On the **HOME tab**, in the **Paragraph group**, click the **Bullets button arrow**. Click **Checkmark Bullets**. Compare your screen with Figure 4.34.

FIGURE 4.34

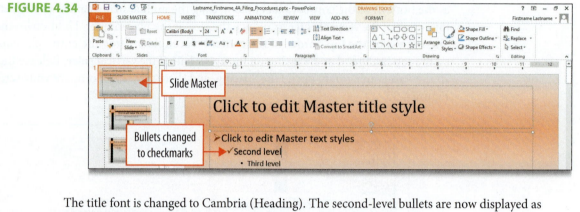

The title font is changed to Cambria (Heading). The second-level bullets are now displayed as checkmarks. Recall that changes made to the first thumbnail affect all slides.

4 On the **SLIDE MASTER tab**, in the **Close group**, click **Close Master View**. On the **SLIDE SHOW tab**, in the **Start Slide Show group**, click **From Beginning**. View the entire slide presentation.

🔁 **ANOTHER WAY**   Press F5 to start a slide show from the beginning.

Because you changed the second-level bullet to checkmarks on the slide master, all slides have checkmarks instead of square bullets. Changing the bullet style on the master slide saved you the time it would take to change the bullets on each slide.

5 Save 🖫 your presentation. Print **Handouts 3 Slides**, or submit your presentation electronically as directed by your instructor.

The change that you made to the bullets affects only this presentation. The original meeting template still uses the square bullets. If you want the change to be permanent on the template, you should open the template and make the change in that file.

6 Click **Close** ☒ to close the presentation and **Exit** PowerPoint.

7 Submit **Lastname_Firstname_4A_Meeting_Template** and **Lastname_Firstname_4A_Filing_ Procedures** as directed by your instructor.

END | You have completed Project 4A

PROJECT ACTIVITIES

In Activities 4.11 through 4.20, you will use reviewing comments to provide feedback to a presentation created by a colleague at the Thompson Henderson Law Partners firm. You will use editing tools, such as the thesaurus. You will compare two versions of a presentation to view the differences between the presentations. Then you will publish your presentation in both PDF and XPS formats. These formats preserve the document formatting and enable file sharing. You will save the presentation as Word handouts for the audience. Finally, you will check your presentation for compatibility with previous versions of PowerPoint and mark the presentation as final. You will password protect your presentation. Your completed presentation will look similar to Figure 4.35.

PROJECT FILES

For Project 4B, you will need the following files:

p04B_Entertainment_Basics.pptx
p04B_Entertainment_Basics2.pptx

You will save your presentations as:

Lastname_Firstname_4B_Entertainment_Basics.pptx
Lastname_Firstname_4B_Entertainment_Basics.pdf
Lastname_Firstname_4B_Entertainment_Basics.xps
Lastname_Firstname_4B_Entertainment_Basics.docx

PROJECT RESULTS

Figure 4.35 Project 4B Commented Presentation

Video P4-3

A **comment** is a note that you can attach to a letter or word on a slide or to an entire slide. People use comments to provide feedback on a presentation. A **reviewer** is someone who adds comments to the presentation to provide feedback.

Activity 4.11 | Adding Comments

In this activity, you will add comments to your meeting presentation. Comments may be added by the person who created the presentation, or other persons who are invited to provide suggestions.

1 Start PowerPoint. Locate and open the file **p04B_Entertainment_Basics.pptx** Navigate to the location where you are storing your folders and projects for this chapter, and then **Save** the file as **Lastname_Firstname_4B_Entertainment_Basics**

2 Make **Slide 2** the active slide. Click the **REVIEW tab**. In the **Comments group**, point to each of the buttons, and read the **ScreenTips**. Compare your screen with Figure 4.36. For a complete explanation of each of these buttons, see Figure 4.37.

FIGURE 4.36

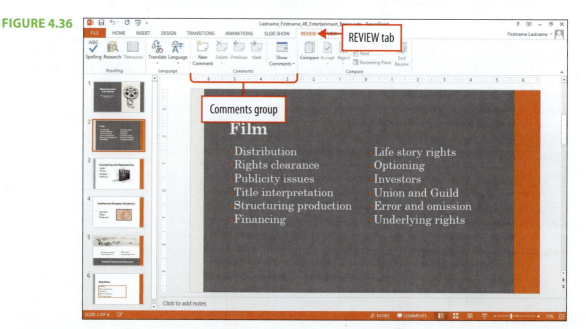

FIGURE 4.37

REVIEWING ELEMENTS	
SCREEN ELEMENT	**DESCRIPTION**
Comments group	
New Comment	Add a note about this part of the document.
Delete	Delete the selected comment.
Previous	Jump to the previous comment.
Next	Jump to the next comment.
Show Comments – Comments Pane	Show the Comments pane to view, add, and delete comments. Comments are not displayed during a slide show.
Show Comments – Show Markup	Show comments and other annotations.

3 In the **Comments group**, click **New Comment**. In the space provided in the Comments pane, type **Comprehensive List!** In the Comments group, all buttons become active. Compare your screen with Figure 4.38.

FIGURE 4.38

When there are no comments in the file, two buttons in the Comments group are active—New Comment and Show Comments which provides access to the Comments Pane. When a comment is added, the relevant buttons become active. When no placeholder or text is selected before adding a comment, by default the comment icon displays at the upper left corner of the slide. The comment displays in the Comments pane. The name of the person that entered the comment displays in the upper left corner of the comment box and the date or time displays in the upper right corner.

More Knowledge   **Comments**

The Comments pane allows you to view and track comments next to the text being discussed, see who replied to who and when, similar to a threaded style conversation. Additional participants can reply and join the conversation.

---

4 Make **Slide 3** the active slide. Click at the end of the third bulleted item, after *Directors*. In the **Comments** pane, click **New**. Type **What kind of directors?** Click outside the comment to deselect it. Compare your screen with Figure 4.39.

Placing the insertion point within a specific area of the slide will position the comment box at that place.

FIGURE 4.39

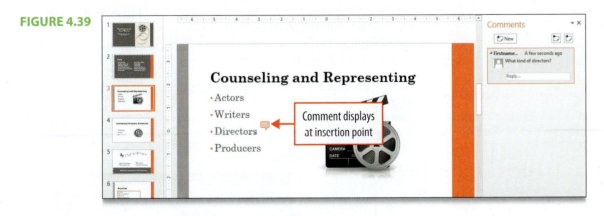

5 Make **Slide 4** the active slide. Select the word *Copyright*. Use the procedure explained in the previous steps to add this comment: **Add short definitions.** Click outside the comment to deselect it.

When you add a comment to selected text, the comment is displayed near the selected text.

6 Select **Slide 5**, and then enter this comment: **Is the word "agreements" necessary?** Click outside the comment. Drag the comment so it is positioned under the words "*Production agreements.*" Compare your screen with Figure 4.40.

When you add a new comment, the default location is the upper left corner of the slide unless you specify otherwise. You can drag a comment box to any position on the slide. Note that bold, underline, and italic are not available in the comment box.

 BY TOUCH   Tap New Comment. Type this comment: **Is the word "agreements" necessary?** Click outside the comment, and then use your finger to drag the comment so it is positioned directly below the last line, under the word Production.

FIGURE 4.40

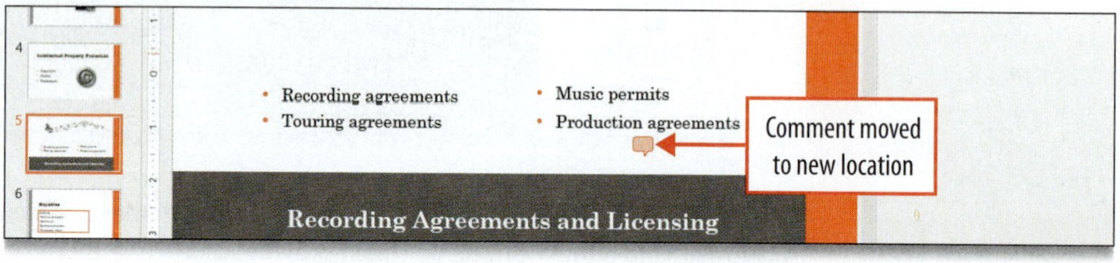

Recording agreements   Music permits
Touring agreements   Production agreements

Comment moved to new location

Recording Agreements and Licensing

7 Save the presentation.

Activity 4.12 | Reading Comments

In this activity, you will learn how to navigate among the comments entered in a presentation.

1 On **Slide 2**, with the **REVIEW tab** selected, in the **Comments group**, click the **Show Comments arrow**, and then click **Show Markup**. Notice that the comment disappears and the **Comments** pane closes. Click the **Show Comments arrow**, and then click **Show Markup** again to redisplay the comment on the slide. Click the **Show Comments arrow**, and then click **Comments Pane** to redisplay the **Comments** Pane.

The Show Comments button Comments Pane and Show Markup options display a check mark when activated.

2 Make **Slide 1** the active slide. In the **Comments group**, click **Next**. The first comment displays in the **Comments** pane so you can read it. Click **Next** again to read the second comment, which is on **Slide 3**. Continue clicking **Next** until you see the message *PowerPoint reached the end of the presentation. Do you want to continue from the beginning?* Compare your screen with Figure 4.41. Click **Cancel**.

FIGURE 4.41

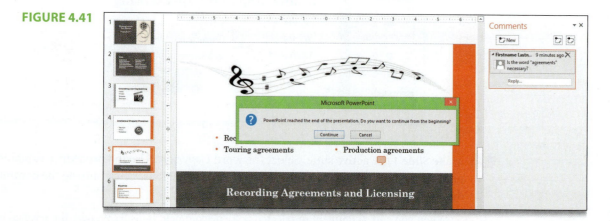

3 In the **Comments group**, click **Previous** to read the previous comment. Continue clicking **Previous** until you receive this message: *PowerPoint reached the beginning of the presentation. Do you want to continue from the end?* Click **Cancel**.

Use the Next and Previous buttons to read the comments in your presentation.

Activity 4.13 | Editing Comments

In this activity, you will learn how to edit a comment and how to delete a comment.

1 On **Slide 2**, in the **Comments** pane, under the first comment, click in the **Reply** box, and then type **Allow time to cover these**. Click outside the comment to close it. Compare your screen with Figure 4.42.

An additional comment by the same author is added in the Comments pane. The author's identifying information displays with the date and time of the comment. Two comment icons display in the upper left portion of the slide.

FIGURE 4.42

2 Click **Next** until you reach the comment on **Slide 4**. In the **Comments group**, click the **Delete button arrow**, and then read the three options: *Delete, Delete All Comments and Ink on This Slide,* and *Delete All Comments and Ink in This Presentation*. Compare your screen with Figure 4.43.

FIGURE 4.43

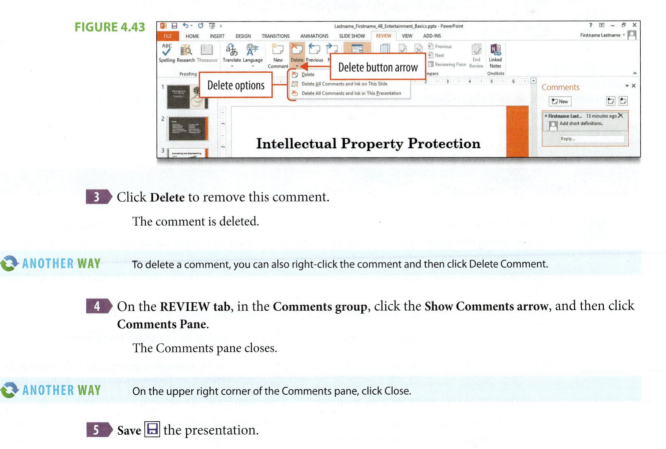

3 Click **Delete** to remove this comment.

The comment is deleted.

ANOTHER WAY   To delete a comment, you can also right-click the comment and then click Delete Comment.

4 On the **REVIEW tab**, in the **Comments group**, click the **Show Comments arrow**, and then click **Comments Pane**.

The Comments pane closes.

ANOTHER WAY   On the upper right corner of the Comments pane, click Close.

5 **Save** 🖫 the presentation.

Activity 4.14 | Using the Thesaurus

You can use the Thesaurus to replace a word in a presentation with a *synonym*—a word having the same or nearly the same meaning as another.

 Display **Slide 5**. In the content placeholder on the right, in the second column, locate the word *permits*.

2 Right-click **permits**, and then on the shortcut menu, point to **Synonyms**. Compare your screen with Figure 4.44.

A list of words with the same meaning as *permits* displays.

FIGURE 4.44

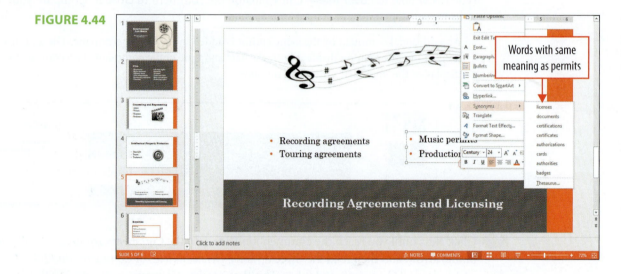

3 Click **licenses** to change the word *permits* to *licenses*.

4 Save 💾 your presentation.

More Knowledge   The Thesaurus

When a word is selected, you can display the Thesaurus pane by clicking on Thesaurus on the REVIEW tab, in the Proofing group, by pressing Shift + F7 , or by clicking Thesaurus on the Synonyms submenu on the shortcut menu. The Thesaurus pane displays a complete Thesaurus of synonyms and *antonyms*—words with an opposite meaning.

Objective 4   Compare and Combine Presentations

Video P4-4

PowerPoint offers a way to compare and combine presentations by merging them into a single presentation, highlighting and listing the differences. You can then manually review the changes and choose the edits for the final presentation. This feature is useful if you work with others on presentations, or if you just want to see what differences exist between two versions of a presentation.

Activity 4.15 | Comparing and Combining Presentations

In this activity, you will view two versions of a presentation to compare their differences.

1 Click **Slide 1** to make it active. On the **REVIEW tab**, in the **Compare group**, click **Compare**. In the **Choose File to Merge with Current Presentation** dialog box, navigate to your student data files for this chapter, and then click **p04B_Entertainment_Basics2**, and then click **Merge**.

The Revisions pane opens on the right side of the slide. The Revisions pane is used to locate all instances in which the two presentations differ.

2 ▶ In the **Revisions** pane, verify that the **DETAILS tab** displays in orange, and if necessary, make it the active tab. Compare your screen with Figure 4.45.

The Revisions pane DETAILS tab is divided into two sections—Slide Changes and Presentation Changes. The Slide Changes section indicates differences between the two presentations for the active slide. The Presentation Changes section lists entire slides that were added or removed when the two presentations were merged.

FIGURE 4.45

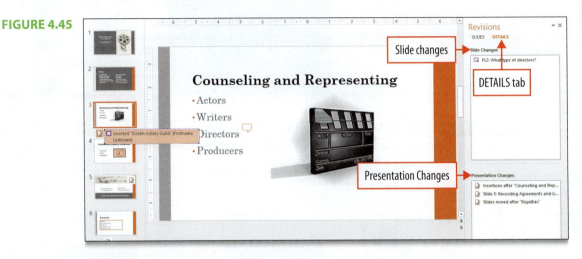

3 ▶ In the **Revisions** pane, under **Presentation Changes**, click **Insertions after "Counseling and Rep…"** to display a **Revisions** check box in the **Slides and Outline** pane on the left. Compare your screen with Figure 4.46.

You can use the Revisions check box to accept or reject the addition of the slide. Your Lastname_Firstname_p04B_Entertainment_Basics presentation does not include this suggested revision; the slide is in the p04B_Entertainment_Basics2 presentation.

FIGURE 4.46

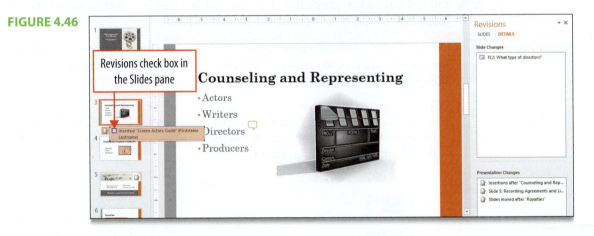

4 ▶ Select the **Revisions** check box that says *Inserted "Screen Actors Guild"*. Compare your screen with Figure 4.47.

The slide is inserted in your presentation. If the Revisions check box is left blank, the slide is not inserted.

FIGURE 4.47

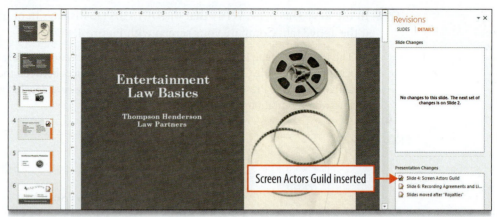

> **5** Display **Slide 2** and notice that a **Revisions button** 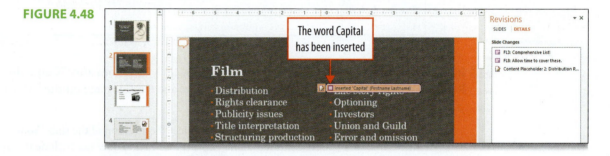 displays on the slide. Click the **Revisions** button to display the **Revisions** check box. Compare your screen with Figure 4.48.

> This revision indicates that the word Capital has been inserted from the p04B_Entertainment_Basics2 presentation.

FIGURE 4.48

> **6** Select the **Revisions** check box that indicates *Inserted "Capital"* to accept the change and insert the word *Capital* in the last bullet of column 1.

> **7** Display **Slide 6**. In the **Revisions** pane, under **Presentation Changes**, click **Slide 6: Recording Agreements and Li…** to display a **Revisions** check box in the **Slides and Outline** pane on the left. Compare your screen with Figure 4.49.

> You can use the Revisions check box to accept or reject the move of the "Recording Agreements and Licensing" slide after Slide 7: "Royalties". Your Lastname_Firstname_p04B_Entertainment_Basics presentation does not include this suggested revision; the slide moved is in the p04B_Entertainment_Basics2 presentation.

FIGURE 4.49

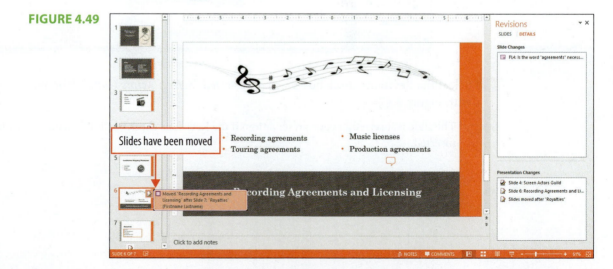

8 Do *not* select the **Revisions** check box on the **Slide 6** thumbnail.

9 In the **Revisions** pane, under **Presentation Changes**, click **Slides moved after "Royalties"** to display a **Revisions** check box under **Slide 7** in the **Slides and Outline** pane on the left. Do *not* select the **Revisions** check box under the **Slide 7** thumbnail.

> The revisions to Slides 6 and 7 are not accepted.

10 On the **REVIEW tab,** in the **Compare group**, click **End Review**, and then in the **Microsoft PowerPoint** dialog box, click **Yes. Save** 💾 your presentation.

> The presentation is now merged with the selected changes, the revisions to Slides 6 and 7 are not included, and the Revisions pane closes. The unapplied changes were discarded.

More Knowledge | **View Multiple Presentations**

You can view two presentations side by side to see the differences between them. On the VIEW tab, in the Window group, click Arrange All. The presentations display side by side on the screen.

Objective 5 | Prepare a Presentation for Distribution

Video P4-5

PowerPoint offers several ways to share, or distribute, a presentation. A common way is to create a PDF document that people who have Adobe Reader installed on their computers can read. You can also create an XPS document that people who have an XPS viewer can read. Another way to share a presentation is to create handouts in Microsoft Word.

Activity 4.16 | Publishing a Presentation in PDF and XPS Format

In this activity, you will save a presentation in PDF and XPS file formats. Adobe's ***Portable Document Format (PDF)*** preserves document formatting and enables file sharing. The PDF format is also useful if you intend to use commercial printing methods. ***XML Paper Specification (XPS)*** is Microsoft's electronic paper format, an alternative to the PDF format that also preserves document formatting and enables file sharing. When an XPS or PDF file is viewed online or printed, it retains the format that you intended, and the data in the file cannot be easily changed.

1 Open **Lastname_Firstname_4B_Entertainment_Basics**, if necessary. On the **INSERT tab**, in the **Text group**, click **Header & Footer** to display the **Header and Footer** dialog box. Click the **Notes and Handouts tab**. Under **Include on page**, select the **Date and time** check box, and then select **Fixed** and type today's date, if necessary. Clear the **Header** check box, if necessary, and then select the **Page number** and **Footer** check boxes. In the **Footer** box, using your own name, type **Lastname_Firstname_4B_Entertainment_Basics** and then click **Apply to All**.

2 Make **Slide 1** active. Click **FILE**, and then click **Export**. Under **Export**, **Create PDF/XPS Document** is selected. On the right side of your screen, read the explanation of a PDF/XPS document. Compare your screen with Figure 4.50.

> Presentations saved as PDF/XPS documents are saved in a fixed format. The document looks the same on most computers. Fonts, formatting, and images are preserved. Because content cannot be easily changed, your document is more secure. To view a PDF or XPS file, you must have a viewer installed on your computer. Free viewers are available on the web to view PDF and XPS documents.

FIGURE 4.50

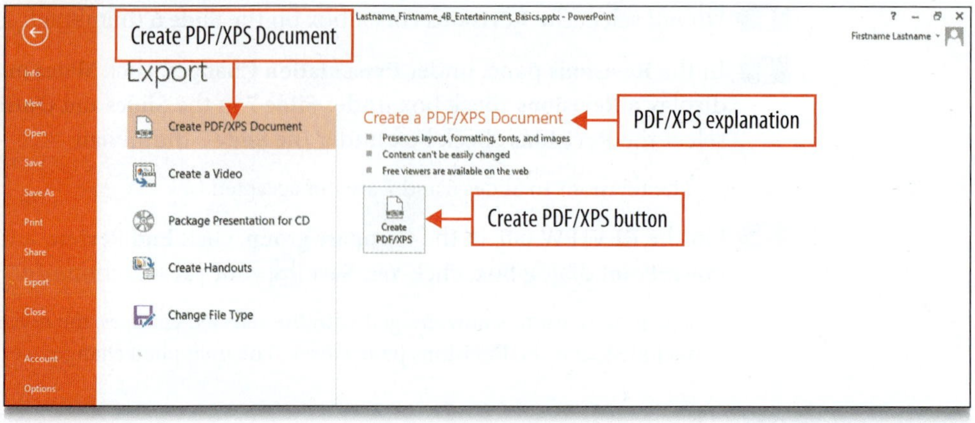

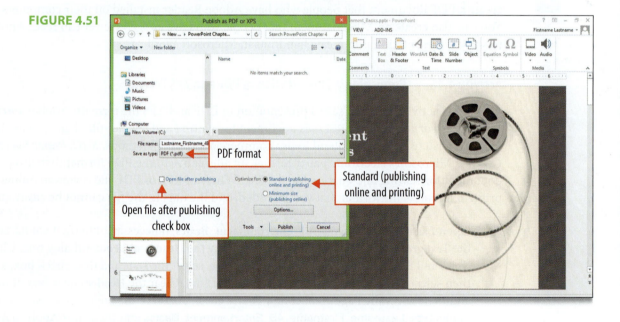

3 Click **Create PDF/XPS**. In the **Publish as PDF or XPS** dialog box, click the **Save as type arrow** to see the two file formats—PDF (*.pdf) and XPS Document (*.xps). Click **PDF (*.pdf)**. If necessary, click the option button for **Standard (publishing online and printing)** to select the print quality. If necessary, clear the **Open file after publishing** check box. Compare your screen with Figure 4.51.

> Choose Standard (publishing online and printing) if the presentation requires high print quality. If the file size is more important than the print quality, click Minimum size (publishing online).

FIGURE 4.51

4 In the **Publish as PDF or XPS** dialog box, click **Options** located in the lower right area of the dialog box.

5 In the **Options** dialog box under **Publish options**, click the **Publish what arrow** to see the choices—Slides, Handouts, Notes pages, and Outline view. Click **Handouts**, and then on the right side of the dialog box, click the **Slides per page arrow**. Click **3**, and then view the preview showing how the printed page will look. Select the **Include comments and ink markup** check box. Compare your screen with Figure 4.52.

> The options to publish a presentation as a PDF file are the same as the options to print the file.

FIGURE 4.52

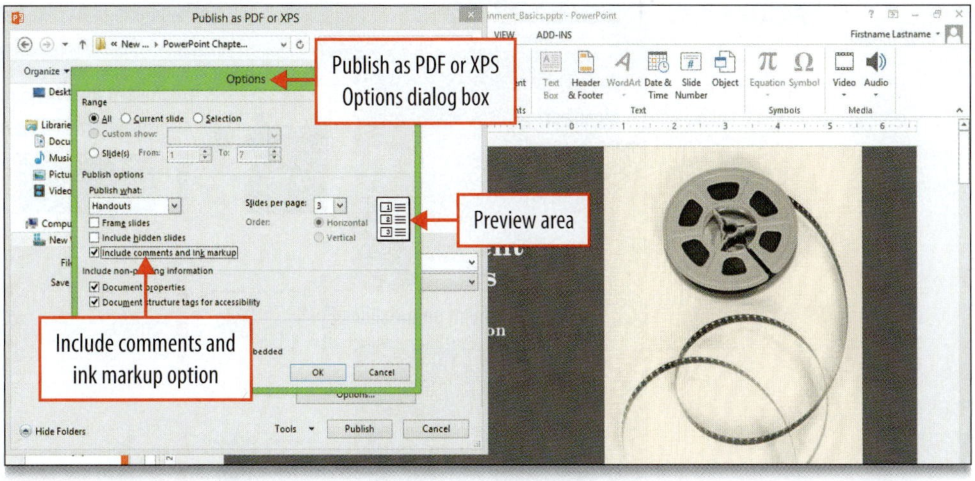

Publish as PDF or XPS Options dialog box

Preview area

Include comments and ink markup option

🔄 **ANOTHER WAY**   Enter the page number in the text box to change pages in the PDF.

---

6 ▶ Click **OK**. Click **Publish**. The document is published (saved) in PDF format in the location where you are saving your work.

Lastname_Firstname_4B_Entertainment_Basics.pdf is located in the same folder as your original PowerPoint presentation file.

N O T E	**Reading PDF Files**

A common application used to open PDF files is Adobe Reader. If you don't have Adobe Reader on your computer, you can download it free from www.adobe.com.

---

7 ▶ Click **FILE**, and then click **Export**. Under **Export**, **Create PDF/XPS Document** is selected. Click **Create PDF/XPS**. In the **Publish as PDF or XPS** dialog box, change the file type to **XPS Document (*.xps)**. Click **Options**. Click the **Publish what arrow**, and then click **Handouts**. Click **Include comments and ink markup**. Click **OK**. Select the **Open file after publishing** check box. Click **Publish**. The presentation is saved as an XPS document and opens in the XPS Viewer. Maximize your window and press Ctrl + N to view all 6 slides on one page. The menu bar on the XPS Viewer provides options to set permissions and digitally sign a document. Compare your screen with Figure 4.53.

The handouts are displayed with 6 slides per page. The comment numbers are displayed on the slides. Your file is saved on your storage media as Lastname_Firstname_4B_Entertainment_Basics. xps in the same folder as your original PowerPoint presentation file. You can only view XPS documents with an XPS Viewer, such as the one provided in Microsoft Windows. You can also download a free copy of the XPS Viewer at www.microsoft.com. Only presentations formatted in PowerPoint 2000 or later versions can be saved and viewed in the XPS Viewer.

FIGURE 4.53

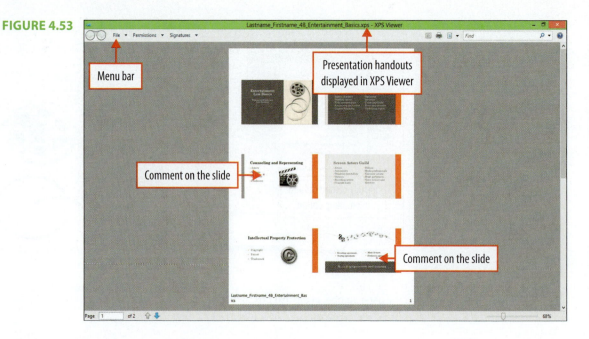

> Menu bar

> Presentation handouts displayed in XPS Viewer

> Comment on the slide

> Comment on the slide

8 ▸ Click **File**, and then click **Exit** to close the file and XPS Viewer.

🔄 **ANOTHER WAY**   To close the file and the viewer, press [Alt] + [F4].

Activity 4.17 | Creating Handouts in Microsoft Word

In this activity, you will create handouts that open in Microsoft Word.

1 ▸ In **PowerPoint**, click **FILE**, click **Export**, and then under **Export**, click **Create Handouts**. At the right, under **Create Handouts in Microsoft Word**, read the explanation. Compare your screen with Figure 4.54.

The handout is a document that contains the slides and notes from the presentation. You can use Word to change the layout and format and even add additional content to the handout. If you link the handout file to your presentation, changes in your presentation will automatically update the handout content.

FIGURE 4.54

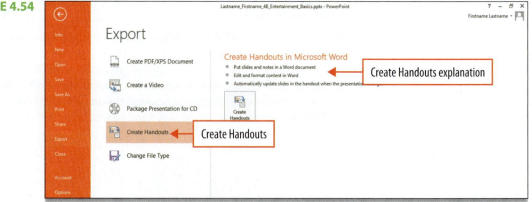

> Create Handouts explanation

> Create Handouts

2 ▸ Click **Create Handouts** to display the **Send to Microsoft Word** dialog box. Under **Add slides to Microsoft Word document**, click **Paste link**. Compare your screen with Figure 4.55.

> To ensure that any changes you make to the PowerPoint presentation are reflected in the Word document, use Paste link. Each time you open the Word document, you will be prompted to accept or reject the changes. The link for the Word file and the PowerPoint file will be broken if either of the files are moved from their folder location.

FIGURE 4.55

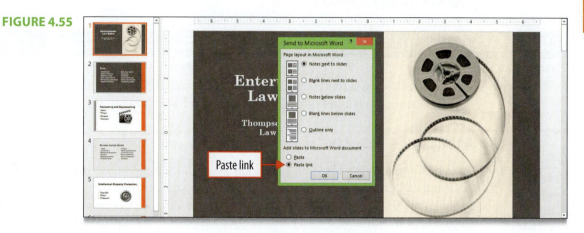

3 ▸ Click **OK**. Click **Word** on the taskbar to see the presentation slides displayed in a new Word document. Compare your screen with Figure 4.56.

FIGURE 4.56

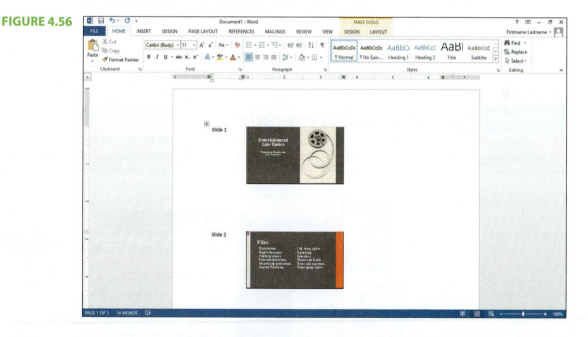

4 ▸ In the Word document, click the **INSERT tab**. In the **Header & Footer group**, click **Footer**, and then click **Edit Footer**. At the left, type **Lastname_Firstname_4B_Entertainment_Basics** Press the Tab key two times, and then type the current date. On the **DESIGN tab**, in the **Close group**, click **Close Header and Footer**.

5 ▸ Press F12 to display the **Save As** dialog box. Navigate to the location where you are saving your work, and then save the Word file as **Lastname_Firstname_4B_Entertainment_Basics Close** the Word document and return to the presentation file.

6 ▸ Click the **FILE tab** to display **Backstage** view. On the right, at the bottom of the **Properties** list, click **Show All Properties**.

7 ▸ On the list of **Properties**, click to the right of **Tags** to display an empty box, and then type **mission, agreements, licensing, film, royalties**

8 ▸ Click to the right of **Subject** to display an empty box, and then type your course name and section number. In the **Author** box, right-click the existing author name, click **Edit Property**, replace the existing text with your first and last name, click outside text box to deselect, and then click **OK**.

9 ▸ **Save** 💾 the presentation.

Objective 6 │ Protect a Presentation

Video P4-6

In the following activities, you will check the compatibility of your file with previous versions of PowerPoint as well as mark your presentation as final and then save it as read-only.

Activity 4.18 │ Using the Compatibility Checker

The *Compatibility Checker* locates any potential compatibility issues between PowerPoint 2013 and earlier versions of PowerPoint. It will prepare a report to help you resolve any issues. PowerPoint 2013 files are compatible with 2007 and 2010 files because they use the same file format (.pptx). However, PowerPoint 2013 does not support saving files to PowerPoint 95 or earlier. If necessary, you can save the presentation in *compatibility mode*, which means to save it as a PowerPoint 97-2003 Presentation.

1 ▸ Click **FILE**. To the left of **Inspect Presentation**, click **Check for Issues**, and then click **Check Compatibility**. Read the report displayed in the **Microsoft PowerPoint Compatibility Checker** dialog box. Compare your screen with Figure 4.57.

The Compatibility Checker summary identifies parts of the presentation that cannot be edited in earlier versions because those features are not available.

More Knowledge │ **Saving Presentations in Other File Formats**

If you exchange PowerPoint presentations with other people, you may save the presentation in other formats. Click FILE, click Export, click Change File Type, and then you may change the file type to PowerPoint 97-2003 Presentation. Other options include PowerPoint Show and PowerPoint Picture Presentation.

FIGURE 4.57

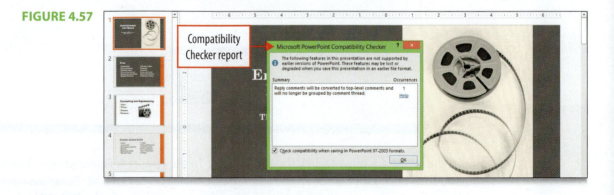

2 ▸ Click **OK**.

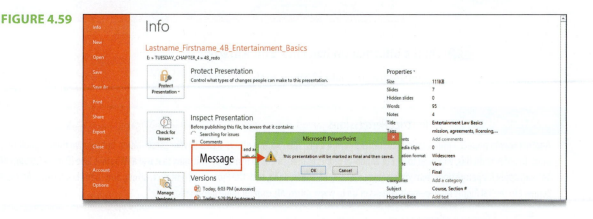 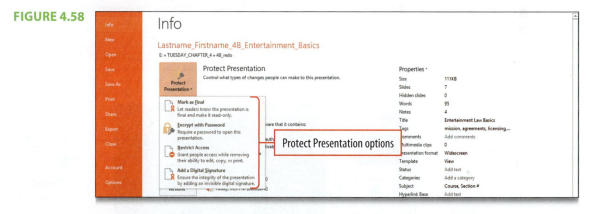

More Knowledge | **Check Accessibility**

You can check the presentation for content that people with disabilities might find difficult to read. To access this, on the Info tab, click the Check for Issues arrow, and then click Check Accessibility. An Accessibility Checker pane displays Inspection Results. You can then select and fix each issue listed in the pane to make the document accessible for people with disabilities. For example, you can add alternative text to describe a picture on the slide.

Activity 4.19 | **Marking a Presentation as Final**

In this activity, you will use the **Mark as Final** command to make your presentation document read-only in order to prevent changes to the document. Additionally, the Status property of the document is set to Final and the Mark as Final icon displays in the status bar.

1 Click **FILE**. Notice that Protect Presentation allows you to: *Control what types of changes people can make to this presentation.* Under **Info**, click the **Protect Presentation arrow**, and then examine the Protect Presentation options. Compare your screen with Figure 4.58.

The options to protect a presentation are Mark as Final, Encrypt with Password, Restrict Access, and Add a Digital Signature.

FIGURE 4.58

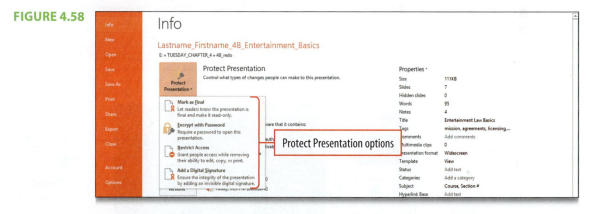

2 Click **Mark as Final**. Notice in the **Microsoft PowerPoint** dialog box that the presentation will be marked as final and then saved. Compare your screen with Figure 4.59.

The Mark as Final command helps prevent reviewers or readers from accidentally making changes to the document. Because the Mark as Final command is not a security feature, anyone who receives an electronic copy of a document that has been marked as final can edit that document by removing Mark as Final status from the document.

FIGURE 4.59

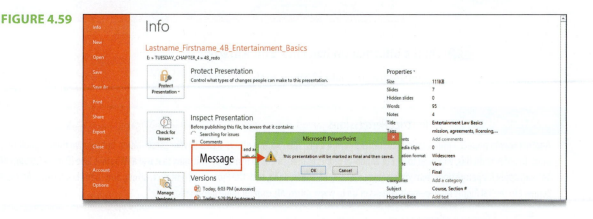

3 Click **OK**. A **Microsoft PowerPoint** dialog box displays that reminds you that the document will be saved as final. The message also tells you that a **Mark as Final** icon will display in the status bar. Compare your screen with Figure 4.60.

FIGURE 4.60

4 Click **OK**. Note the information bar at the top and the **Marked as Final** icon at the bottom left on the status bar. Compare your screen with Figure 4.61.

The information bar provides the option to edit the file even though you marked it as final, so be aware that others will be able to make changes. Marking the presentation as final tells others that you encourage them not to do this.

FIGURE 4.61

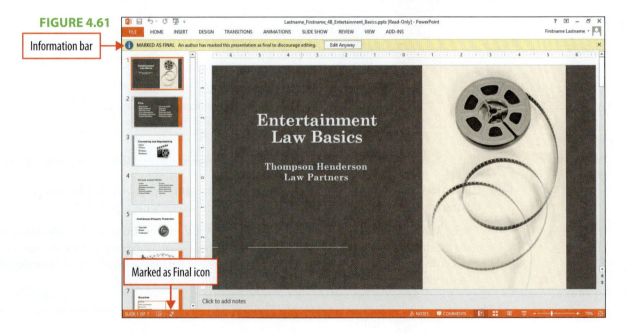

5 On the information bar, click **Edit Anyway**.

You are free to make changes to the document.

More Knowledge   **Restrict Permissions**

Another way to protect a presentation is to restrict permissions. You can give others access to your presentation but remove their capability to edit, copy, or print. In order to do this, you need to install Windows Rights Management to restrict permissions that use a Windows Live ID or a Microsoft Windows account. You can apply for permissions from within PowerPoint—on the Info tab, click the Protect Presentation arrow, and then click Restrict Access. You can then connect to Digital Rights Management Servers or go to www.microsoft.com for more information.

Activity 4.20 | Changing the Presentation Password

In this activity, you will password protect the presentation.

1 Click **FILE**. Under **Info**, click the **Protect Presentation arrow**, and then click **Encrypt with Password**.

2 In the **Encrypt Document** dialog box, in the **Password** box, type **Go** and then click **OK**. Compare your screen with Figure 4.62.

FIGURE 4.62

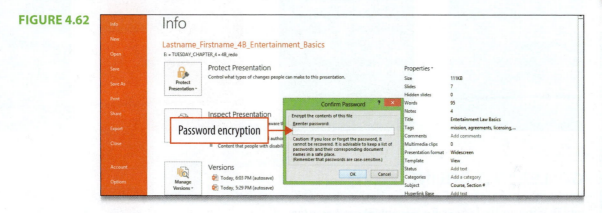

3 In the **Confirm Password** dialog box, type **Go** and then click **OK**. **Save** 🖫 the file. **Close** ☒ the file.

4 **Open** your **Lastname_Firstname_4B_Entertainment_Basics** file.

The Password dialog box displays and you are prompted to enter the password.

5 In the Password dialog box, type **Go** and then click **OK** to open the presentation.

More **Knowledge**   **Remove a Password**

To remove a password from an encrypted PowerPoint presentation, display the Encrypt Document dialog box, highlight the contents of the Password box, and then press Delete or Backspace. Click OK to accept the change.

---

6 Click **FILE**, click **Print**, and then under **Settings**, click the **Full Page Slides button arrow** to display the **Print Layout** gallery. Click **Handouts 3 Slides**. Display the **Print Layout** gallery again, and then check **Print Comments and Ink Markup** if necessary. Print the slides. If requested, submit your presentation electronically as directed by your instructor instead of printing.

7 Click **Close** ☒ to close the presentation, and then **Exit** PowerPoint.

END | You have completed Project 4B

END OF CHAPTER

SUMMARY

You designed a PowerPoint template containing formats, shapes, and images on the master pages; you then created a presentation based on this template; and you entered text for a meeting on the presentation.

You added comments into the presentation and practiced navigating through the presentation to read, edit, and delete comments in the presentation. You used the Thesaurus tool to edit your presentation.

You edited Handout and Notes Masters. You compared two versions of a presentation to view the differences between the presentations. You then merged the two presentations into a single presentation.

You prepared a presentation for distribution by publishing it in PDF and XPS formats. You checked the compatibility of the file, marked the presentation as Final, and password protected the presentation.

GO! LEARN IT ONLINE

Review the concepts and key terms in this chapter by completing these online challenges, which you can find at **www.pearsonhighered.com/go**.

Matching and Multiple Choice:
Answer matching and multiple choice questions to test what you learned in this chapter. MyITLab®

Crossword Puzzle:
Spell out the words that match the numbered clues, and put them in the puzzle squares.

Flipboard:
Flip through the definitions of the key terms in this chapter and match them with the correct term.

END OF CHAPTER

REVIEW AND ASSESSMENT GUIDE FOR POWERPOINT CHAPTER 4

Your instructor may assign one or more of these projects to help you review the chapter and assess your mastery and understanding of the chapter.

	Review and Assessment Guide for PowerPoint Chapter 4		
Project	**Apply Skills from These Chapter Objectives**	**Project Type**	**Project Location**
4C	Objectives 1–2 from Project 4A	**4C Chapter Review** A guided review of the skills from Project 4A.	On the following pages
4D	Objectives 3–6 from Project 4B	**4D Chapter Review** A guided review of the skills from Project 4B.	On the following pages
4E	Objectives 1–2 from Project 4A	**4E Mastery (Grader Project)** A demonstration of your mastery of the skills in Project 4A with extensive decision making.	In MyITLab and on the following pages
4F	Objectives 3–6 from Project 4B	**4F Mastery (Grader Project)** A demonstration of your mastery of the skills in Project 4B with extensive decision making.	In MyITLab and on the following pages
4G	Objectives 1–6 from Projects 4A and 4B	**4G Mastery (Grader Project)** A demonstration of your mastery of the skills in Projects 4A and 4B with extensive decision making.	In MyITLab and on the following pages
4H	Combination of Objectives from Projects 4A and 4B	**4H GO! Fix It** A demonstration of your mastery of the skills in Projects 4A and 4B by creating a correct result from a document that contains errors you must find.	Online
4I	Combination of Objectives from Projects 4A and 4B	**4I GO! Make It** A demonstration of your mastery of the skills in Projects 4A and 4B by creating a result from a supplied picture.	Online
4J	Combination of Objectives from Projects 4A and 4B	**4J GO! Solve It** A demonstration of your mastery of the skills in Projects 4A and 4B, your decision-making skills, and your critical thinking skills. A task-specific rubric helps you self-assess your result.	Online
4K	Combination of Objectives from Projects 4A and 4B	**4K GO! Solve It** A demonstration of your mastery of the skills in Projects 4A and 4B, your decision-making skills, and your critical thinking skills. A task-specific rubric helps you self-assess your result.	On the following pages
4L	Combination of Objectives from Projects 4A and 4B	**4L GO! Think** A demonstration of your understanding of the chapter concepts applied in a manner that you would outside of college. An analytic rubric helps you and your instructor grade the quality of your work by comparing it to the work an expert in the discipline would create.	On the following pages
4M	Combination of Objectives from Projects 4A and 4B	**4M GO! Think** A demonstration of your understanding of the chapter concepts applied in a manner that you would outside of college. An analytic rubric helps you and your instructor grade the quality of your work by comparing it to the work an expert in the discipline would create.	Online
4N	Combination of Objectives from Projects 4A and 4B	**4N You and GO!** A demonstration of your understanding of the chapter concepts applied in a manner that you would in a personal situation. An analytic rubric helps you and your instructor grade the quality of your work.	Online

GLOSSARY

Antonyms Words with an opposite meaning.

Comment A note that you can attach to a letter or word on a slide or to an entire slide. People use comments to provide feedback on a presentation.

Compatibility Checker A feature that locates potential compatibility issues between PowerPoint 2013 and earlier versions of PowerPoint.

Compatibility mode Saves a presentation as PowerPoint 97-2003 presentation. It also ensures that no new or enhanced features in PowerPoint 2013 are available while you work with a document, so that people who are using previous versions of PowerPoint will have full editing capabilities.

Gradient fill A gradual progression of several colors blending into each other or shades of the same color blending into each other.

Gradient stop Allows you to apply different color combinations to selected areas of the background.

Handout Master Includes the specifications for the design of presentation handouts for an audience.

Mark as Final Makes a presentation file read-only in order to prevent changes to the document. Adds a Marked as Final icon to the status bar.

Notes Master Includes the specifications for the design of the speaker's notes.

Office Theme Slide Master A specific slide master that contains the design, such as the background, that displays on all slide layouts in the presentation.

.potx The file extension for a PowerPoint template.

.pptx The file extension for a PowerPoint presentation.

Portable Document Format (PDF) A file format that creates an image that preserves the look of your file, but that cannot be easily changed; a popular format for sending documents electronically, because the document will display on most computers.

Reviewer A person who inserts comments into a presentation to provide feedback.

Slide Master Part of a template that stores information about the formatting and text that displays on every slide in a presentation. There are various slide master layouts.

Synonym A word having the same or nearly the same meaning as another.

Template A predefined layout for a group of slides saved as a .potx file.

XML Paper Specification (XPS) Microsoft's file format that preserves document formatting and enables file sharing. Files can be opened and viewed on any operating system or computer that is equipped with Microsoft XPS Viewer. Files cannot be easily edited.

CHAPTER REVIEW

Apply 4A skills from these Objectives:

1 Create a Custom Template by Modifying Slide Masters

2 Apply a Custom Template to a Presentation

Skills Review | Project 4C Contract

In the following Skills Review, you will create a template that Thompson Henderson Law Partners will use to prepare presentations for the initial meeting with a client. You will use the template to create a presentation for the musical group Billy and the Night Owls. Your completed presentation will look similar to Figure 4.63.

Build from Scratch

PROJECT FILES

For Project 4C, you will need the following files:

New blank Powerpoint presentation
p04C_Contract.jpg

You will save your files as:

Lastname_Firstname_4C_Contract_Template.potx
Lastname_Firstname_4C_Night_Owls.pptx

PROJECT RESULTS

Billy and the Night Owls

Thompson Henderson Law Partners

Performance Contract Basics

❖A contract includes:
 ▪ Performance agreement outline
 ▪ Document of agreement
❖The contractee is the party for whom the performance service is provided
❖The contractor is the party that performs the service

Cross Licensing

❖Cross licensing is a legal agreement
❖Two or more parties may share rights to a performance
❖A royalty fee exchange may be included
❖Performance recording rights may be included

Africa Studio/Fotolia

FIGURE 4.63

(Project 4C Contract continues on the next page)

CHAPTER REVIEW

1 Start PowerPoint, and then click **Blank Presentation**. Press F12 to display the **Save As** dialog box. Navigate to the location where you are saving your work, click the **Save as type box arrow**, and then click **PowerPoint Template (*.potx)**. **Save** your file as **Lastname_Firstname_4C_Contract_Template**

2 Click the **VIEW tab**. In the **Master Views group**, click **Slide Master**.

a. Scroll up, and then click the first thumbnail—**Office Theme Slide Master**. From the **SLIDE MASTER tab**, in the **Background group**, click **Background Styles**. In the **Background Styles gallery**, select **Style 9**.

b. Click the second thumbnail—**Title Slide Layout**. Click the dashed border on the Master title style placeholder, and then on the **HOME tab**, change the font size to **48 point**.

3 Click the **Office Theme Slide Master** thumbnail.

a. On the **SLIDE MASTER tab**, in the **Background group**, click **Background Styles**, and then click **Format Background**. Under **Fill**, click **Gradient fill**, if necessary. Click the **Type arrow**, and then click **Radial**.

b. Click **Add gradient stop** once, and then position the stop at **80%**.

c. Click the **Color arrow**, and then in the eighth column in the second row, click **Gold, Accent 4, Lighter 80%**.

d. Click **Apply to All**. **Close** the **Format Background** pane.

4 Click the **Title Slide Layout** thumbnail.

a. Click the **VIEW tab**. In the **Show group**, click the **Ruler** checkbox to display the horizontal and vertical rulers, if necessary.

b. Click the **INSERT tab**. In the **Illustrations group**, click **Shapes**. Under **Basic Shapes**, click the **Diamond** shape. At **2 inches on the right side of the horizontal ruler** and **3 inches on the upper half of the vertical ruler**, click to insert the shape.

c. On the ribbon, on the **DRAWING TOOLS FORMAT tab**, in the **Shapes Styles group**, click **Shape Effects**, point to **Preset**, and then click **Preset 2**. In the **Shapes Styles group**, click the **Shape Outline button arrow**, and then click **No Outline**.

d. With the diamond still selected, in the **Size group**, change the **Shape Height** to **1.5"** and the **Shape Width** to **1.5"**.

e. In the **Shape Styles group**, click **Shape Fill**, and then click **Picture**. **From a file** click **Browse**, navigate to the location where your data files are stored and then select **p04C_Contract.jpg** Click **Insert**.

f. With the shape still selected, in the **Arrange group**, click **Align**. Click **Align Center**. Click **Align** again, and then click **Align Bottom**.

g. On the ribbon, on the **PICTURE TOOLS FORMAT tab**, in the **Adjust group**, click **Color**. Under **Recolor**, click the second row, sixth color—**Blue, Accent color 5 Dark**.

h. With the shape still selected, on the **HOME tab**, in the **Clipboard group**, click **Copy**. Click the **Title and Content Layout** thumbnail. In the **Clipboard group**, click **Paste**.

i. Under the **DRAWING TOOLS FORMAT tab**, in the **Size group**, change the **Shape Height** to **1"** and the **Shape Width** to **1"**.

j. With the shape still selected, press the Shift key, and then click the content placeholder. In the **Arrange group**, click **Align**, and then select **Align Right**. Click **Align**, and then select **Align Top**.

5 Click the **Title Slide Layout** thumbnail.

a. Press the Shift key, and then drag the Master title placeholder up so the top aligns at **3 inches on the upper half of the vertical ruler**. Release the Shift key, and then click outside the placeholder. Press the Shift key, and then drag the Master subtitle placeholder up so the top aligns with **0 inch mark on the upper half of the vertical ruler**. Release the Shift key.

b. With the subtitle placeholder still selected, drag the **bottom middle sizing handle to 1 inch on the lower half of the vertical ruler**.

c. Click the shape, and then drag the entire shape so the top aligns with **1.5 inches on the lower half of the vertical ruler**. On the **DRAWING TOOLS FORMAT tab**, in the **Arrange group**, click **Align**, and then click **Align Center**.

6 With the **Title Slide Layout** selected, on the **VIEW tab**, in the **Show group**, select the **Guides** check box to

(Project 4C Contract continues on the next page)

display the horizontal and vertical guides, if necessary. At the top of the slide, move your mouse pointer over the orange dotted line until the mouse pointer changes into a double arrow ⬍. Click the light orange dotted **vertical guide line** and drag to the left to **5.50 inches on the left side of the horizontal ruler**.

a. Click the **INSERT tab**. In the **Illustrations group**, click **Shapes**. Under **Rectangles**, click the **Rectangle** shape. Position the pointer at **6 inches on the left side of the horizontal ruler**, aligning it with the top edge of the slide. Click and **drag across the top edge of the slide .5 inch to 5.5 inches on the horizontal ruler** to the edge of the vertical guide line, continue holding, and then **drag down along the vertical guide line** to the bottom edge of the slide, and then release. With the shape still selected, on the **DRAWING TOOLS FORMAT tab**, in the **Shapes Styles group**, click **Colored Fill – Black, Dark 1**.

b. Click the **INSERT tab**. In the **Illustrations group**, click **Shapes**. Under **Basic Shapes**, click the **Diamond** shape. Click on the black line shape to insert the diamond shape. If necessary, with the diamond still selected, in the **Size group**, change the **Shape Height to 1"** and the **Shape Width to 1"**. With the shape still selected, in the **Size group**, click the **dialog launcher**. Click **Position** to expand. In the **Horizontal position box**, type 0.41 and then press Enter. In the **Vertical position box**, type 0.74 and then press Enter.

c. With the shape still selected, on the **DRAWING TOOLS FORMAT tab**, in the **Shapes Styles group**, click **More**. In the fourth row, click the sixth item— **Subtle Effect – Blue, Accent 5**. With the shape still selected, on the **DRAWING TOOLS FORMAT tab**, in the **Shapes Styles group**, click **Shape Effects**. Click **Glow**, and then under **Glow Variations**, in the fifth column, click the last item—**Blue, 18 pt glow, Accent color 5**. On the **VIEW tab**, in the **Show group**, select the **Guides** check box to deselect the box.

7 ▶ Click the **Title and Content Layout** thumbnail.

a. Click anywhere in the first bulleted line. Click the **HOME tab**. In the **Paragraph group**, click the **Bullets button arrow**, and then click **Bullets and Numbering**. In the **Bullets and Numbering** dialog box, click the

Bulleted tab if necessary. Click **Star Bullets**. Then click the **Color button arrow**. Under **Standard Colors**, click **Purple**. Click **OK**.

b. Click anywhere in the second bulleted line. Display the **Bullets and Numbering** dialog box. Click the **Filled Square Bullets**. Click the **Color button arrow**. Under **Standard Colors**, click **Purple**. Click **OK**.

8 ▶ Click the first thumbnail, the **Office Theme Slide Master**.

a. At the bottom left on the slide, click anywhere on the dashed border of the date placeholder.

b. With the **HOME tab** selected, change the **font size** to **10** and **Center** the date.

c. Click the **SLIDE MASTER tab**. In the **Close group**, click **Close Master View**.

9 ▶ On the **INSERT tab**, in the **Text group**, click **Header & Footer** to display the **Header and Footer** dialog box. Click the **Notes and Handouts tab**. Under **Include on page**, select the **Date and time** check box, and then select **Fixed** and type today's date. If necessary, clear the **Header** check box, and then select the **Page number** and **Footer** check boxes. In the **Footer** box, using your own name, type **Lastname_Firstname_4C_Contract_Template** and then click **Apply to All**.

10 ▶ Click the **FILE tab**, and then in the lower right portion of the screen, click **Show All Properties**. In the **Tags** box, type **template** and in the **Subject** box type your course name and section number. In the **Author** box, right-click the existing author name, click **Edit Property**, replace the existing text with your first and last name, click outside textbox to deselect, and then click **OK**.

11 ▶ Print **Handouts 4 Slides Horizontal**, or submit your presentation electronically as directed by your instructor.

12 ▶ Save the template.

13 ▶ Press F12 to display the **Save As** dialog box. If necessary, navigate to the location where you are saving your files, and then click the **Save as type box arrow**. Click **PowerPoint Presentation (*.pptx),** and then **Save** the file as **Lastname_Firstname_4C_Night_Owls** in your storage location.

(Project 4C Contract continues on the next page)

CHAPTER REVIEW

14 Click **Slide 1**. In the title placeholder, type **Billy and the Night Owls** In the subtitle placeholder, type **Thompson Henderson Law Partners**

a. On the **HOME tab**, in the **Slides group**, click the **New Slide button arrow**, and then click **Title** and **Content**.

b. In the title placeholder, type **Performance Contract Basics**

c. In the content placeholder, type the following bulleted items, using the **Increase** and **Decrease List Level** buttons as needed to increase the second and third bulleted lines only:

> **A contract includes:**
>> **Performance agreement outline**
>> **Document of agreement**
>
> **The contractee is the party for whom the performance service is provided**
>
> **The contractor is the party that performs the service**

15 In the **Slides group**, click the **New Slide button arrow**, and then click **Title and Content** to add a third slide.

a. In the title placeholder, type **Cross Licensing** and then press Ctrl + Enter.

b. Type the following bulleted items in the content placeholder:

> **Cross licensing is a legal agreement**
>
> **Two or more parties may share rights to a performance**
>
> **A royalty fee exchange may be included**
>
> **Performance recording rights may be included**

16 **Save** your presentation.

17 Click the **VIEW tab**. In the **Master Views group**, click **Handout Master**. In the **Page Setup group**, click **Slides Per Page**. Click **3 Slides**.

18 Click the **VIEW tab**. In the **Master Views group**, click **Notes Master**. In the **Placeholders group**, remove the **Body**.

19 In the **Close group**, click **Close Master View**.

20 On the **INSERT tab**, in the **Text group**, click **Header & Footer** to display the **Header and Footer** dialog box. Click the **Notes and Handouts tab**. In the **Footer** box, change the name to: **Lastname_Firstname_4C_Night_Owls** and then click **Apply to All**.

21 Click the **FILE tab**, and then in the lower right portion of the screen, click **Show All Properties**. In the **Tags** box, select any existing text, and then type **royalty, rights** If necessary, in the **Subject** box type your course name and section number. In the **Author** box, right-click the existing author name, click **Edit Property**, replace the existing text with your first and last name, click outside textbox to deselect, and then click **OK**.

22 Print **Handouts 4 Slides Horizontal**, or submit your presentation electronically as directed by your instructor.

23 **Save** the presentation. **Exit** PowerPoint.

END | You have completed Project 4C

CHAPTER REVIEW

Apply 4B skills from these Objectives:

3 Create and Edit Comments

4 Compare and Combine Presentations

5 Prepare a Presentation for Distribution

6 Protect a Presentation

Skills Review Project 4D Athlete Taxes

In the following Skills Review, you will modify a presentation created by Thompson Henderson Law Partners as a brief overview of taxation issues to present to Finley Nagursky, who is a professional football player. You will add comments to the presentation, compare and combine presentations, prepare the document for distribution, and then password protect it. Your completed presentation will look similar to Figure 4.64.

PROJECT FILES

For Project 4D, you will need the following files:

p04D_Athlete_Taxes.pptx
p04D_Athlete_Taxes2.pptx

You will save your files as:

Lastname_Firstname_4D_Athlete_Taxes.pptx
Lastname_Firstname_4D_Athlete_Taxes.pdf
Lastname_Firstname_4D_Athlete_Taxes.xps

PROJECT RESULTS

Pix by Marti/Fotolia; Africa Studio/Fotolia; Netfalls/Fotolia; Stefano Tiraboschi/Fotolia; Brocreative/Fotolia; stockshoppe/Fotolia

FIGURE 4.64

(Project 4D Athlete Taxes continues on the next page)

CHAPTER REVIEW

1 Start PowerPoint. Locate and open the file **p04D_Athlete_Taxes.pptx** Navigate to the location where you are storing your folders and projects for this chapter, and then **Save** the file as **Lastname_Firstname_4D_Athlete_Taxes**

2 Make **Slide 2** the active slide. Click the **REVIEW tab**. In the **Comments group**, click **New Comment**. In the space provided, on the **Comments** pane, type **It would be a good idea to add a couple more examples.**

3 Make **Slide 3** the active slide. Click at the end of the bulleted item that ends with *commission income*. In the **Comments group**, click **New Comment**. Type **I am glad you added this one.** Click outside the comment to close it.

4 Make **Slide 4** the active slide. In the last bulleted item, select the word *Deductions*. Use the procedure explained in the previous steps to add this comment: **Is this clear enough for the client to understand?**

5 Make **Slide 2** the active slide. In the **Comments** pane, click in the **Reply** box, and then type **Ask sports agents for more examples.**

6 Click **Next** until you reach the comment on **Slide 3**. In the **Comments group**, click **Delete** to remove this comment. **Close** the **Comments** pane.

7 On the **REVIEW tab**, in the **Compare group**, click **Compare**. In the **Choose File to Merge with Current Presentation** dialog box, navigate to your student data files for this chapter, and then click **p04D_Athlete_Taxes2**, and then click **Merge**.

a. In the **Revisions** pane, under **Presentations Changes**, click **Slide 2: Direct Taxes** to display a **Revisions** check box in the **Slides and Outline pane** on the left. Do *not* select the **Revisions** check box on **Slide** 2.

b. In the **Revisions** pane, under **Presentations Changes**, click **Slides moved after "Indirect Taxes"** to display a **Revisions** check box in the **Slides and Outline** pane on the left. Do *not* select the **Revisions** check box on **Slide 3**.

c. On **Slide 3** notice that a **Revisions** icon displays on the slide. Click the **Revisions** icon to display the **Revisions** check box. Select the **Revisions** check box that indicates *Inserted "all"* to accept the change and insert the word *all*.

d. In the **Revisions** pane, under **Presentations Changes**, click **Insertions after "Athlete Tax"** to display a

Revisions check box in the **Slides and Outline** pane on the left. Select the **Revisions** check box that indicates *Inserted "Accounting & Tax Services for Athletes"* to accept the change and insert the slide into the presentation.

e. On the **REVIEW tab**, in the **Compare group**, click **End Review**, and then click **Yes**.

8 Make **Slide 2** the active slide. Locate the word *sportspersons*. Right-click *sportspersons*, and then on the shortcut menu, point to **Synonyms**. Click **athletes** to change the word *sportspersons* to *athletes*.

9 On the **INSERT tab**, in the **Text group**, click **Header & Footer** to display the **Header and Footer** dialog box. Click the **Notes and Handouts tab**. If necessary, under **Include on page**, select the **Date and time** check box, and then select **Fixed**. If necessary, clear the **Header** check box, and then select the **Page number** and **Footer** check boxes. In the **Footer** box, select the existing text, and then using your own name, type **Lastname_Firstname_4D_Athlete_Taxes** and then click **Apply to All**.

10 Click the **FILE tab**, and then in the lower right portion of the screen, click **Show All Properties**. In the **Tags** box, type **direct taxes, athlete tax, indirect taxes** and in the **Subject** box type your course name and section number. In the **Author** box, right-click the existing author name, click **Edit Property**, replace the existing text with your first and last name, click outside textbox to deselect, and then click **OK**. **Save** the presentation.

11 Print **Handouts 4 Slides Horizontal**, or submit your presentation electronically as directed by your instructor.

12 Click **FILE**, and then click **Export**. Under **Export**, **Create PDF/XPS Document** is selected.

a. Click **Create PDF/XPS**. Click the **Save as type**, and then click **PDF(*.pdf)**. If necessary, select the option button **Standard (publishing online and printing)**. Clear **Open file after publishing** check box.

b. Click **Options**. Click the **Publish what arrow**, and then select **Handouts**. Click the **Slides per page arrow**, and then select **4**. Select the check box for **Include comments and ink markup**. Click **OK**.

c. Click **Publish**.

13 Click **FILE**, Click **Export**, **Create PDF/XPS Document** is selected.

(Project 4D Athlete Taxes continues on the next page)

CHAPTER REVIEW

a. Click **Create PDF/XPS**. Change the file type to **XPS Document (*.xps)**.

b. Click **Options**. Click the **Publish what arrow**, and then select **Handouts**. Click the **Slides per page arrow**, and then select **4**. Select the check box for **Include comments and ink markup**. Click **OK**. Select the **Open file after publishing** check box.

c. Click **Publish**.

d. **Close** the XPS file and viewer.

14 Click **FILE**, with **Info** selected, and then click **Protect Presentation arrow**, and then select **Mark as Final**. Click **OK**. Click **OK**.

15 Click **Edit Anyway**, click **FILE**, and then click **Protect Presentation arrow**. Click **Encrypt with Password**.

a. In the **Encrypt Document** dialog box, in the **Password** box, type **Go** and then click **OK**.

b. In the **Confirm password** dialog box, type **Go** and then click **OK**. **Save** the file. **Close** the file.

c. **Open** your **Lastname_Firstname_4D_Athlete_Taxes** file. The **Password** dialog box displays in which you are prompted to enter the password.

d. Type **Go** and then click **OK** to open the presentation.

16 **Close** the file. **Exit** PowerPoint. Submit your presentations electronically as directed by your instructor for:

| Lastname_Firstname_Athlete_Taxes.pptx |
| Lastname_Firstname_Athlete_Taxes.pdf |
| Lastname_Firstname_Athlete_Taxes.xps |

END | You have completed Project 4D

CONTENT-BASED ASSESSMENTS

Mastering PowerPoint Project 4E Sports Law

In the following Mastering PowerPoint project, you will edit a presentation you already prepared to explain the aspects of Title IX in Collegiate Sports Law and then save it as a template. You will use the template to personalize it for a presentation to Hugh Appleton, who is a College Athletic Director. Your completed presentation will look similar to Figure 4.65.

Apply 4A from these Objectives:

1 Create a Custom Template by Modifying Slide Masters

2 Apply a Custom Template to a Presentation

PROJECT FILES

For Project 4E, you will need the following files:

p04E_Sports_Law.pptx
p04E_Sports1.jpg

You will save your files as:

Lastname_Firstname_4E_Sports_Template.potx
Lastname_Firstname_4E_Sports_Law.pptx

PROJECT RESULTS

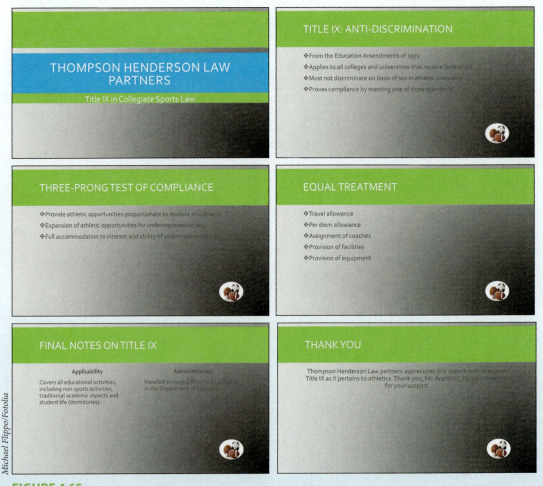

FIGURE 4.65

(Project 4E Sports Law continues on the next page)

CONTENT-BASED ASSESSMENTS

1 Start PowerPoint. Locate and open the file **p04E_Sports_Law.pptx** Save the file as a **PowerPoint Template** in your **PowerPoint Chapter 4** folder, using the file name **Lastname_Firstname_4E_Sports_Template**

2 Click the **VIEW tab**, and then click **Slide Master**. Scroll up and click the **Banded Slide Master** thumbnail. Apply Background **Style 10**. Format the background with a **Radial Gradient fill**, and then apply it to all slides. On the first bulleted item, change the font size to **24**.

3 On the **Title Slide Layout** thumbnail, change the Master title style placeholder **font size** to **48 pts**. Change the Master subtitle style placeholder **font size** to **32 pts**.

4 On the **Title and Content Layout** thumbnail, insert an **Oval** shape and set the **Height** to **1.0"** and the **Width** to **1.25"**. Fill the shape with **p04E_Sports1.jpg** located in the student data files. Remove the **Shape Outline**, and then position the shape at the bottom right corner of the content placeholder.

5 Copy the shape to the **Two Content Layout** thumbnail.

6 Remove the Header from the **Handout Master**, and then **Close Master View**.

7 On the **INSERT tab**, in the **Text group**, click **Header & Footer** to display the **Header and Footer** dialog box. Click the **Notes and Handouts tab**. Under **Include on page**, select the **Date and time** check box, and then select **Fixed**. If necessary, clear the **Header** check box, and then select the **Page number** and **Footer** check boxes. In the **Footer** box, using your own name, type **Lastname_Firstname_4E_Sports_Template** and then click **Apply to All**.

8 Revise the document properties. In the **Author** box, right-click the existing author name, click **Edit Property**, replace the existing text with your first and last name,

click outside textbox to deselect, and then click **OK**. In the **Subject** box, type your course name and section number, and then in the **Tags** box, type **template**

9 **Save** the template. Print **Handouts 6 Slides Horizontal**, or submit your presentation electronically as directed by your instructor.

10 **Close** the template.

11 Create a **new presentation** using your template. **Save** the file as **Lastname_Firstname_4E_Sports_Law** in your storage location.

12 On **Slide 5**, in the left column, remove the bullet, center *Applicability*, and then add bold. Repeat the formatting for *Administration* in the second column.

13 Add a **Title and Content** slide. In the title placeholder, type **Thank You** In the content placeholder, type **Thompson Henderson Law Partners appreciates this opportunity to explain Title IX as it pertains to athletics. Thank you, Mr. Appleton, for your time and for your support.** Remove the bullet and center the text.

14 On the **Slide Master**, change the first-level bullets to **Star Bullets**. **Close** the Master View.

15 Change the footer on the handouts to include **Lastname_Firstname_4E_Sports_Law** and then click **Apply to All**.

16 Edit the document properties. In the **Author** box, add your Firstname Lastname. In the **Subject** box, type your course name and section number, and then in the **Tags** box, type **Title IX, discrimination**

17 **Save** the presentation. Print **Handouts 6 Slides Horizontal**, or submit your presentation electronically as directed by your instructor.

18 **Close** the presentation.

END | You have completed Project 4E

CONTENT-BASED ASSESSMENTS

Apply 4B skills from these Objectives:

3 Create and Edit Comments

4 Compare and Combine Presentations

5 Prepare a Presentation for Distribution

6 Protect a Presentation

In the following Mastering PowerPoint project, you will complete a presentation that covers various aspects of contracts in the entertainment industry, including royalties, minors, and advances. You will review the presentation and add comments, compare and combine presentations before preparing it for distribution. Your completed presentation will look similar to Figure 4.66.

PROJECT FILES

For Project 4F, you will need the following files:

p04F_Contract_Aspects.pptx
p04F_Contract_Aspects2.pptx

You will save your files as:

Lastname_Firstname_4F_Contract_Aspects.pptx
Lastname_Firstname_4F_Contract_Aspects.pdf
Lastname_Firstname_4F_Contract_Aspects.xps

PROJECT RESULTS

Dmitry Ersler/Fotolia; Iurii Sokolov/Fotolia; Shawn Hempel/Fotolia

FIGURE 4.66

(Project 4F Contract Aspects continues on the next page)

CONTENT-BASED ASSESSMENTS

1 Start PowerPoint. Locate and open the file **p04F_Contract_Aspects**. **Save** the file as **Lastname_Firstname_4F_Contract_Aspects**

2 Make **Slide 3** the active slide. At the end of the first bulleted item, add a comment, and then type **Are there any other points that should be added?**

3 On **Slide 4**, select *Intermediaries*, and then add this comment: **I think this term needs to be defined.**

4 On **Slide 5**, add this comment: **Excellent content!** Drag the comment so it is positioned right after *Advances*.

5 Edit the comment on **Slide 3**. Click in the *Reply* box, and then type **Should minor be defined?**

6 Delete the comment on **Slide 4**.

7 **Compare** and **Merge** the presentation with **p04F_Contract_Aspects2** from your student data files for this chapter. Accept the inserted slide **"Hold the Key to Your Future"**. **End Review.**

8 Change the word *payment* to *compensation* on **Slide 3**.

9 Insert a **Footer** on Notes and Handouts that includes the fixed date and time, page number, and file name.

10 Revise the document properties. In the **Author** box, replace the existing text with your first and last name. In the **Subject** box, type your course name and section number, and then in the **Tags** box, type **entertainment, royalties, minors, advances**

11 **Save** the presentation.

12 **Publish** the presentation as a **PDF** file. Set options to **Include comments and ink markup**, **Handouts, 6 slides per page**, and **Horizontal**.

13 **Print** the PDF file, or submit your presentation electronically as directed by your instructor.

14 **Publish** the presentation as an **XPS** file using the same options as the PDF file. **Print** the XPS file, or submit your presentation electronically as directed by your instructor.

15 **Save** the file in your PowerPoint Chapter 4 folder. Mark your presentation as **Final**.

16 **Close** the presentation, and then **Exit** PowerPoint.

END | You have completed Project 4F

CONTENT-BASED ASSESSMENTS

MyITLab®
grader

Mastering PowerPoint   Project 4G Film Production

In the following Mastering PowerPoint project, you will open a presentation explaining the legal aspects of film production and modify the slide masters. Frequently, Thompson Henderson Law Partners presents this information to college classes, so you will save the presentation as a template. Then you will create a presentation from the template and personalize it for the Film Production course at the local university. You will add some comments for other partners to see, edit it, save the presentation as an XPS file for the participants, and then password protect the presentation. Your completed presentation will look similar to Figure 4.67.

Apply 4A and 4B skills from these Objectives:

1 Create a Custom Template by Modifying Slide Masters

2 Apply a Custom Template to a Presentation

3 Create and Edit Comments

4 Compare and Combine Presentations

5 Prepare a Presentation for Distribution

6 Protect a Presentation

PROJECT FILES

For Project 4G, you will need the following files:

p04G_Film_Production.pptx
p04G_Film.jpg

You will save your files as:

Lastname_Firstname_4G_Film_Template.potx
Lastname_Firstname_4G_Film_Production.pptx
Lastname_Firstname_4G_Film_Production.xps

PROJECT RESULTS

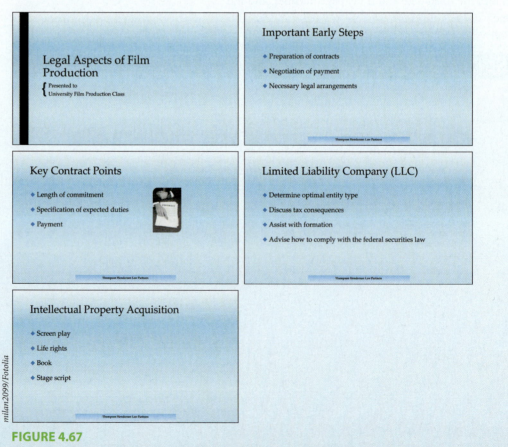

FIGURE 4.67

(Project 4G Film Production continues on the next page)

1 Start PowerPoint. Locate and open the file **p04G_ Film_Production.pptx**, and then save it as a template with the name **Lastname_Firstname_4G_Film_Template**

2 In **Slide Master View**, on the Office Theme Slide Master, change the background to **Style 2**. Format the background with a **Gradient fill**, **Linear type**. Set gradient **stop 2** to **25%** and gradient **stop 3** to **75%**. Set the **stop 3** color to **Blue, Accent 1, Lighter 80%**, and then apply to all slides. Change the color of the first bullet to **Blue, Accent 5**.

3 Click the **Title Slide Layout** thumbnail. On the **VIEW tab**, in the **Show group**, click the **Guides** box. At the top of the slide, move your mouse pointer over the orange dotted line until the mouse pointer changes into a double arrow ⟺. Click the light orange dotted **vertical guide line** and drag to the left to **5.75 inches on the left side of the horizontal ruler**. On the **INSERT tab**, click **Shapes**, under **Rectangles**, click the **Rectangle** shape. Position the pointer at the **6.25 inches on the left side of the horizontal ruler**, aligning it with the top edge of the slide. Click and **drag across the top edge of the slide .5 inch to 5.75 inches on the horizontal ruler** to the edge of the vertical guide line, continue holding, and then **drag down along the vertical guide line** to the bottom edge of the slide, and then release. Apply the shape style **Colored Fill – Black, Dark 1**. Deselect the **Guides** check box.

4 Click the **Title and Content Layout** thumbnail. Insert a **Text Box** in the lower left corner of the content placeholder. Inside the shape, type **Thompson Henderson Law Partners** Change the font to **Palatino Linotype, 12 pt, Bold**, and then **Center** the text. **Select** the text, and then change the **Height** to **0.5"** and the **Width** to **6.0"**. Use a **Shape Fill** to add **Gradient** with a **Light Variations** of **Linear Down**. **Align** the text box at the **center** and **bottom** of the slide.

5 Remove the Header on the **Handout Master**, and then **Close Master View**.

6 Insert the **Header & Footer**. On the **Notes and Handouts tab**, include a **Fixed** date and the **Page number** and **Footer**. In the **Footer** box, using your own name, type **Lastname_Firstname_4G_Film_Template** and then click **Apply to All**.

7 Revise the document properties. In the **Author** box, replace the existing text with your first and last name. In the **Subject** box, type your course name and section number, and then in the **Tags** box, type **template**

8 Print **Handouts 6 Slides Horizontal**, or submit your presentation electronically as directed by your instructor.

9 **Save** the template file, and then **Close** the template.

10 Create a new document from existing template **Lastname_Firstname_4G_Film_Template.potx**, and then save it as **Lastname_Firstname_4G_Film_Production.pptx**

11 On **Slide 1**, after *Presented to,* press Enter, and then type **University Film Production Class**

12 In **Slide Master View**, on the **Title and Content Layout** slide, select all of the text in the first bulleted item, change the line spacing to **1.5**, and then **Close Master View**.

13 On **Slide 4**, after the third bulleted item, add this comment: **Maybe clarify that you mean the formation of an LLC.**

14 On **Slide 5**, select *Life rights*, and then add this comment: **Explain how life rights is considered intellectual property.**

15 On **Slide 4**, delete the comment.

16 On **Slide 2**, use the Thesaurus, to change *compensation* to *payment*.

17 On **Slide 3**, insert the picture file, **p04G_Film. jpg**, Crop to Shape using the Round Diagonal Corner Rectangle under Rectangles. Change the shape Height to 2.53", and position it to the right of the three bullet points. **Recolor** the picture to **Grayscale**.

18 Update the filename in the **Notes and Handouts Footer** to **Lastname_Firstname_4G_Film_Production** and then update the **Properties** with your name as the Author, and then in the **Tags** box, select the existing text, and then type **film production, LLC, intellectual property**

19 Print **Handouts 6 Slides Horizontal**, or submit your presentation electronically as directed by your instructor.

20 **Save** the presentation.

21 **Publish** the presentation as an **XPS file**, including the comments and ink markup and specifying handouts 6 slides per page. **Close** the XPS Viewer. **Print** the XPS file, or submit the file electronically as directed by your instructor.

22 Mark the presentation as **Final**, and then **Close** the file. **Exit** PowerPoint.

END | You have completed Project 4G

CONTENT-BASED ASSESSMENTS

Apply a combination of the **4A** and **4B** skills.

GO! Fix It	Project 4H Labor Issues	Online
GO! Make It	Project 4I Consignment Contracts	Online
GO! Solve It	Project 4J Legal Guide	Online
GO! Solve It	Project 4K Actor Advice	

PROJECT FILES

For Project 4K, you will need the following files:

p04K_Actor_Advice.pptx

p04K_Cinema.jpg

You will save your files as:

Lastname_Firstname_4K_Actor_Template.potx

Lastname_Firstname_4K_Actor_Advice.pptx

Lastname_Firstname_4K_Actor_Advice.pdf

Open **p04K_Actor_Advice** and save it as a template **Lastname_Firstname_4K_Actor_ Template** Examine the slide content, and then modify the appropriate slide master with a background style or a theme. Adjust colors and fonts as needed. Insert a shape on the appropriate slide master so the shape displays only on Slide 1, and then insert **p04K_ Cinema.jpg** in the shape, recolor it, and place it where it is visually pleasing on the slide. Add additional shape(s) for attractive style and color to the title slide to add interest. Change the bullet style for levels of bullets that are used. On the Notes and Handouts, insert the fixed date and time, page number, and a footer with the file name. Add your name, your course name and section number, and the tag **template** to the Properties.

Create a new presentation based on the template. Personalize the presentation for Julia Simpson. Save the presentation **as Lastname_Firstname_4K_Actor_Advice.pptx** On Slide 2, insert a comment. Update the Notes and Handouts footer with the correct file name, add the tags **contracts, paparazzi, media** and then change the author in the Properties. Save the presentation in a PDF file as handouts, including the comments. Mark the presentation as Final and save it. Print or submit electronically as directed by your instructor.

(Project 4K Actor Advice continues on the next page)

CONTENT-BASED ASSESSMENTS

Performance Level

	Exemplary	Proficient	Developing
Customized Office Theme Slide Master with a background or theme and bullet styles	Slide master was customized correctly with a background or theme and with bullet styles. Maintained good contrast.	Slide master was not customized with a background or theme and with bullet styles. Customization done on other slide masters.	No slide master customization was completed.
Inserted a shape with the picture on the Title Slide Layout master and recolored it	Shape was inserted on the slide master and was sized, recolored and placed in an appropriate position.	The shape was not inserted or recolored on the appropriate slide master.	The shape was not inserted or recolored.
Created and personalized a presentation. Saved presentation as PDF with comments and marked as Final	Presentation file was created, personalized, and included comments. Saved as PDF handouts with comments and marked as Final.	Presentation file was created, but was not personalized. May or may not have been saved as PDF and marked as Final.	A presentation file was not created from the template.

Performance Criteria (left vertical label)

END | You have completed Project 4K

POWERPOINT 4

OUTCOMES-BASED ASSESSMENTS

RUBRIC

The following outcomes-based assessments are *open-ended assessments*. That is, there is no specific correct result; your result will depend on your approach to the information provided. Make *Professional Quality* your goal. Use the following scoring rubric to guide you in *how* to approach the problem and then to evaluate *how well* your approach solves the problem.

The *criteria*—Software Mastery, Content, Format and Layout, and Process—represent the knowledge and skills you have gained that you can apply to solving the problem. The *levels of performance*—Professional Quality, Approaching Professional Quality, or Needs Quality Improvements—help you and your instructor evaluate your result.

	Your completed project is of Professional Quality if you:	Your completed project is Approaching Professional Quality if you:	Your completed project Needs Quality Improvements if you:
1-Software Mastery	Choose and apply the most appropriate skills, tools, and features and identify efficient methods to solve the problem.	Choose and apply some appropriate skills, tools, and features, but not in the most efficient manner.	Choose inappropriate skills, tools, or features, or are inefficient in solving the problem.
2-Content	Construct a solution that is clear and well organized, contains content that is accurate, appropriate to the audience and purpose, and is complete. Provide a solution that contains no errors in spelling, grammar, or style.	Construct a solution in which some components are unclear, poorly organized, inconsistent, or incomplete. Misjudge the needs of the audience. Have some errors in spelling, grammar, or style, but the errors do not detract from comprehension.	Construct a solution that is unclear, incomplete, or poorly organized; contains some inaccurate or inappropriate content; and contains many errors in spelling, grammar, or style. Do not solve the problem.
3-Format & Layout	Format and arrange all elements to communicate information and ideas, clarify function, illustrate relationships, and indicate relative importance.	Apply appropriate format and layout features to some elements, but not others. Overuse features, causing minor distraction.	Apply format and layout that does not communicate information or ideas clearly. Do not use format and layout features to clarify function, illustrate relationships, or indicate relative importance. Use available features excessively, causing distraction.
4-Process	Use an organized approach that integrates planning, development, self-assessment, revision, and reflection.	Demonstrate an organized approach in some areas, but not others; or, use an insufficient process of organization throughout.	Do not use an organized approach to solve the problem.

OUTCOMES-BASED ASSESSMENTS

Apply a combination of the 4A and 4B skills.

Build from Scratch

GO! Think Project 4L Workshops

PROJECT FILES

For Project 4L, you will need the following file:

New blank PowerPoint presentation

You will save your files as:

Lastname_Firstname_4L_Venue_Template.potx
Lastname_Firstname_4L_Venue_Risks.pptx
Lastname_Firstname_4L_Venue_Risks.pdf

In this project, you will create a PowerPoint template for Thompson Henderson Law Partners to educate colleges, universities, and other sports venues about safety and security.

Create a template named **Lastname_Firstname_4L_Venue_Template.potx** Customize the slide masters, applying formatting as needed. In the Notes and Handouts, include the fixed date and time, page number, and file name in the footer. Add your name, course name and section number, and the tag **template** to the Properties.

Create a new presentation based on the template that addresses safety and security concerns. Save the presentation as **Lastname_Firstname_4L_Venue_Risks.pptx** Add three slides, each using a different layout. **Add** two comments. Update the Notes and Handouts footer with the new file name. Update your name, course name and section number, and the tags **venue, sports, risk** to the Properties. Export the presentation as Handouts 6 slides per page in a PDF file, including the comments. Mark the PowerPoint presentation as Final. Print or submit electronically as directed by your instructor.

END | You have completed Project 4L

OUTCOMES-BASED ASSESSMENTS

Build from
Scratch

GO! Think! Project 4M Intellectual Property **Online**

Build from
Scratch

You and GO! Project 4N Copyright **Online**

Applying Advanced Graphic Techniques and Inserting Audio and Video

GO! to Work
Video P5

5 POWERPOINT 2013

PROJECT 5A

OUTCOMES
Edit and format pictures and add sound to a presentation.

OBJECTIVES
1. Use Picture Corrections
2. Add a Border to a Picture
3. Change the Shape of a Picture
4. Add a Picture to a WordArt Object and Merge Shapes
5. Enhance a Presentation with Audio and Video

PROJECT 5B

OUTCOMES
Create and edit a photo album and crop pictures.

OBJECTIVES
6. Create a Photo Album
7. Edit a Photo Album and Add a Caption
8. Crop a Picture

vizafoto/Fotolia

In This Chapter

PowerPoint provides a variety of methods for formatting and enhancing graphic elements. PowerPoint provides sophisticated tools for changing the brightness, contrast, and shape of a picture; adding a border; and cropping a picture to remove unwanted areas. PowerPoint allows you to include audio and video effects in presentations, although the resulting files are quite large. You might want to introduce a slide with an audio effect or music, or have an audio effect or music play when the slide or a component on the slide, such as text or a graphic, is clicked. The inclusion of audio and video can enhance a presentation.

Cross Oceans Music produces and distributes recordings of innovative musicians from every continent in genres that include Celtic, jazz, New Age, reggae, flamenco, calypso, and unique blends of all styles. Company scouts travel the world attending world music festivals, concerts, performances, shows, and small local venues to find their talented roster of musicians and performers. These artists create new and exciting music using traditional and modern instruments and technologies. Cross Oceans' customers are knowledgeable about music and demand the highest quality digital recordings provided in state-of-the-art formats.

Enhance a Presentation with Graphics and Media

PROJECT ACTIVITIES

In Activities 5.01 through 5.11, you will change the sharpness or softness and the brightness and contrast of pictures. You will also add borders and change the outline shape of pictures. You will change the shape of a picture, add a WordArt object, and embed a picture and merge shapes. You will insert linked video files and add a trigger to the audio and video. Your completed presentation will look similar to Figure 5.1.

PROJECT FILES

For Project 5A, you will need the following files:

p05A_Cross_Oceans.pptx
p05A_Building.jpg
p05A_Island.jpg
p05A_mp3.jpg
p05A_Smooth_Jazz.wav
p05A_New_Age.wav
p05_Music_Video.avi

You will save your presentation as:

Lastname_Firstname_5A_Cross_Oceans.pptx

PROJECT RESULTS

Iapas77/Fotolia; qingwa/Fotolia; Giulio Meinardi/Fotolia; VanHart/Fotolia; RLG/Fotolia; Tsiumpa/Fotolia; Warren Goldswain/ Fotolia; Pakhnyushchyy/Fotolia

FIGURE 5.1 Project 5A Cross Oceans Music

Video P5-1

Pictures can be corrected to improve the brightness, contrast, or sharpness. For example, you can use Sharpen/Soften to enhance picture details or make a picture more appealing by removing unwanted blemishes. When you *sharpen* an image, the clarity of an image increases. When you *soften* an image, the picture becomes fuzzier. You can use *Presets* to choose common, built-in sharpness and softness adjustments from a gallery. You can also use a slider to adjust the amount of blurriness, or you can enter a number in the box next to the slider.

Another way to correct pictures is to use Brightness and Contrast. *Brightness* is the perceived radiance or luminosity of an image, and *contrast* is the difference between the darkest and lightest area of a picture. You can use *Presets* to choose common, built-in brightness and contrast combinations from a gallery, or you can use a slider to adjust the amount of brightness and contrast separately.

When you change the overall lightening and darkening of the image, you change the individual pixels in an image. *Pixel* is short for *picture element* and represents a single point in a graphic image. To increase brightness, more light or white is added to the picture by selecting positive percentages. To decrease brightness, more darkness or black is added to the image by selecting negative percentages.

Changing the contrast of a picture changes the amount of gray in the image. Positive percentages increase the intensity of a picture by removing gray; negative percentages decrease intensity by adding more gray.

When you *recolor* a picture, you change all colors in the image into shades of one color. This effect is often used to stylize a picture or make the colors match a background.

Activity 5.01 │ Using Sharpen/Soften on a Picture

In this activity, you will change the sharpness of a picture so the text on the slide will have greater emphasis. You will also use the Presets, which allows you to apply one of five standard settings.

1 Start PowerPoint. Locate and open the file **p05A_Cross_Oceans** Press F12 to display the **Save As** dialog box, and then navigate to the location where you are storing your projects for this chapter. Create a new folder named **PowerPoint Chapter 5** and then in the **File name** box and using your own name, save the file as **Lastname_Firstname_5A_Cross_Oceans** Click **Save** or press Enter.

2 Make **Slide 1** the active slide, if necessary, and then click to select the picture.

3 On the **PICTURE TOOLS FORMAT tab**, in the **Arrange group**, click the **Send Backward button arrow**, and then click **Send to Back**.

> **ANOTHER WAY**　To move a picture behind all components on the slide, right-click the picture, point to Send to Back, and then click Send to Back.

The slide title words are now displayed in front of the picture so you can read the words. When you click Send Backward, there are two options. Send Backward moves the picture behind the subtitle text. Send to Back moves the picture behind both the title and subtitle text.

> **ALERT!**　**Is the Text Visible?**
>
> If you cannot read the text in front of a picture that has been sent to the back, move the picture or change the text color.

4 Compare your screen with Figure 5.2, and then take a moment to study the descriptions of the picture adjustment settings, as shown in the table in Figure 5.3.

FIGURE 5.2

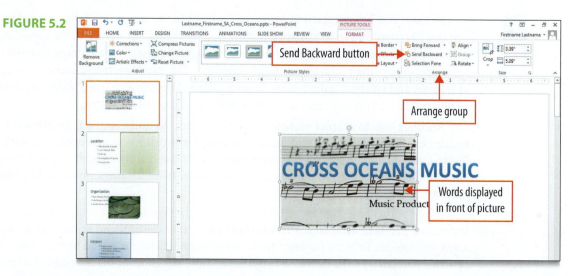

FIGURE 5.3

PICTURE ADJUSTMENT OPTIONS	
SCREEN ELEMENT	**DESCRIPTION**
Remove Background	Automatically remove unwanted portions of the picture. If needed, use marks to indicate areas to keep or remove from the picture.
Corrections	Improve the brightness, contrast, or sharpness of the picture.
Color	Change the color of the picture to improve quality or match document content.
Artistic Effects	Adds an artistic effect to a picture to make it look like a sketch or painting. You can access the Artistic Effects Options from this menu.
Compress Pictures	Compress pictures in the document to reduce its size. Reduces the image resolution and picture quality to make the file size smaller. There are two compression options: Apply only to this picture. The default is to compress the selected picture, but you can uncheck this option to compress all pictures in the document. Delete cropped areas of pictures. If you have cropped a picture, you can delete the cropped area to reduce the file size. However, if you want to undo the cropping, you have to insert the picture again. Provides four target output methods: Print (220 ppi): excellent quality on most printers and screens Screen (150 ppi): good for webpages and projectors E-mail (96 ppi): minimizes document size sharing Use document resolution (selected by default)
Change Picture	Change to a different picture, preserving the formatting and size of the current picture.
Reset Picture	Discards all formatting changes made to the picture.

5 On the **PICTURE TOOLS FORMAT tab**, in the **Adjust group**, click **Corrections**, and then click **Picture Corrections Options** to display the **Format Picture** pane. Under **Picture Corrections**, under **Sharpen/Soften**, drag the **Sharpness** slider to the left to **-100%** and observe the fuzzy effect on the picture. Drag the **Sharpness** slider to the right to **100%** and notice the sharpness of the picture.

6 Under **Sharpen/Soften**, click the **Presets arrow**. Compare your screen with Figure 5.4.

Five presets of variable sharp or soft picture corrections display.

FIGURE 5.4

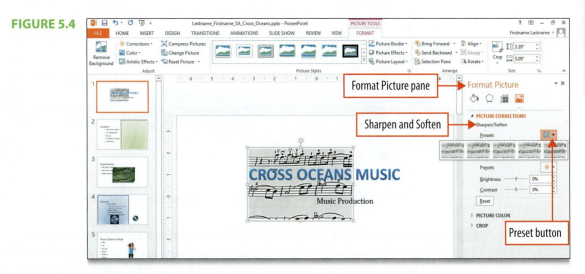

7 Click the fifth option—**Sharpen: 50%**.

The slider is now set at +50%, meaning that the picture is now sharper than the original picture.

> **More Knowledge** | **Using Picture Presets**
>
> The default for Sharpen/Soften is 0%. The Presets range from Soften: 50% to Sharpen: 50%. The slider settings range from -100% to +100%. Soften: 50% in Presets is the same as -50% on the slider.

---

8 Save 💾 the presentation.

Activity 5.02 | Changing the Brightness and Contrast of a Picture

In this activity, you will change the brightness and the contrast of a picture. You will also use the Presets, which allows you to select a combination of brightness and contrast settings.

1 With the image selected, on the **Format Picture** pane, under **Brightness/Contrast**, drag the **Brightness** slider to the left and then to the right. Watch how the picture brightness changes. In the **Brightness** box, select the text, type **20** and then press Enter.

2 Under **Brightness/Contrast**, drag the **Contrast** slider to the left and then to the right. Watch how the picture contrast changes. In the **Contrast** box, select the text, type **20** and then press Enter. Compare your screen with Figure 5.5.

The picture is enhanced so the slide title displays with more prominence.

FIGURE 5.5

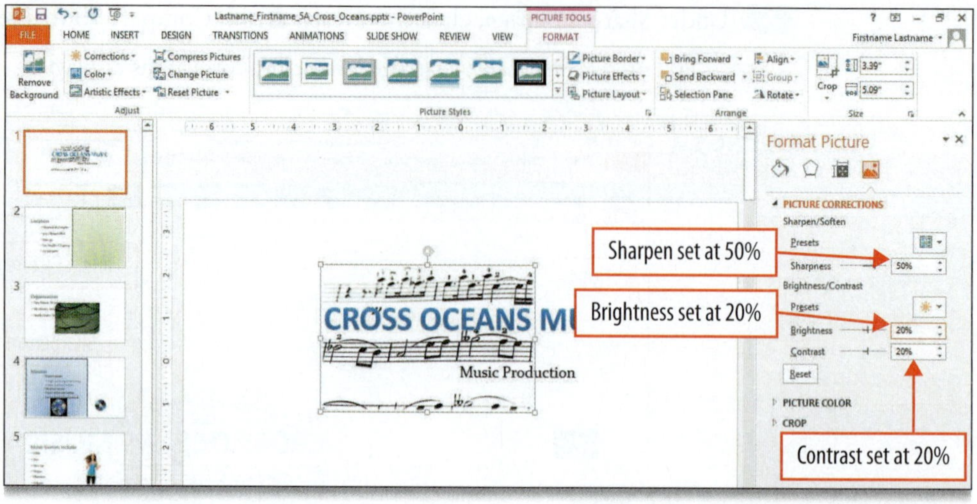

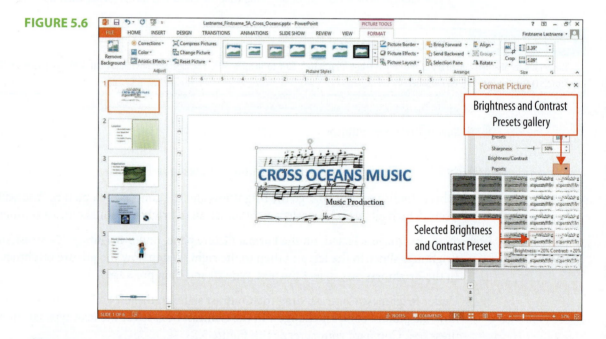

3 In the **Format Picture** pane, under **Brightness/Contrast**, click the **Presets arrow**. In the gallery, in the fourth row, fourth column, point to **Brightness: +20% Contrast: +20%** which is a combination of brightness and contrast you set. Compare your screen with Figure 5.6.

If you prefer, you may change brightness and contrast with one of the presets. The gallery displays the results on your picture to help you make a decision.

FIGURE 5.6

4 Click outside the **Brightness and Contrast** gallery to collapse it. **Close** the **Format Picture** pane, and then **Save** 🖬 your changes.

Activity 5.03 | Recoloring a Picture

In this activity, you will recolor and reposition a picture.

1 Make **Slide 2** the active slide and click the **green shape**. On the **DRAWING TOOLS FORMAT tab**, in the **Shape Styles group**, click the **Shape Fill arrow**, and then click **Picture**. Navigate to the location where your student files are stored, and then insert the picture **p05A_Building.jpg**. Compare your screen with Figure 5.7.

The picture is aligned within the green shape and all of the text on the slide is visible.

FIGURE 5.7

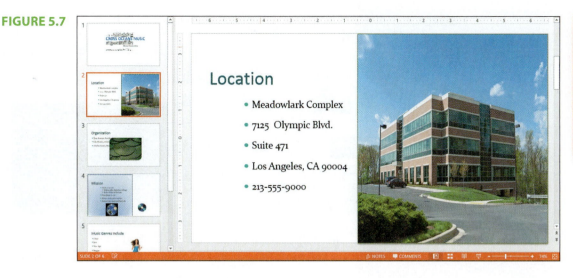

2 ▶ On the **PICTURE TOOLS FORMAT tab**, in the **Adjust group**, click the **Color arrow**. Under **Recolor**, in the third row, second column, locate **Blue, Accent color 1 Light**, and then click to select it. Compare your screen with Figure 5.8.

🔄 **ANOTHER WAY**   On the Ribbon, click the PICTURE TOOLS FORMAT tab, in the Adjust group, click Color, and then click Picture Color Options to display the Format Picture pane.

FIGURE 5.8

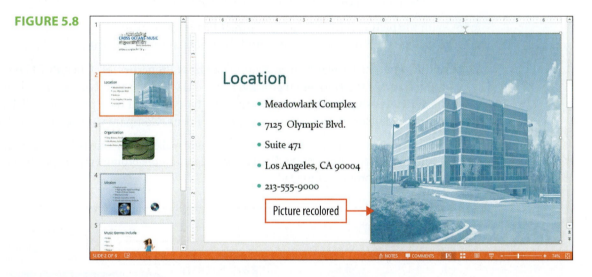

Picture recolored

3 ▶ With the picture on **Slide 3** selected, click the **VIEW tab**. In the **Show group**, select the **Gridlines** check box. Compare your screen with Figure 5.9.

The gridlines help you align objects at specific locations on the ruler.

FIGURE 5.9

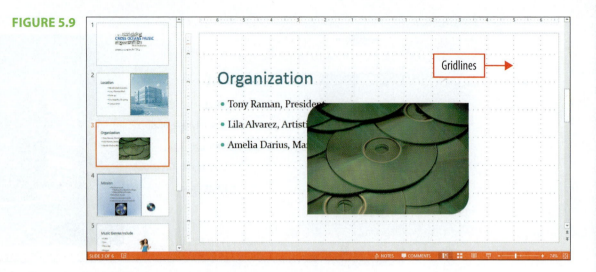

4 On **Slide 3**, click to select the picture. On the **PICTURE TOOLS FORMAT tab**, in the **Arrange group**, click the **Send Backward button arrow**, and then click **Send to Back**.

5 With the picture selected, on the **PICTURE TOOLS FORMAT tab**, in the **Adjust group**, click the **Corrections arrow**, and then click **Picture Corrections Options**. On the **Format Picture** pane, under **PICTURE CORRECTIONS**, in the **Contrast** spin box, select the text, type **80** and then press Enter.

> This amount of contrast adds glare to the picture and makes the bulleted items difficult to read.

6 With the picture selected and the **Format Picture** pane displaying, use the method you prefer to change the **Brightness** to **+40%** and the **Contrast** to **20%**. Change the **Sharpness** to **50%**.

7 At the top of the **Format Picture** pane, click **Size & Properties** . Click **POSITION** to expand, if necessary. In the **Horizontal position** spin box, select the text, type **4.7** and then press Enter. In the **Vertical position** spin box, select the text, type **1.75** and then press Enter. Click outside the picture to deselect it. **Close** the **Format Picture** pane. Compare your screen with Figure 5.10.

> Reducing the contrast and softness of the picture makes the picture fade into the background, allowing the content of the bulleted items to appear more prominently. Repositioning the picture makes the words easier to read.

FIGURE 5.10

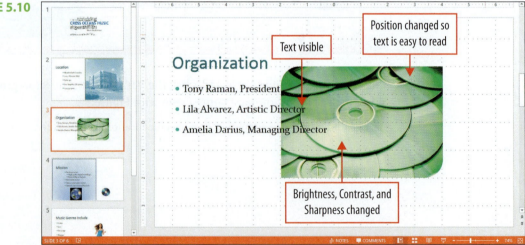

8 ▶ Select the picture. On the **PICTURE TOOLS FORMAT tab**, in the **Arrange group**, click **Selection Pane** to display the **Selection** pane. Compare your screen with Figure 5.11. Click **Content Placeholder 2** to select the content placeholder including the three names. Click **Title 1** to select the title placeholder—*Organization*. Click **Picture** 3 to select the picture on the slide.

The Selection pane displays the shapes on the slide, making it easy to select the desired shape.

FIGURE 5.11

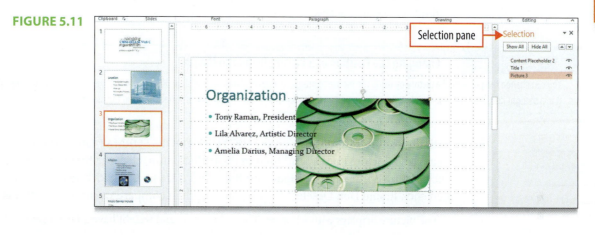

9 ▶ On the **PICTURE TOOLS FORMAT tab**, in the **Arrange group**, click the **Selection Pane** to close it.

🔄 **ANOTHER WAY**   On the Selection pane, click Close ⊠ to close the Selection Pane.

10 ▶ **Save** 💾 your changes.

Objective 2 | Add a Border to a Picture

Video P5-2

After you insert a picture into a slide, you can add a ***border***, which is actually a frame, around the picture. It is possible to edit the color of the border and the line weight. The ***line weight*** is the thickness of the line measured in points (abbreviated as pt), similar to font sizes. It is sometimes also called line width.

You can also select the ***line style***, which is how the line displays, such as a solid line, dots, or dashes. You can also change Line Width, Compound type, Dash type, Cap type, and Join type. Compound type is a line style composed of double or triple lines. Dash type is a style composed of various combinations of dashes. Cap type is the style you apply to the end of a line, and Join type is the style you specify to be used when two lines intersect at the corner.

Activity 5.04 | Adding a Border to a Picture

In this activity, you will add borders to pictures and then customize those borders by changing the color, line weight, and line style.

1 Make **Slide 4** the active slide. Right-click on the picture of the **CD**, and then click **Size and Position**. On the **Format Picture** pane, click **POSITION** to expand, if necessary. In the **Horizontal position** spin box, select the text, type **9.7** and then press [Enter]. In the **Vertical position** spin box, select text, type **5.5** and then press [Enter].

The picture location changes and moves to the right side of the slide. Because the picture was selected, the title of the pane is Format Picture. The pane title is context sensitive depending on what type of object is selected. For example, if a shape has been selected, the pane title would display as Format Shape.

More Knowledge   **Changing the Position of a Picture Using the Mouse**

You can change the position of a picture by using the mouse to drag it to a new location on the slide. Hold down the [Shift] key before dragging a picture to move it in a straight line directly to the new location. You can also use the arrow keys and the gridlines to help position the picture.

---

2 With the picture still selected, on the **PICTURE TOOLS FORMAT tab**, in the **Picture Styles group**, click **Picture Border**, and then in the fifth column, click the first item—**Blue, Accent 1**. Click **Picture Border**, click **Weight**, and then click **2 1/4 pt**. Click **Picture Border**, click **Dashes**, and then click **Round Dot**. Deselect the picture, and then compare your screen with Figure 5.12.

The picture displays with a border. The color, style, and weight have all been set.

More Knowledge   **Removing a Picture Border**

To remove the border on a picture, click to select the picture. On the PICTURE TOOLS FORMAT tab, in the Picture Styles group, click Picture Border, and then click No Outline.

FIGURE 5.12

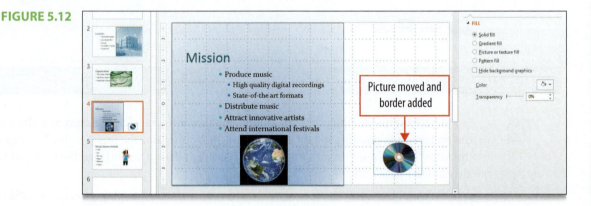

3 Click to select the picture of the globe. On the **Format Picture** pane, at the top, click **Size & Properties**; in the **Horizontal position** spin box, select the text, type **9.7** and then press [Enter]. In the **Vertical position** spin box, select the text, type **3** and then press [Enter].

4 With the globe picture selected, on the **FORMAT tab**, in the **Picture Styles group**, click **Picture Border**, and then under **Standard Colors**, click **Yellow**. Click **Picture Border**, point to **Weight**, and then click **4 ½ pt**.

↻ **ANOTHER WAY**   To change the picture border color, on the Format Picture pane, at the top, click Fill & Line ◇, and then under Line, select the Solid line option, and then click the Color arrow. To change the border weight, click the Width spin box.

---

5 Click the **INSERT tab**. In the **Images group**, click **Pictures**. Navigate to the location where your student files are stored, and then insert the picture **p05A_mp3.jpg**. On the **Format Picture** pane, under **Size**, in the **Height** spin box, select the text, type **1.6** and then press Enter.

The picture is sized proportionately.

🔁 **ANOTHER WAY**   To size a picture proportionately, select the picture, and then drag a corner diagonally to the desired height or width.

6 Under **POSITION**, in the **Horizontal position** spin box, select the text, type **9.7** and then press Enter. In the **Vertical position** spin box, select the text, type **0.5** and then press Enter.

7 With the picture selected, on the **FORMAT tab**, in the **Picture Styles group**, click **Picture Border**, and then in the fifth column, click the last item—**Blue, Accent 1, Darker 50%**. Click **Picture Border**, point to **Weight**, and then click **More Lines** to display the **Format Picture** pane with the **Fill** and **Line** options displayed.

Recall that the Format Picture pane displays the picture formatting types. The Line Style option is selected because you displayed the Picture Border first and then clicked More Lines.

8 Under **LINE**, in the **Width** spin box, select the text, type **9** and then press Enter. Scroll down as necessary, and then, click the **Join type arrow**, and then click **Miter**. Compare your screen with Figure 5.13.

A *mitered* border is a border with corners that are square. The default is rounded corners. The Format Picture pane allows you to enter borders wider than the maximum 6 pt listed when you click Picture Border and select Weight.

FIGURE 5.13

9 With the bordered picture of the MP3 player selected, on the **FORMAT tab**, in the **Picture Styles group**, click **Picture Effects**, point to **Reflection**, and then under **Reflection Variations**, click the first variation—**Tight Reflection, touching**. Deselect the picture, and then compare your screen with Figure 5.14.

🔁 **BY TOUCH**   Tap the FORMAT tab. In the Picture Styles group, tap Picture Effects, point to Reflection, and then under Reflection Variations, tap the first variation—Tight Reflection, touching.

The corners of the border are mitered borders, and a reflection is displayed below the picture.

FIGURE 5.14

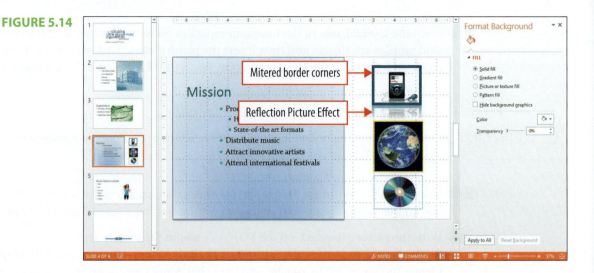

10 ▶ Click the **CD picture** and then hold down Shift, and then click the other two pictures. Release the Shift key. All three pictures should be selected. On the **FORMAT tab**, in the **Arrange group**, click **Align** 🖳, and then click **Align Right**. Click anywhere off the slide to deselect the pictures.

The border of the mp3 player extends farther to the right than the other two pictures.

NOTE **Aligning Pictures**

Use the alignment options on the FORMAT tab in the Arrange group to align pictures evenly. When you select Align Right, the selected pictures will align at the right side of the picture that is farthest to the right. Make sure that all pictures are selected before applying the alignment. The border size is not included in the alignment.

---

11 ▶ Click the picture of the **MP3 player**, and then press ← four times to nudge the picture border so that it is aligned with the other pictures. Deselect the picture, and then compare your screen with Figure 5.15.

Because the MP3 player picture has a wide border, it is now aligned better with the other pictures.

FIGURE 5.15

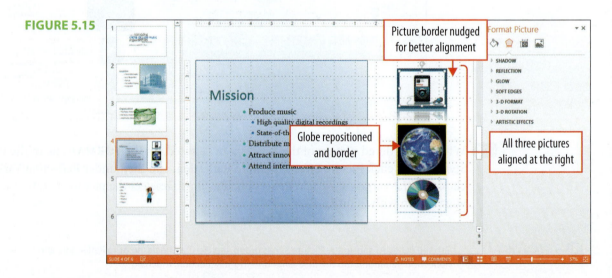

12 ▶ On **Slide 5**, click to select the picture of the dancer. On the **FORMAT tab**, ln the **Picture Styles group**, click **Picture Effects**, point to **Glow**, and then under **Glow Variations**, in the fourth row, click the first column—**Blue, 18 pt glow, Accent color 1**. Compare your screen with Figure 5.16.

The Picture Effect added a different kind of border.

FIGURE 5.16

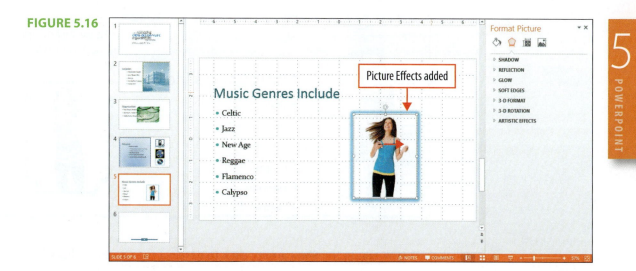

13 **Save** your changes.

Objective 3   Change the Shape of a Picture

Video P5-3

After you have inserted a picture, you can change the outline shape of the image. This is possible with or without the addition of a border. A large selection of shapes is available in PowerPoint. We apply several formatting techniques in this project so you can experiment with different options. Keep in mind, however, that applying too many formatting techniques can distract from the content of the presentation.

Activity 5.05 │ Changing the Shape of a Picture

In this activity, you will change a picture on your slide to a shape and then add a border.

1 With **Slide 5** as the active slide, on the **Format Picture** pane, at the top, click **Size & Properties** ▦. In the **Horizontal position** spin box, select the text, type **7.7** and then press Enter. In the **Vertical position** spin box, select the text, type **1.8** and then press Enter.

2 On the **PICTURE TOOLS FORMAT tab**, in the **Size group**, click the **Crop button arrow**, and then point to **Crop to Shape**. Under **Basic Shapes**, in the second row, point to the ninth symbol—**Plaque**, and then compare your screen with Figure 5.17.

FIGURE 5.17

3 Click the **Plaque** shape. On the **PICTURE TOOLS FORMAT tab**, in the **Picture Styles group**, click **Picture Border**, and then in the fifth column, click the fifth row—**Blue, Accent 1, Darker 25%**. Click **Picture Border**, point to **Weight**, and then click **3 pt**. **Close** the **Format Picture** pane. Click to deselect the picture, and then compare your screen with Figure 5.18.

Without the border, applying the shape is confusing. Adding the border emphasized the shape.

FIGURE 5.18

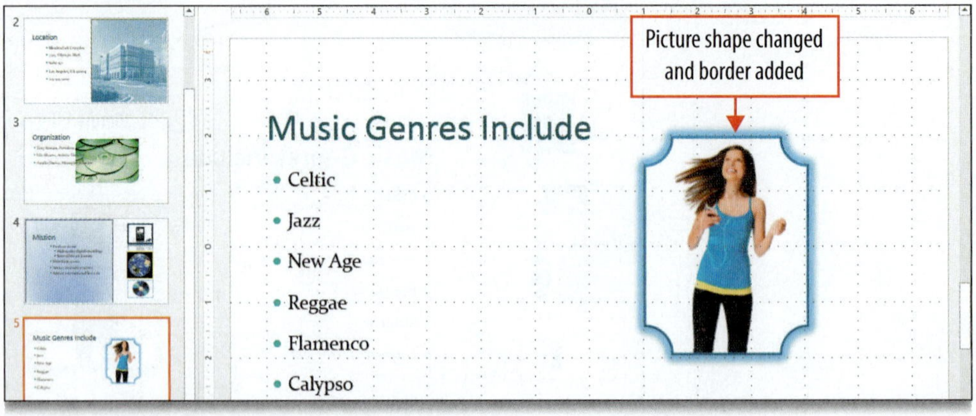

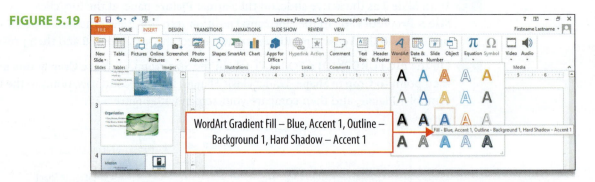

> **4** Click the **VIEW tab**. In the **Show group**, click to deselect the **Gridlines** check box.

> **5** **Save** 🖫 your changes.

Objective 4   Add a Picture to a WordArt Object and Merge Shapes

Video P5-4

A WordArt object may have a picture fill to add interest to a presentation. After adding the WordArt text, insert a picture fill that complements the WordArt message.

Activity 5.06   Adding a WordArt Object and Embedding a Picture

In this activity, you will add a WordArt object containing text. Then you will insert a picture as a fill for the object. You will also recolor the picture.

> **1** Click **Slide 6**. On the **INSERT tab**, in the **Text group**, click **WordArt**. In the third row, point to the third item—**Fill – Blue, Accent 1, Outline – Background 1, Hard Shadow – Accent 1**, and then compare your screen with Figure 5.19.

FIGURE 5.19

> **2** Click **Fill – Blue, Accent 1, Outline – Background 1, Hard Shadow – Accent 1**. In the **WordArt** object, with the text selected, type **Cross Oceans** and then press Enter. Type **Music** on the second line.

> **3** On the **DRAWING TOOLS FORMAT tab**, in the **Arrange group**, click **Align** 🖫, and then select **Align Middle**. Deselect the **WordArt**, and then compare your screen with Figure 5.20.

FIGURE 5.20

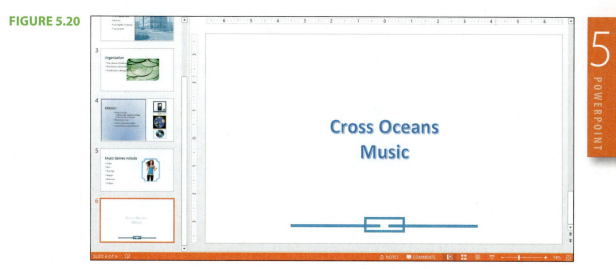

> 4 ▸ Click to select the WordArt object. On the **DRAWING TOOLS FORMAT tab**, in the **Shape Styles group**, click **Shape Fill**, and then click **Picture**. Navigate to the location where you are storing your files, click **p05A_Island.jpg**, and then click **Insert**. Compare your screen with Figure 5.21.

🔄 **ANOTHER WAY**   Double-click the file name to insert a picture.

FIGURE 5.21

Picture file inserted as Shape Fill

> 5 ▸ With the WordArt object selected, on the **PICTURE TOOLS FORMAT tab**, in the **Adjust group**, click **Color**. Under **Recolor**, in the first row, in the fourth column, click **Washout**.

> 6 ▸ Right-click on the WordArt, and then click **Format Picture**. At the top, click **Size & Properties** 🔳. Under **SIZE**, under **Scale Width**, select the **Lock aspect ratio** check box. Under **SIZE**, in the **Height** spin box, select the text, type **2.5** and then press ⏎. Compare your screen with Figure 5.22.

> When *Lock aspect ratio* is selected, you can change one dimension (height or width) of an object, such as a picture, and the other dimension will automatically be changed to maintain the proportion.

FIGURE 5.22

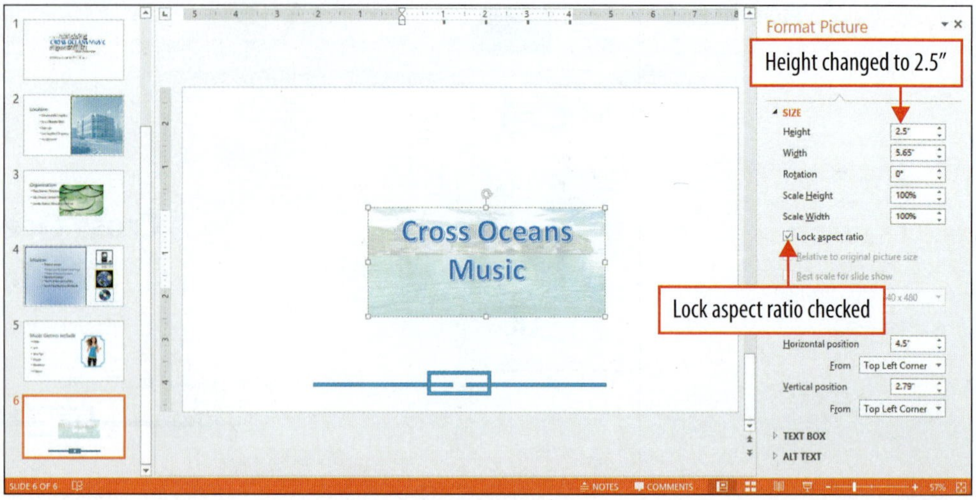

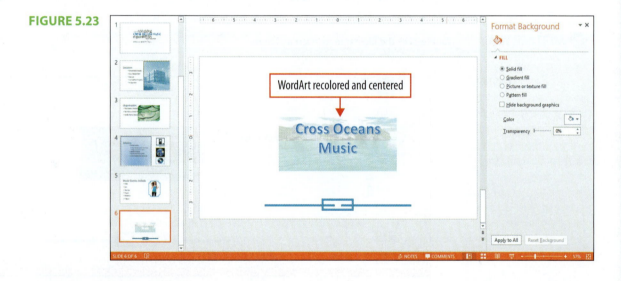

7 ▶ On the **PICTURE TOOLS FORMAT tab**, in the **Arrange group**, click **Align**, and then select **Align Center**. Deselect the **WordArt**, and then compare your screen with Figure 5.23.

FIGURE 5.23

8 ▶ **Save** your changes.

Activity 5.07 │ Merging Shapes

On occasion, the shape you want or need isn't listed in the Illustrations group. You can draw your own shapes and merge them together to create a new shape. In this activity, you will merge three separate shapes into one contiguous shape, move it to a new location, and then center the merged shape.

1 ▶ With **Slide 6** selected, at the bottom of the slide, hold down the Ctrl key and click to select the three blue shapes—a line, a frame box, and a line. Compare your screen with Figure 5.24.

FIGURE 5.24

2 ▶ On the **DRAWING TOOLS FORMAT tab**, in the **Insert Shapes group**, click **Merge Shapes**, and then click **Union**. Compare your screen with Figure 5.25.

The three shapes merge into one shape.

FIGURE 5.25

3 ▶ On the **Format Shape** pane, at the top, click **Size & Properties** 🔲. Under **POSITION**, in the **Horizontal position** spin box, select the text, type **3** and then press Enter. In the **Vertical position** spin box, select the text, type **6** and then press Enter. **Close** the **Format Shape** pane. Compare your screen with Figure 5.26.

The merged shape is repositioned.

FIGURE 5.26

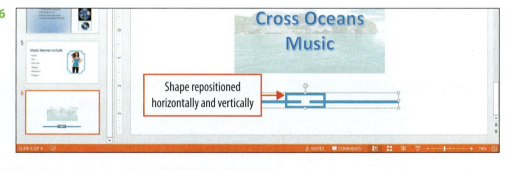

4 ▶ **Save** 💾 your changes.

Video P5-5

To further enhance a presentation, you can add audio and video. After you have applied audio and/or video to a presentation, you can control how you would like the files to play. A file can be set to play one time and then stop, or to *loop*, meaning the audio or video file will play repeatedly from start to finish until it is stopped manually. A *track*, or song, from a CD can also play during a slide show. Audio and video can be embedded or linked to the presentation. To *embed* is to save a presentation so that the audio or video file becomes part of the presentation file. To *link* is to save a presentation so that the audio or video file is saved separately from the presentation. Be sure to obtain permission to link or embed audio and video to a presentation to avoid violating the copyright.

ALERT!	Do You Have Permission to Use Audio in the Classroom?

If you are not allowed to play audio in your classroom or lab, use a headset for these activities. If you do not have a headset, ask your instructor how to proceed.

Activity 5.08 | Adding an Embedded Audio to a Presentation

In this activity, you will add audio to a presentation by embedding audio files and customizing how they will play.

1 Click **Slide 5**, and then click the **INSERT tab**. In the **Media group**, click the **Audio button arrow**, and then compare your screen with Figure 5.27.

FIGURE 5.27

2 Take a moment to study the options available for inserting audio into a presentation, as shown in the table in Figure 5.28.

FIGURE 5.28

SOUND OPTIONS	
SCREEN ELEMENT	**DESCRIPTION**
Online Audio	Displays the **Office.com** Clip Art pane so that you can search for royalty-free sound clip audio files in the Microsoft Office collection, both locally and online.
Audio on My PC	Enables you to insert audio clips such as music, narration, or audio bites from your computer or other computers that you are connected to. Compatible audio file formats include .mid or .midi, .mp3, and .wav.
Record Audio	Enables you to insert audio by recording the audio through a microphone and then naming and inserting the recorded audio.

3 From the displayed menu, click **Audio on My PC** to display the **Insert Audio** dialog box.

Above **Cancel**, click the **Audio Flies down arrow** to display the audio files supported by PowerPoint 2013, and then compare your screen with Figure 5.29. Take a moment to study the description of the Audio File Formats Supported in PowerPoint 2013, as shown in the table in Figure 5.30.

FIGURE 5.29

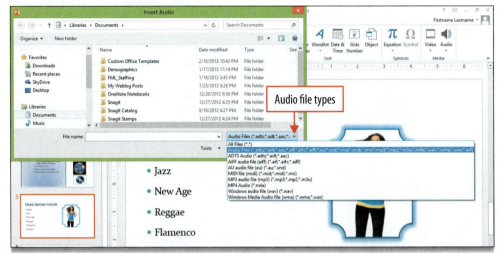

FIGURE 5.30

AUDIO FILE FORMATS SUPPORTED IN POWERPOINT 2013 SUPPORTED AUDIO FORMATS	
FILE FORMAT	**EXTENSION**
AIFF audio file	.aiff
AU audio file	.au
MIDI file	.mid or .midi
MP3 audio file	.mp3
MP4 audio	.m4a
Windows audio file	.wav
Windows Media Audio file	.wma

More **Knowledge** | **For the Best Audio and Video Playback Experience**

PowerPoint 2013 allows you to play back in several different video and audio file formats. For the best video playback experience, it is recommended that you use .mp4 videos encoded with H.264 video (a.k.a. MPEG-4 AVC) and AAC audio. For the best audio playback, it is recommended that you use .m4a files encoded with AAC audio. These formats are recommended for use with PowerPoint 2013 and for use with PowerPoint 2013 Web App.

---

5 Navigate to the location where your student files are stored, and click to select **p05A_Smooth_Jazz.wav**. At the bottom right of the **Insert Audio** dialog box, click the **Insert button arrow**, and then click **Insert**.

The AUDIO TOOLS tab displays on the Ribbon with the FORMAT and PLAYBACK tabs located under it. The PLAYBACK tab contains the Preview, Bookmarks, Editing, Audio Options, and Audio Styles groups. A speaker icon displays on the screen with Playback controls—Play/Pause, Move Back, Move Forward, Time, Mute/Unmute.

More Knowledge — Embedded Sounds versus Linked Sounds

The audio files used in this activity are *.wav* files. These files are embedded in the PowerPoint presentation, meaning that the object, or audio file, is inserted into the presentation and becomes part of the saved presentation file. Because the audio is stored within the presentation file, this guarantees that the audio will play from any audio-enabled computer that you use to show the presentation.

The other method of inserting audio into a presentation is to link the audio file. When you link the audio file, it is stored outside the presentation. If your presentation includes linked files, you must copy both the presentation file and the linked files to the same folder if you want to show the presentation on another computer.

You can use the Optimized Media Compatibility feature, on the FILE Info tab, to make it easier to share your PowerPoint 2013 presentation that contains an audio file with others or to show this presentation on another computer.

6 ▶ On the **AUDIO TOOLS PLAYBACK** tab, in the **Audio Options group**, select the **Hide During Show** check box. Click the **Volume button arrow**, and then click **Medium**. In the **Start** box, select **Automatically**. Compare your screen with Figure 5.31.

ANOTHER WAY To adjust the audio volume, on the Windows taskbar, on the right side, click the Speakers icon, and then adjust the volume.

FIGURE 5.31

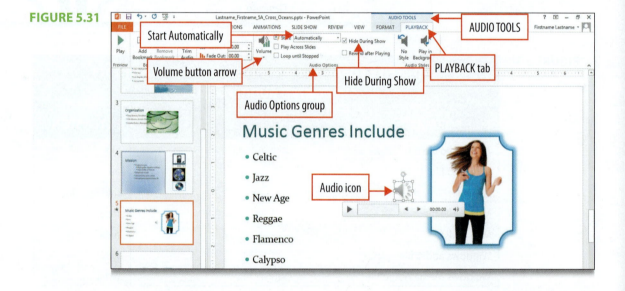

7 ▶ With **Slide 5** as the active slide, click the **SLIDE SHOW tab**. In the **Start Slide Show group**, click **From Current Slide**.

During a slide show presentation, the audio starts automatically when the slide displays. The audio plays one time and then stops. Because the audio icon is hidden, it does not display on the slide during the presentation of a slide show.

You can stop the audio by clicking the slide, by pressing Enter to advance to the next slide, or by pressing Esc.

More Knowledge — Play an Audio File for the Duration of Your Slide Show

You can play a song for the duration of your PowerPoint presentation slide show by selecting Play Across Slides in Audio options on the AUDIO TOOLS PLAYBACK tab. Often, this sets the mood while your audience views your slide show. Music downloaded from the Internet should be saved to your computer's hard drive first, and then inserted into your PowerPoint presentation. Adding audio will increase your file size. If file size is an issue, you can compress the audio file, keeping in mind that this will affect audio quality. On the FILE tab, under Info, click Compress Media, and then select the audio quality.

8 Press [Esc] to end the slide show and return to **Normal** view.

It is possible to play sounds in Normal view. In the Slides and Outline pane, a small star-shaped icon displays to the left of the slide thumbnail. This is the *Play Animations button*. Click this small button to play the sound. Click the Play Animations button again to stop the sound or press [Esc].

9 Make **Slide 1** the active slide. Click the **INSERT tab**, and then in the **Media group**, click the **Audio arrow**. Click **Audio on My PC**. Navigate to the location where your student files are stored, click **p05A_New_Age.wav**, and then click **Insert**. Right-click the **Audio icon** 🔊 and then click **Size and Position**. Click **POSITION** to expand, if necessary. In the **Horizontal position** spin box, select the text, type **9** and then press [Enter]. In the **Vertical position** spin box, select the text, type **6** and then press [Enter].

> **NOTE**   Moving a Sound Icon
>
> You can move the audio icon away from the main content of the slide so that the icon is easier for the presenter to locate. Avoid placing the icon where it interferes with the text the audience is viewing.

---

10 **Close** the Format Picture pane.

11 On the **AUDIO TOOLS PLAYBACK tab**, to the right of **Start**, select **On Click**, if necessary. On the slide, on the **Sound Control Panel**, click **Play** ▶ to listen to the audio clip, and then click **Pause** ⏸ to stop the audio clip.

> **ALERT!**   Is the Audio Not Audible? Is the Sound Control Panel Missing?
>
> Your PC may not have audio capability. If you know for a fact that your PC has audio capability, on the lower right side of the Windows taskbar, in the Notification area, click Speakers. To adjust speaker volume, drag the slider up to increase the volume. Make sure that the audio has not been muted. If the audio is muted, there will be a red stop symbol beside the speaker icon. Click the speaker icon and unmute the audio. Finally, make sure that you have your speakers turned on. If you cannot see the Sound Control Panel, click the speaker icon.

---

12 On the **AUDIO TOOLS PLAYBACK tab**, in the **Audio Options group**, select the **Hide During Show** check box, and then compare your screen with Figure 5.32.

FIGURE 5.32

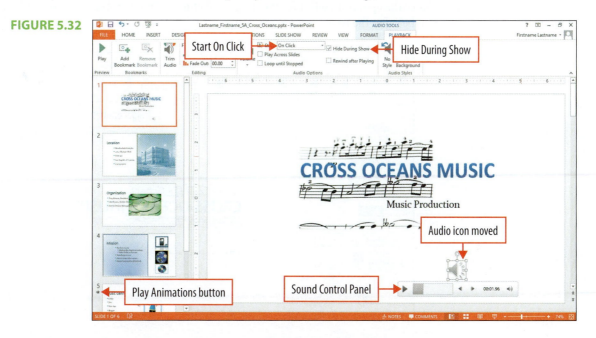

13 Click the **SLIDE SHOW tab**. In the **Start Slide Show group**, click **From Beginning**. Click the slide, and notice that no audio plays. Instead, it takes you to the next slide.

NOTE | Hiding the Sound Icon during a Slide Show

Hiding the audio icon during the slide show works only when the audio is set to play Automatically. If you select On Click, the icon must display. If you select Hide During Show, the audio will not play when you click the slide unless you create a specific trigger.

14 ▶ Press [Esc] to end the slide show and return to **Normal** view.

15 ▶ Click **Slide 1**. Click to select the audio icon. Under **AUDIO TOOLS**, click the **PLAYBACK tab**.

16 ▶ In the **Audio Options group**, deselect the **Hide During Show** check box. Click the **SLIDE SHOW tab**. In the **Start Slide Show group**, click the **From Current Slide** button. Point to the **Audio** icon. On the control panel, click **Play**. Alternatively, you can click the top part of the audio icon to hear the sound.

   After the slide show is started, there may be a delay before the mouse pointer becomes active.

17 ▶ Press [Esc].

18 ▶ **Save** 🖫 your changes.

Activity 5.09 | Setting a Trigger for an Embedded Audio in a Presentation

In this activity, you will set a trigger for an embedded audio. A *trigger* is a portion of text, a graphic, or a picture that, when clicked, causes the audio or video to play. You will display the Animation Pane to help you locate the trigger. The *Animation Pane* is an area used for adding and removing effects.

1 ▶ With **Slide 1** as the active slide, click to select the audio icon, if necessary.

2 ▶ Click the **ANIMATIONS tab**. In the **Advanced Animation group**, click **Animation Pane** to display the **Animation Pane** on the right side of the window. In the **Animation Pane**, the audio file name is displayed in the list.

3 ▶ In the **Advanced Animation group**, click the **Trigger button arrow**, and then point to **On Click of**. Compare your screen with Figure 5.33.

   Notice the options to select for the trigger—Picture 8, Title 1, Subtitle 2 or the file name. The number after the trigger option may vary.

FIGURE 5.33

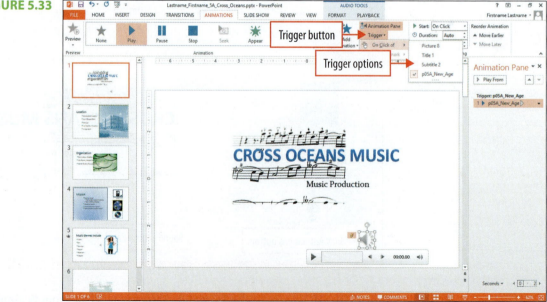

4 ▶ Click **Title 1**. Compare your screen with Figure 5.34.

At the right, in the Animation Pane, *Trigger: Title 1: Cross Oceans ...* is displayed at the top of the list. Notice that it is identified as the trigger.

FIGURE 5.34

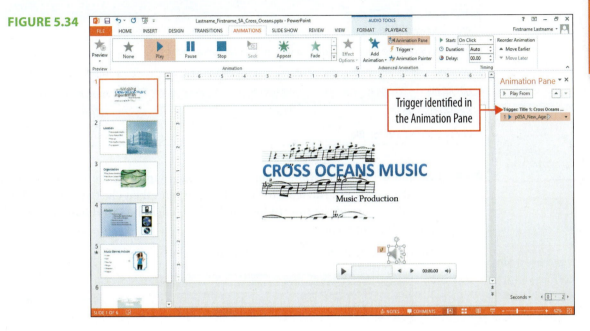

Trigger identified in the Animation Pane

5 ▶ **Close** ☒ the **Animation Pane**. With the **Audio icon** 🔊 selected, on the **AUDIO TOOLS PLAYBACK tab**, in the **Audio Options group**, select the check box for **Hide During Show.**

6 ▶ Click the **SLIDE SHOW tab**. In the **Start Slide Show group**, click **From Current Slide**. Click the title *Cross Oceans Music* to start the audio. Press Esc.

The mouse pointer changes from an arrow to a hand and then back to an arrow when you move off the title.

7 ▶ **Save** 🖫 your changes.

Activity 5.10 │ Adding a Linked Video to a Presentation

In this activity, you will link a video to your presentation. A presentation with a linked video is smaller in file size than a presentation with an embedded video. To prevent possible problems with broken links, it is a good idea to copy the video into the same folder as your presentation and then link to it from there. Both the video file and the presentation file must be available when presenting your slide show.

1 ▶ In the location where your data files are stored, locate **p05_Music_Video.avi**, and then copy it into your **PowerPoint Chapter 5** folder. Take a moment to study the description of the Video File Formats Supported in PowerPoint 2013, as shown in the table in Figure 5.35.

> **N O T E**   Copying a File
>
> To copy a file on your storage device, display File Explorer and locate the file you want, right-click the file name, and then click Copy. Next, open the folder where you are saving your completed files, right-click, and then click Paste.

FIGURE 5.35

VIDEO FILE FORMATS SUPPORTED IN POWERPOINT 2013 SUPPORTED VIDEO FORMATS	
FILE FORMAT	**EXTENSION**
Windows Media file	.asf
Windows Video file (Some .avi files may require additional codecs)	.avi
MP4 Video file	.mp4, .m4v, .mov
Movie file	.mpg or .mpeg
Adobe Flash Media	.swf
Windows Media Video file	.wmv

2 ▶ Click **Slide 6**. Click the **INSERT tab**. In the **Media group**, click the **Video button arrow**, and then click **Video on My PC**. Navigate to your data files, and then click **p05_Music_Video.avi**. In the lower right corner of the **Insert Video** dialog box, click the **Insert button arrow**. Compare your screen with Figure 5.36.

The two options on the Insert list are Insert and Link to File.

FIGURE 5.36

3 ▶ Click **Link to File**. With the video selected, on the **VIDEO TOOLS FORMAT tab**, in the **Size group**, change the **Video Height** to **1.5"**. Right-click the video, and then click **Size and Position** to display the **Format Video** pane. Click **POSITION** to expand, if necessary. In the **Horizontal position** spin box, select the text, type **5.5** and then press [Enter]. In the **Vertical position** spin box, select the text, type **0.5** and then press [Enter]. Compare your screen with Figure 5.37.

Moving and resizing the video allows you to see the content of the slide better.

FIGURE 5.37

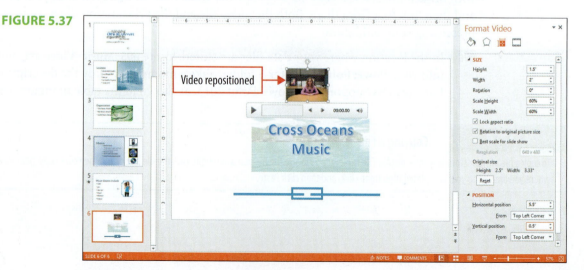

4 Close the **Format Video** pane. **Save** 🖫 your changes.

Activity 5.11 | Changing the Trigger for a Linked Video in a Presentation

In this activity, you will use the Animation Pane to change the trigger that will play the video file from the video image to the WordArt shape. You will also set the video so it plays in full screen.

1 With **Slide 6** as the active slide, click to select the video, if necessary.

2 Click the **ANIMATIONS tab**. In the **Advanced Animation group**, click **Animation Pane** to display the **Animation Pane** on the right side of the window.

In the Animation Pane, the video file name is displayed in the list.

3 Click the **Trigger button arrow**, and then point to **On Click of**. Compare your screen with Figure 5.38.

Notice the options to select for the trigger—Freeform 6, Rectangle 1, and p05_Music_Video.avi. Rectangle represents the WordArt shape. The numbers after Freeform and Rectangle may vary.

FIGURE 5.38

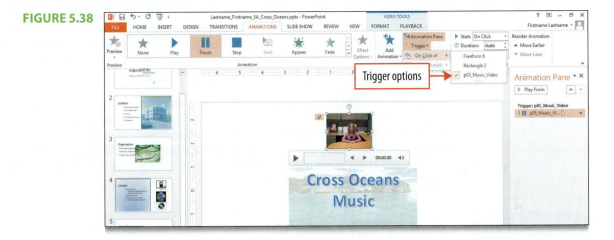

4 Click **Rectangle 1** (the number after Rectangle may vary). Compare your screen with Figure 5.39.

Rectangle refers to the WordArt.

FIGURE 5.39

5 On the **ANIMATIONS tab**, in the **Advanced Animation group**, click **Animation Pane** to close the **Animation Pane**. On the **VIDEO TOOLS PLAYBACK tab**, in the **Video Options group**, select the check box for **Hide While Not Playing**. Select the check box for **Play Full Screen**. Compare your screen with Figure 5.40.

FIGURE 5.40

Hide While Not Playing checked

Play Full Screen checked

6 ▶ Click the **SLIDE SHOW tab**. In the **Start Slide Show group**, click **From Current Slide**. Click the *Cross Oceans Music* WordArt to start the video. After the video plays, press Esc.

> The video plays in full screen. Allow the video to play completely. If you stop the video, the video will display on the slide. For that reason, you might want to resize the video to a smaller size.

7 ▶ In the **Start Slide Show group**, click **From Beginning** to view the entire presentation. Click the trigger on **Slide 1** to hear the audio. Click the trigger on **Slide 6** to view the video. Press Esc.

8 ▶ In **File Explorer**, display the contents of your **PowerPoint Chapter 5** folder. On the **View tab**, in the **Layout group**, click **Details**. Observe the size of the presentation file is larger than the size of the video file, however, the presentation file size would be substantially larger if the video had been linked instead of embedded. Take a moment to study the description of the Compression Quality Comparison, as shown in the table in Figure 5.41.

> Because the presentation file contains a link to the video file, the actual video file is not a part of the presentation file size. For example, the video for this presentation is about 3,100 KB and the presentation file is about 7,500 KB. Therefore, if you had embedded the video in the presentation instead of linking it, the presentation file would be about 10,500 KB. If you send this presentation electronically or transfer it to another location such as a USB drive, be sure to place both files in the same folder before sending or moving them.

More Knowledge   **Compressing Your Presentation Files**

If you are concerned about the size of your files or need to transmit them electronically, you may wish to consider using one of the compression methods. To display your options, on the FILE tab, under Info, click Compress Media. Refer to Figure 5.41 for an explanation of compression qualities. Under Media Size and Performance, the total file size of the media files in the presentation displays. These options will not display on the FILE Info tab unless you have a media file embedded in the presentation.

FIGURE 5.41

COMPRESSION QUALITY COMPARISON	
COMPRESSION METHOD	**DESCRIPTION**
No Compression	The original size of the presentation.
Presentation Quality	Save space while maintaining overall audio and video quality.
Internet Quality	Quality will be comparable to media which is streamed over the Internet.
Low Quality	Use when space is limited, such as when sending presentations via email.

ALERT!   **Did You Change the Name of the Video File after Linking It to a Presentation?**

If you change the name of a video file after you link it to a presentation, the video will not play. You will have to link the file again.

9 Return to the PowerPoint presentation. On the **INSERT tab**, in the **Text group**, click **Header & Footer** to display the **Header and Footer** dialog box. Click the **Notes and Handouts tab**. Under **Include on page**, select the **Date and time** check box, and then select **Fixed**. If necessary, clear the **Header** check box, and then select the **Page number** and **Footer** check boxes. In the **Footer** box, using your own name, type **Lastname_Firstname_5A_Cross_Oceans** and then click **Apply to All**.

10 Click the **FILE tab**, and then in the lower right portion of the screen, click **Show All Properties**. In the **Tags** box, type **mission, genres** and in the **Subject** box type your course name and section number. In the **Author** box, right-click the existing author name, click **Edit Property**, replace the existing text with your first and last name, click outside text box to deselect, and then click **OK**.

11 Save 🖫 your changes. Print **Handouts 4 Slides Horizontal**, or submit your presentation electronically as directed by your instructor.

12 **Close** the presentation, and then **Exit** PowerPoint.

END | You have completed Project 5A

PROJECT ACTIVITIES

In Activities 5.12 through 5.14, you will create a PowerPoint photo album to display business photos of jazz musicians promoted and recorded by Cross Oceans Music. You will insert photos, add an attention-getting theme, and select a layout. You will also add frames to the photos and provide captions. You will reorder pictures in a photo album, adjust the rotation of a photo album image, and change a photo album layout. You will experiment with tools that allow you to enter and format text in a text box and crop a photo to emphasize a key area of the photo. Your completed presentation will look similar to Figure 5.42.

PROJECT FILES

Build from Scratch

For Project 5B, you will need the following files:

New blank PowerPoint presentation
p05B_Jazz1.jpg
p05B_Jazz2.jpg
p05B_Jazz3.jpg
p05B_Jazz4.jpg
p05B_Jazz5.jpg
p05B_Jazz6.jpg
p05B_Jazz7.jpg

You will save your presentation as:

Lastname_Firstname_5B_Jazz_Album.pptx

PROJECT RESULTS

brongkie/Fotolia; Andrey Kiselev/Fotolia; Tomasz Trojanowski/Fotolia; herll/Fotolia; Chad McDermott/Fotolia; Stanislav Komogorov/Fotolia; mkm3/Fotolia

FIGURE 5.42 Project 5B Jazz Album

Video P5-6

In the following activity, you will create a PowerPoint photo album. In PowerPoint, a *photo album* is a stylized presentation format to display pictures; you can display 1, 2, or 4 photos on a slide. The format may include a title or caption for the photo(s). A placeholder is inserted with each photo when the photo is added to the album. PowerPoint provides an easy and powerful tool to aid you in creating an exciting photo album.

Activity 5.12 | Creating a Photo Album

In this activity, you will create a photo album by inserting and customizing photos and selecting a theme. Each picture will be placed on its own slide.

1 ▶ Start PowerPoint. Click **Blank Presentation**. Click the **INSERT tab**. In the **Images group**, click the **Photo Album button arrow**, and then click **New Photo Album**. Compare your screen with Figure 5.43.

> The Photo Album dialog box provides an easy and convenient way to insert and remove pictures; rearrange and rotate pictures; apply brightness and contrast; insert captions; and select a layout, theme, and frame shape.

FIGURE 5.43

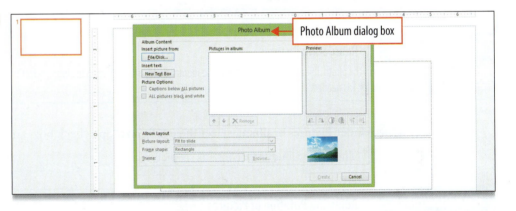

2 ▶ Under **Insert picture from**, click **File/Disk** to display the **Insert New Pictures** dialog box. Navigate to the location where your student files are stored, click **p05B_Jazz1.jpg**, and then click **Insert**. Compare your screen with Figure 5.44.

> The file name displays as the first picture in the album, under Pictures in album, with a preview of the photograph.

🔁 **ANOTHER WAY**   When inserting pictures in the Photo Album dialog box, you can double-click the picture file name to insert it.

FIGURE 5.44

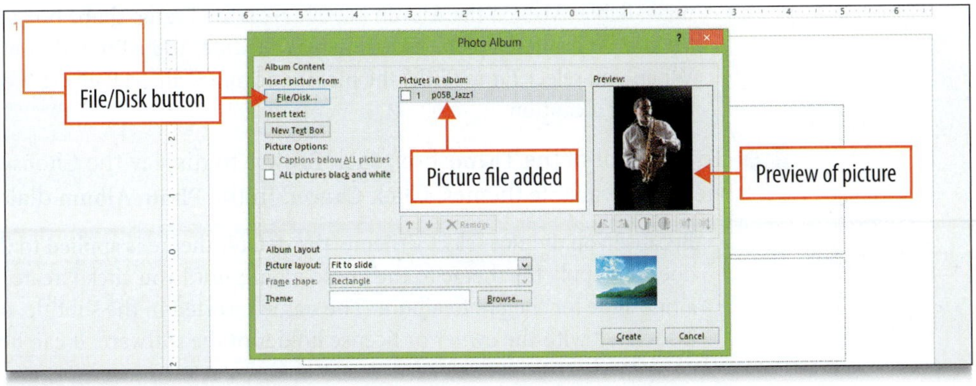

3 Using the technique you practiced, insert **p05B_Jazz2.jpg**, **p05B_Jazz3.jpg**, **p05B_Jazz4.jpg**, **p05B_Jazz5.jpg**, **p05B_Jazz6.jpg**, and **p05B_Jazz7.jpg**. Compare your screen with Figure 5.45.

FIGURE 5.45

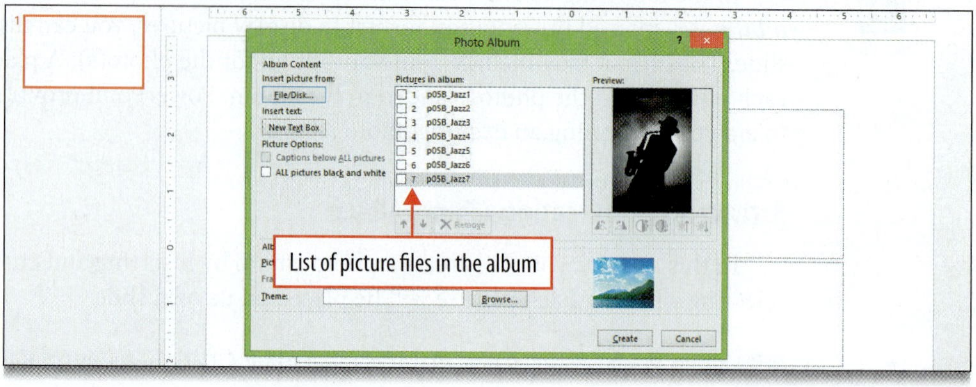

N O T E   Inserting a Picture in the Photo Album Task Pane

If the pictures you want to insert into your photo album are listed in a sequence on your storage location, you can click on the first file name in the list, hold down the Shift key and click on the last picture in the list, and then click Insert. If the pictures are not in a sequence, you can hold down the Ctrl key while clicking the pictures individually, and then click Insert.

More **Knowledge**   Reordering Pictures

PowerPoint inserts pictures in the photo album in alphabetical order. To reorder them, under Pictures in album, select the picture check box, and then click the Move up or Move down ⬇ as needed.

4 Under **Pictures in album**, select the **p05B_Jazz7.jpg** check box, and then click **Remove**.

The photo album now contains six pictures.

More **Knowledge**   Adjusting Rotation of Pictures

Pictures display in either horizontal or vertical orientation in the Preview pane. If you wish to change the orientation, click the rotate left icon 🔄 or rotate right icon 🔄 to rotate the image in 90-degree increments located below the Preview pane.

5 Under **Album layout**, click the **Picture layout arrow** to display the options.

You can choose to insert 1, 2, or 4 pictures on a slide, with or without a title, or you can choose Fit to Slide.

6 Click **Fit to Slide**, if necessary.

In the Album Content area, the Captions below ALL pictures check box is dimmed and therefore unavailable. Also, in the Album Layout area, the Frame shape box is unavailable. In a photo album, the border around a picture is known as a *frame*, and a limited number of styles are available. When you select *Fit to Slide*, the picture occupies all available space on the slide with no room for a frame or a caption.

7 To the right of the **Theme** box, click **Browse** to display the **Choose Theme** dialog box. Scroll to view the available themes. Click **Cancel**. In the **Photo Album** dialog box, click **Create**.

Because you did not select a theme, the default theme is applied to the Photo Album. PowerPoint does not apply the theme to the photo album until you click Create. Notice that PowerPoint creates a title slide for the photo album. The name inserted in the subtitle, on the title slide, is the name associated with the owner or license holder of the software. It can be changed on the slide.

8 ▶ With **Slide 1** active, select the text in the subtitle placeholder, and then press Delete. Click the top edge of the subtitle placeholder to select it, and the press Delete.

9 ▶ In the title placeholder, click placing the insertion point to the left of the word *Photo*. Type **Jazz** and then press Spacebar. Click placing the insertion point to the right of the word *Album*. Press Enter. Type **Cross Oceans Music**

10 ▶ Select the text *Cross Oceans Music*. On the mini toolbar, change the font size to **24**. Select the text *Jazz Photo Album*. On the mini toolbar, change the font size to **54**. Select all the text in the title placeholder. On the mini toolbar, click **Bold**, and then click the **Font Color button arrow** . Under **Standard** colors, click the first color—**Dark Red**. On the mini toolbar, click **Align Left**. On the **HOME tab**, in the **Paragraph group**, click the **Align Text arrow**, and then click **Top**. Click outside the placeholder to deselect. Compare your screen with Figure 5.46.

The title and subtitle font color, font size, and alignment are changed.

FIGURE 5.46

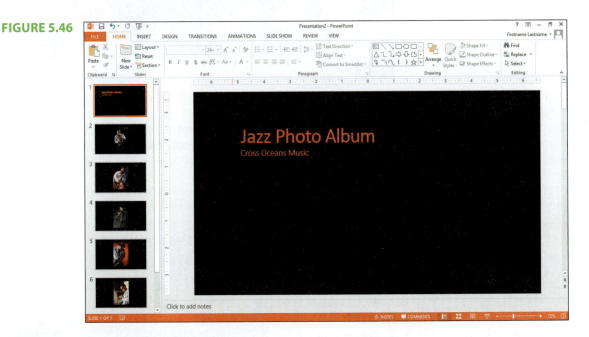

11 ▶ Press F12 to display the **Save As** dialog box, and then navigate to the location where you are storing your projects for this chapter. Using your own name, save the file as **Lastname_Firstname_5B_Jazz_Album**

Because PowerPoint creates the photo album in a new presentation, you should wait until you click Create before saving the photo album.

Objective 7 Edit a Photo Album and Add a Caption

Video P5-7

After you create a PowerPoint photo album, it is possible to format the background of the title slide by adding and customizing a caption for each photo. A ***caption*** is text that helps to identify or explain a picture or graphic.

Activity 5.13 | Editing a Photo Album and Adding a Caption

In this activity, you will edit a photo album, change the picture layout, and add captions.

1 ▶ With **Slide 1** as the active slide, right-click the first thumbnail in the pane on the left to display the shortcut menu, and then click **Format Background**. In the **Format Background** pane, under **Fill**, select **Picture or texture fill**.

2 Under **Insert picture from**, click **File**. Navigate to the location where your student files are stored, click **p05B_Jazz7.jpg**, and then click **Insert**. Compare your screen with Figure 5.47.

This applies the background picture to the title slide only. Notice that the top of the picture is off the slide.

FIGURE 5.47

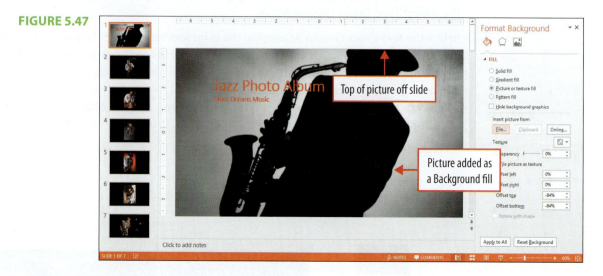

3 In the **Format Background** pane, in the **Offset top** spin box, select the text, type **-40**, and then press **Enter**. In the **Offset bottom** spin box, select the text, type **-60**, and then press **Enter**. **Close** the **Format Background** pane. Compare your screen with Figure 5.48.

This lowers the background silhouette to make the top visible on the slide. Because only the top and bottom offset were changed, the picture is a little distorted.

A L E R T !   **Did Format Background Appear on the Context-Sensitive Menu?**

If you did not see Format Background as a choice when you right-clicked the slide, you probably clicked on the Title or Subtitle placeholder. Right-click in another place on the slide, and you should see the appropriate options.

FIGURE 5.48

4 Click the **SLIDE SHOW tab**. In the **Start Slide Show group**, click **From Beginning**. Click through all the slides. Press **Esc** to return to **Normal** view.

The pictures fit to the slide and do not allow room for a caption.

5 Click the **INSERT tab**. In the **Images group**, click the **Photo Album button arrow**, and then click **Edit Photo Album** to display the **Edit Photo Album** dialog box. Under **Album Layout**, click the **Picture layout arrow** to display the options, and then click **1 picture**. Click the **Frame shape arrow**, to display the options, and then click **Simple Frame, White**.

6 In the **Album Content** area, under **Picture Options**, select the **Captions below ALL pictures** check box, and then compare your screen with Figure 5.49.

FIGURE 5.49

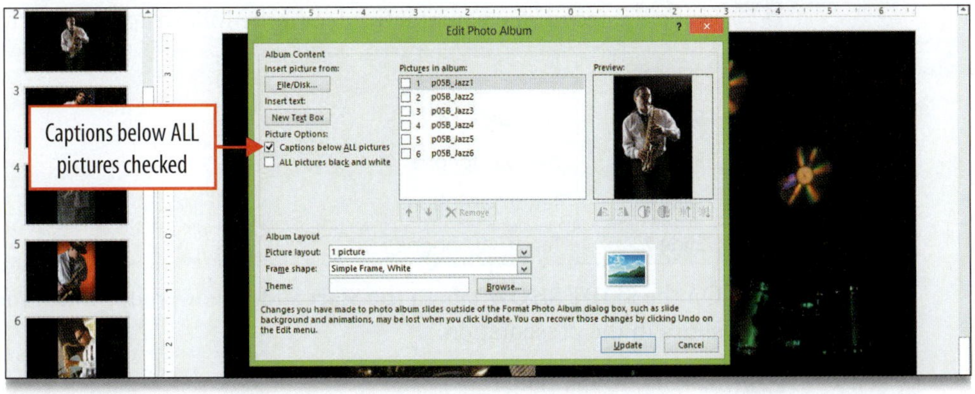

Captions below ALL pictures checked

7 Click **Update**, and then make **Slide 2** the active slide. Compare your screen with Figure 5.50.

Notice that, by default, the file name displays as the caption.

FIGURE 5.50

File name is default caption

8 With **Slide 2** as the active slide, click to select the picture caption placeholder. Double-click to select the caption, and then type **Alto Saxophone** Compare your screen with Figure 5.51.

FIGURE 5.51

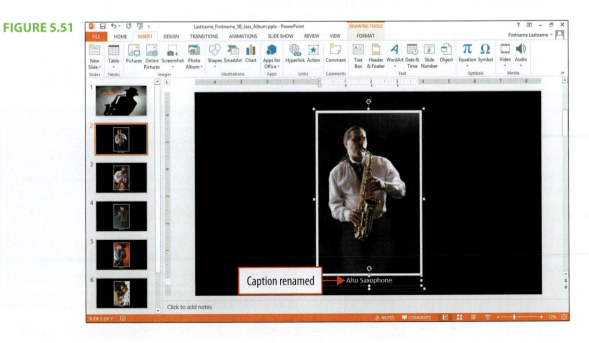
Caption renamed

9 Using the technique you practiced, add the following captions to **Slides 3, 4, 5, 6,** and **7:**

Slide 3	Bass
Slide 4	Trumpet
Slide 5	Alto Saxophone
Slide 6	Tenor Saxophone
Slide 7	Tenor Saxophone

10 On the **SLIDE SHOW tab**, in the **Start Slide Show group**, click **From beginning** to view the slides in the presentation.

11 Save 🖫 your changes.

Objective 8 | Crop a Picture

Video P5-8

In the following activity, you will edit the PowerPoint photo album you created by cropping the picture. When you **crop** a picture, you remove unwanted or unnecessary areas of a picture. Images are often cropped to create more emphasis on the primary subject of the image. Recall that the Compress Picture pane provides the option to delete the cropped area of a picture. Deleting the cropped area reduces file size and also prevents people from being able to view the parts of the picture that you have removed. The **crop handles** are used like sizing handles to crop a picture, and the **Crop tool** is the mouse pointer used when removing areas of a picture.

Activity 5.14 | Cropping a Picture and Inserting a Textbox

1 Make **Slide 7** the active slide, if necessary. Click the picture one time to select the placeholder, and then click again to select the picture.

> Because the placeholder is inserted at the time the picture is inserted, you must click the picture two times in order to gain access to the crop feature.

2 On the **PICTURE TOOLS FORMAT tab**, in the **Size group**, click the **Crop arrow**, and then point to **Crop**. Compare your screen with Figure 5.52.

<table>
<tr><td>**ALERT!**</td><td>**Is the Crop Inactive?**</td></tr>
<tr><td colspan="2">If you cannot display the Crop tool and crop lines, click the picture two times.</td></tr>
</table>

FIGURE 5.52

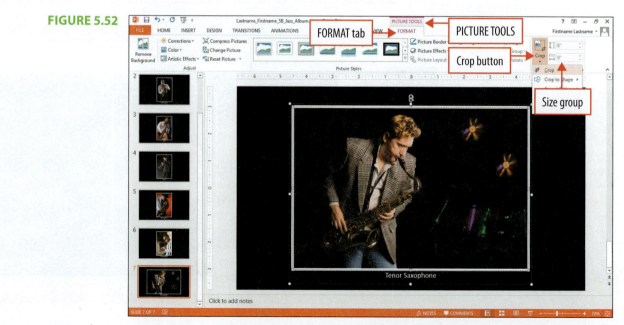

3 Click **Crop**. Position the **Crop pointer** 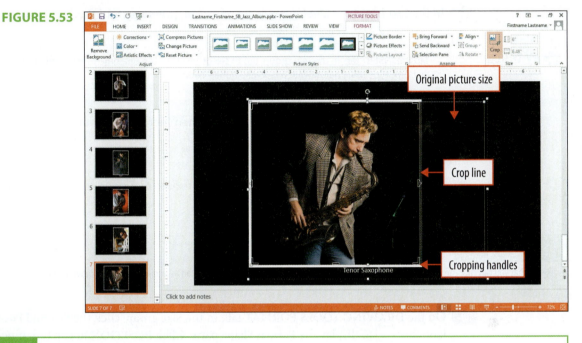 just inside the middle cropping handle on the right edge of the picture.

> The mouse pointer assumes the shape of the crop line, in this case a straight vertical line with a short horizontal line attached.

4 Drag the pointer to the left until the right edge of the picture aligns with approximately the **2-inch mark to the right of 0** on the **horizontal ruler**, and then release the mouse button. Compare your screen with Figure 5.53.

> The dark area to the right represents the area that will be removed. The caption is no longer centered under the picture.

FIGURE 5.53

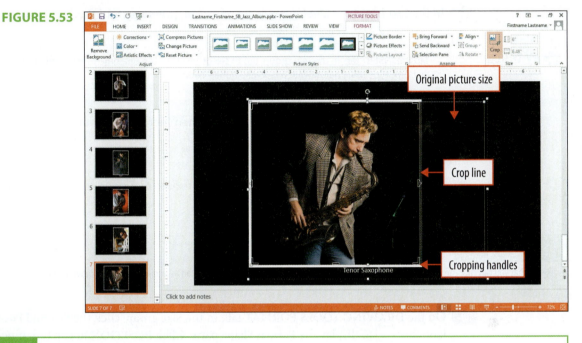

NOTE   **Does the Ruler Display?**

If the ruler does not display, on the VIEW tab, in the Show group, select the Ruler check box.

---

5 Click outside the picture to turn off cropping.

🔄 **ANOTHER WAY**   You can also turn off the cropping button by pressing Esc or by clicking Crop.

---

6 Under the picture, select the caption. On **the DRAWING TOOLS FORMAT tab**, in the **Size group**, in the **Width** spin box, select the text, type **6.5** and then press Enter.

> The caption is now centered under the cropped picture.

7 Click the **INSERT tab**. In the **Text group**, click **Text Box**, and then click one time to the right of the picture. Compare your screen with Figure 5.54.

FIGURE 5.54

Text box

8 ▸ In the text box, type **Meet our newest musician,** press [Enter], and then type **James Todd.**

🔄 **BY TOUCH**   Tap the INSERT tab. In the Text group, tap to select Text Box. Tap one time to the right of the picture. In the text box, type **Meet our newest musician, James Todd**.

9 ▸ Select both lines of text in the text box, and then increase the font size to **24. Center** ☰ the text.

🔄 **BY TOUCH**   Tap the HOME tab. In the Font group, slide the arrow to select the font size to 24. In the Paragraph group, tap Center to center the text.

> **NOTE**   **Selecting Text in Placeholders**
>
> Recall that you can click the border of a placeholder to select text. When the border is displayed as a solid border, you know the text is selected.

10 ▸ On the **DRAWING TOOLS FORMAT tab,** in the **Size group,** click the **Size and Position** dialog launcher ⬛ to display the **Format Shape** pane. Click **POSITION** to expand, if necessary. In the **Horizontal position** spin box, select the text, type **9** and then press [Enter]. In the **Vertical position** spin box, select the text, type **3** and then press [Enter]. Compare your screen with Figure 5.55.

FIGURE 5.55

Text added and text box repositioned

11 ▸ **Close** the Format Shape pane. Click the **SLIDE SHOW tab.** In the **Start Slide Show group,** click **From Beginning,** and then view the presentation. Press [Esc] to return to **Normal** view.

🔄 **ANOTHER WAY**   To start the slide show from the beginning, make Slide 1 the active slide, and then press the F5 key or the Slide Show icon on the status bar.

More Knowledge | Create Multiple Columns in a Single Shape—Text Box

To create multiple columns in a single shape, such as a Text Box, select the text box, and then on the Format Shape pane, click TEXT OPTIONS. Under TEXT OPTIONS, click Textbox, Wrap text in shape, and then click Columns. In the Number spin box, select the text, type in the number of desired columns, and then click OK or press ⏎Enter. The typed text will appear in columns.

12 On the **INSERT tab**, in the **Text group**, click **Header & Footer** to display the **Header and Footer** dialog box. Click the **Notes and Handouts tab**. Under **Include on page**, select the **Date and time** check box, and then select **Fixed**. If necessary, clear the **Header** check box, and then select the **Page number** and **Footer** check boxes. In the **Footer** box, using your own name, type **Lastname_Firstname_5B_Jazz_Album** and then click **Apply to All**.

13 Click the **FILE tab**, and then in the lower right portion of the screen, click **Show All Properties**. In the **Tags** box, type **jazz, photo, album** and in the **Subject** box type your course name and section number. In the **Author** box, right-click the existing author name, click **Edit Property**, replace the existing text with your first and last name, click outside text box to deselect, and then click **OK**.

14 Save 🖫 your changes. Print **Handouts 4 Slides Horizontal**, or submit your presentation electronically as directed by your instructor.

15 **Close** the presentation, and then **Exit** PowerPoint.

END | You have completed Project 5B

END OF CHAPTER

SUMMARY

In this chapter, you practiced completing a PowerPoint presentation by inserting and modifying pictures and images, and by changing the sharpness and softness as well as the brightness and contrast.

Next, you added borders to images. You added a mitered border, a colored border, and a weighted border. You recolored pictures, merged three shapes into one, and added audio and video to a slide show.

You added a WordArt object to the presentation and embedded a picture. You changed the method by which audio and video play in a slide show and created triggers for starting them. You added a video link.

You created and edited a photo album using the fit to slide layout option. You practiced cropping a picture using the crop tool to remove areas of a picture. You added captions to photos to add clarity.

GO! LEARN IT ONLINE

Review the concepts and key terms in this chapter by completing these online challenges, which you can find at **www.pearsonhighered.com/go.**

Matching and Multiple Choice:
Answer matching and multiple choice questions to test what you learned in this chapter. MyITLab®

Crossword Puzzle:
Spell out the words that match the numbered clues, and put them in the puzzle squares.

Flipboard:
Flip through the definitions of the key terms in this chapter and match them with the correct term.

REVIEW AND ASSESSMENT GUIDE FOR POWERPOINT CHAPTER 5

Your instructor may assign one or more of these projects to help you review the chapter and assess your mastery and understanding of the chapter.

	Review and Assessment Guide for PowerPoint Chapter 5		
Project	**Apply Skills from These Chapter Objectives**	**Project Type**	**Project Location**
5C	Objectives 1–5 from Project 5A	**5C Skills Review** A guided review of the skills from Project 5A.	On the following pages
5D	Objectives 6–8 from Project 5B	**5D Skills Review** A guided review of the skills from Project 5B.	On the following pages
5E	Objectives 1–5 from Project 5A	**5E Mastering PowerPoint (Grader Project)** A demonstration of your mastery of the skills in Project 5A with extensive decision making.	In MyITLab and on the following pages
5F	Objectives 6–8 from Project 5B	**5F Mastering PowerPoint (Grader Project)** A demonstration of your mastery of the skills in Project 5B with extensive decision making.	In MyITLab and on the following pages
5G	Objectives 1–8 from Projects 5A and 5B	**5G Mastering PowerPoint (Grader Project)** A demonstration of your mastery of the skills in Projects 5A and 5B with extensive decision making.	In MyITLab and on the following pages
5H	Combination of Objectives from Projects 5A and 5B	**5H GO! Fix It** A demonstration of your mastery of the skills in Projects 5A and 5B by creating a correct result from a document that contains errors you must find.	Online
5I	Combination of Objectives from Projects 5A and 5B	**5I GO! Make It** A demonstration of your mastery of the skills in Projects 5A and 5B by creating a result from a supplied picture.	Online
5J	Combination of Objectives from Projects 5A and 5B	**5J GO! Solve It** A demonstration of your mastery of the skills in Projects 5A and 5B, your decision-making skills, and your critical thinking skills. A task-specific rubric helps you self-assess your result.	Online
5K	Combination of Objectives from Projects 5A and 5B	**5K GO! Solve It** A demonstration of your mastery of the skills in Projects 5A and 5B, your decision-making skills, and your critical thinking skills. A task-specific rubric helps you self-assess your result.	On the following pages
5L	Combination of Objectives from Projects 5A and 5B	**5L GO! Think** A demonstration of your understanding of the chapter concepts applied in a manner that you would outside of college. An analytic rubric helps you and your instructor grade the quality of your work by comparing it to the work an expert in the discipline would create.	On the following pages
5M	Combination of Objectives from Projects 5A and 5B	**5M GO! Think** A demonstration of your understanding of the chapter concepts applied in a manner that you would outside of college. An analytic rubric helps you and your instructor grade the quality of your work by comparing it to the work an expert in the discipline would create.	Online
5N	Combination of Objectives from Projects 5A and 5B	**5N You and GO!** A demonstration of your understanding of the chapter concepts applied in a manner that you would in a personal situation. An analytic rubric helps you and your instructor grade the quality of your work.	Online

GLOSSARY

GLOSSARY OF CHAPTER KEY TERMS

.wav (waveform audio data) A sound file that may be embedded in a presentation.

Animation Pane The area used for adding and removing effects.

Border A frame around a picture.

Brightness The perceived radiance or luminosity of an image.

Caption Text that helps to identify or explain a picture or a graphic.

Contrast The difference between the darkest and lightest area of a picture.

Crop Remove unwanted or unnecessary areas of a picture.

Crop handles Used like sizing handles to crop a picture.

Crop tool The mouse pointer used when removing areas of a picture.

Embed Save a file so that the audio or video file becomes part of the presentation file.

Fit to Slide The photo album option that allows the picture to occupy all available space on a slide with no room for a frame or caption.

Frame The border around a picture in a photo album.

Line style How the line displays, such as a solid line, dots, or dashes.

Line weight The thickness of a line measured in points.

Link Save a presentation so that the audio or video file is saved separately from the presentation.

Lock aspect ratio When this option is selected, you can change one dimension (height or width) of an object, such as a picture, and the other dimension will automatically be changed to maintain the proportion.

Loop The audio or video file plays repeatedly from start to finish until it is stopped manually.

Mitered A border with corners that are square.

Photo album A stylized presentation format to display pictures.

Pixel The term, short for picture element, represents a single point in a graphic image.

Play Animations button A small star-shaped icon that displays to the left of the slide thumbnail.

Presets Built-in sharpness and softness adjustments from a gallery.

Recolor The term used to change all the colors in the image to shades of one color.

Sharpen Increase the clarity of an image.

Soften Decrease the clarity of an image or make it fuzzy.

Track A song from a CD.

Trigger A portion of text, a graphic, or a picture that, when clicked, causes the audio or video to play.

CHAPTER REVIEW

Apply 5A skills from these Objectives:

1 Use Picture Corrections
2 Add a Border to a Picture
3 Change the Shape of a Picture
4 Add a Picture to a WordArt Object and Merge Shapes
5 Enhance a Presentation with Audio and Video

Skills Review | Project 5C Celtic Instruments

In the following Skills Review, you will modify pictures in a presentation about the instruments used in the Celtic music genre for the Cross Oceans Music company. You will change the brightness, contrast, and shapes of pictures and add borders to some pictures for emphasis. You will add WordArt and merge a shape. You will also add audio files that demonstrate the various instruments used in this type of music and a video file. Your completed presentation will look similar to Figure 5.56.

PROJECT FILES

For Project 5C, you will need the following files:

p05C_Celtic_Instruments.pptx
p05C_Flute.wav
p05_Music_Video.avi
p05C_Sheet_Music.jpg

You will save your presentation as:

Lastname_Firstname_5C_Celtic_Instruments.pptx

PROJECT RESULTS

daboost/Fotolia; Hedgehog/Fotolia; scalaphotography/Fotolia; mitay20/Fotolia; Klaus Eppele/Fotolia; miketea88/Fotolia

FIGURE 5.56

(Project 5C Celtic Instruments continues on the next page)

CHAPTER REVIEW

1 Start PowerPoint. Locate and open the file **p05C_Celtic_Instruments**. Using your own first and last name, save the file as **Lastname_Firstname_5C_Celtic_Instruments** in your **PowerPoint Chapter 5** folder.

2 Click **Slide 1**, if necessary, and then click to select the picture.

a. On the **PICTURE TOOLS FORMAT tab**, in the **Size group**, click the **Crop button arrow**, and then click **Crop to Shape**. Under **Flowchart**, locate and click **Flowchart: Punched Tape**, which is in the second row, fourth from the left.

b. In the **Adjust group**, click the **Corrections arrow**, and then click **Picture Corrections Options** to display the **Format Picture** pane. Under **Sharpen/Soften**, in the **Sharpness** spin box, select the text, type **-100** and then press Enter. Under **Brightness/Contrast**, click the **Presets arrow**, and then in the last row, third column, click **Brightness: 0% (Normal) Contrast: +40%**.

c. In the **Arrange group**, click the **Send Backward button arrow**, and then click **Send to Back**.

d. On **Format Picture** pane, at the top, click **Size & Properties**, and then click **POSITION** to expand, if necessary. To the right of **Horizontal position**, in the spin box, select the text, type **1** and then press Enter. To the right of **Vertical position**, in the spin box, select the text, type **2** and then press Enter. **Close** the Format Picture pane.

3 Make **Slide 2** the active slide, and then select the picture.

a. On the **PICTURE TOOLS FORMAT tab**, in the **Arrange group**, click **Selection Pane**, and then in the **Selection** pane, click **Picture 6** (your picture number may vary), if necessary. In the **Adjust group**, click the **Corrections arrow**. Under **Brightness/Contrast**, locate and click **Brightness: 0% (Normal) Contrast: +20%**, which is in the fourth row, third column.

b. In the **Arrange group**, click the **Send Backward button arrow**, and then click **Send to Back**.

c. **Close** the **Selection** pane.

4 Make **Slide 3** the active slide.

a. Click the **picture on the left**—the **flute**. On the **FORMAT tab**, in the **Size group**, click the **Crop button arrow**, and then click **Crop to Shape**. Under **Rectangles**, click the second rectangle—**Rounded Rectangle**.

b. In the **Picture Styles group**, click **Picture Border**, and under **Theme** colors, click the first column, last row—**White, Background 1, Darker 50%**. In the **Pictures Styles group**, click **Picture Border**, click **Weight**, and then click **2 ¼ pt**.

c. Click the **picture in the center**—the **accordion**. On the **FORMAT tab**, in the **Picture Styles group**, click the **More arrow**. Locate and click **Perspective Shadow, White**, which is in the third row, fourth column.

d. Click the **picture on the right**—the **harp**. On the **FORMAT tab**, in the **Picture Styles group**, click the **More arrow**. Locate and click **Simple Frame, Black**, which is in the second row, second column.

5 Make **Slide 3** the active slide, if necessary.

a. Click the **INSERT tab**. In the **Media group**, click the **Audio button arrow**, and then click **Audio on My PC**.

b. Navigate to the location where your student files are stored. Locate and insert **p05C_Flute.wav**.

c. On the **AUDIO TOOLS PLAYBACK tab**, click the **Start button arrow**, and then click **Automatically**. Click the **Hide During Show** check box.

d. Move the speaker icon so it is on the left side of the picture of the accordion.

6 Make **Slide 4** the active slide.

a. On the **INSERT tab**, in the **Text group**, click the **WordArt arrow**. In the second row, fifth column, click **Fill – Green, Accent 4, Sharp Bevel**.

b. Type **Celtic Instruments** Press Enter, and then type **Presented by** Press Enter, and then type **Cross Oceans Music**

c. Select the lines of text. On the **HOME tab**, in the **Font group**, click the **Font Color button arrow**. In the sixth column, fifth row, click **Green, Accent 2, Darker 25%**.

d. On the **DRAWING TOOLS FORMAT tab**, in the **Size group**, click the **Size and Position** dialog launcher. In the **Format Shape** pane, to the right of **Horizontal position**, select the text, type **3.5** in the spin box, and then press Enter. In the **Format Shape** pane, to the right of **Vertical position**, select the text, type **1.0** in the spin box, and then press Enter.

(Project 5C Celtic Instruments continues on the next page)

CHAPTER REVIEW

e. On the **FORMAT tab**, in the **Shape Styles group**, click **Shape Fill**, and then click **Picture**. Navigate to the location where your student files are stored. Locate and click **p05C_Sheet_Music.jpg**, and then click **Insert**.

f. On the **PICTURE TOOLS FORMAT tab**, in the **Adjust group**, click **Color**. Under **Recolor**, locate and click **Green, Accent color 2 Light**. On the **PICTURE TOOLS FORMAT tab**, in the **Picture Styles group**, click the **Picture Effects arrow**, point to **Soft Edges**, and then click **10 Point**. Click to deselect the picture.

g. With **Slide 4** still selected, at the bottom of the slide, hold down the Ctrl key and click to select the **four green shapes** of the shamrock. On the **DRAWING TOOLS FORMAT tab**, in the **Insert Shapes group**, click **Merge Shapes**, and then click **Union**. Right-click the merged shape, and then click **Size and Position** to display the **Format Shape** pane. In the **Vertical position** spin box, select the text, type **5** and then press Enter. In the **Arrange group**, click the **Align button arrow**, and then click **Align Center**. **Close** the **Format Shape** pane.

7 In the location where your data files are stored, locate **p05_Music_Video.avi**, and then copy it into your **PowerPoint Chapter 5** folder.

8 Click **Slide 4**, and then click the **INSERT tab**. In the **Media group**, click the **Video button arrow**, and then click **Video on My PC**.

a. Navigate to the location where your student files are stored, click **p05_Music_Video.avi**, and then click the **Insert button arrow**. Click **Link to File**.

b. On the **VIDEO TOOLS FORMAT tab**, in the **Size group**, change the **Video Height** to **1.5"**.

c. On the **VIDEO TOOLS PLAYBACK tab**, select the check boxes for **Play Full Screen** and **Hide While Not Playing**.

d. Click the **ANIMATIONS tab**. In the **Advanced Animation group**, click the **Trigger** button, point to **On Click of**, and then click **Rectangle 5** (your Rectangle number may vary).

e. On the **Format Video** pane, at the top, click **Size & Properties**, click POSITION, to expand, if necessary. In the **Horizontal position** spin box, select the text, type **1** and then press Enter. In the **Vertical position** spin box, select the text, type **4.5** and then press Enter.

9 Click the **SLIDE SHOW tab**. In the **Start Slide Show group**, click **From Beginning**. Listen for the audio file, and then click the **WordArt** on **Slide 4** to view the video. Click **Esc** to exit the slide show.

10 On the **INSERT tab**, in the **Text group**, click **Header & Footer** to display the **Header and Footer** dialog box. Click the **Notes and Handouts tab**. Under **Include on page**, select the **Date and time** check box, and then select **Fixed**. If necessary, clear the **Header** check box, and then select the **Page number** and **Footer** check boxes. In the **Footer** box, using your own name, type **Lastname_Firstname_5C_Celtic_Instruments** and then click **Apply to All**.

11 Click the **FILE tab**, and then in the lower right portion of the screen, click **Show All Properties**. In the **Tags** box, type **Celtic, instruments, Ireland, Scotland** and in the **Subject** box type your course name and section number. In the **Author** box, right-click the existing author name, click **Edit Property**, replace the existing text with your first and last name, click outside the text box to deselect, and then click **OK**.

12 **Save** the presentation. Print **Handouts 4 Slides Horizontal**, or submit your presentation electronically as directed by your instructor. **Exit** PowerPoint.

END | You have completed Project 5C

CHAPTER REVIEW

Apply 5B skills from these Objectives:

6 Create a Photo Album

7 Edit a Photo Album and Add a Caption

8 Crop a Picture

Skills Review | Project 5D Celtic Album

In the following Skills Review, you will create a photo album for the Cross Oceans Music company. You will insert photos of musicians who record Celtic music and are represented by Cross Oceans. You will add captions and crop unwanted areas of photos. Your completed presentation will look similar to Figure 5.57.

Build from Scratch

PROJECT FILES

For Project 5D, you will need the following files:

New blank PowerPoint presentation
p05D_Mandolinist.jpg
p05D_Flautist.jpg
p05D_Harpist.jpg
p05D_Violinist.jpg
p05D_Bagpiper.jpg

You will save your presentation as:

Lastname_Firstname_5D_Celtic_Album.pptx

PROJECT RESULTS

Alexander Egorin/Fotolia; mocker_bat/Fotolia; leschnyhan/Fotolia; Yuri Arcurs/Fotolia; Elnur/Fotolia

FIGURE 5.57

(Project 5D Celtic Album continues on the next page)

CHAPTER REVIEW

1 Start PowerPoint, and then click **Blank Presentation**. Click the **INSERT tab**. In the **Images group**, click the **Photo Album button arrow**, and then click **New Photo Album**.

2 In the **Photo Album** dialog box, in the **Album Content** area, under **Insert picture from**, click **File/Disk** to display the **Insert New Pictures** dialog box. Navigate to the location where your student files are stored, click **p05D_Violinist.jpg**, and then click **Insert**.

3 Using the technique you practiced, insert the following pictures into the photo album in this order: **p05D_Flautist.jpg**, **p05D_Harpist.jpg**, **p05D_Mandolinst. jpg**, and **p05D_Bagpiper.jpg**.

4 Under **Album Layout**, click the **Picture layout arrow** to display the selections. Click **1 picture**.

5 Click the **Frame shape arrow** to display the frame shape selections, and then click **Rounded Rectangle**.

6 To the right of the **Theme** box, click the **Browse** button to display the **Choose Theme** pane. Click **Wisp**, and then click **Select**. In the **Photo Album** dialog box, click **Create**.

7 Press **F12** to display the **Save As** dialog box, and then navigate to the location where you are storing your projects for this chapter and save the file as **Lastname_Firstname_5D_Celtic_Album**

8 Click **Slide 1** in the Slides and Outline pane, if necessary. Right-click to display the shortcut menu.

a. Click **Format Background** to display the Format Background pane.

b. Select the **Gradient Fill** option, if necessary, and then click the **Type arrow** and select **Rectangular**.

c. Click **Color**. In the ninth column, first row, click **Olive Green, Accent 5**.

d. Click the **Direction** button. Locate and click **From Bottom Left Corner**.

e. Under Gradient stops, click **Stop 2**. In the **Position** spin box, type **75** and then press **Enter**. Click **Apply to All**, and then **Close** the pane.

9 Position the insertion point to the left of *Photo Album*.

a. Type **Celtic Music** and then press **Enter**.

b. Select both lines of the title—*Celtic Music Photo Album*. Click the **FORMAT tab**. In the **WordArt Styles group**, click the **Text Fill arrow**, and then click the ninth column, last item—**Olive Green, Accent 5, Darker 50%**.

c. Click **Text Effects**, point to **Shadow**, and then under **Perspective**, click **Perspective Diagonal Upper Left**.

d. Increase the size of the title to **72 pts**.

10 Delete the subtitle text and replace it with **Cross Oceans Music**

11 Click the **INSERT tab**. In the **Images group**, click the **Photo Album button arrow**, and then click **Edit Photo Album**. In the **Edit Photo Album** dialog box, in the **Album Content** area, under **Picture Options**, select the **Captions below ALL pictures** check box, and then click **Update**.

12 Make **Slide 2** the active slide, and then click to select the caption. Select the text *p05D_* and then press **Delete**. The caption should now read *Violinist*

13 Using the technique you practiced, edit the captions for **Slides 3, 4, 5,** and **6** as follows:

Flautist

Harpist

Mandolinist

Bagpiper

14 On **Slide 6**, click two times to select the **picture of the Bagpiper**. On the **PICTURE TOOLS FORMAT tab**, in the **Size group**, click **Crop**.

a. Drag the right middle cropping handle left to the **1.5-inch mark to the right of 0** on the **horizontal ruler**.

b. Repeat the procedure to crop the left side to the **1.5-inch mark to the left of 0** on the **horizontal ruler**.

c. Click **Crop** to turn off cropping.

15 Click the **SLIDE SHOW tab**. In the **Start Slide Show group**, click **From Beginning**. View the slide show, and then press **Esc** to exit.

(Project 5D Celtic Album continues on the next page)

CHAPTER REVIEW

16 On the **INSERT tab**, in the **Text group**, click the **Header & Footer** button to display the **Header and Footer** pane. Click the **Notes and Handouts tab**. Under **Include on page**, select the **Date and time** check box, and then select **Fixed**. If necessary, clear the **Header** check box, and then select the **Page number** and **Footer** check boxes. In the **Footer** box, using your own name, type **Lastname_ Firstname_5D_Celtic_Album** and then click **Apply to All**.

17 Click the **FILE tab**, and then in the lower right portion of the screen, click **Show All Properties**. In the **Tags** box, type **Celtic, music, album** and in the **Subject** box type your course name and section number. In the **Author** box, right-click the existing author name, click **Edit Property**, replace the existing text with your first and last name, click outside the text box to deselect, and then click **OK**.

18 **Save** the presentation. Print **Handouts 4 Slides Horizontal**, or submit your presentation electronically as directed by your instructor. Then **Close** your presentation, **Close** the **Blank Presentation**, and then **Exit** PowerPoint.

END | You have completed Project 5D

CONTENT-BASED ASSESSMENTS

MyITLab® grader

Mastering PowerPoint   Project 5E Reggae Music

In the following Mastering PowerPoint project, you will modify pictures in a presentation used in educational seminars hosted by Cross Oceans Music. The presentation highlights Reggae music and its roots in jazz and rhythm and blues. You will add WordArt and a merged shape to the presentation. You will also add an audio file that represents this genre of music and format it to play across the slides in the slide show. You will also add a video file. Your completed presentation will look similar Figure 5.58.

Apply 5A skills from these Objectives:

1 Use Picture Corrections
2 Add a Border to a Picture
3 Change the Shape of a Picture
4 Add a Picture to a WordArt Object and Merge Shapes
5 Enhance a Presentation with Audio and Video

PROJECT FILES

For Project 5E, you will need the following files:

p05E_Reggae_Music.pptx
p05E_Reggae.wav
p05E_Music.jpg
p05_Music_Video.avi

You will save your presentation as:

Lastname_Firstname_5E_Reggae_Music.pptx

PROJECT RESULTS

luisapuccini/Fotolia; Alex White/Fotolia; satori/Fotolia; Lisa F. Young/Fotolia; megastocker/Fotolia; Pookeyman/Fotolia; miketea88/Fotolia

FIGURE 5.58

(Project 5E Reggae Music continues on the next page)

CONTENT-BASED ASSESSMENTS

1 Start PowerPoint. Locate and open the file **p05E_Reggae_Music**. Save the file in your chapter folder, using the file name **Lastname_Firstname_5E_Reggae_Music**

2 On the **title slide**, click to select the picture, click the **FORMAT tab**, and then set the **Sharpness** to **25%**. Set **Brightness** to **+20%** and **Contrast** to **-20%**.

3 Make **Slide 2** the active slide, and then click to select the **picture of the Jamaican flag**. On the **FORMAT tab**, click the **Crop button arrow**, and then crop the picture to the **Wave** shape, which is under Stars and Banners, in the second row, seventh shape.

4 Make **Slide 3** the active slide. Click the **picture**, and then send the picture to the back. In the **Adjust group**, click **Color**, and then under **Recolor**, in the first row, fourth column, click **Washout**.

5 Make **Slide 4** the active slide, and then click the picture. Set the **Brightness** to **+20%** and the **Contrast** to **+20%**. Change the picture border to **Turquoise, Accent 3, Darker 50%**. Crop the picture to an **Oval** shape.

6 Make **Slide 5** the active slide, and then click to select the **picture of the flag of Trinidad**. Use **Crop to Shape**, and then under **Stars and Banners**, change the picture shape to **Double Wave**, which is in the second row, the last shape.

7 Make **Slide 6** the active slide, and then click to select the picture. Set the **Brightness** to **25%**, and then **Send to Back**.

8 Make the **title slide** the active slide. Display the **Insert Audio** dialog box. From your student files, insert the audio file **p05E_Reggae.wav**. On the **PLAYBACK tab**, set the audio to **Hide During Show** and to start **Automatically**.

9 Make **Slide 7** the active slide. Insert **WordArt** with **Fill - Aqua, Accent 2, Outline - Accent 2**. Type **Reggae Music** on one line, type **Presented by** on the next line, and then type **Cross Oceans Music** on the third line. Change the **Font Color** to **Turquoise, Accent 3, Darker 25%**. With the **WordArt** selected, on the **DRAWING TOOLS FORMAT tab**, in the **Size group**, click the **Size and Position** dialog launcher. Click **POSITION** to expand, if necessary. Change the **Horizontal position** to **3** and the **Vertical position** to **1 Close** the Format Shape pane.

10 With **Slide 7** as the active slide, with **WordArt** selected, use **Shape Fill** to insert from your data files the picture **p05E_Music.jpg**. On the **PICTURE TOOLS FORMAT tab**, recolor the picture to **Aqua, Accent color 2 Light**. Set the **Sharpness** at **-100%**.

11 In the location where your data files are stored, locate **p05_Music_Video.avi**, and then copy it into your **PowerPoint Chapter 5** folder.

12 With **Slide 7** as the active slide, from your data files, insert **p05_Music_Video.avi** as a linked video. On the **PLAYBACK tab**, select the check boxes for **Play Full Screen** and **Hide While Not Playing**. On the **ANIMATIONS tab**, set a trigger for the video to play **On Click of Rectangle 3,** which is the WordArt shape. If necessary, use the **Selection** pane to identify the WordArt rectangle for the trigger. Right-click, and then click **Size and Position** to display the **Format Video** pane. Change the **Horizontal position** to **.05** and **Vertical position** to **4** Deselect the video. **Close** the Format Video pane.

13 With **Slide 7** selected, at the bottom of the slide, hold down the Ctrl key and click to select the **three turquoise shapes of the drum and each drum stick. Merge** the shapes using the **Union** option. Display the **Format Shape** pane. Click **POSITION** to expand, if necessary. Change the **Horizontal position** to **5.5** and the **Vertical position** to **4.5 Close** the Format Shape pane. Click to deselect the shape.

14 Start the slide show from the beginning. Listen for the audio file, and then click the **WordArt** on **Slide 7** to view the video.

15 Insert a footer on the notes and handouts, which includes a fixed date and time, the page number, and the file name.

16 Click the **FILE tab**, and then in the lower right portion of the screen, click **Show All Properties**. In the **Tags** box, type **Reggae, music** and in the **Subject** box type your course name and section number. In the **Author** box, right-click the existing author name, click **Edit Property**, replace the existing text with your first and last name, click outside the text box to deselect, and then click **OK**.

17 **Save** the presentation. Print **Handouts 4 Slides Horizontal**, or submit your presentation electronically as directed by your instructor. **Close** your presentation and **Exit** PowerPoint.

END | You have completed Project 5E

CONTENT-BASED ASSESSMENTS

Mastering PowerPoint Project 5F CD Cover

In the following Mastering PowerPoint project, you will create a photo album of pictures of island settings for a CD entitled *Reggae Revisited*. One of these cover designs will be chosen by Cross Oceans Music to be the cover of the soon-to-be-released CD of Reggae and Jamaican music. Your completed presentation will look similar to Figure 5.59.

Apply 5B skills from these Objectives:

6 Create a Photo Album

7 Edit a Photo Album and Add a Caption

8 Crop a Picture

Build from Scratch

PROJECT FILES

For Project 5F, you will need the following files:

New blank PowerPoint presentation
p05F_Island1.jpg
p05F_Island2.jpg
p05F_Island3.jpg
p05F_Island4.jpg
p05F_Island5.jpg

You will save your presentation as:

Lastname_Firstname_5F_CD_Cover.pptx

PROJECT RESULTS

*pavel Chernobrivets/*Fotolia; PHB.cz/Fotolia; efred/Fotolia*

FIGURE 5.59

(Project 5F CD Cover continues on the next page)

1 Start a new **Blank Presentation** in PowerPoint. Click the **INSERT tab**. In the **Images group**, click the **Photo Album button arrow**, and then click **New Photo Album**.

2 From the student data files, insert the following pictures into the photo album: **p05F_Island1.jpg**, **p05F_Island2.jpg**, **p05F_Island3.jpg**, **p05F_Island4.jpg**, and **p05F_Island5.jpg**. In the **Picture layout** list, select **1 picture**. Select the **Ion** theme. **Create** a new **Photo Album**.

3 **Edit** the **Photo Album**, and remove the last two pictures, **p05F_Island4** and **p05F_Island5**, from the album. Change the **Picture layout** to **1 picture with title** and the **Frame shape** to **Simple Frame, White**.

4 Save the file in your chapter folder, using the file name **Lastname_Firstname_5F_CD_Cover**

5 Make the **title slide** the active slide. Change the subtitle text to **Cross Oceans Music** Apply **Bold**, and then change the font size to **24**.

6 Select the title text, *Photo Album*, and then change the font size to **48**. Delete the title text, *Photo Album*, and type **Design Entries for CD Cover** Press [Enter], and then type **Reggae & Jamaican Music** With both lines selected, on the **FORMAT tab**, in the **WordArt Styles group**, click the **More** button. In the second row, click the third style—**Gradient Fill – Green, Accent 4, Outline – Accent 4**.

7 Make **Slide 2** active. Change the title to **Design 1** Right-click the picture, and then click **Size and Position**. On the **Format Picture** pane, change the **Horizontal position** to **2** and the **Vertical position** to **2**.

8 Insert a text box in the blank area to the right of the picture. In the text box, type **Reggae** press [Enter], and then type **Revisited** Change the font to **Bauhaus 93** and the font size to **72**. On the **Format Shape** pane, change the **Horizontal position** to **7** and the **Vertical position** to **3**.

9 Make **Slide 3** active. Change the title to **Design 2** Select the picture, and then on the **Format Picture** pane, change the **Horizontal position** to **8** and the **Vertical position** to **2**.

10 Insert a text box in the blank area to the left of the picture. In the text box, type **Reggae** press [Enter], and then

type **Revisited** Change the font to **Brush Script MT** and the font size to **88**. Apply **Bold** and **Text Shadow**. On the **Format Shape** pane, change the **Horizontal position** to **2** and the **Vertical position** to **2.5**.

11 Make **Slide 4** active, and then change the title to **Design 3** Select the picture, and on the **Format Picture** pane, change the **Horizontal position** to **8** and the **Vertical position** to **2**.

12 Insert a text box in the middle of the slide, to the left of the picture. In the text box, type **Reggae** press [Enter], and then type **Revisited** Change the font to **Algerian** and the font size to **60**. Apply **Bold**, **Italic**, and **Text Shadow**. With the text box selected, on the **FORMAT tab**, in the **WordArt Styles group**, click **More**, and then in the second row, click the third column—**Gradient Fill - Green, Accent 4, Outline - Accent 4**. Select the **text box**, and then on the **Format Shape** pane, change the **Horizontal position** to **2** and the **Vertical position** to **3**.

13 Make **Slide 2** the active slide. Select the picture. On the **FORMAT tab**, click the **Crop** button, and then drag the left middle cropping handle to the **4-inch mark to the left of 0** on the **horizontal ruler**. Click outside the picture to deselect.

14 Review your presentation from the beginning.

15 Insert a footer on the notes and handouts, which includes a fixed date and time, the page number, and the file name.

16 Click the **FILE tab**, and then in the lower right portion of the screen, click **Show All Properties**. In the **Tags** box, type **design, CD, entries** and in the **Subject** box type your course name and section number. In the **Author** box, right-click the existing author name, click **Edit Property**, replace the existing text with your first and last name, click outside the text box to deselect, and then click **OK**.

17 **Save** the presentation. Print **Handouts 4 Slides Horizontal**, or submit your presentation electronically as directed by your instructor. **Close** your presentation, **Close** the **Blank Presentation**, and then **Exit** PowerPoint.

END | You have completed Project 5F

CONTENT-BASED ASSESSMENTS

Mastering PowerPoint | Project 5G Jazz Origins and Percussion Album

MyITLab®
grader

Apply 5A and 5B skills from these Objectives:

1 Use Picture Corrections

2 Add a Border to a Picture

3 Change the Shape of a Picture

4 Add a Picture to a WordArt Object and Merge Shapes

5 Enhance a Presentation with Audio and Video

6 Create a Photo Album

7 Edit a Photo Album and Add a Caption

8 Crop a Picture

Build from Scratch

In the following Mastering PowerPoint project, you will edit a short presentation about the origins and elements of jazz by changing the brightness, contrast, and shape of pictures and adding a border and merging a shape. You will also format the presentation to play a short jazz video across slides during the slide show. Finally, you will create a photo album showing some of the percussion instruments used in Cross Oceans Music jazz recordings. The album will contain an audio clip of music. Your completed presentations will look similar to Figure 5.60.

PROJECT FILES

For Project 5G, you will need the following files:

Presentation:
p05G_Jazz_Origins.pptx
p05_Music_Video.avi

Photo Album:
New blank PowerPoint presentation
p05G_Drums1.jpg
p05G_Drums2.jpg
p05G_Drums3.jpg
p05G_Drums4.jpg
p05G_Drums.wav

You will save your presentations as:

Lastname_Firstname_5G_Jazz_Origins.pptx
Lastname_Firstname_5G_Percussion_Album.pptx

PROJECT RESULTS

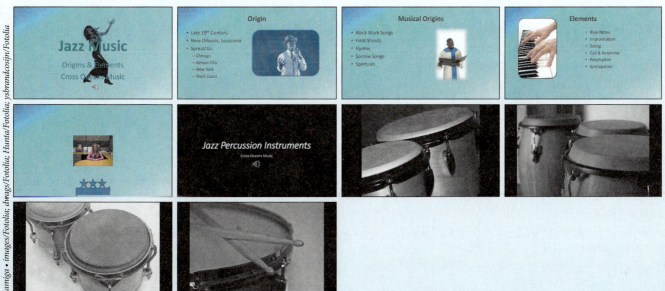

Ken Hurst/Fotolia; Sandra van der Steen/Fotolia; Michal Adamczyk/Fotolia; oilslo/Fotolia; jamiga • images/Fotolia; dwags/Fotolia; Hunta/Fotolia; ysbrandcosijn/Fotolia

FIGURE 5.60

(Project 5G Jazz Origins and Percussion Album continues on the next page)

1 Start PowerPoint. Locate and open the file **p05G_Jazz_Origins**, and then save the file as **Lastname_Firstname_5G_Jazz_Origins**

2 On **Slide 1**, insert the audio **p05G_Jazz.wav**. Move the audio file icon below the subtitle on the slide. Change to **Start Automatically** and **Hide During Show**. View the slide show **From Beginning** and test the sound.

3 On **Slide 2**, change the picture color to **Blue, Accent color 1 Light**, found under **Recolor** in the third row. **Crop** the picture to a **Rounded Rectangle** shape, found under **Rectangles**. Apply a **Picture Border—Blue, Accent 1**, found in the first row, fifth column. Set the border weight (also known as width) to **4 ½ pt**.

4 On **Slide 3**, on the picture, change the **Picture Effects** to **Soft Edges, 25 Point**.

5 Display **Slide 4**. On the **picture**, apply **+20% Brightness**. Change the picture shape to **Flowchart: Alternate Process**, found under **Flowchart**, in the first row. Add a picture border that is **Dark Blue, Background 2, Darker 50%**, found in the third column, last row of the gallery. Set the border weight (also known as width) to **2¼ pt**.

6 On **Slide 5**, at the bottom of the slide, hold down the Ctrl key, and then click to select the four blue shapes of the banner and stars. **Merge Shapes** using **Union** style. Right-click and then click **Size and Position** to display the **Format Shape** pane. Change the **Horizontal position** to **5.25** and the **Vertical position** to **6.0**.

7 With **Slide 5** selected, insert as a linked video **p05_Music_Video.avi**. Set it to play **Automatically**, **Hide While Not Playing**, and **Play Full Screen**. View your presentation from the beginning.

8 Insert a footer on the notes and handouts, which includes a fixed date and time, the page number, and the file name.

9 Click the **FILE tab**, and then in the lower right portion of the screen, click **Show All Properties**. In the **Tags** box, type **jazz, origins** and in the **Subject** box type your course name and section number. In the **Author** box, right-click the existing author name, click **Edit Property**, replace the existing text with your first and last name, click outside the text box to deselect, and then click **OK**.

10 **Save** the presentation. Print **Handouts 6 Slides Horizontal**, or submit your presentation electronically as directed by your instructor. **Close** your presentation.

11 Start PowerPoint, if necessary. Start a new **Blank Presentation**, and insert a **New Photo Album**. From the student data files, insert the following pictures into the photo album: **p05G_Drums1.jpg**, **p05G_Drums2.jpg**, **p05G_Drums3.jpg**, and **p05G_Drums4.jpg**.

12 Set the **Picture layout** to **Fit to Slide**. Do not add a theme so the default theme will be applied. Click to select the box **ALL pictures black and white**, and then create the photo album. In the location where you are storing your projects, save the file as **Lastname_Firstname_5G_Percussion_Album**

13 Make **Slide 1** the active slide. Replace the title—*Photo Album*—with **Jazz Percussion Instruments** Select the title, and then apply **Bold** and **Italics**.

14 Click to select the subtitle. Delete the subtitle text and replace it with **Cross Oceans Music**

15 On **Slide 1**, insert the audio file **p05G_Drums.wav**. Move the audio file icon below the subtitle on the slide. Change to **Start Automatically, Play Across Slides** and **Hide During Show**. View the slide show **From Beginning** and test the sound.

16 Insert a footer on the notes and handouts, which includes a fixed date and time, the page number, and the file name.

17 Click the **FILE tab**, and then in the lower right portion of the screen, click **Show All Properties**. In the **Tags** box, type **jazz, percussion** and in the **Subject** box type your course name and section number In the **Author** box, replace the existing text with your first and last name, if necessary.

18 **Save** the presentation. Print **Handouts 6 Slides Horizontal**, or submit your presentation electronically as directed by your instructor.

19 **Close** the presentation, and then **Exit** PowerPoint. Submit your work as directed for both **Lastname_Firstname_5G_Jazz_Origins** and **Lastname_Firstname_5G_Percussion_Album**.

END | You have completed Project 5G

CONTENT-BASED ASSESSMENTS

Apply a combination of the 5A and 5B skills.

| **GO! Fix It** | Project 5H Caribbean Music and Strings Album | Online |

Build from Scratch

| **GO! Make It** | Project 5I Salsa Music and Latin Album | Online |

Build from Scratch

| **GO! Solve It** | Project 5J Flamenco Music and Brass Album | Online |

Build from Scratch

| **GO! Solve It** | Project 5K New Age Music and Asian Album |

PROJECT FILES

For Project 5K, you will need the following files:

Presentation:
p05K_NewAge_Music.pptx
p05K_Piano.wav
p05_Music_Video.avi

Photo Album:
New blank PowerPoint presentation
p05K_Cymbals.jpg
p05K_Flute.jpg
p05K_Hand_Drum.jpg
p05K_Lute.jpg

You will save your presentations as:

Lastname_Firstname_5K_NewAge_Music.pptx
Lastname_Firstname_5K_Asian_Album.pptx

In this presentation project, you will modify a short presentation that describes the elements of New Age music and create a photo album on Asian music. You will demonstrate your knowledge of the skills you have covered in this chapter.

Open **p05K_NewAge_Music**, and then save it as **Lastname_Firstname_5K_NewAge_Music** Improve the presentation by modifying the photos in the slides. Add the provided audio and video files and set the playback options.

Using the graphic files provided, create a photo album to highlight Asian musical instruments, and add captions or titles, if necessary. Save the album as **Lastname_Firstname_5K_Asian_Album**

For both presentations, insert a header and footer on the Notes and Handouts that includes the fixed date and time, the page number, and a footer with the file name. Add your name, course name and section number, and appropriate tags to the Properties. Print Handouts 6 slides per page or submit electronically as directed by your instructor.

(Project 5K New Age Music and Asian Album continues on the next page)

CONTENT-BASED ASSESSMENTS

Performance Level

Performance Criteria		Exemplary	Proficient	Developing
	Modified photos in NewAge_Music.	Used a variety of picture corrections, shapes, and borders that enhanced the presentation.	Used some picture corrections, shapes, and borders to enhance the presentation.	Used few or no picture corrections, shapes, and borders to enhance the presentation.
	Added audio and video files and applied playback options.	Inserted audio and video files in appropriate places and applied playback options. Both played correctly. May have used a trigger.	Inserted the audio, but either the playback options were not set or the audio did not play back correctly. May have used a trigger.	Inserted the audio, but the playback options were not set and the audio did not play back correctly.
	Created a photo album—Asian Album, inserted pictures, added appropriate captions or titles.	The photo album had a theme, and the pictures were inserted. Used captions and titles as necessary and completed title slide.	The pictures were inserted, but there was no theme. Presentation and captions lacked consistency.	The photo album was not created.

END | You have completed Project 5K

OUTCOMES-BASED ASSESSMENTS

RUBRIC

The following outcomes-based assessments are *open-ended assessments*. That is, there is no specific correct result; your result will depend on your approach to the information provided. Make *Professional Quality* your goal. Use the following scoring rubric to guide you in *how* to approach the problem and then to evaluate *how well* your approach solves the problem.

The *criteria*—Software Mastery, Content, Format and Layout, and Process—represent the knowledge and skills you have gained that you can apply to solving the problem. The *levels of performance*—Professional Quality, Approaching Professional Quality, or Needs Quality Improvements—help you and your instructor evaluate your result.

	Your completed project is of Professional Quality if you:	Your completed project is Approaching Professional Quality if you:	Your completed project Needs Quality Improvements if you:
1-Software Mastery	Choose and apply the most appropriate skills, tools, and features and identify efficient methods to solve the problem.	Choose and apply some appropriate skills, tools, and features, but not in the most efficient manner.	Choose inappropriate skills, tools, or features, or are inefficient in solving the problem.
2-Content	Construct a solution that is clear and well organized, contains content that is accurate, appropriate to the audience and purpose, and is complete. Provide a solution that contains no errors in spelling, grammar, or style.	Construct a solution in which some components are unclear, poorly organized, inconsistent, or incomplete. Misjudge the needs of the audience. Have some errors in spelling, grammar, or style, but the errors do not detract from comprehension.	Construct a solution that is unclear, incomplete, or poorly organized; contains some inaccurate or inappropriate content; and contains many errors in spelling, grammar, or style. Do not solve the problem.
3-Format & Layout	Format and arrange all elements to communicate information and ideas, clarify function, illustrate relationships, and indicate relative importance.	Apply appropriate format and layout features to some elements, but not others. Overuse features, causing minor distraction.	Apply format and layout that does not communicate information or ideas clearly. Do not use format and layout features to clarify function, illustrate relationships, or indicate relative importance. Use available features excessively, causing distraction.
4-Process	Use an organized approach that integrates planning, development, self-assessment, revision, and reflection.	Demonstrate an organized approach in some areas, but not others; or, use an insufficient process of organization throughout.	Do not use an organized approach to solve the problem.

OUTCOMES-BASED ASSESSMENTS

Apply a combination of the 5A and 5B skills.

Build from Scratch

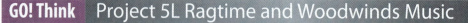

GO! Think Project 5L Ragtime and Woodwinds Music

PROJECT FILES

For Project 5L, you will need the following files:

Presentation:
p05L_Ragtime_Music.pptx
p05_Music_Video.avi
p05L_Entertainer.wav

Photo Album:
New blank PowerPoint presentation
p05L_Bass_Clarinet.jpg
p05L_Bassoon.jpg
p05L_Clarinet.jpg
p05L_Flute.jpg
p05L_Oboe.jpg
p05L_Saxophone.jpg

You will save your presentations as:

Lastname_Firstname_5L_Ragtime_Music.pptx
Lastname_Firstname_5L_Woodwinds_Album.pptx

In this project, you will edit a presentation about the history and structure of Ragtime music. Open **p05L_Ragtime_Music** and save it as **Lastname_Firstname_5L_Ragtime_Music** Modify the images on the slides. Add audio and video to the presentation. Set the audio file to start automatically and play across slides. Set the video to trigger On Click of Title.

Create a photo album using the provided pictures. Rotate, crop, and resize images as needed. Save it as **Lastname_Firstname_5L_Woodwinds_Album** Insert appropriate headers and footers, and then update the Properties on both files. Submit your files as directed.

END | You have completed Project 5L

Build from Scratch

GO! Think Project 5M Classical Music and Renaissance Album **Online**

You and GO! Project 5N Swing Origins **Online**

Build from Scratch

Delivering a Presentation

GO! to Work
Video P6

PROJECT 6A

OUTCOMES
Apply slide transitions and custom animation effects.

PROJECT 6B

OUTCOMES
Insert hyperlinks, create custom slide shows, and view presentations.

OBJECTIVES

1. Apply and Modify Slide Transitions
2. Apply Custom Animation Effects
3. Modify Animation Effects

OBJECTIVES

4. Insert Hyperlinks
5. Create Custom Slide Shows
6. Present and View a Slide Presentation

Kzenon/Fotolia

In This Chapter

Microsoft PowerPoint provides a wide range of tools that can turn a lackluster presentation into one that captivates the attention of the audience. Animation can be applied to individual slides, a slide master, or a custom slide layout. Transitions and other animation effects can be applied to all slides or to selected slides. In addition, you can insert hyperlinks into a presentation to quickly link to a webpage, another slide, or a document. You may also want to create a custom show composed of selected slides. PowerPoint includes an annotation tool that enables you to write or draw on slides during a presentation.

Penn Liberty Motors has one of eastern Pennsylvania's largest inventories of popular new car brands, sport utility vehicles, hybrid cars, and motorcycles. Its sales, service, and finance staff are all highly trained and knowledgeable about Penn Liberty's products, and the company takes pride in its consistently high customer satisfaction ratings. Penn Liberty also offers extensive customization options for all types of vehicles through its accessories division. Custom wheels, bike and ski racks, car covers, and chrome accessories are just a few of the ways Penn Liberty customers make personal statements with their cars.

Penn Liberty Motors

PROJECT
6A

MyITLab®
Project 6A Training

PROJECT ACTIVITIES

In Activities 6.01 through 6.08, you will add slide transitions and animation effects to a presentation that outlines the organizational structure and location of Penn Liberty Motors. Your completed presentation will look similar to Figure 6.1.

PROJECT FILES

For Project 6A, you will need the following files:

p06A_Penn_Liberty.pptx
p06A_Tada.wav

You will save your presentation as:

Lastname_Firstname_6A_Penn_Liberty.pptx

PROJECT RESULTS

Sarunyu_foto/Fotolia; adisa/Fotolia; muro/Fotolia; zavsyg/Fotolia; Christopher Dodge/Fotolia

FIGURE 6.1 Project 6A Penn Liberty

Video P6-1

Transitions are motion effects that occur when a presentation moves from slide to slide in Slide Show view and affect how the content is revealed. When referring to transitions, *animation* is any type of motion or movement that occurs as the presentation moves from slide to slide. Different transitions can be applied to selected slides, or the same transition can be applied to all slides. *Animation* is also used in a second context in this chapter, meaning a special visual effect or sound effect that is added to text or an object.

You can modify the transitions by changing the *transition speed*, which is the timing of the transition between all slides or between the previous slide and the current slide. It is also possible to apply a *transition sound* that will play as slides change from one to the next. Transition sounds are prerecorded sounds that can be applied and will play as the transition occurs.

Setting up a slide show also includes determining how you will advance the slide show from one slide to the next. You can set up the presentation to display each slide in response to the viewer clicking the mouse button or pressing the Enter key. You can also design the slide show so that the slides advance automatically after a set amount of time.

> ### NOTE   Applying Transitions
>
> In this project, you will learn how to apply and modify several kinds of transitions so that you are aware of how they work. When creating a presentation for an audience, however, you do not want to use too many transitions because they can be distracting and may destroy the professional appearance of your slide show. Remember, apply transitions in moderation.

Activity 6.01 | Applying and Modifying Slide Transitions

Slide transitions can be applied to all slides or to specific slides, and different transitions can be applied in one slide show. In this activity, you will modify slide transitions. In this case, modifications include changing the transition speed and sounds to be played during transitions.

1 Start PowerPoint. Locate and open the file **p06A_Penn_Liberty**. In the location where you are saving your work, create a new folder named **PowerPoint Chapter 6** and then **Save** the file as **Lastname_Firstname_6A_Penn_Liberty**

2 Make the **title slide** the active slide. Click the **TRANSITIONS tab**. In the **Transition to This Slide group**, click **More** ⌄ to display the **Transitions** gallery, and then compare your screen with Figure 6.2.

The Transitions gallery includes the following types of slide transitions: Subtle, Exciting, and Dynamic Content.

FIGURE 6.2

3 Under **Subtle**, click the fifth selection—**Wipe**.

The preview of the Wipe transition plays on Slide 1.

4 In the **Timing group**, click **Apply To All**. On the **TRANSITIONS tab**, in the **Preview group**, click **Preview**. Compare your screen with Figure 6.3.

🔄 **ANOTHER WAY**   To preview a slide transition, in the Slide pane, click the Play Animations icon that displays to the left of the slide thumbnail.

The Wipe transition plays on Slide 1. In the Slides/Outline pane, a Play Animations icon displays next to every slide.

FIGURE 6.3

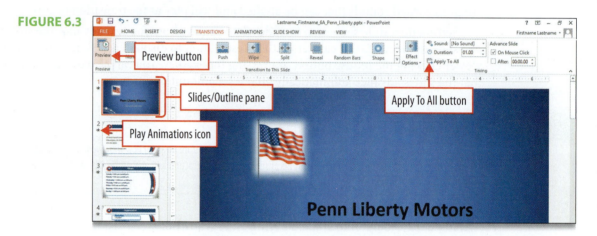

5 Click the **SLIDE SHOW tab**. In the **Start Slide Show group**, click **From Beginning**. Press ⎆Enter⎆ five times to view the entire slide show, and then press ⎆Enter⎆ or ⎆Esc⎆ to return to **Normal** view.

Because you selected Apply To All, the transition occurred between each slide.

6 Make **Slide 2** the active slide. Click the **TRANSITIONS tab**. In the **Transition to This Slide group**, click **More** ⎆▾⎆.

7 In the **Transitions** gallery, under **Exciting**, in the second row, click **Clock**.

By not clicking Apply To All, the Clock transition will apply to Slide 2 only.

8 Using the technique you practiced, view the slide show **From Beginning**. When you are finished viewing the slide show, press ⎆Enter⎆ or ⎆Esc⎆ to return to **Normal** view.

The Clock transition occurs between Slide 1 and Slide 2. The transition between all the other slides remains set to Wipe.

🔄 **BY TOUCH**   Tap to select the SLIDE SHOW tab. In the Start Slide Show group, tap From Beginning.

More Knowledge   **Animated GIFs and JPGs**

Many images are **GIF** (Graphics Interchange Format) or **JPG** (Joint Photographic Experts Group, also JPEG) files. GIFs are usually drawings, and JPGs are typically photos. GIF files are smaller in size and display faster than JPGs. Because of this, GIFs are frequently used on webpages. The image of the waving flag on the title slide is known as an ***animated GIF***. An animated GIF is a file format made up of a series of frames within a single file. Animated GIFs create the illusion of movement by displaying the frames one after the other in quick succession. They can loop endlessly or present one or more sequences of animation and then stop.

9 If necessary, make **Slide 2** the active slide. Click the **TRANSITIONS tab**. In the **Timing group**, click in the **Duration** box, type **3** press **Enter**, and then compare your screen with Figure 6.4.

The number of seconds it takes to reveal the slide content is now three seconds, which is longer than the default value of one second.

FIGURE 6.4

10 In the **Preview group**, click **Preview**.

The transition is displayed one time with the new speed setting. Slide 1 is displayed first and then three seconds later, Slide 2 appears.

11 Make **Slide 5** the active slide. Click the **Duration spin box up arrow** to display **05.00**. On the **SLIDE SHOW tab**, in the **Start Slide Show group**, click **From Beginning**. Click or press **Enter** to view the slides. Click or press **Esc** when finished.

Notice that when you clicked Slide 4 to advance to Slide 5, the transition duration was five seconds. Choose a speed that best displays the content.

12 If necessary, make **Slide 5** the active slide. On the **TRANSITIONS tab**, in the **Timing group**, click the **Sound button arrow**, and then compare your screen with Figure 6.5.

From the displayed list, you can choose from various prerecorded sound effects, choose your own sound effect by clicking Other Sound, or choose [No Sound] to remove a sound effect that was applied.

FIGURE 6.5

13 Click to select **Drum Roll**. In the **Preview group**, click **Preview**.

The Drum Roll plays on Slide 4 before Slide 5 is displayed. The overuse of any animation effects or sound effects can distract the audience from the content of the presentation. Keep your audience and your intent in mind. Whereas animations may enhance a light-hearted presentation, they can also trivialize a serious business presentation or cause viewer discomfort.

ALERT! | **Is the Sound Not Audible?**

There are several possible explanations if you are unable to hear the sound. For example, your computer may not have sound capability or speakers. If, however, you know that your computer has sound capability, first check that your speakers are turned on. If they are on, click the lower right side of the Windows taskbar; in the Notification area, click Speakers. To adjust speaker volume, drag the slider up to increase the volume. Make sure that the audio has not been muted. If the audio is muted, there will be a red stop symbol beside the speaker icon. Click the speaker icon and unmute the audio.

14 ▸ Make the **title slide** the active slide. On the **TRANSITIONS tab**, in the **Timing group**, click the **Sound arrow**, and then from the displayed list, click **Other Sound**.

15 ▸ In the displayed **Add Audio** dialog box, navigate to the location where your student files are stored, click **p06A_Tada.wav**, and then click **OK**. View the slide show **From Beginning**. Press Enter or click to advance each slide. Click or press Esc when finished.

> The Wipe transition plays on all slides except Slide 2. The Clock transition plays on Slide 2. Sound occurs on Slides 1 and 5. The transition duration on Slide 2 is three seconds, and the transition duration on Slide 5 is five seconds. Transitions affect how the slide reveals on the screen.

16 ▸ **Save** 🖫 your changes.

Activity 6.02 | Advancing Slides Automatically

In this activity, you will customize a slide show by changing the Advance Slide method to advance slides automatically after a specified number of seconds.

1 ▸ Make **Slide 2** the active slide. Click the **TRANSITIONS tab**. In the **Timing group**, under **Advance Slide**, clear the **On Mouse Click** check box.

> By clearing the On Mouse Click check box, viewers will no longer need to press Enter or click to advance the slide show. The slide show will advance automatically.

2 ▸ In the **Timing group**, under **Advance Slide**, click the **After spin box up arrow** to display **00:10.00**. Compare your screen with Figure 6.6.

🔄 **ANOTHER WAY**   To enter the time in the After box, click once in the box to select the current time, type 10, and then press Enter.

> The time is entered in number of seconds. This automatic switching of slides is only effective if no one is providing an oral presentation along with the slides.

FIGURE 6.6

3 ▸ View the slide show **From Beginning**—press Enter one time to advance the slide show to **Slide 2**. Wait 10 seconds for the third slide to display. When **Slide 3** displays, press Esc.

NOTE | **Previewing Slides**

Previewing a slide will not advance to the next slide. Play the slide show From Beginning or From Current Slide in order to verify the time it takes to display the next slide.

4 Make **Slide 2** the active slide. On the **TRANSITIONS tab**, in the **Timing group**, change number in the **After** box to **5**. Compare your screen with Figure 6.7.

> If no person is speaking, set the number of seconds to allow people sufficient time to read the content. However, you may need to consider adding time to allow a speaker to make key points.

FIGURE 6.7

After timing changed to 5 seconds

5 Save 💾 your changes.

Objective 2   Apply Custom Animation Effects

Video P6-2

Like other effects that you can customize in PowerPoint, you can customize animation effects. In this context, *animation* refers to a special visual effect or sound effect added to text or an object. You can add animation to bulleted items, text, or other objects such as charts, graphics, or SmartArt graphics.

Animation can be applied as an **Entrance effect**, which occurs as the text or object is introduced into the slide during a slide show, or as an **Exit effect**, which occurs as the text or object leaves the slide or disappears during a slide show. For example, bulleted items can fly into, or move into, a slide and then fade away.

Animation can take the form of a **Motion Paths effect**, which determines how and in what direction text or objects will move on a slide. Examples of an **Emphasis effect** include making an object shrink or grow in size, change color, or spin on its center.

The **Animation Pane** is the area that contains a list of the animation effects added to your presentation. From this pane, you can add or modify effects.

Activity 6.03 | Adding Entrance Effects

In this activity, you will add entrance effects to text and objects by making them move in a specific manner as the text or graphic enters the slide.

1 Make **Slide 3** the active slide, and then click to select the content placeholder. Click the **ANIMATIONS tab**. In the **Advanced Animation group**, click **Add Animation**, and then compare your screen with Figure 6.8. Scroll the list to see all of the animation effects. Refer to Figure 6.9 for more information.

> There are four animation groups—Entrance, Emphasis, Exit, and Motion Paths. You have to scroll the list to see the Motion Paths animations.

FIGURE 6.8

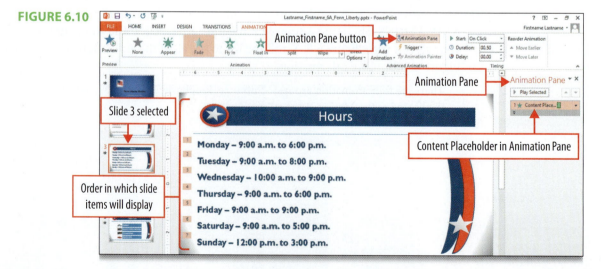

FIGURE 6.9

ANIMATION EFFECTS	
ANIMATION EFFECTS	**EXAMPLES**
Entrance	Fade gradually into focus, fly onto the slide from an edge, or bounce into view
Emphasis	Shrink or grow in size, change color, or spin on its center
Exit	Fly off the slide, disappear from view, or spiral off the slide
Motion Paths	Move up or down, left or right, or in a star or circular pattern

2 ▸ Under **Entrance**, click **Fade**.

Clicking Fade sets the text on the slide to display the various bulleted items one after the other, in order from top to bottom. Choose an animation that enhances the content of the slide.

3 ▸ In the **Advanced Animation group**, click **Animation Pane**, and then compare your screen with Figure 6.10.

The Animation Pane displays with the results of the animation you applied on Slide 3. In this case, the Animation Pane displays with the effect applied to the content placeholder selected. Each item on the slide content placeholder displays with a number next to it to indicate the order in which the items will display.

FIGURE 6.10

ALERT!   **Do You Have Extra Items Displayed in the Animation Pane?**

If you clicked on an effect instead of pointing at it, you will have an extra item in the Animation Pane. Click the unwanted item in the Animation Pane, and then click the arrow and select Remove. If the item arrow does not display, click the correct placeholder on the slide or the item in the Animation Pane to make the item active.

ANOTHER WAY   To remove an effect in the Animation Pane, right-click the effect to display the options, and then select Remove. You can also just click on the effect and press the Delete key.

4 In the **Animation Pane**, below *Content Placeholder*, point to the **expand chevron** ⏬ to display the ScreenTip *Click to expand contents*. Compare your screen with Figure 6.11.

The *chevron* is a V-shaped pattern that indicates that more information or options are available.

FIGURE 6.11

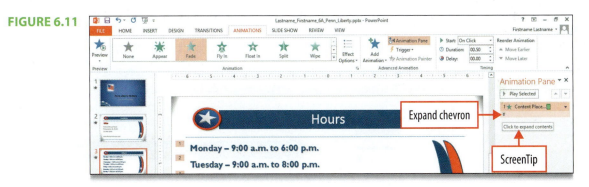

5 Click the **chevron** ⏬ one time to expand the contents, and then compare your screen with Figure 6.12.

The numbers to the left of the items on the slide correspond with the item numbers in the Animation Pane.

FIGURE 6.12

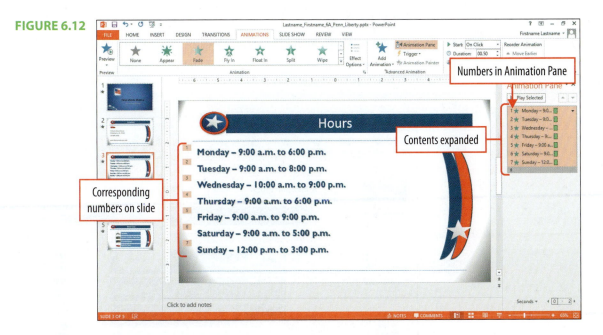

6 Right-click the **first entrance effect** for the content placeholder, and then, if necessary, click **Show Advanced Timeline.** In the **Animation Pane,** click **Play From** to test the animation.

At the bottom of the Animation Pane, a *timeline* displays the number of seconds the animation takes to complete.

ALERT! **Did the Timeline Display?**

If you cannot see the timeline at the bottom of the Animation Pane, right-click the entrance effect for the content placeholder, and then click Show Advanced Timeline. If the timeline is visible, the option is displayed as Hide Advanced Timeline.

---

7 Click the **hide chevron** to hide the contents. Click on **Slide 3,** and then under **Play All,** point to *Content Place…,* read the ScreenTip, *On Click Fade: Content Placeholder 2: Monday – 9:00 a.m. to 6:00…,* and then compare your screen with Figure 6.13.

The ScreenTip identifies the start setting, which is On Click, and the Effect, which is Fade.

FIGURE 6.13

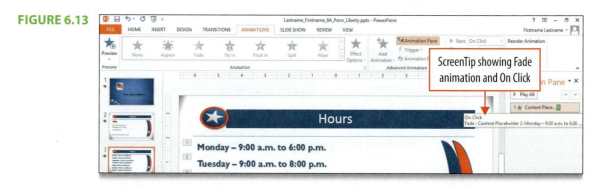

8 Make **Slide 5** the active slide. Click the **SmartArt graphic** containing the cars. On the **ANIMATIONS tab,** in the **Advanced Animation group,** click **Add Animation.** Under **Entrance,** click **Float In.**

The ANIMATIONS tab is inactive until a slide element is selected.

9 In the **Animation group,** click **Effect Options,** and then compare your screen with Figure 6.14.

After an animation effect is applied, the Effect Options becomes active. The sequence options are As One Object, All at Once, or One by One.

FIGURE 6.14

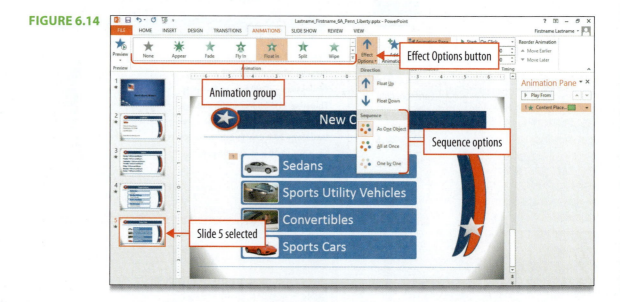

10 ▶ Under **Sequence**, click **One by One**.

Clicking One by One sets the shapes in the SmartArt graphic on Slide 5 as individual objects that display one at a time.

11 ▶ Make the **title slide** the active slide, and then click to select the title placeholder—*Penn Liberty Motors*. In the **Advanced Animation group**, click **Add Animation**, and then click **More Entrance Effects**. In the **Add Entrance Effect** dialog box, under **Moderate**, scroll if necessary, click **Rise Up**, and then compare your screen with Figure 6.15.

A preview of the Rise Up effect displays on the slide. The Add Entrance Effect dialog box provides additional effects.

FIGURE 6.15

> **N O T E** **Automatic Preview**
>
> To see the automatic preview of the effect more easily, you may want to move the dialog box to the side of the slide.

12 ▶ Click **OK**.

13 ▶ Click the **subtitle** placeholder. In the **Advanced Animation group**, click **Add Animation**, and then click **More Entrance Effects**. In the **Add Entrance Effect** dialog box, under **Moderate**, scroll if necessary, and then click **Rise Up**. Click **OK**. Compare your screen with Figure 6.16. In the **Animation Pane**, click **1 Title 1: Penn L…**, and then click **Play From** to test the animation.

The entrance effect for Slide 1 displays in the Animation Pane. The number 1 corresponds with the title placeholder. The number 2 corresponds with the subtitle placeholder. The numbers that appear on the slide in Normal view do not appear when you play the presentation.

FIGURE 6.16

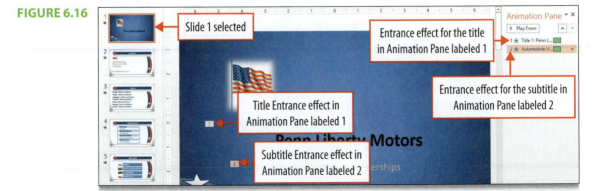

14 ▶ **Save** 🖫 your changes.

Activity 6.04 | Adding Emphasis Effects

In this activity, you will add emphasis effects to text and graphics. These effects make the text or graphics move or change in a specified manner when you click the mouse or press Enter while the text or graphic is displayed on the slide. You will also reorder the effects.

1 With the **title slide** as the active slide, click to select the title placeholder—*Penn Liberty Motors*. On the **ANIMATIONS tab**, in the **Advanced Animation group**, click **Add Animation**, and then click **More Emphasis Effects** to display the **Add Emphasis Effect** dialog box.

The Add Emphasis Effect dialog box includes more emphasis effects than the Add Animations gallery and organizes them into groups—Basic, Subtle, Moderate, and Exciting effects. Use this dialog box if you do not find the effect you want in the gallery.

2 In the **Add Emphasis Effect** dialog box, under **Subtle**, click **Pulse**, and then click **OK**. In the **Animation Pane**, click **Play From** to see the **Pulse** effect on the title. Compare your screen with Figure 6.17.

A third item is displayed in the Animation Pane. The first one is for the entrance effect for the title placeholder, Penn Liberty Motors. The second one is for the entrance effect for the subtitle placeholder, Automobile Dealerships. The third one is for the emphasis effect for the title. The Pulse effect for the title is set to occur when the presenter clicks the mouse button. To make an item in the Animation Pane active, click the item or click on the placeholder on the slide. Notice that the numbers to the left of the title and subtitle on the slide correspond with the numbers for the effects in the Animation Pane.

FIGURE 6.17

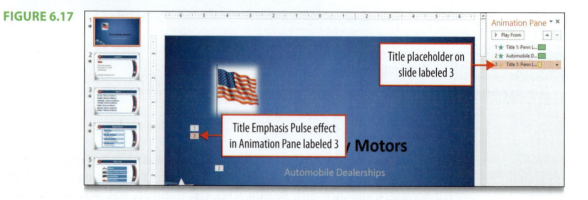

3 On the **SLIDE SHOW tab**, in the **Start Slide Show group**, click **From Current Slide**. Click to see the **title entrance** effect, click to see the **subtitle entrance** effect, and then click to see the **title emphasis** effect. Press Esc.

The sound effect played, the title moved up, the subtitle moved up, and then the title displayed the Pulse emphasis.

4 In the **Animation Pane**, click the third effect, the **emphasis** effect for the title—*3 Title1: Penn L....* At the top of the **Animation Pane**, on the right side, click the **Reorder move up arrow**. Compare your screen with Figure 6.18.

FIGURE 6.18

5 In the **Animation Pane**, click the first effect for the title—*1 Title1: Penn L...*, click **Play From**.

The order that the effects play is changed. The title moved up and displayed with the Pulse emphasis, and then the subtitle displayed.

6 Make **Slide 4** the active slide, and then click to select the title placeholder—*Organization*. Using the technique you practiced, display the **Add Emphasis Effect** dialog box. Under **Subtle**, click **Bold Flash**, and then click **OK**. In the **Animation Pane**, point to the animation to display the ScreenTip *On Click Bold Flash: Title 1: Organization*. Compare your screen with Figure 6.19.

FIGURE 6.19

7 On **Slide 4**, click to select the **SmartArt graphic**. On the **ANIMATIONS tab**, in the **Advanced Animation group**, click **Add Animation**, under **Entrance**, click **Zoom**. In the **Animation group**, click **Effect Options**. Click **Level at Once**. On the **Animation Pane**, click **Play Selected**.

The SmartArt levels display the names and then the organization titles.

8 In the **Animation Pane**, right-click on **Content Place...** and then click **Effect Options**. In the **Zoom** dialog box, click the **SmartArt Animation tab**, select the **Reverse order** check box, and then click **OK**. On the **Animation Pane**, click **Play Selected**.

Because the Reverse check box is selected, the SmartArt levels display the organization titles and then the names.

9 On the **SLIDE SHOW tab**, in the **Start Slide Show group**, click **From Current Slide**. Click to test the title emphasis effect. Click two times to test the **SmartArt Zoom** entrance effect. Click again to display **Slide 5.** When it appears, press (Esc).

The title is displayed immediately. After the mouse click, the title blinks once and then returns to normal. The SmartArt levels displayed the organization titles first and then the names.

BY TOUCH   Tap the SLIDE SHOW tab. In the Start Slide Show group, tap From Current Slide. Tap to test the title emphasis effect. Tap again to display Slide 5. When it appears, press (Esc).

ALERT!   **Did the Title Blink More Than Once?**

If the title blinked again on the second mouse click instead of advancing to Slide 5, you have applied the blink emphasis effect more than once. In the Animation Pane, right-click the extra effect, and then select Remove. Test the animation again.

10 Save 🖫 your changes.

Activity 6.05 | Adding Exit Effects

In this activity, you will add exit effects to text and graphics. These effects make the text or graphics move or change in a specified manner when you click the mouse or press (Enter) while the text or graphic is displayed on the slide.

1 With the **title slide** as the active slide, click to select the **subtitle** placeholder. On the **ANIMATIONS tab**, in the **Advanced Animation group**, click **Add Animation**. From the displayed list, under **Exit**, scroll, if necessary to see the entire list. In the first row, click the third effect—**Fly Out**.

2 On the **SLIDE SHOW tab**, view the slide show **From Current Slide**. Click to display the title **Rise Up** entrance effect. Continue clicking to see the title **Pulse** emphasis effect, the subtitle **Rise Up** entrance effect, and then the subtitle **Fly Out** exit effect. Press Esc. In the **Animation Pane**, point to the fourth effect to see the ScreenTip *On Click Fly Out: Automobile Dealerships*. Compare your screen with Figure 6.20.

The order in which the effects play is determined by the sequence shown in the Animation Pane.

FIGURE 6.20

3 In the **Animation Pane**, right-click the fourth animations effect, which is the subtitle **Fly Out** exit effect. From the options list, select **Remove** to remove the effect.

4 Select the **subtitle** placeholder on the **Slide 1** again. On the **ANIMATIONS tab**, in the **Advanced Animation group**, click **Add Animation**. Click **More Exit Effects**. Under **Moderate**, scroll if necessary, and then click **Sink Down** to see the **Sink Down** exit effect. Notice that the **Preview Effect** check box is selected. Click **OK**. In the **Animation Pane**, point to the fourth effect to see the ScreenTip *On Click Sink Down: Automobile Dealerships*. Compare your screen with Figure 6.21.

In the Animation Pane, the entrance effect for the title is marked with a green star, the emphasis effect for the title is marked with a gold star, the entrance effect for the subtitle is marked with a green star, and the exit effect for the subtitle is marked with a red star. The stars are displayed with different actions to help define the pattern selected. The ScreenTip clarifies what specific effect was applied.

FIGURE 6.21

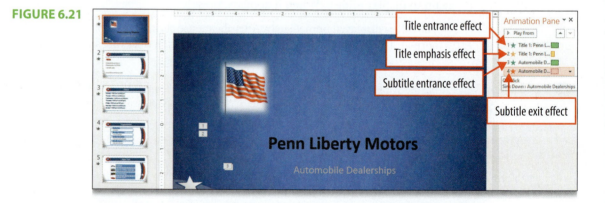

5 View the slide show **From Current Slide**. Click four times to activate the title entrance, the title emphasis, the subtitle entrance, and the subtitle exit effects, and then press Esc.

Slide 1 is displayed with the sound effect. With each click, the title enters in an upward direction, the title blinks, the subtitle enters, and finally the subtitle exits.

6 With **Slide 5** as the active slide, click the **content placeholder** to select the **SmartArt** graphic. On the **ANIMATIONS tab**, click **Add Animation**, and then click **More Exit Effects**. Under **Basic**, click **Wipe**, and then click **OK**. Compare your screen with Figure 6.22.

The first effect in the Animation Pane identifies the entrance effect for the SmartArt. Because there are four items in the SmartArt, the items are numbered 1 through 4 on the slide. The second effect in the Animation Pane identifies the exit effect for the SmartArt. The corresponding numbers on the slide are 5 through 8.

FIGURE 6.22

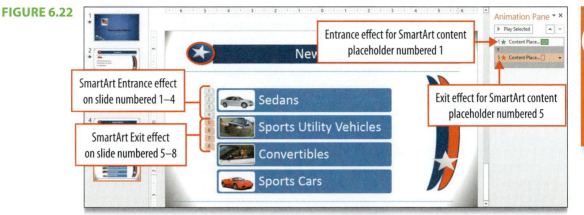

SmartArt Entrance effect on slide numbered 1–4

SmartArt Exit effect on slide numbered 5–8

Entrance effect for SmartArt content placeholder numbered 1

Exit effect for SmartArt content placeholder numbered 5

Sedans

Sports Utility Vehicles

Convertibles

Sports Cars

7 In the **Animation Pane**, click **1 Content Place…**. Click **Play Selected** to see the entrance effects. Click **5 Content Place…** and then click **Play Selected** to the exit effects.

Each item in the SmartArt graphic entered separately with the Float In entrance, and then the items exited separately with the Wipe exit.

8 View the slide show **From Current Slide**. After the sound effect and Wipe transition are complete, click **four times** to see the cars enter, and then click **four more times** to see them exit. Click **two more times** to return to **Normal** view.

Because you are viewing the slide as it would be displayed in a slide show, you need to click or press [Enter] in order to see the results.

9 **Save** 🖫 your changes.

NOTE	**Selecting Effects**

Entrance, Emphasis, Exit, and Motion Paths effects may be selected from the Add Animation gallery or from the Add Effect dialog boxes. The Add Effect dialog box specific to each type of effect contains additional effects, which are categorized as Basic, Subtle, Moderate, and Exciting.

Activity 6.06 | Adding Motion Paths

Motion paths can also be applied to graphics. Built-in motion paths enable you to make text or a graphic move in a particular pattern, or you can design your own pattern of movement.

1 Make **Slide 2** the active slide. Click to select the **title** placeholder—*Location*. On the **ANIMATIONS tab**, in the **Advanced Animation group**, click **Add Animation**, and then click **More Motion Paths**. In the **Add Motion Path** dialog box, scroll down, and then under **Lines_Curves**, click **Left**, and click **OK**. Compare your screen with Figure 6.23.

The motion path graphic displays on the slide with a green dot at the beginning of the motion path, with a red dot at the end of the motion path, and with a dotted line in between.

FIGURE 6.23

Lines option

Location

Left motion path

2 View the slide show **From Current Slide**. Wait for the title to move to the left. When **Slide 3** displays, press Esc.

The transition on Slide 2 displayed first, and then the title moved to the left. Use motion paths very sparingly. They can be distracting, and the audience may watch the path of the text or graphic instead of listening to the presenter.

3 With **Slide 2** selected, in the **Animation Pane**, point to the **Motion Path** effect to display the **ScreenTip**. Compare your screen with Figure 6.24.

The ScreenTip displays *On Click Left: Title 1: Location*. On the slide, the title placeholder displays a motion path graphic showing the direction of the movement.

FIGURE 6.24

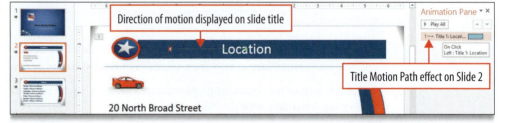

Direction of motion displayed on slide title

Location

20 North Broad Street

Title Motion Path effect on Slide 2

4 Click to select the **red car** picture. On the **ANIMATIONS tab**, in the **Advanced Animation group**, click **Add Animation**, and then click **More Motion Paths**. In the **Add Motion Path** dialog box, scroll down, and then under **Lines_Curves**, click **Right**. Click **OK**. Compare your screen with Figure 6.25.

A motion path displays. The original car picture stays in place and a "ghost" image displays at the endpoint of the motion path. A green dot displays on the original image, a dotted line displays along the motion path, and a red dot displays on the "ghost" image at the endpoint of the motion path.

FIGURE 6.25

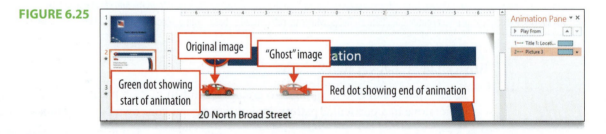

Original image

"Ghost" image

Green dot showing start of animation

Red dot showing end of animation

20 North Broad Street

More Knowledge — **Relocating the Endpoint of a Motion Path**

You can change the location of the endpoints of the motion path by selecting and dragging an endpoint to a new location. Hold the Shift key to ensure that that the motion path remains in a straight line.

5 Save your changes.

Video P6-3

Entrance, Emphasis, and Exit effects as well as Motion Paths can be modified or customized by changing how they start, the speed at which they occur, and their direction. Effect settings such as timing delays and the number of times an effect is repeated can also be added. Effects can be set to start after a previous effect or simultaneously.

On Click allows you to start the animation effect when you click the slide or a trigger on the slide. On Click also allows you to display animation such as a motion path because the animation is triggered by the mouse click or, in some instances, by pressing ⌤Enter. Changing an animation start method to *After Previous* allows the animation effect to start immediately after the previous effect in the list finishes playing. Changing the start method to *With Previous* starts the animation effect at the same time as the previous effect in the list.

Activity 6.07 | Modifying Animation Effects

In this activity, you will modify the start method of some of the animation effects you added. You will also modify their speed and timing.

1 Click the **SLIDE SHOW tab**. In the **Start Slide Show group**, click **From Beginning**. Return to **Normal** view when finished.

On the title slide, you had to click for the title to enter, click for the title to blink, click for the subtitle to enter, and then click for the subtitle to exit. After clicking Slide 1, Slide 2 displayed after three seconds. The title moved to the left and the car picture moved to the right with each click. Slide 3 advanced automatically after five seconds. On Slide 3, the hours of each day of the week displayed one by one as you clicked the mouse or pressed ⌤Enter. On Slide 4, the title effect occurred when you clicked the mouse. On Slide 4, the SmartArt levels display the names and then the organization titles with two separate clicks.

On Slide 5, each type of vehicle displayed with separate mouse clicks, and each one exited with separate mouse clicks.

2 Make the **title slide** the active slide, and then click to select the **subtitle** placeholder.

🔄 **ANOTHER WAY**   If animation has been applied to a placeholder or to an object such as a picture or graphic, you can select the object or placeholder by clicking the small number that displays on the slide. This number corresponds with the list of objects in the Animation Pane.

The title slide subtitle is displayed with two numbers. Number 3 represents the entrance effect, and number 4 represents the exit effect. Numbers 1 and 2 are for the title placeholder.

3 In the **Animation Pane**, click on the fourth item in the list to select it, and then right-click the **subtitle Exit** effect, the fourth effect in the list. Compare your screen with Figure 6.26. The Start Options are defined in the table in Figure 6.27.

FIGURE 6.26

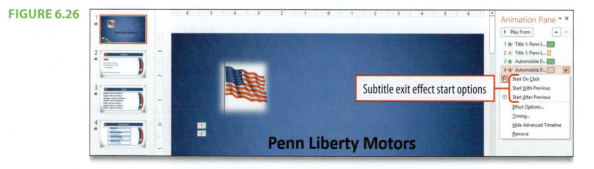

Subtitle exit effect start options

FIGURE 6.27

START OPTIONS	
SCREEN ELEMENT	**DESCRIPTION**
Start On Click	Animation begins when the slide is clicked. Displays with a mouse icon in the option list.
Start With Previous	Animation begins at the same time as the previous effect. One click executes all animation effects applied to the object. Displays with no icon in the option list.
Start After Previous	Animation begins after the previous effect in the list finishes. No additional click is needed. One click executes all animation effects applied to the object. Displays with a clock icon in the option list.

4 Click **Start After Previous**. View the slide show **From Current Slide**. Click three times to display the title entrance, the title emphasis, and then the subtitle entrance and exit effects. Press Esc.

 ANOTHER WAY   To select a start method, on the ANIMATIONS tab, in the Timing group, click the Start arrow, and then select the method.

By changing On Click to After Previous, it was not necessary to click the mouse to initiate the subtitle exit effects. On the ANIMATIONS tab, in the Timing group, the Start box now displays After Previous. The exit effects applied to the subtitle displayed automatically. Notice that number 4 disappeared from the exit effect in the Animation Pane.

5 Make **Slide 3** the active slide. In the **Animation Pane**, right-click the **entrance effect** for the content placeholder, and then click **Effect Options**. In the **Fade** dialog box, click the **Timing tab**, and then click the **Start arrow**. Click **After Previous**.

6 Click the **Duration arrow**, and then select **1 seconds (Fast)**. Compare your screen with Figure 6.28.

The Fade dialog box is a context-sensitive dialog box for the entrance effect applied to the title. The name of the dialog box reflects which effect you are modifying. In this dialog box, you can modify more than one setting.

FIGURE 6.28

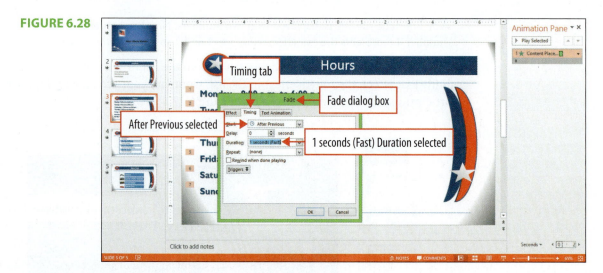

7 Click **OK**, and then view the slide show **From Current Slide**. After the last day displays, press Esc.

Each day displayed automatically without any mouse clicks.

8 Make **Slide 2** the active slide, and then click to select the content placeholder. On the **ANIMATIONS tab**, in the **Advanced Animation group**, click **Add Animation**, and then click **More Entrance Effects**. Under **Basic**, click **Fly In**, and then click **OK**. View the slide show **From Current Slide**, and then press Esc to return to **Normal** view.

The title is displayed and then moved to the left. The red car picture moved to the right. The items in the content placeholder fly in from the bottom one after the other. No mouse clicks were required.

9 Make **Slide 5** the active slide. In the **Animation Pane**, click **Play All**, and then view the slide show **From Current Slide**. After Wipe transition completes, click the mouse eight times. Press Esc.

The Play button displays all animations associated with the slide, in Normal view, regardless of how the animation is set to start. However, From Beginning or From Current Slide plays all animations applied to the slide in Slide Show view, and it displays them the way they will display in a slide show. If you are testing the effects with the Slide Show button and the animation is set to start On Click, you must click the mouse or press Enter to begin the animation.

10 In the **Animation Pane**, right-click the entrance effect for the SmartArt—the first effect. Click **Effect Options** to display the **Float Up** dialog box. On the **Timing tab**, click the **Start arrow**, and then select **After Previous**. Change the **Duration** to **0.5 seconds (Very Fast)**. Click **OK**. View the slide show **From Current Slide**. Press Esc to return to **Normal** view.

The SmartArt items enter without mouse clicks. To view the exit effect, you have to click the mouse for each one. The Duration speed was 0.5 seconds, which may be a little fast for a presentation, but appropriate for you to see the effect. Always choose a time suitable for your audience.

11 In the **Animation Pane**, right-click the exit effect for the SmartArt—the second effect. Click **Effect Options** to display the **Wipe** dialog box. On the **Timing tab**, click the **Start arrow**, and then select **After Previous**. If necessary, change the **Duration** to **0.5 seconds (Very Fast)**. Click **OK**. View the slide show **From Current Slide**. Press Esc.

The SmartArt items entered and exited without mouse clicks. Notice that the pictures entered and exited separately from the descriptions. The Duration speed was 0.5 seconds, which may be a little fast for a presentation, but appropriate for you to see the effect. Always choose a time suitable for your audience.

12 Save 🖫 your changes.

Activity 6.08 | Setting Effect Options

In this activity, you will set effect options that include having an animation disappear from the slide after the animation effect, setting a time delay, and animating text.

1 With **Slide 2** as the active slide, in the **Animation Pane**, right-click the third effect, the **entrance effect** for the content placeholder, and then click **Effect Options** to display the **Fly In** dialog box.

The Fly In dialog box has three tabs—Effect, Timing, and Text Animation. On the Effect tab, you can change the Settings and the Enhancements. You can change the direction of the Fly In, add sound, and change the way text is animated.

2 On the **Effect tab**, under **Settings**, click the **Direction arrow**, and then click **From Left**.

3 ▶ Under **Enhancements**, click the **After animation arrow**. Compare your screen with Figure 6.29.

You can apply a color change to the animated text or object. You can also automatically hide the animated object after the animation takes place or hide the animated object on the next mouse click. Don't Dim is selected by default.

FIGURE 6.29

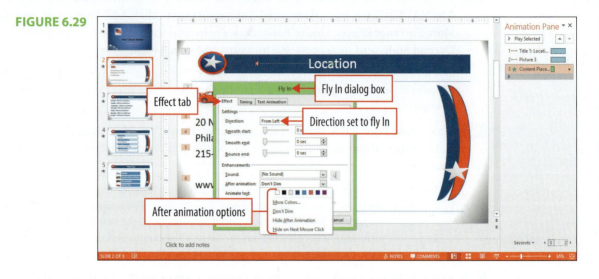

4 ▶ In the row of colors, click the fifth color—**Light Blue**. Click **OK**. View the slide show **From Current Slide**. When **Slide 3** displays, press Esc.

The animation changes display automatically one at a time.

5 ▶ With **Slide 2** selected, in the **Animation Pane**, right-click the effect for the content placeholder, and then click **Effect Options**. In the **Fly In** dialog box, click the **Timing tab**. Click the **Duration arrow**, and then click **2 seconds (Medium)**. Compare your screen with Figure 6.30.

By using the Timing tab, you can change how the animation will start. You can also set a delay, in seconds, from when the slide displays until the text displays. You can select the speed and how many times you would like the animation to repeat. Selecting the *Rewind when done playing* check box will cause the animated text or object to disappear from the slide after the animation is completed, as opposed to remaining on the slide. From this tab you can also set a ***trigger***, which is a portion of text, a graphic, or a picture that, when clicked, produces a result. Recall that in Chapter 5 you practiced inserting sounds into slides and selecting a placeholder or object that would start the sound when clicked. Triggers are created for animation purposes using the same technique.

FIGURE 6.30

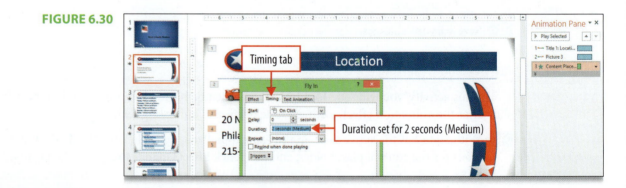

NOTE **Repeating an Animated List of Items**

In the Fly In dialog box, on the Timing tab, if you elect to repeat a list of items that have animation applied to them, typing a number in the Repeat box will cause each line of text or each bulleted item to repeat before the next item displays. Repeating a list of two or three bulleted items might be used in a presentation as a special effect to emphasize the points but may produce unexpected and unwanted results, so be very cautious about using this option.

6 ▶ In the **Fly In** dialog box, click the **Text Animation tab**. Click the **Group text arrow**.

You can treat a list as one object and animate all paragraphs of text simultaneously. If your bulleted list has several levels of bulleted items, you can select how you want to animate the items. Use the Text Animation tab to set a delay in seconds, animate an attached shape, or reverse the order of the items.

7 ▶ If necessary, click **By 1st Level Paragraphs**, and then click **OK**.

8 ▶ On the **ANIMATIONS tab**, in the **Animation group**, click **Effect Options**, and then compare your screen with Figure 6.31.

 ANOTHER WAY   To set the direction and sequence of bullet points, use the Effect Options button in the Animation group.

FIGURE 6.31

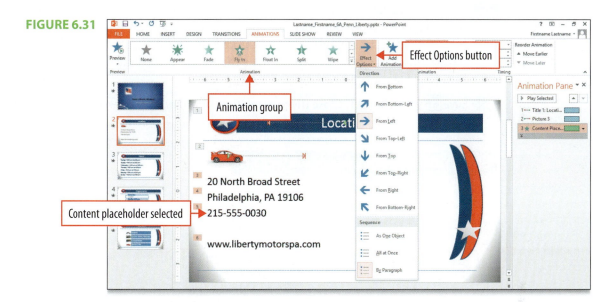

9 ▶ Click **From Bottom**. In the **Animation Pane**, click **Play Selected**.

The lines of text on the slide display from the bottom. On the ANIMATIONS tab, in the Animation group, the Effect Options button now points up, which means the items are coming from the bottom and moving upward.

10 ▶ With **Slide 2** active, click the **title** placeholder—*Location*. At the top of the **Animation Pane**, on the right side, click the **Reorder down-pointing arrow** two times. Click the **top item** in the list—**1 Picture 3**, and then click **Play From**. Compare your screen with Figure 6.32.

The order of the effects is changed. The car, address, and website are displayed first. The motion effect on the title is displayed last because the order of the effects was changed in the Animation Pane. You can easily reorder the list of animation sequences by selecting a placeholder and then clicking the reorder arrows at the top of the Animation Pane.

 ANOTHER WAY   To reorder effects in the Animation Pane, you can click on the effect, and then drag it to the new position.

FIGURE 6.32

11 Click **2 Content Place....** Under the **Content Placeholder**, click the **chevron** ⬇, and then click **Play Selected** and watch the timeline. Click the **chevron** ⬆ to hide the contents.

12 View the slide show **From Beginning**. Click when necessary to advance the slides.

13 On the **ANIMATIONS tab**, in the **Advanced Animation group**, click the **Animation Pane** to close the pane.

14 On the **INSERT tab**, in the **Text group**, click **Header & Footer** to display the **Header and Footer** dialog box. Click the **Notes and Handouts tab**. Under **Include on page**, select the **Date and time** check box, and then select **Fixed**. If necessary, clear the **Header** check box, and then select the **Page number** and **Footer** check boxes. In the **Footer** box, using your own name, type **Lastname_Firstname_6A_Penn_Liberty** and then click **Apply To All**.

15 Click **the FILE tab**, and then in the lower right portion of the screen, click **Show All Properties**. In the **Tags** box, type **hours, cars** and then in the **Subject** box, type your course name and section number. In the **Author** box, right-click the existing author name, click **Edit Property**, replace the existing text with your first and last name, click outside textbox to deselect, and then click **OK**.

16 Save 🖫 your changes. **Close** the presentation, and then **Exit** PowerPoint. Submit your work as directed.

END | You have completed Project 6A

PROJECT 6B Penn Liberty Motors Advertisement

PROJECT ACTIVITIES

In Activities 6.09 through 6.20, you will insert various types of hyperlinks into a presentation created by Penn Liberty Motors as an advertisement for the company. The focus of the ad is the location of Penn Liberty Motors in Philadelphia. You will create two custom slide shows from a single presentation to appeal to two different audiences. You will also annotate the presentation. Finally, you will organize your slides into sections and print selections from a presentation. Your completed presentation will look similar to Figure 6.33.

PROJECT FILES

For Project 6B, you will need the following files:

p06B_Advertisement.pptx
p06B_Blue_Car.jpg

You will save your files as:

Lastname_Firstname_6B_Advertisement.pptx
Lastname_Firstname_6B_History.docx

PROJECT RESULTS

FIGURE 6.33 Project 6B Advertisement

Video P6-4

In the following activities, you will insert hyperlinks into a PowerPoint presentation. Recall that *hyperlinks* are text or objects such as clip art, graphics, WordArt, or pictures that, when clicked, will move you to a webpage, an email address, another document or file, or another area of the same document. In a PowerPoint presentation, hyperlinks can also be used to link to a slide in the presentation, to a slide in a different presentation, or to a custom slide show.

Activity 6.09 | Inserting a Hyperlink to Webpage

In this activity, you will insert a hyperlink into a slide that will connect to the Penn Liberty Motors webpage.

1 Start PowerPoint. Locate and open the file **p06B_Advertisement**. Navigate to the **PowerPoint Chapter 6** folder you created, and then **Save** the file as **Lastname_Firstname_6B_Advertisement**

2 Make the **Slide 5** the active slide. Click to select the textbox containing the webpage address *www.philadelphiazoo.org* and select the web address text.

3 Click the **INSERT tab**. In the **Links group**, click **Hyperlink** to display the **Insert Hyperlink** dialog box. If necessary, under **Link to**, click **Existing File or Web Page**. Compare your screen with Figure 6.34.

The Insert Hyperlink dialog box provides an easy and convenient way to insert hyperlinks. You can link to an Existing File or Web Page (the default setting), a Place in This Document, Create New Document, or an E-mail Address. You can also browse the web, browse for a file, or change the text that displays in the ScreenTip.

FIGURE 6.34

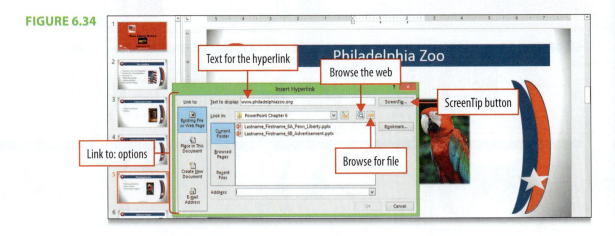

4 Click **ScreenTip**. In the **Set Hyperlink ScreenTip** dialog box, type **Philadelphia Zoo** Compare your screen with Figure 6.35.

FIGURE 6.35

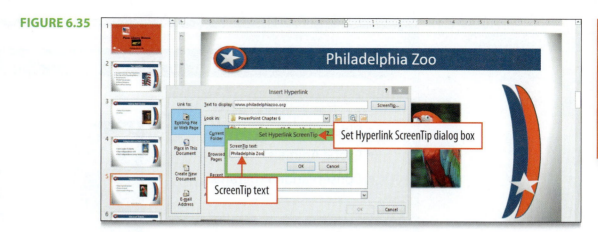

5 ▸ Click **OK**. In the **Address** box, delete the existing text, if any, and then type **http://www.philadelphiazoo.org** Compare your screen with Figure 6.36.

The text you typed is a *URL*, or *Uniform Resource Locator*. A URL defines the address of documents and resources on the web.

FIGURE 6.36

More **Knowledge** | **Understanding Uniform Resource Locators**

A Uniform Resource Locator, or URL, generally consists of the protocol and the IP address or domain name. The first part of the address is the *protocol*. A protocol is a set of rules. *HyperText Transfer Protocol (HTTP)* is the protocol used on the World Wide Web to define how messages are formatted and transmitted. It also instructs the *Web browser* software how to display webpages. Web browsers, such as Internet Explorer, format webpages so that they display properly. The protocol is followed by a colon (:) and two forward slashes (/). The *www* stands for *World Wide Web*. The World Wide Web is a collection of websites. This is followed by the *domain name*. The domain name is a user friendly name that represents an *IP address*. An IP address, or Internet Protocol address, is a unique set of numbers, composed of a network ID and a machine ID, that identifies the web server where the webpage resides. The *suffix* part of the domain name, the portion after the dot (.), is the *high level domain name (HLDN)* or top level domain name, such as *.com*, *.org*, or *.gov*. This is the upper level domain to which the lower level domain belongs.

6 ▸ Click **OK**.

The webpage address now displays with an underline and takes on the appearance of a hyperlink.

7 ▸ Start the slide show **From Current Slide**. On **Slide 5**, without clicking, point to the address *www.philadelphiazoo.org*, and then compare your screen with Figure 6.37.

The Link Select pointer displays. A ScreenTip displays with the text you typed.

FIGURE 6.37

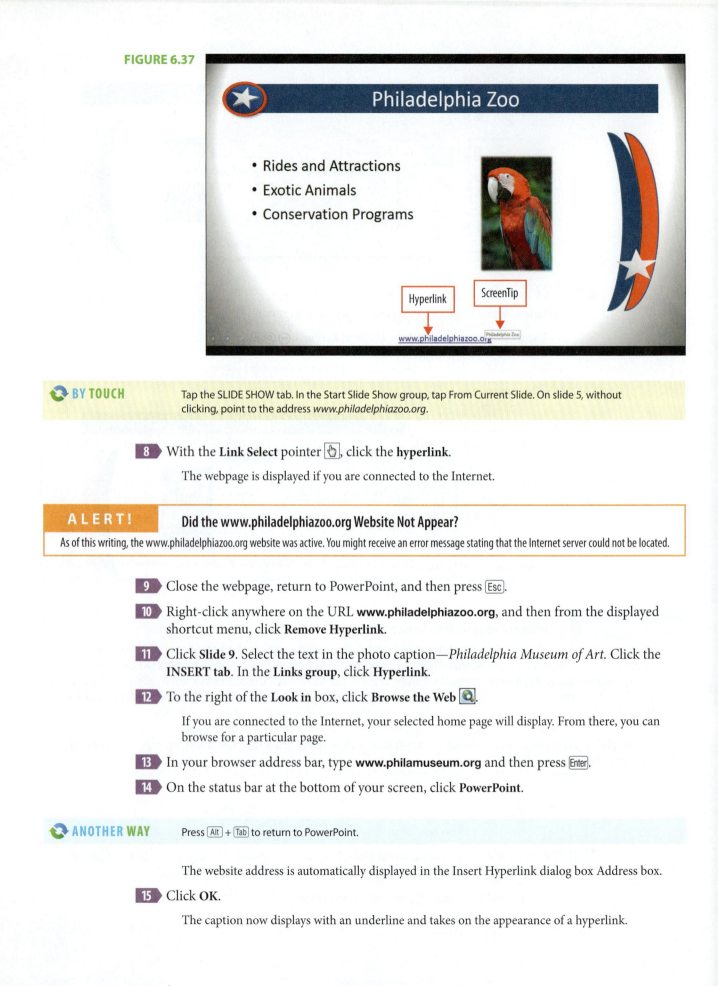

BY TOUCH   Tap the SLIDE SHOW tab. In the Start Slide Show group, tap From Current Slide. On slide 5, without clicking, point to the address *www.philadelphiazoo.org*.

8 With the **Link Select** pointer 🖑, click the **hyperlink**.

The webpage is displayed if you are connected to the Internet.

ALERT! **Did the www.philadelphiazoo.org Website Not Appear?**

As of this writing, the www.philadelphiazoo.org website was active. You might receive an error message stating that the Internet server could not be located.

9 Close the webpage, return to PowerPoint, and then press Esc.

10 Right-click anywhere on the URL **www.philadelphiazoo.org**, and then from the displayed shortcut menu, click **Remove Hyperlink**.

11 Click **Slide 9**. Select the text in the photo caption—*Philadelphia Museum of Art*. Click the **INSERT tab**. In the **Links group**, click **Hyperlink**.

12 To the right of the **Look in** box, click **Browse the Web** 🔍.

If you are connected to the Internet, your selected home page will display. From there, you can browse for a particular page.

13 In your browser address bar, type **www.philamuseum.org** and then press Enter.

14 On the status bar at the bottom of your screen, click **PowerPoint**.

ANOTHER WAY   Press Alt + Tab to return to PowerPoint.

The website address is automatically displayed in the Insert Hyperlink dialog box Address box.

15 Click **OK**.

The caption now displays with an underline and takes on the appearance of a hyperlink.

16 Start the slide show **From Current Slide**. Point to the caption—*Philadelphia Museum of Art*, and then compare your screen with Figure 6.38.

> It is not necessary to format the webpage hyperlink text in URL format as long as it is linked correctly to the webpage address. Any text or object can serve as a hyperlink.

FIGURE 6.38

17 Click to test your hyperlink. When you are finished, **Close** the webpage and return to PowerPoint. Press Esc to return to your presentation screen.

ALERT!   **Did the www.philamuseum.org Website Not Appear?**

As of this writing, the **www.philamuseum.org** website was active. You might receive an error message stating that the Internet server could not be located.

---

18 Save 💾 your changes.

Activity 6.10 | Inserting a Hyperlink to a Slide in Another Presentation

In this activity, you will insert a hyperlink into a presentation that will link to the New Cars slide in a previously created presentation.

1 In **Normal** view, make **Slide 12** the active slide. Select the text in the picture caption—*Penn Liberty Motors New Car Selections*. Click the **INSERT tab**. In the **Links group**, click **Hyperlink** to display the **Insert Hyperlink** dialog box.

2 If necessary, under **Link to**, click to select **Existing File or Web Page**, and then navigate to the **PowerPoint Chapter 6** folder, if necessary, and click **Lastname_Firstname_6A_Penn_Liberty**. Compare your screen with Figure 6.39.

FIGURE 6.39

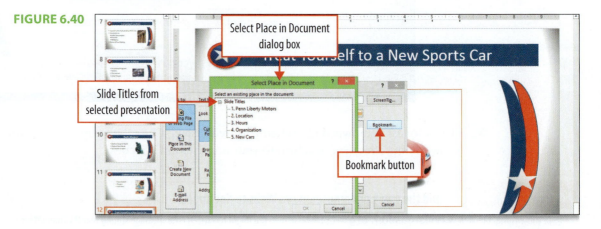

3 ▶ In the **Insert Hyperlink** dialog box, click **Bookmark** to display the **Select Place in Document** dialog box. Compare your screen with Figure 6.40.

Notice that the slides from Lastname_Firstname_6A_Penn_Liberty are listed.

FIGURE 6.40

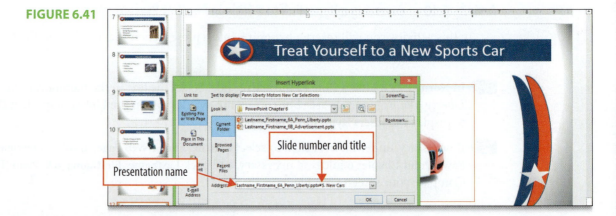

4 ▶ In the **Select Place in Document** dialog box, click the fifth slide—*New Cars*—and then click **OK**. Compare your screen with Figure 6.41.

The Address box contains the name of the presentation and the number and title of the slide.

FIGURE 6.41

5 ▶ Click **OK**. Click the **SLIDE SHOW tab**, and then in the **Set Up group**, click **Set Up Slide Show**. If necessary, in the **Set Up Show** dialog box, under **Show type**, select the **Presented by a speaker (full screen)** option button. If necessary, under **Advance slides**, click the **Manually** option button. Click **OK**.

6 Start the slide show **From Current Slide**, and then click the hyperlink. The hyperlink will move you to **Slide 5** of the other presentation. When the animations finish playing, press ⎋Esc to return to **Slide 12** of the current slide show. Press ⎋Esc to return to **Normal** view.

Because you selected Presented by a speaker (full screen), you were able to view Slide 5 from the Penn Liberty presentation.

7 Save your changes.

Activity 6.11 | Inserting a Hyperlink to an Email Address

In this activity, you will insert a hyperlink that will open an email client and insert the recipient's email address and subject.

1 Make **Slide 6** the active slide. Select the text *Contact Us*. Click the **INSERT tab**. In the **Links group**, click **Hyperlink**.

2 In the **Insert Hyperlink** dialog box, under **Link to**, click to select **E-mail Address**.

3 In the **E-mail address** box, type **kevin@libertymotors.com**

4 In the **Subject** box, type **Discount Tickets** and then compare your screen with Figure 6.42.

The word *mailto:* displays before the email address. This is an *HTML* attribute instructing the Web browser software that this is an email address. HTML stands for *HyperText Markup Language* and is the language used to code webpages. The recently used email addresses with the associated subject also display for easy selection. You may not have any in your list.

FIGURE 6.42

5 Click **OK**.

<table>
<tr><td>**A L E R T !**</td><td>**Do You Have an Email Client to Use?**</td></tr>
</table>

If you do not have an email client that is configured to a mail service, skip the following steps in this activity. Instead, save your changes and proceed to the next activity.

6 Start the slide show **From Current Slide**, and when the slide show displays, click the hyperlink. Compare your screen with Figure 6.43.

An email program opens with the email address you typed in the To box. In this case, *Microsoft Outlook* opens. Microsoft Outlook is the program, or *email client*, that facilitates the sending and receiving of electronic messages. This enables you to type an email message and click Send from within the PowerPoint presentation. An email client is a software program that enables you to compose and send an email message.

FIGURE 6.43

A L E R T !   **Does Your Screen Differ?**

If the email client on the computer you are using is not Microsoft Outlook, the Discount Tickets window that displays will differ from the one shown in Figure 6.43. If you do not have an email client, you will not be able to do this. If you get a startup screen when you click on the email link, that means your client has not been configured.

> **7** **Close** the email program without saving changes to the email message, and then press Esc.
>
> **8** **Save** 🖫 your changes.

Activity 6.12 | Inserting a Hyperlink to a New File

In this activity, you will insert a hyperlink that will allow you to create a new file.

> **1** In **Normal** view, make the **title slide** the active slide. Click to select the image of the flag. Click the **INSERT tab**. In the **Links group**, click **Hyperlink**.
>
> **2** Under **Link to**, click to select **Create New Document**. Compare your screen with Figure 6.44.
>
> When Create New Document is selected, the Insert Hyperlink dialog box allows you to create a new document from PowerPoint. The file can be a document, a spreadsheet, or a presentation.

FIGURE 6.44

N O T E   **Insert a Hyperlink to an Existing File**

If you have created a file that you want to link to, click Existing File or Web Page (the default setting) and navigate to the file.

> **3** In the **Name of new document** box, substitute your own first name and last name, and then type **Lastname_Firstname_6B_History.docx** Make sure that you type the file extension—.docx

4 ▶ If necessary, click **Change**, and then navigate to your **PowerPoint Chapter 6** folder and click **OK**.

In this case, you are creating a Microsoft Word document. The *file extension* or file type identifies the format of the file or the application that was used to create it. If the *full path* listed is incorrect, click Change, and then navigate to the PowerPoint Chapter 6 folder you created. The full path includes the location of the drive, the folder, and any subfolders in which the file is contained.

N O T E   **File Name and File Extension**

Typing the file extension with the file name in the Name of new document box is the only way that Windows recognizes which application to start. If you do not type a file extension in the Name of new document box, Windows will assume you are creating a presentation and will start a new PowerPoint presentation because you are currently using PowerPoint.

---

5 ▶ Under **When to edit**, make sure the **Edit the new document now** option button is selected, and then compare your screen with Figure 6.45.

FIGURE 6.45

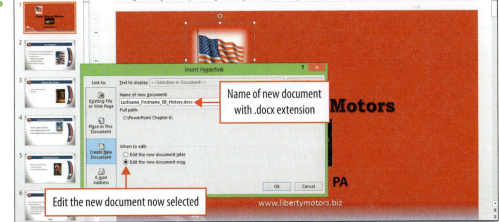

6 ▶ Click **OK** to open a new Microsoft Word file named **Lastname_Firstname_6B_History.docx**.

A L E R T !   **Did You Have Trouble Displaying the Word Document?**

If you made an error in the process of creating the hyperlink to create a new document and tried to do it again, you may find that the Word document does not display. If that happens, look in your chapter folder. If a file named Lastname_Firstname_6B_History.docx displays, delete the file. Return to PowerPoint, and then enter the hyperlink again.

---

7 ▶ Type **Penn Liberty Motors was founded in 1903 by Martin Rau.** Press Enter two times, and then type **Lastname_Firstname_6B_History.docx** Compare your screen with Figure 6.46.

FIGURE 6.46

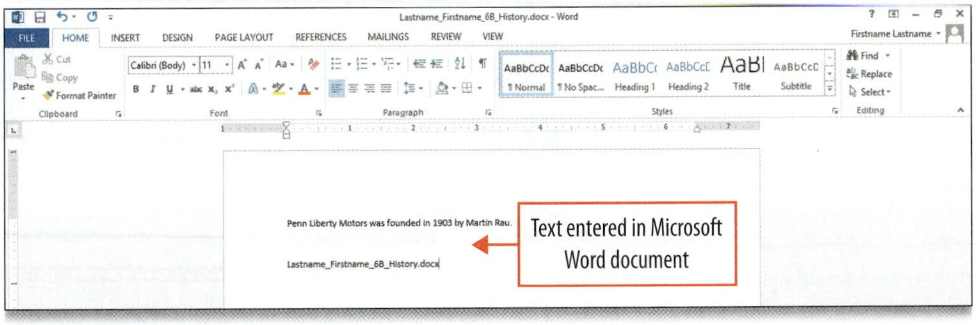

8 Save ⊟ the document, and then **Exit** ✕ Microsoft Word.

9 Start the slide show **From Current Slide**, and when the slide show displays, click the flag image to display the Word document.

The flag image contains the hyperlink to the Word document.

10 **Exit** Word ✕. Press `Esc` to return to **Normal** view.

11 Save ⊟ your changes.

Activity 6.13 | Creating an Action Button

An *action button* is a built-in button shape that you can add to your presentation and then assign an action to occur upon the click of a mouse or with a mouse over. It is a type of hyperlink, created by inserting an action button from the list of shapes. Action buttons have built-in actions or links associated with them, or you can change the action that occurs when the action button is clicked. Action buttons are generally used in self-running slide shows.

1 In **Normal** view, make **Slide 5** the active slide. Click the **INSERT tab**. In the **Illustration group**, click **Shapes**.

2 At the bottom of the list, under **Action Buttons**, click the fourth button—**Action Button: End**.

3 Position the ✚ pointer at the lower right corner—at the **3-inch mark to the right of 0** on the **horizontal ruler** and at the **3-inch mark below 0** on the **vertical ruler**. Click once to display the **Action Settings** dialog box.

The Action Settings dialog box displays. Because the action associated with the End button is to link to the last slide in the presentation, *Last Slide* displays in the Hyperlink to box. The action button on the slide is too large, but you will resize it later.

4 Click the **Hyperlink to: arrow**, and then scroll to review the list of options, which includes other slides in the presentation, a custom show, a URL, other files, and other PowerPoint presentations. Click **Last Slide** to close the list, and then compare your screen with Figure 6.47.

There are two tabs in the Action Settings dialog box. You can set the action to occur on a Mouse Click or *Mouse Over*. Mouse Over means that the action will occur when the presenter points to (hovers over) the action button. It is not necessary to click.

FIGURE 6.47

5 ▶ Click the **Mouse Over tab**. Click the **Hyperlink to:** option, click the **Hyperlink to: arrow**, and then select **Last Slide**. Select the **Play sound** check box, click the **Play sound check box arrow**, scroll down, and then click **Chime**. Click **OK**.

6 ▶ With the action button still selected, on the **DRAWING TOOLS FORMAT tab**, in the **Size group**, change the **Shape Height** 📏 to **0.5"**. Change the **Shape Width** 📐 to **0.5"**. Compare your screen with Figure 6.48.

The action button is displayed at the bottom right of the slide.

FIGURE 6.48

7 ▶ Start the slide show **From Current Slide**, and then move the mouse over the action button.

The chime effect is played when the mouse was over the action button, and then the last slide in the presentation is displayed.

8 ▶ Press [Esc], and then **Save** 💾 your changes.

Objective 5 | Create Custom Slide Shows

Video P6-5

A ***custom slide show*** displays only the slides you want to display to an audience in the order you select. You still have the option of running the entire presentation in its sequential order. Custom shows provide you with the tools to create different slide shows to appeal to different audiences from the original presentation.

There are two types of custom shows—basic and hyperlinked. A ***basic custom slide show*** is a separate presentation saved with its own title containing some of the slides from the original presentation. A ***hyperlinked custom slide show*** is a quick way to navigate to a separate slide show from within the original presentation. For example, if your audience wants to know more about a topic, you could have hyperlinks to slides that you could quickly access when necessary.

Activity 6.14 | Creating a Basic Custom Slide Show

In this activity, you will create basic custom slide shows from an existing presentation. You will then save them as separate custom shows that can be run from the SLIDE SHOW tab.

1 ▶ Make the **title slide** the active slide. On the **SLIDE SHOW tab**, in the **Start Slide Show group**, click **Custom Slide Show button arrow**, and then click **Custom Shows** to display the **Custom Shows** dialog box.

2 ▶ Click **New** to display the **Define Custom Show** dialog box, In the **Slide show name** box, delete the text, and then type **Historic** Compare your screen with Figure 6.49.

From the Define Custom Show dialog box, you can name a custom slide show and select the slides that will be included in the slide show. All the slides in the current presentation are displayed in the Slides in presentation box. The slides you want to include in the custom show will display in the Slides in custom show box.

FIGURE 6.49

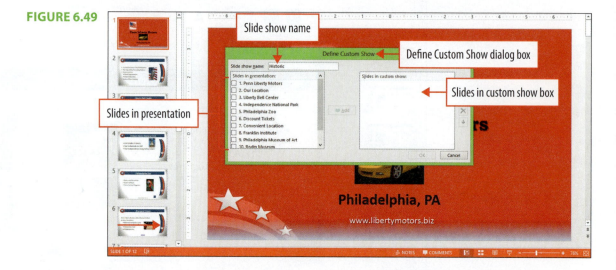

3 ▶ Under **Slides in presentation**, click to select **Slide 1**. Using the same technique, click to select **Slides 2, 3, 4, 5,** and **6**. Compare your screen with Figure 6.50.

FIGURE 6.50

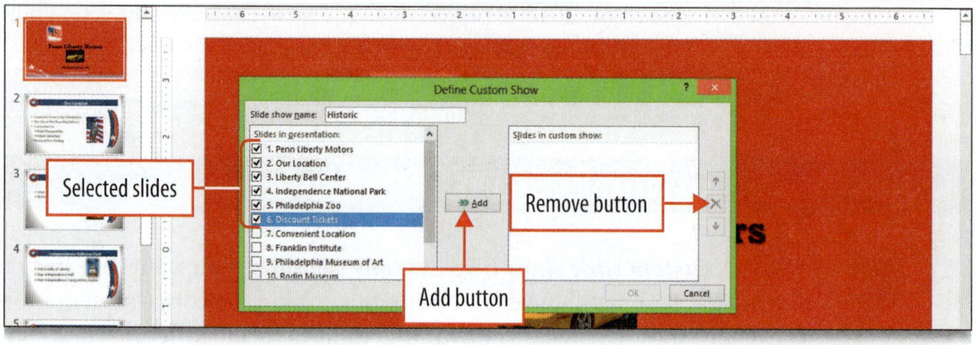

4 ▶ Click **Add**. Under **Slides in presentation**, click to select **Slide 12** and add it to the custom show. Compare your screen with Figure 6.51.

Slide 12 is renumbered as Slide 7 in the custom show.

FIGURE 6.51

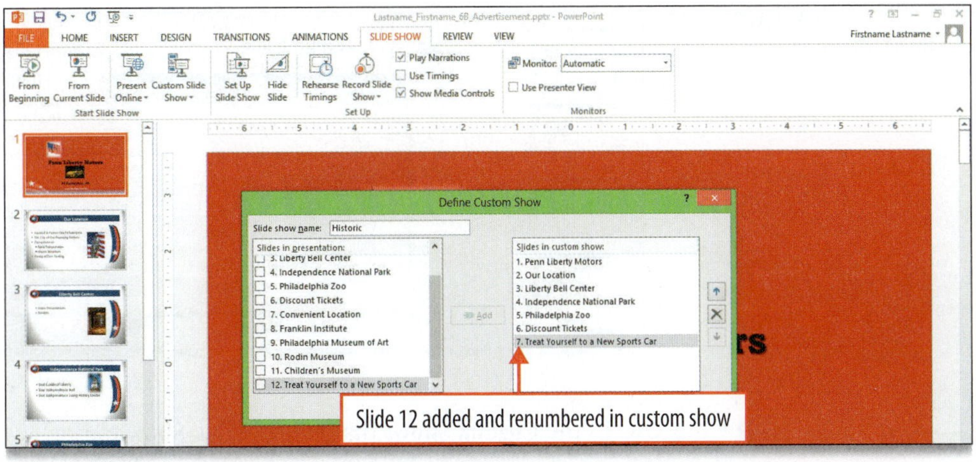

Slide 12 added and renumbered in custom show

5 Click **OK**. Compare your screen with Figure 6.52.

FIGURE 6.52

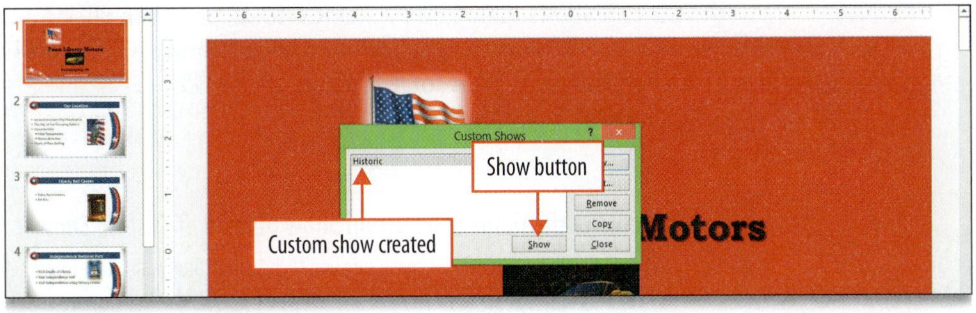

Show button

Custom show created

6 In the **Custom Shows** dialog box, click **Show** to preview your custom show. Click through the slides. When you are finished viewing the slide show, press Esc.

The Historic custom slide show included only seven slides.

A L E R T ! **Did the Presentation Not Display?**

If the first slide of the presentation did not display automatically, press Esc. On the SLIDE SHOW tab, in the Set Up group, click the Set Up Slide Show. In the Set Up Show dialog box, select the *Presented by a speaker (full screen)* option button, and then click OK.

---

7 On the **SLIDE SHOW tab**, in the **Start Slide Show group**, click **Custom Slide Show arrow**.

The custom show—Historic—displays, and you can start the show from this list also.

8 Click **Historic** to view the slide show again. When you are finished viewing the slide show, press Enter or Esc.

9 Click **Custom Slide Show arrow** again. Click **Custom Shows** to display the **Custom Shows** dialog box, and then click **New**. In the **Slide show name** box, delete the text, and type **Cultural**

10 Under **Slides in presentation**, click to select **Slides 6, 7, 8, 9, 10, 11,** and **12**. Click **Add**. Under **Slides in presentation**, click to select **Slide 1,** and then add it to the custom slide show.

Slide 1 is now Slide 8 in the Cultural custom show.

11 Under **Slides in custom show**, click **Slide 8**. Click the **Up arrow** seven times to move **Slide 8** so it is in the **Slide 1** position in the custom show, and then compare your screen with Figure 6.53.

FIGURE 6.53

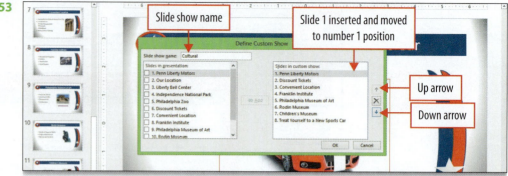

12 ▶ Click **OK**. In the **Custom Shows** dialog box, click **Show** to preview your custom show. When you are finished viewing the slide show, press Enter or Esc.

> Eight slides displayed.

13 ▶ In the **Start Slide Show group**, click **Custom Slide Show arrow**. Click **Custom Shows** to display the **Custom Shows** dialog box. Click **Cultural**, and then click **Edit**. In the **Slides in custom show** list, click **2. Discount Tickets**, and then click **Remove**. Click **OK**. In the **Custom Shows** dialog box, click **Show**. Press Enter or Esc when you are done.

> Seven slides displayed.

ALERT!   **Did You Click the Name of a Custom Show Instead of Custom Shows?**

To edit a specific custom show, when you click Custom Slide Show, make sure you click Custom Shows to allow you to select the show and edit it. If you clicked a custom show by accident, press Esc and try again.

---

14 ▶ Click **Custom Slide Show arrow**, and then click **Custom Shows** to display the **Custom Shows** dialog box. Click **New**. In the **Slide show name** box, delete the text, and then type **Location**

15 ▶ In the **Slides in presentation** box, click to select **Slides 2, 3, 4, 5,** and **6**. Click **Add**. Click **OK**.

16 ▶ In the **Custom Shows** dialog box, click **Show** to preview your custom show. When you are finished viewing the slide show, press Enter, or Esc.

17 ▶ In the **Start Slide Show group**, click **Custom Slide Show arrow**. Compare your screen with Figure 6.54.

> Three custom shows are displayed in the list—Historic, Cultural, and Location.

FIGURE 6.54

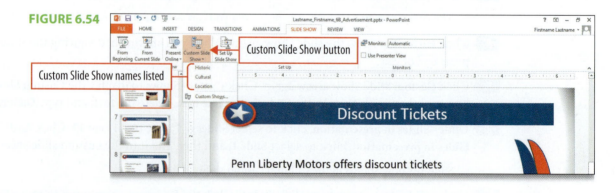

18 ▶ **Save** 🖫 your changes.

Activity 6.15 | Creating a Hyperlinked Custom Slide Show

In this activity, you will create a hyperlinked custom slide show from an existing presentation by selecting the slides that will be shown in the custom show. These slides can be hyperlinked to the original presentation.

1 In **Normal** view, make the **title slide** the active slide. Click to select the picture of the car.

2 On the **INSERT tab**, in the **Links group**, click **Hyperlink**. In the **Insert Hyperlink** dialog box, under **Link to:**, click **Place in This Document**. In the **Insert Hyperlink** dialog box, under **Select a place in this document:**, scroll down to display the **Custom Shows**.

3 Under **Select a place in this document**, below **Custom Shows**, click **Location**, and then select the **Show and return** check box. Compare your screen with Figure 6.55.

FIGURE 6.55

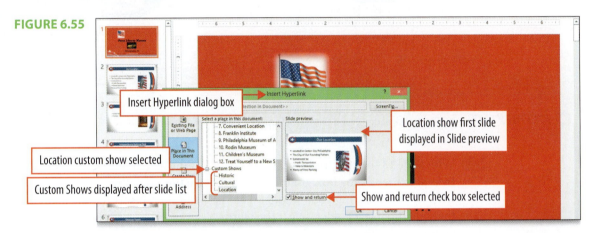

4 Click **OK**. Start the slide show **From Beginning**, and then click the picture of the **car** on the title slide. When the presentation returns to the title slide, press Esc.

The slides in the custom show—Location—will display, and after the last slide, the presentation will return to the title slide.

5 Save  your changes.

Objective 6 Present and View a Slide Presentation

Video P6-6

In the following activities, you will use the navigation tools included with PowerPoint to view slide shows. You can start a slide show from the beginning or from any slide you choose. The *navigation tools* include buttons that display on the slides during a slide show that enable you to perform actions such as move to the next slide, the previous slide, the last viewed slide, or the end of the slide show. Additionally, you can add an *annotation*, which is a note or a highlight that can be saved or discarded.

Activity 6.16 | Duplicating and Hiding a Slide

In this activity, you will duplicate one slide at the end of the presentation. You will hide two slides so that they do not display during the slide show and unhide one slide.

1 Make **Slide 12** the active slide. On the **HOME tab**, in the **Slides group**, click the **New Slide arrow**, and then from the displayed list, click **Duplicate Selected Slides**. Compare your screen with Figure 6.56.

FIGURE 6.56

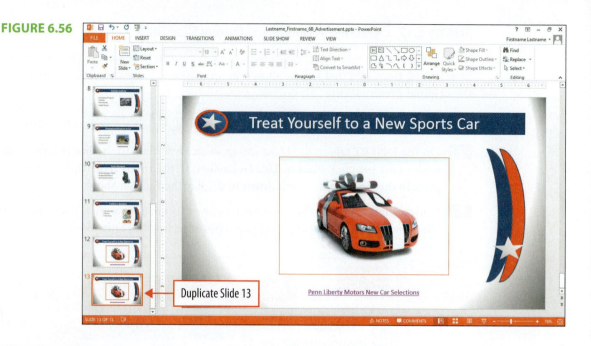

Duplicate Slide 13

🔄 **ANOTHER WAY**   Right-click Slide 13, and then click Duplicate Slide.

2 ▸ With **Slide 13** selected, right-click the picture of the car, and then click **Change Picture**. In the **Insert Pictures** dialog box, on the right of **From a file**, click **Browse**. Navigate to the location where you are storing your student data files, and then insert the file **p06B_Blue_Car.jpg**. In the slide title placeholder, select the words *New Sports Car* and then type **Sedan** Compare your screen with Figure 6.57.

The slide is duplicated and the picture and the slide title are changed.

FIGURE 6.57

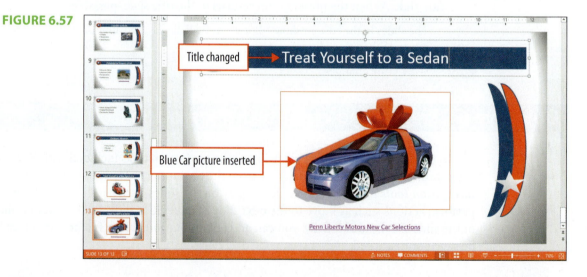

Title changed

Blue Car picture inserted

3 ▸ Make **Slide 6** the active slide. On the **SLIDE SHOW tab**, in the **Set Up group**, click **Hide Slide**. Compare your screen with Figure 6.58.

In the Slides/Outline pane, the number displayed to the left of the slide thumbnail has a diagonal line through it.

FIGURE 6.58

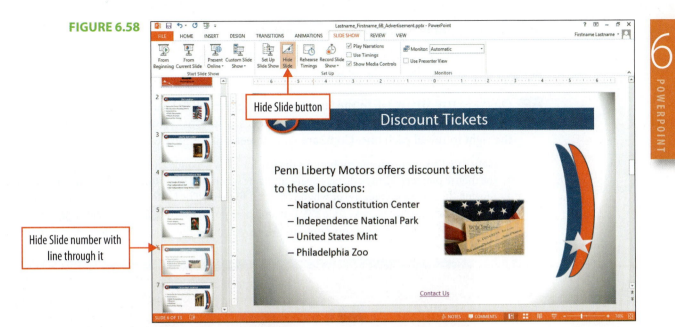

Hide Slide button

Hide Slide number with line through it

4 ▶ Make **Slide 12** the active slide. Right-click the thumbnail for **Slide 12** to display the shortcut menu, and then compare your screen with Figure 6.59.

You can hide a slide from the shortcut menu. Make sure you right-click the thumbnail.

FIGURE 6.59

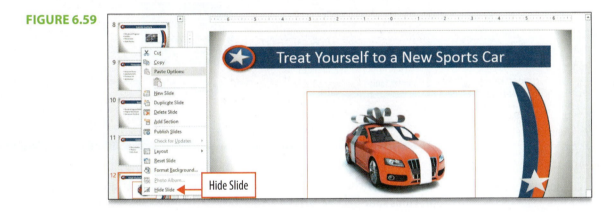

Hide Slide

5 ▶ Click **Hide Slide**.

6 ▶ Right-click the **Slide 6** thumbnail to display the shortcut menu again, and then click **Hide Slide** to unhide **Slide 6**.

Slide 6 is displayed. Only one slide is hidden—Slide 12.

N O T E   **Hiding and Displaying a Slide**

On the SLIDE SHOW tab, in the Setup group, the Hide Slide button is a toggle button. Recall that a toggle button performs an action when clicked and then reverses the previous action when clicked again. In the shortcut menu, Hide Slide is also a toggle command.

---

7 ▶ Save your changes.

Activity 6.17 | **Using the Onscreen Navigation Tools**

In this activity, you will use the onscreen navigation tools and the slide shortcut menu to navigate to a desired slide in the slide show.

1 On the **SLIDE SHOW tab** in the **Start Slide Show group**, click **From Beginning**. Move the mouse to the bottom left corner of the screen to reveal six buttons. Move the mouse pointer to the right to reveal each one. Compare your screen with Figure 6.60.

Notice that six semitransparent buttons display for a few seconds and then disappear. If you move the mouse pointer, they display again for a few seconds. The buttons display as long as you are moving the mouse pointer or when you point to them. The buttons are Return to the previous slide, Advance to the next slide, Pen and laser pointer tools, See all slides, Zoom into the slide, and More slide show options. As you move the mouse over them, they can be seen.

FIGURE 6.60

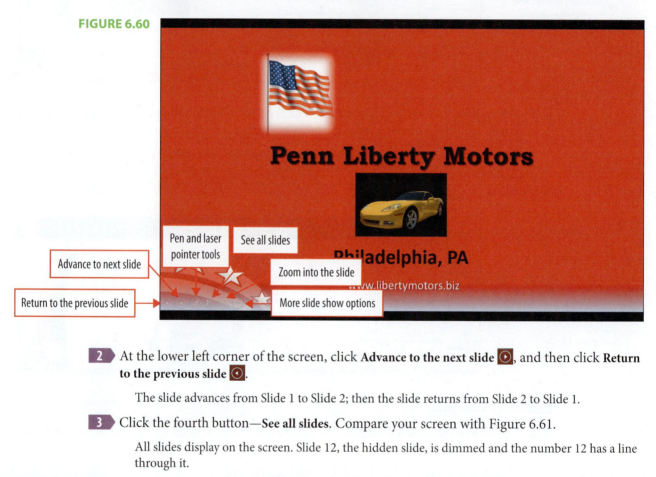

2 At the lower left corner of the screen, click **Advance to the next slide**, and then click **Return to the previous slide**.

The slide advances from Slide 1 to Slide 2; then the slide returns from Slide 2 to Slide 1.

3 Click the fourth button—**See all slides**. Compare your screen with Figure 6.61.

All slides display on the screen. Slide 12, the hidden slide, is dimmed and the number 12 has a line through it.

More Knowledge | **Zoom Slider**

The Zoom Slider in the bottom right corner of the screen allows you to change the zoom level so you can change the number of slides that are visible on the screen at one time.

FIGURE 6.61

Slide 12, the hidden slide is dimmed and a line is through the number 12

4 ► Click **Slide 7** to display it. Right-click anywhere on the slide, click **Custom Show**, and then click **Historic**. Click to view each of the slides in the custom show. When the slide show is finished, press Esc.

> You right-clicked Slide 7 to display the shortcut menu, and then you viewed the Historic custom show.

5 ► On the **SLIDE SHOW tab**, in the **Start Slide Show group**, click **From Beginning**. At the lower left corner of the screen, click **More slide show options** ⊙, and then click **Show Presenter View**. Compare your screen with Figure 6.62.

> Slide Show view changes to Presenter View.

More Knowledge | **Arrow Options**

Arrow Options display on the More slide show options menu. When the Arrow Options is set for Visible, the mouse pointer displays on the Slide show. When the Arrow Options is set for Hidden, the mouse pointer does not display. The default setting is Automatic.

FIGURE 6.62

6 In Presenter View, below the large slide, click **Black or unblack slide show** ⬛. Compare your screen with Figure 6.63.

The large slide changes to black in Presenter View. This is useful when you do not want your presentation to display; for example, before your presentation begins.

FIGURE 6.63

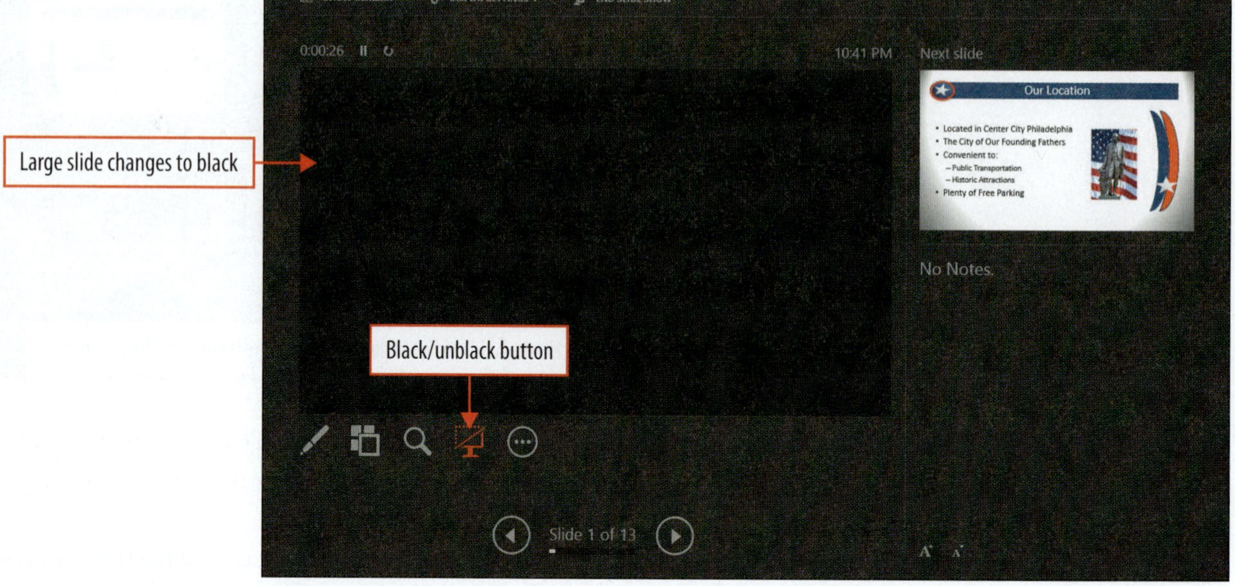

Large slide changes to black

Black/unblack button

7 Click **Black or unblack slide show** ⬛ to make the large slide visible again.

🔄 **ANOTHER WAY**   Click the slide to make the large slide visible again.

More Knowledge   **AutoExtend Feature in Presenter View**

The AutoExtend feature in Presenter View allows you to project to a second screen. The Swap Presentation View and Slide Show is located in the DISPLAY SETTINGS which allows you to swap the screens that the presentation displays on. The Duplicate Slide Show display setting allows you to display a slide show on more than one monitor.

---

8 Below the large slide, click **More slide show options** ⚫, and then click **Hide Presenter View** to return to the slide show.

Activity 6.18 │ Using the Annotation Tool

In this activity, you will use the Pen and laser tools to highlight and annotate information on a slide.

1 At the lower left corner of the screen, click the third button—**Pen and laser tools**. Compare your screen with Figure 6.64. Take a moment to review the Pen and Laser Pointer Tool options, as described in the table shown in Figure 6.65.

FIGURE 6.64

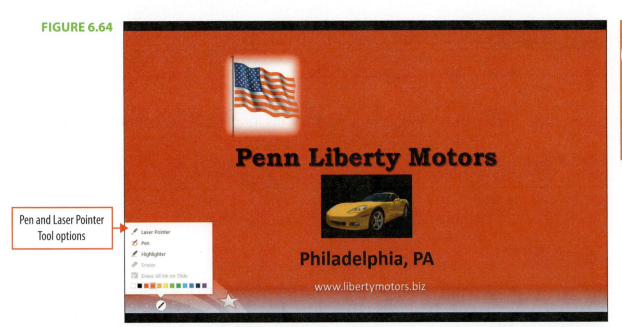

Pen and Laser Pointer Tool options

FIGURE 6.65

PEN AND LASER POINTER TOOLS	
SCREEN ELEMENT	**DESCRIPTION**
Laser Pointer	Changes your mouse pointer into a laser pointer.
Pen	Allows you to write or circle items on the slide.
Highlighter	Allows you to emphasize parts of the slide.
Eraser	Removes areas of an annotation.
Erase All Ink on Slide	Removes all annotations on a slide.
Ink Color	Displays a selection of colors for highlighting or writing with the pen.

2 Click **Laser Pointer** and move the mouse around the screen. Compare your screen with Figure 6.66.

  The mouse pointer displays as a large red dot.

FIGURE 6.66

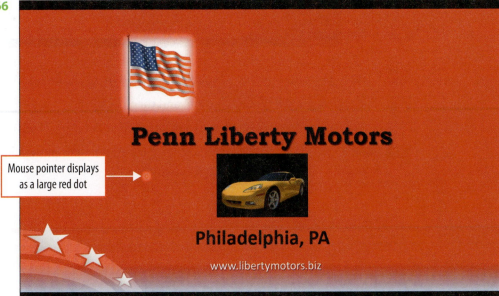

Mouse pointer displays as a large red dot

More Knowledge Laser Pointer Color Options

If you want to change the color of the laser pointer, on the SLIDE SHOW tab, in the Set Up group, click Set Up Slide Show. In the Set Up Show dialog box, under Show options, click the color you want, and then click OK.

3 ▶ Click the **Pen and laser tool** button, and then click **Laser Pointer** to turn off the laser pointer.

ANOTHER WAY   You can also press Esc to turn off the laser pointer and return to the default mouse pointer.

4 ▶ Click the **Advance to next slide** button to go to **Slide 2**. At the lower left corner of the screen, click the third button—**Pen and laser tools** to display the shortcut menu, and then click **Highlighter**.

The mouse pointer displays as a yellow rectangle.

5 ▶ Place the highlighter pointer to the left of the *P* in *Public*, and then click and drag to the right to highlight *Public Transportation*.

6 ▶ Point to the left of *Attractions*, and then click and drag to the right to highlight *Attractions*. Compare your screen with Figure 6.67.

FIGURE 6.67

7 ▶ Click the **Pen and laser tools** button. At the bottom of the list, click the color—**Red**.

8 ▶ Click the **Pen and laser tools** button, and then click **Pen**.

The Pen and laser tool displays as a small red circle or dot.

9 ▶ Point above the word *Parking*, and then click and drag to draw a circle around the word *Parking*. Compare your screen with Figure 6.68.

FIGURE 6.68

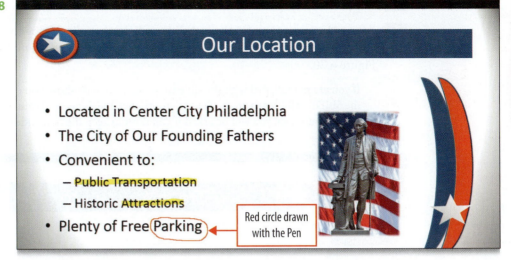

10 ▶ Click the **Pen and laser tools** button, and then click **Eraser**. Click one time on the circle to remove the circle. It is not necessary to drag the eraser.

11 ▶ Click the **Pen and laser tools** button, and then click **Pen**. Using the technique you practiced, draw a circle around the word *Free*.

12 ▶ Press Esc two times. In the displayed dialog box, which prompts you to keep your annotations, click **Keep**.

13 ▶ **Save** 🖫 your changes.

Activity 6.19 | Creating a Self-Running Presentation

In this activity, you will set up a presentation to run without an individual present to run the slide show. Normally, self-running presentations run on a *kiosk*. A kiosk is a booth that includes a computer and a monitor that may have a touchscreen. Usually, kiosks are located in an area such as a mall, a trade show, or a convention—places that are frequented by many people.

1 ▶ With the **title slide** as the active slide, click the **SLIDE SHOW tab**, if necessary. In the **Set Up group**, click **Rehearse Timings**. Compare your screen with Figure 6.69.

The presentation slide show begins, the Recording toolbar displays, and the Slide Time box begins timing the presentation.

FIGURE 6.69

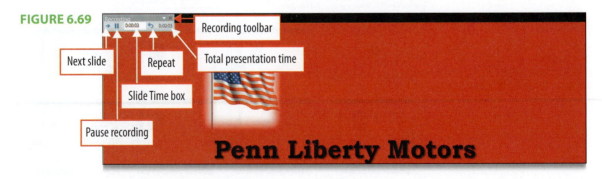

2 ▶ Wait until the **Slide Time** box `0:00:09` displays **10 (seconds)**, and then click **Next** ⬛.

ALERT! **Did Your Time Get Past 10 Seconds?**

If you spent longer on the slide than 10 seconds, you can revise your timing. On the Rehearsal toolbar, click the Repeat button 🔄, and then click Resume Recording to restart recording the time for the current slide.

---

3 Repeat this step for every slide.

4 After you set the time for the last slide, a dialog box displays with the total time for the slide show and prompts you to save the slide timings or discard them. Compare your screen with Figure 6.70.

If you are not satisfied with the slide times for your slide show, you can rehearse the times again. On the SLIDE SHOW tab, in the Set Up group, click the Rehearse Timings button, and time the slides. When you finish, you will be asked if you want to keep the new slide timings. Answer Yes if you do.

FIGURE 6.70

5 Click **Yes**.

ALERT! **Are Your Slide Times Longer Than the Time You Expected?**

If you want your slide times to be an exact number of seconds, click the Next button early. For example, if you want each slide to be 10 seconds, click the Next button when you see 9 in the Slide Time box.

6 On the PowerPoint **status bar,** click **Slide Sorter** . With the slides displayed, drag the **Zoom slider** to **70%**. Compare your screen with Figure 6.71.

Slide Sorter view displays with the time of each slide in the presentation. Your slide times may not be timed at exactly 10 seconds. There is a delay between the click and the actual time, but that is not critical.

FIGURE 6.71

7 On the **SLIDE SHOW tab**, in the **Set Up group**, click **Set Up Slide Show**. Compare your screen with Figure 6.72.

The Set Up Show dialog box displays. The options in the Set Up Show dialog box are described in the table shown in Figure 6.73.

FIGURE 6.72

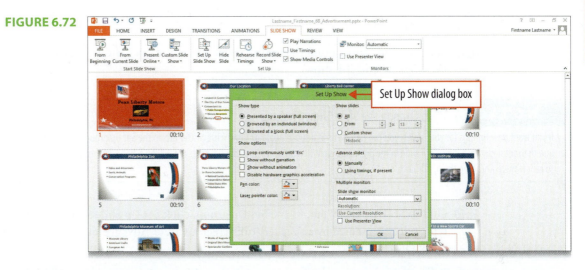

FIGURE 6.73

SET UP SHOW OPTIONS	
SCREEN ELEMENT	**DESCRIPTION**
Show type	Presented by a speaker (full screen) is used to present to a live audience.
	Browsed by an individual (window) enables your audience to view the presentation from a hard drive, CD, or the Internet.
	Browsed at kiosk (full screen) delivers a self-running show that can run without a presenter in an unattended booth or kiosk. You can also send someone a self-running presentation on a CD.
Show options	Loop continuously until the Esc key is pressed is used when the show is unattended.
	Show without narration suppresses any recorded audio in the presentation.
	Show without animation suppresses the animation in the presentation.
	Disable hardware graphics acceleration.
	Pen color allows you to select a pen color for the slide show.
	Laser pointer color allows you to select a laser pointer color for the slide show.
Show slides	All: Shows all of the slides.
	From: Selects a range of slides to view.
	Custom show: Shows a custom show.
Advance slides	Manually lets you advance the slides yourself.
	Using timings, if present, activates the timings you set for each slide.
Multiple monitors	If your computer supports using multiple monitors, a PowerPoint presentation can be delivered on two monitors. Slide show monitor gives you the option to select the monitor that the slide show will display, or you can let PowerPoint select the monitor automatically.
	Resolution allows you to use the current resolution or select another resolution that your monitor supports.
	Use Presenter View allows you to run the PowerPoint presentation from one monitor while the audience views it on a second monitor. This enables you to run other programs that will not be visible to your audience.

8 Under **Advance slides**, click to select **Using timings, if present**. Under **Show type**, select **Browsed at a kiosk (full screen)**.

Under Show options, the Loop continuously until "Esc" check box is selected by default. This option refers to playing a sound file or animation continuously. Advance slides options are disabled.

9 Click **OK**.

10 Start the slide show **From Beginning**. Wait 10 seconds per slide, and then view a few slides. Press Esc to end the show.

| **N O T E** | **To Change the Slide Show Timings** |

If you want new timings for your slides, you can rehearse the timings again. On the SLIDE SHOW tab, in the Set Up group, click the Rehearse Timings button, and then set new timings for each slide in the presentation. When all slides have been timed, you will be asked whether you want to keep the new timings or to cancel them and keep the old timings.

---

11 On the **SLIDE SHOW tab**, in the **Set Up group**, click **Set Up Slide Show** button. Under **Show type**, select **Presented by a speaker (full screen)**. Under **Advance slides**, click **Manually**. Click **OK**.

The timings are saved with the presentation. When you want to use them for a kiosk, click the Set Up Slide Show button, select Using timings, if present and then Browsed at a kiosk (full screen).

12 On the **VIEW tab**, in the **Presentation Views group**, click **Normal**.

Activity 6.20 | Printing Selections from a Presentation

In this activity, you will print selections from a presentation. You will select three slides to print.

1 Hold down Ctrl and click to select **Slides 1, 2**, and **6** thumbnails.

2 On the **FILE tab**, click **Print**. Under **Settings**, click the **Print All Slides arrow**, and then point to **Print Selection**. Compare your screen with Figure 6.74.

The Print All Slides list displays. Print Selection—Only print the selected slides is highlighted.

FIGURE 6.74

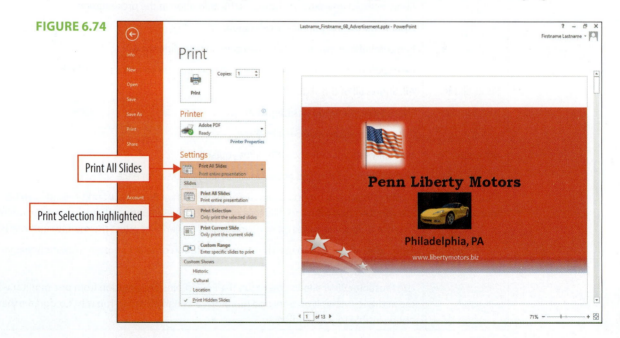

ANOTHER WAY   To print selected files, on the FILE tab, click Print, and then under Setting, in the Slides box, type the numbers of the slides that you want to print. Enter slide numbers and/or slide ranges. For example, 1, 3, 5–12.

3 ▷ Press [Esc] to return to **Normal** view.

4 ▷ On the **INSERT tab**, in the **Text group**, click **Header & Footer** to display the **Header and Footer** dialog box. Click the **Notes and Handouts tab**. Under **Include on page**, select the **Date and time** check box, and then select **Fixed**. If necessary, clear the **Header** check box, and then select the **Page number** and **Footer** check boxes. In the **Footer** box, using your own name, type **Lastname_Firstname_6B_Advertisement** and then click **Apply To All**.

5 ▷ Click **the FILE tab**, and then in the lower right portion of the screen, click **Show All Properties**. In the **Tags** box, type **discount, tourist, attractions** In the **Subject** box, type your course name and section number. In the **Author** box, right-click the existing author name, click **Edit Property**, replace the existing text with your first and last name, click outside textbox to deselect, and then click **OK**.

6 ▷ **Save** 🖫 your changes. **Close** your presentation, and then **Exit** PowerPoint. Submit your work as directed by your instructor.

END | You have completed Project 6B

END OF CHAPTER

SUMMARY

You used techniques related to viewing and presenting a slide show by adding and modifying slide transitions and various animation effects, including entrance, exit, emphasis effects, and motion paths.

Within a slide show, you also inserted hyperlinks to quickly link to a webpage, an email address, another document or file, another area of the same document, and other slides within a slide show.

You practiced hiding slides and creating a basic custom slide show and a hyperlinked custom slide show. You created action buttons, assigned an action to the buttons, and used the onscreen navigation tools.

You practiced using annotation tools such as the pen and laser pointer tools that enabled you to write or draw on slides during a presentation. You also created a self-running slide show that runs in a loop.

GO! LEARN IT ONLINE

Review the concepts and key terms in this chapter by completing these online challenges, which you can find at **www.pearsonhighered.com/go.**

Matching and Multiple Choice:
Answer matching and multiple choice questions to test what you learned in this chapter. MyITLab®

Crossword Puzzle:
Spell out the words that match the numbered clues, and put them in the puzzle squares.

Flipboard:
Flip through the definitions of the key terms in this chapter and match them with the correct term.

REVIEW AND ASSESSMENT GUIDE FOR POWERPOINT CHAPTER 6

Your instructor may assign one or more of these projects to help you review the chapter and assess your mastery and understanding of the chapter.

	Review and Assessment Guide for PowerPoint Chapter 6		
Project	**Apply Skills from These Chapter Objectives**	**Project Type**	**Project Location**
6C	Objectives 1–3 from Project 6A	**6C Skills Review** A guided review of the skills from Project 6A.	On the following pages
6D	Objectives 4–6 from Project 6B	**6D Skills Review** A guided review of the skills from Project 6B.	On the following pages
6E	Objectives 1–3 from Project 6A	**6E Mastery (Grader Project)** A demonstration of your mastery of the skills in Project 6A with extensive decision making.	In MyITLab and on the following pages
6F	Objectives 4–6 from Project 6B	**6F Mastery (Grader Project)** A demonstration of your mastery of the skills in Project 6B with extensive decision making.	In MyITLab and on the following pages
6G	Objectives 1–6 from Projects 6A and 6B	**6G Mastery (Grader Project)** A demonstration of your mastery of the skills in Projects 6A and 6B with extensive decision making.	In MyITLab and on the following pages
6H	Combination of Objectives from Projects 6A and 6B	**6H GO! Fix It** A demonstration of your mastery of the skills in Projects 6A and 6B by creating a correct result from a document that contains errors you must find.	Online
6I	Combination of Objectives from Projects 6A and 6B	**6I GO! Make It** A demonstration of your mastery of the skills in Projects 6A and 6B by creating a result from a supplied picture.	Online
6J	Combination of Objectives from Projects 6A and 6B	**6J GO! Solve It** A demonstration of your mastery of the skills in Projects 6A and 6B, your decision-making skills, and your critical thinking skills. A task-specific rubric helps you self-assess your result.	Online
6K	Combination of Objectives from Projects 6A and 6B	**6K GO! Solve It** A demonstration of your mastery of the skills in Projects 6A and 6B, your decision-making skills, and your critical thinking skills. A task-specific rubric helps you self-assess your result.	On the following pages
6L	Combination of Objectives from Projects 6A and 6B	**6L GO! Think** A demonstration of your understanding of the chapter concepts applied in a manner that you would outside of college. An analytic rubric helps you and your instructor grade the quality of your work by comparing it to the work an expert in the discipline would create.	On the following pages
6M	Combination of Objectives from Projects 6A and 6B	**6M GO! Think** A demonstration of your understanding of the chapter concepts applied in a manner that you would outside of college. An analytic rubric helps you and your instructor grade the quality of your work by comparing it to the work an expert in the discipline would create.	Online
6N	Combination of Objectives from Projects 6A and 6B	**6N You and GO!** A demonstration of your understanding of the chapter concepts applied in a manner that you would in a personal situation. An analytic rubric helps you and your instructor grade the quality of your work.	Online

GLOSSARY

GLOSSARY OF CHAPTER KEY TERMS

Action button A built-in button shape that you can add to your presentation and then assign an action to occur upon the click of a mouse or with a mouse over.

After Previous A custom animation that starts the animation effect immediately after the previous effect in the list finishes playing.

Animated GIF A file format made up of a series of frames within a single file that creates the illusion of animation by displaying the frames one after the other in quick succession.

Animation 1. Any type of motion or movement that occurs as the presentation moves from slide to slide. 2. A special visual effect or sound effect added to text or an object.

Animation Pane The area that contains a list of the animation effects added to your presentation. From this pane, you can add or modify effects.

Annotation A note or a highlight that can be saved or discarded.

Basic custom slide show A separate presentation saved with its own title containing some of the slides from the original presentation.

Chevron A V-shaped symbol that indicates more information or options are available.

Custom slide show Displays only the slides you want to display to an audience in the order you select.

Email client A software program that enables you to compose and send an email message.

Emphasis effect An animation effect that, for example, makes an object shrink or grow in size, change color, or spin on its center.

Entrance effect An animation effect that occurs when the text or object is introduced into the slide during a slide show.

Exit effect An animation effect that occurs when the text or object leaves the slide or disappears during a slide show.

File extension Also called the file type, it identifies the format of the file or the application used to create it.

Full path Includes the drive, the folder, and any subfolders in which a file is contained.

GIF Stands for Graphics Interchange Format. It is a file format used for graphic images, such as drawings.

Hyperlinked custom slide show A quick way to navigate to a separate slide show from within the original presentation.

Hyperlinks Navigation elements that, when clicked, will take you to another location, such as a webpage, an email address, another document, or a place within the same document. In a PowerPoint presentation, hyperlinks can also be used to link to a slide in the presentation, to a slide in a different presentation, or to a custom slide show.

HyperText Markup Language (HTML) The language used to code webpages.

HyperText Transfer Protocol (HTTP) The protocol used on the World Wide Web to define how messages are formatted and transmitted.

JPG (JPEG) Stands for Joint Photographic Experts Group. It is a file format used for photos.

Kiosk A booth that includes a computer and a monitor that may have a touchscreen.

Microsoft Outlook An example of an email client.

Motion path effect An animation effect that determines how and in what direction text or objects will move on a slide.

Mouse Over Refers to an action that will occur when the mouse pointer is placed on (over) an action button. No mouse click is required.

Navigation tools Buttons that display on the slides during a slide show that allow you to perform actions such as move to the next slide, the previous slide, the last viewed slide, or the end of the slide show.

On Click Starts the animation effect when you click the slide or a trigger on the slide.

Protocol A set of rules.

Timeline A graphical representation that displays the number of seconds the animation takes to complete.

Transition sound A prerecorded sound that can be applied and will play as slides change from one to the next.

Transition speed The timing of the transition between all slides or between the previous slide and the current slide.

Transitions Motion effects that occur when a presentation moves from slide to slide in Slide Show view and affect how content is revealed.

Trigger A portion of text, a graphic, or a picture that, when clicked, causes the audio or video to play.

Uniform Resource Locator (URL) Defines the address of documents and resources on the web.

Web browser A software application used for retrieving, presenting, and searching information resources on the World Wide Web. It formats webpages so that they display properly.

With Previous A custom animation that starts the animation effect at the same time as the previous effect in the list.

CHAPTER REVIEW

Skills Review Project 6C Vintage Car

Apply 6A skills from these Objectives:

1 Apply and Modify Slide Transitions
2 Apply Custom Animation Effects
3 Modify Animation Effects

In the following Skills Review, you will modify a PowerPoint presentation advertising the annual Vintage Car Event hosted by Penn Liberty Motors. You will apply slide transitions and custom animation effects to the slide show to generate interest in the event. Your completed presentation will look similar to Figure 6.75.

PROJECT FILES

For Project 6C, you will need the following file:

p06C_Vintage_Cars.pptx

You will save your presentation as:

Lastname_Firstname_6C_Vintage_Cars.pptx

PROJECT RESULTS

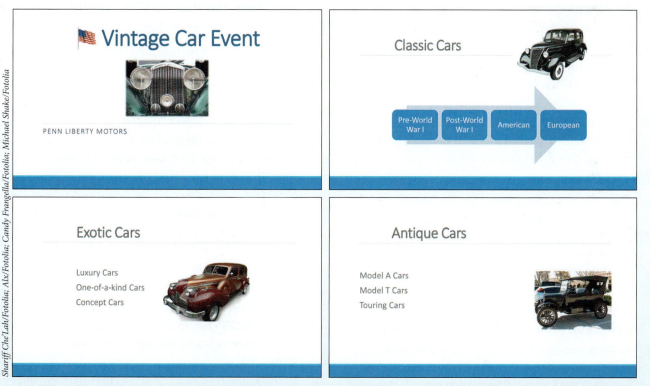

Shariff Che'Lah/Fotolia; Alx/Fotolia; Candy Frangella/Fotolia; Michael Shake/Fotolia

FIGURE 6.75

(Project 6C Vintage Car continues on the next page)

CHAPTER REVIEW

1 Start PowerPoint. Locate and open the file **p06C_Vintage_Cars**. Using your own first and last name, **Save** the file as **Lastname_Firstname_6C_Vintage_Cars** in your PowerPoint Chapter 6 folder.

2 Make the **title slide** the active slide.

a. Click the **TRANSITIONS tab**. In the **Transition to This Slide group**, click **More**. In the **Transitions** gallery, under **Subtle**, in the first row, click **Shape**.

b. In the **Timing group**, click **Apply To All**.

3 Make **Slide 2** the active slide.

a. In the **Transition to This Slide group**, click **More**. In the **Transitions** gallery, under **Subtle**, in the first row, click the fourth transition—**Push**.

b. On the **TRANSITIONS tab**, in the **Timing group**, in the **Duration** box, click **spin box up arrow** to **02.00**, and then in the **Preview group**, click **Preview**.

c. In the **Timing group**, click the **Sound arrow**, and then select **Click**. In the **Preview group**, click **Preview**.

d. In the **Timing group**, under **Advance Slide**, clear the **On Mouse Click** check box. Click once in the **After** spin box, type **3** and then press Enter.

4 Make **Slide 2** the active slide.

a. Select the **SmartArt** graphic. On the **ANIMATIONS tab**, in the **Advanced Animation group**, click **Add Animations**, and then under **Entrance**, click **Zoom**.

b. On the **ANIMATIONS tab**, in the **Animation group**, click **Effect Options**, and then click **One by One**.

c. In the **Advanced Animation group**, click **Animation Pane**. In the **Animation Pane**, click **Play Selected**.

d. In the **Animation Pane**, right-click **Content Place…** and then click **Effect Options**. In the **Zoom** dialog box, click the **SmartArt Animation tab**, select the **Reverse order** check box, and then click **OK**.

5 Make **Slide 3** the active slide.

a. Apply the same Step 3 transition sound, and duration slide settings and advance slide mouse settings that you applied to **Slide 2**.

b. Click the **SLIDE SHOW tab**, and then view the slide show **From Beginning**. Wait for **Slides 2** and **3** to advance after three seconds.

c. On Slide 3, click the **content placeholder**. On the **ANIMATIONS tab**, in the **Advanced Animation group**, click **Add Animation**, and then under **Entrance**, click on **Fly In**.

d. In the **Animation Pane**, below *Content Placeholder*, click the **chevron** to expand the contents. In the **Animation Pane**, click **Play Selected**.

6 Make **Slide 4** the active slide.

a. Select the content placeholder. On the **ANIMATIONS tab**, in the **Advanced Animation group**, click **Add Animation**. Under **Entrance**, click **Wipe**.

b. In the **Animation group**, click **Effect Options**, under **Sequence**, select **All at Once**.

c. In the **Animation Pane**, click **Play Selected**.

7 Make **Slide 1** the active slide.

a. Click to select the subtitle placeholder—*Penn Liberty Motors*. On the **ANIMATIONS tab**, in the **Advanced Animation group**, click **Add Animation**. Under **Emphasis**, in the first row, click **Grow/Shrink**. In the **Animation Pane**, click **Play From**.

b. Click the **subtitle** placeholder. In the **Advanced Animation group**, click **Add Animation**, and then click **More Exit Effects**. Under **Basic**, select **Disappear**. Click **OK**.

c. In the **Animation Pane**, right-click the second effect, which is the exit effect for the subtitle, and then click **Start After Previous**. In the **Preview group**, click **Preview** to view the effect.

8 Make **Slide 4** the active slide.

a. Click to select the content placeholder. On the **ANIMATIONS tab**, in the **Animation group**, click **Effect Options**, under **Sequence**, and then click **By Paragraph**.

b. In the **Animation Pane**, click the **chevron** to expand all effects, if necessary. With all three animations selected, right-click the first effect—**Model A Cars**, and then click **Effect Options** to display the **Wipe** dialog box. On the **Timing tab**, click the **Start arrow**, and then select **After Previous**. Change the **Duration** to **1 seconds (Fast)**. Click **OK**.

c. Click to select the **title** placeholder. In the **Advanced Animation group**, click **Add Animation**. Under **Motion Paths**, scroll if necessary, click **Shapes**.

(Project 6C Vintage Car continues on the next page)

CHAPTER REVIEW

d. Click the **car picture**. On the **ANIMATIONS tab**, in the **Advanced Animation group**, click **Add Animation**, and then click **More Motion Paths**. In the **Add Motion Path** dialog box, scroll down, and then under **Lines_Curves**, click **Left**. Click **OK**.

9 Make **Slide 3** the active slide.

a. Click to select the content placeholder. In the **Animation Pane**, right-click the first entrance effect—*Luxury Cars,* and then select **Effect Options** to display the **Fly In** dialog box. On the **Effect tab**, under the **Settings**, click the **Direction arrow**, and then click **From Bottom-Left**.

b. Under **Enhancements**, click the **After animation arrow**. In the row of colors, click the fifth color—**Teal**. Click the **Animate text arrow**, if necessary, and then click **All at Once**.

c. On the **Timing tab**, click the **Duration arrow**, and then click **1 seconds (Fast)**.

d. On the **Text Animation tab**, click the **Group text arrow,** select **All Paragraphs at Once**, and then click **OK**.

e. Click to select the **title** placeholder. On the **ANIMATIONS tab**, in the **Advanced Animation group**, click **Add Animation**. Under **Emphasis**, select **Pulse**. In the **Animation Pane**, click **Play From**.

f. At the top of the **Animation Pane**, click the **Reorder up arrow** to move the title—*Title 1: Exotic Cars*—to the top of the list. Click **Play From** in the **Animation Pane**.

g. Click on **SLIDE SHOW tab**, and then view the slide show **From Beginning**.

10 **Close** the **Animation Pane**.

11 On the **INSERT tab**, in the **Text group**:

a. Click **Header & Footer** to display the **Header and Footer** dialog box.

b. Click the **Notes and Handouts tab**. Under **Include on page**, select the **Date and time** check box, and then select **Fixed**. If necessary, clear the **Header** check box, and then select the **Page number and Footer** check boxes. In the **Footer** box, using your own name, type **Lastname_Firstname_6C_Vintage_Cars** and then click **Apply To All**.

12 Click the **FILE tab**, and then in the lower right portion of the screen, click **Show All Properties**.

a. In the **Tags** box, type **vintage cars, Penn Liberty** In the **Subject** box, type your course name and section number.

b. In the **Author** box, right-click the existing author name, click **Edit Property**, replace the existing text with your first and last name, click outside text box to deselect, and then click **OK**.

13 Print **Handouts 4 Slides Horizontal**, or submit your presentation electronically as directed by your instructor.

14 **Save** the presentation. **Exit** PowerPoint.

END | You have completed Project 6C

CHAPTER REVIEW

Apply 6B skills from these Objectives:

4 Insert Hyperlinks

5 Create Custom Slide Shows

6 Present and View a Slide Presentation

Skills Review Project 6D Safety

In the following Skills Review, you will modify a PowerPoint presentation that showcases safety features of the cars sold by Penn Liberty Motors. You will insert hyperlinks to a webpage and the email address of the company's safety director. You will also create custom slide shows of standard safety features available on all vehicles and custom safety features available on select vehicles. You will annotate the slide show and then create a self-running version of the presentation for use in a kiosk. Your completed presentation will look similar to Figure 6.76.

PROJECT FILES

For Project 6D, you will need the following files:

p06D_Safety.pptx
p06D_ESC.docx
p06D_Customer_Service.jpg

You will save your files as:

Lastname_Firstname_6D_Safety.pptx
Lastname_Firstname_6D_ESC_Benefits.docx

PROJECT RESULTS

Tsiumpa/Fotolia; Sarunyu_foto/Fotolia; Tomasz Zajda/Fotolia; Toniflap/Fotolia; Eduard Stelmakh/ Fotolia; Monkey Business/Fotolia; Kzenon/Fotolia; Gudellaphoto/Fotolia; Vera Anistratenko/Fotolia;

FIGURE 6.76

(Project 6D Safety continues on the next page)

CHAPTER REVIEW

1   Start PowerPoint. Locate and open the file **p06D_ Safety**. **Save** the file as **Lastname_Firstname_6D_Safety** in your **PowerPoint Chapter 6** folder.

2   Make the **title slide** the active slide.

a. Click to select the picture of the car.

b. Click the **INSERT tab**. In the **Links group**, click **Hyperlink**. In the **Insert Hyperlink** dialog box, under **Link to**, click **Existing File or Web Page**.

c. In the **Address** box, type **www.nhtsa.dot.gov** This is the website for the National Highway Traffic Safety Administration.

d. Click **ScreenTip**. In the **Set Hyperlink ScreenTip** dialog box, type **National Highway Traffic Safety Administration** Click **OK**. Click **OK** again.

3   Confirm that the **title slide** is the active slide.

a. In the subtitle, click and drag to select *Safety Features*.

b. On the **INSERT tab**, in the **Links group**, click **Hyperlink**.

c. Under **Link to**, click **Place in This Document**. Scroll down, click **13. Penn Liberty Motors Safety Team**, and then click **OK**.

4   Make **Slide 13** the active slide.

a. Click and drag to select *Email Your Concerns*. On the **INSERT tab**, in the **Links group**, click **Hyperlink**. Under **Link to**, click **E-mail Address**. In the **Email address** box, type **safetyteam@libertymotors.com** In the **Subject** box, type **Safety First** Click **OK**.

b. Click and drag to select the second bulleted item— *Available to Customers*. Click the **INSERT tab**. In the **Links group**, click **Hyperlink** to display the **Insert Hyperlink** dialog box. Click **Existing File or Web Page**.

c. Navigate to the **PowerPoint Chapter 6** folder and select **Lastname_Firstname_6B_Advertisement**. In the **Insert Hyperlink** dialog box, click **Bookmark** to display the **Select Place in Document** dialog box. Click the last slide—*Treat Yourself to a New Sedan*— and then click **OK**. Click **OK** to close the **Insert Hyperlink** dialog box.

d. Click the **SLIDE SHOW tab**, and then in the **Set Up group**, click **Set Up Slide Show**. In the **Set Up Show** dialog box, under **Show type**, select the **Presented**

by a speaker (full screen) option button, if necessary. Under **Advance slides**, click **Manually**, and then click **OK**.

e. View slide show **From Current Slide**. Click the hyperlinks to test them.

5   Make **Slide 10** the active slide.

a. Click to select the picture of the dashboard. Click the **INSERT tab**. In the **Links group**, click **Hyperlink**. In the **Insert Hyperlink** dialog box, under **Link to**, click **Existing File or Web Page**.

b. Click the **Browse for File**, navigate to the location where your student files are stored, and then double-click **p06D_ESC.docx**. Click **OK**.

6   **Slide 10** should be the active slide.

a. In the title, select (*ESC*). On the **INSERT tab**, in the **Links group**, click **Hyperlink**. In the **Insert Hyperlink** dialog box, click **ScreenTip**. Type **Benefits** Click **OK**.

b. Under **Link to**, click **Create New Document**. In the **Name of new document** box, substitute your own first name and last name and type **Lastname_ Firstname_6D_ESC_Benefits.docx** Make sure the **Edit the new document now** option button is selected, and then click **OK**.

c. When Microsoft Word displays, type **Benefits of ESC** and then press Enter. Type **Save between 6,000 and 11,000 lives annually.** Press Enter. Type **Prevent up to 275,000 injuries each year.** Press Enter two times, and then type **Lastname_Firstname_6D_ESC_ Benefits.docx**

d. **Save** your document in the **PowerPoint Chapter 6** folder, and then **Exit** Microsoft Word.

e. View the slide show **From Current Slide**. Click to test the hyperlink. **Close** Word, and then press Esc to return to **Normal** view.

7   Make **Slide 7** the active slide.

a. Click the **INSERT tab**. In the **Illustrations group**, click **Shapes**.

b. At the bottom of the list, under **Action Buttons**, click the third button—**Action Button: Beginning**.

c. Position the ⊞ pointer at the **4.5-inch mark left of 0** on the **horizontal ruler** and at the **3-inch mark below 0** on the **vertical ruler**, and then click once to insert the shape and display the **Action Settings** dialog box.

(Project 6D Safety continues on the next page)

d. In the **Action Settings** dialog box, click the **Mouse Over tab**. Click the **Hyperlink to** option button, click the **Hyperlink to arrow**, and select **First Slide**. Click the **Play sound** check box, click the **Play sound check box arrow**, and then select **Chime**. Click **OK**.

e. On the **FORMAT tab**, in the **Size group**, change the **Height** to **0.5"** and the **Width** to **0.5"**.

f. View the slide show **From Current Slide**, click or mouse over the **action button** to test it. Press `Esc`.

8 ▶ If necessary, make the **title slide** the active slide.

a. Click the **SLIDE SHOW tab**. In the **Start Slide Show group**, click **Custom Slide Show arrow**, and then click **Custom Shows**. In the **Custom Shows** dialog box, click **New**. In the **Slide show name** box, remove existing text, and type **Standard Safety Features**

b. In the **Slides in presentation** box, click to select **Slides 1, 2, 3, 4,** and **5**. Click **Add**. Scroll to and then click **Slide 13**, and then click **Add** to add it to the slides in the custom show. Click **OK**.

c. Click **Edit**. Under **Slides in presentation**, click **Slide 6** and add it to the custom show. Under **Slides in custom show**, click **Slide 7**, and then click the **up arrow** so the new slide is before the *Penn Liberty Motors Safety Team* slide. Click **OK**.

d. In the **Custom Shows** dialog box, click **New**. In the **Slide show name** box, remove existing text and type **Optional Safety Features**

e. In the **Slides in presentation** box, click to select **Slides 7, 8, 9, 10, 11, 12, and 13**. Click **Add**. Click **OK**, and then **Close** the **Custom Shows** dialog box.

f. In the **Start Slide Show group**, click **Custom Slide Show arrow**. Click **Standard Safety Features**, and then view the slides. Repeat the procedure to view **Optional Safety Features**.

9 ▶ Make the **title slide** the active slide, if necessary.

a. Click to select the picture of the flag. On the **INSERT tab**, in the **Links group**, click **Hyperlink**. In the **Insert Hyperlink** dialog box, under **Link to**, click **Place in This Document**.

b. In the **Insert Hyperlink** dialog box, under **Select a place in this document**, scroll down to display the **Custom Shows**. Select **Optional Safety Features**, and then click the **Show and return** check box. Click **OK**.

c. View the slide show **From Beginning**, and then click the flag to view the custom show. When the **title slide** displays, press `Esc`.

10 ▶ Make **Slide 13** the active slide.

a. On the **HOME tab**, in the **Slides group**, click the **New Slide arrow**, and then from the displayed list, click **Duplicate Selected Slides**.

b. On **Slide 14**, right-click the picture, and then click **Change Picture**. In the **Insert Pictures** dialog box, on the right of **From a file**, click **Browse**. Navigate to the location where you are storing your student data files, and then insert the file **p06D_Customer_Service.jpg**. On the slide title, select the words **Safety Team**, and then type **Customer Service** Place the insertion point before *Customer* and then press `Enter`.

c. Make **Slide 6** the active slide. Click the **SLIDE SHOW tab**. In the **Set Up group**, click **Hide Slide**.

d. Make **Slide 13** the active slide. Right-click the thumbnail for **Slide 13** to display the shortcut menu. Click **Hide Slide**.

e. Right-click the **Slide 6** thumbnail to display the shortcut menu again, and then click **Hide Slide** to unhide **Slide 6**.

11 ▶ On the **SLIDE SHOW tab**, in the **Start Slide Show group**, click **From Beginning**. Move the mouse to the bottom left corner of the screen to reveal the six navigation buttons. Move the mouse pointer to the right to reveal each button.

a. At the lower left corner of the screen, click the **Advance next** button. Click the **Advance previous** button. Click the fourth button—**See all slides.**

b. Click **Slide 7** to display it. Right-click anywhere on the slide, click **Custom Show**, and then click **Standard Safety Features**. Click to view each of the slides in the custom show. When the slide show is finished, press `Esc`.

c. On the **SLIDE SHOW tab**, in the **Start Slide Show group**, click **From Beginning**. At the lower left corner of the screen, click the **More slide show options** button, and then click **Show Presenter View**.

d. In **Presenter View**, below the large slide, click the **Black or unblack slide show** button.

(Project 6D Safety continues on the next page)

CHAPTER REVIEW

e. Click the **Black or unblack slide show** button to make the large slide visible again.

f. Below the large slide, click **See all slides**, and then click **Slide 8**. Click **More slide show options**, and then click **Hide Presenter View**.

12 At the lower left corner of the screen, click the third button—**Pen and laser pointer tools.** Click **Laser Pointer** and move the mouse around the screen. Click the **Pen and laser pointer tools** button, and then click **Laser Pointer** to turn it off.

a. At the lower left corner of the screen, click the third button—**Pen and laser pointer tools,** and then click **Highlighter**.

b. Place the highlighter pointer to the left of the *S* in *Seat-Belt*, and then click and drag to the right to highlight *Seat-Belt Use.*

c. Click the **Pen and laser pointer tools** button, and then click **Pen**. Circle the first bulleted item—*Built-in Sensors Detect.*

d. Click the **Pen and laser pointer tools** button, and then click the second ink color—**Black**. Circle the last bullet—*Includes On-Off Switch.*

e. Click **Pen and laser pointer tools** button, click **Eraser**, and then click to delete the black annotation on the last bulleted item.

f. Press (Esc) two times. In the displayed dialog box, which prompts you to keep your annotations, click **Keep**.

13 Make the **title slide** the active slide.

a. On the **SLIDE SHOW tab**, in the **Set Up group**, click **Rehearse Timings**.

b. In the **Slide Time** display, wait for four seconds, and then click **Next Slide arrow**. Repeat for all slides. When prompted, click **Yes** to save the timings.

c. On the **PowerPoint task bar**, click the **Slide Sorter icon**, and then after the slides display, drag the **Zoom slider** to **70%**.

d. In the **Set Up group**, click **Set Up Slide Show**. In the **Set Up Show** dialog box, under **Advance slides**, select

Using timings, if present. Under **Show type**, select the **Browsed at a kiosk (full screen)** option button. Click **OK**.

e. View the slide show **From Beginning** and view all slides. When **Slide 1** appears again, press (Esc).

f. On the **SLIDE SHOW tab**, in the **Set Up group**, click **Set Up Slide Show**. Under **Show type**, select **Presented by a speaker (full screen)**. Under **Advance slides**, select **Manually**. Click **OK**.

g. On the **VIEW tab**, in the **Presentation Views**, click **Normal** to return to **Normal** view.

14 Hold down (Ctrl) and click thumbnails to select **Slides 1, 2, 3, 4, 5, 6, 7, 8, 9, 10, 11, 12,** and **14.**

a. On the **FILE tab**, click **Print**. Under **Settings**, click the **Print All Slides arrow**, and then point to **Print Selection**. Press (Esc) to return to **Normal** view.

15 On the **INSERT tab**, in the **Text group**:

a. Click **Header & Footer** to display the **Header and Footer** dialog box.

b. Click the **Notes and Handouts tab**. Under **Include on page**, select the **Date and time** check box, and then select **Fixed**. If necessary, clear the **Header** check box, and then select the **Page number and Footer** check boxes. In the **Footer** box, using your own name, type **Lastname_Firstname_6D_Safety** and then click **Apply To All**.

16 Click the **FILE tab**, and then in the lower right portion of the screen, click **Show All Properties**.

a. In the **Tags** box, type **safety, seat belts** If necessary, in the **Subject** box type your course name and section number.

b. In the **Author** box, right-click the existing author name, click **Edit Property**, replace the existing text with your first and last name, click outside textbox to deselect, and then click **OK**.

17 Print **Handouts 9 Slides Horizontal**, or submit your presentation electronically as directed by your instructor.

18 **Save** the presentation. **Exit** PowerPoint.

END | You have completed Project 6D

CONTENT-BASED ASSESSMENTS

Mastering PowerPoint | Project 6E Race Car

In the following Mastering PowerPoint project, you will modify a PowerPoint presentation advertising the Annual Race Car Rally hosted by Penn Liberty Motors. You will apply slide transitions and custom animation effects to the slide show to make the slide show more dynamic. The purpose is to appeal to race car enthusiasts. Your completed presentation will look similar to Figure 6.77.

Apply 6A skills from these Objectives:

1. Apply and Modify Slide Transitions
2. Apply Custom Animation Effects
3. Modify Animation Effects

PROJECT FILES

For Project 6E, you will need the following files:

p06E_Race_Car.pptx   p06E_Tires1.wav

p06E_Fast_Car.wav   p06E_Drag_Race.wav

p06E_Car_Horn.wav

You will save your presentation as:

Lastname_Firstname_6E_Race_Car.pptx

PROJECT RESULTS

FIGURE 6.77

(Project 6E Race Car continues on the next page)

CONTENT-BASED ASSESSMENTS

1 Start PowerPoint. Locate and open the file **p06E_Race_Car**. **Save** the file in your **PowerPoint Chapter 6** folder using the file name **Lastname_Firstname_6E_Race_Car**

2 Make the **title slide** the active slide. Display the **Transitions** gallery, and then under **Subtle**, in the first row, click the third transition—**Fade**. Set the **Duration** to **1.50**, and then click **Apply To All**.

3 Make **Slide 2** the active slide. Click the **content placeholder** to select the **SmartArt** graphic. In the **Add Animation** gallery, under **Entrance**, click **Fly In**. Click **Effect Options**. Under **Sequence**, choose **Level at Once**.

4 Open the **Animation Pane**, right-click the entrance effect for content placeholder, and then click **Effect Options**. Change the **Direction** to **From Left**. On the **Timing tab**, set the **Duration** to **1 seconds (Fast)**.

5 On **Slide 2**, click to select the **car** graphic, and then apply the **Fly In** entrance effect. Change **Direction** to **From Top-Left**, set the **Duration** to **2 seconds (Medium)**, and then set the **Start** to **After Previous**.

6 On the **TRANSITIONS tab**, in the **Timing group**, insert the sound file **p06E_Fast_Car.wav** from the student data files.

7 Make **Slide 3** the active slide. Select the **SmartArt** graphic, and then apply the **Fly In** entrance animation effect. Click **Effect Options**, under **Sequence**, and then select **One by One**. Click **Effect Options** again, and then select **From Top**. Change the **Duration** to **1 seconds (Fast)**.

8 On **Slide 3**, click to select the **car** picture, and then add the **Fly In** entrance effect. In the **Animation Pane**, right-click the entrance effect for the picture, select **Effect Options**, and then change the **Direction** to **From Top-Right**. Under **Enhancements**, add the sound file **p06E_Car_Horn.wav** from your student data files. Change the **Start** to **After Previous** and the **Duration** to **2 seconds (Medium)**.

9 View the slide show **From Current Slide** to test the transition and animation entrance effects on **Slide 3**.

10 Make **Slide 4** the active slide. Click to select the **SmartArt** graphic. Click **Add Animation**, and then click the **Wipe** entrance effect. With the **SmartArt** selected, click **Effect Options**, and then under **Sequence**, click **One by One**. In the **Animation Pane**, right-click **Content Place…** and then click **Effect Options**. In **Wipe** dialog

box, on the **Timing tab**, click the **Start arrow**, and then click **After Previous**. Click the **SmartArt Animation tab**, select the **Reverse order** check box, and then click **OK**.

11 On **Slide 4**, click to select the **car picture**. Click **Add Animation**, and then click **More Exit Effects**. Under **Moderate**, click **Basic Zoom**. In the **Animation Pane**, right-click **Picture 4**, and then click **Effect Options**. Under **Enhancements**, click the **Sound arrow**, and add the sound file **p06E_Tires1.wav** from your student data files.

12 View the slide show **From Current Slide** to test the transition and animation entrance effects on **Slide 4**.

13 Make **Slide 5** the active slide. Select the **title** placeholder. Click **Add Animation**. Select **More Motion Paths**, and then under **Lines_Curves**, select **Arc Up**.

14 On **Slide 5**, select the **car picture**. Click **Add Animation**, under **More Motion Paths**, click **Diagonal Down Right**.

15 On **Slide 5**, select the **SmartArt** graphic. Display the **Animations** gallery. Under **Exit**, click **Fade**. Click **Effect Options,** and then select **One by One**. Click to select the **car picture**, and then apply the **Grow/Shrink** emphasis effect. Click **Effect Options**, and then under **Amount**, select **Smaller**. Select the car graphic if necessary, and then insert the sound file **p06E_Drag_Race.wav** from your student data files.

16 View the slide show **From Current Slide** to test the transition and animation entrance effects on **Slide 5**.

17 Make the **title slide** the active slide. Click to select the **title** placeholder. Display the **Add Animation** gallery, and then click **More Entrance Effects**. Under **Basic**, select **Blinds**. In the **Animation Pane**, right-click the entrance effect for the title, and then click **Effect Options**. Set the **Start** to **With Previous** and the **Duration** to **1 seconds (Fast)**. On the **TRANSITIONS tab**, in the **Timing group**, apply the **Whoosh** sound.

18 Start the slide show **From Beginning**, and then view the animation effects. When you are finished, return to **Normal** view.

19 Insert a footer on the notes and handouts that includes a fixed date and time, the page number, and the file name.

20 Click the **FILE tab**, and then in the lower right portion of the screen, click **Show All Properties**. In the **Tags** box, type **race, exhibition, event** In the **Subject**

(Project 6E Race Car continues on the next page)

CONTENT-BASED ASSESSMENTS

box, type your course name and section number. In the **Author** box, right-click the existing author name, click **Edit Property**, replace the existing text with your first and last name, click outside textbox to deselect, and then click **OK**.

END | You have completed Project 6E

21 ▶ Print **Handouts 6 Slides Horizontal**, or submit your presentation electronically as directed by your instructor.

22 ▶ **Save** the presentation. **Exit** PowerPoint.

CONTENT-BASED ASSESSMENTS

Mastering PowerPoint   Project 6F Custom Detail Aspects

In the following Mastering PowerPoint project, you will modify a PowerPoint presentation listing many of the customization services available at Penn Liberty Motors to give a vehicle a unique appearance. You will insert hyperlinks and create custom slide shows of interior and exterior detailing. You will annotate the slide show and create a self-running version of the presentation for use in the automobile dealership. Your completed presentation will look similar to Figure 6.78.

Apply 6B skills from these Objectives:

4 Insert Hyperlinks

5 Create Custom Slide Shows

6 Present and View a Slide Presentation

PROJECT FILES

For Project 6F, you will need the following file:

p06F_Custom_Detail.pptx

You will save your files as:

Lastname_Firstname_6F_Custom_Detail.pptx
Lastname_Firstname_Dashboard.docx

PROJECT RESULTS

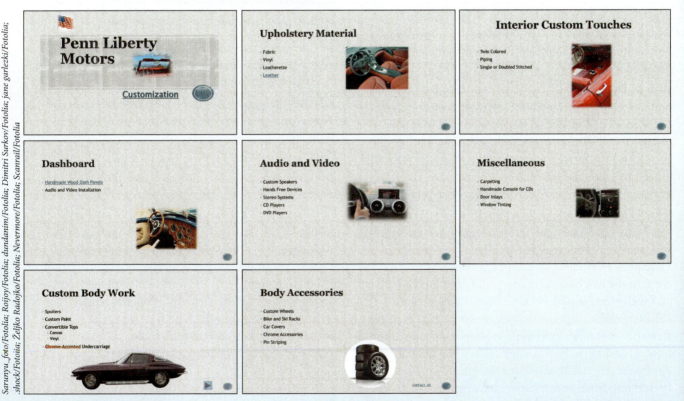

FIGURE 6.78

Sarunyu_foto/Fotolia; Rojoy/Fotolia; dundanim/Fotolia; Dimitri Surkov/Fotolia; jane garlezki/Fotolia; .shock/Fotolia; Željko Radojko/Fotolia; Nevermore/Fotolia; Scanrail/Fotolia

(Project 6F Custom Detail Aspects continues on the next page)

1 Start PowerPoint. Locate and open the file p06F_Custom_Detail. **Save** the file in your **PowerPoint Chapter 6** folder using the file name Lastname_Firstname_6F_Custom_Detail

2 Make the **title slide** the active slide, if necessary. Click to select the picture of the **car**. Display the **Insert Hyperlink** dialog box, and then type the address **www.dmv.state.pa.us** Include the **ScreenTip Pennsylvania Driver and Vehicle Services** View **From Current Slide** and test the hyperlink. Note: As of this writing, the *www.dmv.state.pa.us* website was active. You might receive an error message stating that the Internet server could not be located.

3 Make **Slide 7** the active slide. At the bottom right corner of the slide, insert an **Action Button: Forward or Next**, which is found in the last row of the **Shapes** gallery. Size the button **0.5"** wide and high. View **From Current Slide** and test the hyperlink.

4 Make **Slide 2** the active slide. Select *Leather*. Insert a hyperlink to **Place in This Document**, and then click **3. Interior Custom Touches**. Test the hyperlink.

5 Make **Slide 8** the active slide. Select *Contact Us*, and then add a **Hyperlink** to an **Email Address**. For the email address, type **customteam@libertymotors.com** Include the **ScreenTip**, **Contact us for all your customization needs.** Test the link, and then **Close** the email program. Notice that if you are using a campus computer, the actual email program may not work as it would at home.

6 Make **Slide 4** the active slide. Select the first bulleted item—*Handmade Wood Dash Panels*. Set up a **Hyperlink** to **Create New Document**. In the **Name of new document** box, substitute your own last and first name and type **Lastname_Firstname_6F_Dashboard.docx** Make sure the **Edit the new document now** option button is selected and verify the file will be saved in your **PowerPoint Chapter 6** folder. In the displayed Word document, type **Dash panels are also available in aluminum and carbon fiber.** Press Enter two times, and then type **Lastname_Firstname_6F_Dashboard.docx** Save the document **PowerPoint Chapter 6**, and then **Exit** Word.

7 Create a new custom slide show named **Interior Customization** Add **Slide 1** through **Slide 6**. Create

another custom slide show named **Body Customization** Add **Slide 1**, **Slide 7**, and **Slide 8**. Move the *Body Accessories* slide so it is number 2 in the list. Remove **Slide 1**.

8 Make the **title slide** the active slide. Double-click to select the subtitle *Customization*. Insert a hyperlink to **Place in This Document**. Scroll down to custom shows, and then click **Body Customization**. Select the **Show and return** check box, and then click **OK**. View **From Current Slide** and test the link to view the 2 slides, and then return to the title slide.

9 Hide **Slide 5**.

10 View the slideshow and use the onscreen navigation tools to go to **Slide 7**. Click the **Pen and laser tools** button, and then click **Highlighter**. Change the **Ink Color** to **Red**. In the last bulleted item, highlight *Chrome-Accented*. Highlight the first bulleted item—*Spoilers*.

11 Remove the highlighting on *Spoilers*.

12 **Keep** your ink annotations. Return to **Normal** view.

13 Make the **title slide** the active slide. Set each slide to display for four seconds.

14 Set the presentation to be **Presented by a speaker (full screen)** and then under Advance slides, click **Manually**.

15 Insert a footer on the notes and handouts that includes a fixed date and time, the page number, and the file name.

16 Click the **FILE tab**, and then in the lower right portion of the screen, click **Show All Properties**. In the **Tags** box, type **dashboard, custom, accessories** If necessary, in the **Subject** box type your course name and section number. In the **Author** box, right-click the existing author name, click **Edit Property**, replace the existing text with your first and last name, click outside textbox to deselect, and then click **OK**.

17 Print **Handouts 9 Slides Horizontal**, or submit your presentation electronically as directed by your instructor.

18 **Save** the presentation. **Exit** PowerPoint.

END | You have completed Project 6F

CONTENT-BASED ASSESSMENTS

Mastering PowerPoint | Project 6G Repairs

In the following Mastering PowerPoint project, you will modify a PowerPoint presentation that advertises Penn Liberty Motors' Repair Department and lists the types of repairs performed and the goodwill customer services available. You will apply slide transitions and custom animation effects, insert hyperlinks, and create custom slide shows. You will annotate the slide show and create a self-running version of the presentation. Your completed presentation will look similar to Figure 6.79.

Apply 6A and 6B skills from these Objectives:

1 Apply and Modify Slide Transitions
2 Apply Custom Animation Effects
3 Modify Animation Effects
4 Insert Hyperlinks
5 Create Custom Slide Shows
6 Present and View a Slide Presentation

PROJECT FILES

For Project 6G, you will need the following files:

p06G_Repairs.pptx
p06G_Emergency.docx

You will save your presentation as:

Lastname_Firstname_6G_Repairs.pptx

PROJECT RESULTS

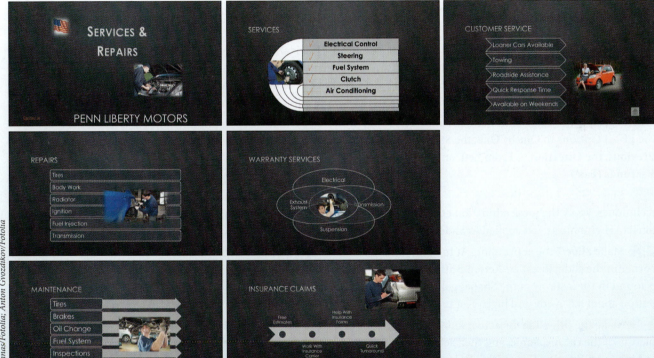

FIGURE 6.79

Sarunyu_foto/Fotolia; Kurhan/Fotolia; loraks/Fotolia; Kadmy/Fotolia; Cyril Comtat/Fotolia; Karin & Uwe Annas/Fotolia; Anton Gvozdikov/Fotolia

(Project 6G Repairs continues on the next page)

CONTENT-BASED ASSESSMENTS

1 Start PowerPoint. Locate and open the file **p06G_Repairs**, and then **Save** the file as **Lastname_Firstname_6G_Repairs**

2 Make the **title slide** the active slide. Apply a **Wipe** transition to all slides.

3 Make **Slide 2** the active slide. Select the **SmartArt** graphic. Add the **Fly In** entrance effect, set the **Effect Options** to **One by One**, and then set the **Start** to **After Previous**. In the **Animation Pane**, select **Effect Options**. Set the **Direction** to **From Left**, and then change the **Duration** to **2 seconds (Medium)**.

4 Make **Slide 3** the active slide. Select the **SmartArt** graphic. Apply the **Fly In** entrance effect, set the **Effect Options** to **As One Object**, and then change the **Direction** to **From Left** and the **Duration** to **2 seconds (Medium)**.

5 Make **Slide 4** the active slide. Select the **SmartArt** graphic, and then add the **Fade** entrance animation effect. Change the **Effect Options** to **One by One**. Change the **Start** to **After Previous**.

6 Make **Slide 5** the active slide. Using the same techniques, apply the same animation entrance effects to the **SmartArt** graphic as you applied to **Slide 4**.

7 Make **Slide 6** the active slide. Select the **SmartArt** graphic. Apply the **Wipe** entrance animation effect. Set the **Effect Options** to **One by One**, the **Start** to **After Previous**, the **Direction** to **From Left**, and the **Duration** to **1 seconds (Fast)**.

8 Make **Slide 7** the active slide. Using the same techniques, apply the same animation effects to the **SmartArt** graphic as you applied to **Slide 6**.

9 Make **Slide 7** the active slide. At the bottom right corner of the slide, insert an **Action Button: Home**, which is found in the last row of the **Shapes** gallery. Size the button about **0.5"** wide and high. Test the hyperlink.

10 Make the **title slide** the active slide. Select the picture of the **car mechanic**, and then set up a **Hyperlink** to **Link to an Existing File or Web Page**. Navigate to the location where your student files are stored, and then

click **p06G_Emergency.docx**. For the **ScreenTip**, type **24-Hour Phone Number** Test the hyperlink.

11 Make **Slide 6** the active slide. Select the picture, and then set up a **Hyperlink** to **Place in This Document**. Select **7. Customer Service**. Test the hyperlink.

12 Make **Slide 1** the active slide. Select *Contact Us*, and then set up a **Hyperlink** to an **E-mail Address**. For the **Address**, type **repairs@libertymotors.com** Test the hyperlink.

13 Set up a new custom slide show named **Warranty and Maintenance** Add **Slides 1, 3, 4**, and **5** to the custom slide show. Set up a second custom slide show named **Insurance Claims** Add **Slide 6** and **Slide 7** to the custom slide show.

14 Make **Slide 2** the active slide. Select the picture. Set up a **Hyperlink** to a **Place in This document**. Scroll down to the custom shows, and then click **Insurance Claims**. Click the **Show and return** check box. Test the hyperlink.

15 View the slide show **From Beginning**. Use the **Navigation tools** to go to **Slide 4**. Click the **Pen and laser pointer tools**, and then click **Pen**. In the gray area before each of the five text line items, draw a check mark. **Keep** the ink annotations.

16 Insert a footer on the notes and handouts that includes a fixed date and time, the page number, and the file name.

17 Click the **FILE tab**, and then in the lower right portion of the screen, click **Show All Properties**. In the **Tags** box, type **insurance, maintenance, warranty** If necessary, in the **Subject** box type your course name and section number. In the **Author** box, right-click the existing author name, click **Edit Property**, replace the existing text with your first and last name, click outside textbox to deselect, and then click **OK**.

18 Print **Handouts 9 Slides Horizontal**, or submit your presentation electronically as directed by your instructor.

19 **Save** the presentation. **Exit** PowerPoint.

END | You have completed Project 6G

CONTENT-BASED ASSESSMENTS

Apply a combination of the **6A** and **6B** skills.

GO! Fix It	Project 6H Staff	Online

GO! Make It	Project 6I Auto Show	Online

GO! Solve It	Project 6J Leasing	Online

GO! Solve It	Project 6K Special Orders	

PROJECT FILES

For Project 6K, you will need the following file:

p06K_Special_Orders.pptx

You will save your presentation as:

Lastname_Firstname_6K_Special_Orders.pptx

In this project, you will customize a slide show showcasing special-order vehicles, such as limousines, motorcycles, and race cars, available at Penn Liberty Motors. You will apply transitions and customized entrance and exit animation effects.

Open **p06K_Special_Orders**, and then save it as **Lastname_Firstname_6K_Special_Orders** Apply transitions and add entrance and exit animation effects. Insert a hyperlink to the Specialized Inventory text for the email address: **custom@libertymotors.com** Use hyperlinks to link the picture of a vehicle to its features. Create at least two basic custom shows to appeal to two different vehicle enthusiasts, and then insert a hyperlink to one of the custom shows. Create an action button.

Insert a Header & Footer on the Notes and Handouts that includes a footer with the text **Lastname_Firstname_6K_Special_Orders** In the Properties, add your name, course name and section number for the subject, and the tags **classic, limousines** Save your presentation. Print Handouts 4 slides per page, or submit electronically as directed by your instructor.

(Project 6K Special Orders continues on the next page)

CONTENT-BASED ASSESSMENTS

Performance Level

Performance Criteria	Performance Element	Exemplary	Proficient	Developing
	Formatted slide show with a variety of transitions and effects.	Slide show included relevant transitions and effects.	Slide show included a variety of transitions and effects, but they were not appropriate for the presentation.	Slide show contained no transitions and effects.
	Inserted hyperlinks to website, to email address, and to place in the slide show.	All hyperlinks worked correctly.	One of the hyperlinks did not work correctly.	Hyperlinks were not created, or they did not work correctly.
	Created two custom slide shows and linked one of them.	Created two custom shows and one was linked correctly.	Created one custom show and did not link.	No custom slide shows were created.
	Created an action button.	The action button produced the intended result.	Action button was created but did not work properly.	No action button was created.

END | You have completed Project 6K

OUTCOMES-BASED ASSESSMENTS

RUBRIC

The following outcomes-based assessments are *open-ended assessments*. That is, there is no specific correct result; your result will depend on your approach to the information provided. Make *Professional Quality* your goal. Use the following scoring rubric to guide you in *how* to approach the problem and then to evaluate *how well* your approach solves the problem.

The *criteria*—Software Mastery, Content, Format and Layout, and Process—represent the knowledge and skills you have gained that you can apply to solving the problem. The *levels of performance*—Professional Quality, Approaching Professional Quality, or Needs Quality Improvements—help you and your instructor evaluate your result.

	Your completed project is of Professional Quality if you:	Your completed project is Approaching Professional Quality if you:	Your completed project Needs Quality Improvements if you:
1-Software Mastery	Choose and apply the most appropriate skills, tools, and features and identify efficient methods to solve the problem.	Choose and apply some appropriate skills, tools, and features, but not in the most efficient manner.	Choose inappropriate skills, tools, or features, or are inefficient in solving the problem.
2-Content	Construct a solution that is clear and well organized, contains content that is accurate, appropriate to the audience and purpose, and is complete. Provide a solution that contains no errors in spelling, grammar, or style.	Construct a solution in which some components are unclear, poorly organized, inconsistent, or incomplete. Misjudge the needs of the audience. Have some errors in spelling, grammar, or style, but the errors do not detract from comprehension.	Construct a solution that is unclear, incomplete, or poorly organized; contains some inaccurate or inappropriate content; and contains many errors in spelling, grammar, or style. Do not solve the problem.
3-Format & Layout	Format and arrange all elements to communicate information and ideas, clarify function, illustrate relationships, and indicate relative importance.	Apply appropriate format and layout features to some elements, but not others. Overuse features, causing minor distraction.	Apply format and layout that does not communicate information or ideas clearly. Do not use format and layout features to clarify function, illustrate relationships, or indicate relative importance. Use available features excessively, causing distraction.
4-Process	Use an organized approach that integrates planning, development, self-assessment, revision, and reflection.	Demonstrate an organized approach in some areas, but not others; or, use an insufficient process of organization throughout.	Do not use an organized approach to solve the problem.

OUTCOMES-BASED ASSESSMENTS

Apply a combination of the 6A and 6B skills.

Build from
Scratch

GO! Think   Project 6L Car Purchase

PROJECT FILES

For Project 6L, you will need the following files:

New blank PowerPoint presentation
p06L_Off_Lease.docx

You will save your presentation as:

Lastname_Firstname_6L_Car_Purchase.pptx

Penn Liberty Motors has launched a new sales initiative to sell used cars. In this project, you will create a presentation with a minimum of six slides comparing the benefits of buying a new car versus buying a used car. In addition, certified lease cars should be part of the presentation. Insert a hyperlink on one slide to hyperlink to the **p06L_Off_Lease.docx** file provided in the student files. Include transitions and custom animation effects in the presentation. Create a self-running slide show.

Insert a Header & Footer on the Notes and Handouts that includes the date and time fixed, the page number, and a footer with the text **Lastname_Firstname_6L_Car Purchase** In Properties, add your name and course information and the tags **certification, lease** Save your presentation. Print Handouts 6 slides per page, or submit electronically as directed by your instructor.

END | You have completed Project 6L

Build from
Scratch

GO! Think   Project 6M Security   Online

Build from
Scratch

You and GO!   Project 6N Digital Sound   Online

Presentations Using Tables and Pie Charts

GO! to Work
Video P7

PROJECT 7A	OUTCOMES
	Create, position, and modify a table.

OBJECTIVES

1. Add a Table to a Presentation
2. Add or Delete Table Rows, Columns, or Cells
3. Move and Size a Table
4. Modify a Table
5. Insert a Section Header

PROJECT 7B	OUTCOMES
	Work with pie charts, create and apply chart templates, and apply animation to charts.

OBJECTIVES

6. Create and Modify Pie Charts
7. Create and Apply a Chart Template
8. Apply Animation to a Chart

vicky/Fotolia

In This Chapter

You can create a table in PowerPoint, use tables created in Microsoft Word or Excel by copying and pasting them into PowerPoint, or create a table by opening an Excel spreadsheet from within PowerPoint. You can modify a table by sizing the table; adding and removing rows, columns, and cells; and splitting and merging cells. You can format a table by applying built-in table styles or changing the border color, line, or weight.

Pie charts are used to show how different categories relate to the whole. You can create professional-looking charts by applying predefined layouts, styles, and animation or saving the chart as a template.

The **Seattle-Tacoma Job Fair** is a nonprofit organization that brings employers and job seekers together in the greater Seattle-Tacoma metropolitan area. Each year, the organization holds a number of targeted job fairs, such as the annual Greater Seattle Job Fair, which draws 2,000 employers in more than 70 industries and registers more than 5,000 candidates. Candidate registration is free; employers pay a nominal fee to display and present at the fairs. Candidate resumes and employer postings are managed by a new database system, allowing participants quick and accurate access to job data and candidate qualifications.

PROJECT 7A

Tabular Presentation

MyITLab®
Project 7A Training

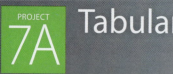

PROJECT ACTIVITIES

In Activities 7.01 through 7.10, you will create, copy, and modify tables and add section headers in a PowerPoint presentation that will be used by the database administrator of the Seattle-Tacoma Job Fair organization for an in-house presentation. Your completed presentation will look similar to Figure 7.1.

PROJECT FILES

For Project 7A, you will need the following files:

p07A_Job_Database.pptx
p07A_Additional_Companies.docx
p07A_Recent_Participants.xlsx

You will save your presentation as:

Lastname_Firstname_7A_Job_Database.pptx

PROJECT RESULTS

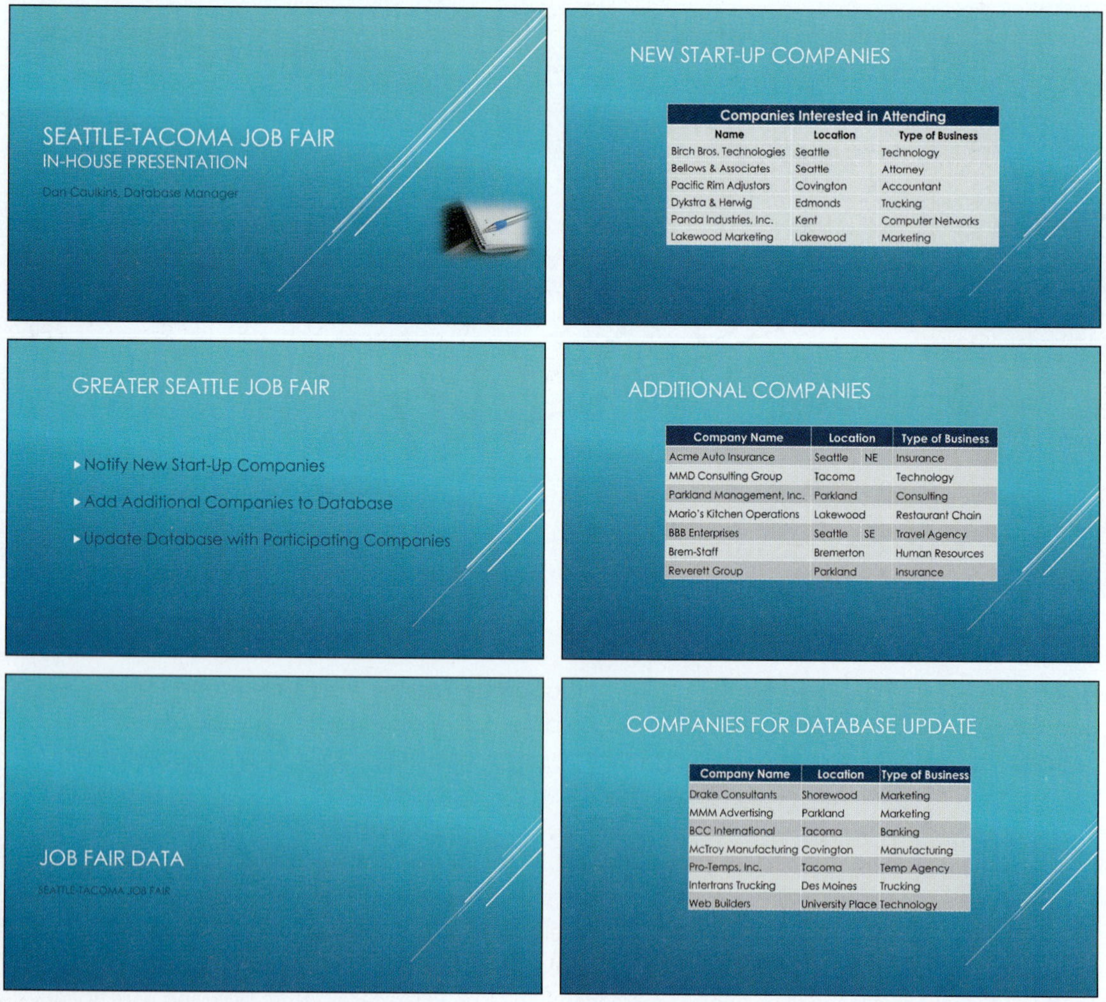

maho/Fotolia

FIGURE 7.1 Project 7A Job Database

Video P7-1

In the following activities, you will add a *table*—a grid of rows and columns—to a PowerPoint presentation in several ways. You will create a table within PowerPoint, and, using the enhanced table feature, copy and paste tables from Microsoft Word and Microsoft Excel into a PowerPoint presentation. When you create a table in PowerPoint, it becomes an *embedded* object. Recall that an embedded object is saved with, and becomes part of, the PowerPoint file. Likewise, when you copy information or an object contained in another file, such as Word or Excel (the *source file*), and then paste it into PowerPoint (the *destination file*), the object becomes part of the destination file. Any changes you make to the embedded object are reflected only in the destination file—the file in PowerPoint.

> **NOTE** **Table Design Variations**
>
> In this project, you will be inserting tables using various methods, styles, and formatting. When creating your own presentations, however, you should maintain a uniform style or theme.

Activity 7.01 | Creating a Table in PowerPoint

In this activity, you will create a table in PowerPoint for new companies to be added to the Seattle-Tacoma Job Fair organization database for use in the upcoming Greater Seattle Job Fair. You will also enter data listing companies, their location, and type of business.

1 Start PowerPoint. Locate and open the file **p07A_Job_Database**. In the location where you are saving your work, create a new folder named **PowerPoint Chapter 7**, and then save the file as **Lastname_Firstname_7A_Job_Database**

2 Make **Slide 3** the active slide. Click the **INSERT tab**. In the **Tables group**, click **Table** to display the **Insert Table** gallery, and then compare your screen with Figure 7.2.

This gallery displays with a grid structure that resembles a table. It also contains three options—Insert Table, Draw Table, and Excel Spreadsheet. The table in Figure 7.3 describes these options.

FIGURE 7.2

FIGURE 7.3

INSERT TABLE OPTIONS	
MENU SELECTION	**DESCRIPTION AND USAGE**
Table Grid	Enables you to select the number of rows and columns for the table by pointing to the individual cells. Live Preview displays the rows and columns on the slide before you click to commit to your selection.
Insert Table…	Displays the Insert Table dialog box, which contains two spin boxes—*Number of columns* and *Number of rows*. Use the spin boxes to enter the number of columns and rows you want in the table.
Draw Table	Enables you to create a customized table by first drawing the outside boundaries of the table, and then creating rows and columns within the table borders.
Excel Spreadsheet	Opens an Excel worksheet for data entry.

3 In the displayed **Table grid**, point to the first cell, and then, without clicking the mouse, move the Select pointer ⌖ to the right to select two cells.

> Moving the pointer to the right selects columns. Above the grid, the words *2×1 Table* display, instead of *Insert Table*.

4 Move the ⌖ pointer down to select seven rows, and then compare your screen with Figure 7.4. Notice that a Live Preview of the table is available in the presentation.

> Moving the pointer downward selects rows and indicates the number of rows to be inserted. The cells are highlighted, and the table size displays at the top of the grid. Live Preview shows the table grid on the slide. This table will have two columns and seven rows—a 2×7 Table.

FIGURE 7.4

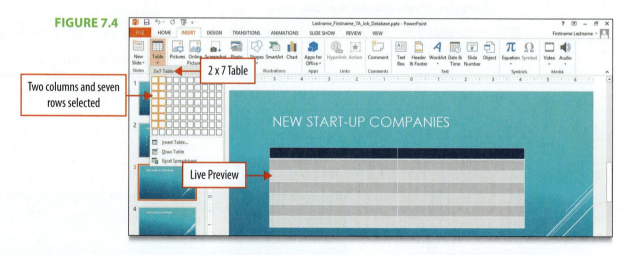

5 Click to create the 2×7 table, and then compare your screen with Figure 7.5.

🔄 **ANOTHER WAY**   To insert a table, you still begin by clicking the INSERT tab and then clicking Table to display the Table gallery. Then, click Insert Table. In the displayed Insert Table dialog box, type the number or use the spin box arrows to enter the number of rows and the number of columns. Click OK. You can also display the Insert Table dialog box by clicking the Insert Table icon in the body text placeholder of a slide that contains a content placeholder.

On the Ribbon, the TABLE TOOLS contextual tab displays, and the DESIGN tab is active. The table displays in the default table design theme. Take a moment to study the options in the DESIGN tab covered in this chapter, as described in the table in Figure 7.6.

FIGURE 7.5

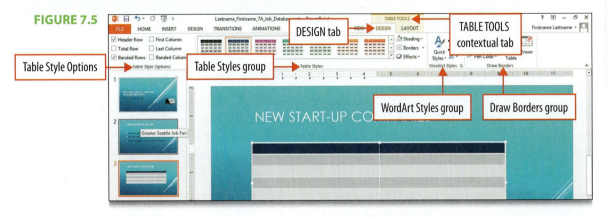

TABLE TOOLS	
SCREEN ELEMENT	**DESCRIPTION AND USAGE**
Table Style Options group	
Header Row	Turns on or off the header row of the table. The *header row* is the top row of the table; this row is formatted differently from the rows containing data.
Total Row	Displays special formatting for the last row of the table. The *total row* is the last row of the table; this row is formatted differently from other rows containing data.
Banded Rows	Displays banded rows, in which even rows are formatted differently from odd rows. This banding can make tables easier to read.
First Column	Displays special formatting for the first column of the table. For example, you may want to list categories or dates in the first column.
Last Column	Displays special formatting for the last column of the table. For example, you may want to list totals in the last column.
Banded Columns	Display banded columns, in which even columns are formatted differently from odd columns. This banding can make tables easier to read.
Table Styles group	
Table Styles	Applies a built-in, predefined style to your table.
Shading	Changes the color behind the selected text, paragraph, or table cell. This is especially useful when you want information to jump off the page. Applies different shading options to columns, rows, or individual cells.
Borders	Customizes the borders of selected cells.
Effects	Add visual effects to the table, such as a shadow or reflection. Applies effects to selected cells, such as a Cell Bevel, Shadow, and Reflection.
WordArt Styles group	
WordArt Quick Styles	Adds some artistic flair by choosing between predefined text styles. Applies a predefined WordArt style to selected text or to all text in a shape.
Text Fill	Fills the text with a solid color, gradient, picture, or texture.
Text Outline	Customizes the outline of your text by choosing the color, width, and line style.
Text Effects	Turns your work into a work of art. Adds a visual effect, such as shadow, glow, or reflection, to your text.

FIGURE 7.6

FIGURE 7.6
(continued)

TABLE TOOLS	
SCREEN ELEMENT	**DESCRIPTION AND USAGE**
Draw Borders group	
Pen Style [———— ▾]	Changes the style of new borders.
Pen Weight	Changes the width of new borders.
Pen Color	Changes the color of new borders.
Draw Table	Design your own table by drawing the cell, row, and column borders yourself. You can even draw diagonal lines and cells within cells.
Eraser	Removes specific borders in a table to create merged cells.

6 ▸ With the insertion point in the first cell, type **Name** and then press ⟮Tab⟯ to move to the second cell in the first row of the table.

The table shown in Figure 7.7 describes various methods of navigating a table.

FIGURE 7.7

NAVIGATING A TABLE	
KEY	**RESULT**
⟮Enter⟯	Inserts a new line within a cell.
⟮Delete⟯ or ⟮Backspace⟯	Deletes text within a cell.
⟮Tab⟯	Moves the insertion point one cell forward. Pressing ⟮Tab⟯ in the last cell in a table inserts a new row.
⟮Shift⟯+⟮Tab⟯	Moves the insertion point one cell backward.
⟮→⟯	Within a cell, moves the insertion point forward one character at a time. When the insertion point is located to the right of the text in a cell, moves the insertion point one cell forward.
⟮←⟯	Within a cell, moves the insertion point backward one character at a time. When the insertion point is located to the left of the text in a cell, moves the insertion point one cell backward.
⟮↑⟯ or ⟮↓⟯	Moves the insertion point one cell up or one cell down in the table.

7 ▸ With the insertion point in the second cell, type **Location**

This row is the header row. The header row is the top row of the table and is formatted differently from the rows containing data.

8 ▸ Press ⟮Tab⟯ to advance to the second row. Type the following information in the corresponding cells, pressing ⟮Tab⟯ or ⟮→⟯ after each entry except the last entry:

Birch Bros. Technologies	**Seattle**
Bellows & Associates	**Seattle**
Pacific Rim Adjustors	**Covington**
Dykstra & Herwig	**Edmonds**
Panda Industries, Inc.	**Kent**
Lakewood Marketing	**Lakewood**

9 Click outside the table to deselect the table. Compare your screen with Figure 7.8.

FIGURE 7.8

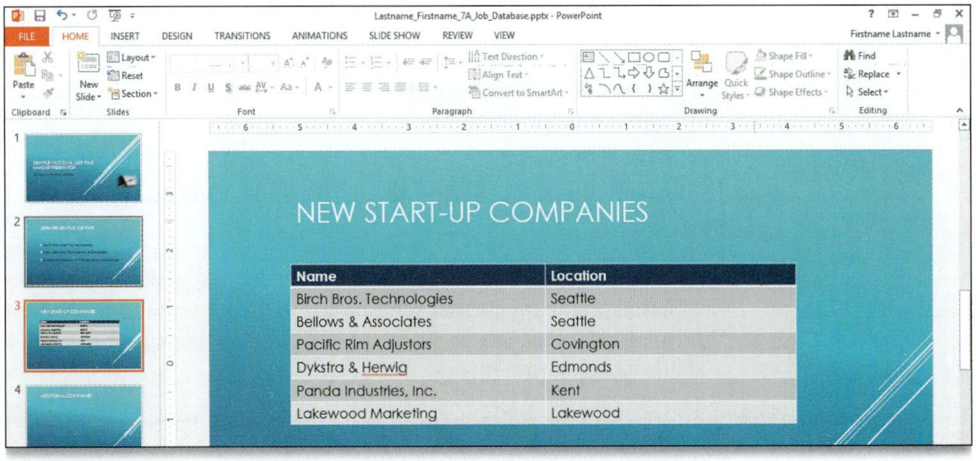

10 Save 🖫 your changes.

Activity 7.02 | Copying a Table from Microsoft Word

In this activity, you will copy a table from a Microsoft Word document to a PowerPoint slide.

1 With the PowerPoint presentation still open, on the keyboard, press the ⊞ to display the Start screen. Scroll to the right, as necessary, locate Microsoft Word 2013, and then click on the Word 2013 tile.

🔁 **ANOTHER WAY** In Windows 8, on the keyboard, press ⊞ +C, and then on the right side of the screen, on the Charms bar, click Search, and then under Apps, in the Search box, type **Word** In the search results, click Word 2013.

N O T E **Copying Tables from Word in Windows 7**

With the PowerPoint presentation still open, on the left side of the Windows 7 taskbar, click Start ⊕. From the displayed Start menu, locate the Word program, and then click Microsoft Office Word 2013.

---

2 In Word, click **Open Other Documents**. Navigate to the location where the student data files are stored, and then open **p07A_Additional_Companies.docx**.

3 In Word, if necessary, click in the table to display the contextual tabs. Under **TABLE TOOLS LAYOUT tab**, in the **Table group**, click the **Select arrow**, and then click **Select Table** to select the entire table. Compare your screen with Figure 7.9.

FIGURE 7.9

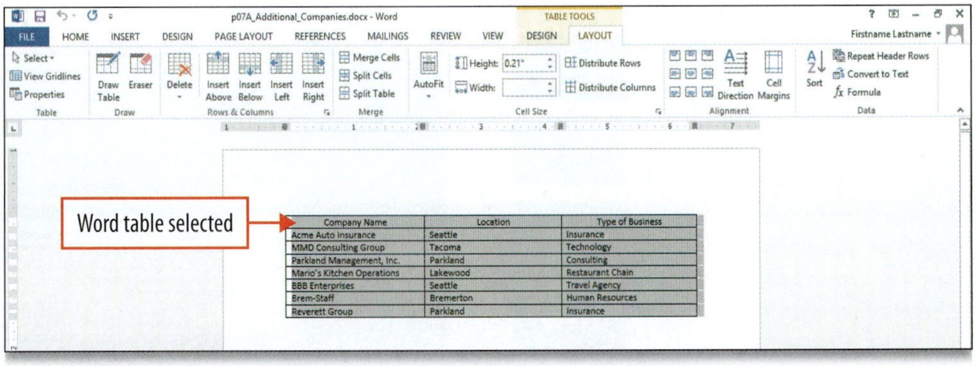

4 Click the **HOME tab**. In the **Clipboard group**, click **Copy** to copy the table to the Office Clipboard.

ANOTHER WAY To copy selected text or data, you can also right-click in the selection to display the shortcut menu, and click Copy. To paste, right-click in the destination and click Paste. You can also use keyboard shortcuts Ctrl + C to Copy and Ctrl + V to Paste.

5 In PowerPoint, make **Slide 4** the active slide. On the **HOME tab**, in the **Clipboard group**, click **Paste** .

The table is pasted into the slide and is formatted with the destination style. The destination style is based on the theme that was applied to the presentation. The first row and the first column are displayed with a dark background with white lettering. The color is determined by the colors used in the presentation theme.

6 Under the lower right corner of the table, click **Paste Options** (Ctrl) ▾ to display the options. Compare your screen with Figure 7.10.

The default paste option is Use Destination Styles. Paste Options provides other options—Keep Source Formatting, Embed, Picture, and Keep Text Only, each of which can be useful in different situations.

FIGURE 7.10

7 Click the first option, which is **Use Destination Styles**, if necessary. Under **TABLE TOOLS**, click the **DESIGN tab**. In the **Table Style Options group**, click the **First Column** check box to remove the check mark. Compare your screen with Figure 7.11.

The shading is removed from the first column. The table is displayed with the same style as the table on Slide 3, except it is smaller.

FIGURE 7.11

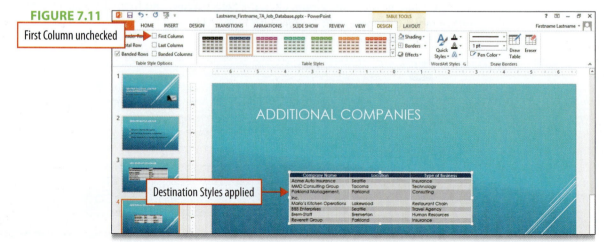

8 Return to Word and **Close** ✖ Word without saving.

9 Return to PowerPoint and **Save** 🖫 your changes.

Activity 7.03 | Copying a Table from Microsoft Excel

In this activity, you will copy a table from a Microsoft Excel worksheet to a PowerPoint slide.

1 With the PowerPoint presentation still open, on the keyboard, press the ⊞ to display the Start screen. Scroll to the right, as necessary, locate Microsoft Excel 2013, and then click on the Excel 2013 tile.

🔄 **ANOTHER WAY**   In Windows 8, on the keyboard, press ⊞ +C, and then on the right side of the screen, on the Charms bar, click Search, and then under Apps, in the Search box, type **Excel** In the search results, click Excel 2013.

> **N O T E**   **Copying Tables from Excel in Windows 7**
>
> With the PowerPoint presentation still open, on the left side of the Windows 7 taskbar, click Start ⊕. From the displayed Start menu, locate the Excel program, and then click Microsoft Office Excel 2013.

2 In Excel, click **Open Other Workbooks**. Navigate to the location where the student data files are stored, and then open **p07A_Recent_Participants.xlsx**.

3 In Excel, click cell **A1**, hold down Shift, and then click cell **D8** to select the entire table. Release Shift. Compare your screen with Figure 7.12.

🔄 **ANOTHER WAY**   To select all the cells in a worksheet, click the first cell, and then drag the mouse to the last cell.

FIGURE 7.12

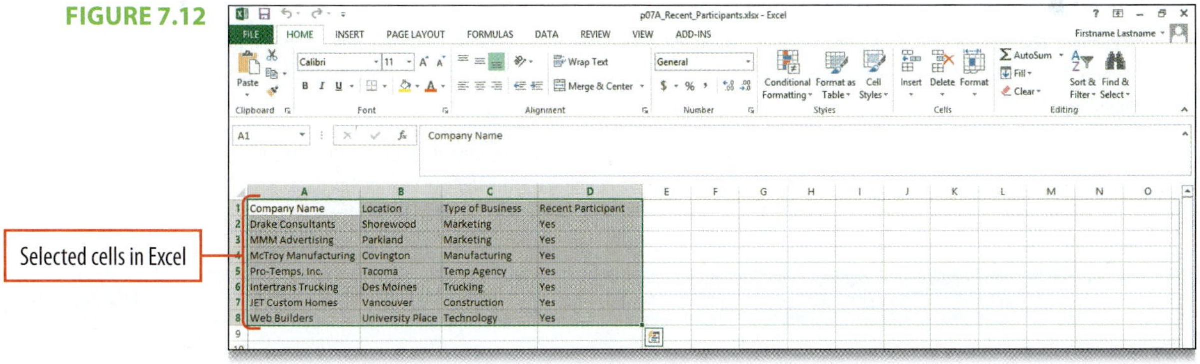

Selected cells in Excel

4 On the **HOME tab**, in the **Clipboard group**, click **Copy** 🗐.

> A moving border displays around the range of cells that has been copied to the Office Clipboard. A *range* of cells is a selection of two or more adjacent or nonadjacent cells.

5 In PowerPoint, make **Slide 5** the active slide. On the **HOME tab**, in the **Clipboard group**, click **Paste** 📋. Under the lower right corner of the table, click **Paste Options** 📋 (Ctrl) ▾ to display the options, and then click the second option—**Keep Source Formatting**. Compare your screen with Figure 7.13.

> All text is formatted in Calibri 11 pt because that is the default font and font size in Excel. You will modify this later.

FIGURE 7.13

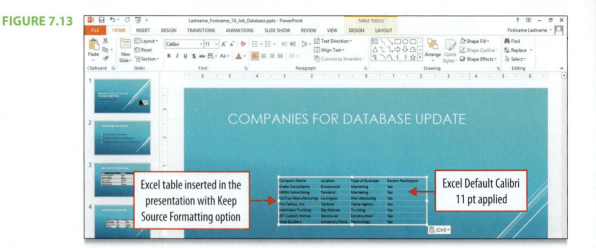

Excel table inserted in the presentation with Keep Source Formatting option

Excel Default Calibri 11 pt applied

COMPANIES FOR DATABASE UPDATE

NOTE **Copying Tables from Word and Excel**

When copying tables from Word and Excel and pasting them into a PowerPoint slide, when you use the Destination Style paste option, the shading does not always match. Select the table. Under TABLE TOOLS, click the DESIGN tab. In the Table Style Options group, you can check the options you want in your table.

6 ▸ Return to Excel and **Close** ✕ Excel without saving.

7 ▸ Return to PowerPoint, click outside the table, and then notice that the source formatting has been kept. **Save** 🖫 the changes.

More **Knowledge** **Inserting a Table Using Microsoft Excel**

To take advantage of the advanced functionality of Excel tables, you can use Microsoft Excel to create a table from within PowerPoint. On the INSERT tab, in the Tables group, click Table, and then click Excel Spreadsheet. An Excel worksheet window opens within PowerPoint. You can enter data in the cells and then click outside the table to deselect it.

In PowerPoint, the newly added spreadsheet becomes an OLE embedded object. OLE stands for Object Linking and Embedding and is the program-integration technology used to share information between Office programs. Integration means that Microsoft Office programs support sharing information through linked or embedded objects.

Therefore, if you change the theme (colors, fonts, and effects) of your presentation, the theme applied to the spreadsheet is not updated. Also, it is not possible to edit the table by using the options in PowerPoint. However, you can double-click the table to change the data.

Objective 2 Add or Delete Table Rows, Columns, or Cells

Video P7-2

In the following activities, you will delete a row and a column from a table, and you will add a row and a column to a table in PowerPoint. The method by which you combine two or more cells into a single cell is to *merge*. You can also add cells to a table when you *split*, or divide, a cell into two or more cells. Cells can be merged or split horizontally or vertically. You will also work with *table gridlines*. Table gridlines differ from the slide gridlines, which are used to position slide elements. Table gridlines are the nonprinting lines between columns and rows in a table.

Activity 7.04 | Adding and Deleting Table Rows

In this activity, you will delete a company name and information from the table by deleting a row. You will then add new company information by adding a row to the table.

1 With **Slide 5** as the active slide, click in the cell that contains *JET Custom Homes*. On the **TABLE TOOLS LAYOUT tab**, in the **Rows & Columns group**, click the **Delete arrow**. Compare your screen with Figure 7.14.

Three options to delete are displayed.

FIGURE 7.14

2 Click **Delete Rows** to delete the selected row.

3 Click in the cell that contains *McTroy Manufacturing*. On the **TABLE TOOLS LAYOUT tab**, in the **Rows & Columns group**, point to **Insert Above**. Compare your screen with Figure 7.15.

You can insert rows above or below the selected row. You can also insert columns to the left or right of the selected column.

FIGURE 7.15

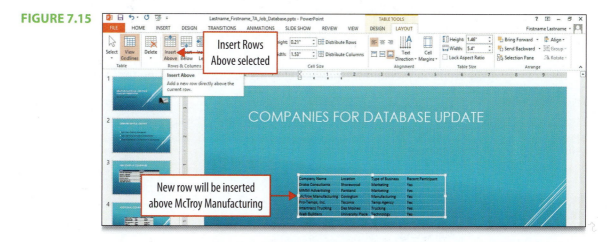

4 Click **Insert Above** to insert a new, blank row above the selected row.

5 Type the following information, pressing Tab or → after each entry:

BCC International	Tacoma	Banking	No

When the row is already selected, it is not necessary to position the insertion point before you begin typing.

6 Save 🖫 your changes.

Activity 7.05 | Adding and Deleting Table Columns

1 With **Slide 5** as the active slide, point above the column header *Recent Participant*, outside of the table, to display the ↓ pointer. Compare your screen with Figure 7.16.

This pointer is called the Select Column pointer. Use this pointer to select an entire table column.

FIGURE 7.16

2 ▶ Right-click to select the column and display the shortcut menu and the mini toolbar. On the mini toolbar, click the **Delete arrow**, and then click **Delete Columns**.

🔄 **ANOTHER WAY**   To delete a column, you can also right-click any cell in the column, and then click the Delete, and then click Delete Column.

The column is removed, and the table is resized to fit the current content.

3 ▶ Make **Slide 3** the active slide. Right-click the cell that contains *Location* to display the shortcut menu and the mini toolbar. On the mini toolbar, click the **Insert arrow**, and then click **Insert Columns to the Right**.

One new column is inserted to the right of the active column. The widths of columns 1 and 2 are adjusted.

4 ▶ In the new column, type the following information, using the ⬇ to move to the next cell:

Type of Business
Technology
Attorney
Accountant
Trucking
Computer Networks
Marketing

5 ▶ Save 💾 your changes.

Activity 7.06 | Merging and Splitting Table Cells

1 ▶ Make **Slide 3** the active slide. In the header row, right-click any cell to display the shortcut menu and the mini toolbar. On the mini toolbar, click the **Insert arrow**, and then click **Insert Rows Above**.

2 ▶ Point to the left of the cell in **column 1, row 1**, outside of the table, to display the ➡ pointer. Compare your screen with Figure 7.17.

This pointer is called the Select Row pointer. Use this pointer to select an entire table row.

FIGURE 7.17

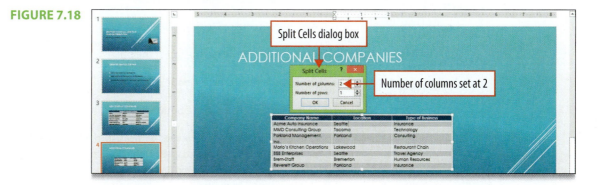

3 ▶ Right-click to display the shortcut menu and the mini toolbar, and then on the shortcut menu, click **Merge Cells**.

🔄 **ANOTHER WAY**   Select the cells you want to merge. On the TABLE TOOLS contextual tab, click the LAYOUT tab, and then in the Merge group, click Merge Cells.

When you right-clicked, the row was selected, and the context-sensitive menu displayed at the same time. All of the cells in the header row are merged into one large cell.

4 ▶ In the new header row, type **Companies Interested in Attending** Right-click the text you typed, and then on the mini toolbar, click **Center** ⌷.

5 ▶ Make **Slide 4** the active slide. In **column 2**, right-click the cell in **row 2**—*Seattle*. From the shortcut menu, click **Split Cells** to display the **Split Cells** dialog box. Compare your screen with Figure 7.18.

The Split Cells dialog box displays with the number *2* in the *Number of columns* spin box. The number that is entered in the *Number of columns* spin box is the number of cells that will result when the cell is split, or divided, vertically.

FIGURE 7.18

6 ▶ Click **OK** to split the cell into two cells that are side-by-side in the same row.

The selected cell is split into two smaller cells.

7 ▶ Take a moment to study the table shown in Figure 7.19, which describes the options available on the **TABLE TOOLS LAYOUT tab**.

FIGURE 7.19

LAYOUT TAB OPTIONS	
SCREEN ELEMENT	**DESCRIPTION AND USAGE**
Table group	
Select	Select the row or column containing the cursor, or select the entire table.
View Gridlines	Show or hide the gridlines in the table.
Rows & Columns group	
Delete	Delete rows, columns, or the entire table.
Insert Above	Add a new row directly above the current row.
Insert Below	Add a new row directly below the current row.
Insert Left	Add a new column directly to the left of the current column.
Insert Right	Add a new column directly to the right of the current column.
Merge group	
Merge Cells	Merge the selected cells into one cell.
Split Cells	Split the current cell into multiple cells.
Cell Size group	
Table Row Height	Set the height of the selected cells; enter a value in the row height spin box.
Table Column Width	Set the width of the selected cells; enter a value in the column width spin box.
Distribute Rows	Distribute the height of the selected rows equally between them.
Distribute Columns	Distribute the width of the selected columns equally between them.
Alignment group	
Align Left	Align text in the cell to the left.
Center	Centers the text horizontally in the cell.
Align Right	Aligns text in the cell to the right.
Align Top	Aligns text in the cell to the top of the cell.
Center Vertically	Centers the text vertically in the cell.
Align Bottom	Aligns text in the cell to the bottom of the cell.
Text Direction	Change the orientation of text to vertical, stacked, or rotated by 90 degrees or 270 degrees. You can also display the Format Shape pane by clicking More Options at the end of the Text Direction menu.
Cell Margins	Specify the margins for the selected cells. The built-in selections are Normal (default), None, Narrow, Wide, or display the Cell Text Layout dialog box by clicking the Custom Margins options to set custom settings.
Table Size group	
Height	Set the height of the table.
Width	Set the width of the table.
Lock Aspect Ratio	Locks the relationship between the width and height of a table. When resizing a table, the height and width of the table change in proportion to each other. If you change the height of a table, the width automatically changes, proportionally, to match the height.

FIGURE 7.19
(continued)

LAYOUT TAB OPTIONS	
SCREEN ELEMENT	**DESCRIPTION AND USAGE**
Arrange group	
Bring Forward	Bring the selected object forward one level so that it's hidden behind fewer objects.
Send Backward	Send the selected object back one level so that it's hidden behind more objects.
Selection Pane	See a list of all your objects. This makes it easier to select objects, change their order, or change their visibility.
Align	Change the placement of your selected objects on the page. This is great for aligning objects to the margins or the edge of the page. You can also align them relative to one another.
Group	Join objects together to move and format them as if they were a single object.
Rotate	Rotate or flip a selected object.

8 ▸ To the right of the *Seattle* cell, click in the new empty cell, and then type **NE** to indicate that the company is located in the northeast section of Seattle.

9 ▸ In **column 2**, click in the cell in **row 6**—*Seattle*. Using the technique you practiced, split the cell into two cells.

10 ▸ Click the new empty cell, and then type **SE** to indicate that the company is located in the southeast section of Seattle. Click outside the table to deselect it, and then compare your screen with Figure 7.20.

FIGURE 7.20

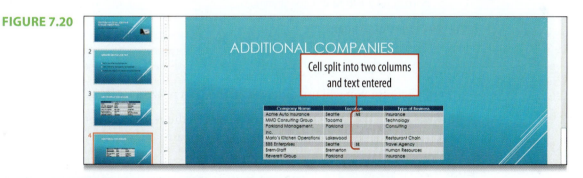

11 ▸ Save 💾 your changes.

Objective 3 | Move and Size a Table

Video P7-3

After you have created a table, you may want to change its position on the slide or resize it. In the following activities, you will move a table and use different methods to resize a table. You will also change the size of a table by changing the size of individual columns and rows.

Activity 7.07 | Moving a Table

1 On the **VIEW tab**, in the **Show group**, click the **Ruler** check box to display the ruler, if necessary. Make **Slide 3** the active slide, and then click anywhere in the table. A border displays around the table.

2 Point to the top border of the table to display the Move pointer. Compare your screen with Figure 7.21.

This pointer is similar to the pointer you have used to move other objects, such as pictures. Be careful not to position the mouse pointer on the *sizing handles*, small squares located in the corners and in the center of table borders. The sizing handles are used to increase or decrease the size of the table.

FIGURE 7.21

3 Hold down Shift, and then drag the table downward until the top of the table aligns on the **upper half of the vertical ruler at 1.5 inches.**

The table is lower on the slide. Because you used the Shift key, as you moved the table, the horizontal position did not change.

4 Save your changes.

Activity 7.08 | Sizing a Table

In this activity, you will use different methods to resize a table.

1 Make **Slide 4** the active slide. In **row 1**, point to the cell border between **column 1** and **column 2** to display the Move Vertical pointer. Compare your screen with Figure 7.22.

FIGURE 7.22

2 With the pointer, double-click to resize the column.

Double-clicking the border between two columns will resize a column to accommodate the largest entry. This feature is called *AutoFit*. It is used to increase the column width if the data does not fit on one line and to decrease the column width if the column is too wide.

3 Point to the border between **row 1** and **row 2** to display the Move Horizontal pointer ⬍. Drag the border down until the displayed dotted line aligns with the border between **row 2** and **row 3**. Without releasing mouse, compare your screen with Figure 7.23.

ANOTHER WAY | To change the height or width of a row or column, you can also click anywhere in the row or column that you want to change. On the TABLE TOOLS LAYOUT tab, in the Cell Size group, use the Table Row Height and Table Column Width spin boxes to enter a specific cell height and width. You can also display the Move Vertical pointer or the Move Horizontal pointer and drag the column or row border, respectively, to manually change the width or height.

FIGURE 7.23

4 Release mouse. The height of **row 1**—the header row—is doubled.

5 On the **TABLE TOOLS LAYOUT tab**, in the **Table Size group**, select the **Lock Aspect Ratio** check box. In the **Table Size group**, click the **Width spin box up arrow** to **7.5"**.

When **Lock aspect ratio** is selected, you can change one dimension (height or width) of an object, such as a picture, and the other dimension will automatically be changed to maintain the proportion.

6 With the table still selected, in the **Arrange group**, click **Align** 🖿. From the displayed list, click **Align Center**. Click **Align** again, and then click **Align Middle**. Compare your screen with Figure 7.24.

The table is centered horizontally and vertically on the slide. The width of the table is increased.

FIGURE 7.24

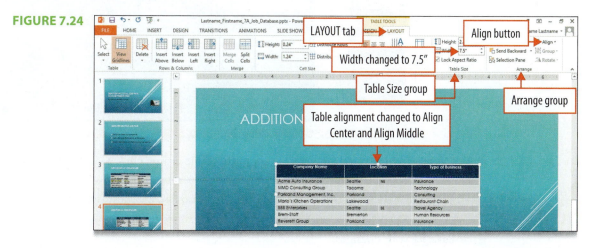

7   Make **Slide 5** the active slide, and then click anywhere in the table. Under **TABLE TOOLS**, on the **LAYOUT tab**, in the **Table group**, click **View Gridlines**, if necessary. In the **Arrange group**, click **Align** 🖃, and then select **Align Center**.

🔁 **ANOTHER WAY**   To select a table, you can right-click anywhere in the table and then click Select Table.

Because there is no formatting on the table you copied from Excel, the gridlines define the cells and do not print. The table is centered horizontally.

8   In the upper right corner of the table, point to the sizing handle ⬚ to display the Diagonal Resize pointer ⬈. Hold down Ctrl, and then drag the pointer up and to the right so that the top edge of the table aligns on the **upper half of the vertical ruler at 1.5 inches** and the right edge aligns on the **right half of the horizontal ruler at 3 inches**.

The squares, located in the corners and in the center of the table borders, are the sizing handles. Sizing handles are used to increase or decrease the size of the table. Because you use the Control key as you resized the table, the center alignment was maintained. The table gridlines define the cells.

9   On the **HOME tab**, in the **Font group**, click the **Font Size button arrow** [20 ▾], and then click **18**. Compare your screen with Figure 7.25.

The table is larger and the font size is increased.

🔁 **BY TOUCH**   Tap the HOME tab; in the Font group, tap the Font Size button arrow, and then tap 18.

FIGURE 7.25

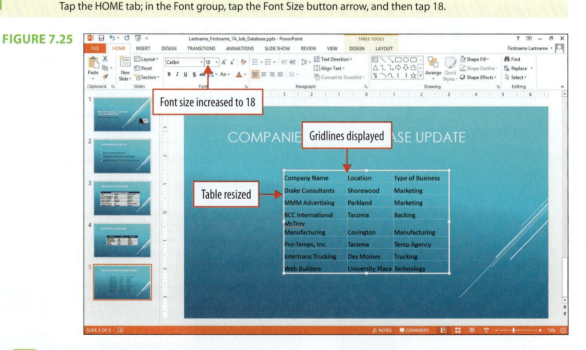

10   On the **TABLE TOOLS LAYOUT tab**, in the **Table group**, click **View Gridlines** to turn them off.

🔁 **BY TOUCH**   Tap the TABLE TOOLS LAYOUT tab, in the Table group, tap View Gridlines to turn them off.

11   **Save** 🖫 your changes.

Objective 4   Modify a Table

Video P7-4

Similar to other PowerPoint objects, you may want to make your table more visually appealing. You can apply a built-in table style; modify an existing style; apply borders, color, shading, and texture to cells; and make the table easier to read by applying banded rows or banded columns.

Activity 7.09 | Modifying a Table

In this activity, you will modify a table by applying a predefined style, adding shading to cells.

1 Make **Slide 3** the active slide, and then click anywhere in the table. On the **TABLE TOOLS DESIGN tab**, in the **Table Style Options group**, click to remove the check mark in the **Banded Rows** check box.

When you select *banded rows*, the odd and even rows of a table are formatted differently. Selecting *banded columns* formats the odd and even columns differently.

2 Outside of the table, point to the left of **row 2** to display the Select Row pointer ➡. Right-click to display the shortcut menu and the mini toolbar. On the mini toolbar, click **Bold** and **Center**. Click outside the table, and then compare your screen with Figure 7.26.

The rows are not banded. The text in row 2 is centered and displayed in bold.

FIGURE 7.26

3 Outside of the table, point to the left of **row 1** to display the ➡ pointer. Right-click to display the mini toolbar. On the mini toolbar, change the **Font Size** to **24**.

4 Position the ↔ pointer on the right border of **column 2**. Drag the border to the left about an inch. Repeat the procedure for **column 3**.

5 On the **TABLE TOOLS LAYOUT tab**, in the **Arrange group**, click **Align**, and then click **Align Center**. Click outside the table, and then compare your screen with Figure 7.27.

FIGURE 7.27

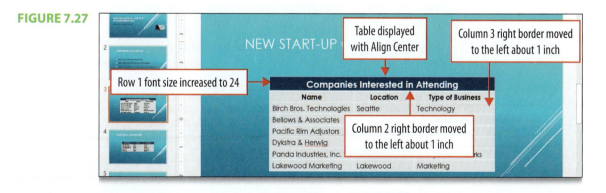

6 Make **Slide 4** the active slide. Right-click anywhere in the table to display the shortcut menu and mini toolbar. On the mini toolbar, click **Select Table**. On the **HOME tab**, in the **Font group**, change the **Font** to **Century Gothic (Body)** and the **Font Size** to **18**.

The cells containing *NE* and *SE* were formatted in Calibri when they were split, so all cells are now displayed in Century Gothic (Body).

7 ▶ Position the ⊞ pointer on the right border of **column 1**, and then double-click to **AutoFit** the contents.

8 ▶ Outside of the table, point to the left of **row 1** to display the Select Row pointer ➡. Right-click to display the shortcut menu and the mini toolbar. On the mini toolbar, change the **Font Size** to **20**.

9 ▶ Right-click anywhere in the table, and then on the shortcut menu, click **Select Table**. On the **HOME tab**, in the **Paragraph group**, click **Line Spacing** ≡▾, and then click **1.5**.

10 ▶ Click the cell for *Location*. Place the ⊞ pointer on the right border, and then drag to the left about a half inch. Click the cell for *Type of Business*. Place the ⊞ pointer on the right border, and then drag to the left about a half inch. If *Type of Business* displays on two lines, use the ⊞ pointer to drag the border to the right until it displays on one line.

11 ▶ Click anywhere in the table. Under **TABLE TOOLS**, click the **LAYOUT tab**, in the **Arrange group**, click **Align**, click **Align Center**. Click **Align** again, and then click **Align Middle**. Click outside the table, and then compare your screen with Figure 7.28.

FIGURE 7.28

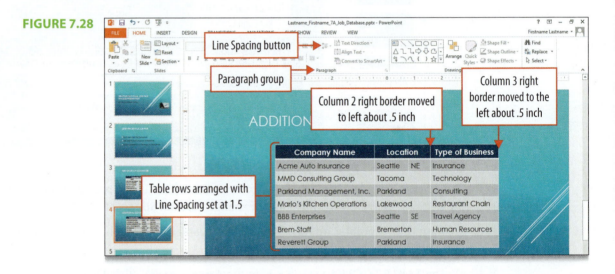

12 ▶ Make **Slide 5** the active slide. Click anywhere in the table. On the **TABLE TOOLS DESIGN tab**, in the **Table Style Options group**, click to place check marks in the **Header Row** and **Banded Rows** check boxes. Compare your screen with Figure 7.29.

Banding for the Header Row and Banded Rows is activated, but will not display until a table style is selected.

FIGURE 7.29

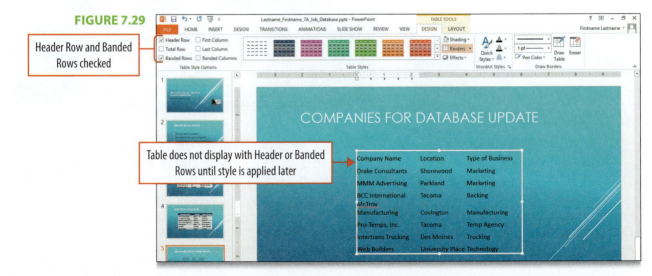

13 In the **Table Styles group**, click **More** to display the **Table Styles** gallery. Under **Medium**, in the second row, point to, but do not click, the second style—**Medium Style 2 – Accent 1**. Compare your screen with Figure 7.30.

FIGURE 7.30

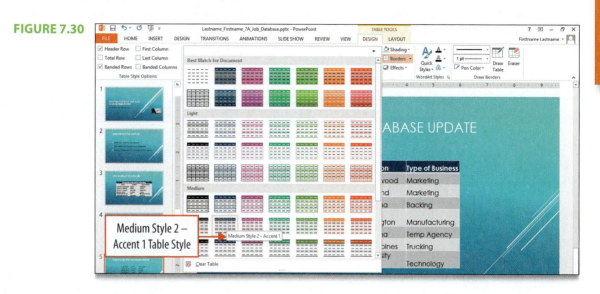

14 Click **Medium Style 2 – Accent 1**.

15 In **row 1**, point to the cell border between **column 1** and **column 2** to display the Move Vertical pointer. Using the Move Vertical pointer, double-click to resize the column. Repeat this procedure between **column 2** and **column 3** and at the **right edge** of the table to AutoFit the columns.

16 Position the pointer to the left of **row 1**, which begins with *Company Name*. Right-click, and then change the **Font Size** to **20** and **Center** the text. Under **TABLE TOOLS**, click the **LAYOUT tab**, if necessary. In the **Alignment group**, click **Center Vertically**. **AutoFit column 3**. In the **Arrange group**, click **Align**, and then click **Align Center**. Click **Align**, and then click **Align Middle**. Compare your screen with Figure 7.31.

> Row 1 is formatted with a larger font size, and the text is centered horizontally and vertically within the each cell. Every other row is shaded. The table style displays the table with the same formatting that is used for the tables on Slides 3 and 4. The default table style for this presentation is Medium Style 2 – Accent 1. Because the table on Slide 5 was pasted using Keep Source Formatting, there was no style applied at that time. Now, all slides use the same style. The table is now centered on the slide.

FIGURE 7.31

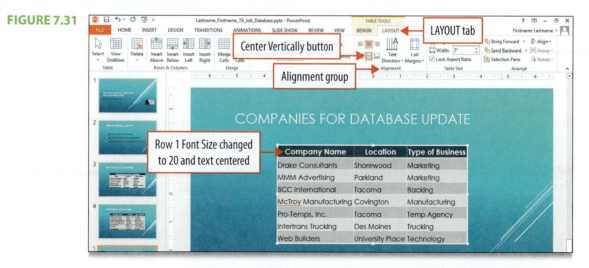

> **NOTE** Formatting Tables
>
> The sequence you follow to change the table and column size and the fonts determines what methods you use. There is no one correct order. For example, you might size the table width before you decide to increase the font size. After increasing the font size, you might have to size the table again. Also, when copying and pasting tables from Word and Excel, the procedure you follow might be different depending on which Paste option you select. Using a theme on a table is easier, but the theme does not always correct sizing problems. In general, it is easier to size and center a table after the text is entered, fonts are changed, and a theme is applied.

Objective 5 | Insert a Section Header

Video P7-5

A *section header* is used to organize slides in meaningful ways. You can use section headers to outline topics, assign slide ownership while collaborating with others, and organize the slides in your presentation.

Activity 7.10 | Inserting a Section Header

In this activity, you will insert and rename a Section, and you will add a Section Header slide.

1 On the left side of the PowerPoint window, click between the **Slide 2** and the **Slide 3** thumbnails. On the **HOME tab**, in the **Slides group**, click the **New Slide arrow**, and then click **Section Header**.

A new slide is inserted and becomes Slide 3.

2 Click in the title placeholder, and then type **JOB FAIR DATA** Click in the subtitle placeholder, and then type **SEATTLE-TACOMA JOB FAIR** Compare your screen with Figure 7.32.

FIGURE 7.32

3 On the left side of the PowerPoint window, click between the **Slide 2** and the **Slide 3** thumbnails. On the **HOME tab**, in the **Slides group**, click the **Section arrow**, and then click **Add Section**. Compare your screen with Figure 7.33.

The Untitled Section displays above Slide 3. The Default Section displays above Slide 1.

ANOTHER WAY Right-click between the Slide 2 and Slide 3 thumbnails, and then click Add Section.

FIGURE 7.33

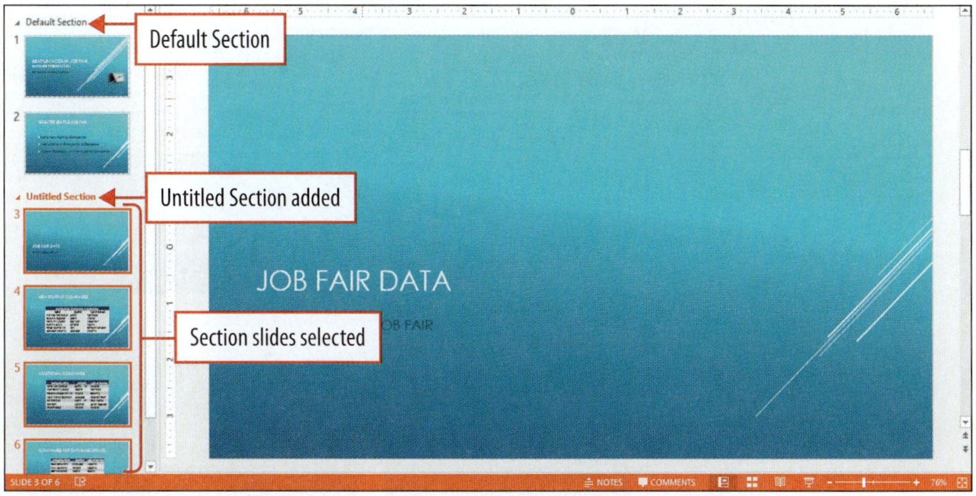

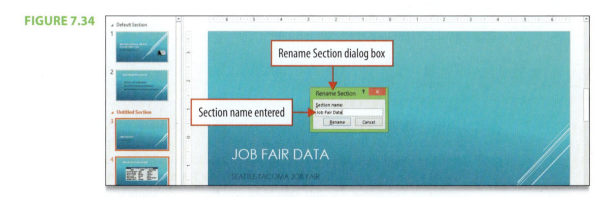

Default Section

Untitled Section added

Section slides selected

JOB FAIR DATA

4 With **Untitled Section** selected and highlighted in orange, on the **HOME tab**, in **the Slides group**, click the **Section arrow**, and then click **Rename Section**. In the **Rename Section** dialog box, under **Section name**, with the **Untitled Section** text selected, type **Job Fair Data** Compare your screen with Figure 7.34.

ANOTHER WAY   On the left side of the PowerPoint slide, right-click Untitled Section, and then click Rename Section.

FIGURE 7.34

Default Section

Rename Section dialog box

Section name entered

JOB FAIR DATA

SEATTLE-TACOMA JOB FAIR

5 Click **Rename**.

The renamed section, *Job Fair Data*, displays above the Slide 3 thumbnail.

6 On the **VIEW tab**, in the **Presentation Views**, click **Slide Sorter**. Notice *the Job Fair Data* section in **Slide Sorter View**. Compare your screen with Figure 7.35.

The Default Section displays before Slide 1. The section, *Job Fair Data*, displays between Slides 2 and 3. Slides 3, 4, 5, 6 display under the *Job Fair Data* section. Clicking the Job Fair Data section arrow collapses and expands the section to hide or display the slides in the section. This can be useful when you have multiple sections and you want to rearrange the order of the sections.

ANOTHER WAY   On the PowerPoint taskbar, click Slide Sorter.

FIGURE 7.35

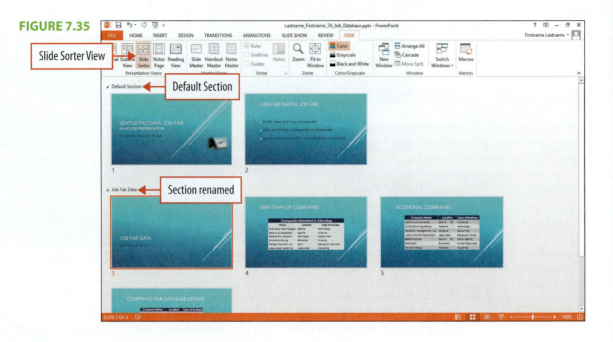

More **Knowledge**   **Move or Remove a Section Header**

To move a section header to a new location, right-click the section name that you want to move, and then click Move Section Up or Move Section Down, as necessary. To remove a section header, right-click the section name that you want to remove, and then click Remove Section.

7 On the **VIEW tab**, in the **Presentation Views group**, click **Normal**.

ANOTHER WAY   On the PowerPoint taskbar, click Normal.

8 On the **INSERT tab**, in the **Text group**, click **Header & Footer** to display the **Header and Footer** dialog box. Click the **Notes and Handouts tab**. Under **Include on page**, select the **Date and time** check box, and then select **Fixed**. If necessary, clear the **Header** check box, and then select the **Page number** and **Footer** check boxes. In the **Footer** box, using your own name, type **Lastname_Firstname_7A_Job_Database** and then click **Apply to All**.

9 Click the **FILE tab**, and then in the lower right portion of the screen, click **Show All Properties**. In the **Tags** box, type **database, job fair** and in the **Subject** box type your course name and section number. In the **Author** box, right-click the existing author name, click **Edit Property**, replace the existing text with your first and last name, click outside text box to deselect, and then click **OK**.

10 Save 🖫 your changes. **Close** the presentation, and then **Exit** PowerPoint. Submit your work as directed.

END | You have completed Project 7A

PROJECT ACTIVITIES

In Activities 7.11 through 7.15, you will add pie charts to a presentation describing the demographics of the attendees at the Seattle-Tacoma Job Fair. You will modify the pie charts and view a chart in grayscale. You will also save a chart as a chart template for future use, and you will apply animation to charts. Your completed presentation will look similar to Figure 7.36.

PROJECT FILES

For Project 7B, you will need the following file:

p07B_Fair_Demographics.pptx

You will save your files as:

Lastname_Firstname_7B_Fair_Demographics.pptx
Lastname_Firstname_7B_Pie.crtx

PROJECT RESULTS

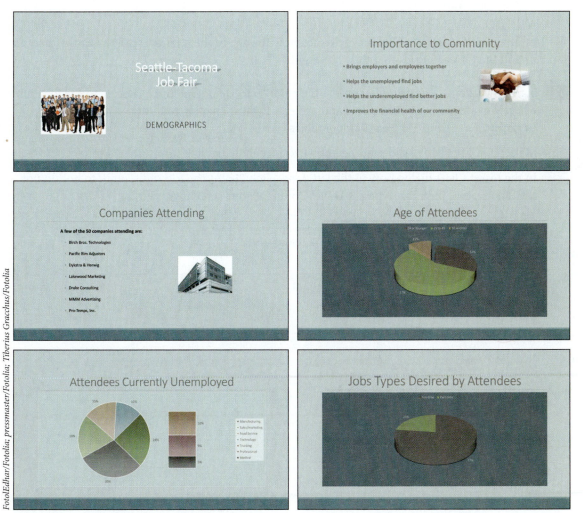

FotolEdhar/Fotolia; pressmaster/Fotolia; Tiberius Gracchus/Fotolia

FIGURE 7.36 Project 7B Fair Demographics

Video P7-6

In the following activities, you will add pie charts to a PowerPoint presentation. Used to plot a single data series, a *pie chart* shows the relationship of parts to a whole. Categories, or *slices*, in a pie chart represent the contribution of each value to the total. As a rule of thumb, limit the number of categories you use on a pie chart to no more than seven. The categories on a pie chart can also be displayed as percentages and should not be negative or zero values. Recall that in an Excel worksheet, a *data series* is a set of values arranged in one column or row only.

Pie charts may be displayed as two- or three-dimensional (3-D) charts. To emphasize a slice of the pie, you can manually pull out, or *explode*, the slice so that it stands away from the pie. There is also a type of pie chart known as an *exploded pie chart*, which displays all of the slices disconnected, or exploded, from each other. You can change the pie explosion setting for all slices and individual slices, but you cannot move the slices of an exploded pie manually. If you want to pull out the slices manually, consider using a pie or pie in 3-D chart instead.

NOTE | **Chart Design Variations**

In this project, you will be inserting charts using various methods, styles, and formatting. When creating your own presentations, however, you should maintain a uniform style or theme.

Activity 7.11 | Creating Pie Charts

In this activity, you will create pie charts to show the age of the attendees at the Seattle-Tacoma Job Fair and the job categories that they represent.

1 ▶ Start PowerPoint. Locate and open the file **p07B_Fair_Demographics**. Navigate to the location where you are storing your folders and projects for this chapter, and then save the file as **Lastname_Firstname_7B_Fair_Demographics**

2 ▶ Make **Slide 4** the active slide. In the body text placeholder, click **Insert Chart** .

3 ▶ In the **Insert Chart** dialog box, in the left pane, click **Pie**. At the top right, point to but do not click the second pie chart type—**3-D Pie**. Compare your screen with Figure 7.37.

🔄 **ANOTHER WAY** | To display the Insert Chart dialog box, you can also go to the INSERT tab, and in the Illustrations group, click Chart. You can choose a chart type from the displayed list.

FIGURE 7.37

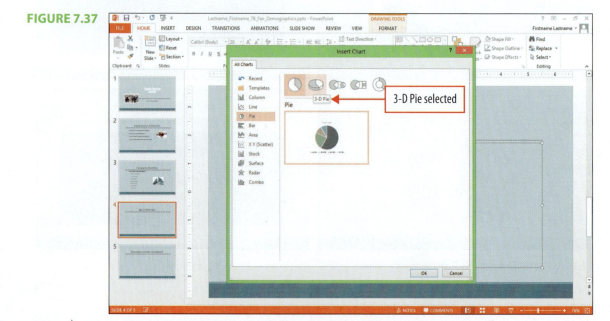

4 Click **3-D Pie**. Click **OK**.

An Excel worksheet and a sample pie chart in PowerPoint are displayed. You may need to move the Excel worksheet to see the pie chart, which uses the sample data in the Excel worksheet. You will enter your own data in the worksheet. Cells A1 through A5 have a purple border around them; cell B1 has a red border around it; cells B2 though B5 have a blue border around them. You may click in the cells and type over the existing words and numbers.

5 Click cell **B1**, type **Age of Attendees** to replace *Sales*, and then press Enter.

In cell B1, *Age of Attendees* replaces the word *Sales* and also appears on the PowerPoint slide.

6 In cell **A2**, type **24 or Younger** and then press Enter. In cell **A3**, type **25 to 49** and then press Enter. In cell **A4**, type **50 or Older** and then press Enter.

As you type the new data in Excel, the pie chart in PowerPoint adjusts to reflect your data.

7 Position the Move Columns pointer ⊕ on the border between **column A** and **column B**. Double-click to resize **column A**. Double-click the border between **column B** and **column C** to resize **column B**.

8 Right-click cell **A5** to display the shortcut menu, click **Delete**, and then point to **Table Rows**. Compare your screen with Figure 7.38.

🔁 **ANOTHER WAY**   You can also delete a row by pointing to the row number to display the Select Row icon ➡, right-clicking to display a shortcut menu, and then click Delete.

You can delete columns and rows from the shortcut menu.

FIGURE 7.38

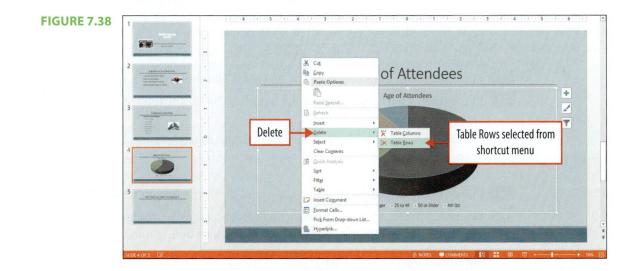

9 Click **Table Rows** to delete the row.

The sample data in cell A5 is not a part of your chart, so it is removed. The Excel worksheet range adjusts to include only cells A1 through B4, and the chart on the slide also adjusts. On the PowerPoint slide, a *legend* on the chart identifies the patterns or colors that are assigned to the pie slices, also known as the categories.

NOTE   **Deleting a Category**

To delete a category, you must use the Delete command on the shortcut menu to delete a table row. If you select a cell or a range of cells and then press Delete, you may not delete the category from the legend, and the marker may still display with no corresponding category label.

---

10 ▶ Click in cell **B2**. Type **32%** and then press Enter. Type **57%** and then press Enter. Type **11%** and then press Enter. Compare your screen with Figure 7.39.

FIGURE 7.39

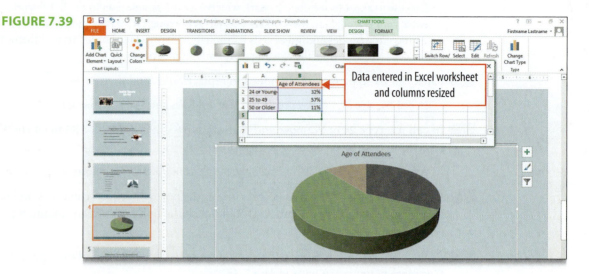

11 ▶ **Close** the Excel worksheet and, if necessary, return to PowerPoint.

More Knowledge   **Import Charts From External Sources**

Recall that you can copy and paste a *table* created in Word or Excel into a PowerPoint presentation. You can copy and paste a *chart* created in Excel into a PowerPoint presentation. Use Destination Theme & Link Data or Keep Source Formatting & Link Data if you want to keep the chart linked to the original source worksheet. If you don't want to keep the chart linked to the original source worksheet but want to keep the data, Use Destination Theme & Embed Workbook or Keep Source Formatting & Embed Workbook. You can paste the chart as a Picture, but then you will not be able to edit the data. You can also copy and paste charts created in Word documents. However, you will not be able to link to the data in the Word document.

---

12 ▶ Make **Slide 5** the active slide. In the body text placeholder, click **Insert Chart** .

13 ▶ In the **Insert Chart** dialog box, at the left, click **Pie**. At the top right, click the fourth pie chart type—**Bar of Pie**. Click **OK**.

A *Bar of Pie chart* emphasizes one slice of the pie by representing the slice as a bar showing how the data in the slice are further divided. A similar chart, *Pie of Pie chart*, displays the emphasized data as a pie instead of a bar.

14 ▶ In the worksheet, click cell **B1**—*Sales*— and then type **Event Statistics** Press Enter.

15 ▶ Beginning in cell **A2**, type the following data, pressing Tab to move from cell to cell. Press Enter after the last cell—*5%*. As you type, watch the chart build on the slide.

Manufacturing	30%
Sales/Marketing	19%
Food Service	15%
Technology	12%
Trucking	10%
Professional	9%
Medical	5%

You did not press Tab after the last entry because you do not want to create another category. Instead, you should press Enter or click in any cell.

16 Click to position the ⊞ pointer on the border between **column A** and **column B**. Double-click to resize **column A**. Using the same procedure, resize **column B**. Compare your screen with Figure 7.40.

It is not necessary to resize the columns in Excel because PowerPoint will display the words and numbers correctly. Resizing the columns helps you see the data in the worksheet better and correct any mistakes you might make. As you enter data in the Excel worksheet, the worksheet will auto scroll.

FIGURE 7.40

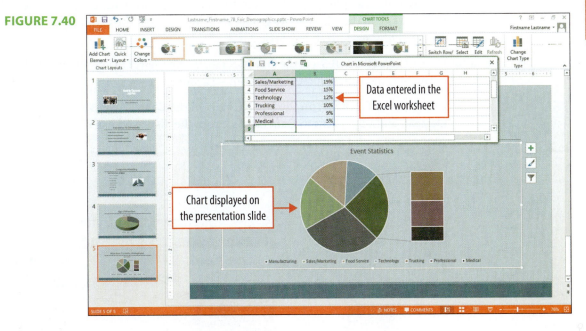

17 **Close** the Excel worksheet and, if necessary, return to PowerPoint. Compare your screen with Figure 7.41.

The legend at the right identifies the patterns or colors that are assigned to the pie slices. The chart is divided into five slices. The slice used for the Bar of Pie represents the three categories with the lowest values—Trucking, Professional, and Medical.

FIGURE 7.41

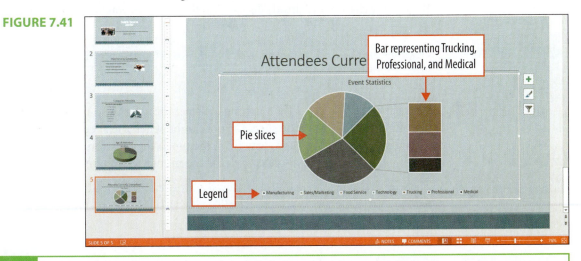

NOTE **Correcting Data Errors**

If you need to correct or change the data for your chart once you are working in PowerPoint, click the Chart Area. Under CHART TOOLS, on the DESIGN tab, in the Data group, click the Edit Data arrow, and then click Edit Data. Make the changes in the worksheet, and then close the worksheet.

18 **Save** 🖫 the changes to your presentation.

In this activity, you will modify the pie charts you created by applying a layout and style and by customizing the background.

 Make **Slide 4** the active slide. Click to the left of the chart title, *Age of Attendees*, which is displayed with a light gray font color, to select the **Chart Area**. Under **CHART TOOLS**, on the **DESIGN tab**, in the **Chart Styles group**, click **More** ⬇. In the **Chart Styles** gallery, in the first row, click the seventh style—**Style 7**.

2 Under **CHART TOOLS**, on the **DESIGN tab**, in the **Chart Layouts group**, click the **Quick Layout arrow**, and then click the second layout—**Layout 2**.

3 Under **CHART TOOLS**, on the **DESIGN tab**, in the **Chart Layouts group**, click the **Add Chart Element**, and then point to **Data Labels**. From the displayed list, click **Outside End**. Compare your screen with Figure 7.42.

FIGURE 7.42

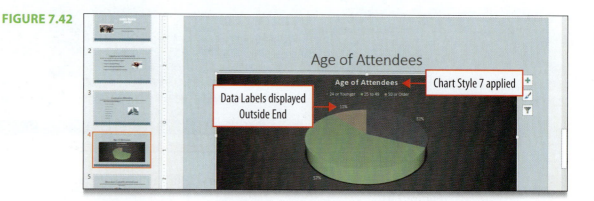

4 In the **Chart Layouts group**, click **Add Chart Element**, and then point to **Chart Title**. From the displayed list, click **None**.

Because the chart title is already displayed in the slide title, you do not need a chart title.

> 🔄 **ANOTHER WAY**   Click in the chart, and then on the right side of the chart, click Chart Elements ➕ , and then click Chart Title to remove the check mark.

5 Click the pie slice labeled *11%* one time to select the chart, and then click the slice a second time to select only the slice. Do not double-click the slice. When the Move 🔁 pointer displays, drag the slice away from the pie to the location shown in Figure 7.43— approximately 0.25 inch—and then release the mouse. Compare your screen to Figure 7.43.

The selected pie slice is exploded, or moved away from the pie, and the entire pie is resized. You needed to click the slice two times. The first click selects the entire pie chart, and the second click selects only the desired slice.

> 🔄 **ANOTHER WAY**   Click the pie slice labeled *11%* one time. Click the pie slice again. Right-click, and then on the shortcut menu, click Format Data Point to display the Format Data Point pane. On Format Data Point pane, under Series Options, drag the Point Explosion slider to the right to move the pie slice away from the pie.

FIGURE 7.43

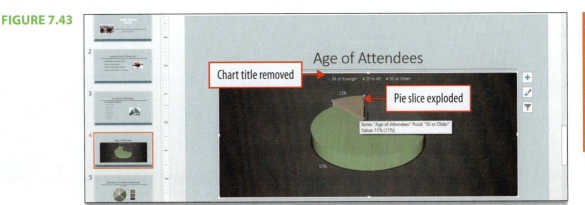

Chart title removed

Age of Attendees

Pie slice exploded

A L E R T !   **Why Did the Format Data Series Pane Display?**

If you double-click the pie slice, you will display the Format Data Series pane. This pane is different from the Format Data Point pane, which only modifies the individual pie slice. The Format Data Series pane modifies the entire pie chart. In the Format Series pane, you can change the Pie Explosion, but all the pie slices will explode instead of a single pie slice. If you did not intend to use the Format Data Series pane, click Close and try selecting the pie slice again. Be sure to click the slice one time to select the chart, pause, and then click the slice a second time to select only the slice. You can then drag the slice away from the other slices or use the Format Data Point pane to reposition the pie slice.

---

6 ▶ Point to the top left edge of the dark gray area and look for the Chart Area ScreenTip, and then click to select the **Chart Area**. Do not click the **Plot Area**. Under **CHART TOOLS**, click the **FORMAT tab**. In the **Shape Styles group**, click the **Shape Fill button arrow**, and then point to **Gradient**. Click **More Gradients** to display the **Format Chart Area** pane. Under **Fill**, click **Solid fill**.

A L E R T !   **Did You Select the Chart Area?**

If you clicked the Plot Area instead of the Chart Area, the Solid fill will not appear in the correct place. Click Undo. Point the mouse in the dark gray area, look for the Chart Area ScreenTip, and then retry applying the Solid fill.

🔄 **ANOTHER WAY**   On the **CHART TOOLS FORMAT tab**, in the **Current Selection group**, click the **Chart Elements arrow** and then click **Chart Area** from the list of chart elements.

---

7 ▶ Click the **Color arrow** to display the gallery. From the displayed list, in the third column, fourth row, locate **Ice Blue, Background 2, Darker 50%**. Before clicking, compare your screen with Figure 7.44.

FIGURE 7.44

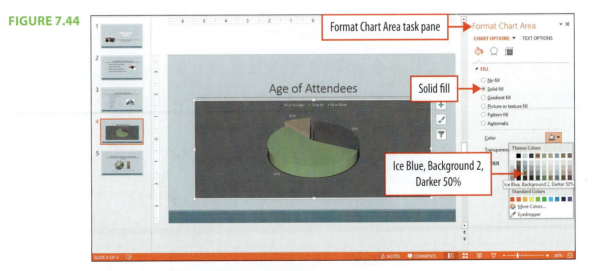

Format Chart Area task pane

Age of Attendees

Solid fill

Ice Blue, Background 2, Darker 50%

---

8 ▶ Click **Ice Blue, Background 2, Darker 50%**. **Close** the pane. Click outside the slide, and then compare your screen with Figure 7.45.

FIGURE 7.45

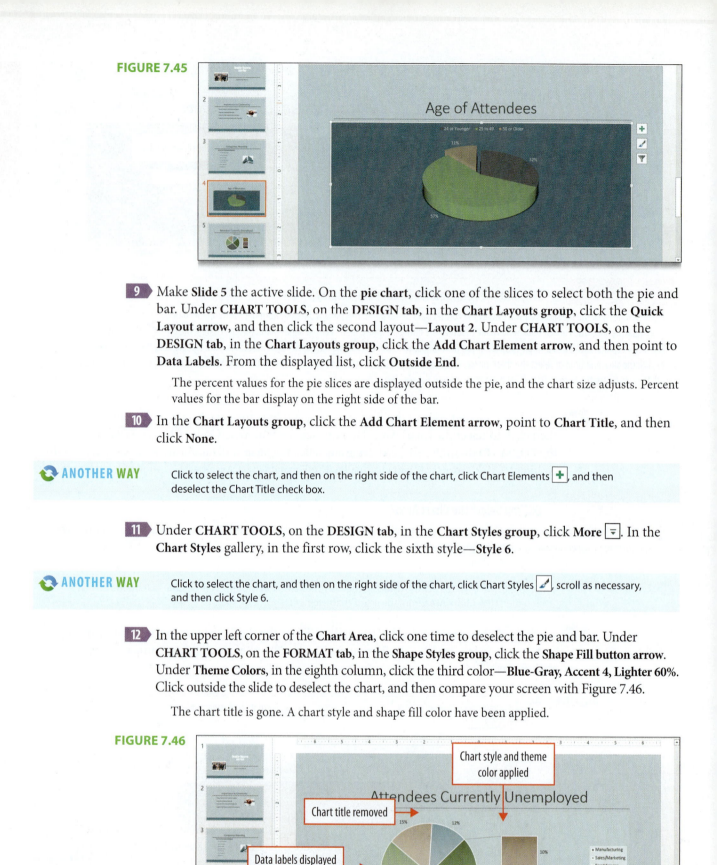

FIGURE 7.45

> **9** ▶ Make **Slide 5** the active slide. On the **pie chart**, click one of the slices to select both the pie and bar. Under **CHART TOOLS**, on the **DESIGN tab**, in the **Chart Layouts group**, click the **Quick Layout arrow**, and then click the second layout—**Layout 2**. Under **CHART TOOLS**, on the **DESIGN tab**, in the **Chart Layouts group**, click the **Add Chart Element arrow**, and then point to **Data Labels**. From the displayed list, click **Outside End**.

> The percent values for the pie slices are displayed outside the pie, and the chart size adjusts. Percent values for the bar display on the right side of the bar.

> **10** ▶ In the **Chart Layouts group**, click the **Add Chart Element arrow**, point to **Chart Title**, and then click **None**.

ANOTHER WAY   Click to select the chart, and then on the right side of the chart, click Chart Elements ✚ , and then deselect the Chart Title check box.

> **11** ▶ Under **CHART TOOLS**, on the **DESIGN tab**, in the **Chart Styles group**, click **More** ▾ . In the **Chart Styles** gallery, in the first row, click the sixth style—**Style 6**.

ANOTHER WAY   Click to select the chart, and then on the right side of the chart, click Chart Styles 🖌 , scroll as necessary, and then click Style 6.

> **12** ▶ In the upper left corner of the **Chart Area**, click one time to deselect the pie and bar. Under **CHART TOOLS**, on the **FORMAT tab**, in the **Shape Styles group**, click the **Shape Fill button arrow**. Under **Theme Colors**, in the eighth column, click the third color—**Blue-Gray, Accent 4, Lighter 60%**. Click outside the slide to deselect the chart, and then compare your screen with Figure 7.46.

> The chart title is gone. A chart style and shape fill color have been applied.

FIGURE 7.46

Chart style and theme color applied

Attendees Currently Unemployed

Chart title removed

Data labels displayed outside pie slices

13 ▶ Click to select the chart. On the **VIEW tab**, in the **Color/Grayscale group**, click **Grayscale**.

The entire presentation displays in grayscale, showing how the colors would translate into grayscale. The GRAYSCALE tab displays Grayscale options that can be applied to selected objects in the presentation. If an option cannot be applied to an object, it will be disabled. Grayscale is useful to see how a chart will look when printed on a black and white printer.

14 ▶ On the **GRAYSCALE tab**, in the **Close group**, click **Back To Color View**.

The chart displays in the previously selected colors.

 **BY TOUCH**   Tap the VIEW tab. In the Color/Grayscale group, tap Grayscale. On the GRAYSCALE tab, in the Close group, tap Back To Color View.

15 ▶ **Save** 🖫 your changes.

Objective 7   Create and Apply a Chart Template

Video P7-7

A *chart template* is a predefined layout or format that can be used to create a chart. After you have made changes in the layout, formatting, and style of a chart, it is possible to save your changes in a chart template and apply it to future charts. This eliminates the need to recreate your modifications.

In the following activities, you will save a customized chart as a chart template, and then apply the template to another chart.

> **ALERT!**   **Do You Have Time to Complete Objective 7 without Interruption?**
>
> Because you will be saving a chart template on the computer you are currently using, it is important that you complete Objective 7 before moving to another computer.

Activity 7.13 │ Creating a Chart Template

In this activity, you will select one of the pie charts you created and save it as a template and use it for another pie chart.

1 ▶ Make **Slide 4** the active slide, and then click to select the **Chart Area**.

> **ALERT!**   **Are You Allowed to Save Locally on Your Computer?**
>
> If you are working in a lab that does not allow you to save to the computer hard drive, either go to a computer where you can do this, use a USB drive, or just read the directions.

2 ▶ In the **Chart Area**, right-click, and then on the shortcut menu, click **Save As Template…** to display the **Save Chart Template** dialog box. In the **File name** box, type **Lastname_Firstname_7B_Pie.crtx** Compare your screen with Figure 7.47.

Chart templates are saved using the file extension *.crtx*. The chart was saved in the Charts folder on your computer, not in your chapter folder. You will move it later.

FIGURE 7.47

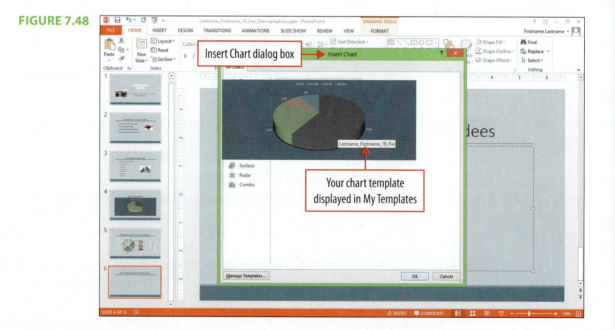

> **Chart folder on computer**
>
> **Chart file name**
>
> **Chart Template file type with .crtx extension**

3 Click **Save**.

4 Save 🖫 your changes.

Activity 7.14 | Applying a Chart Template

1 Make **Slide 5** the active slide. On the **HOME tab**, in the **Slides group**, click the **New Slide button arrow**, and then click **Title and Content**.

2 On **Slide 6**, in the title placeholder, type **Job Types Desired by Attendees** Drag to select the text. On the **HOME tab**, in the **Paragraph group**, click **Center** ≣.

3 In the body text placeholder, click **Insert Chart** 📊. In the **Insert Chart** dialog box, click **Templates** to display **My Templates**. Point to the thumbnail of the template you created, and then compare your screen with Figure 7.48.

> When you point to the thumbnail, the ScreenTip *Lastname_Firstname_7B_Pie* will display with your name.

FIGURE 7.48

> **Insert Chart dialog box**
>
> **Your chart template displayed in My Templates**

4 Select the template, and then click **OK**.

NOTE   Chart Template Location

Unless you specify a different folder, the template file (.crtx) will be saved in the Charts folder on your computer, and the template becomes available under Templates in the Insert Chart dialog box. If a chart template is located in a folder other than the Charts folder, click Manage Templates, locate the chart template, and then copy or move it to the Charts folder under Templates.

5 Beginning in cell **A2**, type the following data, pressing [Tab] to move from cell to cell. As you type, watch the chart build on the slide.

Full-Time	77%
Part-Time	23%

6 Right-click cell **A5**, and then from the shortcut menu, point to **Delete**. Click **Table Rows**. Repeat for cell **A4**.

7 Right-click cell **D1**, and then from the shortcut menu, point to **Delete**. Click **Table Columns**. Repeat for cell **C1**.

ANOTHER WAY   To hide unused categories, click to select the chart, and then on the right side of the chart, click Chart Filters 🔻. On the VALUES tab, under Categories, deselect the Category 3 and Category 4 check boxes, and then click Apply. Categories 3 and 4 are hidden on the displayed chart. However, the categories continue to exist in the spreadsheet. Because the chart type is a pie chart, only Series 1 is selected on Chart Filters VALUES tab under SERIES.

8 **Close** the worksheet and return to the presentation.

9 In PowerPoint, on **Slide 6**, click outside the slide to deselect the **Chart Area**. Compare your screen with Figure 7.49.

Because you selected the chart template, you do not have to format this slide, unless you want to make some modifications. Slides 4 and 6 display with the same formatting. There is no exploded pie slice here, however, because there are only two slices in the pie. The chart template was made from a chart that had three slices.

FIGURE 7.49

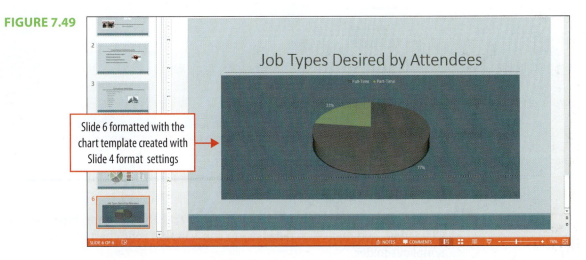

Slide 6 formatted with the chart template created with Slide 4 format settings

10 **Save** 💾 your changes.

11 On **Slide 6**, click the **Chart Area** to select it. Under **CHART TOOLS**, on the **DESIGN tab**, in the **Type group**, click **Change Chart Type**. In the **Change Chart Type** dialog box, click **Templates**, and then at the bottom left, click **Manage Templates** to display the **Charts** folder on your computer. Locate your chart template file—*Lastname_Firstname_7B_Pie.crtx*. See Figure 7.50.

FIGURE 7.50

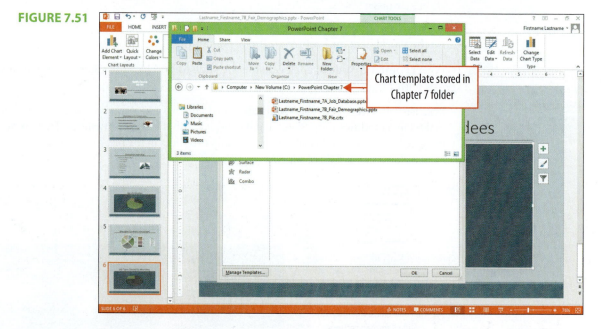

12 ▶ Right-click the chart template file, and then click **Cut**. Navigate to your **PowerPoint Chapter 7** folder, right-click, and then click **Paste**. See Figure 7.51.

The chart template is stored in your chapter folder and has been deleted from the computer you were using.

FIGURE 7.51

13 ▶ **Close** File Explorer ⊠ , and then return to the presentation. In the **Change Chart Type** dialog box, click **Cancel** to close it.

14 ▶ In PowerPoint, under **CHART TOOLS** on the **DESIGN tab**, in the **Type group**, click **Change Chart Type**, and then click **Templates** to confirm that your chart template is not in the templates folder.

15 ▶ Click **Cancel**.

More Knowledge | **Applying a Chart Template in Another Presentation**

A chart template contains the chart format and stores the colors that are in use when you save the chart as a template. When you use a chart template to create a chart in another presentation, the new chart uses the colors of the chart template—not the colors of the current presentation. To use the colors of the current presentation, right-click the Chart Area, and then click Reset to Match Style.

Objective 8 | Apply Animation to a Chart

Video P7-8

Recall that animation can be applied to text, pictures, clip art, and SmartArt to create dynamic slide shows. Animation can also be applied to individual chart elements. Charts can display all at once or by category, and you can control the elements to display automatically or by mouse click.

Activity 7.15 | Applying Animation to a Chart

1 Make **Slide 6** the active slide, if necessary. Click the **pie chart** one time to select all of the slices in the pie.

2 Click the **ANIMATIONS tab**. In the **Animation group**, click **More** ⬇. Under **Entrance**, click **Fade**. Click **Effect Options**, and then click **By Category**.

3 In the **Timing group**, click the **Start box arrow**, and then click **After Previous**.

4 In the **Preview group**, click **Preview** to view the animation effect.

5 On the **SLIDE SHOW tab**, in the **Start Slide Show group**, click **From Beginning** to view your entire presentation. Press Enter to advance the slides. Press Esc when the slide show is finished.

6 On the **INSERT tab**, in the **Text group**, click **Header & Footer** to display the **Header and Footer** dialog box. Click the **Notes and Handouts tab**. Under **Include on page**, select the **Date and time** check box, and then select **Fixed**. If necessary, clear the **Header** check box, and then select the **Page number** and **Footer** check boxes. In the **Footer** box, using your own name, type **Lastname_Firstname_7B_Fair_Demographics** and then click **Apply to All**.

7 Click the **FILE tab**, and then in the lower right portion of the screen, click **Show All Properties**. In the **Tags** box, type **attendee, unemployment** and in the **Subject** box type your course name and section number. In the **Author** box, right-click the existing author name, click **Edit Property**, replace the existing text with your first and last name, click outside text box to deselect, and then click **OK.**

8 **Save** 🖫 your changes, and then **Exit** PowerPoint. Submit your work as directed.

END | You have completed Project 7B

END OF CHAPTER

SUMMARY

You practiced adding tables to a Microsoft PowerPoint presentation using several different methods. You created a table and copied tables from other applications, including Word 2013 and Excel 2013.

You practiced moving and sizing tables, merging and splitting table cells, and adding and removing table columns and rows. You used pie charts to show how different categories relate to the whole.

You created professional-looking charts by applying a predefined layout and style. You added visual interest to tables by applying predefined styles, fill color, weight, shading, and color of borders.

You customized charts by adding effects and modifying chart elements. You saved a customized chart as a chart template and applied animation to chart elements. You added and renamed a slide section.

GO! LEARN IT ONLINE

Review the concepts and key terms in this chapter by completing these online challenges, which you can find at **www.pearsonhighered.com/go**

Matching and Multiple Choice:
Answer matching and multiple choice questions to test what you learned in this chapter. MyITLab®

Crossword Puzzle:
Spell out the words that match the numbered clues, and put them in the puzzle squares.

Flipboard:
Flip through the definitions of the key terms in this chapter and match them with the correct term.

END OF CHAPTER

Your instructor may assign one or more of these projects to help you review the chapter and assess your mastery and understanding of the chapter.

	Review and Assessment Guide for PowerPoint Chapter 7		
Project	**Apply Skills from These Chapter Objectives**	**Project Type**	**Project Location**
7C	Objectives 1–5 from Project 7A	**7C Skills Review** A guided review of the skills from Project 7A.	On the following pages
7D	Objectives 6–8 from Project 7B	**7D Skills Review** A guided review of the skills from Project 7B.	On the following pages
7E	Objectives 1–5 from Project 7A	**7E Mastering PowerPoint (Grader Project)** A demonstration of your mastery of the skills in Project 7A with extensive decision making.	In MyITLab and on the following pages
7F	Objectives 6–8 from Project 7B	**7F Mastering PowerPoint (Grader Project)** A demonstration of your mastery of the skills in Project 7B with extensive decision making.	In MyITLab and on the following pages
7G	Objectives 1–8 from Projects 7A and 7B	**7G Mastering PowerPoint (Grader Project)** A demonstration of your mastery of the skills in Projects 7A and 7B with extensive decision making.	In MyITLab and on the following pages
7H	Combination of Objectives from Projects 7A and 7B	**7H GO! Fix It** A demonstration of your mastery of the skills in Projects 7A and 7B by creating a correct result from a document that contains errors you must find.	Online
7I	Combination of Objectives from Projects 7A and 7B	**7I GO! Make It** A demonstration of your mastery of the skills in Projects 7A and 7B by creating a result from a supplied picture.	Online
7J	Combination of Objectives from Projects 7A and 7B	**7J GO! Solve It** A demonstration of your mastery of the skills in Projects 7A and 7B, your decision-making skills, and your critical thinking skills. A task-specific rubric helps you self-assess your result.	Online
7K	Combination of Objectives from Projects 7A and 7B	**7K GO! Solve It** A demonstration of your mastery of the skills in Projects 7A and 7B, your decision-making skills, and your critical thinking skills. A task-specific rubric helps you self-assess your result.	On the following pages
7L	Combination of Objectives from Projects 7A and 7B	**7L GO! Think** A demonstration of your understanding of the chapter concepts applied in a manner that you would apply them outside of college. An analytic rubric helps you and your instructor grade the quality of your work by comparing it to the work an expert in the discipline would create.	On the following pages
7M	Combination of Objectives from Projects 7A and 7B	**7M GO! Think** A demonstration of your understanding of the chapter concepts applied in a manner that you would apply them outside of college. An analytic rubric helps you and your instructor grade the quality of your work by comparing it to the work an expert in the discipline would create.	Online
7N	Combination of Objectives from Projects 7A and 7B	**7N You and GO!** A demonstration of your understanding of the chapter concepts applied in a manner that you would apply them in a personal situation. An analytic rubric helps you and your instructor grade the quality of your work.	Online

GLOSSARY

GLOSSARY OF CHAPTER KEY TERMS

AutoFit An option that resizes a column to accommodate the largest entry.

Banded columns A table setting that enables you to format even columns differently from odd columns to make the table easier to read.

Banded rows A table setting that enables you to format even rows differently from odd rows to make the table easier to read.

Bar of Pie chart A type of pie chart that emphasizes one slice of the pie by representing the slice as a bar showing how the data in the slice are further divided.

Chart template A predefined layout or format that can be used to create a chart.

.crtx The file extension for a chart template.

Data series In an Excel worksheet, a set of values arranged in one column or row only.

Destination file The file into which information or an object is copied.

Embedded A type of object that is saved with, and becomes a part of, a PowerPoint file.

Explode Manually pull out a slice of a pie chart so that it stands away from the pie in order to emphasize it.

Exploded pie chart A type of pie chart that displays all of the slices disconnected from each other. The slices cannot be manipulated individually.

Header row The top row of the table; this row is formatted differently from the rows containing data.

Legend In a pie chart, identifies the patterns or colors that are assigned to the pie slices.

Lock Aspect Ratio Locks the relationship between the width and height of a table. When resizing a table, the height and width of the table change in proportion to each other.

Merge To combine two or more cells into a single cell.

Pie chart Used to plot a single data series, this chart type shows the relationship of parts to a whole.

Pie of Pie chart A type of pie chart that emphasizes one slice of the pie by representing the slice as another pie showing how the data in the slice are further divided.

Range A selection of two or more adjacent or nonadjacent cells.

Section header Used to organize slides in meaningful ways.

Sizing handles Small squares, located in the corners and in the center of table borders, that are used to increase or decrease the size of the table by dragging.

Slices Categories in a pie chart that represent parts of the whole and show the contribution of each value to the total.

Source file A file from which information or an object is copied.

Split To divide a cell into two or more cells.

Table A grid of rows and columns.

Table gridlines Nonprinting lines between columns and rows in a table.

Total row The last row of a table; this row is formatted differently from other rows containing data.

CHAPTER REVIEW

Apply 7A skills from these Objectives:

1 Add a Table to a Presentation
2 Add or Delete Table Rows, Columns, or Cells
3 Move and Size a Table
4 Modify a Table
5 Insert a Section Header

Skills Review | Project 7C Job Fairs

In the following Skills Review, you will complete a PowerPoint presentation that includes the various job fairs that the organizers of the Seattle-Tacoma Job Fair will attend in the coming year. You will create a table and insert tables from Microsoft Word and Microsoft Excel. Your completed presentation will look similar to Figure 7.52.

PROJECT FILES

For Project 7C, you will need the following files:

p07C_Job_Fairs.pptx
p07C_Locations_Dates.xlsx
p07C_Registration.docx

You will save your presentation as:

Lastname_Firstname_7C_Job_Fairs.pptx

PROJECT RESULTS

FIGURE 7.52

(Project 7C Job Fairs continues on the next page)

CHAPTER REVIEW

1 Start PowerPoint. Locate and open the file **p07C_Job_Fairs**. Using your own first and last name, save the file as **Lastname_Firstname_7C_Job_Fairs** in your chapter folder.

2 Make **Slide 5** the active slide.

a. On the **INSERT tab**, in the **Tables group**, click **Table**.

b. In the displayed **Table** grid, point to the first cell and, without pressing mouse, move the Select pointer to the right to select three cells. Then move the Select pointer down to select five cells. Click the left mouse button one time to create a 3×5 table.

c. With the insertion point in the first cell, type **Job Fair** Press Tab or press →. In the second cell, type **Location** and then press Tab. In the third cell, type **Date** and then press Tab.

d. At the beginning of **row 2**, type the following information, pressing Tab or → after each entry except the last entry:

Sales & Retail	Seattle	March 19-21
Transportation	Redmond	April 16-18
Food Service & Restaurant	Tacoma	October 8-10
Construction Industry	Covington	November 12-14

3 With the PowerPoint presentation still open, on the keyboard, press the ⊞ to display the Start screen. Scroll to the right, as necessary, locate Microsoft Word 2013, and then click on the Word 2013 tile.

a. Click **Open Other Documents**. Navigate to the location where the student data files are stored, and then open **p07C_Registration.docx**.

b. In Word, click anywhere in the table to select it, if necessary. Under **TABLE TOOLS**, click the **LAYOUT tab**.

c. In the **Table group**, click **Select**, and then click **Select Table** to select the entire table.

d. On the **HOME tab**, in the **Clipboard group**, click **Copy**.

4 In PowerPoint, make **Slide 4** the active slide.

a. On the **HOME tab**, in the **Clipboard group**, click **Paste**.

b. Under **TABLE TOOLS**, click the **DESIGN tab**. In the **Table Style Options group**, remove the check mark in the **First Column** check box.

c. **Close** Word without saving, and then return to the presentation slide.

5 With the PowerPoint presentation still open, on the keyboard, press the ⊞ to display the Start screen. Scroll to the right, as necessary, locate Microsoft Excel 2013, and then click on the Excel 2013 tile.

a. Click **Open Other Workbooks**. Navigate to the location where the student data files are stored, and then open **p07C_Locations_Dates.xlsx**.

b. Click cell **A1**, press Shift, and then click **C8**.

c. On the **HOME tab**, in the **Clipboard group**, click **Copy**.

6 In PowerPoint, make **Slide 3** the active slide.

a. On the **HOME tab**, in the **Clipboard group**, click **Paste**.

b. Under the lower right corner of table, click **Paste Options**. Click the second option, **Keep Source Formatting**.

c. **Close** Excel without saving, and then return to the presentation slide.

7 With **Slide 3** still active:

a. Click anywhere in the table.

b. Under **TABLE TOOLS**, on the **LAYOUT tab**, in the **Table group**, click **View Gridlines**, if necessary, to display the gridlines.

c. Right-click in the cell that contains *Dayton Technology*, click **Delete**, and then click **Delete Rows**.

d. Right-click in the cell that contains *Alternative Date*, click **Delete**, and then click **Delete Columns**.

e. Right-click in the cell that contains *Job Fair*, click **Insert**, and then click **Insert Columns to the Right**.

f. In the new column beginning in **row 1**, type the following, pressing ↓ after each entry except the last entry:

Location
Seattle
Shorewood
University Place
Parkland
Edmonds
Bellevue

(Project 7C Job Fairs continues on the next page)

8 With **Slide 3** still active:

a. Right-click the cell that contains *Job Fair*, click **Insert**, and then click **Insert Rows Above**.

b. Point to the left of the new blank row, outside of the table to display the Select Row pointer, and then right-click to display the shortcut menu. Select **Merge Cells**. In the new row, type **Currently Scheduled**

c. Right-click the text you just typed. On the Mini toolbar, click **Center**.

9 With **Slide 3** still active:

a. Right-click in the cell containing *Seattle*.

b. Click **Split Cells**, accept the default of **2** columns, and then click **OK**.

c. In the new cell, type **SE**

d. On the **VIEW tab**, in the **Show group**, click the **Ruler** check box to display the ruler, if necessary.

e. In the cell for *Shorewood Healthcare*, point to the cell border between **column 1** and **column 2** to display the Move Vertical pointer, and then double-click to **AutoFit** the column.

f. Point to the bottom border of **row 1**—*Currently Scheduled*—and then drag the border down until the Move Horizontal pointer is between **row 2** and **row 3**.

10 Make **Slide 5** the active slide.

a. Click anywhere in the table.

b. Position the Move Vertical pointer to the cell border between **column 1** and **column 2**. Double-click to resize **column 1**.

c. Using the same procedure, double-click the border between **column 2** and **column 3** to resize **column 2**. Position the Move Vertical pointer to the edge of the last column, and then double-click to **AutoFit**.

d. Right-click anywhere in the table, and then click **Select Table**. Under **TABLE TOOLS**, on the **LAYOUT tab**, in the **Arrange group**, click **Align**, and then click **Align Center**. Click **Align** again, and then click **Align Middle**.

11 Make **Slide 4** the active slide.

a. Right-click in the table, and then click **Select Table**.

b. In upper right corner of the table, point to the sizing handle to display the Diagonal Resize pointer. Hold down Ctrl and drag so the top edge of the table aligns on the **upper half of the vertical ruler at 1 inch** and on the **right half of the horizontal ruler at 3 inches**.

c. On the **HOME tab**, in the **Font group**, change the **Font Size** to **18**, if necessary.

d. Position the Move Vertical pointer between **column 1** and **column 2**, and then double-click to use the **AutoFit** feature.

e. Under **TABLE TOOLS**, on the **LAYOUT tab**, in the **Arrange group**, click **Align**, and then click **Align Center**.

f. Hold down Shift and drag the entire table so the top is aligned at **1.5 inches on the upper half of the vertical ruler**.

12 Make **Slide 3** the active slide.

a. Click anywhere in the table.

b. Under **TABLE TOOLS**, on the **DESIGN tab**, in the **Table Style Options group**, click to place check marks in the **Banded Rows** and **Header Row** check boxes.

c. In **Table Styles group**, click **More** to display the **Table Style** gallery. Under **Medium**, in the first row, click the second style—**Medium Style 1 – Accent 1**.

d. On the **LAYOUT tab**, in the **Table Size group**, click the **Lock Aspect Ratio** check box to display a check mark, and then change the **Width** to **7"**.

e. Right-click in the table, and then click **Select Table**. On the **HOME tab**, change the **Font Size** to **18**.

f. Position the Select Row pointer to the left of **row 1**, and then right-click to select the row. Change the **Font Size** to **24**. Under **TABLE TOOLS**, on the **LAYOUT tab**, in the **Alignment group**, click **Center Vertically**.

g. Using the Select Row pointer, select **row 2**, right-click, and then on the mini toolbar, click **Bold**.

h. Right-click anywhere in the table, and then click **Select Table**. Under **TABLE TOOLS**, on the **LAYOUT tab**, in the **Arrange group**, click **Align**, and then click **Align Center**. Click **Align** again, and then click **Align Middle**.

(Project 7C Job Fairs continues on the next page)

CHAPTER REVIEW

13 On the left, click between the **Slide 2** and the **Slide 3** thumbnails.

a. On the **HOME tab**, in the **Slides group**, click the **New Slide arrow**, and then click **Section Header**.

b. Click in the title placeholder, and then type **JOB FAIR DATA** Click in the subtitle placeholder, and then type **SEATTLE-TACOMA JOB FAIR**

c. On the left, click between the **Slide 2** and the **Slide 3** thumbnails. On the **HOME tab**, in the **Slides group**, click the **Section arrow**, and then click **Add Section**.

d. On the left, with **Untitled Section** selected and highlighted in orange, on the **HOME tab**, in **the Slides group**, click the **Section arrow**, and then click **Rename Section**. In the **Rename Section** dialog box, under **Section name**, with the **Untitled Section** text selected, type **Job Fair Data** Click **Rename**.

e. On the **VIEW tab**, in the **Presentation Views**, click **Slide Sorter**. Notice *the Job Fair Data* section in **Slide Sorter View**. On the **VIEW tab**, in the **Presentation Views**, click **Normal**.

14 On the **SLIDE SHOW tab**, in the **Start Slide Show group**, click **From Beginning** to view your entire presentation.

15 On the **INSERT tab**, in the **Text group**:

a. Click **Header & Footer** to display the **Header and Footer** dialog box.

b. Click the **Notes and Handouts tab**. Under **Include on page**, select the **Date and time** check box, and then select **Fixed**. If necessary, clear the **Header** check box, and then select the **Page number** and **Footer** check boxes. In the **Footer** box, using your own name, type **Lastname_Firstname_7C_Job_Fairs** and then click **Apply to All**.

16 Click the **FILE tab**, and then in the lower right portion of the screen, click **Show All Properties**. In the **Tags** box, type **job, fair, Seattle** and in the **Subject** box type your course name and section number. In the **Author** box, right-click the existing author name, click **Edit Property**, replace the existing text with your first and last name, click outside text box to deselect, and then click **OK**.

17 Print **Handouts 6 Slides Horizontal**, or submit your presentation electronically as directed by your instructor.

18 **Save** your changes, **Close** the presentation, and then **Exit** PowerPoint. Submit your work as directed.

END | You have completed Project 7C

CHAPTER REVIEW

Apply 7B skills from these Objectives:

6 Create and Modify Pie Charts

7 Create and Apply a Chart Template

8 Apply Animation to a Chart

Skills Review | Project 7D Attendee Survey

In the following Skills Review, you will complete a PowerPoint presentation regarding a recent Seattle-Tacoma Job Fair and those who attended. The survey represents both unemployed and underemployed individuals who are looking for a position. You will add pie charts to emphasize the data collected. You will modify the pie charts and view a chart in grayscale. You will also create a pie chart template and apply it to give your presentation a consistent look and feel. Your completed presentation will look similar to Figure 7.53.

PROJECT FILES

For Project 7D, you will need the following file:

p07D_Attendee_Survey.pptx

You will save your files as:

Lastname_Firstname_7D_Attendee_Survey.pptx

Lastname_Firstname_7D_Attendees.crtx

PROJECT RESULTS

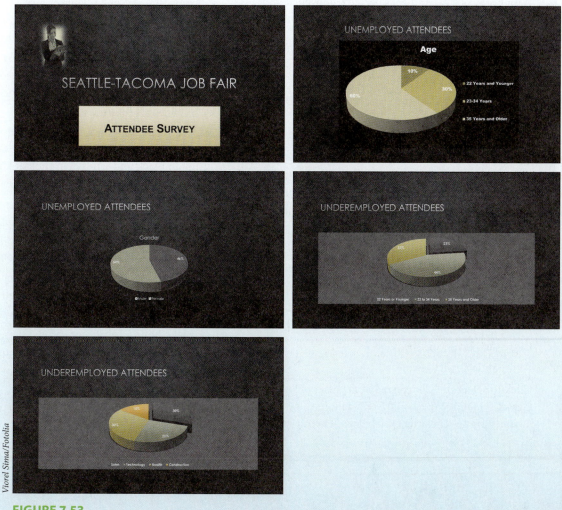

Viorel Sima/Fotolia

FIGURE 7.53

(Project 7D Attendee Survey continues on the next page)

CHAPTER REVIEW

1 Start PowerPoint. Locate and open the file **p07D_Attendee_Survey**. Using your own first and last name, save the file as **Lastname_Firstname_7D_Attendee_Survey** in your chapter folder.

2 Make **Slide 3** the active slide.

a. In the content placeholder, click the **Insert Chart** icon, and then click **Pie**. Click the second pie chart type—**3-D Pie**, and then click **OK**.

b. In the Excel worksheet, click in cell **B1**, and then type **Gender** and then press Enter. Click in cell **A2**, type **Male** and then press Enter. In cell **A3**, type **Female** and then press Enter.

c. In cell **B2**, type **46%** and then press Enter In cell **B3**, type **54%** and then press Enter.

d. Click to select cell **A4**, and then drag to select cell **A5**. With both cells **A4** and **A5** selected, right-click and from the shortcut menu, point to **Delete**, and then click **Table Rows**.

e. **Close** the Excel worksheet.

3 Make **Slide 4** the active slide.

a. Click the **Insert Chart** icon, click **Pie**, click **3-D Pie**, and then click **OK**.

b. In the Excel worksheet, click in cell **A2**, and then type **22 Years and Younger** and then press Enter. In cell **A3**, type **23 to 34 Years** and then press Enter. In cell **A4**, type **35 Years and Older** and then press Enter.

c. Position the Move Column pointer between **column A** and **column B**, and then double-click to **AutoFit column A**.

d. In **column B**, in cell **B2**, type **23%** in cell **B3**, type **44%** and then in cell **B4**, type **33%**

e. Select cell **A5**, right-click, point to **Delete**, and then click **Table Rows**.

f. **Close** the Excel worksheet.

4 With **Slide 4** still active:

a. Click to select the **Chart Area**, if necessary. Under **CHART TOOLS**, on the **DESIGN tab**, in the **Chart Layouts group**, click the **Quick Layout arrow**, and then click the third layout—**Layout 3**.

b. In the **Chart Styles group**, click **More**. In the **Chart Styles** gallery, and then in the last row, click the last style—**Style 10**.

c. Under **CHART TOOLS**, on the **DESIGN tab**, in the **Chart Layouts group,** click the **Add Chart Element arrow**, point to **Data Labels**, and then select **Inside End**. On the **HOME tab**, click **Bold**.

d. Click the pie slice labeled *23%* one time. Click the slice once more. Do not double-click the slice. Drag the slice out approximately **.25 inch**. Click outside the slide to deselect it.

5 With **Slide 4** still active:

a. Click to select the **Chart Area**, if necessary.

b. Under **CHART TOOLS**, click the **FORMAT tab**. In the **Shapes Styles group**, click **Shape Fill**. Under **Theme Colors**, in the fifth column, last row, click **Gray-50%, Accent 1, Darker 50%**.

6 Make **Slide 3** the active slide. Click to select the pie chart. Under **CHART TOOLS**, on the **DESIGN tab**, in the **Chart Layouts group**, click the **Add Chart Element arrow**, point to **Data Labels**, and then select **Inside End**. Click to select the **54% and 46%** data labels, and then on the **HOME tab**, click **Bold**.

7 On the **VIEW tab**, in the **Color/Grayscale group**, click **Grayscale** to view the presentation as shown when printing in black and white. On the **GRAYSCALE tab**, in the **Close group**, click **Back To Color View**.

8 Make **Slide 4** the active slide. Select the **Chart Area**. Right-click, and then click **Save As Template…**. In the **Save Chart Template** dialog box, save the template with the name **Lastname_Firstname_7D_Attendees**

9 Make **Slide 4** the active slide, if necessary. On the **HOME tab**, in the **Slides group**, click **New Slide arrow**. Click **Title and Content**.

10 Make **Slide 5** the active slide, if necessary.

a. In the title placeholder, type **UNDEREMPLOYED ATTENDEES**

b. In the body placeholder, click the **Insert Chart** icon. In the **Insert Chart** dialog box, click **Templates**, and then click the **Lastname_Firstname_7D_Attendees** chart thumbnail. Click **OK**.

(Project 7D Attendee Survey continues on the next page)

CHAPTER REVIEW

c. In Excel, type the following in **column A**, beginning with cell **A2**:

| Sales |
| Technology |
| Health |
| Construction |

d. Position the Move Column pointer between **column A** and **column B**, and then double-click to **AutoFit column A**.

e. Type the following in **column B**, starting with cell **B2**:

| 30% |
| 25% |
| 30% |
| 15% |

f. Delete **column C** and **column D**.

g. **Close** the Excel worksheet.

11 On **Slide 5**, click the chart border, if necessary.

a. Under **CHART TOOLS**, on the **DESIGN tab**, in the **Type group**, click **Change Chart Type**. In the **Change Chart Type** dialog box, click **Templates**, and then click **Manage Templates** to display the **Charts** folder on your computer. Locate your chart template file—*Lastname_Firstname_7D_Attendees.crtx*.

b. Right-click the chart file, and then click **Cut**. Navigate to your chapter folder, right-click, and then click **Paste**.

c. **Close** File Explorer, and then return to the presentation.

d. In the **Change Chart Type** dialog box, click **Cancel**.

12 With **Slide 5** active:

a. Click to select the **Chart Area**, if necessary. Click the **ANIMATIONS tab**. In the **Animation group**, click **More**. Under **Entrance**, click **Float In**. Click **Effect Options**. Under **Sequence**, click **By Category**.

b. In the **Timing group**, click the **Start box arrow**, and then click **After Previous**.

13 On the **SLIDE SHOW tab**, in the **Start Slide Show group**, click **From Beginning** to view the presentation.

14 On the **INSERT tab**, click **Header & Footer** to display the **Header and Footer** dialog box. Click the **Notes and Handouts tab**. Under **Include on page**, select the **Date and time** check box, and then select **Fixed**. If necessary, clear the **Header** check box, and then select the **Page number** and **Footer** check boxes. In the **Footer** box, using your own name, type **Lastname_Firstname_7D_Attendee_Survey** and then click **Apply to All**.

15 Click the **FILE tab**, and then in the lower right portion of the screen, click **Show All Properties**. In the **Tags** box, type **attendees, unemployed** and in the **Subject** box type your course name and section number. In the **Author** box, right-click the existing author name, click **Edit Property**, replace the existing text with your first and last name, click outside text box to deselect, and then click **OK**.

16 **Save** your changes. Print **Handouts 6 Slides Horizontal**, or submit your presentation electronically as directed by your instructor. **Close** the presentation, and then **Exit** PowerPoint.

END | You have completed Project 7D

CONTENT-BASED ASSESSMENTS

Mastering PowerPoint   Project 7E Surveys

In the following Mastering PowerPoint project, you will complete a PowerPoint presentation by creating and inserting tables of data that have been collected. The Seattle-Tacoma Job Fair organization is conducting surveys in preparation for the upcoming job fairs. Your completed presentation will look similar to Figure 7.54.

Apply 7A skills from these Objectives:

1 Add a Table to a Presentation

2 Add or Delete Table Rows, Columns, or Cells

3 Move and Size a Table

4 Modify a Table

5 Insert a Section Header

PROJECT FILES

For Project 7E, you will need the following files:

p07E_Surveys.pptx

p07E_Staffing_Survey.xlsx

p07E_New_Hires.docx

You will save your presentation as:

Lastname_Firstname_7E_Surveys.pptx

PROJECT RESULTS

FIGURE 7.54

(Project 7E Surveys continues on the next page)

CONTENT-BASED ASSESSMENTS

1 Start PowerPoint. Locate and open the file **p07E_Surveys**. Save the file in your chapter folder, using the file name **Lastname_Firstname_7E_Surveys**

2 Make **Slide 3** the active slide. Insert a 3×8 table. In **row 1**, type the following text. In the third column, press Enter after *Minimum* before typing *Employees*.

Job Fair	Location	Minimum Employees

3 Type the following information in the corresponding cells, beginning in **row 2**:

Greater Seattle	Seattle	500
Bellingham Technology	Bellingham	20
Shorewood Healthcare	Shorewood	100
Vancouver Paints	Vancouver	75
Auburn Technology	Auburn	150
Edmonds Healthcare	Edmonds	100
Human Resources	Marysville	50

4 Select the **Header Row**. Center the text both horizontally and vertically.

5 Apply the **Medium Style 3 – Accent 1** design to the table.

6 In **column 3**, center the cells with numerical values.

7 **AutoFit** between **columns 2** and **3**.

8 Move the table down until the top border aligns on the **upper half of the vertical ruler at 0.75 inch**. Set the alignment to **Align Center**.

9 In Excel, open **p07E_Staffing_Survey.xlsx**. Copy the Excel table, and then paste it on **Slide 4**. **Close** Excel and return to PowerPoint.

10 Delete **column 4**. Click the **Lock Aspect Ratio** check box, if necessary. Change the table width to **8"**.

11 Move the table up so it is aligned on the **upper half of the vertical ruler at 0.75 inch**. Set the alignment to **Align Center**.

12 On the **TABLE TOOLS DESIGN tab**, select the **Header Row** check box.

13 Split the *Advertising/Public Relations* cell into two columns. In the new cell, type **Public Relations** In the original cell, delete */Public Relations*.

14 Split the *Engineering/Architect* cell into two columns. In the new cell, type **Architect** In the original cell, delete */Architect*

15 Drag to select all the text in the table, and then change the **Font** to **Garamond (Body)** with **Font Size 18**. **Center** the numbers in **column 3**.

16 **Center** the text in **row 1**, and then increase the **Font Size** to **20**.

17 In Word, open **p07E_New_Hires.docx**. Copy the table, and then paste it on **Slide 5**. **Close** Word and return to PowerPoint.

18 Delete the *Location* column. **AutoFit column 1** and **column 2**. Lock the Aspect Ratio, if necessary, and then increase the table width to **7.5"** Drag to select all the text in the table, and then change the font size to **18**. **AutoFit column 1** and **column 2** again. **Center** the numbers in **column 3**.

19 Move the table up until the top of the table aligns on the **upper half of the vertical ruler at 0.75 inch**. Set the table alignment to **Align Center**.

20 Remove the dark coloring from the first column.

21 Add a **Section Header slide** between **Slides 2** and **3**. Add the title **JOB FAIR DATA** and the subtitle **SEATTLE-TACOMA JOB FAIR**

22 Add a **Section** between **Slides 2** and **3** and rename it **Job Fair Data** View the presentation in **Slide Sorter View**, and then return to **Normal View**.

23 On the **SLIDE SHOW tab**, view your presentation **From Beginning**.

24 Insert a footer on the notes and handouts that includes a fixed date and time, the page number, and the file name.

25 Click the **FILE tab**, and then in the lower right portion of the screen, click **Show All Properties**. In the **Tags** box, type **survey, industry** and in the **Subject** box type your course name and section number. In the **Author** box, right-click the existing author name, click **Edit Property**, replace the existing text with your first and last name, click outside text box to deselect, and then click **OK**.

26 **Save** your changes, and then print **Handouts 6 Slides Horizontal**, or submit your presentation electronically as directed by your instructor. **Close** the presentation, and then **Exit** PowerPoint.

END | You have completed Project 7E

CONTENT-BASED ASSESSMENTS

Mastering PowerPoint | Project 7F Statistics

In the following Mastering PowerPoint project, you will complete a PowerPoint presentation by modifying a pie chart and saving it as a template. You will then apply the chart template to another pie chart showing the statistics of the people who attended the Seattle-Tacoma Job Fair. The presentation also highlights the ten largest represented employment areas by industry type. Your completed presentation will look similar to Figure 7.55.

Apply 7B skills from these Objectives:

6 Create and Modify Pie Charts

7 Create and Apply a Chart Template

8 Apply Animation to a Chart

PROJECT FILES

For Project 7F, you will need the following file:

p07F_Statistics.pptx

You will save your files as:

Lastname_Firstname_7F_Statistics.pptx
Lastname_Firstname_7F_Statistics.crtx

PROJECT RESULTS

FIGURE 7.55

(Project 7F Statistics continues on the next page)

CONTENT-BASED ASSESSMENTS

1 Start PowerPoint. Locate and open the file **p07F_Statistics**. Navigate to the location where you are storing your folders and projects for this chapter, and then save the file as **Lastname_Firstname_7F_Statistics**

2 Make **Slide 3** the active slide. Remove the **Chart Title**.

3 Set the **Data Labels** to display as **Outside End**.

4 Using the **Chart Styles** gallery, apply **Style 8**—in the first row, the eighth style.

5 **Explode** the pie slice labeled *22%* by approximately **0.25 inch**.

6 Set the entrance animation of the chart to **Fade**, **By Category**, and then set the **Start** to **After Previous**.

7 Save the chart template in the **Charts** folder using the name **Lastname_Firstname_7F_Statistics**

8 Make **Slide 2** the active slide, and then insert the chart template you just saved.

9 In cell **A2**, type **Male** and in then cell **A3**, type **Female**

10 In cell **B2**, type **42%** and then in cell **B3**, type **58%**

11 Delete **column C** and **column D**. Delete **row 4** and **row 5**. **Close** the Excel worksheet.

12 Add a new **Title and Content** slide as **Slide 4**. Insert a **Pie of Pie** chart. In Excel, beginning in cell **A2**, type the following information:

Healthcare	250
Food Service	250
Retail	200
Manufacturing	150
Technology	100
Education	90

13 Exit Excel. On **Slide 4**, type **Number of Jobs Forecasted** as the title of the slide. Delete the chart title. Set the **Data Labels** to display as **Outside End**.

14 On the **CHART TOOLS DESIGN tab**, click **Change Chart Type**, under **Templates**, click **Manage Templates**. Using **Cut** and **Paste**, move the template file to your chapter folder.

15 Return to PowerPoint, and then view your presentation **From Beginning**.

16 Insert a footer on the notes and handouts that includes a fixed date and time, the page number, and the file name.

17 Click the **FILE tab**, and then in the lower right portion of the screen, click **Show All Properties**. In the **Tags** box, type **employers, job, fair** and in the **Subject** box type your course name and section number. In the **Author** box, right-click the existing author name, click **Edit Property**, replace the existing text with your first and last name, click outside text box to deselect, and then click **OK**.

18 **Save** your changes.

19 Print **Handouts 4 Slides Horizontal**, or submit your presentation electronically as directed by your instructor. **Close** the presentation, and then **Exit** PowerPoint.

END | You have completed Project 7F

CONTENT-BASED ASSESSMENTS

In the following Mastering PowerPoint project, you will modify a presentation by adding pie charts and tables highlighting the many job fairs in the state and the local industries that are participating in the Seattle-Tacoma Job Fair. Your completed presentation will look similar to Figure 7.56.

PROJECT FILES

For Project 7G, you will need the following files:

p07G_Fair_Types.pptx
p07G_Industry_Specifics.xlsx

You will save your files as:

Lastname_Firstname_7G_Fair_Types.pptx
Lastname_Firstname_7G_Fair_Types.crtx

PROJECT RESULTS

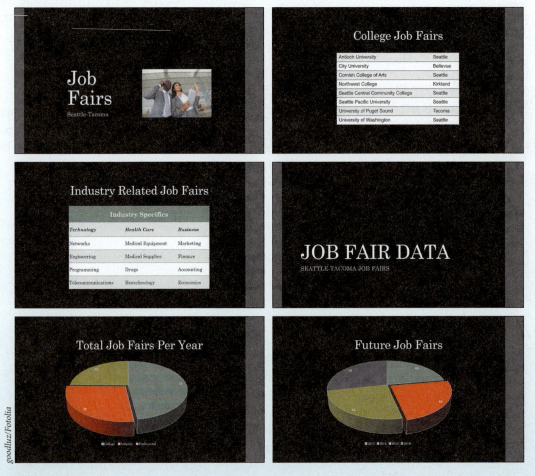

goodluz/Fotolia

FIGURE 7.56

(Project 7G Fair Types continues on the next page)

CONTENT-BASED ASSESSMENTS

1 Start PowerPoint. Locate and open the file **p07G_Fair_Types**. Using your own first and last name, save the file as **Lastname_Firstname_7G_Fair_Types** in your chapter folder.

2 Make **Slide 2** the active slide. Insert a **2×7** table.

3 Insert a new row—**row 8**.

4 Beginning in the first row, type the following data:

Antioch University	Seattle
City University	Bellevue
Cornish College of Arts	Seattle
Northwest College	Kirkland
Seattle Central Community College	Seattle
Seattle Pacific University	Seattle
University of Puget Sound	Tacoma
University of Washington	Seattle

5 In the **Table Styles Options**, clear the **Header Row** check box.

6 Change the **Table Style** to **Medium Style 1**. **AutoFit column 1** and **AutoFit column 2**. With **Lock Aspect Ratio** checked, size the table width to **6.5"**. Move the table down so it is aligned on the **upper half of the vertical ruler at 1.5 inches**. Set the table alignment to **Align Center**.

7 Copy the table in **p07G_Industry_Specifics.xlsx**, and then paste it on **Slide 3**. **Close** Excel and return to PowerPoint.

8 Delete **column 4**. Merge the three cells in **row 1**. **Center** and **Bold** the text *Industry Specifics*.

9 On the **TABLE TOOLS DESIGN tab**, select **Header Row** and **Banded Rows**. Change the **Table Style** to **Medium Style 1 – Accent 1**. **AutoFit column 2** and **AutoFit column 3**.

10 Display the Diagonal Resize pointer, hold down Ctrl, and then resize the table so the top edge aligns on the **upper half of the vertical ruler at 1.5 inches** and the right edge aligns on the **right half of the horizontal ruler at 2.5 inches**.

11 Select the table, and then change the **Font Size** to **18**.

12 Center the text in the table rows vertically. Change the **Font Size** for the Header Row to **24**. Select the second row, and then apply **Bold** and **Italic**. Set the table alignment for **Align Center**.

13 Make **Slide 4** the active slide, and then insert a **3-D Pie** chart. In cell **B1**, type **Seattle Tacoma Area**

14 Beginning in cell **A2**, type the following:

College	35
Industry	20
Professional	18

15 Delete **row 5**, and then **Close** the Excel worksheet.

16 Set the **Data Labels** to display **Inside End**. Select the **18** label on the pie chart, and then add **Bold**. Remove the **Chart Title**. Click outside the chart to see the result.

17 **Explode** the *Industry* slice by approximately **0.25 inch**.

18 Save the Slide 4 chart design as a template in the **Charts** folder, using the name **Lastname_Firstname_7G_Fair_Types**

19 Make **Slide 5** the active slide. Insert a chart using the template you saved. In cell **B1**, type **Total Projection by Year**

20 Beginning in cell **A2**, type the following:

2013	55
2014	60
2015	62
2016	70

21 Delete **column C** and **column D**.

22 **Close** the Excel worksheet.

23 Using **Manage Templates**, cut the chart template, and then paste it into your **Chapter 7** folder.

24 On **Slide 5**, apply the **Wipe** entrance animation effect to display **By Category**, and then set the **Start** to **After Previous**.

25 Add a **Section Header slide** between **Slide 3** and **Slide 4**. Add the title **JOB FAIR DATA** and the subtitle **SEATTLE-TACOMA JOB FAIRS**

26 Add a **Section** between **Slide 3** and **Slide 4** and rename it **Job Fair Data** View the presentation in **Slide Sorter View**, and then return to **Normal View**.

27 View the slide show **From Beginning**.

(Project 7G Fair Types continues on the next page)

CONTENT-BASED ASSESSMENTS

28 Insert a footer on the notes and handouts that includes a fixed date and time, the page number, and the file name.

29 Click the **FILE tab**, and then in the lower right portion of the screen, click **Show All Properties**. In the **Tags** box, type **college, industry, job** and in the **Subject** box type your course name and section number. In the **Author** box, right-click the existing author name, click **Edit Property**, replace the existing text with your first and last name, click outside text box to deselect, and then click **OK**.

30 **Save**. Print **Handouts 6 slides per page**, or submit electronically as directed by your instructor.

END | You have completed Project 7G

CONTENT-BASED ASSESSMENTS

Apply a combination of the **7A** and **7B** skills.

GO! Fix It	Project 7H Job Portfolio	Online
GO! Make It	Project 7I Interview Primer	Online
GO! Solve It	Project 7J Richards Consulting	Online
GO! Solve It	Project 7K Career Development	

Build from
Scratch

PROJECT FILES

For Project 7K, you will need the following files:

New blank PowerPoint presentation
p07K_Values.xlsx

You will save your presentation as:

Lastname_Firstname_7K_Career_Development.pptx

In this project, you will create a presentation to present at the next Greater Seattle Job Fair as part of a Career Development Workshop. The purpose is to highlight the importance of career development whether the job applicant is a recent graduate or a seasoned professional. The presentation is to have an attractive format and an appropriate theme to keep the audience interested.

Create a presentation and save the file as **Lastname_Firstname_7K_Career_Development** with a minimum of six slides, practicing the activities of this chapter by adding tables and pie charts. Insert the table in the Excel file **p07K_Values** into one of the slides. Use data of your choice and create two pie charts. Include coverage on topics such as: workshop goals, breakout sessions, education requirements, available jobs by industry, or others of your choice.

Insert a Header and Footer on the Notes and Handouts that includes fixed date and time, page number, and a footer with the text **Lastname_Firstname_7K_Career_Development** In the Properties, add your name, course name and section information, and the tags **career, education**

Save your presentation. Print Handouts 6 slides per page, or submit electronically as directed by your instructor.

(Project 7K Career Development continues on the next page)

CONTENT-BASED ASSESSMENTS

GO! Solve It Project 7K Career Development (continued)

Performance Level

Performance Elements	Exemplary	Proficient	Developing
Performance Element	You consistently applied the relevant skills. (5 points)	You sometimes, but not always, applied the relevant skills. (3 points)	You rarely or never applied the relevant skills. (0 or 1 point)
Formatted tables	Tables are accurate and professionally formatted. Inserted Excel table content onto one of the slides.	Tables need to have more formatting.	Tables are not completed.
Inserted two pie charts	Pie charts are completed, and data given are correct. Chart is easy to read, and all sections show.	Pie charts are present, but information is not accurate or difficult to read.	Pie charts are incomplete, and the data are inaccurate.
Maintained a professional appearance	Presentation is free from spelling and grammar errors, and contains appropriate amount of text per slide.	Few spelling and grammar errors, and appropriate amount of information per slide.	Spelling and grammar errors exist, and too much information is on each slide.
Added required elements	Notes and Handouts footer and Properties are completed correctly.	Completed all required items but one.	Failed to complete two or more required items correctly.

END | You have completed Project 7K

OUTCOMES-BASED ASSESSMENTS

RUBRIC

The following outcomes-based assessments are *open-ended assessments*. That is, there is no specific correct result; your result will depend on your approach to the information provided. Make *Professional Quality* your goal. Use the following scoring rubric to guide you in *how* to approach the problem and then to evaluate *how well* your approach solves the problem.

The *criteria*—Software Mastery, Content, Format and Layout, and Process—represent the knowledge and skills you have gained that you can apply to solving the problem. The *levels of performance*—Professional Quality, Approaching Professional Quality, or Needs Quality Improvements—help you and your instructor evaluate your result.

	Your completed project is of Professional Quality if you:	Your completed project is Approaching Professional Quality if you:	Your completed project Needs Quality Improvements if you:
1-Software Mastery	Choose and apply the most appropriate skills, tools, and features and identify efficient methods to solve the problem.	Choose and apply some appropriate skills, tools, and features, but not in the most efficient manner.	Choose inappropriate skills, tools, or features, or are inefficient in solving the problem.
2-Content	Construct a solution that is clear and well organized, contains content that is accurate, appropriate to the audience and purpose, and is complete. Provide a solution that contains no errors in spelling, grammar, or style.	Construct a solution in which some components are unclear, poorly organized, inconsistent, or incomplete. Misjudge the needs of the audience. Have some errors in spelling, grammar, or style, but the errors do not detract from comprehension.	Construct a solution that is unclear, incomplete, or poorly organized; contains some inaccurate or inappropriate content; and contains many errors in spelling, grammar, or style. Do not solve the problem.
3-Format & Layout	Format and arrange all elements to communicate information and ideas, clarify function, illustrate relationships, and indicate relative importance.	Apply appropriate format and layout features to some elements, but not others. Overuse features, causing minor distraction.	Apply format and layout that does not communicate information or ideas clearly. Do not use format and layout features to clarify function, illustrate relationships, or indicate relative importance. Use available features excessively, causing distraction.
4-Process	Use an organized approach that integrates planning, development, self-assessment, revision, and reflection.	Demonstrate an organized approach in some areas, but not others; or, use an insufficient process of organization throughout.	Do not use an organized approach to solve the problem.

OUTCOMES-BASED ASSESSMENTS

Apply a combination of the 7A and 7B skills.

Build from Scratch

| GO! Think | Project 7L Advertising Strategy |

PROJECT FILES

For Project 7L, you will need the following files:

New blank PowerPoint presentation
p07L_Recommendations.xlsx

You will save your files as:

Lastname_Firstname_7L_Advertising_Strategy.pptx
Lastname_Firstname_7L_Advertising_Strategy.crtx

In this project, you will create a presentation of at least four slides that details the new advertising campaign being developed by the Seattle-Tacoma Job Fair organization to reach a wider audience for the upcoming job fairs. Items you should bring into your presentation include identifying the specific audience and determining where to advertise.

Create a table with popular job categories that includes seven areas such as government, retail, healthcare, and information technology. Insert the Excel file **p07L_Recommendation.xlsx**, which lists various promotional media recommendations from advertising agencies, as a table. Select an attractive theme, and then format the slides appropriately. Create a slide with a pie chart, and then save it as a template with file name **Lastname_Firstname_7L_Advertising_Strategy.crtx** and move the template file to your student folder. Use this template to insert another pie chart on a new slide. Change the pie chart to view in grayscale and then change it back to view in color.

Update the Notes and Handouts footer with the new file name and the author name in the Properties. Save the presentation. Print or submit electronically as directed by your instructor.

END | You have completed Project 7L

Build from Scratch

| GO! Think | Project 7M Security Jobs | Online |

| You and GO! | Project 7N IT Salaries | Online |

Build from Scratch

Presentations Using Tables and Publishing Presentations

GO! to Work
Video P8

PROJECT 8A

OUTCOMES
Draw tables, modify a table using draw features, create and modify a text box.

OBJECTIVES

1. Draw Tables
2. Modify a Table Using the Draw Borders Features
3. Modify a Text Box

PROJECT 8B

OUTCOMES
Insert outline text, create a video, and copy the presentation to a CD, DVD, network, or local drive and save a presentation in other formats.

OBJECTIVES

4. Insert Outline Text from Another Program into a PowerPoint Presentation
5. Save a Presentation in Other Formats
6. Create a Video
7. Copy a Presentation to a CD, DVD, Network, or Local Drive

Riccardo Piccinini/Fotolia

In This Chapter

PowerPoint provides different ways to add a table to a presentation. With the Draw Table feature, you can use the Draw pointer to draw the table shape directly on the slide. In this chapter, you also will create and modify a text box.

You have the option of creating a video of your presentation that can be used to include on a website or send as an email attachment. You will save a presentation in other formats—Picture, Show, and Outline. Another feature of PowerPoint is the Package for CD feature, which enables you to copy a presentation along with linked files to a CD, a network drive, a local drive, or a flash drive.

Laurel County Community College (LCCC) is located in eastern Pennsylvania and serves urban, suburban, and rural populations. The college offers this diverse area a broad range of academic and vocational programs, including associate degrees, certificate programs, and noncredit continuing education and personal development courses. LCCC makes positive contributions to the community through cultural and athletic programs and partnerships with businesses and nonprofit organizations. The college also provides industry-specific training programs for local businesses through its Workforce and Economic Development Center.

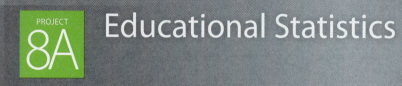

MyITLab®
Project 8A Training

PROJECT ACTIVITIES

In Activities 8.01 through 8.11, you will create and modify tables and modify and format text boxes in a PowerPoint presentation that will be used by the administration to present enrollment statistics for Laurel County Community College. Your completed presentation will look similar to Figure 8.1.

PROJECT FILES

For Project 8A, you will need the following files:

p08A_Educational_Statistics.pptx
p08A_Money.jpg

You will save your presentation as:

Lastname_Firstname_8A_Educational_Statistics.pptx

PROJECT RESULTS

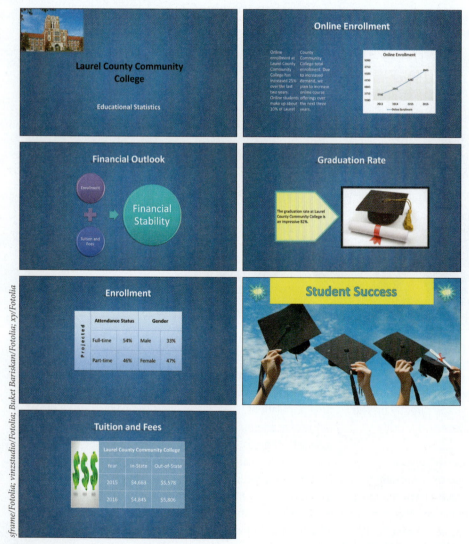

sframe/Fotolia; vinzstudio/Fotolia; Buket Bariskan/Fotolia; xy/Fotolia

FIGURE 8.1

Objective 1 Draw Tables

In the following activities, you will use the Draw Tool and the Table Tools contextual tab to create and modify tables in a PowerPoint presentation. Recall that you have already created tables using the Insert table feature.

Video P8-1

Activity 8.01 | Creating Tables Using the Draw Tool

In this activity, you will use the *Draw pointer* to create a table in PowerPoint and enter data in the cells. The Draw pointer is a pen-shaped pointer that is used to create table borders. This method is an alternate way to create a table that you may prefer to use.

1 Start PowerPoint. Locate and open the file **p08A_Educational_Statistics**. In the location where you are saving your work, create a new folder named **PowerPoint Chapter 8**, and then save the file as **Lastname_Firstname_8A_Educational_Statistics**

2 Make **Slide 2** the active slide. On the **INSERT tab**, in the **Illustrations group**, click **SmartArt**. If an error message displays, click **OK**.

3 In the **Choose a SmartArt Graphic** dialog box, at the left, click **Relationship**. Scroll to the sixth row, and then click **Vertical Equation**. Compare your screen with Figure 8.2.

Three shapes are displayed—two smaller ovals on the left and one larger one at the right. The purpose of this slide is to serve as an introduction to the next slides that you will create.

FIGURE 8.2

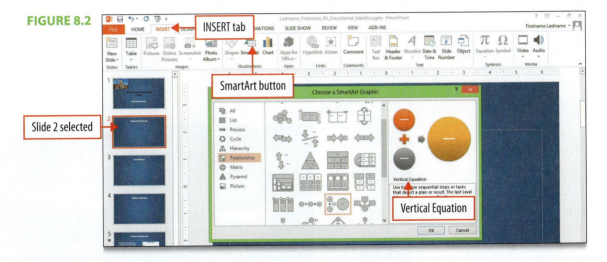

4 Click **OK**. In the top circle at the left, type **Enrollment** In the lower left circle, type **Tuition and Fees** In the larger circle on the right, type **Financial Stability**

More Knowledge	Move Text within SmartArt Shapes and Reverse Order

You can change the position of text within SmartArt using features on the HOME tab in the Paragraph group. The features include Align Text—Top, Middle, Bottom; Text Direction—Horizontal, Rotate all text 90°, Rotate all text 270°, Stacked; Align—Left, Right, Center, Justify; and Line Spacing—1.0, 1.5, 2.0, 2.5, 3.0. You can reverse the order of the SmartArt graphic using features on the SMARTART TOOLS DESIGN tab, in the Create Graphic group. The features include Promote, Demote, Right to Left, Left to Right, Move Up, and Move Down.

---

5 Under **SMARTART TOOLS**, on the **DESIGN tab**, in the **SmartArt Styles group**, click **Change Colors**. Under **Colorful**, click the fourth pattern—**Colorful Range – Accent Colors 4 to 5**. In the **SmartArt Styles group**, click **More** ⬇. Under **3-D**, in the first row, click the second pattern—**Inset**.

6 Click outside the SmartArt, and then compare your screen with Figure 8.3.

FIGURE 8.3

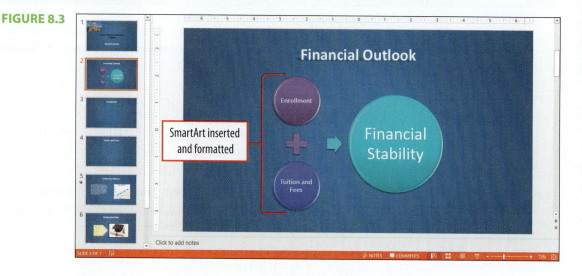

7 On the **VIEW tab**, in the **Show group**, select the **Ruler** check box, if necessary, to display the horizontal and vertical rulers.

8 Make **Slide 3** the active slide. On the **INSERT tab**, in the **Tables group**, click **Table**, and then click **Draw Table**. Move the mouse pointer to the content placeholder. Do not click the placeholder. Compare your screen with Figure 8.4.

The pointer changes to a pen shape.

FIGURE 8.4

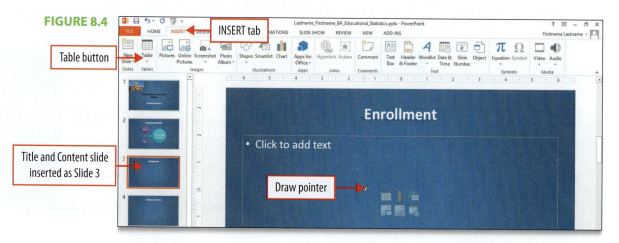

9 Position the Draw pointer ✎ on the **left half of the horizontal ruler at 4 inches** and on the **upper half of the vertical ruler at 1 inch**. Drag the pointer to **4 inches on the right half of the horizontal ruler** and **2 inches on the lower half of the vertical ruler**. Release the mouse. Compare your screen with Figure 8.5.

A table with one cell is displayed on the slide. The TABLE TOOLS tab becomes active. Under TABLE TOOLS, the DESIGN and LAYOUT tabs are displayed. The DESIGN tab is active. The Draw pointer returns to a Text Select pointer ⌶ inside the table. When you draw the table, the width of the table is displayed on the ruler in white. The numbers on the ruler change to display the width of the table.

FIGURE 8.5

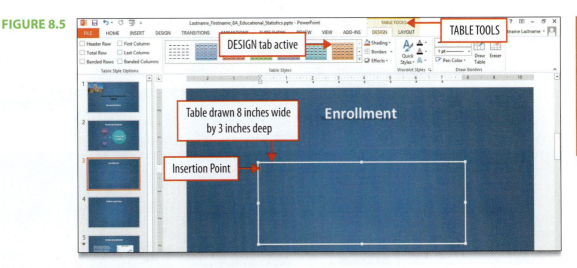

Figure labels: TABLE TOOLS · DESIGN tab active · TABLE TOOLS · Table drawn 8 inches wide by 3 inches deep · Insertion Point · Enrollment

---

ALERT! Do You Want to Draw Your Table Again?

If you had trouble drawing your table, click Undo 🔄 to remove the table. On the INSERT tab, in the Tables group, click Table, and then click Draw Table to activate the Draw pointer. Draw the table again.

---

10 ▶ On the **VIEW tab**, in the **Show group**, select the **Gridlines** check box to display the gridlines.

The gridlines are dotted lines that can help you draw cell borders within the table. These lines do not print.

11 ▶ Under **TABLE TOOLS**, on the **DESIGN tab**, in the **Draw Borders group**, click **Draw Table** to display the Draw pointer ✏️.

12 ▶ In the table, position the Draw pointer ✏️ a little below the top border of the table, on the vertical gridline that aligns **on the horizontal ruler** a little to the left of **2 inches**. Using the gridlines as your guide, click and drag the Draw pointer ✏️ down to create a column. If you need to draw the border again, click Undo 🔄, and try again.

You had to draw only a short distance to create the column border. The Draw pointer had to be a little below the top of the table border. The Draw Table button is active.

ALERT! Did You Draw Another Table instead of a Border?

If you start drawing a border too close to the outside border of a table, you might draw another table. If you do, click Undo, and try again.

---

13 ▶ In the table, position the Draw pointer ✏️ on the vertical gridline that aligns **on the horizontal ruler** a little to the left of **4 inches**. Using the gridlines as a guide, click and drag the Draw pointer ✏️ down to create another column border. Following the same procedure, draw another column border **2 inches to the right**. The columns do not have to be even.

The table is divided into four columns. The insertion point is in the third column. When you click in each of the columns, the width of the column is displayed on the ruler in white. The numbers on the ruler change.

14 ▶ In the table, using the gridlines as a guide, position the Draw pointer a little inside the table border on the **lower half of the vertical ruler at 1 inch**, and then click and drag to the right border of the table to create the row border. In the table, draw another row border on the **lower half of the vertical ruler at 2 inches**. Press [Esc] to turn off the Draw pointer. Compare your screen with Figure 8.6.

A table of four columns and three rows is displayed. You will adjust the sizes later.

FIGURE 8.6

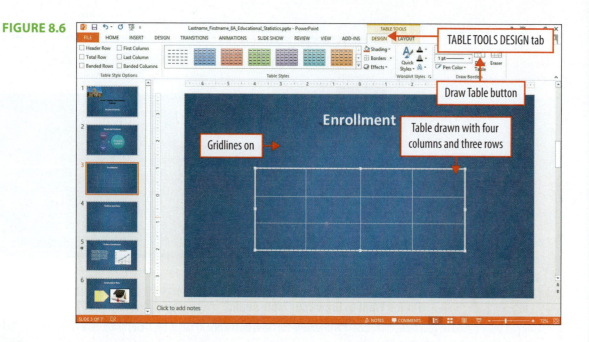

TABLE TOOLS DESIGN tab

Draw Table button

Gridlines on

Table drawn with four columns and three rows

NOTE   Turning the Draw Pointer On or Off

To draw the initial table, on the INSERT tab, in the Tables group, click Table, and then select Draw Table to make the Draw pointer active. It is also turned on when you select a pen style, weight, or color. When you click inside the table, the TABLE TOOLS contextual DESIGN and LAYOUT tabs are active. On the DESIGN tab, in the Draw Borders group, click Draw Table to turn the Draw pointer on or off. Or, to turn off the Draw pointer, press ⎋ Esc.

15 ▶ On the **VIEW tab**, in the **Show group**, click the **Gridlines** check box to remove the check mark.

The gridlines do not display. The gridlines provide assistance in positioning the borders, but it is not necessary to have them on.

16 ▶ Type the following information in the corresponding cells, pressing ⎯Tab⎯ or ⟶ after each entry except the last entry:

Attendance Status		Gender	
Full-time	54%	Male	53%
Part-time	46%	Female	47%

17 ▶ Click outside the table to deselect the table. Compare your screen with Figure 8.7.

FIGURE 8.7

18 ▶ Save 💾 your changes.

More Knowledge | **Changing the Pen Style, Weight, and Color**

Under TABLE TOOLS, on the DESIGN tab, in the Draw Borders group, you can change the pen style, the weight in points, and the color before drawing your borders.

Activity 8.02 | Merging Table Cells Using TABLE TOOLS

In this activity, you will merge cells in a table.

1 On **Slide 3**, click in the cell for *Attendance Status*, and then drag to the right to select the next cell. Under **TABLE TOOLS**, on the **LAYOUT tab**, in the **Merge group**, click **Merge Cells**.

2 Click in the cell for *Gender*, drag to the right to select the next cell, and then click **Merge Cells**. Compare your screen with Figure 8.8.

FIGURE 8.8

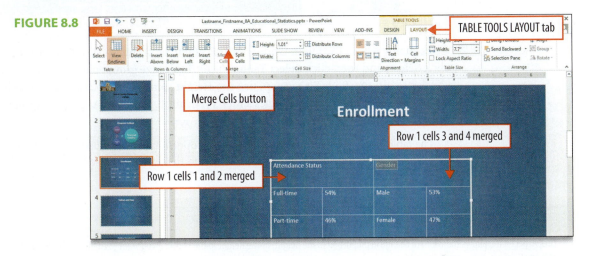

3 **Save** your changes.

Activity 8.03 | Adjusting Column Widths and Table Size

In this activity, you will change column widths by using the options on the LAYOUT tab. You will also change the size of the entire table.

1 Make **Slide 3** the active slide, if necessary. In the second row, click in the cell for *Full-time*. Under **TABLE TOOLS**, on the **LAYOUT tab**, in the **Cell Size group**, use the **Table Column Width button spin arrows** to change the width to **2"**. Repeat this procedure to change the width of the second column to **1.5"**, the third column to **1.5"**, and the last column to **1.5"**. Compare your screen with Figure 8.9.

The columns are resized.

FIGURE 8.9

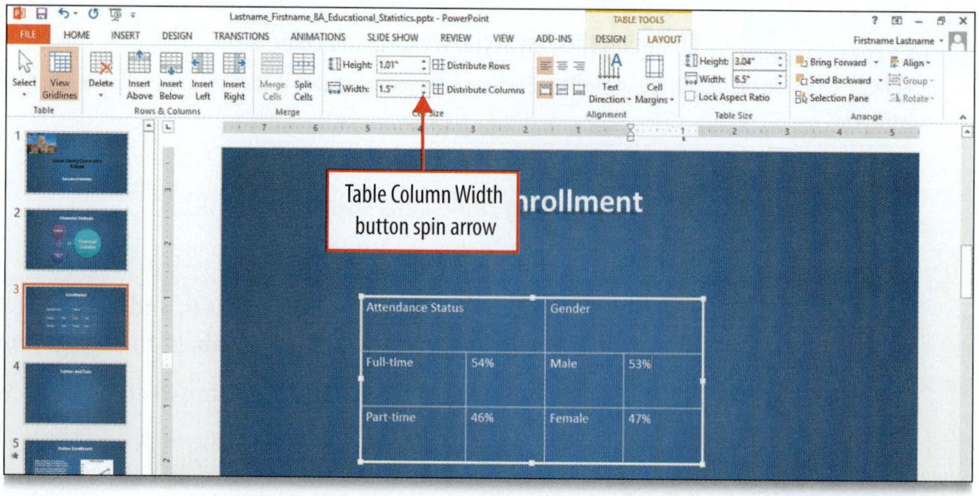

2 ▶ Click in any cell in the table. Under **TABLE TOOLS**, on the **LAYOUT tab**, in the **Table group**, click **Select**, and then click **Select Table**. In the **Table Size group**, click the **Lock Aspect Ratio** check box. In the **Table Size group**, use the **Height spin arrows** to change the table height to **3.5"**. In the **Alignment group**, click **Center Vertically** ⊟. In the **Alignment group**, click **Cell Margins**, and then select **Wide**.

> The table rows and columns are sized larger proportionately. The text in all cells is centered vertically. The space between the cell border and the text is increased, which is noticeable in cells that are aligned at the left.

N O T E   **Using Lock Aspect Ratio**

Lock Aspect Ratio allows the width to change in proportion to the height, or the height to the width. If you want to change only the width or only the height of a table, do not click Lock Aspect Ratio.

---

3 ▶ Click in the cell for *Attendance Status*. Under **TABLE TOOLS**, on the **LAYOUT tab**, in the **Table group**, click **Select**, and then click **Select Row**. On the **HOME tab**, in the **Font group**, click **Bold** ⓑ. In the **Paragraph group**, click **Center** ≡.

4 ▶ Click in the cell for *54%*, and then click **Center** ≡. Using the same procedure, center the three cells containing *46%, 53%,* and *47%*. Under **TABLE TOOLS**, click the **LAYOUT tab**, and then compare your screen with Figure 8.10.

> Row 1 is formatted with bold, and the text is centered horizontally. The cells containing percentages are all centered horizontally.

FIGURE 8.10

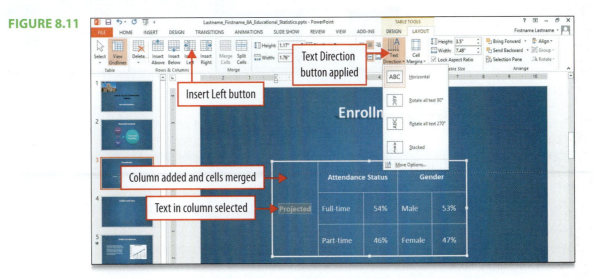

5 Save your changes.

Activity 8.04 | Changing Text Direction

In this activity, you will insert a column, merge the cells, enter text, and then format and change the direction of the text.

1 Click in the cell for *Attendance Status*. Under **TABLE TOOLS**, on the **LAYOUT tab**, in the **Rows & Columns group**, click **Insert Left** to insert a new column. In the **Merge group**, click **Merge Cells**.

The cells in column 1 are merged.

2 In the new column, type **Projected** Double-click to select *Projected*. On the **LAYOUT tab**, in the **Alignment group**, click **Text Direction**. Compare your screen with Figure 8.11.

FIGURE 8.11

3 Click **Rotate all text 270°**. With the text still selected, on the **HOME tab**, in the **Font group**, click **Character Spacing** [AV▾], and then click **Very Loose**. Under **TABLE TOOLS**, on the **LAYOUT tab**, in the **Cell Size group**, click the **Table Column Width spin arrow** 🖼 to **1"**.

The column width is reduced, and the text is rotated 270° and displayed with very loose character spacing.

4 Click the cell for *Full-time*. In the **Cell Size group**, click the **Table Column Width spin arrow** 🖼 to **1.6"**.

The column with *Full-time* and *Part-time* is resized. You might find it easier to make final column size adjustments after adding a column.

5 Click in the cell for *Attendance Status*. Under **TABLE TOOLS**, on the **LAYOUT tab**, in the **Arrange group**, click **Align** 🖼, and then select **Align Center**. Click **Align** again, and select **Align Middle**.

6 Under **TABLE TOOLS**, on the **DESIGN tab**, in the **Table Styles group**, click **More** ⮟. Under **Best Match for Document**, in the first row, click the second pattern—**Themed Style 1 – Accent 1**.

7 Click in the cell for *Attendance Status*, if necessary. Under **TABLE TOOLS**, on the **LAYOUT tab**, in the **Table group**, click **Select**, and then click **Select Row**. Press Ctrl + B to add bold. Click outside the table, and then compare your screen with Figure 8.12.

When you applied the theme, the bold was removed. Because the first column is one merged cell, the entire column was included when you selected the first row.

FIGURE 8.12

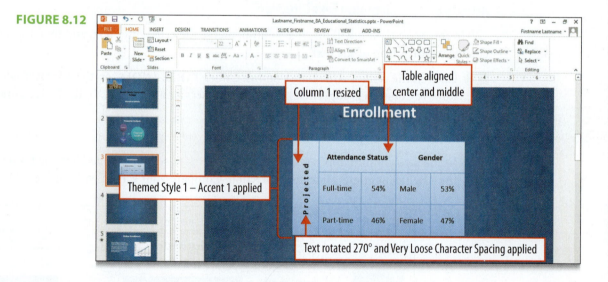

8 Save 🖫 your changes.

Objective 2 | Modify a Table Using the Draw Borders Features

Video P8-2

In the following activities, you will draw and format a table on a title only slide. You will use Draw Table to create new cells and the Eraser to remove and merge cells. You will also fill a cell with a picture.

Activity 8.05 | Inserting a Table on a Title Only Slide

1 Make **Slide 4** the active slide. Notice that this is a Title Only slide.

The Title Only slide Layout does not have a content placeholder. If you do not intend to enter any bulleted items, you can use this Layout for a table.

2 On the **INSERT tab**, in the **Tables group**, click **Table**, and then click **Draw Table**. Position the Draw pointer on the **left half of the horizontal ruler at 3 inches** and on the **upper half of the vertical ruler at 1 inch**. Drag the pointer to **3 inches on the right half of the horizontal ruler** and then **2 inches on the lower half of the vertical ruler**. Release the mouse. Compare your screen with Figure 8.13.

FIGURE 8.13

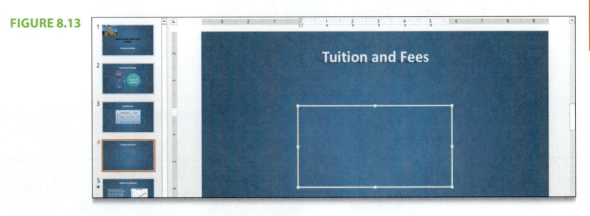

3 **Save** your changes.

Activity 8.06 | Applying Borders to a Table Using the Draw Table Feature

1 On the **VIEW tab**, in the **Show group**, click the **Gridlines** check box to display the gridlines.

2 Click inside the table. Under **TABLE TOOLS**, on the **DESIGN tab**, in the **Draw Borders group**, click **Draw Table**. In the table, position the Draw pointer on the **horizontal ruler at 2 inches**. Using the gridlines as your guide, click and drag the pointer down to create a column. If you need to draw the border again, click Undo , and then try again.

3 In the table, position the Draw pointer on the **horizontal ruler at 4 inches**, and then draw another column border.

4 In the table, position the Draw pointer on the **vertical ruler at 1 inch**, and then click and drag to the right border of the table to create a row border. In the table, draw another row border on the **lower half of the vertical ruler at 2 inches**. Press Esc to turn off the Draw pointer. Click outside the table, and then compare your screen with Figure 8.14.

A table with three columns and three rows is displayed.

FIGURE 8.14

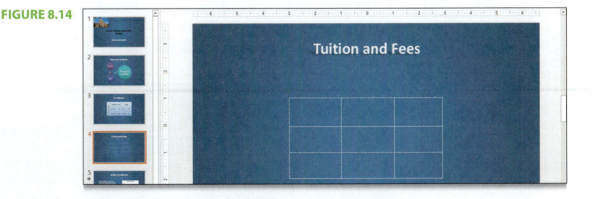

5 On the **VIEW tab**, in the **Show group**, click the **Gridlines** check box to remove the gridlines.

6 Type the following information in the corresponding cells, pressing [Tab] or → after each entry except the last entry:

Year	In-State	Out-of-State
2015	$4,663	$5,578
2016	$4,845	$5,806

7 Compare your screen with Figure 8.15.

FIGURE 8.15

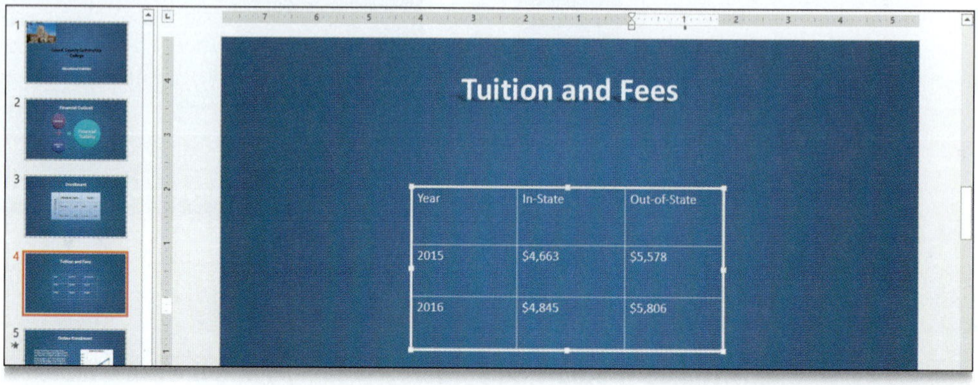

FIGURE 8.15

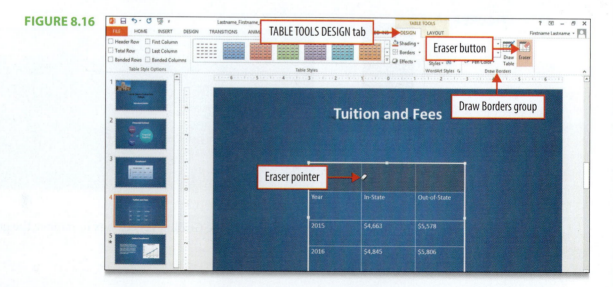

8 Save 🖫 your changes.

Activity 8.07 | Merging Cells Using the Eraser

In this activity, you will use the Eraser pointer to remove borders in a table in order to merge cells. The *Eraser* is a pointer that looks like an eraser.

1 Click in the cell containing *Year*. Under **TABLE TOOLS**, on the **LAYOUT tab**, in the **Rows & Columns group**, click **Insert Above** to insert a new row.

A new row with three cells is added.

2 Under **TABLE TOOLS**, on the **DESIGN tab**, in the **Draw Borders group**, click **Eraser**. With the Eraser pointer 🖉, point to the first vertical border in the new row, and then compare your screen with Figure 8.16.

FIGURE 8.16

3 In **row 1**, click the first border to remove it. In **row 1**, click the second border to remove it. In the **Draw Borders group**, click **Eraser** to turn off the **Eraser**. Type **Laurel County Community College**

↻ **ANOTHER WAY**   You can turn off the Eraser pointer by pressing [Esc].

The cells in row 1 are merged into one cell, and text has been added.

4 Under **TABLE TOOLS**, on the **LAYOUT tab**, in the **Table group**, click **Select**, and then click **Select Table**. In the **Alignment group**, click **Center Vertically** and **Center**. Compare your screen with Figure 8.17.

Because you selected the table, all cell text is centered vertically and horizontally.

FIGURE 8.17

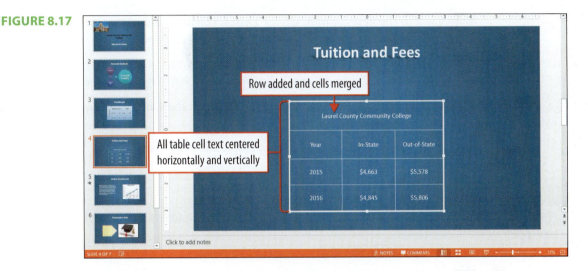

5 On the **HOME tab**, in the **Font group**, change the **Font size** to **24**. Under **TABLE TOOLS**, on the **LAYOUT tab**, in the **Table Size group**, remove the check mark in the **Lock Aspect Ratio** check box, and then change the **Width** to **6.5"**. Compare your screen with Figure 8.18.

Only the width of the table increased. The height did not change.

FIGURE 8.18

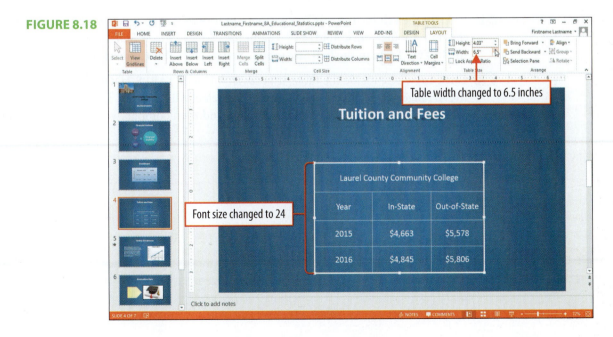

N O T E   Selecting a Table

To select a table, you can click on a border of the table. However, you might find it easier to use Select Table, which is located under TABLE TOOLS on the LAYOUT tab, in the Table group.

6 Save 🖫 your changes.

Activity 8.08 │ Filling a Cell with a Picture

1 Click in the cell that contains *Year*. Under **TABLE TOOLS**, on the **LAYOUT tab**, in the **Rows & Columns group**, click **Insert Left**. Under **TABLE TOOLS**, on the **DESIGN tab**, in the **Draw Borders group**, click **Eraser**. Click the three borders inside the new column to merge the cells. Press Esc to turn off the **Eraser**.

2 Click in the new column. Under **TABLE TOOLS**, on the **DESIGN tab**, in the **Table Styles group**, click the **Shading button arrow** 🖾, and then click **Picture**. Navigate to your data files, click **p08A_Money.jpg**, and then click **Insert**.

> The image fills the cell. It will display proportional to the size of the cell.

3 Under **TABLE TOOLS**, on the **LAYOUT tab**, in the **Cell Size group**, click the **Table Column Width spin arrow** 🖽 to **1.7"**.

> The column is wider to adjust the proportion of the picture.

N O T E   Sizing a Picture in a Cell

The size of a cell determines the size of a picture that you insert into the cell. To avoid unwanted distortion of a picture, increase the size of the cell or column until you are satisfied with the result.

4 Under **TABLE TOOLS**, on the **DESIGN tab**, in the **Table Styles group**, click the **Shading button arrow**, and then click **Table Background**. Under **Theme Colors**, in the fifth column, the fourth row, click **Blue, Accent 1, Lighter 40%**.

> The background of all cells is lighter. You changed the table background instead of using a Table Style so the picture will be visible.

5 Click in the cell for *Laurel County Community College*. Drag to select the text, and then on the mini toolbar, click **Bold** ❘**B**❘. Click in the cell for *Out-of-State*. Under **TABLE TOOLS**, on the **LAYOUT tab**, in the **Cell Size group**, change the **Table Column Width** to **2"**.

6 Click anywhere inside the table, if necessary. Under **TABLE TOOLS**, on the **LAYOUT tab**, in the **Arrange group**, click **Align** 🖼, and then select **Align Center**. Click **Align** again, and then select **Align Middle**. Click outside the table, and then compare your screen with Figure 8.19.

FIGURE 8.19

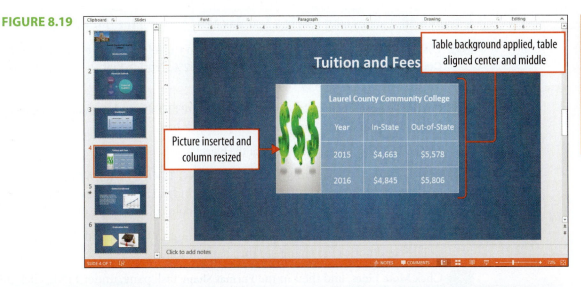

Picture inserted and column resized

Table background applied, table aligned center and middle

Objective 3 | Modify a Text Box

Video P8-3

Activity 8.09 | Adding Columns to a Presentation and Setting Internal Margins

In this activity, you will add columns to a presentation and set internal margins in a *text box*—a drawn object which is used to position text anywhere on a slide.

1 ▶ Display **Slide 5**, and then right-click the placeholder containing text on the left side of the slide. On the shortcut menu, click **Format Shape**.

2 ▶ In the **Format Shape** task pane, at the top, click **TEXT OPTIONS**, and then click **Textbox** 🔲. Click the **Columns** button. In the **Columns** dialog box, replace the value in the **Number** box with **2**, and then click **OK**.

The text in the text box displays in two columns.

3 ▶ In the **Format Shape** task pane, under **TEXT BOX**, change the **Left margin** and **Right margin** values to **0.4** Notice that there is additional spacing between the dashed border of the text box and the text. Compare your screen with Figure 8.20.

You can change internal margins to modify the space between the text and the text box border.

FIGURE 8.20

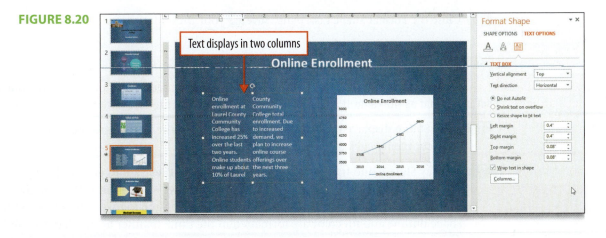

Text displays in two columns

4 ▶ **Save** 💾 the presentation.

Activity 8.10 | Wrapping Text in a Text Box and Changing the Outline Style

1 Display **Slide 6**, and then click in the shape on the left. Type **The graduation rate at Laurel County Community College is an impressive 82%.** Notice that the text in the shape extends outside the boundaries of the shape.

2 On the **Format Shape** task pane, click **TEXT OPTIONS**, and then click **Textbox** 🄰. Under **TEXT BOX**, select the **Wrap text in shape** check box.

The text is wrapped to the shape of the object.

3 With the shape still selected, on the **DRAWING TOOLS FORMAT tab**, in the **Shape Styles group**, click the **Shape Outline button arrow**. Under **Theme Colors**, in the ninth column, click the first color—**Aqua, Accent 5** to change the color of the shape outline.

4 Click the **Shape Outline button arrow** again, point to **Weight**, and then point to each of the line weights and notice the change to the shape outline.

5 Click **More Lines**, and then in the **Format Shape** task pane, under **LINE**, click the **Compound type arrow**. Click the last style—**Triple**. Select the value in the **Width** box, type **10** and then press Enter. Compare your screen with Figure 8.21.

The outline style of the shape is changed. Use this technique to change the outline style of a text box, shape, or picture.

FIGURE 8.21

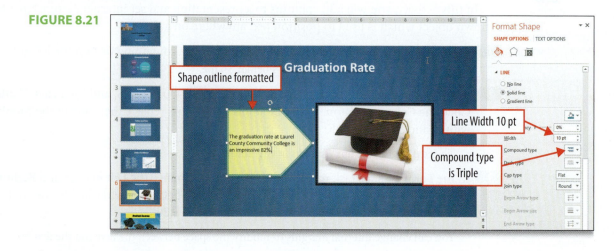

6 **Close** the **Format Shape** task pane. **Save** 🖫 your presentation.

Activity 8.11 | Setting Shape Default Formatting

If you plan to apply the same formatting to several shapes, you can format the first shape and set its format as the default so that new shapes you insert are formatted in the same manner.

1 With **Slide 6** displayed, point to the outside edge of the shape, and then right-click. On the shortcut menu, click **Set as Default Shape**.

2 Display **Slide 7**, and then on the **INSERT tab**, in the **Illustrations group**, click the **Shapes** button. Under **Stars and Banners**, click the first shape—**Explosion 1**. Position the pointer near the upper left corner of the slide, and then click one time to insert the shape. Notice that the shape outline and fill color are formatted in the same manner as the shape on **Slide 6**.

3 With the shape selected, press Ctrl + **D** to make a duplicate of the shape. Drag the new shape to the upper right corner of the slide. Click outside the shape to deselect. Compare your screen with Figure 8.22.

FIGURE 8.22

Shape inserted

Shape inserted

4 ▶ On the **SLIDE SHOW tab**, in the **Start Slide Show group**, view your presentation **From Beginning**.

5 ▶ **Save** 🖫 your presentation.

6 ▶ On the **INSERT tab**, in the **Text group**, click **Header & Footer** to display the **Header and Footer** dialog box. Click the **Notes and Handouts tab**. Under **Include on page**, select the **Date and time** check box, and then select **Fixed**. If necessary, clear the **Header** check box, and then select the **Page number** and **Footer** check boxes. In the **Footer** box, using your own name, type **Lastname_Firstname_8A_Educational_Statistics** and then click **Apply to All**.

7 ▶ Click the **FILE tab**, and then in the lower right portion of the screen, click **Show All Properties**. In the **Tags** box, type **education, statistics** and in the **Subject** box type your course name and section number. In the **Author** box, right-click the existing author name, click **Edit Property**, replace the existing text with your first and last name, click outside text box to deselect, and then click **OK**.

8 ▶ **Save** 🖫 your changes.

9 ▶ **Close** your presentation, and then **Exit** PowerPoint. Submit your work as directed.

END | You have completed Project 8A

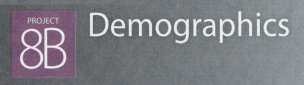

MyITLab®
Project 8B Training

PROJECT ACTIVITIES

In Activities 8.12 through 8.17, you will insert slides from an outline created in Word, and then create a video file of the presentation. You will also distribute the presentation using the Package Presentation for CD feature. You will save a Slide as a Picture, Save the Presentation as Show, and Save a Presentation as an Outline. Your completed results will look similar to Figure 8.23.

PROJECT FILES

For Project 8B, you will need the following files:

p08B_Demographics.pptx
p08B_Educational_Importance.docx
p08B_Workforce_Value.doc

You will save your files as:

Lastname_Firstname_8B_Demographics.pptx
Lastname_Firstname_8B_Outline.rtf
Lastname_Firstname_8B_Show.ppsx
Lastname_Firstname_8B_Video.mp4
Lastname_Firstname_8B_Picture.jpg
FML_Demographics (folder)

PROJECT RESULTS

FIGURE 8.23 Project 8B Demographics

Video P8-4

If content has been created in a program other than PowerPoint, it is often possible to bring that content into PowerPoint instead of retyping all of the information. For example, you can create slides in a PowerPoint presentation based on an outline created in Microsoft Word.

If a program supports the use of heading styles, the outline can be inserted into Microsoft PowerPoint. A *heading style* is a set of formatting characteristics, such as font name, size, color, paragraph alignment, and spacing, that is saved and used to quickly format selected text. An outline from a Microsoft Word document (.docx or .doc), text file (.txt), or *Rich Text Format (RTF) file* can be used to create slides. A text file may be one created with a program like Notepad. A Rich Text Format file is a non-application-specific file format used to transfer formatted text documents between applications. The RTF format enables the transfer of documents between different platforms, such as Microsoft Windows computers and Apple computers. The extension for files saved in RTF format is *.rtf*. A *platform* is the combination of hardware and software used on a computer.

If the source file—the document from which the outline is obtained—contains no heading styles, such as a plain text file, PowerPoint will create an outline based on *paragraphs*. In this case, a paragraph is any text that has a *hard return* after it. A hard return is created by pressing the Enter key to start a new line. PowerPoint will also treat each item in a bulleted or numbered list, a title, and a subtitle as a paragraph. Each Level 1 paragraph is treated as a title on a separate slide when the file is inserted into PowerPoint.

Activity 8.12 | Inserting Outline Text from Another Program into a PowerPoint Presentation

In this activity, you will create Title and Content slides by inserting an outline created in Microsoft Word.

1 Start PowerPoint. Locate and open the file **p08B_Demographics**. Navigate to the **PowerPoint Chapter 8** folder you created, and then save the file as **Lastname_Firstname_8B_Demographics** Click **Minimize** ─.

You have reduced PowerPoint to an icon displaying on the taskbar.

2 Press ⊞ to display the **Start** screen, and then locate and start **Microsoft Word**. Navigate to the location where your student files are stored, and then locate and open the file **p08B_Educational_Importance.docx**.

3 On the **VIEW tab**, in the **Show group**, select the **Navigation Pane** check box, if necessary. In the **Views group**, click **Outline**. In the **navigation pane**, click the **HEADINGS tab**, if necessary, and then compare your screen with Figure 8.24.

This document is an outline created with Word 2013. Notice that Word is in *Outline view* with a Navigation bar at the left. Outline view is a document view in Microsoft Word that distinguishes the importance of data by the heading styles that have been applied. For example, text formatted with a Heading 1 style is displayed at the left margin, is identified as Level 1, and becomes the title of a slide. Text formatted with a Heading 2 style is indented and identified as Level 2. Text formatted with a Heading 3 style is further indented and identified as Level 3. Levels 2 and 3 will be displayed in the content placeholder as different levels of bulleted items. Outline view uses formatting to convey hierarchy and offers a clear way to view data. It is similar to the way the Outline tab in the PowerPoint Outline pane displays the hierarchy of the various levels of content. The navigation pane helps you see the levels better.

FIGURE 8.24

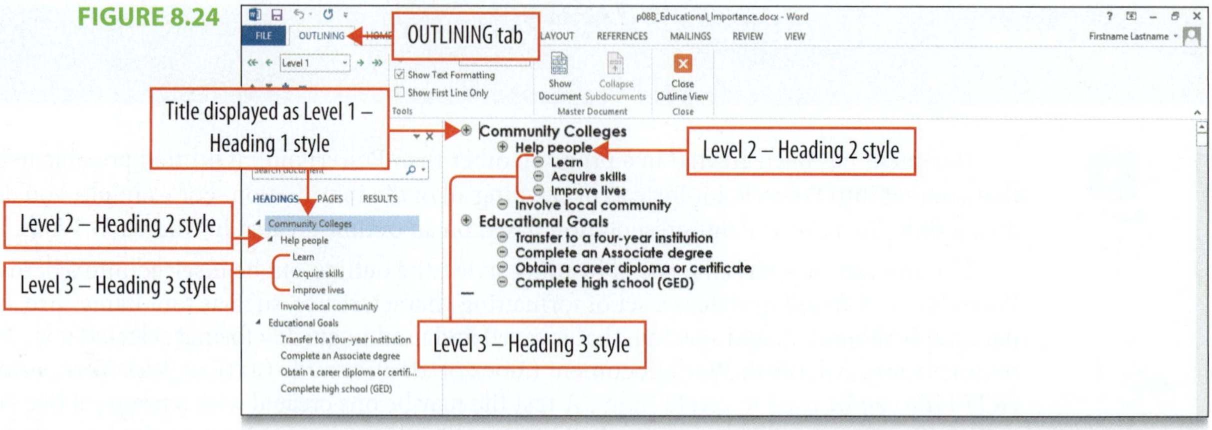

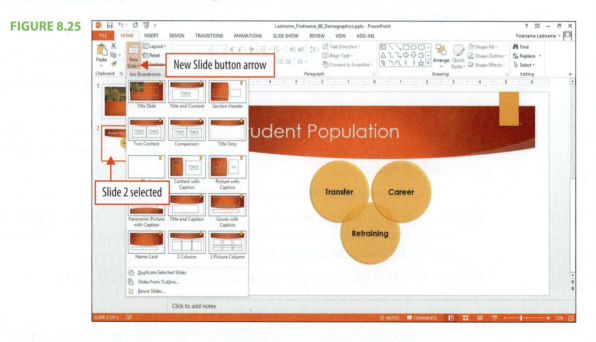

4 ▶ Click the **FILE tab** to display **Backstage** view, click **Close** to close the Word document, and then **Minimize** ⬛ Word.

The Word file is closed, and Word has been reduced to an icon at the bottom of your screen. Your PowerPoint presentation should be minimized on the taskbar.

5 ▶ Restore **PowerPoint** to return to the presentation. Make **Slide 2** the active slide. On the **HOME tab**, in the **Slides group**, click the **New Slide button arrow** to display the **New Slide** gallery. Compare your screen with Figure 8.25.

FIGURE 8.25

6 ▶ Click **Slides from Outline**. In the **Insert Outline** dialog box, navigate to the location where your student files are stored, and then click **p08B_Educational_Importance.docx**. Compare your screen with Figure 8.26.

The Insert Outline dialog box displays, and the Files of type arrow is set to All Outlines.

FIGURE 8.26

Insert Outline dialog box

Word data file selected

File types set to All Outlines

Open button changed to Insert button

7 ▸ Click **Insert**.

PowerPoint creates two new slides using the content from the Word 2013 outline. Two slides are created because there are two Level 1 data items in the outline. Each Level 1 data item displays as the title of a slide, and the lower level data items display as the bulleted items. These slides use the Title and Text Layout.

> **ALERT!** **Did You Receive an Error Message?**
>
> If you received an error message telling you that you cannot open the outline file, click OK. The message means that you have the Word outline open. Restore (return to) Word, close the document, return to PowerPoint, and then insert the slides again.

8 ▸ Make **Slide 4** the active slide. **Minimize** ⎯ PowerPoint, and then restore **Word**.

9 ▸ Click the **FILE tab**, and then click **Open**. Navigate to your student files, and then open **p08B_Workforce_Value.doc.**

On the Word title bar, after the file name, [Compatibility Mode] is added as indicated by the file extension .doc. *Compatibility mode* ensures that no new or enhanced features in Word 2013 are available while you work with a document, so that people who are using previous versions of Word will have full editing capabilities. For example, if you create the document in Word 2013, you can save it as the file type Word 97-2003 Document, and the file name will have .doc as the extension. When saving a document created with Word 2013, you can also select *Maintain compatibility with previous versions of Word*, and the file extension will be .docx.

> **ALERT!** **Did You Close Word?**
>
> If you closed Word instead of minimizing it, start Word again, and then open the data file.

10 ▸ On the **VIEW tab**, in the **Show group**, select the **Navigation Pane** check box, if necessary. Under **HEADINGS**, click *Impact to Community*, if necessary. On the **HOME tab**, in the **Styles group**, notice that the **Heading 1** style is active. Compare your screen with Figure 8.27.

This time, the Word document is displayed in Print Layout view. Paragraphs 2 and 3 are formatted as Heading 2. Paragraph 4 is formatted as Heading 1, and Paragraphs 5 to 7 are formatted as Heading 2. The file, p08B_Workforce_Value.doc, can be used as an outline to create slides because it was created using the Heading 1 and Heading 2 styles.

FIGURE 8.27

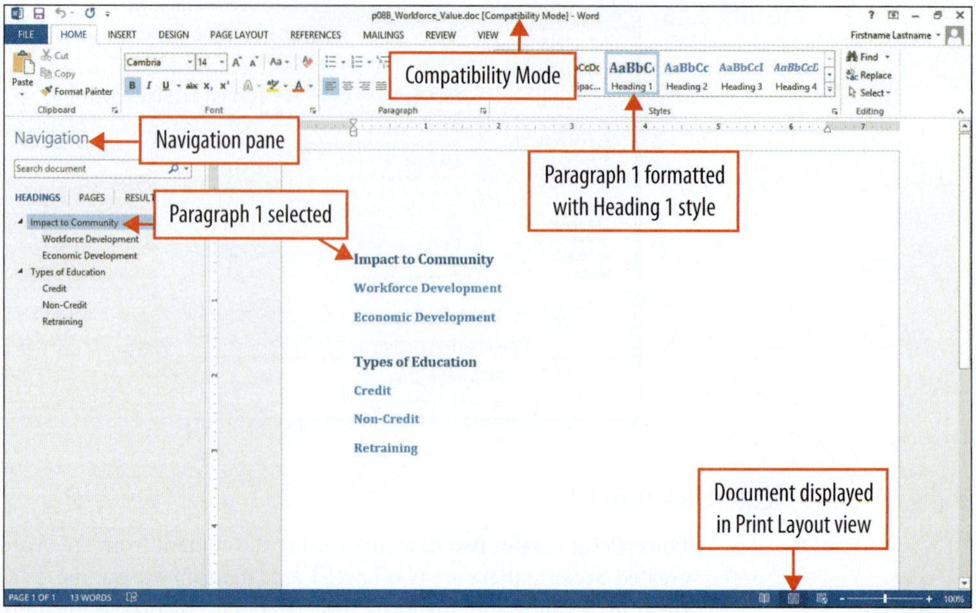

NOTE   Displaying Word Document in Outline View

Usually Word documents display in Normal view. If you have trouble inserting slides so the slide title and bulleted items are positioned correctly, you may want to open the Word document, turn on the Outline view, and then check the file. On the VIEW tab, in the Views group, click Outline to display the Outline view. In the Close group, click Close Outline View to return to Print Layout view.

11 On the **VIEW tab**, in the **Show group**, remove the check mark in the **Navigation Pane** check box. Close **Word** without saving.

12 From the taskbar, restore **PowerPoint**, and then make **Slide 4** the active slide, if necessary. On the **HOME tab**, in the **Slides group**, click the **New Slide button arrow**. In the **New Slide**, gallery click **Slides from Outline**.

13 In the **Insert Outline** dialog box, navigate to the location where your student files are stored, and then click **p08B_Workforce_Value.doc**. Click **Insert**. Click **Slide 5**, and then compare your screen with Figure 8.28.

PowerPoint creates two new slides—Slide 5 and Slide 6—using the content from the document saved in compatibility mode. The slides are added after the active slide. These slides use the Title and Text Layout. The formatting is based on the heading styles of the original document, or source document. The line *Impact to Community* was formatted in Word with the Heading 1 style and is displayed in the title placeholder. The other two lines—*Workforce Development and Economic Development*—were formatted with the Word Heading 2 style and are displayed as bulleted items in the content placeholder.

FIGURE 8.28

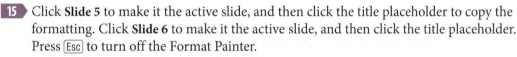

Heading 1 style displays text as the slide title → **Impact to Community**

Heading 2 style displays text as bulleted items

▸ Workforce Development
▸ Economic Development

Slide 5 selected

Slides 5 and 6 selected

Click to add notes

SLIDE 5 OF 6

NOTES   COMMENTS   72%

ALERT!   **Did the Slides Appear in the Wrong Place?**

If the slides do not appear as Slides 5 and 6, click Undo, and then insert them again. You could also move the slides to the correct place.

---

14 ▸ Make **Slide 4** the active slide. Click the title placeholder, and then click a border of the placeholder to change the border to a solid line. On the **HOME tab**, in the **Clipboard group**, double-click **Format Painter** 🖌.

15 ▸ Click **Slide 5** to make it the active slide, and then click the title placeholder to copy the formatting. Click **Slide 6** to make it the active slide, and then click the title placeholder. Press Esc to turn off the Format Painter.

> The Font color changed from blue to black. The formatting in the title placeholders on Slides 5 and 6 is the same formatting as in Slide 4. When bringing in content from other sources, you should adjust the formatting so all slides have the same look.

ALERT!   **Did the Formatting Not Appear on the Slide 6 Title?**

If the formatting on the slide titles on Slides 5 and 6 does not match the formatting on the title on Slide 4, you may not have selected the border of the slide title on Slide 4 before using Format Painter. If the formatting appeared on Slide 5 but not on Slide 6, you may not have double-clicked Format Painter so you could copy the formatting more than one time.

---

16 ▸ Make **Slide 4** the active slide. Click the content placeholder, and then click a border of the placeholder to change the border to a solid line. On the **HOME tab**, in the **Clipboard group**, double-click **Format Painter** 🖌.

17 ▸ Click **Slide 5** to make it the active slide, and then click the content placeholder to copy the formatting. Click **Slide 6** to make it the active slide, and then click the content placeholder. Press Esc to turn off the Format Painter. Click outside the content placeholder to deselect, and then compare your screen with Figure 8.29.

> All slides are formatted with Century Gothic, which is the font that was used on Slide 1 through Slide 4. You copied the formatting for the title placeholder first, and then you copied the formatting for the content placeholder.

FIGURE 8.29

Types of Education

- Credit
- Non-Credit
- Retraining

Slide 6 content placeholder

Inserted Slides 3–6 formatted with Century Gothic

More Knowledge **Formatting Slides**

Slides inserted from a Word outline retain the format from the Word file. Because the inserted slides do not adjust to the formatting in a slide master, it is easier to copy the formats with the Format Painter.

---

18 On the **SLIDE SHOW tab**, in the **Start Slide Show group**, view your presentation **From Beginning**. At the end of the presentation, press Esc.

19 On the **INSERT tab**, in the **Text group**, click **Header & Footer** to display the **Header and Footer** dialog box. Click the **Notes and Handouts tab**. Under **Include on page**, select the **Date and time** check box, and then select **Fixed**. If necessary, clear the **Header** check box, and then select the **Page number** and **Footer** check boxes. In the **Footer** box, using your own name, type **Lastname_Firstname_8B_Demographics** and then click **Apply to All**.

20 Click the **FILE tab**, and then in the lower right portion of the screen, click **Show All Properties**. In the **Tags** box, type **education, demographics** and in the **Subject** box type your course name and section number. In the **Author** box, right-click the existing author name, click **Edit Property**, replace the existing text with your first and last name, click outside the text box to deselect, and then click **OK**.

21 Save 💾 your changes.

Objective 5 | Save a Presentation in Other Formats

Video P8-5

Activity 8.13 | Saving a Presentation as an Outline

In this activity, you save a presentation as an Outline with the .rtf extension.

1 With the **Lastname_Firstname_8B_Demographics** presentation open, press F12 to display the **Save As** dialog box.

2 Click the **Save as type arrow**, and then click **Outline/RTF**. In the **File name** box, type **Lastname_Firstname_8B_Outline** and then click **Save**.

3 Start Word and then click **Open Other Documents**. Navigate to your **PowerPoint Chapter 8** folder, and then click your **Lastname_Firstname_8B_Outline** file. Click **Open** to view the file. Compare your screen with Figure 8.30.

The Word document text is formatted in the same font and font size as in PowerPoint. The Heading 1 style is applied to the slide titles and the Heading 2 style is applied to the bulleted text. Objects such as pictures, charts, SmartArt, and shapes do not display when a PowerPoint file is saved as an Outline. Thus, the SmartArt graphic on Slide 2 does not display in the Word document. The title on Slide 2 does display.

FIGURE 8.30

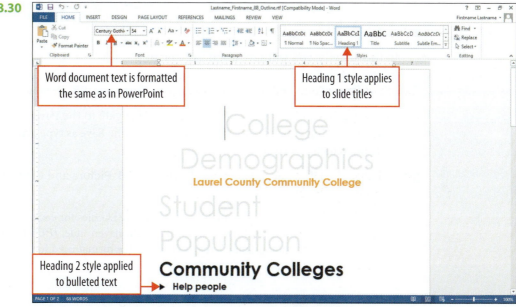

4 **Exit** Word without saving.

Activity 8.14 | Saving the Presentation as a Show

You can save a PowerPoint presentation as a Show with the **.ppsx** file extension so that it opens in Slide Show view.

1 Start PowerPoint, and open your **Lastname_Firstname_8B_Demographics** file, if necessary. Press F12 to display the **Save As** dialog box. Navigate to your **PowerPoint Chapter 8** folder. Click the **Save as type arrow**, and then point to **PowerPoint Show**. Compare your screen with Figure 8.31.

FIGURE 8.31

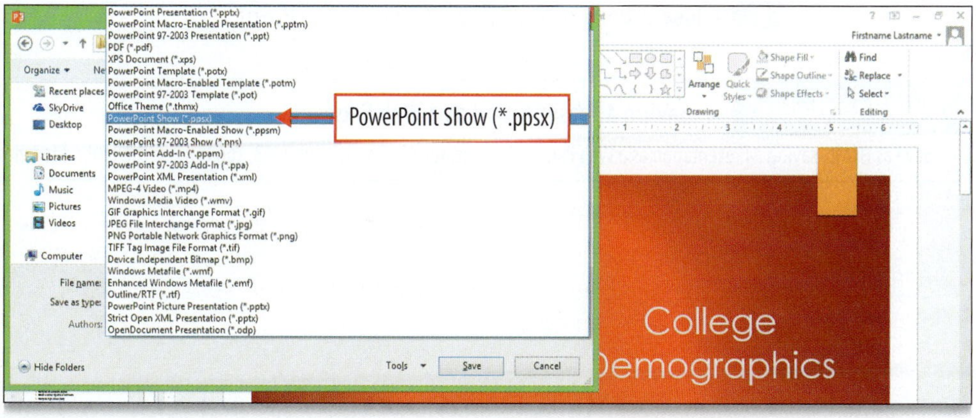

2 Click **PowerPoint Show**. In the **File name** box, type **Lastname_Firstname_8B_Show** and then click **Save**.

3 **Close** the presentation and **Exit** PowerPoint.

 4 In **Windows**, using **File Explorer**, navigate to your **PowerPoint Chapter 8** folder, where you saved the file, and then double-click your **Lastname_Firstname_8B_Show** file.

The presentation opens in Slide Show View.

 5 Press Esc to close the presentation.

To edit a presentation saved as a Show, do not open the file using File Explorer. Open the file in PowerPoint.

Activity 8.15 | Saving a Slide as a Picture

In this activity, you will save a slide as a picture.

 1 Start PowerPoint and open your **Lastname_Firstname_8B_Demographics** file. Display **Slide 2**.

 2 Press F12 to display the **Save As** dialog box. Navigate to the **PowerPoint Chapter 8** folder where you are storing your files for this project. Click the **Save as type arrow**, and then click **JPEG File Interchange Format**.

 3 Change the **File name** to **Lastname_Firstname_8B_Picture** and then click **Save**. Compare your screen with Figure 8.32.

The *All Slides* option creates a folder containing JPEG files for each slide in the presentation. The *Just This One* option creates a JPEG file of the displayed slide. *JPEG (or .jpg)* is an abbreviation that stands for Joint Photographic Experts Group: a file format used for photos and including the .jpg and .jpeg extensions.

FIGURE 8.32

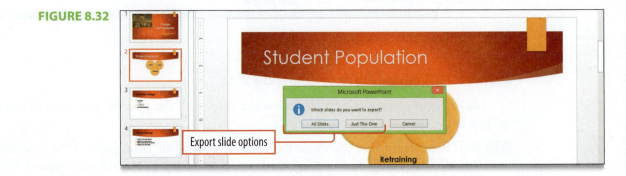

 4 In the displayed message box, click **Just This One**.

 5 **Close** the presentation and **Exit** PowerPoint.

> *More* **Knowledge** **Saving a Presentation as a Web Page**
>
> Save as HTML, saving a Presentation as a Web Page, is discontinued in PowerPoint 2013. You can use the embedded viewer on SkyDrive instead.

Objective 6 | Create a Video

Video P8-6

Activity 8.16 | Creating a Video

In this activity, you will create a video of a presentation. The video will be saved as a **MP4 video file (.mp4)**, the default file type when saving a video in PowerPoint 2013. A video player needs to be set up on your computer in order to play the video.

1 Start PowerPoint. Open **Lastname_Firstname_8B_Demographics**. Click the **FILE tab** to display **Backstage** view, and then click **Export**. Under **Export**, click **Create a Video**. Compare your screen with Figure 8.33.

A full-fidelity video from your presentation can be created and distributed by using a disc, the web, or email. If selected, the video incorporates all recorded timings, narrations, and laser pointer gestures; includes all slides not hidden in the slide show; and preserves animations, transitions, and media. Click the arrow to the right of *Computer & HD Displays* to see the options for saving the video. Click the arrow to the right of *Don't Use Recorded Timings and Narrations* to see the options for including timings and audio that may have been included in the presentation. Use the spin arrow to select the time you want each slide to display. The default number of seconds is 5 seconds.

FIGURE 8.33

2 To the right of **Seconds spent on each slide**, use the **spin arrows** to change the number of seconds to **3.00**, and then click **Create Video**. In the **Save As** dialog box, navigate to your **PowerPoint Chapter 8** folder, change the **File name** to **Lastname_Firstname_8B_Video** and click **Save.** Wait for the video export to complete.

A status bar displays on the PowerPoint task bar—Creating video Lastname_Firstname_8B_Video. mp4 that indicates the presentation is being exported to video. The video file is automatically saved in the same folder with the presentation file, and then the presentation file displays on your screen. Each slide was timed for 3 seconds.

3 Save your presentation. **Minimize** PowerPoint.

4 In **File Explorer**, display the contents of your **PowerPoint Chapter 8** folder. Double-click **Lastname_Firstname_8B_Video.mp4** to start the video. When the video is finished, press ⊞ + **D**, to return to the Windows desktop. **Close File Explorer**, and then restore **PowerPoint**.

Because the slides were set for 3 seconds per slide, the slide show displayed each slide for 3 seconds before advancing to the next slide. PowerPoint saved the file with an .mp4 (MP4 Video) extension.

ALERT! **If The Video Did Not Play...**

If the video not play, most likely you do not have a default video play set up on your computer. Right-click on the .mp4 file and then click Open with to view the list of installed video players on your computer.

Video P8-7

If the computer you are using has a writable CD or DVD drive, you can copy your presentation to a **CD-R**, **DVD-R**, **CD-RW**, or **DVD-RW** disc. A writable CD or DVD drive not only plays CDs and DVDs, but also enables you to save files to CDs and DVDs. You can write to a CD-R or DVD-R—media that can be written to, or saved to, only once—or to a CD-RW or DVD-RW—media that can be written to, or saved to, multiple times.

A PowerPoint feature known as **Package Presentation for CD** creates a package of a presentation and related files on a CD. It can also be used to copy and save your presentation on a **network drive**, a **local drive**, or a **flash drive**. A network drive is a common drive on another computer, such as a server, that is available to others working on the network. A local drive is a drive on your computer, such as the C: drive. A flash drive, another useful replacement for the floppy disk, is a compact removable drive that plugs into the USB port of the computer.

When you use Package Presentation for CD, the PowerPoint presentation, including all embedded and linked items—such as fonts, videos, sounds, Excel spreadsheets, and charts—is copied.

Activity 8.17 | Copying a Presentation Using Package Presentation for CD

In this activity, using the Package Presentation for CD feature, you will copy a presentation to your student folder.

1 With **Lastname_Firstname_8B_Demographics** open, click the **FILE tab** to display **Backstage** view, and then click **Export**. Under **Export**, click **Package Presentation for CD**, and then click the **Package for CD button**. The **Package for CD** dialog box displays.

2 In the **Package for CD** dialog box, in the **Name the CD** box, substituting your own first, middle, and last initials for *FML*, type **FML_Demographics** in the **Name the CD** box. Compare your screen with Figure 8.34.

Because CD names have a maximum character length, you are saving the name with your initials instead of your first and last names. Make sure you entered your own initials, not FML.

FIGURE 8.34

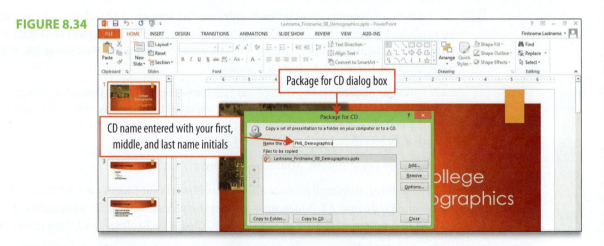

3 Click **Add**. In the displayed **Add Files** dialog box, navigate to your **PowerPoint Chapter 8** folder, click **Lastname_Firstname_8A_Educational_Statistics**, and then click **Add**.

4 In the **Package for CD** dialog box, click **Lastname_Firstname_8B_Demographics**, and then click the **down arrow** to change the play order so that it follows *Lastname_Firstname_8A_Educational_Statistics*. Compare your screen with Figure 8.35.

Both Lastname_Firstname_8A_Educational_Statistics and Lastname_Firstname_8B_Demographics will be copied. You can add as many presentations as you want. You can also remove a file or a presentation by selecting the presentation and then clicking Remove.

FIGURE 8.35

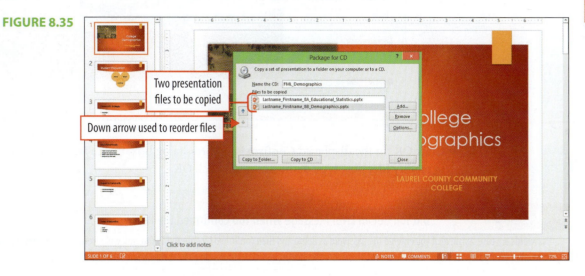

5 Click **Options** to display the **Options** dialog box.

6 Under **Include these files**, make sure the **Linked files** and the **Embedded TrueType fonts** check boxes are selected.

You can include embedded TrueType fonts if they are not included in the presentation. *TrueType* is the scalable font technology built into Microsoft Windows and Apple Macintosh.

More Knowledge   **Embed Fonts in a Presentation**

You can embed fonts within a presentation so that other people who open the presentation can view and use the fonts, even if the fonts are not installed on their computer. Only TrueType and OpenType fonts can be embedded. Settings to embed a font in a presentation file are located in PowerPoint Options. To set an option, click the FILE tab; click Options, to display the PowerPoint Options dialog box; and then on the left, click Save, to display the options for Embed fonts in the file. The options are: Embed only the characters used in the presentation (best for reducing file size) and Embed all characters (best for editing by other people).

---

7 Under **Enhance security and privacy**, in the second box—**Password to modify each presentation**, type **demo** Make sure that you do not request a password to open each presentation.

Requiring a password to modify a presentation prevents others from altering or editing a presentation unless they know the password. You may, if you wish, require a password to open the presentation. For this exercise, you will not do that.

8 Near the bottom of the **Options** dialog box, select the **Inspect presentations for inappropriate or private information** check box. Compare your screen with Figure 8.36.

Hidden information may include your name as the presentation's creator, a company name, or other confidential information you may not want others to view.

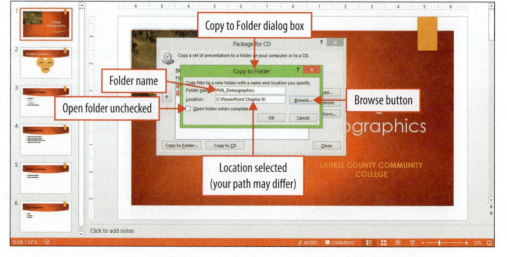

FIGURE 8.36

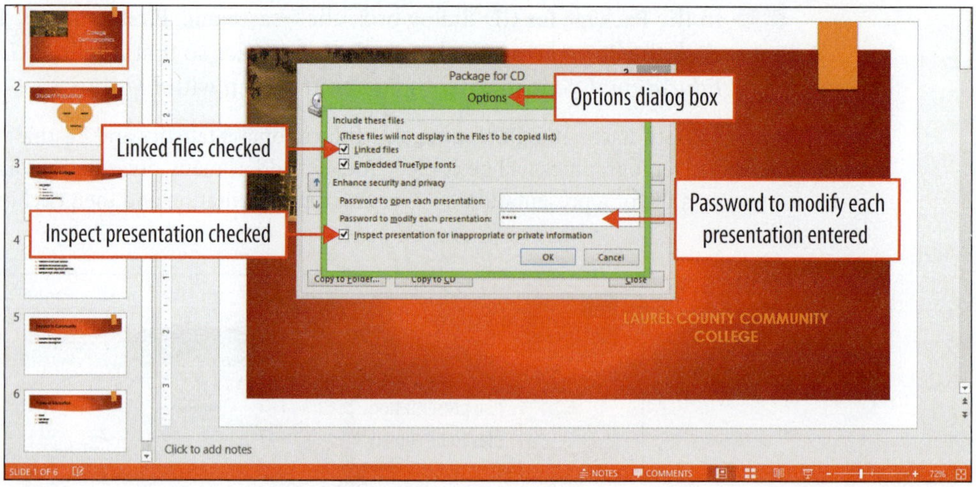

---

9 ▶ Click **OK**. In the displayed **Confirm Password** dialog box, in the **Reenter the password required to modify files** box, type **demo** and then click **OK**.

A L E R T !   **Did You Get an Error Message When You Confirmed the Password?**

Passwords are case sensitive. If you entered the password as demo and then confirmed by entering Demo, you will receive an error message. Make sure you remember your password.

---

10 ▶ In the **Package for CD** dialog box, click **Copy to Folder**.

In this activity, you are copying files to a folder in your PowerPoint Chapter 8 folder. If you are copying files to a CD, you have the option of clicking Copy to Folder, and then locating your CD drive or clicking Copy to CD.

11 ▶ In the **Copy to Folder** dialog box, in the **Folder name** box, you should see your CD folder name. To the right of the **Location** box, click **Browse**, and then in the **Choose Location** dialog box, navigate to your **PowerPoint Chapter 8** folder. Click **Select**. In the **Copy to Folder** dialog box, clear the check box for **Open folder when complete**. Compare your screen with Figure 8.37.

FIGURE 8.37

12 ▶ Click **OK**. A warning dialog box displays, prompting you to include linked files only if you trust the source of each linked file.

Because you either created or know the origins of the files that will be linked to your presentation, it is safe to click Yes. Linked files can be used to transport viruses to your computer or to a network where these files are saved.

13 ▶ Click **Yes**. The **Document Inspector** dialog box displays. Compare your screen with Figure 8.38.

The **Document Inspector** is a PowerPoint feature that allows you to review a presentation for hidden data or personal information that may be stored in the presentation or in the document properties, and then provides the option to remove the information. This information may not be immediately visible when viewing the presentation as a slide show, but it may be possible for others to retrieve this information.

Both of the files in your package will be inspected for Comments and Annotations, Document Properties and Personal Information, Task Pane Apps, Custom XML Data, Invisible On-Slide Content, and Presentation Notes. Off-Slide Content refers to objects such as graphics or tables that you may have moved off the slide. Because these objects are not visible on the slide, they do not display in the slide show. By default, this option is not checked.

FIGURE 8.38

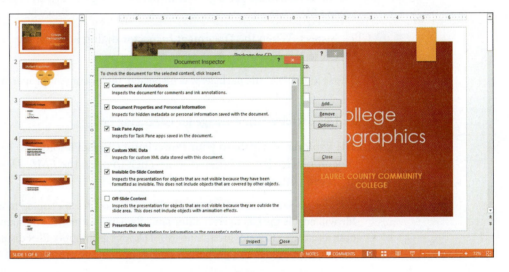

14 ▶ Click **Inspect**, and then compare your screen with Figure 8.39.

The Document Inspector dialog box displays. Under Review the inspection results, check marks appear to the left of all categories inspected in which no information was located. An exclamation point appears to the left of Document Properties and personal information, indicating that some information was located. That information is listed. To the right of Document Properties and Personal Information, a Remove All button is displayed. This information includes the content you added to the document properties earlier.

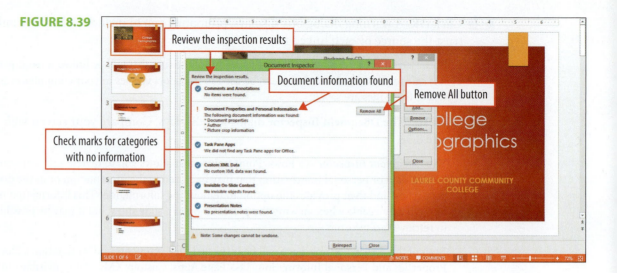

FIGURE 8.39

15 ▸ Click **Remove All**, and then click **Close**.

> The first file in the package was inspected, the document properties were removed, and then the file was copied to the package. The Inspector dialog box displays again so you can inspect the second file.

16 ▸ Click **Inspect**. When the **Document Inspector** dialog box displays again, click **Remove All**. Click **Close**.

> The second file in the package was inspected, the document properties were removed, and then the file was copied to the package.

17 ▸ Click **Close** to close the **Package for CD** dialog box.

18 ▸ In **File Explorer**, navigate to your **PowerPoint Chapter 8** folder to locate the *FML_Demographics* folder, and then double-click to open the *FML_Demographics* folder. Compare your screen with Figure 8.40.

> A folder for PresentationPackage displays. If these files are copied to a CD, the AUTORUN.INF file will enable the CD to start automatically. The Lastname_Firstname_8A_Educational_Statistics. pptx and the Lastname_Firstname_8B_Demographics.pptx files display. The document inspector removed the header and properties information in the presentation files.

More Knowledge | **How to View a PowerPoint Presentation If You Do Not Have PowerPoint 2013 Installed**

If you give the CD to someone who doesn't have PowerPoint 2013 installed on his or her computer, that person can use the PowerPoint Web App to view the presentation.

FIGURE 8.40

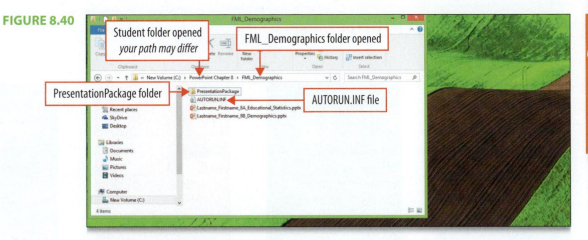

FIGURE 8.40

19 **Save** 🖫 your changes in the PowerPoint presentation, **Close** the presentation, and then **Exit** PowerPoint. Submit your work as directed.

END | You have completed Project 8B

END OF CHAPTER

SUMMARY

You added a SmartArt object to your slide show and then practiced creating, modifying, and formatting tables using the Draw Tool Draw pointer to create table borders and use other insert Table Tools.

You modified a text box to wrap into columns. You used outlines to create slides for a presentation, inserting content instead of retyping the information. You saved a presentation slide as a Picture.

You saved your presentation as a video. You used the Package for CD feature to create a self-running presentation that could be copied to a CD, a flash drive, a network drive, or a local hard drive.

You saved a presentation as an Outline in Rich Text Format with file extension .rtf. This format can be read on different platforms. You also saved a presentation as a Show with file extension .ppsx.

GO! LEARN IT ONLINE

Review the concepts and key terms in this chapter by completing these online challenges, which you can find at **pearsonhighered.com/go**.

Matching and Multiple Choice:
Answer matching and multiple choice questions to test what you learned in this chapter. MyITLab®

Crossword Puzzle:
Spell out the words that match the numbered clues, and put them in the puzzle squares.

Flipboard:
Flip through the definitions of the key terms in this chapter and match them with the correct term.

END OF CHAPTER

REVIEW AND ASSESSMENT GUIDE FOR POWERPOINT CHAPTER 8

Your instructor may assign one or more of these projects to help you review the chapter and assess your mastery and understanding of the chapter.

Review and Assessment Guide for PowerPoint Chapter 8			
Project	**Apply Skills from These Chapter Objectives**	**Project Type**	**Project Location**
8C	Objectives 1–3 from Project 8A	**8C Skills Review** A guided review of the skills from Project 8A.	On the following pages
8D	Objectives 4–7 from Project 8B	**8D Skills Review** A guided review of the skills from Project 8B.	On the following pages
8E	Objectives 1–3 from Project 8A	**8E Mastering PowerPoint (Grader Project)** A demonstration of your mastery of the skills in Project 8A with extensive decision making.	In MyITLab and on the following pages
8F	Objectives 4–7 from Project 8B	**8F Mastering PowerPoint (Grader Project)** A demonstration of your mastery of the skills in Project 8B with extensive decision making.	In MyITLab and on the following pages
8G	Objectives 1–7 from Projects 8A and 8B	**8G Mastering PowerPoint (Grader Project)** A demonstration of your mastery of the skills in Projects 8A and 8B with extensive decision making.	In MyITLab and on the following pages
8H	Combination of Objectives from Projects 8A and 8B	**8H GO! Fix It** A demonstration of your mastery of the skills in Projects 8A and 8B by creating a correct result from a document that contains errors you must find.	Online
8I	Combination of Objectives from Projects 8A and 8B	**8I GO! Make It** A demonstration of your mastery of the skills in Projects 8A and 8B by creating a result from a supplied picture.	Online
8J	Combination of Objectives from Projects 8A and 8B	**8J GO! Solve It** A demonstration of your mastery of the skills in Projects 8A and 8B, your decision-making skills, and your critical thinking skills. A task-specific rubric helps you self-assess your result.	Online
8K	Combination of Objectives from Projects 8A and 8B	**8K GO! Solve It** A demonstration of your mastery of the skills in Projects 8A and 8B, your decision- making skills, and your critical thinking skills. A task-specific rubric helps you self-assess your result.	On the following pages
8L	Combination of Objectives from Projects 8A and 8B	**8L GO! Think** A demonstration of your understanding of the chapter concepts applied in a manner that you would apply them outside of college. An analytic rubric helps you and your instructor grade the quality of your work by comparing it to the work an expert in the discipline would create.	On the following pages
8M	Combination of Objectives from Projects 8A and 8B	**8M GO! Think** A demonstration of your understanding of the chapter concepts applied in a manner that you would apply them outside of college. An analytic rubric helps you and your instructor grade the quality of your work by comparing it to the work an expert in the discipline would create.	Online
8N	Combination of Objectives from Projects 8A and 8B	**8N You and GO!** A demonstration of your understanding of the chapter concepts applied in a manner that you would apply them in a personal situation. An analytic rubric helps you and your instructor grade the quality of your work.	Online

GLOSSARY

GLOSSARY OF CHAPTER KEY TERMS

.ppsx The PowerPoint file extension that allows a file to open in Slide Show view.

.rtf The extension for a file that is saved in Rich Text Format.

CD-R Removable media (CD) that can be written to, or saved to, only one time.

CD-RW Removable media (CD) that can be written to, or saved to, to multiple times.

Compatibility mode Ensures that no new or enhanced features in Word 2013 are available while you work with a document, so that people who are using previous versions of Word will have full editing capabilities.

Document Inspector A PowerPoint feature that allows you to review a presentation for hidden data or personal information that may be stored in the presentation or in the document properties and then provides the option to remove the information.

Draw pointer A pen-shaped pointer that is used to create table borders.

DVD-R Removable media (DVD) that can be written to, or saved to, only one time.

DVD-RW Removable media (DVD) that can be written to, or saved to, multiple times.

Eraser A pointer that is used to remove table borders.

Flash drive A compact removable drive that plugs into the USB port of the computer.

Hard return Created by pressing the Enter key to start a new line.

Heading style A set of formatting characteristics, such as font name, size, color, paragraph alignment, and spacing, that is used to quickly format selected text.

JPEG (or .jpg) An abbreviation that stands for Joint Photographic Experts Group: a file format used for photos and including the .jpg and .jpeg extensions.

Local drive A drive on your computer, such as the C: drive.

MP4 video file (.mp4) The default file type when saving a video in PowerPoint 2013.

Network drive A common drive on another computer, usually a server, that is available to others working on the network.

Outline view A document view in Microsoft Word that distinguishes the importance of data by the heading styles that have been applied.

Package Presentation for CD A PowerPoint feature that creates a package of a presentation and related files on a CD.

Paragraphs Any text that has a hard return at the end of it.

Platform The combination of hardware and software used on a computer.

Rich Text Format (RTF) file A non-application-specific file format used to transfer formatted text documents between applications.

Text box A drawn object that is used to position text anywhere on a slide.

TrueType The scalable font technology built into Microsoft Windows and Apple Macintosh.

CHAPTER REVIEW

Apply 8A skills from these Objectives:

1 Draw Tables
2 Modify a Table Using the Draw Borders Features
3 Modify a Text Box

Skills Review | Project 8C Recruiting

In the following Skills Review, you will complete a PowerPoint presentation to help administration more clearly understand the current and potential enrollment from high school students. You will create and modify tables and modify and format textboxes using several methods. Your completed presentation will look similar to Figure 8.41.

PROJECT FILES

For Project 8C, you will need the following files:

p08C_Recruiting.pptx
p08C_Books.jpg

You will save your presentation as:

Lastname_Firstname_8C_Recruiting.pptx

PROJECT RESULTS

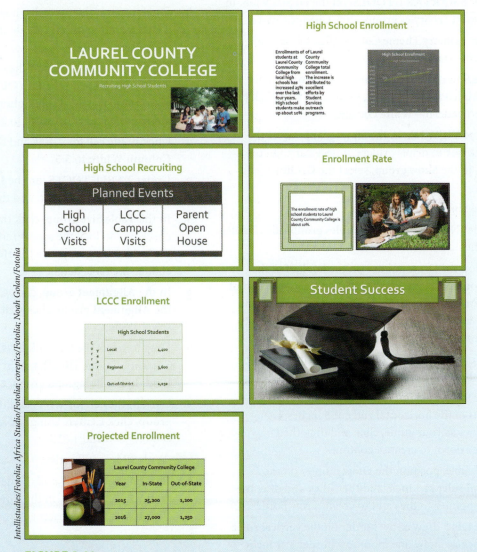

Intellistudies/Fotolia; Africa Studio/Fotolia; corepics/Fotolia; Noah Golan/Fotolia

FIGURE 8.41

(Project 8C Recruiting continues on the next page)

CHAPTER REVIEW

1 ▶ Start PowerPoint. Locate and open the file **p08C_Recruiting**. Using your own first and last name, save the file as **Lastname_Firstname_8C_Recruiting** in your **PowerPoint Chapter 8** folder.

2 ▶ Make **Slide 2** the active slide.

a. On the **INSERT tab**, in the **Illustrations group**, click **SmartArt**. If you receive an error message, click **OK**. In the **Choose a SmartArt Graphic** dialog box, at the left, click **List**. In the eighth row, click the pattern— **Table List**. Click **OK**.

b. Click the top rectangle shape, and then type **Planned Events** In the left box below, type **High School Visits** In the middle box, type **LCCC Campus Visits** In the right box, type **Parent Open House**

c. Under **SMARTART TOOLS**, on the **DESIGN tab**, in the **SmartArt Styles group**, click **Change Colors**.

d. Under **Primary Theme Colors**, click the second pattern—**Dark 2 Outline**.

e. In the **SmartArt Styles group**, click **More**. Under **Best Match for Document**, in the first row, click the second pattern—**White Outline**.

3 ▶ On the **VIEW tab**, in the **Show group**, select the **Ruler** check box to display rulers, if necessary. On the **VIEW tab**, in the **Show group**, select the **Gridlines** check box.

4 ▶ Make **Slide 3** the active slide.

a. On the **INSERT tab**, in the **Tables group**, click **Table**, and then click **Draw Table**.

b. Position the Draw pointer on the **left half of the horizontal ruler at 3 inches** and on the **upper half of the vertical ruler at 1 inch**. Drag the pointer to the **right half of the horizontal ruler at 3 inches** and to the **lower half of the vertical ruler at 3 inches**.

c. Under **TABLE TOOLS**, on the **DESIGN tab**, in the **Draw Borders group**, click **Draw Table**.

d. In the table, position the Draw pointer a little to the left of the **horizontal ruler at 3 inches**. Using gridlines as your guide, click and drag the Draw pointer down to create a column.

e. In the table, position the Draw pointer on the **vertical ruler at 1 inch**, and then click and drag the Draw pointer to the right to create a row border.

f. In the table, draw a row border on the **vertical ruler at 2 inches**. Draw one more row border at **1 inch**

below the previous horizontal border. Press Esc to turn off the Draw pointer.

g. On the **VIEW tab**, in the **Show group**, click the **Gridlines** check box to turn off gridlines.

5 ▶ With **Slide 3** active:

a. Type the following information in the corresponding cells, pressing Tab or → after each entry except the last entry:

High School Students	
Local	4,400
Regional	3,600
Out-of-District	1,050

b. Drag to select the two cells in **row 1**. Under **TABLE TOOLS**, on the **LAYOUT tab**, in the **Merge group**, click **Merge Cells**.

c. In the second row, click in the cell for *Local*. Under **TABLE TOOLS**, on the **LAYOUT tab**, in the **Cell Size group**, use the **Table Column Width button spin arrows** to change the width to **3.5"**.

d. Click in the cell for *4,400*, and then change the **Table Column Width** to **3.5"**.

e. Under **TABLE TOOLS**, on the **LAYOUT tab**, in the **Table group**, click **Select**, and then click **Select Table**.

f. In the **Table Size group**, click the **Lock Aspect Ratio** check box to lock the aspect ratio, if necessary. In the **Table Size group**, use the **Height** spin buttons to change the table height to **4"**.

g. In the **Alignment group**, click **Center Vertically**. In the **Alignment group**, click **Cell Margins**, and then select **Wide**.

h. Drag to select the text in the cell for *High School Students*. On the **HOME tab**, in the **Font group**, click **Bold**. In the **Paragraph group**, click **Center**.

i. Click in the cell for *4,400*, and then in the **Paragraph group**, click **Center**. Using the same procedure, center *3,600* and *1,050*.

6 ▶ With **Slide 3** still active:

a. Click in the cell for *Local*. Under **TABLE TOOLS**, on the **LAYOUT tab**, in the **Rows & Columns group**, click **Insert Left** to insert a new column.

(Project 8C Recruiting continues on the next page)

b. In the **Merge group**, click **Merge Cells**. In the new column, type **Current Year**

c. On the **LAYOUT tab**, in the **Alignment group**, click **Text Direction**, and then click **Stacked**. Select the text. On the **HOME tab**, in the **Font group**, click **Character Spacing**, and then click **Very Tight**.

d. Under **TABLE TOOLS**, on the **LAYOUT tab**, in the **Cell Size group**, change the **Table Column Width** to 1.2".

e. Under **TABLE TOOLS**, on the **LAYOUT tab**, in the **Table group**, click **Select**, and then click **Select Table**. Under **TABLE TOOLS**, on the **DESIGN tab**, in the **Table Styles group**, click **More**. Under **Medium**, in the fourth row, click the second pattern—**Medium Style 4 – Accent 1**.

f. With the table still selected, on the **HOME tab**, in the **Font group**, click **Font Color**, and then click **Green, Accent 1, Darker 50%**, which is in the fifth column, the sixth row. Click **Bold**.

g. With the table still selected, under **TABLE TOOLS**, click the **LAYOUT tab**. In the **Arrange group**, click **Align**, and then click **Align Center**.

h. Select *High School Students*, and then on the **HOME tab**, change the **Font Size** to **24**.

7 Make **Slide 4** the active slide.

a. On the **INSERT tab**. In the **Tables group**, click **Table**, and then click **Draw Table**.

b. Position the Draw pointer on the **left half of the horizontal ruler at 3 inches** and on the **upper half of the vertical ruler at 1 inch**. Drag the pointer to the **right half of the horizontal ruler at 3 inches** and to the **lower half of the vertical ruler at 2 inches**.

c. On the **VIEW tab**, in the **Show group**, click the **Gridlines** check box to display gridlines, if necessary.

d. Under **TABLE TOOLS** on the **DESIGN tab**, in the **Draw Borders group**, click **Draw Table**. In the table, position the Draw pointer on the **horizontal ruler at 2**. Using the gridlines as a guide, click and drag the Draw pointer down to draw a column border. In the table, position the Draw pointer on the **horizontal ruler at 4 inches**, and then draw another column border.

e. In the table, position the Draw pointer on the **vertical ruler at 1 inch**, and then click and drag to the right border of the table to create a row border. Draw another row border on the **vertical ruler at 2 inches**.

f. On the **VIEW tab**, in the **Show group**, remove the check mark from the **Gridlines** check box.

g. Press [Esc] to turn off the Draw pointer, and then type the following information:

Year	In-State	Out-of State
2015	25,200	1,200
2016	27,000	1,250

8 With **Slide 4** as the active slide, click inside the cell containing the text *In-State*.

a. Under **TABLE TOOLS**, on the **LAYOUT tab**, in the **Rows & Columns group**, click **Insert Above**.

b. Under **TABLE TOOLS**, on the **DESIGN tab**, in the **Draw Borders group**, click **Eraser**. Click the two borders that divide **row 1** to merge the cells. Press [Esc] to turn off the **Eraser**.

c. In the new row, type **Laurel County Community College**

d. Under **TABLE TOOLS**, on the **LAYOUT tab**, in the **Table group**, click the **Select button**, and then click **Select Table**. On the **LAYOUT tab**, in the **Alignment group**, click **Center Vertically** and **Center**.

e. On the **HOME tab**, in the **Font group**, change the **Font size** to **24**. Under **TABLE TOOLS**, on the **LAYOUT tab**, in the **Table Size group**, remove the check mark in the **Lock Aspect Ratio** check box, and then change the **Width** to 7.7".

9 With **Slide 4** still active:

a. Click in the first row of the table. Under **TABLE TOOLS**, on the **LAYOUT tab**, in the **Rows & Columns group**, click the **Insert Left button** to insert a column.

b. Under **TABLE TOOLS**, on the **DESIGN tab**, in the **Draw Borders group**, click **Eraser**. Click on the three row borders in the new column to merge the cells. Press [Esc] to turn off the **Eraser**.

c. Click in the new column. Under **TABLE TOOLS**, on the **DESIGN tab**, in the **Table Styles group**, click the **Shading button arrow**, and then click **Picture**. Navigate to your data files, click **p08C_Books.jpg**, and then click **Insert**. Under the **TABLE TOOLS** on the **LAYOUT tab**, in the **Cell Size group**, change the

(Project 8C Recruiting continues on the next page)

cell size for the first column to **Table Column Width** to **2.5"**.

d. On the **TABLE TOOLS DESIGN tab**, in the **Table Styles group**, click the **Shading button arrow**, and then click **Table Background**. Under **Theme Colors**, in the fifth column, the fourth row, click **Green, Accent 1, Lighter 40%**.

e. Click a border to select the table. Press Ctrl + B to add bold.

f. Click in the cell for *Out-of-State*. Under **TABLE TOOLS**, on the **LAYOUT tab**, in the **Cell Size group**, change the **Table Column Width** to **2.2"**. In the **Arrange group**, click **Align**, and then select **Align Center**.

10 Display **Slide 5**, and then right-click the placeholder containing text on the left side of the slide. On the shortcut menu, click **Format Shape**.

a. In the **Format Shape** task pane, at the top, click **TEXT OPTIONS**, and then click **Textbox**. Click the **Columns** button. In the **Columns** dialog box, replace the value in the **Number** box with **2**, and then click **OK**.

b. In the **Format Shape** task pane, under **TEXT BOX**, change the **Left margin** and **Right margin** values to **0.4**

11 Display **Slide 6**, and then click the border to select the shape on the left. Type **The enrollment rate of high school students to Laurel County Community College is about 10%.**

a. On the **Format Shape** task pane, click **TEXT OPTIONS**, and then click **Textbox**. Under **TEXT BOX**, select the **Wrap text in shape** check box.

b. With the shape still selected, on the **DRAWING TOOLS FORMAT tab**, in the **Shape Styles group**, click the **Shape Outline button arrow**. Under **Theme Colors**, in the fifth column, click the fifth color— **Green, Accent 1, Darker 25%**.

c. Click the **Shape Outline button arrow** again, point to **Weight**, and then point to each of the line weights and notice the change to the shape outline.

d. Click **More Lines**, and then in the **Format Shape** task pane, click the **Compound type arrow**. Click the

second style—**Double**. Select the value in the **Width** box, type **10** and then press Enter. **Close** the **Format Shape** task pane.

12 With **Slide 6** displayed, point to the outside edge of the shape on the left, and then right-click. On the shortcut menu, click **Set as Default Shape**.

a. Display **Slide 7**, and then on the **INSERT tab**, in the **Illustration group**, click **Shapes**. Under **Stars and Banners**, in the second row, click the fifth shape— **Vertical Scroll**. Position the pointer near the upper left corner of the slide, and then click one time to insert the shape.

b. With the shape selected, press Ctrl + D to make a duplicate of the shape. Drag the new shape to the upper right corner of the slide as shown in Figure 8.41. Click outside the shape to deselect.

c. On the **SLIDE SHOW tab**, in the **Start Slide Show group**, view your presentation **From Beginning**.

13 On the **INSERT tab**, in the **Text group**:

a. Click **Header & Footer** to display the **Header and Footer** dialog box.

b. Click the **Notes and Handouts tab**. Under **Include on page**, select the **Date and time** check box, and then select **Fixed**. If necessary, clear the **Header** check box, and then select the **Page number** and **Footer** check boxes. In the **Footer** box, using your own name, type **Lastname_Firstname_8C_Recruiting** and then click **Apply to All**.

14 Click the **FILE tab**, and then in the lower right portion of the screen, click **Show All Properties**. In the **Tags** box, type **enrollment, recruiting** and in the **Subject** box type your course name and section number. In the **Author** box, right-click the existing author name, click **Edit Property**, replace the existing text with your first and last name, click outside the text box to deselect, and then click **OK**.

15 Print **Handouts 4 Slides Horizontal**, or submit your presentation electronically as directed by your instructor.

16 **Save** your changes, **Close** the presentation, and then **Exit** PowerPoint. Submit your work as directed.

END | You have completed Project 8C

CHAPTER REVIEW

Skills Review Project 8D Academics

Apply 8B skills from these Objectives:

4 Insert Outline Text from Another Program into a PowerPoint Presentation

5 Save a Presentation in Other Formats

6 Create a Video

7 Copy a Presentation to a CD, DVD, Network, or Local Drive

In the following Skills Review, you will complete a PowerPoint presentation for the Laurel County Community College that gives an overview of programs and academics. You will create slides from outlines created in Word. You will save the presentation as an Outline, as a Show, and as a Picture. You will also create and view a video of the presentation and copy the presentation to a CD or DVD. The completed presentation will look similar to Figure 8.42.

PROJECT FILES

For Project 8D, you will need the following files:

p08D_Academics.pptx
p08D_Academic_Departments.doc
p08D_Educational_Opportunities.docx

You will save your files as:

Lastname_Firstname_8D_Academics.pptx
Lastname_Firstname_8D_Outline.rtf
Lastname_Firstname_8D_Show.ppsx
Lastname_Firstname_8D_Video.mp4
Lastname_Firstname_8D_Picture.jpg
FML_Academics (folder)

PROJECT RESULTS

FIGURE 8.42

(Project 8D Academics continues on the next page)

CHAPTER REVIEW

1 ▶ Start PowerPoint. Locate and open the file **p08D_Academics**. Navigate to the **PowerPoint Chapter 8** folder you created, and then save the file as **Lastname_Firstname_8D_Academics**

2 ▶ Make **Slide 2** the active slide.

a. On **HOME tab**, in the **Slides group**, click the **New Slide button arrow**. In the **New Slides** gallery, click **Slides from Outline**.

b. In the **Insert Outline** dialog box, navigate to the student data files, if necessary, click **p08D_Educational_Opportunities.docx**, and then click **Insert**.

3 ▶ Make **Slide 4** the active slide.

a. On **HOME tab**, in the **Slides group**, click the **New Slide button arrow**. In **New Slides** gallery, click **Slides from Outline**.

b. In the **Insert Outline** dialog box, navigate to the student data files, if necessary, click **p08D_Educational_Opportunities.docx**, and then click **Insert**.

4 ▶ Make **Slide 5** the active slide.

a. Click the title placeholder, and then click a border of the placeholder to change the border to a solid line. On the **HOME tab**, in **Clipboard group**, double-click **Format Painter**.

b. Click **Slide 4** to make it the active slide, and then click the title placeholder to apply the format.

c. Click **Slide 3** to make it the active slide, and then click the title placeholder to apply the format. Press `Esc` to turn off **Format Painter**.

5 ▶ Make **Slide 5** the active slide.

a. Click the content placeholder, and then click a border of the placeholder to change the border to a solid line. On the **HOME tab**, in **Clipboard group**, double-click **Format Painter**.

b. Click **Slide 4** to make it the active slide, and then click the content placeholder to apply the format.

c. Click **Slide 3** to make it the active slide, and then click the content placeholder to apply the format. Press `Esc` to turn off **Format Painter**.

6 ▶ On the **INSERT tab**, in the **Text group**, click **Header & Footer** to display the **Header and Footer** dialog box. Click the **Notes and Handouts tab**. Under **Include on page**, select the **Date and time** check box, and then

select **Fixed**. If necessary, clear the **Header** check box, and then select the **Page number** and **Footer** check boxes. In the **Footer** box, using your own name, type **Lastname_ Firstname_8D_Academics** and then click **Apply to All**.

7 ▶ Click the **FILE tab**, and then in the lower right portion of the screen, click **Show All Properties**. In the **Tags** box, type **academics, workforce** and in the **Subject** box type your course name and section number. In the **Author** box, right-click the existing author name, click **Edit Property**, replace the existing text with your first and last name, click outside the text box to deselect, and then click **OK**.

8 ▶ **Save** the presentation.

9 ▶ With the **Lastname_Firstname_8D_Academics** presentation open, press `F12` to display the **Save As** dialog box.

a. Click the **Save as type arrow**, and then click **Outline/ RTF**. In the **File name** box, type **Lastname_ Firstname_8D_Outline** and then click **Save**.

b. Start Word and then click **Open Other Documents**. Navigate to your **PowerPoint Chapter 8** folder, and then click your **Lastname_Firstname_8D_Outline** file. Click **Open** to view the file.

c. **Exit** Word.

10 ▶ Start PowerPoint, and open your **Lastname_ Firstname_8D_Academics** file, if necessary. Press `F12` to display the **Save As** dialog box. Navigate to your **PowerPoint Chapter 8 folder**. Click the **Save as type arrow**, and then click **PowerPoint** Show.

a. In the **File name** box, type **Lastname_Firstname_8D_ Show** and then click **Save**.

b. **Close** the presentation and **Exit** PowerPoint.

c. In **Windows**, using **File Explorer**, navigate to your **PowerPoint Chapter 8** folder, where you saved the file, and then double-click your **Lastname_ Firstname_8D_Show** file.

d. **Close** PowerPoint. Open **File Explorer** and navigate to your chapter folder. View the .ppsx presentation file just created. Press `Esc` to close the presentation.

11 ▶ Start PowerPoint and open your **Lastname_ Firstname_8D_Academics** file. Display **Slide 2**.

a. Press `F12` to display the **Save As** dialog box. Navigate to the **PowerPoint Chapter 8** folder where you are

(Project 8D Academics continues on the next page)

storing your files for this project. Click the **Save as type arrow**, and then click **JPEG File Interchange Format**.

b. Change the **File name** to **Lastname_Firstname_8D_Picture** and then click **Save**.

c. In the displayed message box, click **Just This One**.

12 With **Lastname_Firstname_8D_Academics** still open in PowerPoint, click the **FILE tab** to display **Backstage** view, and then click **Export**.

a. Under **Export**, click **Create a Video**.

b. To the right of **Seconds spent on each slide**, change the number of seconds to **3.00**.

c. Click **Create Video**. Navigate to your **PowerPoint Chapter 8** folder, and in the **File Name** box, type **Lastname_Firstname_8D_Video.mp4** and then click **Save**.

d. In **File Explorer**, display the contents of your **PowerPoint Chapter 8** folder. Double-click **Lastname_Firstname_8D_Video.mp4** to start the video.

e. When the video is finished, press the ⊞ + **D** to return to the Windows desktop, and then return to PowerPoint.

13 Click the **FILE tab** to display **Backstage** view, click **Export**, click **Package Presentation for CD**, and then under the *Package Presentation for CD* description, click **Package for CD**.

14 In the **Package for CD** dialog box, in the **Name the CD** box, substituting your own first, middle, and last initials for *FML*, type **FML_Academics**

15 Click **Options**. In the **Options** dialog box, under **Include these files**, make sure the **Linked files** and the **Embedded TrueType fonts** check boxes are selected. Under **Enhance security and privacy**, in the **Password to modify each presentation** box, type **LCCC** Near the bottom of the **Options** dialog box, select the **Inspect presentations for inappropriate or private information** check box. Click **OK**.

16 In the **Confirm Password** dialog box, in the **Reenter the password required to modify files** box, type **LCCC** and then click **OK**.

17 In the **Package for CD** dialog box, click **Copy to Folder**.

18 In the **Copy to Folder** dialog box, click **Browse**, and then in the **Choose Location** dialog box, navigate to your **PowerPoint Chapter 8** folder. Click **Select**. Clear the check box for **Open folder when complete**. Click **OK**.

19 In the **Microsoft PowerPoint** warning box, click **Yes**. In the displayed **Document Inspector** dialog box, click **Inspect**. Click **Remove All**. Click **Close**.

20 Click **Close** to close the **Package for CD** dialog box.

21 Print **Handouts 6 Slides Horizontal**, or submit your presentation electronically as directed by your instructor.

22 **Save** your changes, **Close** the presentation, and then **Exit** PowerPoint. Submit your work as directed.

END | You have completed Project 8D

CONTENT-BASED ASSESSMENTS

Mastering PowerPoint   Project 8E Retention Rates

In the following Mastering PowerPoint project, you will complete a PowerPoint presentation by creating tables of data that have been collected. The Laurel County Community College is in the process of analyzing the retention rates of the college. Your completed presentation will look similar to Figure 8.43.

Apply 8A skills from these Objectives:

1 Draw Tables
2 Modify a Table Using the Draw Borders Features
3 Modify a Text Box

PROJECT FILES

For Project 8E, you will need the following files:

p08E_Retention_Rates.pptx
p08E_Success.jpg

You will save your presentation as:

Lastname_Firstname_ 8E_Retention_Rates.pptx

PROJECT RESULTS

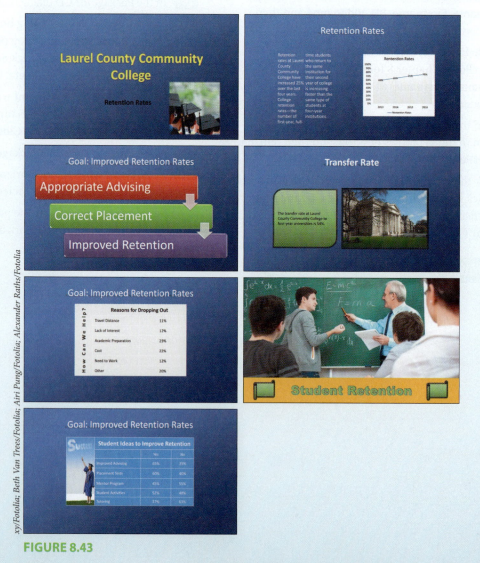

xy/Fotolia; Beth Van Trees/Fotolia; Airi Pung/Fotolia; Alexander Raths/Fotolia

FIGURE 8.43

(Project 8E Retention Rates continues on the next page)

1 Start PowerPoint. Locate and open the file **p08E_Retention_Rates**. Navigate to the **PowerPoint Chapter 8** folder you created, and then save the file as **Lastname_Firstname_8E_Retention_Rates**

2 Make **Slide 2** the active slide. Insert a **Staggered Process SmartArt Graphic**, which is in the **Process** group. If an error message displays, click **OK**. In the top box, type **Appropriate Advising** In the next box, type **Correct Placement** In the bottom box, type **Improved Retention**

3 With the **SmartArt Graphic** still active, change the color, under **Colorful** to the first pattern, **Colorful – Accent Colors**. Apply the **3-D Polished** SmartArt style.

4 Make **Slide 3** the active slide. Draw a table that is about **8 inches wide** by **3.5 inches deep**. Divide the table into two columns and seven rows.

5 Beginning in **row 1**, type the following:

Reasons for Dropping Out	
Travel Distance	11%
Lack of Interest	12%
Academic Preparation	23%
Cost	22%
Need to Work	12%
Other	20%

6 **Merge** the cells in **row 1**, and then **Center** the text.

7 Select the table. In the **Alignment group**, apply **Center Vertically**. Change the **Cell Margins** to **Wide**. **Center** the cells containing percentages.

8 Click the cell for *Reasons for Dropping Out*. Insert a column to the left, and then **Merge Cells**. Type **How Can We Help? Rotate all text 270°.** Select the text, and then add **Character Spacing, Very Loose**. Change the **Table Column Width** to **1"**.

9 Select the table, and then apply the table style **Medium Style 2**, which is under **Medium**, in the second row.

10 Select **row 1**. Add **Bold**, and then change the **Font size** to **24**.

11 On the **LAYOUT tab**, remove the check mark in the **Lock Aspect Ratio** check box, if necessary, and then

change only the width of the table to 7". Use **Align Center** and **Align Middle** to position the table on the slide.

12 On **Slide 4**, draw a table that is about **8 inches wide** by **3.5 inches deep**. Divide the table into three columns and seven rows.

13 Beginning in **row 1**, type the following:

Student Ideas to Improve Retention		
	Yes	No
Improved Advising	65%	35%
Placement Tests	60%	40%
Mentor Program	45%	55%
Student Activities	52%	48%
Tutoring	37%	63%

14 Click in the cell for *Student Ideas to Improve Retention*, and then use **Eraser** to merge the cells in the top row. **Center** the text. Click in the cell for *Improved Advising*, and then adjust the **Table Column Width** to 3.5".

15 Select the table, and then change the **Alignment** to **Center Vertically**. **Center** the cells containing *Yes* and *No* and the cells containing percentages.

16 Click in the cell for *Improved Advising*, and then insert a column to the left. Use the **Eraser** to merge the cells. On **DESIGN tab**, click **Shading**, and then click **Picture**. Navigate to **p08E_Success.jpg**, and then **Insert** the picture. Change the **Table Column Width** to 1.5".

17 With the **Lock Aspect Ratio** check box checked, **increase the width of the table to 8.0"**.

18 Select the table. On the **DESIGN tab**, click the **Shading button arrow**. Change the **Table Background** to **Dark Blue, Background 2, Lighter 40%**, which is under **Theme Colors**, in the third column, fourth row.

19 Select *Student Ideas to Improve Retention*, increase the **Font Size** to **28**, and then add **Bold**. Use **Align Center** and **Align Middle** to position the table.

20 Make **Slide 5** the active slide. In the text box on the left, change the text to **2** columns and left and right margin values to **0.4**

21 Make **Slide 6** the active slide. In the text box on the left, type **The transfer rate at Laurel County Community College to four-year universities is 54%.** and then

(Project 8E Retention Rates continues on the next page)

CONTENT-BASED ASSESSMENTS

wrap text in shape. Change the shape outline to **Theme Colors—Black, Background 1**, and the **Weight**, to **Double, Width** value **5**

22 With **Slide 6** displayed, point to the outside edge of the shape, right-click, and then click **Set as Default Shape**.

23 Make **Slide 7** the active slide. Insert the **Horizontal Scroll** shape under **Stars and Banners** and position it near the lower left corner of the slide. Duplicate the shape, and position it near the lower right corner of the slide.

24 View the slide show **From Beginning**.

25 Insert a footer on the notes and handouts, which includes a fixed date and time, the page number, and the file name.

26 Click the **FILE tab**, and then in the lower right portion of the screen, click **Show All Properties**. In the **Tags** box, type **improved, retention rate** and in the **Subject** box type your course name and section number. In the **Author** box, right-click the existing author name, click **Edit Property**, replace the existing text with your first and last name, click outside the text box to deselect, and then click **OK**.

27 **Save** your changes. Print **Handouts 4 Slides Horizontal**, or submit your presentation electronically as directed by your instructor. **Close** the presentation, and then **Exit** PowerPoint.

END | You have completed Project 8E

CONTENT-BASED ASSESSMENTS

Mastering PowerPoint | Project 8F LCCC Staffing

In the following Mastering PowerPoint project, you will complete a PowerPoint presentation by adding slides from outlines created in Microsoft Word. You will publish the presentation as a video so Laurel County Community College can share information on their website about faculty and staff. You will create a CD package and save the presentation as a Show. Your completed presentation will look similar to Figure 8.44.

Apply 8B skills from these Objectives:

4 Insert Outline Text from Another Program into a PowerPoint Presentation

5 Save a Presentation in Other Formats

6 Create a Video

7 Copy a Presentation to a CD, DVD, Network, or Local Drive

PROJECT FILES

For Project 8F, you will need the following files:

p08F_LCCC Staffing.pptx
p08F_Staff_Positions.docx

You will save your files as:

Lastname_Firstname_8F_LCCC_Staffing.pptx
Lastname_Firstname_8F_Video.mp4
Lastname_Firstname_8F_Show.ppsx
FML_Staffing (folder)

PROJECT RESULTS

FIGURE 8.44

(Project 8F LCCC Staffing continues on the next page)

CONTENT-BASED ASSESSMENTS

1 Start PowerPoint. Locate and open the file **p08F_LCCC_Staffing**. Navigate to the **PowerPoint Chapter 8** folder you created, and then save the file as **Lastname_Firstname_8F_LCCC_Staffing**

2 Make **Slide 2** the active slide. Display the **New Slide** gallery, and then click **Slides from Outline**. Navigate to your student files, and then insert **p08F_Staff_Positions.docx**.

3 Use the **Format Painter** to copy the formatting from the title placeholder on **Slide 2** to the title placeholders on **Slides 3, 4**, and **5**. Turn off **Format Painter**.

4 Make **Slide 5** the active slide, if necessary. Select the content placeholder, and then change the **Font color** to **Green, Accent 1, Darker 25%**, which is in the fifth column, the fifth row. Use the **Format Painter** to copy the formatting from the content placeholder on **Slide 5** to the content placeholders on **Slides 2, 3**, and **4**.

5 Insert a footer on the notes and handouts, which includes a fixed date and time, the page number, and the file name.

6 Modify the **Properties**. Replace the text in the **Author** box with your own name; in the **Subject** box, type your course name and section number; and then in the **Tags** box, type **faculty, staffing**

7 **Save** the presentation.

8 With **Lastname_Firstname_8F_LCCC Staffing** still open, create a **Video** that is timed for **3.00** seconds for each slide. Save it in your **PowerPoint Chapter 8** folder with the file name **Lastname_Firstname_8F_Video.mp4**

9 Create a **Package Presentation for CD**. Using your own first, middle, and last initials for *FML*, name the Package **FML_Staffing**

10 Under **Options**, enter a **Password to modify each presentation**. For the password, type **staffing** Select **Inspect presentation for inappropriate or private information.**

11 Copy the package to your **PowerPoint Chapter 8** folder. Uncheck **Open folder when complete**. Include linked files and embedded TrueType fonts in your package.

12 Inspect the document, and then **Remove All** properties and personal information. Close the **Document Inspector** dialog box, and then close the **Package for CD** dialog box.

13 With the **Lastname_Firstname_8F_LCCC_Staffing** file open, press F12 to display the **Save As** dialog box. Navigate to your **PowerPoint Chapter 8** folder. Click the **Save as type arrow**, and then click **PowerPoint Show**. In the **File name** box, type **Lastname_Firstname_8F_Show** and then click **Save**. **Exit** PowerPoint.

14 In **Windows**, using **File Explorer**, navigate to your **PowerPoint Chapter 8** folder, where you saved the file, and then double-click your **Lastname_Firstname_8F_Show** file to view the presentation.

15 Print **Handouts 6 Slides Horizontal**, or submit your presentation electronically as directed by your instructor.

END | You have completed Project 8F

CONTENT-BASED ASSESSMENTS

Mastering PowerPoint   Project 8G Student Clubs

In the following Mastering PowerPoint project, you will create a PowerPoint presentation highlighting the various student clubs at Laurel County Community College. You will draw a table with columns and rows for the presentation and enter data into the table plus create slides from a text outline created in another application. The presentation will also be published as a video. You will create a CD package and save the presentation as a Show. Your completed presentation will look similar to Figure 8.45.

Apply 8A and 8B skills from these Objectives:

1 Draw Tables
2 Modify a Table Using the Draw Borders Features
3 Modify a Text Box
4 Insert Outline Text from Another Program into a PowerPoint Presentation
5 Save a Presentation in Other Formats
6 Create a Video
7 Copy a Presentation to a CD, DVD, Network, or Local Drive

PROJECT FILES

For Project 8G, you will need the following files:

p08G_Student_Clubs.pptx
p08G_Club_Sponsors.docx
p08G_LCCC_Clubs.docx

You will save your files as:

Lastname_Firstname_8G_Student_Clubs.pptx
Lastname_Firstname_8G_Video.mp4
Lastname_Firstname_8G_Show.ppsx
FML_Clubs (folder)

PROJECT RESULTS

Student Clubs
Laurel County Community College

LCCC Student Clubs
- Agriculture Club
- Chemistry Club
- French Club
- Jazz Club
- International Club
- Phi Theta Kappa
- Veteran's Club

Meeting Locations

Laurel County Community College

Club Name	Building*
Agriculture Club	Agriculture Bldg.
Chemistry Club	Logan Hall
French Club	Sangamon Bldg.
Jazz Club	Fine Arts Center
International Club	Logan Hall
Phi Theta Kappa	Menendez Hall
Veteran's Club	Wright Hall

*Check website for meeting room changes

Club Sponsors
- Agriculture Club – Mr. Roth
- Chemistry Club – Dr. Rogers
- French Club – Ms. Dubois
- Jazz Club – Mr. Smith
- International Club – Dr. Eng
- Phi Theta Kappa – Mr. Hamilton
- Veteran's Club – Mr. Romano

FIGURE 8.45

(Project 8G Student Clubs continues on the next page)

CONTENT-BASED ASSESSMENTS

1 Start PowerPoint. Locate and open the file **p08G_Student_Clubs**. Navigate to the **PowerPoint Chapter 8** folder you created, and then save the file as **Lastname_Firstname_8G_Student_Clubs**

2 Insert **p08G_LCCC_Clubs.docx** as slides from an outline. On **Slide 2**, select the title placeholder, and then change the **Font Color** to **White, Background 1**. Select the content placeholder, and then change the **Font Color** to **Turquoise, Accent 1**.

3 With **Slide 2** as the active slide, insert a new slide with the **Title Only Layout**. On the new slide, in the title placeholder, type **Meeting Locations**

4 On **Slide 3**, draw a table to the right of the title placeholder that is about **7 inches wide** by **4.5 inches deep**. Divide the table into two columns and nine rows. Type the following into the table:

Club Name	Building*
Agriculture Club	Agriculture Bldg.
Chemistry Club	Logan Hall
French Club	Sangamon Bldg.
Jazz Club	Fine Arts Center
International Club	Logan Hall
Phi Theta Kappa	Menendez Hall
Veteran's Club	Wright Hall
*Check website for meeting room changes	

5 **Merge** the cells in the last row. Select the table, and apply **Center Vertically** to table text.

6 Click in the cell for *Club Name*. Insert a column to the left, and then **Merge** the cells. Type **Laurel County Community College** Select the text, **Rotate all text 270°**, and then apply **Character Spacing, Very Loose**. Change the **Table Column Width** to **1.5"**.

7 Select the table, and then apply the **Medium Style 2** table design and change the font size for all text to **18**.

8 Select **row 1**, and then add **Bold** and **Center**.

9 Select the table. With the **Lock Aspect Ratio** check box checked, change the table size **Width** to **7.5"**. Click in the cell for *Club Name*, and then increase the **Table Row Height** to **.8"**.

10 Apply **Align Middle** to the table position on the slide.

11 With **Slide 3** as the active slide, insert **p08G_Club_Sponsors.docx** as Slides from Outline.

12 Make **Slide 2** the active slide. Select the title placeholder. Use the **Format Painter** to copy the formats to the title placeholder on **Slide 4**. Follow the same procedure to copy the content placeholder formats on **Slide 2** to the content placeholder on **Slide 4**.

13 Insert a footer on the notes and handouts, which includes a fixed date and time, the page number, and the file name.

14 Click the **FILE tab**, and then in the lower right portion of the screen, click **Show All Properties**. In the **Tags** box, type **student, clubs** and in the **Subject** box type your course name and section number. In the **Author** box, right-click the existing author name, click **Edit Property**, replace the existing text with your first and last name, click outside the text box to deselect, and then click **OK**.

15 **Save** the presentation.

16 Create a video of your presentation with **3.00** seconds on each slide. Save the file as **Lastname_Firstname_8G_Video.mp4**

17 Create a **Package Presentation for CD**. Using your own first, middle, and last initials for *FML*, name the file **FML_Clubs** Include a **Password to modify each presentation**. For the password, type **clubs** Select **Inspect presentation for inappropriate or private information**. Copy the package to your **PowerPoint Chapter 8** folder. Uncheck **Open folder when complete**.

18 Include linked files in the package. Inspect the document, and then **Remove All** properties and personal information. Close the **Document Inspector** dialog box, and then **Close** the **Package for CD** dialog box.

19 With the **Lastname_Firstname_8G_Student_Clubs** file open, press **F12** to display the **Save As** dialog box. Navigate to your **PowerPoint Chapter 8** folder. Click the **Save as type arrow**, and then click **PowerPoint Show**. In the **File name** box, type **Lastname_Firstname_8G_Show** and then click **Save**.

20 **Exit** PowerPoint.

21 Print **Handouts 4 Slides Horizontal**, or submit your presentation electronically as directed by your instructor.

END | You have completed Project 8G

CONTENT-BASED ASSESSMENTS

Apply a combination of the 8A and 8B skills.

GO! Fix It	Project 8H Service Learning	Online
GO! Make It	Project 8I Enrollment Trends	Online
GO! Solve It	Project 8J Distance Learning	Online
GO! Solve It	Project 8K Curriculum Enrollment	

Build from
Scratch

PROJECT FILES

For Project 8K, you will need the following files:

New blank PowerPoint presentation
p08K_Curriculum_Areas.docx

You will save your files as:

Lastname_Firstname_8K_Curriculum_Enrollment.pptx
Lastname_Firstname_8K_Video.mp4
Lastname_Firstname_8K_Picture.jpg
FML_Curriculum (folder)

In this project, you will create a presentation for Laurel County Community College to use to justify hiring more full-time faculty in the programs with the highest enrollments. You are to create a presentation with a minimum of four slides and practice the activities of this chapter by creating and formatting a minimum of two tables. Add the outline, **p08K_Curriculum_Areas**, to the presentation after the title slide. Create a video and create a Package Presentation for CD. For the password, use **areas** The presentation is to be professional and appealing to the audience. Apply a table style to your tables. Save one slide as a Picture—JPEG.

Save the presentation as **Lastname_Firstname_8K_Curriculum Enrollment** Check the presentation for spelling and grammar errors, and then save the changes. Insert a Header & Footer on the Notes and Handouts, which includes the date and time fixed, the page number, and a footer with the text **Lastname_Firstname_8K_Curriculum_Enrollment** In the Properties, add your name and course information and the tags **students, enrollment**

Save your presentation. Print Handouts 4 slides per page, or submit electronically as directed by your instructor.

(Project 8K Curriculum Enrollment continues on the next page)

CHAPTER REVIEW

Performance Level

Performance Criteria		Exemplary	Proficient	Developing
	Inserted slide from outline	Text from Word document appears on the slide and is formatted correctly.	Text from Word document appears on the slide but is not formatted correctly.	Slides from outline are not visible.
	Created a video	Video runs with no errors.	Video is saved but has a few errors.	Video does not run.
	Created and formatted two tables	Tables are used effectively with appropriate formatting and are error free.	Tables are not used effectively but are error free.	Tables are not used effectively, are inappropriately formatted, and contain errors.
	Maintained a professional appearance	Presentation is free from spelling and grammar errors, and slides contain appropriate amount of text per slide.	Presentation has few spelling and grammar errors and an appropriate amount of information per slide.	Spelling and grammar errors exist, and too much or too little information is on each slide.
	Added the required elements	Completed all items correctly: file name, fixed date, page number, handouts, footer, and tags.	Completed all required items but one.	Failed to complete two or more required elements correctly.

END | You have completed Project 8K

OUTCOMES-BASED ASSESSMENTS

RUBRIC

The following outcomes-based assessments are *open-ended assessments*. That is, there is no specific correct result; your result will depend on your approach to the information provided. Make *Professional Quality* your goal. Use the following scoring rubric to guide you in *how* to approach the problem and then to evaluate *how well* your approach solves the problem.

The *criteria*—Software Mastery, Content, Format and Layout, and Process—represent the knowledge and skills you have gained that you can apply to solving the problem. The *levels of performance*—Professional Quality, Approaching Professional Quality, or Needs Quality Improvements—help you and your instructor evaluate your result.

	Your completed project is of Professional Quality if you:	Your completed project is Approaching Professional Quality if you:	Your completed project Needs Quality Improvements if you:
1-Software Mastery	Choose and apply the most appropriate skills, tools, and features and identify efficient methods to solve the problem.	Choose and apply some appropriate skills, tools, and features, but not in the most efficient manner.	Choose inappropriate skills, tools, or features, or are inefficient in solving the problem.
2-Content	Construct a solution that is clear and well organized, contains content that is accurate, appropriate to the audience and purpose, and is complete. Provide a solution that contains no errors in spelling, grammar, or style.	Construct a solution in which some components are unclear, poorly organized, inconsistent, or incomplete. Misjudge the needs of the audience. Have some errors in spelling, grammar, or style, but the errors do not detract from comprehension.	Construct a solution that is unclear, incomplete, or poorly organized; contains some inaccurate or inappropriate content; and contains many errors in spelling, grammar, or style. Do not solve the problem.
3-Format & Layout	Format and arrange all elements to communicate information and ideas, clarify function, illustrate relationships, and indicate relative importance.	Apply appropriate format and layout features to some elements, but not others. Overuse features, causing minor distraction.	Apply format and layout that does not communicate information or ideas clearly. Do not use format and layout features to clarify function, illustrate relationships, or indicate relative importance. Use available features excessively, causing distraction.
4-Process	Use an organized approach that integrates planning, development, self-assessment, revision, and reflection.	Demonstrate an organized approach in some areas, but not others; or, use an insufficient process of organization throughout.	Do not use an organized approach to solve the problem.

OUTCOMES-BASED ASSESSMENTS

Apply a combination of the **8A** and **8B** skills.

Build from Scratch

GO! Think Project 8L Faculty

PROJECT FILES

For Project 8L, you will need the following files:

New blank PowerPoint presentation
p08L_Programs.docx

You will save your files as:

Lastname_Firstname_8L_Faculty.pptx
Lastname_Firstname_8L_Video.mp4
Lastname_Firstname_8L_Faculty.ppsx
FML_CD (folder)

In this project, you will create a presentation showing the levels of education of the full-time faculty teaching at Laurel County Communication College.

You will insert the file **p08L_Programs** near the beginning of the presentation. This presentation should include at least four slides. Be sure to use tables that are appropriately created and formatted. The presentation is to be professional and appealing to the audience. Also create a video of the presentation and a PowerPoint Show.

Save the presentation as **Lastname_Firstname_8L_Faculty** Check the presentation for spelling and grammar errors, and then save any changes.

Update the Notes and Handouts footer with the new file name and the author name in the Properties. Save the presentation. Print or submit electronically as directed by your instructor.

END | You have completed Project 8L

Build from Scratch

GO! Think Project 8M Anticipated Openings   Online

Build from Scratch

You and GO! Project 8N LCCC Faculty   Online

Glossary

.crtx The file extension for a chart template.

.potx The file extension for a PowerPoint template.

.ppsx The PowerPoint file extension that allows a file to open in Slide Show view.

.pptx The file extension for a PowerPoint presentation.

.rtf The extension for a file that is saved in Rich Text Format.

.wav (waveform audio data) A sound file that may be embedded in a presentation.

Action button A built-in button shape that you can add to your presentation and then assign an action to occur upon the click of a mouse or with a mouse over.

Address bar (Internet Explorer) The area at the top of the Internet Explorer window that displays, and where you can type, a URL—Uniform Resource Locator—which is an address that uniquely identifies a location on the Internet.

Address bar (Windows) The bar at the top of a folder window with which you can navigate to a different folder or library, or go back to a previous one.

After Previous An animation option that begins the animation sequence for the selected slide element immediately after the completion of the previous animation or slide transition. A custom animation that starts the animation effect immediately after the previous effect in the list finishes playing.

Alignment The placement of text or objects relative to the left and right margins.

Alignment guides Green lines that display when you move an object to assist in alignment.

Animated GIF A file format made up of a series of frames within a single file that creates the illusion of animation by displaying the frames one after the other in quick succession.

Animation 1. Any type of motion or movement that occurs as the presentation moves from slide to slide. 2. A special visual effect or sound effect added to text or an object. A visual or sound effect added to an object or text on a slide.

Animation Painter A feature that copies animation settings from one object to another.

Animation Pane The area that contains a list of the animation effects added to your presentation. From this pane, you can add or modify effects. The area used for adding and removing effects.

Annotation A note or a highlight that can be saved or discarded. Includes the specifications for the design of presentation handouts for an audience.

Antonyms Words with an opposite meaning.

App The term that commonly refers to computer programs that run from the device software on a smartphone or a tablet computer—for example, iOS, Android, or Windows Phone—or computer programs that run from the browser software on a desktop PC or laptop PC—for example Internet Explorer, Safari, Firefox, or Chrome.

App for Office A webpage that works within one of the Office applications, such as Excel, and that you download from the Office Store.

Apps for Office 2013 and SharePoint 2013 A collection of downloadable apps that enable you to create and view information within your familiar Office programs.

Artistic effects Formats applied to images that make pictures resemble sketches or paintings.

Aspect ratio The ratio of the width of a display to the height of the display.

AutoFit An option that resizes a column to accommodate the largest entry.

Background Removal A feature that removes unwanted portions of a picture so that the picture does not appear as a self-contained rectangle.

Background style A predefined slide background fill variation that combines theme colors in different intensities or patterns.

Backstage tabs The area along the left side of Backstage view with tabs to display screens with related groups of commands.

Backstage view A centralized space for file management tasks; for example, opening, saving, printing, publishing, or sharing a file. A navigation pane displays along the left side with tabs that group file-related tasks together.

Banded columns A table setting that enables you to format even columns differently from odd columns to make the table easier to read.

Banded rows A table setting that enables you to format even rows differently from odd rows to make the table easier to read.

Bar of Pie chart A type of pie chart that emphasizes one slice of the pie by representing the slice as a bar showing how the data in the slice are further divided.

Basic custom slide show A separate presentation saved with its own title containing some of the slides from the original presentation.

Black slide A slide that displays after the last slide in a presentation indicating that the presentation is over.

Body font A font that is applied to all slide text except slide titles.

Border A frame around a picture.

Brightness The perceived radiance or luminosity of an image.

Caption Text that helps to identify or explain a picture or a graphic.

Category labels Text that displays along the bottom of a chart to identify the categories of data.

CD-R Removable media (CD) that can be written to, or saved to, only one time.

CD-RW Removable media (CD) that can be written to, or saved to, multiple times.

Cell The intersection of a column and row in a table.

Cell reference The intersecting column letter and row number that identify a cell.

Center alignment The alignment of text or objects that is centered horizontally between the left and right margins.

Chart A graphic representation of numeric data.

Chart elements The various components of a chart, including the chart title, axis titles, data series, legend, chart area, and plot area.

Chart Elements button A button that displays options for adding, removing, or changing chart elements.

Chart Filters button A button that displays options for changing the data displayed in a chart.

Chart style A set of predefined formats applied to a chart, including colors, backgrounds, and effects.

Chart Styles button A button that displays options for setting the style and color scheme for a chart.

Chart template A predefined layout or format that can be used to create a chart.

Chevron A V-shaped symbol that indicates more information or options are available.

Click The action of pressing and releasing the left button on a mouse pointing device one time.

Clip A single media file, such as art, sound, animation, or a movie.

Clip art Downloadable predefined graphics available online from Office.com and other sites.

Clipboard A temporary storage area that holds text or graphics that you select and then cut or copy.

Cloud computing Refers to applications and services that are accessed over the Internet, rather than to applications that are installed on your local computer.

Cloud storage Online storage of data so that you can access your data from different places and devices.

Collaborate To work with others as a team in an intellectual endeavor to complete a shared task or to achieve a shared goal.

Collaboration The action of working with others as a team in an intellectual endeavor to complete a shared task or achieve a shared goal.

Column chart A type of chart used for illustrating comparisons among related numbers.

Commands An instruction to a computer program that causes an action to be carried out.

Comment A note that you can attach to a letter or word on a slide or to an entire slide. People use comments to provide feedback on a presentation.

Common dialog boxes The set of dialog boxes that includes Open, Save, and Save As, which are provided by the Windows programming interface, and which display and operate in all of the Office programs in the same manner.

Compatibility Checker A feature that locates potential compatibility issues between PowerPoint 2013 and earlier versions of PowerPoint.

Compatibility mode Saves a presentation as PowerPoint 97-2003 presentation. It also ensures that no new or enhanced features in PowerPoint 2013 are available while you work with a document, so that people who are using previous versions of PowerPoint will have full editing capabilities. Ensures that no new or enhanced features in Word 2013 are available while you work with a document, so that people who are using previous versions of Word will have full editing capabilities.

Compressed file A file that has been reduced in size and thus takes up less storage space and can be transferred to other computers quickly.

Compressed folder A folder that has been reduced in size and thus takes up less storage space and can be transferred to other computers quickly; also called a *zipped* folder.

Context menus Menus that display commands and options relevant to the selected text or object; also called *shortcut menus*.

Context-sensitive commands Commands that display on a shortcut menu that relate to the object or text that you right-clicked.

Contextual tabs Tabs that are added to the ribbon automatically when a specific object, such as a picture, is selected, and that contain commands relevant to the selected object.

Contiguous slides Slides that are adjacent to each other in a presentation.

Contrast The difference between the darkest and lightest area of a picture.

Copy A command that duplicates a selection and places it on the Clipboard.

Crop A command that removes unwanted or unnecessary areas of a picture.

Crop handles Handles used to remove unwanted areas of a picture. Used like sizing handles to crop a picture.

Crop pointer The pointer used to crop areas of a picture.

Crop tool The mouse pointer used when removing areas of a picture.

Crosshair pointer The pointer used to draw a shape.

Custom slide show Displays only the slides you want to display to an audience in the order you select.

Cut A command that removes a selection and places it on the Clipboard.

Data marker A column, bar, area, dot, pie slice, or other symbol in a chart that represents a single data point.

Data point A chart value that originates in a worksheet cell.

Data series In an Excel worksheet, a set of values arranged in one column or row only. A group of related data points.

Default The term that refers to the current selection or setting that is automatically used by a computer program unless you specify otherwise.

Deselect The action of canceling the selection of an object or block of text by clicking outside of the selection.

Desktop In Windows, the screen that simulates your work area.

Desktop app The term that commonly refers to a computer program that is installed on your computer and requires a computer operating system like Microsoft Windows or Apple OS to run.

Destination file The file into which information or an object is copied.

Dialog box A small window that contains options for completing a task.

Dialog Box Launcher A small icon that displays to the right of some group names on the ribbon, and which opens a related dialog box or pane providing additional options and commands related to that group.

Document Inspector A PowerPoint feature that allows you to review a presentation for hidden data or personal information that may be stored in the presentation or in the document properties and then provides the option to remove the information.

Document properties Details about a file that describe or identify it, including the title, author name, subject, and keywords that identify the document's topic or contents; also known as *metadata*.

Drag The action of holding down the left mouse button while moving your mouse.

Draw pointer A pen-shaped pointer that is used to create table borders.

DVD-R Removable media (DVD) that can be written to, or saved to, only one time.

DVD-RW Removable media (DVD) that can be written to, or saved to, multiple times.

Edit The process of making changes to text or graphics in an Office file.

Editing The process of modifying a presentation by adding and deleting slides or by changing the contents of individual slides.

Ellipsis A set of three dots indicating incompleteness; an ellipsis following a command name indicates that a dialog box will display if you click the command.

Email client A software program that enables you to compose and send email message.

Embed Save a file so that the audio or video file becomes part of the presentation file.

Embedded A type of object that is saved with, and becomes a part of, a PowerPoint file.

Emphasis effect An animation effect that, for example, makes an object shrink or grow in size, change color, or spin on its center. Animation that emphasizes an object or text that is already displayed.

Enhanced ScreenTip A ScreenTip that displays more descriptive text than a normal ScreenTip.

Entrance effect An animation effect that occurs when the text or object is introduced into the slide during a slide show. Animation that brings a slide element onto the screen.

Eraser A pointer that is used to remove table borders.

Exit effect An animation effect that occurs when the text or object leaves the slide or disappears during a slide show. Animation that moves an object or text off the screen.

Explode Manually pull out a slice of a pie chart so that it stands away from the pie in order to emphasize it.

Exploded pie chart A type of pie chart that displays all of the slices disconnected from each other. The slices cannot be manipulated individually.

Extract To decompress, or pull out, files from a compressed form.

Eyedropper A tool that captures the exact color from an object on your screen and then applies the color to any shape, picture, or text.

File A collection of information stored on a computer under a single name, for example, a Word document or a PowerPoint presentation.

File Explorer The program that displays the files and folders on your computer, and which is at work anytime you are viewing the contents of files and folders in a window.

File extension Also called the *file type*, it identifies the format of the file or the application used to create it.

Fill The inside color of an object.

Fill color The inside color of text or of an object.

Fit to slide The photo album option that allows the picture to occupy all available space on a slide with no room for a frame or caption.

Flash drive A compact removable drive that plugs into the USB port of the computer.

Folder A container in which you store files.

Folder window In Windows, a window that displays the contents of the current folder, library, or device, and contains helpful parts so that you can navigate the Windows file structure.

Font A set of characters with the same design and shape.

Font styles Formatting emphasis such as bold, italic, and underline.

Footer Text that displays at the bottom of every slide or that prints at the bottom of a sheet of slide handouts or notes pages. A reserved area for text or graphics that displays at the bottom of each page in a document.

Formatting The process of establishing the overall appearance of text, graphics, and pages in an Office file—for example, in a Word document. The process of changing the appearance of the text, layout, and design of a slide.

Formatting marks Characters that display on the screen, but do not print, indicating where the Enter key, the Spacebar, and the Tab key were pressed; also called *nonprinting characters*.

Frame The border around a picture in a photo album.

Full path Includes the drive, the folder, and any subfolders in which a file is contained.

Gallery An Office feature that displays a list of potential results instead of just the command name.

GIF Stands for Graphics Interchange Format. It is a file format used for graphic images, such as drawings.

Gradient fill A gradual progression of several colors blending into each other or shades of the same color blending into each other. A fill effect in which one color fades into another.

Gradient stop Allows you to apply different color combinations to selected areas of the background.

Groups On the Office ribbon, the sets of related commands that you might need for a specific type of task.

Handout Master Includes the specifications for the design of presentation handouts for an audience.

Hard return Created by pressing the Enter key to start a new line.

Header A reserved area for text or graphics that displays at the top of each page in a document. Text that prints at the top of each sheet of slide handouts or notes pages.

Header row The top row of the table; this row is formatted differently from the rows containing data.

Heading style A set of formatting characteristics, such as font name, size, color, paragraph alignment, and spacing, that is used to quickly format selected text.

Headings font A font that is applied to all slide title text.

Hyperlinked custom slide show A quick way to navigate to a separate slide show from within the original presentation.

Hyperlinks Navigation elements that, when clicked, will take you to another location, such as a webpage, an email address, another document, or a place within the same document. In a PowerPoint presentation, hyperlinks can also be used to link to a slide in the presentation, to a slide in a different presentation, or to a custom slide show.

HyperText Markup Language (HTML) The language used to code webpages.

HyperText Transfer Protocol (HTTP) The protocol used on the World Wide Web to define how messages are formatted and transmitted.

Info tab The tab in Backstage view that displays information about the current file.

Insertion point A blinking vertical line that indicates where text or graphics will be inserted.

JPEG (or .jpg) An abbreviation that stands for Joint Photographic Experts Group. It is a file format used for photos and includes the .jpg and .jpeg extensions.

JPG (JPEG) Stands for Joint Photographic Experts Group. It is a file format used for photos.

Keyboard shortcut A combination of two or more keyboard keys, used to perform a task that would otherwise require a mouse.

KeyTip The letter that displays on a command in the ribbon and that indicates the key you can press to activate the command when keyboard control of the ribbon is activated.

Keywords Custom file properties in the form of words that you associate with a document to give an indication of the document's content; used to help find and organize files. Also called *tags*.

Kiosk A booth that includes a computer and a monitor that may have a touchscreen.

Landscape orientation A page orientation in which the paper is wider than it is tall.

Layout The arrangement of elements, such as title and subtitle text, lists, pictures, tables, charts, shapes, and movies, on a slide.

Layout Options A button that displays when an object is selected and that has commands to choose how the object interacts with surrounding text.

Legend A chart element that identifies the patterns or colors that are assigned to the data series in the chart. In a pie chart, identifies the patterns or colors that are assigned to the pie slices.

Line chart A type of chart commonly used to illustrate trends over time.

Line style How the line displays, such as a solid line, dots, or dashes.

Line weight The thickness of a line measured in points.

Link Save a presentation so that the audio or video file is saved separately from the presentation.

List level An outline level in a presentation represented by a bullet symbol and identified in a slide by the indentation and the size of the text.

Live Preview A technology that shows the result of applying an editing or formatting change as you point to possible results—*before* you actually apply it.

Local drive A drive on your computer, such as the C: drive.

Location Any disk drive, folder, or other place in which you can store files and folders.

Lock aspect ratio When this option is selected, you can change one dimension (height or width) of an object, such as a picture, and the other dimension will automatically be changed to maintain the proportion. Locks the relationship between the width and height of a table. When resizing a table, the height and width of the table change in proportion to each other.

Loop The audio or video file plays repeatedly from start to finish until it is stopped manually.

Mark as Final Makes a presentation file read-only in order to prevent changes to the document. Adds a Marked as Final icon to the status bar.

Merge To combine two or more cells into a single cell.

Metadata Details about a file that describe or identify it, including the title, author name, subject, and keywords that identify the document's topic or contents; also known as *document properties.*

Microsoft Office 365 A set of secure online services that enables people in an organization to communicate and collaborate by using any Internet-connected device—a computer, a tablet, or a mobile phone.

Microsoft Outlook An example of an email client.

Mini toolbar A small toolbar containing frequently used formatting commands that displays as a result of selecting text or objects.

Mitered A border with corners that are square.

Motion Path effect An animation effect that determines how and in what direction text or objects will move on a slide.

Mouse Over Refers to an action that will occur when the mouse pointer is placed on (over) an action button. No mouse click is required.

MP4 video file (.mp4) The default file type when saving a video in PowerPoint 2013.

MRU Acronym for *most recently used,* which refers to the state of some commands that retain the characteristic most recently applied; for example, the Font Color button retains the most recently used color until a new color is chosen.

Navigate The process of exploring within the organizing structure of Windows.

Navigation pane In a folder window, the area on the left in which you can navigate to, open, and display favorites, libraries, folders, saved searches, and an expandable list of drives.

Navigation tools Buttons that display on the slides during a slide show that allow you to perform actions such as move to the next slide, the previous slide, the last viewed slide, or the end of the slide show.

Network drive A common drive on another computer, usually a server, that is available to others working on the network.

Noncontiguous slides Slides that are not adjacent to each other in a presentation.

Nonprinting characters Characters that display on the screen, but do not print, indicating where the Enter key, the Spacebar, and the Tab key were pressed; also called *formatting marks.*

Normal view The primary editing view in PowerPoint where you write and design your presentations.

Notes Master Includes the specifications for the design of the speaker's notes.

Notes page A printout that contains the slide image on the top half of the page and notes that you have created on the Notes pane in the lower half of the page.

Notes pane An area of the Normal view window that displays below the Slide pane with space to type notes regarding the active slide.

Notification bar An area at the bottom of an Internet Explorer window that displays information about pending downloads, security issues, add-ons, and other issues related to the operation of your computer.

Object A text box, picture, table, or shape that you can select and then move and resize.

Office Theme Slide Master A specific slide master that contains the design, such as the background, that displays on all slide layouts in the presentation.

Office Web Apps The free online companions to Microsoft Word, Excel, PowerPoint, Access, and OneNote.

On Click An animation option that begins the animation sequence for the selected slide element when the mouse button is clicked or the Spacebar is pressed. Starts the animation effect when you click the slide or a trigger on the slide.

Open dialog box A dialog box from which you can navigate to, and then open on your screen, an existing file that was created in that same program.

Option button In a dialog box, a round button that enables you to make one choice among two or more options.

Options dialog box A dialog box within each Office application where you can select program settings and other options and preferences.

Outline view A document view in Microsoft Word that distinguishes the importance of data by the heading styles that have been applied. A PowerPoint view that displays the presentation outline to the left of the Slide pane.

Package Presentation for CD A PowerPoint feature that creates a package of a presentation and related files on a CD.

Pane A separate area of a window.

Paragraph symbol The symbol ¶ that represents the end of a paragraph.

Paragraphs Any text that has a hard return at the end of it.

Paste The action of placing text or objects that have been copied or cut from one location to another location.

Paste Options gallery A gallery of buttons that provides a Live Preview of all the Paste options available in the current context.

Path A sequence of folders that leads to a specific file or folder.

PDF The acronym for Portable Document Format, which is a file format that creates an image that preserves the look of your file; this is a popular format for sending documents electronically because the document will display on most computers.

Photo album A stylized presentation format to display pictures.

Pie chart Used to plot a single data series, this chart type shows the relationship of parts to a whole.

Pie of Pie chart A type of pie chart that emphasizes one slice of the pie by representing the slice as another pie showing how the data in the slice are further divided.

Pixel The term, short for picture element, represents a single point in a graphic image.

Placeholder A box on a slide with dotted or dashed borders that holds title and body text or other content such as charts, tables, and pictures.

Platform The combination of hardware and software used on a computer.

Play Animations button A small star-shaped icon that displays to the left of the slide thumbnail.

Point The action of moving your mouse pointer over something on your screen.

Pointer Any symbol that displays on your screen in response to moving your mouse.

Points A measurement of the size of a font; there are 72 points in an inch.

Portable Document Format (PDF) A file format that creates an image that preserves the look of your file, but that cannot be easily changed; a popular format for sending documents electronically, because the document will display on most computers.

Portrait orientation A page orientation in which the paper is taller than it is wide.

Presets Built-in sharpness and softness adjustments from a gallery.

Print Preview A view of a document as it will appear when you print it.

Progress bar In a dialog box or taskbar button, a bar that indicates visually the progress of a task such as a download or file transfer.

Protected View A security feature in Office 2013 that protects your computer from malicious files by opening them in a restricted environment until you enable them; you might encounter this feature if you open a file from an email message or download files from the Internet.

Protocol A set of rules.

pt The abbreviation for *point*; for example, when referring to a font size.

Quick Access Toolbar In an Office program window, the small row of buttons in the upper left corner of the screen from which you can perform frequently used commands.

Range A selection of two or more adjacent or nonadjacent cells.

Reading view A view in PowerPoint that displays a presentation in a manner similar to a slide show but in which the taskbar, title bar, and status bar remain available in the presentation window.

Read-only A property assigned to a file that prevents the file from being modified or deleted; it indicates that you cannot save any changes to the displayed document unless you first save it with a new name.

Recolor The term used to change all the colors in the image to shades of one color.

Reviewer A person who inserts comments into a presentation to provide feedback.

RGB A color model in which the colors red, green, and blue are added together to form another color.

Ribbon A user interface in both Office 2013 and File Explorer that groups the commands for performing related tasks on tabs across the upper portion of the program window.

Rich Text Format (RTF) file A non-application-specific file format used to transfer formatted text documents between applications.

Right-click The action of clicking the right mouse button one time.

Rotation handle A circular arrow that provides a way to rotate a selected image.

Ruler guides Dotted red vertical and horizontal lines that display in the rulers indicating the pointer's position.

Sans serif font A font design with no lines or extensions on the ends of characters.

ScreenTip A small box that displays useful information when you perform various mouse actions such as pointing to screen elements or dragging.

Scroll bar A vertical or horizontal bar in a window or a pane to assist in bringing an area into view, and which contains a scroll box and scroll arrows.

Scroll box The box in the vertical and horizontal scroll bars that can be dragged to reposition the contents of a window or pane on the screen.

Section header A type of slide layout that changes the look and flow of a presentation by providing text placeholders that do not contain bullet points. Used to organize slides in meaningful ways.

Selecting Highlighting, by dragging with your mouse, areas of text or data or graphics, so that the selection can be edited, formatted, copied, or moved.

Serif font A font design that includes small line extensions on the ends of the letters to guide the eye in reading from left to right.

Shape A slide object such as a line, arrow, box, callout, or banner.

SharePoint Collaboration software with which people in an organization can set up team sites to share information, manage documents, and publish reports for others to see.

Sharpen Increase the clarity of an image.

Shortcut menu A menu that displays commands and options relevant to the selected text or object; also called a *context menu*.

Sizing handles Small squares surrounding a picture that indicate that the picture is selected. Small squares, located in the corners and in the center of table borders, that are used to increase or decrease the size of the table by dragging.

SkyDrive Microsoft's free cloud storage for anyone with a free Microsoft account.

Slices Categories in a pie chart that represent parts of the whole and show the contribution of each value to the total.

Slide A presentation page that can contain text, pictures, tables, charts, and other multimedia or graphic objects.

Slide handout Printed images of slides on a sheet of paper.

Slide Master Part of a template that stores information about the formatting and text that displays on every slide in a presentation. There are various slide master layouts.

Slide pane A PowerPoint screen element that displays a large image of the active slide.

Slide Sorter view A presentation view that displays thumbnails of all of the slides in a presentation.

Slide transitions Motion effects that occur in Slide Show view when you move from one slide to the next during a presentation.

Smart guides Dashed lines that display on your slide when you are moving an object to assist you with alignment.

SmartArt graphic A visual representation of information that you create by choosing from among various layouts to communicate your message or ideas effectively.

SmartArt Styles Combinations of formatting effects that you can apply to SmartArt graphics.

Soften Decrease the clarity of an image or make it fuzzy.

Source file A file from which information or an object is copied.

Split To divide a cell into two or more cells.

Split button A button divided into two parts and in which clicking the main part of the button performs a command and clicking the arrow opens a menu with choices. A type of button in which clicking the main part of the button performs a command and clicking the arrow opens a menu, list, or gallery.

Start search The search feature in Windows 8 in which, from the Start screen, you can begin to type and by default, Windows 8 searches for apps; you can adjust the search to search for files or settings.

Status bar The area along the lower edge of an Office program window that displays file information on the left and buttons to control how the window looks on the right.

Style A group of formatting commands, such as font, font size, font color, paragraph alignment, and line spacing that can be applied to a paragraph with one command. A collection of formatting options that you can apply to a picture, text, or an object.

Subfolder A folder within a folder.

Synchronization The process of updating computer files that are in two or more locations according to specific rules—also called *syncing*.

Syncing The process of updating computer files that are in two or more locations according to specific rules—also called *synchronization*.

Synonym A word having the same or nearly the same meaning as another.

Table A format for information that organizes and presents text and data in columns and rows. A grid of rows and columns.

Table gridlines Nonprinting lines between columns and rows in a table.

Table style A format applied to a table that is consistent with the presentation theme.

Tabs (ribbon) On the Office ribbon, the name of each activity area.

Tags Custom file properties in the form of words that you associate with a document to give an indication of the document's content; used to help find and organize files. Also called *keywords*.

Taskbar The area along the lower edge of the desktop that displays buttons representing programs.

Team A group of workers tasked with working together to solve a problem, make a decision, or create a work product.

Template A preformatted document that you can use as a starting point and then change to suit your needs. A predefined layout for a group of slides saved as a .potx file.

Text alignment The horizontal placement of text within a placeholder.

Text box A drawn object that is used to position text anywhere on a slide.

Text effects Formats applied to text that include shadows, reflections, glows, bevels, and 3-D rotations.

Theme A predesigned combination of colors, fonts, and effects that look good together and is applied to an entire document by a single selection.

A set of unified design elements that provides a look for your presentation by applying colors, fonts, and effects.

Theme colors A set of coordinating colors that are applied to the backgrounds, objects, and text in a presentation.

Theme fonts The fonts applied to two types of slide text—headings and body.

Thumbnails Miniature images of presentation slides.

Timeline A graphical representation that displays the number of seconds the animation takes to complete.

Timing options Animation options that control when animated items display in the animation sequence.

Title bar The bar at the top edge of the program window that indicates the name of the current file and the program name.

Title slide A slide layout—most commonly the first slide in a presentation—that provides an introduction to the presentation topic.

Toggle button A button that can be turned on by clicking it once, and then turned off by clicking it again.

Toolbar In a folder window, a row of buttons with which you can perform common tasks, such as changing the view of your files and folders or burning files to a CD.

Total row The last row of a table; this row is formatted differently from other rows containing data.

Track A song from a CD.

Transition sound A prerecorded sound that can be applied and will play as slides change from one to the next.

Transition speed The timing of the transition between all slides or between the previous slide and the current slide.

Transitions Motion effects that occur when a presentation moves from slide to slide in Slide Show view and affect how content is revealed.

Trigger A portion of text, a graphic, or a picture that, when clicked, causes the audio or video to play.

Trim A command that deletes parts of a video to make it shorter.

Triple-click The action of clicking the left mouse button three times in rapid succession.

TrueType The scalable font technology built into Microsoft Windows and Apple Macintosh.

Trusted Documents A security feature in Office that remembers which files you have already enabled; you might encounter this feature if you open a file from an email message or download files from the Internet.

Uniform Resource Locator (URL) An address that uniquely identifies a location on the Internet. Defines the address of documents and resources on the web.

URL The acronym for Uniform Resource Locator, which is an address that uniquely identifies a location on the Internet.

USB flash drive A small data storage device that plugs into a computer USB port.

Variant A variation on the presentation theme style and color.

Web browser A software application used for retrieving, presenting, and searching information resources on the World Wide Web. It formats webpages so that they display properly.

Window A rectangular area on a computer screen in which programs and content appear, and which can be moved, resized, minimized, or closed.

With Previous An animation option that begins the animation sequence at the same time as the previous animation or slide transition. A custom animation that starts the animation effect at the same time as the previous effect in the list.

WordArt A gallery of text styles with which you can create decorative effects, such as shadowed or mirrored text.

XML Paper Specification (XPS) A Microsoft file format that creates an image of your document and that opens in the XPS viewer. Microsoft's file format that preserves document formatting and enables file sharing. Files can be opened and viewed on any operating system or computer that is equipped with Microsoft XPS Viewer. Files cannot be easily edited.

XPS The acronym for XML Paper Specification—a Microsoft file format that creates an image of your document and that opens in the XPS viewer.

Zipped folder A folder that has been reduced in size and thus takes up less storage space and can be transferred to other computers quickly; also called a *compressed* folder.

Zoom The action of increasing or decreasing the size of the viewing area on the screen.

Index